A DIARY
OF THE
CENTURY

BOOKS BY EDWARD ROBB ELLIS

A DIARY OF THE CENTURY
  Tales from America's Greatest Diarist (1995)
ECHOES OF DISTANT THUNDER
  Life in the United States, 1914–1918 (1975)
A NATION IN TORMENT
  The Great American Depression, 1929–1939 (1970)
THE EPIC OF NEW YORK CITY
  A Narrative History (1966)
THE TRAITOR WITHIN
  Our Suicide Problem (with George N. Allen, 1961)

A DIARY

OF THE

CENTURY

TALES FROM AMERICA'S

GREATEST DIARIST

EDWARD ROBB ELLIS

CARICATURES BY THE AUTHOR
INTRODUCTION BY PETE HAMILL

KODANSHA INTERNATIONAL
New York · Tokyo · London

Kodansha America, Inc.
114 Fifth Avenue, New York, New York 10011,
U.S.A.

Kodansha International Ltd.
17-14 Otowa 1-chome, Bunkyo-ku, Tokyo 112, Japan

Published in 1995 by Kodansha America, Inc.

Library of Congress Cataloging-in-Publication Data

Ellis, Edward Robb.
    A diary of the century : tales from America's
greatest diarist / Edward Robb Ellis ; caricatures by
the author ; introduction by Pete Hamill.
        p.   cm.
    Includes index.
    ISBN 1-56836-080-0
        1. United States—History—20th century.
2. Ellis, Edward Robb—Diaries.   3.
Journalists—United States—Diaries.   I. Title.
E741.E43   1995
973.9—dc20   95-12798

Book design by Debbie Glasserman

Printed in the United States of America

95 96 97 98 99   RRD/H   10 9 8 7 6 5 4 3 2 1

To my daughter,
Sandra Gail Ellis,
and my granddaughters
Shine and Orion Emelio

The life of a single man
may make us in a vivid
though limited fashion
the contemporary of a
perished age.

THE AUTOBIOGRAPHY OF
JOHANN WOLFGANG VON GOETHE

Three passions, simple but
overwhelmingly strong, have
governed my life: the longing
for love, the search for
knowledge, and unbearable
pity for the suffering of
mankind.

THE AUTOBIOGRAPHY OF
BERTRAND RUSSELL

There was so much to write.
He had seen the world change;
not just the events; although
he had seen many of them and
had watched the people, but he
had seen the subtler change and
he could remember how the people
were at different times. He had
been in it and he had watched
it and it was his duty to write
of it.

ERNEST HEMINGWAY,
THE SNOWS OF KILIMANJARO

CONTENTS

Photographs follow pages 228 and 420.

LIST OF ILLUSTRATIONS

INTRODUCTION

Pete Hamill

The diarist has one essential goal: to freeze time. With each entry, he or she says that on this day, a day that will never again occur in the history of the world, *I lived.* I lived in this city or that town, upon which the sun shone warmly or the rain fell steadily. I ate breakfast, walked city streets or country roads, drove a car or entered a subway. I worked. I dreamed. Other human beings said witty things to me, or stupid things, or brutal things; or I did the same to them. I laughed. I wept. The newspapers told me about the fevers of politics, distant wars, and who won the ballgames. I experienced a work of art or read a novel or heard music that would not leave my mind. I was bored. I was afraid. I was brave. I was cowardly. I endured a headache. I broke my leg. I loved someone who did not love me back. I suffered the death of a loved one. This day will never come again, but here, in this diary, I will have it forever. Casual reader, listen: I, too, have lived.

The greatest diaries, from those of André Gide to those of the superb Japanese writer Kafu Nagai, are ruled by this principle. They are records of lone human beings attempting to be still in the flux of time. In the beginning, that impulse was also the engine of the extraordinary achievement that became the diaries of Edward Robb Ellis. He began writing his entries as a boy, in a year before there were sound movies or jet planes or television; he would witness, up close or at a distance, the bewildering storm of economic, social, and technological changes that have made up the twentieth century. In his first boyish jottings, made in composition books in the 1920s, his style has a naive charm and his innocence is almost total. Even in a small town in the Midwest, time moved swiftly, but the boy wanted to hold on to it, to examine the world and himself through the magical act of putting words on paper.

Later, as the young man determined to be a newspaperman, the diary began to serve other purposes. Recording the present gave him a sense of the past (decades later he would carry this into superb works of narrative history) and desire for the pleasures of the future. He records his hopes and plans for women, friendships, books, as if writing a first draft of his life. This was not unique to Eddie Ellis. Thomas Mann once described his own diary keeping as "this process by which each passing day is captured, not only its impressions, but also, at least by suggestion, its intellectual direction and content as well, less for the purpose of rereading and remembering than for taking stock, reviewing, maintaining awareness, achieving perspective."

Eddie Ellis and Thomas Mann are very different writers, of course, although they had a brief encounter in 1946 in Chicago, as recorded in this book. The young newspaperman stares at the seventy-one-year-old Nobel Prize winner, the product of so much European darkness and human hope, and seems to realize that the newspaper interview is an inadequate medium for the task of understanding him or his high art. Ellis chooses instead to etch a portrait of the great writer's face and presence, as if to say the books are there in the cool eyes, the "barbed wire of his salty mustache," the hint of vanity in the pompadour fashion of his hair. Strangers to each other, they have only one thing in common: their diaries are part of a similar project.

The basic thread of those diaries—of most diaries—is the capture of each passing day, and that includes the way history forces its attentions on the individual. In addition to notes about his marriage, his sexual desires, his social life and artistic goals, Mann grapples with the rise of fascism, the coming of Hitler, the brutal arrival of night and fog. Eddie Ellis lived a completely different life in a much different country. As we follow him from the small town where he grew up to the University of Missouri to thirty-five years of newspapering in New Orleans, Oklahoma City, Peoria, Chicago, and, finally, New York, we also feel the steady, intrusive pressure of the larger world. As reporter and citizen, an American living an American life, he ponders the meaning of the Great Depression, Hitler, Pearl Harbor, the war, McCarthyism, the murders of John F. Kennedy and Martin Luther King, Vietnam and Watergate, and the collapse of the Soviet Union. For a newspaperman, this is unusual. Very few journalists actually keep journals; the record of most newspapermen's presence in the world can be found only in the yellowed clippings in newspaper morgues. In addition, even the best journalists are often drawn to their trade to avoid dealing with the personal. It is easier to deal with the problems of strangers than the mysteries of the self. But in his bald, unaffected style, Ellis insists on the primacy of the self. "A diarist," he says, "is a writer who watches himself watching himself."

Sometimes he is a participant in the life of his times, hitching a freight car with the unemployed, seeing the way the Great Depression took the heart out of his stepfather, going off to the navy during the war and witnessing its terrible aftermath. As a young reporter he has a hilarious encounter with Huey Long when that smart, dangerous man was the Kingfish of Louisiana. He has breakfast with a hangman in a prison near New Orleans and witnesses the death of a small-time gangster in the electric chair in Sing Sing. He interviews a variety of celebrities, from the writer Will Durant to the comic genius Jimmy Durante. He describes a marvelous afternoon in the 1950s with the songwriter Irving Berlin, who almost never gave interviews, and a heated encounter with a homegrown New York anti-Semite who thought Hitler was right. As a feature writer for the now-vanished *New York World-Telegram & Sun*, he covered fires and murders and a terrible plane crash in New York. He never becomes the calloused newspaper veteran, sworn to the impossible codes of dispassionate objectivity; he expresses what he could never write in a newspaper: his horror, his fear, his uncertainty, his revulsion. And, over and over again, day after day, he tries to make sense of what he has witnessed.

But the diary is not simply a record of what he covered and who he met. In what Mann calls "the prayer-like communion" of the diary, he also tells his own story, as it happens, unmediated by nostalgia or the facile, treacherous editing of time. His need for love is a constant theme across the decades. His parents divorced when he was twenty months old, and for the rest of his life he searched for a father figure, an older man who had attained some wisdom. But he never found what he was looking for. He tried to connect with a professor in college and, decades later, with the philosopher John Dewey, and along the way, many others. But most of his father figures were dead, living on in books. In the diaries, we find another connecting theme: a man learning to be his own father.

The need for love drove him to a string of youthful romances, encounters in bars, unabashed expressions of longing for women. All are recorded with a kind of baffled naïveté. He lists his favorite songs, as if each reminded him of a woman; he describes the talents of his young women for kissing and, finally, for sex. Watching himself watching himself, he agonizes over the need to choose between women while hoping that they will choose him. He gets engaged to a young woman from Mississippi, but she breaks the engagement to marry an engineer. He falls in love with another young woman, a musician, and on the eve of World War II, he marries her. They have a daughter. He worries about the war but has been told he will not be drafted because he has a hernia. He loves his daughter and believes he is happy. Alas, the hernia is not a hernia; he is drafted in

1943, goes off to boot camp in the West, carrying with him a copy of *The Brothers Karamazov*. The diary is forbidden; so is Dostoyevski. He sends letters home to his wife instead of writing in his diary. He is enraged by what he considers to be mindless, dehumanizing discipline. As a proud atheist, he is angered by the navy's rule that the only permitted book is the Bible. Boot camp ends. He comes home on a brief leave before being assigned to the Pacific, and his wife asks him for a divorce. The moment is shocking to the reader of the entry; a half-century later, Ellis is still baffled and hurt.

The divorce is postponed until after the war, but Ellis is miserable. Then in 1947, he comes to New York, when that city was a great big wonderful town. He has a job as a reporter and feature writer for the *World-Telegram & Sun*, one of seven New York dailies. The city itself seems to cure his personal grief. "I should have been born here," he exults in the diary. After work, he roams bars and bookshops. He makes friends. He meets a wonderful woman named Ruth Kraus, who works as an executive secretary for the *Herald-Tribune*. He marries her. They are, by the testimony of the diary entries, deliriously happy together. Sometimes he drinks too much, in mind-obliterating binges. Sometimes he is frustrated by the limitations of newspaper writing and gives in to anger. His beloved Ruthie always stands by him. The years move swiftly; their details, some banal, some hilarious, go into the diary. When Ellis quits the newspaper, enraged by a humiliating clash with an editor, he sits down and goes to work writing *The Epic of New York City*, the best one-volume history of the metropolis. Ruthie helps in the project, doing research, typing, even taking dictation from Ellis. He feels his talent and his life growing; watching himself watching himself, he makes elaborate plans for future work. Then, in the most harrowing entries of this selection, his wife, as the Irish say, dies on him.

He is beyond consolation. He weeps, drinks, rages. He stops seeing cherished friends. For the first time in his life, he has writer's block. He begins to go to pieces. And then the diary leads him out of the darkness, the diary that has been the metronome of his life. He chooses to live.

In the almost three decades that pass after the death of Ruth Kraus, the palette of the diary grows darker. Ellis is searching now for meaning. The atheist becomes an agnostic. He explores mysticism. He gives up alcohol but starts smoking pot; his accounts of marijuana visions are among the best in the literature of mind-altering drugs. He also looks outward and broods about the decline of his country and the world. Racism, greed, incivility, violence: all are on the increase. He loathes Richard Nixon, hates the bullying American style in international affairs. His love affair with New York begins to cool. Bookstores close. Friends are assaulted. A young woman, the daughter of a friend, comes to visit him and is robbed at knifepoint outside his door as she leaves. In the Reagan era, homeless men drift through the streets; he gives some of them his old coats, but even his liberal friends have begun to grow calluses around the heart.

He examines the erosions of age: his paunch, his lined face, his short-ness of breath from emphysema. But desire remains alive. At seventy, he has a sexual affair with a woman half his age. At eighty, he sees a woman with beautiful legs in a restaurant and wishes he were forty. He has become known now for his diary. Interviewers come to see him. He wor-ries, publicly amd privately, about the fate of his diary and his vast library. In the search for meaning, he reads the eighteen volumes of the work of Carl Jung and turns back to the classics, to the Greeks, to Marcus Aurelius. He utters to himself the most familiar human lament, that life had gone by "so fast, so fast." In one startling image, he says that "death looks like a ship emerging from fog."

But these diaries will survive the death of their author, whenever that happens, and because so many of their pages are about him, Eddie Ellis will survive too. They are a great resource for historians, of course, but they have another value: like certain great novels, they speak intimately to the reader and allow that reader to live for a while in another person's shoes. To be sure, they don't compare in literary insight to the journals of André Gide or the notebooks of Henry James. They don't contain the tormented insights found in the diaries of Cesare Pavese, or display the dedicated industry of Arnold Bennett, the pathos of Anne Frank, the evil brilliance of Joseph Goebbels, to mention only a few of the century's most famous diar-ists. Eddie Ellis was not an insider in the lurid theater of great interna-tional affairs, as was, for example, Count Galeazzo Ciano, Mussolini's son-in-law and foreign minister, and dozens of other statesmen and gener-als who left their diaries to history. He wasn't involved in a literary revolu-tion, as were Virginia Woolf and Ezra Pound. Eddie Ellis is an ordinary American who worked at the newspaper trade and has lived a long and decent life, sometimes with ringside tickets for the big show. That is no small accomplishment.

If his diaries have an American precedent, it can be found in the nine-teenth century, in the great diary-making enterprises of Philip Hone and George Templeton Strong. They, too, were decent men and New Yorkers, trying to make sense of the dailiness of their lives. Much of what we know about their time—about the way human beings actually lived—we know from them. There are human beings not yet born who will be helped in understanding our times through the diaries of Edward Robb Ellis. That is his accomplishment. That is his triumph.

New York
February 1995

PREFACE

This is the story of my life and times as told in my diary from 1927 to 1995. I was born in 1911. This means I am 83 years old as I write these lines.

I have kept my diary 67 years, or more than 24,000 days.

It has more than 20 million words. The *Encyclopedia Brittanica* has 44 million words. This book represents about 1 percent of the entire diary.

As a newspaper reporter I saw interesting events and met famous people. As a man I met thousands of people socially and wrote about most of them. My diary contains the plots of scores of short stories and dozens of novels.

I worked for newspapers and wire services in New Orleans, Oklahoma City, Peoria, Chicago, and New York. During World War II I edited a navy newspaper on Okinawa. Most of my life has been lived in New York City.

I am driven by curiosity. I want to know everything about everything, but realize this is an impossible dream. I always carry pen and paper to jot notes to use when I type my journal. I look and I listen and I pay attention to details.

There is a character named Autolycus in *The Winter's Tale*. Shakespeare calls him "a snapper-up of unconsidered trifles." This is what I call myself. However, I agree with Goethe, who said there is no such thing as a trifle. A single detail may reveal the universal in the particular.

To write this book I had to read my diary and thus relive my life in more detail than is possible with most people. I was astonished at how much I had forgotten. I felt anguished by my many sins.

I have not changed facts to make myself look better, although I did try to improve my style. Years ago I enjoyed the diary of Anais Nin. Recently, though, I learned she was a liar who wrote many untruths. I felt betrayed. I agree with the many writers who say it is the duty of the artist to tell the truth.

This does not mean, however, that I will wallow in my sins to produce a sensational book. Nonetheless, within these pages you will learn: I drank too much, became an alcoholic, gave up booze. I smoked too much, now suffer from emphysema, gave up cigarets. I got stoned on marijuana, became fascinated with mysticism, never used any hard drugs. I had 18 months of psychoanalysis.

When I was a reporter all reporters were underpaid because journalism was so exciting that a publisher could easily replace any man who quit. My career was no more spectacular than those of other big-city reporters, but I kept a diary and they didn't.

I remember . . .

Barbra Streisand and I sat alone in a bar on 8th Avenue in Manhattan . . . Cary Grant telephoned me at my home . . . I chatted with Grace Kelly . . . I saw Helen Hayes clutch to her breast one of the books I wrote . . . I spent an afternoon with Irving Berlin, helped Jimmy Durante fill out a form in the marriage license bureau . . . was a guest of Mrs. Clark Gable at her husband's ranch . . .

I watched Mae West ogle Mr. America . . . I danced with Miss America . . . Henry Ford and I exchanged a few words . . . I broke my foot covering a subway accident in Manhattan and talked with a man who was in love with the Brooklyn Bridge . . .

I flunked out of college but went back and got my degree . . . I was fired from newspaper jobs but always got better ones . . . I covered bloody auto accidents and airplane crashes, listened to insane people in mental hospitals . . . I flew in a B-24 over Korea and lived through a typhoon with wind blowing at 200 miles an hour . . . As a college student I touched the arm of President Franklin D. Roosevelt . . . later got drunk with his son Elliott . . . without meaning to, used Eleanor Roosevelt as a messenger . . . I shook hands with General Douglas MacArthur in his suite in the Waldorf Towers, was astonished when an emperor's son lit my cigaret, spent an afternoon with a Bowery bum . . .

I took morning walks with President Harry Truman, interviewed President Herbert Hoover in his apartment in the Waldorf Towers, watched Dwight Eisenhower inaugurated as president of Columbia University, covered a speech made by President John F. Kennedy in the Waldorf-Astoria hotel . . .

I listened to a woman confess to murder one foggy morning in a police station in New Orleans . . . spent an evening with Huey Long . . . watched cops chase hungry people during the Depression . . . covered the trial of bank robber Willie Sutton, witnessed an electrocution at Sing Sing . . .

Edward R. Murrow and I swapped stories over drinks in a cocktail lounge, Pete Hamill and I discussed writing in my home, I watched Norman Mailer sign copies of one of his books, I sat 20 feet from Toscanini as he conducted the NBC Symphony Orchestra in Carnegie Hall, and I caricatured E. E. Cummings in his home in Greenwich Village . . .

Nothing interests me so much as the human mind. For this reason I am fascinated by something Mark Twain wrote in his autobiography:

The last quarter of a century of my life has been pretty constantly and faithfully devoted to the study of the human race—that is to say, the study of myself, for in my individual person I am the entire human race compacted together. I have found that there is no ingredient of the race which I do not possess in either a small way or a large way . . .

The shades of difference between other people and me serve to make variety and prevent monotony, but that is all; broadly speaking, we are all alike; and so by studying myself carefully and comparing myself with other people and noting the divergences I have been enabled to acquire a knowledge of the human race. . . .

Edward Robb Ellis
New York
November 1994

ACKNOWLEDGMENTS

My wife, Ruth Kraus Ellis, helped me more than anyone else in my entire life. She was the wisest person I ever knew because she was the kindest person I ever knew. She was so generous she reminded me of a little girl standing by a country road, smiling, her apron filled with apples and giving them to every passerby. She died of a heart attack in 1965.

After her death I was buoyed up by the friendship and help of another kind lady, Selma Seskin Pezaro. She came down with Parkinson's disease and died a lingering death that finally ended in 1992.

The best editor I ever had was Boyd Lewis. He hired me for the Chicago bureau of the United Press, and he also did more than others to advance my career in journalism. An amateur artist, he painted me in oils; the portrait is at the University of Wyoming, where my diary was stored awhile.

I am indebted to Dr. Gene M. Gressley, former archivist at the University of Wyoming, for housing my diary in fireproof vaults and for analyzing its worth. I thank Ed Gildea, publisher and editor of *Diarist's Journal,* for publishing excerpts of my diary in his unique magazine. I am grateful to William G. Kerr, who has a doctorate in history from Cambridge University, for helping me realize the value of my diary.

The past few years I have been heartened and helped by my friend Peter F. Skinner, a man of quick sympathy and wide scholarship. I chose him to edit my journal after my death. He introduced me to Rita Rosenkranz, now my fond friend and literary agent. We three are a team.

I thank Philip Turner, senior editor at Kodansha America, for sensing the value of my diary when shown excerpts by Ms. Rosenkranz. He made this book possible.

I thank Laura Stein and Gene Wolsk for initiating the process that found a home for my diary. When I die it will become part of the Fales Library at New York University.

Here, in alphabetical order, are the names of others who helped me:

George N. Allen, Romare Bearden, Kathryn Ellis Burton, Robert Burton, Phyllis Calderaro, Carmen Capalbo, Walter Cowan, Claire Cox,

Deborah Crawford, Vara Crawford, Lorna Doone Dawson, Chris Downing, Jack Ellis, Virginia Ellis, Ellise Fuchs, Paul Good, Harry Gordon, Ken Gray, David Hall, Dr. Lionel Heiden, Herbert Kamm, Joseph Nathan Kane, Doris Wedge Kent, Jerry Lacy, Eliz Irwin Logan, Jim Lucas, Dr. Louis Marino, Jr., Colins MacLean, John McGuire, Paul Meskil, Jim Moran, June Morgan, Joe Peebles, Gabe Pressman, Carmen Quesada, Selwyn Raab, B. Michael Rubin, Thomas Sancton, Leslie Evan Schlytter, Sallie Shulman O'Donnell, Shirley Jones Shilgalis, Patricia B. Soliman, Janet Steinberg, Barbara Steinman, Joe Stocker, Chris Squires, Nace Strickland, Anna Walinska, Ed Wallace, Harvey Wang, Jack Waugh and Lucy Wind.

A Note to the Reader

I have changed the names of some people in this book to protect their privacy.

E.R.E.

A DIARY
OF THE
CENTURY

CHAPTER 1

I begin this book with what I wrote on my 50th birthday. I don't want you to wade through all the stuff I wrote when I was a teenage kid. I'll leave in just enough of it to let you know something about my background.

WEDNESDAY, FEBRUARY 22, 1961 ■ This is my 50th birthday. Today I became a half-century old in a universe five billion years old. I exist on a planet of 197 million square miles in a single galaxy amid billions of galaxies—a dot in space, a nanosecond in time.

Obviously, it is not of the slightest importance whether I pause to evaluate my life, but so strong is the ego of this atom I feel impelled to do so.

Dictating to my wife, Ruth, at her electric typewriter, I lounge on a green sofa in the study of our apartment on the 26th floor of the Hotel Master at 310 Riverside Drive in the city of New York, county of New York, state of New York, the federal republic of the United States, western hemisphere, earth, solar system, the universe.

I am five feet eight and a half inches tall and weigh 160 pounds. My ancestors were born in Wales, England, Scotland, and Ireland. Ellis is a Welsh name. I have a ruddy complexion, hazel eyes, brown hair, and a moustache flecked with white hairs. Only about half my teeth are my own; I think I still have all my marbles. I broke my right foot covering a subway accident and my belly is scarred by an appendectomy.

How do I feel upon becoming 50 years old? Surprised. Surprised that I should live so long. Surprised that it should seem so short. Surprised that I am not famous. Surprised that I should be surprised because I am not famous.

However, when I feel the years in my bones I do not feel them so painfully as I had feared I would. Once the second-best ballroom dancer at the University of Missouri, I'm no longer so graceful, although I still have a spring to my step and walk faster than most men by age. Blessed with high energy inherited from my father, I am quick and darting in my movements. I become tired faster than before, but my friends say I look 10 years younger than I am.

I was born at 5 A.M., Wednesday, February 22, 1911, in my paternal grandfather's Victorian house in Kewanee, Illinois, population 16,000, some 135 miles southwest of Chicago. Grandfather John Ellis was a millionaire, while my father was a playboy who squandered the family fortune. My parents separated when I was one year old and soon thereafter divorced. My elder sister, Kathryn, and I lived alone with our mother until she married a second time, when I was seven years old.

All my life I have been motivated by curiosity. I wonder why? My mother wasn't curious. Although my grandfather died before I was born, judging from what I've heard about him, read about him, and from the books he left, I think it possible I inherited my curiosity from him. Born in England of Welsh parents, he came to America alone when he was only 16 years old.

I was born across the street from the public library, and in my memory it remains my favorite spot in my home town. When I was six I learned to read. From the beginning, language seemed like magic to me. Recently I read that Freud said "words and magic were in the beginning one and the same thing, and even today words retain much of their magical power."

During the Christmas season of 1927, when I was a sophomore in high school, I hung out at the local "Y" with other kids my age. The weather was so harsh we played indoors, and after swimming and running and tumbling, we became bored. I suggested we hold a contest to see who could keep a diary the longest. My challenge was accepted by two of my friends. One wrote his diary for two weeks, the other three months, and here I am, still writing mine. It has taught me that one way to find the truth is to tell the truth.

At the age of 50 my mind is better than ever—surprise, surprise! I can concentrate with the intensity of a beam of sunshine focused through a magnifying glass. Guilt and passion disrupt my attention far less frequently. Slowly I begin to perceive the relationships among everything I have experienced and read. My analyses and judgments seem sounder than before. My curiosity burns brighter. Problems once mysterious now seem obvious.

And yet—! Every new answer breeds a dozen new questions. What I know, compared with what I do not know, is like a grain of sand by the sea. I am not sure whether there is any absolute. Recently I read that even the constancy of the speed of light is being questioned by physicists and astronomers. While I believe I am alive, I am unable to say exactly what this phrase means. Maybe the atoms now comprising my body existed before I was born, and maybe they will continue to exist after my body decays.

A few people consider me egotistical. Actually, I am humble. I was lucky to have been born with a fairly good mind, and I have spent years polishing this instrument I inherited. I'll admit I become impatient when confronted with ignorance. However, I know my limitations even better than I recognize my capabilities. At times I feel overwhelmed by my own ignorance.

I can find no meaning in life. I believe that the individual life can be suffused with meaning only through reciprocal love and work of one's choice. My wife is a more valuable person than I because she has an infinite capacity for loving others. She is a genius at loving. I am a genius at nothing. When she dies an ocean of tears will flow. I admire her without envying her.

When I was a boy of 14 I knew I wanted to become a reporter and then an author. Well, now I am an experienced reporter and next fall my first book will be published. The fact that I say *first* proves that I am optimistic about my career. I believe that the next decade of my life will become the most fruitful one. Perhaps my only really valuable creation is this diary.

My 10 months of psychoanalysis have helped me learn how to forgive myself. I'm more at peace with myself now than at any time in the past. Nevertheless, I'm aware I haven't identified all my psychological conflicts, let alone resolved them. Bertrand Russell says there are three major conflicts: 1) Man against his environment; 2) man against man; 3) man against himself. In my opinion, the conflict of man with himself is the most troublesome.

Carved on the temple of Delphi was "Know thyself." I think I know myself better than most people because I spend more time studying myself than anything else. A diarist is a writer who watches himself watching himself. If I can learn to know myself well, then I'll be able to know others as well.

Human beings are more alike than different. By paying close attention to whatever I feel and think, I can learn what others feel and think. Fortunately, it is the differences among people that make them interesting.

Now that I've shed much of my guilt, now that I am less rigid about what I expect from myself, I get along better with others because I expect less from them, too. Life hurts. For years I've realized I'm an eccentric, without understanding exactly what I meant by this word. Now I know: An eccentric is one who insists upon being himself regardless of the opinion of others, provided he does not injure them or himself. If everyone in the world were as eccentric, meaning if everyone accepted himself, there would be no more war.

However, I am too much of a realist to believe that humanity ever will tolerate, let alone applaud, the uniqueness of every individual. Life is strife. War is normal. Peace is abnormal. In every seemingly peaceful meadow there is savage carnage occurring beneath every leaf. The only sane persons are those addicted to reality.

Both the teetotaler and the alcoholic have compulsive personalities. I deplore the fact that I am a compulsive drinker. While I do not drink every day, every two or three weeks I begin drinking and cannot stop until I become drunk, often embarrassing Ruthie. I began therapy in the hope of curing my spree-drinking, and now I see some improvement. Now I am less an oak than a willow, in that under pressure I tend to bend rather than break.

While I no longer demand perfection from myself, I still am a compulsive worker. Of Puritan heritage, I have flouted almost every Puritanical ethic except the work ethic. I keep telling Ruthie that my ambition is not so much to become a famous author as to become a wise old man. What do I mean by this? I'm not sure. No longer do I expect greatness from myself. I just want to be myself.

Now that I have lived a half-century, do I have any regrets? Sure. I regret that I was slow to mature. I regret that I did not become a psychoanalyst. Although I am not sorry I decided to become a journalist, I wish that early on I had chosen to become a therapist. Why? Because nothing fascinates me so much as human nature.

We are left with two frontiers. One is outer space. The other is inner space. While I lack the interest and ability to probe outer space, I'm rather well equipped to probe the mysteries of the human mind.

My half-brother, an inventor with several patents to his credit, is perhaps the world's leading expert about shock absorbers. But he and I cannot communicate about them. I have no technical knowledge of his specialty. He cannot explain it in simple language. This is an example of the failure of communication between the specialist and the layman. This breakdown is spreading. It is as though nerve endings had lost touch with one another. For lack of communication we may come to the end of our civilization.

Civilization is a web of agreements among people. We call these agreements *institutions*. For example, there is the Roman Catholic Church, with millions of people around the world agreeing among themselves to honor the dogmas of this faith. The Australian aborigines also have their own agreements, their own institutions. In their own ways they are as civilized as we. An institutional agreement results in social rapport.

But wherever I look in the world I see agreements unravelling. Because of the population explosion, the technological revolution, the threat of nuclear holocaust, the maldistribution of wealth, greed and racism, there is a global increase in tensions—which may finally explode. I hope I will not be around when this explosion occurs. In some ways it is comforting to be 50 years old, to know that not too many years hence a little trap-door will open and deposit me in eternity.

1927

KEWANEE, ILLINOIS, HOG CAPITAL OF THE WORLD, TUESDAY, DECEMBER 27, 1927
■ *This was the first entry I ever wrote in my diary, misspelling and all.* ■
Well Christmas is past and everyone happy. I got a wristwatch, billfold, DeMolay pin, and the usual hetregeneous collection of sox, ties and hand-kerchiefs. Went to the students' dance at the Kewanee Club last night. Took Barbara. Not so hot. Had fun there, though. Am reading a book about the World War. Had trouble with Tom Pierce about ushering at the theater. All right now. I'm paid 25 cents afternoons and 50 cents evenings.

1928

SUNDAY, JANUARY 6, 1928 ■ In Congregational Sunday School this morning Mrs. Hayward asked each of us what we want to be when we grow up. I said that first I want to become a newspaper reporter and then an author.

FRIDAY, JANUARY 20, 1928 ■ When I was ten years old I got my first real job—taking papers out of the press in the basement of the *Kewanee Star-Courier*. I also delivered a paper route on my bicycle. I remember one day I had a cold. Just as I approached a house I had to spit. So what did I do? I threw the paper toward the street and spat on the front porch. Then I laughed so hard that I fell off my bike.

TUESDAY, JANUARY 24, 1928 ■ Gee, I've been keeping this diary nearly a month. That's a good start, isn't it? Today in school I saw Agnes and remembered the nite I had a date with her. She's keen looking! The weather was warm and we walked to that little park behind my house and sat on a bench behind bushes and began necking. Then, for the first time in my life, I kissed a girl's breast—and got a nosebleed. Oh, gosh, it was awful! I dripped red blood all over her white breast! I wanted to die! But Agnes said it was okay and pulled out a hankie and wiped my blood off her skin. Oh, it was terrible!

WEDNESDAY, FEBRUARY 1, 1928 ■ Stayed home tonight and finished reading *The Plastic Age*. Gee, this book is so different from any other I've ever read—and I've read walls of books in the Kewanee Public Library. It's pleasing to sit here all alone in my room, just reading. I don't know what I'd do if it wasn't for my books. They're like periscopes I use to look beyond the horizon and this dinky burg!

THURSDAY, FEBRUARY 2, 1928 ■ Today is Grandpa Robb's 69th birthday. He's really a good old scout! When I was a kid I'd show up at a certain drug store at eleven o'clock because I knew Gramps would be there drinking a malted milk. I'd pretend I just happened to drop in, but he would ask whether I wanted a malt and I'd think a moment and then say yes. Grandpa doesn't swear or smoke or drink booze. He's a Puritan and so, of course, is my mother. They seem to believe that if something feels good it's bad. The way I understand the history of this town, it was settled by Puritans from Connecticut.

MONDAY, FEBRUARY 13, 1928 ■ Eddie Meier is one of my best friends. Lately, he and I have been doing something interesting. Every Sunday we go to a different church and take notes of the sermon preached by the minister or priest. After the service is over, Eddie and I go to the den in the basement of his house, where we study our notes. The stuff said from the pulpits doesn't make any sense. The hell with religion! Eddie and I have become atheists.

TUESDAY, FEBRUARY 28, 1928 ■ I don't play the piano, of course, but today I sat down on the piano bench and began fooling around with the keys, striking chords. Suddenly I struck a chord in a minor key. Even I know a minor chord when I hear it. The funny thing is that the sound of that chord reminded me of the color brown. Then I was reminded of the Brownies—cartoon characters I read about when I was a kid. What in hell happened?

TUESDAY, MARCH 20, 1928 ■ Tonight in the Peerless Theater I saw Greta Garbo in *The Divine Woman*. Oh, it was wonderful, simply wonderful. The acting was perfect. Greta Garbo is hot stuff.

MONDAY, MARCH 26, 1928 ■ Not many people came to the theater tonight so I didn't have to do much ushering. All I did was lie on the sofa and think. I do a lot of thinking lately, imagining things. I guess I take myself seriously while no one else does—except maybe Janet. I felt rather blue and don't know why. When I feel this way, I easily could commit suicide.

MONDAY, APRIL 2, 1928 ▦ Mamma didn't ask me where I was last night. Maybe she didn't know how late I got in 'cause I took off my shoes & tip-toed upstairs. At school today I was nominated for editor of our annual, *The Kewanite*. It's one of the highest offices in school—president of the Student Federation, president of the senior class & editor of *The Kewanite*. I sure hope I get it!

WEDNESDAY, APRIL 11, 1928 ▦ At school this morning we voted on *The Kewanite* staff, and I won on a vote of 70 to 37. Gee, I'm glad I'm going to be editor.

SATURDAY, APRIL 21, 1928 ▦ This is a great day, a great day! Today marks the beginning of a second composition book of my diary. As yet no living person has gazed upon the pages of my diary although several persons have asked for that privilege. At first I put down only the things I wouldn't be ashamed of, but as time went on I began to record all, or nearly all, of my thoughts, actions and desires, be they good or bad.

SUNDAY, APRIL 29, 1928 ▦ While I was visiting Knox College in Galesburg a guy from Rock Island sent me a letter and Mamma opened it. When I got home she gave me hell because it had a dirty joke in it. I don't think she has any right to open my mail.

TUESDAY, MAY 1, 1928 ▦ I'm writing down all the words I don't know the meaning of, so I can look them up later.

THURSDAY, JULY 12, 1928 ▦ Well, I've really done *It!* Borrowed Dale's car, wasn't as great as expected. Some experience, though. Can't say more here.

FRIDAY, JULY 13, 1928 ▦ Like a dummy, I stuck my diary under my bed to let the ink dry. I had just written about last night's sexual adventure. Used clothes pins to keep open the pages of the composition book. Well, today Mamma dusted under my bed and found my diary and read it, read about what I did last night. She screamed: "You're totally worthless! You're totally worthless!" I feel awful!

TUESDAY, AUGUST 21, 1928 ■ My diary is just about the only hobby I have. My faithfulness to it for nearly eight months, without a day lost, proves it. Nothing I have ever done has proved so fascinating as the daily recording of not only events but the psychological side of my life. At this stage of life everything appears strange and peculiar. I am only now starting to think as I have never thought before. All the mystery and why of everything is disturbing, to say the least, and I constantly am finding myself immeshed in the tangle of circumstances called life. George Meredith struck the keynote of our perplexities when he cried: "Ah, what a dusty answer gets the soul when hot for certainties in this, our Life!"

TUESDAY, NOVEMBER 6, 1928 ■ Presidential election day. Herbert Hoover, Republican, vs. Al Smith, Democrat. Everyone all hot and bothered. Before going to school I walked to the *Star-Courier* and asked Mr. Upton for a job as a reporter. He said he might be able to use me this evening when the election returns start coming in. I was there with Jimmy Fulton at the time. When we got bulletins from the Associated Press we used thick black pens to write the returns on hunks of newsprint, which we hung in the front window. A crowd of maybe 500 people gathered in front of the *Courier* building so I suggested to Mr. Upton that I circulate among them, listen to what they are saying and then write a story about it. He said okay. I drifted through groups of townspeople and listened to their chatter. Sure were some crazy remarks made. Saw one fight. When the mob left I walked up to the newsroom and started to type my story with one finger, but Mrs. Upton saw me and shoved me aside and told me to dictate to her. I did. She's a swell lady. Mr. Adler, the editor, saw my article and said I had good possibilities as a reporter. Also said he would put the write-up in Wednesday's paper.

WEDNESDAY, NOVEMBER 7, 1928 ■ Right after school I ran to the *Courier* & got a paper from the press to see if my article was in it. Sure, enough, there it was on page 5. The headline read *Crowd Gossip as Interesting as Election.* Grandpa Robb called to congratulate me. My very first newspaper story! Herbert Hoover won the election.

MONDAY, DECEMBER 3, 1928 ■ This evening Barney Lundberg drove me down to Peoria so that we might see and hear a talkie movie. It is called *The Singing Fool* and it stars Al Jolson. We went to the Madison Theater and had to wait in line about 20 minutes & then could get only single seats. This is the first feature-length movie with sound that I ever heard.

Gee, it sure is different and wonderful! Al Jolson sang "Sonny Boy" and "I'm Sitting on Top of the World" and other songs. Man, how he can sing! He half talks & half sings it, getting very sentimental and dramatic. All minor noises, like the snapping of fingers & the clapping of hands, were distinctly heard.

THURSDAY, DECEMBER 27, 1928 ▪ *This entry was written in red ink.* ▪ Well, I have accomplished my one great purpose—to keep a diary one whole year without a single day missed! And if I can do that thing so faithfully for one year, surely I should be able to continue it the rest of my life.

1929

MONDAY, JANUARY 14, 1929 ▪ Some of my favorite songs right now are: *Dream House . . . That's How I Feel About You, Sweetheart . . . I Faw Down Go Boom! . . . Avalon Town . . . Blue Shadows . . . Spell of the Blues . . . Sally of My Dreams.*

WEDNESDAY, JANUARY 16, 1929 ▪ I have been intending to have the five volumes of my first diary bound professionally but haven't had the money to do it. Mamma read in one volume, and you know the hell that caused! So, until I can have them bound, I've tied them together with string and then dropped hot tallow on the knot. This was not so much to keep them together but a means of knowing if Mamma or anyone else reads them. I read some of this diary before sealing it and it struck me that in only a few years much of what I wrote will seem silly & childish to me. This should not be so, but perhaps it will. Therefore, Edward Robb Ellis of the future, whatever age you may attain, whatever honors may be yours, whatever depths you may sink to, whatever your general condition, please remember that all I now write & have written has been done in an earnest spirit and with the attitude of a fellow my age. Don't laugh at any of it, for it *was* you and *shall be* you until this diary is destroyed. I mean each and every word of this. At this period of my life (17 yrs. old) I am beginning to form a philosophy and creed and of course some of my conceptions and ideas are faulty, but you must consider all this. So please remember, Mr. Ellis, that this Eddie Ellis did his best. Judge accordingly.

FRIDAY, FEBRUARY 15, 1929 ▪ The crime wave in Chicago is something terrible now, seven men being killed yesterday by a gang. They were lined up against a garage wall and executed with shotguns and machine guns.

Joe Kavolus actually saw a gangster killed by another one when he was in Chicago last summer.

This was the infamous "St. Valentine's Day massacre." Seven members of the George (Bugs) Moran gang were rubbed out in a garage on North Clark Street as mobsters vied for control of the bootlegging trade. In 1929 Chicago had 498 reported homicides.

MONDAY, MARCH 4, 1929 ■ Herbert Hoover became President today. I ran home from school this noon and heard him sworn into office and part of his inaugural address—and then the radio went dead!

TUESDAY, MARCH 19, 1929 ■ Hemming's dad let him use the family Ford and he got two other guys and me and drove to Davenport, Iowa. We ate a good dinner that cost 30 cents each. Then we went to the Capital Theater, where we saw five acts of vaudeville and a movie—all for 25 cents apiece.

SATURDAY, APRIL 6, 1929 ■ Today I shaved for the first time.

SATURDAY, APRIL 13, 1929 ■ At the Peerless Theater we're getting ready for talking pictures.

TUESDAY, APRIL 30, 1929 ■ I'm fascinated by high places. Ever since I was a kid I've climbed to the top of water towers and stores and every church in town, I believe. Danger is exciting. Well, last summer, down on the south side of town, a new and very tall water tower was built, and I hadn't climbed it yet. Late this afternoon I walked down there. After sneaking past a watchman I began climbing the narrow ladder and at first it was scary. It seemed to take a long time to reach the thin balcony around the base of the tank itself. I edged my way to the western side just as the sun started to sink behind the horizon. I felt flushed with joy because I was alone and higher than Kewanee, and then I remembered something from *The Rubaiyat of Omar Khayyam.* In Islamic nations muezzins stand in tall minarets to pray. Okay, so I'll pray! I stood erect, held my arms as high as possible, palms to the west, and prayed aloud, "Oh, when in hell am I going to get the hell out of this jerkwater town?"

FRIDAY, MAY 31, 1929 ■ Tonight I graduated from Kewanee High School. We assembled in the social room and marched to the gym at 8:00 all garbed in gray caps and gowns. Scholastically I did not cover myself with glory, for I graduated 49th in a class of 115 kids. However, I was the cheer-

leader, was voted the most active boy in my class, was editor of *The Kewanite* and learned this evening that I won the $50 Lay Prize. This is given to
the boy who "made the greatest improvement upon his opportunity while
a student in Kewanee High School." I really don't think I deserve it, but
appreciate it nonetheless. When my name was announced I looked down
into the audience and saw Mamma. She was crying. Maybe now she
doesn't think I am totally worthless.

MONDAY, JUNE 17, 1929   ▨   This morning I went over to see Fred Glidden,
because he goes to the University of Missouri. It has the first school of
journalism ever established in this country and, of course, I want to study
journalism. Fred is a student in that school. He gave me a good description of it.

*Fred Glidden became a famous Western novelist, using the pen name of
Luke Short. He was one of President Eisenhower's favorite authors.*

WEDNESDAY, JUNE 19, 1929   ▨   For a long time now the thing I wanted most
is a big dictionary. The one I own now is greatly inferior. I'm trying to put
together five bucks to buy a really good dictionary. Today I had to go to the
hospital to have my tonsils taken out. Doc Oliver did the dirty work, using
only a local anesthetic. He jabbed me four or five times before he hit the
right spot. I was scared but don't believe it showed. I'm afraid that I am a
coward.

THURSDAY, JULY 11, 1929   ▨   Got a letter from the University of Missouri
stating definitely that I am eligible to enter there on September 9. After
reading the letter I bounded up, jumping, I'll bet, three feet in the air. All
sorts of visions are possessing me, as to how the campus will look and how
I'll like it.

FRIDAY, SEPTEMBER 5, 1929   ▨   Last day at home. Spent most of the day
packing my big trunk. Went to town in the afternoon to say a few goodbyes
and then some at the school, too. Excited about going to college, of
course! The folks drove me to the station.

CHAPTER 2

UNIVERSITY OF MISSOURI, SUNDAY, SEPTEMBER 7, 1929 ■ This morning two fellows took me out in their car and offered me the chance to pledge Kappa Sigma. I didn't rush into it, but asked all about it—expenses, etc. Finally I consented and was given a button and then all the fellows congratulated me.

SATURDAY, SEPTEMBER 14, 1929 ■ Haase and Schaff barged into my room, pushed me into a chair, made me take a big chew from a plug of tobacco, then light a cigaret. They ordered me to chew, spit, smoke and talk, all at the same time. I swallowed some of the tobacco juice and vomited about six times.

This hazing of freshmen is so stupid and cruel that I should have stormed out of the fraternity house bellowing "Screw you!" at those sadistic bastards. I did not do so because my ego was so weak I wanted to be liked and accepted. I also let myself be paddled. However, when I became a sophomore, I refused to paddle any freshmen. It did not take long for me to become disenchanted with fraternity life.

FRIDAY, OCTOBER 4, 1929 ■ My second date with Cora. Not only does she have a great shape, but she has the most beautiful lips I've ever seen. She does not use lipstick because her lips really are as red as cherries. We strolled onto the campus and sat down on a bench under trees and began necking. Cora knows how to kiss better than any other girl I ever knew. She also seems to have power over me, because she took my hand and led it up to her breast.

THURSDAY, OCTOBER 10, 1929 ■ Nervous as hell in classes. I'm flunking Spanish and astronomy while getting high marks in English and writing essays for other guys at a buck a throw. Such psychic turmoil! Near our frat house there is a bridge with steel girders and today I walked along the thin railing—a damned dangerous thing to do.

FRIDAY, OCTOBER 18, 1929   Fathers of Kappa Sig members have been invited here for the weekend and the house is full of men. Wish I had a real dad to bring here.

MONDAY, OCTOBER 21, 1929   Today I read something by Seneca: "Think how long you have done the same things; a man may wish to die, not so much because he is brave or wretched, but because he is tired of living."

TUESDAY, OCTOBER 29, 1929   I'm just a damned fool in more ways than one! For one thing, I'm spending money as though I were rich. For another thing, I don't study. This afternoon I was in my pajamas writing letters when Cora called and asked me to meet her, which I did. When I got back I tried to study Spanish but grew discouraged with my lack of concentration. Damn, how I hate Spanish!

This was the day of the Wall Street crash that triggered the Great Depression, but I was so self-centered that my diary doesn't even mention this historic event. After my parents were divorced, my father gave me money which my mother saved for my college education, but soon my hometown bank failed and I was left penniless. I had to start working my way through college by waiting tables, jerking sodas, and clerking in a book store. This was what I wrote on that memorable day.

MONDAY, NOVEMBER 11, 1929   This is Armistice Day. The World War ended 11 years ago today. This evening I was in such a peculiar mood that I walked to Stephens College, a junior college for girls, to serenade them. Choosing one dormitory near the street, I leaned against a lamp post, stuck my hands in my pockets and began singing. I opened up with *Am I Blue,* went to *St. Louis Blues* and on to *Big City Blues.* Dozens of girls came to the windows, leaned out to look down at me, then applauded. I asked if there were any requests. One voice pleaded for *The Pagan Love Song* and later another girl wanted to hear *One Alone.* I sang both requests and then sang *Ah! Sweet Mystery of Life.* The girls clapped after each selection. Suddenly I saw an elderly man watching me from across the street. Guessing that he was the college prexy, I asked whether I had better move along, but he said I might sing one more number. Instead, I sang four more ballads and then bowed to my hidden but highly appreciative audience.

KEWANEE, ILLINOIS, THURSDAY, DECEMBER 26, 1929   Home for the holidays. Got Gramp's car tonite to have a date with Barbara. I drove to Galva and parked on a side road, where we made love. Afterwards, as I turned the car around, it got stuck in a ditch and I had to rouse a farmer & his three sons to push us out for $1.

1930

THURSDAY, MARCH 6, 1930 ■ Had a conference with both my Spanish and geology teachers. Guess I'm flunking both subjects.

SATURDAY, MARCH 8, 1930 ■ I have three ambitions: I want to see the world, become a successful author, and fall in love.

WEDNESDAY, MARCH 19, 1930 ■ I brought Dorothy Edwards to a dinner in our Kappa Sig house this evening. We decided to see a movie, so I called a cab and we got in and headed west, then turned north on Garth St. Dorothy and I were chatting, so we did not see what happened—another car crashed head-on into our taxi. Suddenly we were thrown to one side of the car and next, jolted to the floor.

I grabbed Dorothy and screamed: "Are you hurt? Are you hurt?"

Her eyes were dazed. She said: "No, I'm all right! I'm all right!"

I opened the door on the righthand side and stepped out—and fell. My right knee had been injured. Dorothy managed to crawl out. It was true that she had not been hurt. She was worried about me because already I was in intense pain. Our cab driver ran away. Jim McKay happened to drive up with a date, so we asked him to take us back to the frat house.

There I hobbled upstairs, took off my pants and looked at my knee. There was nothing to be seen on the skin, but I was unable to straighten my leg and the pain got worse. Charlie Wilde rubbed liniment on the knee, told me I had to go to the hospital, helped me on with my pants and back downstairs. Dorothy went with us to the hospital. No doctor was on duty. A nurse advised me to check myself in and go to bed, but I insisted upon going to the movie theater. We saw Janet Gaynor and Charles Parrell in *Sunny Side Up*. Sure glad we didn't let my knee keep us away. Took another cab home.

The next day the pain became so intense that I went to the university hospital to be examined by doctors and have X-rays taken. I was told I had to have an operation on my knee, so a couple of days later I underwent surgery. Before I emerged from the general anesthetic, they put a plaster cast on my right leg from the hip down to my foot. The next three months I walked on crutches, becoming so expert with them that I could tap-dance on them. For awhile I was unable to attend classes so later, when I flunked out, I rationalized that this accident was to blame.

MONDAY, MAY 12, 1930 ▨ A week or so ago the Pi Phi house mother caught one of her girls having sex on the kitchen table with some Sigma Nu fellow. She demanded that the girl be expelled from the sorority at the next chapter meeting. But when the matter was aired at that meeting, 18 girls stood up to reveal that they were not virgins and that the girl had done nothing wrong but get caught. I admire them.

THURSDAY, MAY 29, 1930 ▨ I have flunked out of college!
Part of it was due to my absence from classes because of my bum leg. But—I never really did study.
I'm out—a failure.
Laugh, Eddie, laugh.
I hate like hell to have to go back to Kewanee, because everybody in town will know I flunked out of college.

KEWANEE, ILLINOIS, MONDAY, JUNE 2, 1930 ▨ Harvey Keach called and asked me to see him at his confectionery store. When I got there he offered me a job at $14 a week, so now I'll be a soda jerker, hey, hey. I'm glad to get a job, because jobs are scarce these days.

FRIDAY, JUNE 13, 1930 ▨ I'm trying to read *The Art of Thinking* by Abbe Ernest Dimnet, but it's pretty hard going. I'm also reading *The Mansions of Philosophy* by Will Durant.

SUNDAY, JUNE 15, 1930 ▨ Barney has a radio in his car. Certainly was a novelty to listen to music as we rode along.

WEDNESDAY, JUNE 25, 1930 ▨ In Keach's this morning Joe told me about an affair he had with Phyllis. He knocked her up and then took her to Galesburg where she had an abortion costing $30. I asked what he'd have done if she had not agreed to this operation. He said; "I'd have killed her!" When he saw the look of horror in my eyes he said he didn't really mean what he said—but I'm not sure.

THURSDAY, AUGUST 28, 1930 ▨ This nation is in a furor. Instead of the predicted prosperity, there is a business depression that affects everyone. Food prices are the lowest they have been in six years, but jobs are scarce.

Unemployment is the chief problem with which our government has to contend. Men are being laid off everywhere, and riots and bread lines are the result. When I was at the University of Missouri I was unaware of this, but now I am back in Kewanee, a manufacturing center, and I see just how hard times are. I was beginning to worry about my reduced job at Harvey's, but today I got a job clerking in Roy's Clothing Store.

SUNDAY, NOVEMBER 30, 1930 ■ Eddie Meier and I share a new hobby. We sit in his den in the basement of his house, and there we blow soap bubbles. They're fascinating because they are so beautiful.

MONDAY, DECEMBER 15, 1930 ■ Today my sister Doris is four years old. I gave her two small gifts & was more than rewarded when her sweet little face lit up and she lisped: "Thank you, Eddie!"

1931

THURSDAY, JANUARY 1, 1931 ■ This is the fourth year I've kept my diary. It has gotten me into trouble with my mother, who found and read only the worst parts. Now she thinks I'm a sinner roaring down the primrose path to Hell! She is a woman of strict morals and she doesn't understand me. She divorced my father when I was only 21 months old, so all my life I've had to live without the influence and love of a father. Mother made a sissy out of me. She kept me so clean and neat that she and her women friends called me "The Candy Kid." I hated it!

THURSDAY, JANUARY 8, 1931 ■ Eddie Meier said he began keeping a diary because I urged him to do so. Johnny Appleseed roamed the Ohio valley scattering seeds that became apple trees. In the minds of my friends I plant the idea of keeping a diary.

UNIVERSITY OF MISSOURI, FRIDAY, JANUARY 23, 1931 ■ Well, I'm back on the campus again and tonight I had a date with Cora. Lousy trip getting here.

MONDAY, MARCH 2, 1931 ■ I'm reading the life of Buddha in *The Outline of History* and on my desk I have a cheap metal statue of him. Here's what he believed:

    1—Birth and death bring grief, and life is vain.
    2—The vanity of life is caused by desire.
    3—The only cure is to kill desire.

FRIDAY, MAY 29, 1931   ▦   Here are some of my favorite songs: *Little Joe* . . . *Do You Want to Take a Walk?* . . . *I Surrender, Dear* . . . *The One Man Band* . . . *Out of Nowhere* . . . *Dream a Little Dream of Me* . . . *The Waltz You Saved for Me* . . . *Just a Gigolo* . . . *Reaching for the Moon* . . . *Dark Eyes* . . . *With All My Heart.*

SATURDAY, MAY 30, 1931   ▦   End of the semester, and I survived. Got an M (medium) in geology and Spanish.

PEORIA, ILLINOIS, TUESDAY, JUNE 2, 1931   ▦   I got a ride from Columbia to East St. Louis and from there I hitchhiked to Peoria, where my sister Kay works in the public library. A friend of hers got me a job with the Palmolive Soap Co. I'm one of six guys who will walk from house to house handing out soap coupons to housewives. We have a crew manager and we'll go to several towns in Illinois. I'm lucky to get any kind of job in these hard times.

TUESDAY, JUNE 9, 1931   ▦   We began in Peoria and walked about 25 miles in the heat. I've been through the slums of Peoria and its whorehouse district. One of our guys had a knife pulled on him. The slums are appalling! If I had to live the way these people do, I'd commit suicide. For my week's work I was paid $19.25.

MONDAY, JUNE 22, 1931   ▦   When I knocked on the screen door of one home the housewife appeared and took one look at me and squealed: "Ohhh, my Gawd! You're Douglas Fairbanks, Jr.!" I said: "No, ma'am, I'm not. Other people have said I look like him, but I work for the Palmolive Soap Company, and . . ."

SPRINGFIELD, ILLINOIS, SATURDAY, JUNE 27, 1931   ▦   Our soap coupons failed to arrive, so we didn't work today. I found a peach of a bookstore and had a long talk about books with the girl who works there. She is very intelligent. When I asked for a date, she said she could see me tomorrow.

SUNDAY, JUNE 28, 1931   ▦   I walked to Daphne's home and found her waiting for me. She owns a Whippet roadster named for some Greek goddess—I forget which one. Anyway, according to Daphne, this goddess lived her life in hell. We drove to the public swimming pool where I tried to impress my date with some fancy high-diving. When dusk came, we drove back to her house to sit on the porch swing and talk, talk, talk. I didn't touch her. When it was time for me to leave I walked her to the door and said: "Daphne, you're the most intelligent woman I ever met!" She snapped; "So *that's* what you think of me?" With a sinking heart, I led her back to the swing, where we sat down, and then I kissed her.

SATURDAY, JULY 18, 1931 ▥ I knew that Vachel Lindsay, the famous poet, lives in Springfield. My home-town paper has published some feature stories I wrote in college, so I thought I'd try to interview the poet and sell another article. I telephoned his home and spoke to his wife, who invited me to join them this evening. Wild with joy, I dashed to the store where Daphne works and bought a volume of Lindsay's collected poems.

Now 52 years old, he is called The Vagabond Poet because he has tramped through the south and west, trading his verses for food and lodgings. His poems have a visionary, rhapsodic quality, and I've heard that when he reads them from a lecture platform he does so very dramatically. Eleven years ago Lindsay became the first American poet to lecture at Oxford University.

Because of his fame, I was a little scared this evening, but his wife made me feel comfortable from the start. Lindsay was born in Springfield and lives in a 100-year-old house often visited by Abraham Lincoln. As I entered the frame house on 5th Street I saw a big picture that hangs in the parlor. It is a pen drawing illustrating Lindsay's much-loved poem called "Abraham Lincoln Walks at Midnight". Lindsay himself is a man with rugged features, enthusiasm and an air of informality.

Saying that the evening was warm, he suggested I pick up a chair and carry it out to the back lawn, where his wife was setting up other chairs. She lighted a candle on a table, he lit a cigarette, and he continued to smoke as he told story after story. Then he played some Victrola recordings made as he recited some of his most popular poems, such as "The Congo" and "The Chinese Nightingale." It felt eerie to hear his voice coming from that machine as I saw his face fading and emerging in the candlelight.

I spent about two hours with Lindsay and his wife. Before I left he autographed that book of his poetry I bought today. Exciting!

What I did not know that night is that for years Vachel Lindsay had been depressed by the waning of his creative powers. On December 5, 1931, he killed himself.

My article about Lindsay was published in the Kewanee Star-Courier, *and this time I was paid — two dollars. This is the first money I ever received for my writing.*

BLOOMINGTON, ILLINOIS, MONDAY, AUGUST 24, 1931 ▨ Now that our Palmolive crew has reached Bloomington, I searched for and found Billy Bishop, the Kewanee poet, because I knew he had moved here. I'm not the only one who believes in his talent. Billy now has a patron who lets him live in a garage apartment for free with the understanding that he must continue to write poems. The two of us had a wonderful reunion. He told me about the hunger marchers he saw as they passed through this city on their way from Chicago to the state capital at Springfield. He said they reminded him of the French Revolution.

Billy also found a book bargain so great that he aches to take advantage of it but lacks the money. Saying that since he couldn't have it, he wanted me to have it, he led me to a secondhand store this evening. Displayed there were 60 volumes entitled *World's Greatest Literature*. The set was published in 1901 and the original price was $105. All the volumes were in excellent condition. The price? Nine dollars! With my head whirling in ecstasy, I gave the merchant a ten dollar bill and he handed me a one dollar bill. What a library I'm going to have!

UNIVERSITY OF MISSOURI, WEDNESDAY, SEPTEMBER 16, 1931 ▨ Registration day. The out-of-state fee has been raised from $10 to $15. My total registration fee was $69! I couldn't get the courses I wanted because they were filled. I'm speaking of English Narration, English Exposition and Logic. Instead, I had to sign up for advanced Spanish, Zoology, Sociology and, of course, Military.

MONDAY, OCTOBER 5, 1931 ▨ This morning I got a letter from Mother saying that the First National Bank of Kewanee has closed. That's the bank that has every cent I own. Mother also said that Grandpa Robb had all of his money there, and now Grandma is worried to death. Many of the people in Kewanee stood in front of the closed doors of the bank, weeping and cursing. One of Mother's women friends ran up and down our street, bewailing the fact that her family has lost everything. Now I must think twice before spending so much as a nickel. I can't afford to belong to Kappa Sig. Here I am at age 20—absolutely penniless!

THURSDAY, OCTOBER 8, 1931 ▨ Tonight I felt very morose. I worry about money and the kind of grades I may get, and I need a girl to love, one who will love me, and my spirits sank so low that I told Nace I feel like getting drunk or killing myself. Mother had some bonds left, so she sends me $10.50 a week and this is supposed to cover everything, but the money won't stretch that far. Nace and I moved out of the frat and room together in a private home and we eat at a boarding house. Things are so bad that there's even talk that the University of Missouri might have to close down. I notice that there are fewer drunks on campus this semester.

KEWANEE, ILLINOIS, WEDNESDAY, DECEMBER 23, 1931 ▓   Back for the Christmas holiday, I feel my hatred for my home town coursing through my veins like poison. Something or other prompted Mother to say to me today: "I believe you're a better boy than you were, now that you're growing older. Daddy said once that the things you did were only done because you thought it cute and were going through a natural stage for boys."

1932

UNIVERSITY OF MISSOURI, SUNDAY, JANUARY 3, 1932 ▓   On my way back here I stopped in St. Louis to pick up Nace, who took me for a drive in his car. Today I saw my first bread line—200 starving men forming a gray line as they waited for food. The sight of them disturbed me.

SATURDAY, JANUARY 9, 1932 ▓   Nace Strickland is the best room mate one could have. Today he told me something that happened when he was a child. Reared in St. Louis, he didn't know much about country life, so he was excited when two of his aunts took him for a drive on back roads. In one pasture he saw a bull mounting a cow, whereupon Nace exclaimed: "Hey, I didn't know those things could milk themselves!"

SATURDAY, JANUARY 23, 1932 ▓   Today I persuaded Nace to start keeping a diary.

WEDNESDAY, JANUARY 27, 1932 ▓   The past three days I've been phoning a girl whom I saw for the first time last Sunday in the College Inn. When I was on the line with her this evening she asked whether I'd care to take her to a friend's house to study. I was willing! I remembered how pretty she is. She lives in town, I walked to her home and for the first time learned her name, a sweet name, Melody Snow. She is so fascinating that instantly I liked her better than any other girl I've met in town. And this evening she let me kiss her repeatedly, almost causing me to swoon in ecstasy. Her lips are so soft, so moist, so delicious.

FRIDAY, FEBRUARY 5, 1932 ▓   This semester I'm studying Logic with Dr. Jay William Hudson. He fascinates me! He is 58 years old, only about five feet tall, has a deep bass voice, smokes a curved Sherlock Holmes pipe seemingly half as large as himself. Finding a biography of him, I learned that he earned his doctorate at Harvard, has served as president of the Western Philosophical Association, is married to a Frenchwoman and has written many books, some fiction, some non-fiction. He is the first certified intellectual I ever met and he scares the hell out of me. He has a dry wit that I admire. The first class I had with him he talked the whole hour, concluding with these words: "I won't always speak as long as I have today. Yet I am glad that I did talk as I did, for if I hadn't taken up all the time by raving on, you folks would have had a chance to say something. I would much rather hear myself talk than listen to you talk. I am really much more interesting to myself than you are to me."

MONDAY, FEBRUARY 22, 1932 ▪ My 21st birthday. What a momentous day! Now, if ever, I am going to have to foster some semblance of manhood and play the part of an intellectual adult. There is one thing of which I am exceedingly conscious on this day, and that is *my own ignorance*. I can claim but a scant share of all the knowledge the world holds. I am woefully lacking any real insight into all those things worth knowing. I am so damned incompetent! However, there is one quality I possess—energy! If I can retain even a part of this youthful zest and joy in living, then perhaps I can conquer the world. Oh, hell, I'm so Goddam pretentious. Twenty-one, indeed! I'm more like a two-year-old. I wonder whether I'm a neurotic. I'm always highstrung and often nervous. In fact, I'm horribly high-strung and at times become irascible toward Melody Snow when she has done nothing to provoke me. Am I abnormal or normal? Am I over-sexed?

WEDNESDAY, MARCH 16, 1932 ▪ For quite awhile now Melody Snow has been saying that she loves me. I love her, too, but not so much, I'm afraid, as she loves me. Today she said something that shocked me into speechlessness.

"I know why I love you, Eddie," she began in a firm voice. "I am sure of myself. Just the other night I was lying awake and it was then that I thought of the proof that I love you. When I was a nurse in Kansas City I worked in the delivery room and watched woman after woman give birth to a child. I saw the agony they had to endure. It was so painful that some fainted, but the doctors would bring them back to consciousness so that they might cooperate in the actual birth. Knowing what torture it is, having seen it so very often, I swore up and down that no man was worth all that, and that never as long as I lived would I go through that for anyone. But, Eddie—"

Her voice softened and I felt her curls touch my forehead.

"—the other evening the thought came to me that I'd suffer that for you, Eddie, I'd endure childbirth for your sake . . . And I would."

All I could do, all I could do was to hug her.

THURSDAY, MARCH 24, 1932 ▣   Since I began going with Melody Snow I have not dated Cora. Today, though, when I was downtown, I heard someone hail me and when I turned around I saw that it was Cora. We exchanged a couple of idle remarks, and then she asked whether I'd had my diary bound recently. I said yes.

"Well," she said, her voice hardening, "a boy I know happened to be up at the bindery and saw your diary lying open on a bench. It happened to be open to some pages that had my name on them. In fact, Eddie, it was open to those pages telling of one particular night—that evening we spent out at the stadium!"

TUESDAY, MAY 24, 1932 ▣   Today I received a letter from my sister Kay. In the first half she wrote about the effect the Depression is having on our family, saying that our step-father "cries all the time and can talk of nothing except financial troubles . . ." The second half of her letter goes this way: "And, brother of mine, do you care if I stick in a little advice as usual. It's in regard to your dearly beloved diary, which you so fondly keep. I want to warn you that you are going to get into a pack of trouble over it if you bring it home. *Don't think for a minute that it isn't read!* And really, Eddie, it's not a thing to your credit to keep a diary such as yours is. Don't you realize that it could absolutely break you, and ruin your reputation if it were found? I know you are thinking 'Yes, but no one *will* get hold of it.' But how do you know? If you were in an accident or died suddenly, it would come to light undoubtedly. Really, dear, you have become a fanatic on the subject, and think it's something of which to be proud, but I assure you, you were never more mistaken . . ."

Well, just because she's my elder sister, and also because she is like Mother, she always thinks she knows what is best for me. Because Kay is a librarian, she should understand the value of a journal. As usual, I'm going to ignore her advice. What must be kept in mind is the fact that someone should have the courage and integrity to put down on paper all his life's happenings precisely as they occurred. It is my belief that the historian of the future will thank me. In these pages he will not find a record of world deeds, mighty achievements, conquest. What he will discover is the drama of the unfolding life of one individual, day after day after day.

KEWANEE, ILLINOIS, SATURDAY, JUNE 11, 1932 ■ Last night l dreamed I held my diary under a shower and was delighted when the words did not wash off. Does this mean I think my diary may make me "immortal"?

WEDNESDAY, JUNE 15, 1932 ■ Today I got a job at the swimming pool in the park on the north side of town. I'm lucky to get any employment, what with grown men looking for work and standing in bread lines. What I do is to hand out baskets to kids to hold their clothes after they're changed into swim suits. After the pool closed this evening the life guards and I practiced high diving.

THURSDAY, JUNE 16, 1932 ■ While working at the pool I had the radio turned on to the Republican national convention in Chicago. Herbert Hoover was renominated for the Presidency. My step-father is a Democrat in this Republican town. Grandpa Robb, though, is so anti-Catholic that he voted against Al Smith and for Hoover in the election of 1928. Grandpa's father was born a Protestant in Ireland, and Gramps hates everything Catholic. He really believes that the Catholics are planning to kill every Protestant in the U.S. I've heard this Goddam nonsense from him ever since I was a kid. Nonetheless, I still love the old guy.

FRIDAY, JULY 1, 1932 ■ Before leaving the university I spent $3 for the one-volume edition of 1,652 pages of *The Rise of American Civilization* by Charles A. Beard and Mary R. Beard. This is what I have been reading since getting home. After dinner this evening I climbed upstairs to my room to read further in this fascinating book, but went back downstairs to listen to the radio about the Democratic national convention, also in Chicago this year. I'd like to call my step-father Frank, but Mother insists that I continue to call him Daddy. Well, tonight *Frank* and I talked politics, a subject both of us like. With pencils and paper the two of us kept tabs with each roll call of the delegates, and on the fourth ballot the winner was Franklin D. Roosevelt, the governor of New York. I'm glad!

MONDAY, JULY 18, 1932 ■ This afternoon as Mother and I sat on the front porch she asked what was poking out my pants pocket. Well, it was a tin box of contraceptives! I'm sure I got red in the face. I mumbled something and walked inside the house. I think she knew what it was.

TUESDAY, JULY 26, 1932 ■ I was walking to work at the pool when I saw a battered old car parked along the road. It had colored chalk scrawled all over it. When I got closer I saw that it held two veterans of the World War. They were driving to Washington, D.C. to join the 22,800 members of the Bonus Expeditionary Army encamped near the capital. They are there to lobby for the immediate payment in cash of the bonus due them. The car near me had on one side this legend: HEROES—1918 . . . BUMS—1932. Curious, I began asking questions of one of the men, who answered me and then suddenly asked: "Say, are you a reporter? What paper yuh with?" I felt flattered, I paid him 10¢ for a copy of the B.E.A. News.

MONDAY, AUGUST 8, 1932   ■   Nace called from St. Louis to yell into the phone: "We're going to California, Ellis!" Then he explained that his uncle knows a rich man in Long Beach who has had an Essex Super Six designed for him. He wants Nace to drive it from St. Louis to the West Coast. Nace wants me to go with him and when we deliver the car we'll be paid $10 each. I exploded in excitement, but had a hard time persuading Mother to let me go. I ran to the Kewanee Star-Courier, where the city editor, Chris Ketridge, gave me a letter of introduction that might get me into the Olympic Games in Los Angeles as a reporter. Since Nace and I will have to hitch-hike back from California, I also went to the police station and the chief wrote a letter vouching for my good character.

CHAPTER 3

TUESDAY, AUGUST 9, 1932 ■ At seven o'clock this morning I left the house with $12.03 in my pocket. I hitched rides to within about 48 miles of St. Louis, and then my luck ran out, so I rode a bus the rest of the way. I'm carrying my diary, this composition book, in my Gladstone bag.

THURSDAY, AUGUST 11, 1932 ■ Nace and I left his home in Webster Groves at 9 A.M. Saw the foothills of the Ozarks.

FRIDAY, AUGUST 12, 1932 ■ Fort Worth, Texas—Today we rode through parts of Missouri, Kansas, Oklahoma and Texas. At Atokee, Okla., we had to make a detour. Christ, what roads! And what back hill country we saw. The plight of those poor farmers and squatters made me realize how lucky I am to have a decent home. Mother thinks we are poverty-stricken, but Christ, she should see these Oklahomans!

SUNDAY, AUGUST 14, 1932 ■ Phoenix, Arizona—Last night we slept in the car near El Paso, so this morning I opened my eyes to a series of hills that almost are mountains, a mission church and adobe huts inhabited by Mexicans. We walked across the border into Mexico, the first time I ever was in a foreign country, and I felt thrilled. Nace and I have named the car Xenophon, after the Greek historian and disciple of Socrates. We got in it, started out again, entered Arizona and drove over Superstition Mountain east of Phoenix. Once we left the car to climb to a peak to look beyond the horizon, Nace saw a rattlesnake and then stepped on a cactus thorn that jabbed through his shoe and into his foot. We were back in the car on the road at sunset, and never in my life have I seen such vivid colors! I wish I were a painter so that I might capture the beauty of this scenery, this sunset. Today I saw more beauty than ever before in my life.

MONDAY, AUGUST 15, 1932 ■ Grand Canyon, Arizona—It was about 2:30 this afternoon when we had our first sight of the Grand Canyon. Breathtaking! For more than two hours Nace and I sat on the edge of a rock, just drinking in the scene. The colors are beyond description and the distances stagger the imagination. We ate outside the Grand Canyon National Park and then returned for a moonlight view of the canyon. We sat with our legs dangling in space, stunned into silence. This is absolutely the most beautiful sight I have ever seen!

TUESDAY, AUGUST 16, 1932 ■ Long Beach, California—All last moonlit night we drove west, taking turns at the wheel, alert to everything around us. As we crossed the Mojave Desert I saw stars that seemed three times larger than they look in Illinois. After the sun came up I drove through a mirage on the road. At last we entered California and as we neared Pasadena I saw orange trees. We stopped to buy six huge oranges for only five cents, and also a big bag of grapes for the same price! And finally I saw the Pacific Ocean! We got a room in a hotel for five nights for $2.50.

WEDNESDAY, AUGUST 17, 1932 ■ Today I swam in the Pacific Ocean for the first time. I also rented a surf board for 10¢ and had my first go at surf-ing—an exciting sport! Nace & I bought our supper at a grocery store and ate in our clean hotel room. We got a dozen oranges for 5¢, two pounds of pears for 10¢, a dozen rolls for 5¢ and a quart of milk for 7¢. What a life!

After frolicking in the ocean a few days, Nace and I began to run out of money. Fortunately, we found a lady professor who wanted someone to drive her to her home in Lubbock, Texas. As the three of us rode through the Impe-rial Valley in California, the temperature hit 123 degrees in the shade! After leaving the lady and her car, Nace and I had to hitchhike our way back. We had bad luck. Adventure is discomfort remembered. Few folks would pick us up. We did get a lift from a toothless old guy in a 1921 Hupmobile, Nace and I paying for the gas, but the car simply disintegrated in slow motion, mile after mile. In desperation, we hopped a freight train and rode in the empty gondola of a coal car, sharing this space with men who were jobless and hopeless, not two college kids on a lark. By the time we reached Kansas City our faces were black and our pockets were empty. All we had left was five cents, and we still had to cross the entire state of Missouri. We were starving. As we stood near a fruit stand we engaged in a whispered debate about the ethics of stealing one apple; our middle-class upbringing forbade this theft. And so we starved.

THURSDAY, SEPTEMBER 1, 1932 ■ Webster Groves, Missouri—I'd some-times wondered what it feels like to be hungry, ravenously hungry, and now I know. It begins in the belly with a burning sensation the size of an apple. Hour after hour without food and the hot spot swells up until it is the size of a grapefruit. Next the stomach feels like a chamois skin dipped in hot water, then stretched taut. Finally, the headache, the relentless headache! A clerk in a YMCA in Kansas City knew a man who wanted a driver to spell him at the wheel as he headed for St. Louis, so we got our last ride. It was early afternoon when we reached this St. Louis suburb, the home of Nace's folks. I think they're rich. They were not home and Nace had no key, but we pried open a window and ran to the kitchen. There we stuffed ourselves with food for the next 20 minutes—then almost vomited.

UNIVERSITY OF MISSOURI, SEPTEMBER 8–SEPTEMBER 19, 1932   Since returning here events have moved so fast I've neglected my diary. One evening Clark Nichols asked whether I'd like to drive to Jefferson City to see and hear Franklin D. Roosevelt, who is campaigning for the Presidency on the Democratic ticket. Would I! When we reached the capital of Missouri we found a crowd of thousands of people awaiting the candidate. Missouri Senator Jim Reed, in his shirt-sleeves, orated a long time while we waited. Roosevelt did not appear until about 10 P.M.

For some reason I both forget and regret, I stopped writing there. Nonetheless, I clearly remember what I saw. Roosevelt arrived in a touring car with its top down; he sat in the back seat, with a man on either side of him. Standing by the car I could see his thin ankles and the braces supporting his legs. With people cheering all around him, he asked the men at his sides to boost him up onto the top of the seat, where all might see him. Now that he was perched higher, Roosevelt broke into a wide grin and threw up both arms to acknowledge the cheers. He fascinated me. Before I left, and after he had resumed his usual place on the rear seat, I reached out and touched the sleeve of his coat.

MONDAY, OCTOBER 31, 1932   The class I like most, and the one in which I get my best grades, is Psychology. I am fascinated by the workings of the human mind. But to come down to earth, today at the bank I learned I have only $5.76 to finish this semester! I'm jerking sodas at a drugstore for 25 cents an hour.

THURSDAY, NOVEMBER 3, 1932   For the first time in my life I cast my vote for the President of the United States—Franklin D. Roosevelt. My ballot was mailed to me from Illinois and I had to mark it in the presence of a notary public. Roosevelt won!

THURSDAY, DECEMBER 1, 1932 ▓ This evening Ross said to me: "It must take an awfully egotistical person to keep a diary." Surprised, I began to defend myself, citing several reasons for maintaining this journal—a chance to practice writing, the opportunity to analyze myself, the value of a diary as a reference volume.

Decades later someone else declared that I must be a narcissist. This remark bothered me so much that I pondered it the next couple of weeks. At long last I found the proper explanation: A narcissist is an individual who considers himself perfect, and therefore does not wish to change. I realize I am imperfect, and therefore want to change.

THURSDAY, DECEMBER 15, 1932 ▓ Last night I dreamed that I stood beside myself, that there were two guys named Eddie Ellis. I was as curious as I was amazed. I stared at myself and saw myself staring at myself. Then both Eddies lifted a hand to finger the face of the other person. Page Dr. Freud!

What the hell—a dash of madness never hurt anybody! I hope. Now that I've been psychoanalyzed I believe I know why I dreamed that dream. Besides dating Melody Snow I had begun going with a beautiful girl from Mississippi named Phoebe. I was half in love with each while wholly in love with neither. Thus was my mind split, for what seemed a very long time, by these two lovely women.

Later I learned that Goethe was riding a horse one day and suddenly saw himself on another horse, approaching himself. The same sort of thing also happened to Abraham Lincoln. One day in his home in Illinois he glanced into a mirror and saw a double image of himself. This phenomena is called a doppelganger, a German word meaning "double goer."

SUNDAY, DECEMBER 18, 1932 ▓ Tonight I went to Melody Snow's house and chatted with her and her mother, who finally went to sleep in her bedroom. This left the two of us alone in Melody's bedroom, and soon we were in bed kissing one another and finally making love. It was sensual and exciting when—

WHAM!

The bed slats broke! A helluva noise! I was sure her mother had been awakened and would come charging in. From the other room we heard a slight groan, but that was all. Pulling on my clothes and buttoning them as fast as possible, I fled into the night. As Melody kissed me the last time, she giggled.

KEWANEE, ILLINOIS, CHRISTMAS, 1932 ▓ This surely was a Depression Christmas. We had no Xmas tree because they cost 50¢ and my step-father said he couldn't afford one. I was so broke that I sent a present to Melody but then was unable to buy gifts for Mother and my two kid sisters. The family came here for dinner at noon and Grandpa Robb was asked to give the blessing. Poor soul. He got about half way through and then stopped. I waited, head bent, then peeked and saw that Gramps was crying. I sure love that old guy. Later we gathered around the radio to listen to Eddie Cantor. Now that we're in a Depression, clowns are important.

1933

UNIVERSITY OF MISSOURI, THURSDAY, JANUARY 5, 1933 ■ Former President Calvin Coolidge died today.

SUNDAY, JANUARY 8, 1933 ■ Holding Melody in my arms, I asked: "If I ever become a big city reporter, will you come live with me?"
   She replied: "Yes, I believe I'd be foolish enough to do that."

TUESDAY, JANUARY 10, 1933 ■ I am totally fascinated by Henry George's classic book *Poverty and Progress.* His style is simple, his analysis profound. He said: "It is not production but unequal distribution which is one great cause of poverty." This evening I switched from Henry George to *The Autobiography of Lincoln Steffens,* the great journalist and muckraker. I was reading along, enjoying page after page, until I found one idea so original that it jolted me as though I had been struck by lightning: *Teach questions, not answers!* I yelled it at the top of my voice. Then I stooped down to kiss the book, straightened up, threw on my heavy winter clothes, charged out into the cold night and paced back and forth, thinking, thinking, thinking.

THURSDAY, JANUARY 12, 1933 ■ In *The Winter's Tale* there is a character named Autolycus, a thief and peddler, whom Shakespeare calls ". . . a snapper-up of unconsidered trifles." In a way, I think I'm like that rogue because I pay attention to things ignored by most people.
   This afternoon members of our Abnormal Psychology class rode a bus to Fulton, Missouri, to visit an insane asylum. One chubby man, who didn't look mad, told us he is 6,000,000 years old, has visited the planet Saturn, founded several universities and had been killed, then brought back to life. Another man thought Greta Garbo is in love with him. Another thought his food is being poisoned. Another trembled so violently that he had to trot around the room to maintain his equilibrium.

SATURDAY, JANUARY 28, 1933   For a long time I've been caricaturing people here on the campus and lately some folks have been talking about me. After a fraternity man saw one of my caricatures he suggested that some evening I go to his chapter house and draw his frat brothers. This evening I went to a small cafe and offered to caricature men or women for 25 cents. Three persons wanted to be drawn, so within a few minutes I earned 75 cents. Why should I jerk sodas for 25 cents an hour when I can get 25 cents for one caricature?

SUNDAY, JANUARY 29, 1933   I've been dating Melody Snow, of course, and at the same time I've been going out with Phoebe, the beautiful co-ed from Mississippi. I have *not* been intimate with Phoebe. This evening she astonished me by saying she thinks she's in love with me! In fact, she continued, she may have fallen in love with me as long ago as last fall when she saw me leading cheers at the Varsity-Freshman football game. She said that the first time I asked her for a date she was thrilled. I was almost awe-struck when she accepted, because she is one of the most popular girls on the campus. Well, now, it seems we have a problem. I admire and respect both Melody and Phoebe and am half in love with both of them, but not wholly in love with either. How does it happen—how *can* it happen—that I, the most worthless of creatures, should be loved by two such lovely girls?

TUESDAY, FEBRUARY 7, 1933   Now that the new semester has begun I'm allowed to take my first journalism courses—reporting, copy reading and promotional advertising. Today I had my first real assignment, covering the Kiwanis Club luncheon in the Tiger Hotel. I've also moved into a new room in a private home at a cost of $6 per month.

THURSDAY, FEBRUARY 16, 1933   Mother wrote to tell me that a third bank in Kewanee has closed its doors. This left my step-father with only the 30 cents in his pockets. He went to a fourth bank, the only one still open, to borrow $25 to buy groceries for the family. In her letter Mother said: "Now all that lies between us & starvation is the hope that Daddy will get a federal appointment as postmaster of Kewanee. I can't see that conditions are getting any better, and the bank closing has caused a great deal more suffering in Kewanee. The Depression has caused so much worry that people are dying of heart trouble, and some are losing their minds. I understand that Mrs. J. B. is losing her mind over it. I thought something was wrong with her when she talked to me at the school house before Christmas. All she talked about was the Depression, and asked me if I thought the Lord had brought this upon the people to make them suffer . . ."

FRIDAY, FEBRUARY 24, 1933 ■ Johnnie Straus is a dear friend of mine. I think his father is rich because he owns an auto agency in St. Louis. The other day on the campus I ran into Johnnie, who knows that I'm broke, and he said he wanted to drive Phoebe, his girl and me to St. Louis—all expenses paid. I'd just become 22 years old, so he grinned and said this was my birthday present. So we left in Johnnie's car, with Phoebe wearing her fur coat. In the city we went to the expensive apartment owned by his parents, where we were waited on by a maid. Phoebe's birthday gift to me was a handsome leatherbound volume of Shakespeare's complete works, a book I had seen and lusted for in the Missouri Book Store. Later the four of us from the university went to the ornate dining room of the Hotel Jefferson to dine and dance to Bobby Meeker's orchestra. A special train called "The 42nd Street Special" had left Hollywood loaded with movie stars en route to Washington to see Franklin D. Roosevelt inaugurated as President, and tonight it stopped in St. Louis. There in the hotel dining room I saw Bette Davis, Eleanor Holmes, Laura La Plante and others. Bette Davis had a fur stole, which she dragged across the floor. Near us stood a Negro captain of waiters; I tried to get his attention by saying "Sir!" Mississippi-born Phoebe snarled: "What did you call that *nigger?*" I looked at her in sudden fury, though I said nothing.

SATURDAY, MARCH 4, 1933 ■ I turned on the radio to hear Roosevelt inaugurated as President in a ceremony held in front of the Capitol building in Washington. I liked the way he stressed "direct action . . . immediate action . . . vigorous action." I recalled with pride that I have touched the right arm of this great man.

MONDAY, MARCH 6, 1933 ■ Our newly installed President Roosevelt has pulled a fast one on us. Two days after taking power he issued a proclamation declaring a national banking holiday, thus closing the doors of every bank in the U.S. until next Friday. Fortunately, a day or two ago, I had cashed a $5 check. I have some change left from this, but that's all. Even when the banks open again I'll be in a bad fix because in my bank account I have only $10 or $15 left to get through the rest of this semester. I'm getting high grades in History.

WEDNESDAY, MARCH 15, 1933 ■ Mr. Gaebler, the owner of the Black and Gold Inn, has offered me a job waiting tables. I agreed to work four hours a day in exchange for three meals. If I have to work my way through college—I must. However, I do not recommend this as an easy way to get an education.

FRIDAY, APRIL 7, 1933   ▪   Beer became legal again today. Five of us went to the University Shop, which was almost full with beer drinkers. Although I don't really like the stuff, I drank three bottles that made me feel lightheaded. A drunk standing next to me said: "Seven bottles of beer and an introvert becomes an extrovert."

THURSDAY, MAY 11, 1933   ▪   I read an article about Hitler in the *Saturday Evening Post.*

SATURDAY, MAY 13, 1933   ▪   Mig Johnson drove me to St. Louis. In the afternoon we drove around and saw a Depression village, called a Hooverville, on the levee. The 1,200 people who camp there are in danger of being flooded by the Mississippi River, which is rising.

KEWANEE, ILLINOIS, TUESDAY, JUNE 6, 1933   ▪   Home for summer vacation. The only part of this town I really like is the Kewanee Public Library, where I went this afternoon to read Plato. There's really a warm spot in my heart for this library.

MONDAY, JUNE 12, 1933   ▪   This morning I began reporting for the *Kewanee Star-Courier.* The managing editor, Chris Ketridge, has taken me on as an apprentice, so I will receive no pay. However, the work is fast and very interesting. There is no other business or profession which I care to follow. It's journalism for me! There's a second apprentice, too, a young man named Walt Nones, who lives in New York City, graduated from Princeton and now is a student at Oxford. He told me he came here to study the Midwest so that he might write about it in a novel. I had a very interesting conversation with him. Soon I'll resume work at the bath house near the pool because I simply must earn some money. I'll get $2.25 per day.

THURSDAY, JUNE 15, 1933   ▪   I wrote a feature story about some circus elephants in Liberty Park. Over my article were these words: "By Eddie Ellis." My first by-line! And when I went to the office of the civic nurse to watch her take care of some babies, she said to their mothers: "We have a reporter with us today."

FRIDAY, JUNE 30, 1933 ■ Walt, the Oxford student, came charging out to my house to wail that he found the Middle West dull. Hell, I could have told him this.

SATURDAY, JULY 1, 1933 ■ As you can see, I'm typing my diary for the first time since I started writing it on December 27, 1927. These days I think better with a typewriter than a pen, although I never did study touch-typing. I don't know how many fingers I use. I taught myself how to type on a typewriter in Grandpa Robb's real estate office.

TUESDAY, JULY 11, 1933 ■ I haven't finished reading *The Mansions of Philosophy* by Durant, but went to the library to get *A Short Introduction to the History of Human Stupidity* by Pitkin. When I'm working at the pool, handing out clothing baskets, I have time to think. My aspiration to make something worthwhile of myself is an ideal that burns brighter every day. There is so much to learn and not enough time in which to learn it.

FRIDAY, JULY 14, 1933 ■ A man named Joe Mickalowski was killed accidentally under the wheels of a coal truck. The editor told me to cover the inquest, so I went to the mortuary, wondering how I'd feel about seeing a corpse. Not as bad as I anticipated. The *Star-Courier* published my article on page one under an eight-column headline—my first banner! I like this work so much I hesitate to call it *work*. However, Phil Adler, who owns the paper, now wants to pay me $5 a week. My job at the pool pays $9, so now I'll earn $14 a week.

SATURDAY, JULY 29, 1933 ■ Because Clarence Schlaver is on vacation I was told to write his Saturday column and today it was published:

DAY BY DAY
WITH THE NEWS
By Eddie Ellis

This is the first time I've had a column in a newspaper! I hardly could wait for the first edition to come off the press. Not one word was changed. One of my paragraphs concerned Senator Huey Long of Louisiana:

The Kingfish continues to snitch his slice of news. Coarse Huey P. Long tiffed it with a cameraman who tried to get a picture of him boarding a train down in New Orleans. His bodyguard, dark-skinned

Joe Messina, pulled his revolver on the photographer while Huey smashed the flashbulb on the camera.

TUESDAY, AUGUST 22, 1933 ▦ When I stopped at Gramp's house I found him sitting on the steps on the back porch. He was watching his Boston Terrier, Bob, frisking in front of him. After I sat down beside Grandpa he surprised me by pulling up his pants to show me that his legs were terribly swollen. Awful! I'm afraid he might die when I'm back at the university.

SATURDAY, SEPTEMBER 2, 1933 ▦ Today my column in the *Star-Courier* contained this paragraph:

DEMOCRACY

"We hold these truths to be self-evident,
that all men are created equal . . ."
Thus reads the Declaration of Independence
of the year 1776. "Twenty-four attendants
keep Cornelius Vanderbilt Whitney's great
race horse, Equipoise, in shape for racing."
Thus reads a Chicago newspaper of the year 1933.

UNIVERSITY OF MISSOURI, MONDAY, SEPTEMBER 25, 1933 ▦ Since returning here I've clerked in the university's Co-Op Book Store in the basement of Jesse Hall. I had to memorize the location of all the books listed on eight pages of copy. My first day I sold $360 worth of goods. Today I was paid $20.68 for my first two weeks of work. I'm scheduled to work only 12 hours a week, and this won't even pay for my meals.

SUNDAY, OCTOBER 22, 1933 ▦ This afternoon when I joined Phoebe I said I'd written her a letter, so her eyes lit up and she ran her hand down into the pocket of a big coat I hadn't worn in a long time. When she brought out her hand she held a small envelope, one containing a condom! I don't think she knew what it was. She stuffed it back in the pocket, found the letter and smiled at me. Ohh, god!

MONDAY, OCTOBER 23 1933 ▦

GRANDPA ROBB DIED YESTERDAY.
I loved that old duffer!

WEDNESDAY, NOVEMBER 29, 1933   ■   Bob Hoover invited Phoebe and me to drive with him to Kansas City to spend Thanksgiving with his parents. I'd heard he is rich, and when we arrived I found that his home truly is luxurious. Mr. Hoover, a very friendly man, led me into his den to show me his private library, hundreds and hundreds of books standing on shelf after shelf. I almost felt ill with envy. Some day I'm going to own a private library as great as this one.

SUNDAY, DECEMBER 3, 1933   ■   All my life I've been afraid of poverty. Grandfather John Ellis, who died before I was born, was a rich man who owned his own bank, and I was born in the handsome four-story Victorian house he built, one of the finest in Kewanee. However, his son — my father, the man my mother divorced — was a playboy who ran through the family fortune. Now we're in a Depression and sometimes when I see a ragged beggar I shudder, actually shudder. On the street the other day I saw a beggar and felt so moved I wrote a poem about him.

1934

SATURDAY, FEBRUARY 17, 1934   ■   Today I read part of Sherwood Anderson's *Winesburg, Ohio*, a collection of tales about "a small town whose inhabitants are warped into grotesques by their unfulfilling lives." If I had been forced to stay in Kewanee I could have written the same kind of book just by listening to Mother gossip about other people. There are tragedies under every roof.

MONDAY, FEBRUARY 19, 1934   ■   Some of my favorite songs: *My Silent Love . . . Lullaby of the Leaves . . . I've Got the South in My Soul . . . Time on My Hands . . . Old Rockin' Chair . . . Piccalo-Pete . . . Harmonica Harry . . . I Kiss Your Hand, Madame . . . Somebody Loves Me . . . I Surrender, Dear . . . Body and Soul . . . All of Me . . . You're My Everything . . . Mona Lisa . . . The Man I Love . . . What Wouldn't I Do for That Man? . . . Mood Indigo.*

SATURDAY, FEBRUARY 24, 1934   ■   Three other reporters and I went to the Socialist headquarters here in Columbia to interview Norman Thomas, who in 1928 and 1932 ran for President on the Socialist ticket. Sitting on a sofa, he let us shoot questions at him for 90 minutes.

He is 50 years old, a lean six feet two, has a round skull, thinning gray hair, gray eyebrows, stark blue eyes, a wide mouth often gaping into a grin, a witty mind, a wide vocabulary and a fondness for slang phrases: ". . . it makes you woosie . . . that kind of stuff . . . they got the gravy . . ."

Alluding to his defeat by Hoover and then Roosevelt, he grinned and said: "It's better to be right than be President—but it doesn't do much good."

Does the Depression worry him?

"Yes," he replied, scratching the left side of his mouth with his glasses. "Something's got to be done, but there's no use sighing for angels. Something's got to be done!"

If the Socialists won political power, what is the first thing they would do?

Norman Thomas answered: "We are not so organized that at ten o'clock tomorrow morning we could take over things. But we would get at the key industries, such as banking, coal, oil, railroads."

How does he regard President Roosevelt?

"Roosevelt personally," Thomas replied, "is a man of great resourcefulness and ability. He is very shrewd and bold."

I asked: "Do you plan to run again for the Presidency?"

Thomas said: "I don't know yet. It's too far away for me to say."

He did run again—four more times, in fact. Although he never became President, he was such a compassionate man that he was called "the conscience of America." Norman Thomas and I were fated to meet again later under exciting circumstances.

THURSDAY, MARCH 15, 1934 ▪ Lately I've realized that in this diary I confess things I otherwise might not even admit doing. Every day I have to face myself and my sins. The style in this saga is not my best because of the haste with which I write, because I write late at night when I am tired, and because I have no chance to rewrite. However, if I were to take the time necessary to rewrite my diary it would be like a snake swallowing its own tail.

WEDNESDAY, APRIL 25, 1934 ▪ I drove from Columbia to Jefferson City to try to get an interview with Max Baer for the *Kewanee Star-Courier*. Baer is a professional boxer who has a June 14 date with Primo Carnera in Madison Square Garden to fight for the heavyweight championship of the world.

This evening in the Jefferson Theater I watched him laugh through two exhibition rounds. I reached his dressing room under the stage before he got out of his blue trunks with the Star of David on them.

"Nice bout," I said.

"Only clowning," he said. "Just foolin' around." Obviously, he didn't want me to think I had seen his best stuff.

"Going to take Carnera?"

"You betcha!" Baer has a grin like a jack-o-lantern.

"Will you use any special punch?"

"Nope . . . Any one will do if he gets in the way of it!"

Max Baer swung at his trainer, Mike Cantwell, pulled the punch before it touched the man.

I had read that Baer has one of the hardest right-hand punches in the boxing business. Last year he knocked out former heavyweight champion Max Schmeling.

Baer, the contender, is 25 years old and weighs 221 pounds. When he emerged from the shower I realized he has the widest shoulders and thinnest hips of any man I ever saw. I also realized, for the first time in my life, that a man's body can be beautiful. His muscles are long curves, like a ski slope.

As he towelled himself, Baer said: "I'm going to give Jack Dempsey seven and a half per cent of what I make on the Carnera fight. Good publicity. People like to hear that sort of thing. But I'm really doing it for Jack because he needs the money, got lots of expenses. Jack's my pal, my best friend."

"Mr. Baer," I asked, "how did you get into boxing?"

"Hey, it's Max, Max! Always Max! . . ." His grin stretched out and his eyes screwed up in amusement. "Well, you see, one night I went to a country dance wearing bell-bottomed pants—you know, the wide ones they used to wear. Had on a sweater with Colleen Moore's picture on it. Now that I'm out in Hollywood I like to kid her about it. She's a real movie star! Class! Anyway, I was standing by some guy who made a crack about me, so I said I'd lick him and he said 'Is that so?' I had a dame with me, so what was I to do? This guy hit me—*zowie!*—on the chin, but I'd leaned back, so he didn't hurt me a bit. Three months later I was fighting—professionally, I mean."

Now he was by a mirror, combing black hair thick with oil.

I asked: "How do you like making movies?"

"Oh, they're all right. I got into them because I needed the dough—$50,000 in twelve weeks. That's a lotta money!"

"How do you train?"

"I do lots of road work. Run, walk, run, walk. Keep at it all the time. Got seven sparring partners."

A small man burst into the dressing room and cried: "For God's sake, Max, get dressed! We're gonna grab that train into Kansas City at ten bells and it's nine-thirty right now!"

"Naw, it isn't," Baer protested. He leaned over my wristwatch and said: "Yep, guess it is."

Now that he had put on a jacket, he stuck a handkerchief in the breast pocket at a jaunty angle.

Another man said: "Yuh oughta have a glass of beer before starting out."

I looked a question at the boxer.

"Yeah," he said, "I drink beer even when I'm training."

"Well," I said, "thanks a lot, Mr. Baer."

"Hey, it's Max, Max, always Max!" Grinning, he looped a friendly arm over my shoulders.

Less than two months later Max Baer became the heavyweight champion of the world by knocking out hulking Primo Carnera in 11 rounds in New York City. Baer's boxing career lasted from 1929 to 1941. He won 65 of 79 fights. After retiring from the ring he appeared in films and on television. He died in 1959 in Hollywood.

By this time I had floundered into a decision I lived to regret: I rejected Melody Snow. Then I became engaged to Phoebe, the beauty from Mississippi. I was so confused by love I did not understand why I made those choices. "Blessed is he," says a maxim, "who knows why he does what he does." I did not know. I hurt both of those lovely women and myself. I had been intimate with Melody but not Phoebe. However, even Phoebe laughed when I quoted one line from a how-to sex book I found in a drawer in my mother's room. It said: "One or two kisses may be permitted an engaged couple if the marriage ceremony is not far distant."

FRIDAY, MAY 25, 1934 ■ Today I attended my last college class. It was, thank God, one taught by Dr. Jay William Hudson, my favorite professor. He spent the hour laughing, philosophizing and bantering with Frank Martin, who is a helluva lot smarter than I am. Dr. Hudson left us with an idea so optimistic that I hope I remember it all my life. He said: "We are all infinite in capacities."

WEDNESDAY, JUNE 6, 1934 ■ Graduation day! Donning my cap and gown, I walked to Jesse Hall to join the journalism students, and then students from all the various colleges marched to the Field House. When I got inside I saw Mother sitting with Phoebe's parents. I didn't pay attention to the main speaker because I was debating with myself whether I loved

Phoebe enough to marry her. I saw a man receive the first doctorate of journalism ever conferred upon anyone, a degree I consider about as useful as an oar in an airplane. After I had the thrill of getting my own sheepskin, after the ceremony broke up, I found Mother and threw my arms around her and thanked her for helping me get through college. She wept softly. Turning, I happened to see Dr. Hudson, so I wormed my way through the crowd and up to him to thank him for inspiring me. I even went so far as to pat him on the shoulder.

CHAPTER 4

Phoebe's father drove me to some southern cities so that I might seek work at newspaper after newspaper. He hoped that when she married me she would live relatively close to her family. Despite the Depression, I got a job with the New Orleans bureau of the Associated Press because the bureau manager said he wanted more lively writing. The salary was $25 a week. I was prepared for the charm of New Orleans, which O. Henry called one of the three romantic cities in the U.S., the others being San Francisco and New York. I was unprepared for the political crisis I met, one so acute that Louisiana seemed on the verge of civil war. Huey P. Long, age 41, was becoming the dictator of the state and let it be known that he wanted to be the President of the United States. He used tactics so ruthless that he was compared to Hitler. President Roosevelt called him a dangerous man. In 1928 Huey was elected governor and then in 1930 in mid-term, he was elected to the U.S. Senate. He did not remain in Washington, but spent most of his time in Louisiana telling his hand-picked successor as governor, O. K. Allen, what to do. Huey was worshipped by the poor whites of Louisiana because he gave them free school books and new roads and bridges and promised to redistribute all the wealth in the nation. "Every man a king!" he proclaimed. Huey was despised by the well-to-do citizens of New Orleans and their political machine, the Old Regulars. Resolving to break this last bastion of opposition, Huey launched a fake probe of vice in New Orleans. City officials, the public and press were barred from the hearing room. Mayor T. Semmes Walmsley, whom Huey called "Turkey Head" Walmsley, alerted the city's 1,400 policemen. Huey called out the state's 4,000 national guardsmen, now his private army. They set up machine guns pointing at City Hall. With armed men in two camps eyeing one another warily, the situation became volatile.

NEW ORLEANS, MONDAY, AUGUST 20, 1934 ▨ This morning I arrived in Union Station, which has a sign saying "New Orleans—America's Most Interesting City." I began walking toward the *Times-Picayune* building on the NE corner of Lafayette Square. The AP office is in this building, adjoining the city room of the *Picayune*. City Hall is also on this square and as I passed it I saw cops guarding it. Directly across the street there was another building, filled with national guardsmen, and with machine guns in place. After reaching the AP office and reporting to the bureau manager, I saw editors and reporters in the *Picayune* run to windows overlooking Lafayette Square. Someone had said he heard gunfire. I, too, ran to a window to stare toward City Hall, but nothing unusual was to be seen. An editor said: "Well, maybe it was just a car, backfiring." He sounded disappointed.

TUESDAY, AUGUST 21, 1934 ▦ An AP reporter is renting me a room in his apartment at 708 Orleans Ave., corner of Royal St. This is the exact center of the French Quarter. From here it is three blocks to the Mississippi River, three blocks to N. Rampart St., six blocks to Esplanade Ave. and six blocks to Canal St. Most exotic place I ever saw!

FRIDAY, SEPTEMBER 7, 1934 ▦ Last night Governor Allen ordered the rest of the national guardsmen to New Orleans to "protect" Huey as he continues his phoney probe of vice in this city. Wherever Huey goes, he is shielded by his personal bodyguard and rifle-carrying guardsmen. From 10 A.M. until 1:30 P.M. today I watched the arrival of more guardsmen at Jackson barracks. The so-called vice investigation is held on the 18th floor of the Canal Bank building, with public and press excluded. In the AP office we sit by a radio to listen as Huey, counsel to the joint legislative committee, asks questions of questionable witnesses. He manages to make them say precisely what he wants said. He is becoming the law in this state.

TUESDAY, SEPTEMBER 18, 1934 ▦ Today I spoke to Huey Long. I met him in the lobby of the Hotel Roosevelt, where he keeps a suite. I asked for his reaction to a political move made by his enemy, Mayor Walmsley. Grinning, striking a pose, Huey orated: "As Victor Hugo said in his *History of a Crime*: 'Oh, danger, irresistible controverter, in his last moments the atheist invokes God, the royalist calls upon the republic!' That's my comment, boy! That's my comment!"
On the next page is a sketch I did of Huey sometime after our first meeting.

THURSDAY, SEPTEMBER 27, 1934 ▦ Today I covered an auction held by society women to raise money with which to fight Huey Long. Some actually let family heirlooms go to the highest bidder.

TUESDAY, NOVEMBER 6, 1934 ▦ Election day. The AP bureau manager sent me to Huey Long's suite on the top floor of the Roosevelt Hotel to

watch him as election returns came in. I arrived at 8:15 and stayed until 11 P.M.

At the door I showed my AP press card to Earle Christenberry, Huey's secretary. He wore no jacket, so I saw the revolver on his left hip. The suite consists of three rooms, one of which was used as a private broadcasting studio. The place was swarming with Huey's stooges, pudgy politicians who treat him as though he were truly a king, not just the "Kingfish." He speaks, they nod vigorous assent. He jokes, they laugh explosively. He asks for a Coke, someone runs to get a bottle. It looked like a Mack Sennett comedy.

Tonight, for a change, Huey was dressed conservatively in a gray silk suit, gray shirt, black sox and black shoes. He is a toucher. Aware that he had nothing to fear from me, he shook hands enthusiastically and from time to time this evening he slapped me on my shoulders. He has the face of a clown—fat nose, fat cheeks, fleshy chin with a deep cleft. He radiates energy and brims with intelligence. He is so brilliant I wish he were on the side of the good guys. Often he has said: "There may be smarter men than me, but they ain't in Louisiana!" Well-read, articulate, he can speak correct English but poses as a common man. I watched him bellow, lick his lips and pick his nose.

Every time a phone rang, Huey would pick up the receiver and yell into it: "Kingfish speaking!" He is a ham actor who is on stage all the time. From all parts of the state he was receiving election returns. Every now and then he would sit down at a microphone in the improvised studio to announce poll figures, denounce his enemies, rejoice at victories, whoop and holler.

Several times when he went on the air I was one of only three men in the room with him—the radio technician, the announcer and myself. Watching our faces, our emotional reactions, Huey played us like an organ. He bellowed into the mike, eyed it suspiciously, denounced some enemy as a jackass. He was clowning and knew he was clowning. If our lips lifted into smiles, Huey would pour it on, and after we laughed and reached a peak of laughter, he would ease up, only to begin another cycle.

Suddenly he sprang up, yelling that he had to take a piss. He beckoned to me to follow him to the bath room, where he left the door open so he could talk to me while urinating. The election returns had been so favorable to him that he felt euphoric. Grinning, he said: "Think I'll go down and take Mexico, next! Do yuh think they'd know it was all in fun?"

Years later I visited Washington, D.C., and in a hall of the Capitol I saw a statue of Huey Long and instantly remembered seeing him relieving himself.

WEDNESDAY, NOVEMBER 7, 1934 ▓ Some of my favorite songs: *Smoke Gets in Your Eyes . . . Cocktails for Two . . . Sophisticated Lady . . . Don't Blame Me . . . Lover . . . True . . . Moonglow . . . The Very Thought of You . . . Love in Bloom . . . Stay as Sweet as You Are . . . Dancing in the Dark . . . Old Man River . . . My Old Flame . . . They Wouldn't Believe Me, Say It Isn't So . . . The Continental . . . Solitude . . . Time on My Hands . . . Stars Fell on Alabama . . . I Only Have Eyes for You.*

THURSDAY, NOVEMBER 8, 1934 ▓ Walter Winchell said in his column the other day: "Miss Louise Schmaltz of New Orleans has been named Miss America . . . Schmaltz? America?"

Tonight I interviewed her in a night club. With her were three men who have taken control of her professional life, buzzing around her as though she were a queen bee. Also with her was one of the saddest guys I ever met—her fiance. Her handlers ignored him, everyone in the club stared at her, nobody even looked at him.

It was no shock to learn her nickname is "Honey." She truly is beautiful! She stands five four, weighs 116 pounds, has creamy skin and oval face and shining eyes. She also seemed perfectly honest and natural. Before becoming Miss America she won ten other beauty contests, the first when she was only fourteen.

"I had been in swimming," she told me. "Didn't know I was going to enter the contest. Well, they wanted me to, so I came out of the water, tied my wet hair back with a ribbon, put on some old shoes and just walked down the boardwalk once. When they told me I won, I couldn't believe it!"

Turning, she smiled at her boy friend. His glum face remained glum.

I asked her to dance and she accepted. Because I am vain about my dancing ability, I wondered how well she dances. Well, Ellis, she dances as gracefully as I do, or better, so there!

TUESDAY, NOVEMBER 13, 1934 ■ Yesterday at work I had an exciting idea about improving the quality of our news coverage. Here's what I wrote to my boss:

Date—November 12
To—Bureau Manager
From—Ellis
Relative to your request for suggestions to improve AP service, I wish to submit the following:

Let us gather facts from people about unemployment and relief.

We get a lot of figures regarding the philosophy and progress of relief measures, but what does the man on the street think about them?

I realize that the AP never crusades. What I'm suggesting is not a crusade. It is an inquiry into the subject of relief as seen through the eyes of those who receive relief. I have no idea what this inquiry might disclose. It may be favorable to the New Deal or it may be adverse, but whichever it is, it will consist of plain facts.

Obviously, what is true here in New Orleans may not be true elsewhere in the U.S. However, the AP would perform a public service in presenting local conditions.

Here are some questions we might ask:

1) Is anyone in New Orleans actually starving? If so, are there now more starving people than in the past few years?

2) How is relief affecting the morale of those being helped?

3) Is there more begging on streets than before?

4) How concerned about the Depression are rich people and people in the middle class?

5) Does anyone in need of help reject it? If so, why?

This is but a beginning. More questions would grow from these, questions which are not being answered by relief agencies.

You know better than I the number of words we move over the AP wires every day. I believe we could complete this inquiry in about two weeks and then move perhaps 150 words daily.

MONDAY, NOVEMBER 26, 1934   ■   Ever since reaching New Orleans I have written to Phoebe in Mississippi and she has written occasional replies. Her letters have become colder and colder, and in yesterday's letter she explained why: She has broken our engagement and plans to marry a chemical engineer from Houston. *I have lost her!* I wanted lots of work today to help me cope with this crisis but didn't get many assignments outside the office. Instead, much of the time I had to file those damned wires from 6 P.M. until 2 A.M., when what I like about journalism is writing. Tonight when I reached the office Norman handed me a letter with the AP insignia in the upper lefthand corner. I was singing *Stay as Sweet as You Are* as I opened the envelope and read:

Dear Ellis:

Possibly you have reached the same conclusion I have that you have not had sufficient newspaper training to properly handle the work in this bureau. I regret having to reach this conclusion, but you have shown no aptitude for Associated Press work and I think it is unfair for you and for the organization to waste further time with the connection. I will give you until December 15th to find another job and I will be glad to aid you in getting another connection.

Sincerely yours,
Chief of Bureau

And I was still singing when I finished reading it. People believe that a person singing or whistling is happy, but this is not necessarily so. I do both when I'm gloomy. So, I lost my girl. I lost my job. Wonderful, wonderful, Mr. Ellis. From now on I'll call this diary *The Autobiography of a Failure.*

MONDAY, DECEMBER 17, 1934   ■   Today I got a job as a reporter for the *New Orleans Item.* To my surprise, the AP bureau chief really did recommend me to the *Item's* city editor, Don Higgins. I think I'm going to like it here. However, my salary has dropped from $25 to only $18 a week.

1935

THURSDAY, JANUARY 3, 1935 ■ Last Monday I watched jobless men and women rally at the railway station as they sent ten delegates to Washington to lobby for the Lundeen unemployment insurance bill. New Orleans cops broke up their meeting four times. The last time a squad car roared up and five burly cops stepped out. The sergeant had the face and manners of a wild boar. He plowed his way through the poorly clad people surrounding a table on which a speaker stood.

"Whatcha talkin' about?" he bellowed.

Some folks cringed and told him.

"Well, ya got a permit?"

They said Police Superintendent Reyer gave them verbal permission to hold a meeting.

"Well, show ut to me!"

They were unable, of course, to meet this illogical demand. The sergeant growled, glowered and then grunted: "I'm-a gonna listen, an' if I doan like what yuh say, I'll break this thing up!"

They stood in front of a fire-gutted warehouse on a side street near the waterfront. An empty street for folks with empty hearts, empty bellies, empty wallets, empty eyes. The police sergeant listened awhile, his head cocked to one side, and suddenly he bellowed: "Okay! That's it! C'mon, break it up! Get the hell out of here or I'll run ya in!"

To my left stood a tall ragged man holding a placard saying "We demand food, not slop!" Softly, suddenly, he said: "I'm goin' ta stay right where I am."

But he left. So did all the others. They began trudging down a street, their shoulders weary, their eyes angry. A few muttered that they ought to stand and fight, but their leaders spoke soothingly to them and they kept walking.

"Make it snappy!" the sergeant yowled. "Ya lookin' fer trouble? Well, I'll give it to ya, all right! Keep on movin' or I'll run ya all in!"

He saw a Negro woman beckoning to someone to follow her.

"Hey, you! Yeah, you! Hey, you black woman! Who you think you are, tellin' anybody to go along with ya? Who ya think you are—a leader? What's yer name?"

She paused, her face frightened, and in a low voice told him her name. And she kept on shuffling forward.

"Well, you get ta hell about your business! If I catch you trying anything, I'm goin' ta run ya in—see?"

I get angry only a couple of times in two or three years. Now I seethed in impotent fury. If I had been a member of that crowd I don't know what I would have done, but I knew what I wanted to do: I wanted to bludgeon that bully across his stupid head!

The men and women made their way to the second floor of the Marine Workers Industrial Union Hall, also near the waterfront. They crammed into a dingy room—Negroes and whites, all ragged, most of them dirty and hungry. They stood and listened to speeches about the rights of man.

There was talk about battles soon to be won and voices said yes while eyes said maybe, and the folks shifted from foot to foot on the dirty floor near the dirty walls. One speaker was tall and thin and mentioned his military service. When he finished talking I followed him out of the room. He knew I was a reporter, and he was willing to talk. He said he was weak from hunger because he hadn't eaten since the previous noon. He told me he had been the fifth most highly decorated man in the Allied Forces during the World War.

To prove what he said, he pulled out a pawn shop ticket saying he had received five dollars for a war medal. Holding this in his hand, one foot propped up on the low windowsill opening onto a dreary roof, he smiled bitterly and said: "This is what price glory—"

His remark was so melodramatic that somebody may believe that I dreamed it up for my diary, but the man actually said what he said. Of course, he was quoting the title of a play about the war.

MONDAY, JANUARY 14, 1935 ■ Today I had a chance to explore the waterfront for the first time. New Orleans, a major world port, has ten miles of wharves and is used by scores of steamship lines and nine railroads. At the Thalia St. wharf I watched as bananas from Central America were unloaded from a ship by sweating Negro longshoremen. They are paid 45 cents an hour and get work only about three days a week. As I sat watching the men, a hairy tarantula almost ran up my pant leg. Looking up, I began watching the sea gulls soaring over the river and ships and docks. Seldom have I seen such beauty. The sleek white birds have black-tipped wings and long necks, tuck their orange feet under them, and some glided so near that I saw their sparkling eyes. They are the essence of grace. I wish I were a poet because poetry is the best medium for describing these lovely lofty creatures. If I believed in reincarnation, I'd like to come back as a sea gull. I am curious about them, just as I am curious about everything. Life without curiosity wouldn't be worth living. Today I remembered the first two lines of a poem:

What is this life if, full of care
We have no time to stand and stare.

TUESDAY, JANUARY 15, 1935 ■ The city editor has given me my first beat. I'm covering the criminal district court building and parish prison at 2700 Tulane Ave. I've also received a police press card. I work from 5 a.m. to noon. In the prison I eat breakfast with the hangman. He is Henry Meyer, an asthmatic old man with gray eyebrows, a blue shirt, no tie, a black vest, and he has executed 54 people.

The cops astonish me. For one thing, most are grossly ignorant. For another thing, some get drunk on duty. In one station house a lieutenant pulled out a bottle of whiskey and urged me to drink. Another cop said menacingly: "There are lots of things you'll see the police do that you won't like—but forget that! You might itch to print something you've seen, but if you do you won't get any cooperation from them."

FRIDAY, JANUARY 18, 1935 ■ This foggy morning, as fog-horns moaned from the river, I stood in the fuzzy glow of a street light eating a peanut butter sandwich and waiting for Alec, a police reporter for the *Times-Picayune*. He has a Ford coupe and he and I are friendly rivals.

When we reached police headquarters a cop grinned and said: "This morning I really got something for you birds!" Then he explained that a woman had been arrested for shooting and killing a city detective named Louis Tridico. She was being held in the second precinct house. We drove there, slowly, slowly, through fog like mushroom soup.

It was about 6 A.M. when we got to the precinct station. The woman is Mrs. Mamie Ragas. She sat in the light from a bulb in a green hood, at a desk with a typewriter on which a sergeant was typing her confession. Earlier she had told her story to an assistant district attorney, Michael E. Culligan, who now stood in the room beyond the slanting line of the light.

She is 40 years old. She isn't beautiful and she isn't ugly, but something in between. Yesterday she became a grandmother. She wore an orange-black checkered dress, a black coat with a brown collar, no hat. Her reddish-brown hair was mussy and her brown eyes were red-rimmed from weeping. She was calm. She told her story softly, without gestures, and waited patiently when the sergeant's typing lagged behind her narrative.

"Louis was a friend of mine once, but I hadn't seen him in about a year and a half. The last time I saw him was when he returned from a trip to Hot Springs with Myrtle DuBuc. About a week later Myrtle called me and asked me if I knew Louis Tridico, and I said yes. She came over and we talked about him . . ."

After that, she continued, she didn't see Tridico until last night when he came to her house to congratulate her upon becoming a grandmother.

"It was after midnight, and my sister, Sophia Welch, answered the bell. It was Louis. He asked for me and she told him I was at Delmonico's restaurant at St. Charles and Erato Streets. He came over there and we had a couple of drinks. Then we returned to my house and he began fumbling in his pockets. He had been drinking. He asked me for his automobile keys. I told him I didn't have them, that he must have lost them. He began calling me a bitch and other things . . ."

She said she ran into her bedroom and reached under the mattress for a .32-calibre revolver and hid it in her bosom. She went back to him and after a few minutes he left, still cursing and mumbling.

"I closed the door, but he returned a few minutes later, still insisting that I had his keys. I called a cab, but when it arrived he refused to leave and chased the cab driver away. All the time he was cursing me."

She said she told him he may have left his keys in Myrtle DuBuc's house, two blocks away, so she was going to go there.

"He grabbed me when I said that, and he slapped me. When he grabbed at me, I pulled the gun out, and had it in my hand, but I didn't use it because I felt sorry for him and his children. He has two such pretty children."

She said she broke away from Tridico and ran down the street to Miss DuBuc's house.

"Myrtle woke up and answered the door. She was mad, too, because I woke her up. I told her to please come to my house and get Louis. We were talking about it and suddenly Louis was standing there on the stairs, sort of weaving."

Miss DuBuc looked at him and asked where his tie was. He said he didn't know, and he also didn't know where his keys were.

"Myrtle opened his coat, found his tie in his left top pocket, and straightened it and his shirt. We all then went into Myrtle's little apartment. Louis looked at me and started cursing me all over again, and said he didn't care what I said to Myrtle, or how I said it. But I hadn't gone over there to make trouble between them—only to try to get him away from my house, my home. He was so drunk. He said he'd make it hot for me. Then he dared me to shoot him, and all the while I had the gun on me. He shouted: 'I'll make you eat that gun!', so I had the gun in my hand and just pulled the trigger. I wasn't going to let him call my bluff in front of Myrtle, no matter what the consequences were! I ain't worryin' none. If I have to kick, it ain't worryin' me.

"Well, I shot him and he kind of stared at me. His eyes opened kind of wide and he swayed and then he lunged toward me, and I thought he was going to grab me, so I shot him again. He was only five or six feet away from me when I shot him. He went down like a ton of bricks, and stayed there. Myrtle screamed that I'd shot her man and she ran out of the room. I knew the police would get there sooner or later, so I just sat on the edge of the bed to wait for them. I'm sorry it had to happen. I'm sorry because of his two little kids. They're beautiful children."

Mamie Ragas, murderess, turned and smiled a half-smile at me. In the glare of the bulb dangling from the ceiling I saw she had an elbow on the table, her face in her hand, and I heard the wail of a fog-horn and I stared at Mamie and she gazed at me with eyes that were soft and I felt sad, very sad.

TUESDAY, JANUARY 22, 1935   ■   Snow fell on roses today in New Orleans. These southern people couldn't have been more excited by the outbreak of another War Between the States.

About 5 A.M. I walked downstairs and met a night watchman on a corner behind St. Louis Cathedral. In the glow of an antique street lamp he held the palm of his hand toward the white sky. A few flakes melted on his skin.

"Lookit that!" he exulted. "Lookit that!" Pointing at himself, he said: "Had a top-coat on when I began duty last night, but—gosh! I sure had to change into this overcoat, even if it does have moth holes in it!"

This is the first snowfall in New Orleans since 1899, according to the old-timers. While they aren't all exactly sure of the date, they agree it has been "some little spell" since the last time.

When I walked into the press room at the criminal court building, a reporter yelled: "Eddie! Is this snow?"

"Why, sure."

"Well," he said slowly, "I wasn't sure whether it was snow or ice."

We got in his car to drive out to get a story and this southern boy exclaimed at almost every snowflake. Excitedly he pointed at what he called snowdrifts—none more than a half inch deep. When we returned he jumped out of his car, scooped up what little snow he could and sprinkled it on his hat and shoulders. Then he yelled to a telephone operator in the building and she threw on a coat and joined us outdoors. She shouted in amazement. We put her under a palm tree, then hammered at the trunk to shake some snow off the fronds and onto her. Proud as a queen in ermine, she ran back inside to show her white collar to her friends.

Later in the day a man on a streetcar told me: "I got my wife and daughter out of bed and we all hurried into the yard. My little girl made a snowball and threw it at her mother. My wife said: 'That's the first time I've ever been hit by a snowball!' "

Instead of working today, these people who never before had seen snow frolicked outdoors or hung around doors and windows to gawk at something they called a miracle. A burly Negro grinned and said: "Man! Tom an' Jerry'll sho catch hell today!" Eleven precincts reported snow. The twelfth precinct reported egg nogs.

THURSDAY, APRIL 4, 1935 ▪ The other day I asked for a raise. God! My heart couldn't have pounded any harder had someone shoved me over Niagara Falls without a barrel. Clarke Salmon, the managing editor, was pleasant. "You're in line for a raise," he said, "but I'm not promising anything. It may come in two months, it may come in six months. I don't know. I do know, however, that your work here is quite satisfactory." Well, words are one thing while my pocketbook is something else. Poverty eats into my flesh like acid.

SATURDAY, JUNE 15, 1935 ▪ This Saturday night I had to work, and when I reached the office at 7:30 the city editor told me to grab a cab and get to Magazine and St. Joseph Streets. "Some fellow's shot himself."

In 15 minutes I was at that corner. A crowd and three cops stood around a Buick roadster. I told one cop I was from the *Item*.

"Okay," he said. "Name's Joe Watkins. Thirty-four. Works E. J. Mothe Company, Algiers. Shot himself. Twenty-two rifle." And the cop showed me a bloody coat.

The man who tried to kill himself was in the car. Suddenly he screamed. I walked over and looked inside. The inside of the car was light enough for me to see that the man was sitting stiffly against the seat, holding his belly. His crumpled shirt was drenched in blood. It seemed true, as another cop had told me, that he had shot himself near the heart.

Turning to the people standing nearby, surprised at my own boldness, I asked: "Is anyone here a friend of this man?" None knew him.

Looking again into the car, I asked: "Joe, why did you do this?"

"I want to die! . . . I don't want to live! . . ."

One bystander said: "Maybe he was goin' huntin'. He's got a rifle."

I asked: "Where were you headed, Joe?"

"I'm headed for hell!" he screamed. "I'm headed for hell!"

I smelled whiskey on his breath.

"Did you do any drinking tonight, Joe?"

"Yeah. . . . My wife's good, but I'm a no good son-of-a-bitch!"

An ambulance from Charity hospital pulled up and two attendants got out and walked over to the car. One attendant tried to place a stethoscope on Joe's gory chest, then the two men conferred and finally they lifted him out of his car and gently placed him on a stretcher.

"Sorry to make all this racket," Joe said as he lay there. Looking up at me, he extended his hand and said: "Shake!"

His hand was covered in blood. Appalled at it, I hesitated, and before I could decide he was whisked away. I hated myself. Refuse to shake hands with a man who might be dying! What a prig you are, Ellis!

FRIDAY, JUNE 21, 1935 ■ Yesterday marked my tenth month in New Orleans, so I think I'll jot down my impressions of this city. I've moved out of the apartment I shared with other guys at 708 Orleans St. and now have my own room and private balcony at 714 Orleans, still behind the gray spires of St. Louis Cathedral. Now I'm covering the waterfront as best I can, considering the fact that it has ten miles of wharves and even more miles where ships tie up. New Orleans is 110 miles from the Gulf of Mexico, and the Mississippi River really is muddy, very muddy, and has a strong current . . . New Orleans is like no other city I ever saw because it has a flavor all its own, not at all American, as Chicago and Kansas City, but continental and carefree, The City That Care Forgot, as they say down here . . . I live in the French Quarter, the oldest part of the city, but the architecture is more Spanish than French . . . the houses are flush with the narrow sidewalks, called *banquettes*, and one walks beneath balconies, called *galleries*, and as I stroll down Royal St. I sometimes dodge water thrown on flowers on the balconies, or the wetness of overhead dogs relieving themselves . . . The buildings, some private homes and some apartment houses, are only three or four stories high, for the most part, and shabby looking on the outside . . . to be let inside is to discover patios fragrant with flowers, alive with the splashing of fountains and as peaceful as paradise . . . in fact, *Paradise* comes from a Persian word meaning an enclosed garden . . . the people themselves are colorful, quaint, individualistic, some of them Creoles, many of them artists such as musicians and painters and writers . . . speaking of writers, William Faulkner lived in the French Quarter a few years ago, and stories of his heavy drinking still reverberate here . . . Ednard Waldo of the *Item* knew Faulkner, called him Bill, and one day saw him stagger into a bar wearing nothing but shorts . . . with him was a woman completely naked, except for some painting on her flesh . . . one nipple was painted green and the word GO was painted on the fleshy part, the other nipple was painted red with the word STOP beneath, and there also were a couple of arrows pointed toward her pubic hair . . . I demanded to know whether Ednard saw this with his own eyes, and he swore he did . . . here in the French Quarter drinking is almost as normal as breathing . . . Bourbon Street, with its many bars, is frenetic almost every hour of the day and night, the sounds of jazz spilling out their doors, drunks wandering in and out . . . in one bar I became paralyzed with pity when I saw an oaf of a bartender spray seltzer water on an old woman begging for food . . . one afternoon I saw Thomas Hart Benton, the painter, served tea in the Arts and Craft Club and noted the look of disgust on his dark face as he peered at the very tiny cup . . . the *Item* has an alcoholic photographer who is drunk all the time, and one day he was sent to the cathedral to take a picture of a visiting archbishop . . . Mac staggered inside, saw a group of priests, raised his camera and banged away . . . an *Item* reporter hurried over to him to whisper that the archbishop was not one of the priests, that he'd have to wait to photograph him . . . in a loud voice Mac said: "Fuck the archbishop!" . . . this city is so flat that in Audubon Park a dirt hill was built so that kids might see what a hill looks like . . . because the water level is high here, dead people are not buried in the ground but are put in small tombs that look like ovens, on top of the ground . . . streetcars have special sections for colored people . . . some street names are long and difficult . . . I've heard that a cop found a dead horse on Tchoupitoulas St., but dragged it around the corner to Canal St. to make it easier to write out his report . . . pushcarts carry huge hunks of ice which the vendor shaves off and sweetens with colored juices, thus making a "snowball" . . . dangling from the pushcarts are sleighbells . . . in this year of the Depression some 8,000 people are going hungry and kids eat out of garbage cans . . . here and there on the streets are "spasm bands" consisting of two or three black urchins playing music with instruments made from tin cans . . . many adults finish a night on the town by sitting in stalls in the French Market, along Decatur St., eating its famous doughnuts and drinking its famous coffee . . . in the Negro sections of town the poverty is depressing . . . one day as I walked to work I was propositioned by five whores, each asking only 50 cents . . . heart-breaking!

MONDAY, JULY 1, 1935 ▪ I owe almost $800 for my college education.

FRIDAY, JULY 12, 1935   I've been told that the *Houston Chronicle* pays its cub reporters $35 a week. Here in New Orleans the *Times-Picayune* reporters get twice as much as those of us on the *Item*. In fact, the *Item* is known throughout the south for its low wage scale. Leonard Hinton, an *Item* editorial writer and a nice guy, explained our publisher's sophistry whenever he tries to justify the coolie wages he pays us: 1) New Orleans has few trade schools; 2) therefore, there are few trained workers; 3) therefore, labor as a whole is not paid well in this city; 4) therefore, the publisher does not wish to embarrass other institutions here by paying high wages on the *Item*.

Oh, yeahhh?

TUESDAY, JULY 23, 1935   Last night I went to the Golden Dragon, a Negro nightclub on South Rampart St., to listen to Louie Armstrong.

Not long ago he came back to New Orleans where he was born, came back in triumph because in England he had played a command performance for King George VI. This is his homecoming, so Louie lifted up his golden trumpet and blew glad notes.

Yowls of joy soared from hundreds of throats: "... Lissen-a-that! ... Lissen-a-that! ... His ole theme song, sure nuff! ..."

Louie was ladling out *When It's Sleepytime Down South.*

South Rampart St. was the place to be last night. One of its own had made good — and made good and made good! Now he was back with them again, grinning his infectious grin, braying the lyrics in his brassy voice, same old Louie. He gave his trumpet one last loving kiss, and then there was Satchelmouth at the microphone. He wore no tie, his shirtsleeves were rolled up, and around his neck he wore a towel, like every other champion. On the fourth finger of his left hand he wore a ring with diamonds that glittered and glinted and vied with one another to shine the best.

Pale moon shinin' on the fields below / Darkies singin' sweet an' low ...

The rasping and gurgling of his voice made my spine feel like a xylophone. He slid from one note to a lower one and then careened down to a guttural bass note lower than my worst sin. As he sang he mopped his face and weaved back and forth, but he kept his black eyes on the mike under his nose, like a serpent hypnotizing a bird. Not until he reached the end of the ballad did he free the mike from his spell, but when he did so he let out one final boom that could have frightened the poor thing to death.

With his towel he swabbed the sweat from his squat face, and grinned and laughed, and the dancers crowded around him, holding up hands to be shaken and things to be autographed. One cinnamon-colored woman begged for his autograph: "Please, Louie baby! Aw, please, Louie boy! C'mon an' write on this here card, woan you?"

Louis signed and sweated and talked with me about his childhood. He was born in a poor part of New Orleans on July 4, 1900, and as a child he was a street singer. When he was twelve he shot off his father's gun on New Year's Eve and was sent to the Colored Waif's Home for Boys. There he was taught to read music and play the drums, bugle and cornet. Later he learned more from Joe (King) Oliver, the greatest cornetist in New Orleans before the war. Louie switched from the cornet to the trumpet, and the gold one he used tonight was given to him in England. After charming the British monarch, Louie crossed over to Europe, where his reputation became phenomenal. Now everybody knows he is the world's greatest jazz musician. He has worn out four trumpets and no welcomes.

He didn't tell me all this in the nightclub, because it was noisy, but I had read about him before getting there. His mother is dead, but his father still lives here. When I said I was from the *Item* he told me he sold copies of the *Item* on the street when he was a kid.

Not only were black people welcoming Louie home again, but white men and women were to be seen amidst the mob of happy people packed into the Golden Dragon. The waiters were having the time of their lives. They jigged and shuffled and bared their teeth in song as they wafted trays of drinks over the heads of the swaying hundreds. One waiter was busy lighting cigarets in his mouth and then handing them out with a flourish to the dusky damsels sitting at a nearby table. It was an adoring audience. Every time Louie picked up his golden trumpet, the folks settled into a trance of expectation, and Louie didn't fail them. Like another Gabriel, he blew his horn and opened the gates to heaven.

SATURDAY, JULY 27, 1935 ■ I need a new typewriter. This old Corona portable has grown rheumatic and stiff. Because of this, I type my diary in the office.

MONDAY, SEPTEMBER 9, 1935 ■ Last night about 11 I was outdoors and heard a newsboy yelling "Extra! . . . Extra!" He was selling copies of the *Tribune*, the morning paper put out by the company that also publishes the *Item*, for which I work. Crossing the street I bought a paper and saw this headline:

HUEY LONG SHOT!

I felt as though I'd been hit by lightning. I ran down the block and found a cab and threw myself into it while yelling: "*Item* office—and make it fast!"

When I charged into the city room it felt like falling into a cement mixer—men yelling, phones ringing, copy boys running, editors barking orders, typewriters clickety-clacking, wide-eyed visitors babbling, more reporters and editors plunging into the rooms. There was blood on the moon tonight, and everyone was a little crazy.

Huey shot? Just last month he announced he was running for the Presidency. I got the story of the shooting in dribs and drabs. Huey was up in Baton Rouge in the state capitol building where he had called a special session of the house. He was planning to curtail New Deal activities in Louisiana, and this evening he was on the floor of the chamber to make sure that his legislative puppets did his bidding.

Also present in the capitol was Charles (Chick) Frampton, an *Item* reporter and my friend who sits at the desk next to mine here in the city room. Many a time had I listened as Chick talked about his unusual relationship with Huey Long. It seems that soon after he became governor he became enraged by attacks made on him by newspapers in cities and large towns. He felt he couldn't trust any of their reporters. He had talked to me before I joined the *Item* because I worked for the AP and Huey knew its reputation for impartiality. The *Item* was one of the many papers criticizing him. Huey, who had an original way of doing everything, telephoned the city editor of the *Item* one day and growled:

"I'm tired of these reporters following me around all the time! Have you got one man there that's got any sense at all, that I can talk with, and I'll clear everything with this one man."

The city editor—I think it was Don Higgins—glanced around the city room and when he saw Chick he told Huey he had such a man.

Huey roared: "Put that son-of-a-bitch on the phone!"

Half-amused, half-angered, Chick took the phone and said to the governor: "Now, look! Before we go any further, I don't want you using that kind of language on me."

Huey chortled: "You'll do! C'mon over here."

That, Chick had told me, was the genesis of his odd arrangement with Huey Long. I wanted to know whether Huey asked him to slant the news in his behalf. No. Did Chick color his stories in favor of Huey? No. Huey just told Chick whatever he wanted to tell him. Chick was the only reporter able to get in touch with Huey at any time. Late one night, Chick told me, he called Huey in his suite in the Roosevelt Hotel in New Orleans. Huey was married and had three children, but he also had a mistress, Alice Lee Grosjean, once married, now divorced, a brunette in her twenties, a very smart lady. That night Chick's call awakened Huey. Chick told him that his secretary of state had just died. Chick heard Huey yell; "Roll over, Alice! You're my new secretary of state!" And, indeed, he gave her that position.

So last night Chick was in the house chamber in the capitol and as Huey walked out he stopped to chat with Chick. It was about 9 P.M., time for the house to adjourn. Chick walked to the governor's office to use a phone, calling long-distance to the *Item* office and speaking with our telegraph editor, George Coad. George told Chick a hurricane had hit Florida and some CCC boys on the keys down there were in danger of drowning. Maybe the senator might wish to comment.

Chick told George to hang on. He would use another phone to reach Huey in the office of the sergeant-at-arms, next to the house chamber, and get a quote. When Chick got Huey on the second line, the senator asked where he was and Chick said in the governor's office.

"Wait there," Huey said. "I'm coming to see you.

On the phone to New Orleans Chick told George to keep the line open.

Huey and his bodyguards left the little office and walked through a marble corridor toward the office of the governor. He paused a moment near the main door to the governor's office. It was 9:20 P.M. At that moment Chick Frampton opened the door to see whether Huey had arrived. Also at that moment a man in a white suit stepped out from behind a pillar and walked up to Huey. He raised his right hand. It held a small pistol. A bodyguard hit his arm the very second the man fired. Huey screamed: "I'm shot!"

He wheeled around and began running toward stairs leading down to the basement.

Huey's bodyguards fired at the gunman again and again and again, shooting off part of his face.

After many chaotic minutes it was learned that the assassination attempt had been made by Dr. Carl Weiss, 29, an idealist, a brilliant doctor, a man who may have believed that Huey had ruined his father, also a physician.

Huey was driven to Our Lady of the Lake Hospital. Chick Frampton ran there from the capitol building. When he reached the side of the wounded man, Huey asked: "Chick, who was that who shot me?"

"Don't you know?" Chick asked in surprise.

A little later a state trooper arrived and said the gunman had been identified as a Dr. Weiss.

Huey muttered: "Weiss . . . Dr. Weiss . . . What did he want to shoot me for?"

TUESDAY, SEPTEMBER 10, 1935 ■ Huey Long died today. He was 42 years old.

WEDNESDAY, NOVEMBER 6, 1935 ■ Ethel Barrymore arrived in New Orleans last night in her private Pullman car and refused to see any reporters or photographers. She is on tour in a play called *The Constant Wife*.

Late this morning in the city room I heard such a hubbub at the city desk that I walked over to see what was happening and found Sue Bryan telling a fascinating story. Sue, an *Item* reporter, is a member of a prominent New Orleans family. She was saying that this morning she waited at the railway station from 7:45 to 10:45 to try to get an interview with Miss Barrymore, but—!

In an excited voice Sue was giving the details to Charlie Campbell, the assistant city editor, with other editors and reporters leaning in to catch her every word. Sue said that at about 10:45 she saw the actress leaving her private railway car and walking toward a taxi.

"Miss Barrymore—" Sue cried, hurrying toward her.

La Barrymore stopped long enough to raise both arms toward heaven in a gesture of supplication. Then—

"I never give interviews!" she screamed at Sue.

Sue now was telling us that Barrymore was drunk, very drunk.

"But, Miss Barrymore! . . . Aw, c'mon, Miss Barrymore!"

"I do *not* give interviews!!"

Sue said her voice was so shrill it frightened pigeons atop the railroad station.

Then the actress added: "—especially to such ignorant young reporters as yourself, you little rat!"

Sue, accustomed to the manners of debutantes, listened in astonishment as Barrymore twice more called her a rat.

"If you call me a rat again," Sue yelled, "I'll knock you down!"

"Oh, you will, will you?" screeched the actress. Screwing up her face and reaching out with stiff fingers, she clawed the air close to Sue's eyes.

In the city room Sue told us: "I actually got scared. She looked like a witch! You can't imagine! Her eyes were sunken in, her hair was black and dishevelled, and her black coat was drawn up around her throat. She was so drunk she hardly could stand up!"

Charlie Campbell told her to go ahead and write the story just as it happened. Staff members cheered and laughed, making so much noise that the publisher, James M. Thomson, shuffed out in his bedroom slippers to ask what all the fuss was about. When he was told, he beckoned Sue into his office. When she came out she mournfully announced that he told her he wouldn't print her story because a friend of his, who knows Miss Barrymore, had called to ask him to treat her well.

"Scoop" Kennedy spoke for all of us when he snarled: "Why, that yellow-livered son-of-a-bitch!"

But the United Press correspondent heard about Sue and asked her to write the yarn for his wire service under her by-line. Great!

MONDAY, DECEMBER 30, 1935   ▓   Again I asked the managing editor for a raise. He said he likes my work and he agreed I'm worth more than I'm paid. He said he'd do what he could with the publisher, James McIlhany Thomson.

1936

Heywood Broun visited New Orleans early in 1936. I was eager to see the founder of the American Newspaper Guild. I listened to him speak and then I attended a private party given in Broun's honor in the French Quarter. Before going to bed that night I wrote six typed pages in my diary. Here are excerpts from my diary of that day—some impressions of Heywood Broun, the crusading journalist, by a cub reporter:

THURSDAY, JANUARY 2, 1936   ▓   Heywood Broun was scheduled to speak at eight o'clock tonight in the Socialist party's local headquarters, 308 Chartres St. I arrived early and, never having visited this Socialist hall before, gazed about with interest. The place had a barren look, its only furniture being several hard chairs, one piano, one phonograph and one table. Spread out on the table, for display and sale, was Socialist literature, such as a brochure by Morris Hillquit entitled "Foundations of Socialism." The walls were decorated with a red flag and placards and photographs, one of them a picture of Eugene V. Debs. Because I got there early I was able to take a seat in the front row, just in front of Broun.

When he was introduced, he ambled over to the piano to rest his right arm upon it. The moment I saw Broun I was reminded of a Roman Senator from the golden age of Pericles, so great was his girth, so curly was his hair. This impression soon faded, however, for Broun was the quintessence of informality, rather than pomposity. He spoke with animation and heat, rivers of sweat coursing down from the highlands of his forehead and spilling over the fat pastures of his cheeks. A dimple in his left cheek fascinated me, for it appeared, disappeared, reappeared—a fleshy twinkle.

At one point Broun said: "I always hate to use the phrase 'white-collar worker' because I'm not always sure about my own." And, his eyes mischievous, he grabbed at his collar which, to tell the truth, was not the cleanest I ever had seen. Then my eyes wandered down from Broun's collar to his shirt-front, which had been patched.

Among other things, Broun remarked that it is difficult for a man to rise in the newspaper field. "The only way to get ahead," he said, "is by being imperfect in the niche where you were put. If you fit perfectly, you have to stay where you are."

To illustrate this point, Broun described his own uneven progress in journalism. He said he started as a copyreader and was fast at this job but not completely accurate. He was transferred to rewrite where, he said, he was no great shakes. Then a baseball writer died and Broun inherited his post, but Broun's ambition was to become a drama critic. The newspaper's veteran drama critic was aware of Broun's dream and, according to Broun, would warn him every now and then: "Don't look at me like that, Heywood! I'm in good health." He wasn't, though, and when he was taken sick Broun finally became a drama critic.

For an hour and a half Heywood Broun talked about the coolie wages paid white-collar workers, the failure of capitalism, the dangers of fascism, the stupidity of war, the death of the *New York World*, the appeal of journalism to young people, and other things. Then the meeting was thrown open to questions.

Someone asked: "Mr. Broun, what is the origin of the policy of underpaying reporters?"

A laugh arose from the crowd, composed mainly of newspaper people, and Broun laughed with them. Grinning like Falstaff, he replied:

"Well, maybe it's because publishers think about reporters in much the way that many people think about Irishmen. The Irishman, you know, is considered a jovial, happy-go-lucky, devil-may-care sort of fellow, always throwing away his money and getting drunk and not caring much about tomorrow.

"It's been pretty much the same way with the newspaperman. Originally, he fell in with the so-called romantic tradition of the press. He liked the work so much he felt he really didn't care how much he was paid.

"But now things are different. Now the reporter may drink as much as ever, he may be just as much a devil-may-care sort of chap, but now he says that when he gets drunk he wants to do it on his own money—not on the bartender's credit!"

THURSDAY, JANUARY 30, 1936   ■   I'm interested in labor affairs because work-ingmen are underdogs, I'm not making much money, and so I also am an underdog. The other night in the French Quarter a ragged man approached me and mumbled: "Mister, I don't want any money but—please! Won't you buy me a cup of coffee?" I paused for a second and then said: "Sure! Where?" He led me to a lunch counter and sat down on a stool. I put a dime on the counter and suggested he get a doughnut, too. His dirty hand over the coin, he looked at me with pleading eyes and begged: ""Do you . . . uh, do you mind if I get some stew instead?" I shuddered.

FRIDAY, FEBRUARY 9, 1936   ■   My salary has been increased from $18 to $21 a week. A weak hurrah. I worked 59 weeks at $18 a week and, believe me, that's marginal living! Maybe I'm supposed to be grateful for this raise, but I'm not. Damn that stupid damn publisher!

MONDAY, MARCH 9, 1936   ■   Today I bought a new suit costing $15. I paid half today and will pay the balance next week.

THURSDAY, MARCH 19, 1936   ■   I saw a woman standing on the sidewalk at the foot of an office building 20 stories high. She held a cup with a few pencils in it. I gazed up the facade of the skyscraper, 20 floors of masonry and metal, a monument to the skill of architects, engineers, contractors, carpenters, hodcarriers and the like. A triumph of mind over matter. Soci-ety can erect an imposing building such as this, but cannot clothe one woman?

WEDNESDAY, MARCH 25, 1936   ■   The telephone operator for the Texas Transport and Terminal Co. is a big blonde, name of Winnie, half-Dutch, 29 years old, always goodnatured. That is, until today. When I went there to get a story her eyes were red and she asked me to wait for her in the hall. Alone together, she told me that today everyone in her office had received a raise, except for one other person and herself. She is divorced and has a four-year-old son. She's trying to better herself by studying secretarial work in a night school. Her company pays her—get this! Her company pays her only $10.51 per week! Damn! This is the kind of thing that makes me want to become a socialist or communist or anarchist or something!

MONDAY, APRIL 13, 1936   ■   This morning on a street I saw a penniless fam-ily of five—father, mother, three children. The kids were begging. The father was carrying one child. Seeing their misery hurt my belly. After I'd walked past them, I just had to call one of the boys to me, so that I might slip a few coins into his small hand. Nonetheless, I felt guilty, as though I were a member of the social class responsible for their plight.

FRIDAY, APRIL 17, 1936   ▦   I'm eating on one dollar a day. The best bargain is a heaping platter of red beans and rice, costing 35 cents. New Orleans is noted for its sea food and famous restaurants, but of course I can't afford to eat in them. Taken to dinner by friends, I've come to like oysters and shrimp and swordfish — delicacies I seldom saw in Illinois.

TUESDAY, MAY 5, 1936   ▦   This evening in an apartment on Bourbon St. some friends and I began talking about poverty. Having a few drinks in me, soon I was pacing the floor and raging about social conditions. When my mother needed a cancer operation at the Mayo Clinic in Rochester, Minn., I wanted to be with her so I had to borrow $50 from the *Item* to get there by train. (Mother was very brave and the operation turned out okay.) Anyway, the *Item* is charging me 20 per cent interest on that loan. Bastards!

FRIDAY, MAY 29, 1936   ▦   Today my friend Charles Richards, who's a staff artist on the *Item*, drew this sketch of me.

WEDNESDAY, JULY 29, 1936 ■ I was sauntering along Commercial Alley when suddenly I saw a new book store. Naturally, I had to look inside, and there I saw the entire *Harvard Classics*, all 51 volumes. Because I am poor I had no intention of buying this famous set but thought it wouldn't hurt to ask its price, and so I asked. The whole dang thing for only $7.50? Gulp. Then I gulped again. It seemed to me that it was my duty as a human being not to let that bargain get away, so I inquired whether it might be purchased on the installment plan. Yes. Yes? Should I buy it? Yes, yes, yes! Could I pay at the rate of one dollar a week? Yes. I thought I heard a heavenly choir. I paid the man a dollar and walked out in a state of delirium. At home in Kewanee I still have that set of 60 books called *World's Greatest Literature*, which I bought in Illinois for only nine dollars. Now, altogether, I own about 400 books.

MONDAY, AUGUST 24, 1936 ■ Ed LeBreton used to be a reporter on the *Item*. Nice guy. Six foot one, skinny, gentle, Phi Beta Kappa. About three months ago he left here to take a job with the *Oklahoma City Times* because it pays $35 a week. Then he came back here to marry Barbara Logan, a lovely lady, and was so rushed I had only ten minutes with him. Nonetheless, he said the city editor of the *Times* wants a new feature writer, and Ed suggested I write the man. The editor's name is Jack Bell. I wrote to ask for a job and today I got a reply from Bell. He offered me a two-week trial and said the paper will pay my railway fare both ways if I'm not accepted there. I became so excited that my hands trembled. Bell said in his letter: "Frankly, I want a man who can write light, frothy stuff, who can take a few facts and dress them up in clever, wise-cracking language . . ." This part bothers me. A long time ago I realized I am neither witty nor clever, I'm just sincere. However, to go from $21 to $35 a week is dreamy stuff, and I do have a vacation coming, so I'll go to Oklahoma City and try out.

SUNDAY, AUGUST 30, 1936 ■ I rode the Illinois Central to Memphis, then the Rock Island to Oklahoma City, reading *Time* magazine and figuring out a novel I want to write. Arriving here at 10:30 P.M., I took a room at the Black Hotel, walked around the business district, saw the flood-lit *Times* building, stared at its facade and muttered to myself: "Veni, vidi, vici!" I hope I spell these words correctly; after all, in high school I did flunk Latin.

Jack Bell, city editor of the Oklahoma City Times, *later left there for Washington, D.C., where he worked for the Associated Press, first covering* the Senate, then the White House. On November 22, 1963, he was in the press car behind John F. Kennedy when the President was assassinated.

OKLAHOMA CITY, FRIDAY, SEPTEMBER 4, 1936 ▪ I can't understand Jack Bell. He never raises his voice, but he's as hard-boiled as they come. I heard him bawl the hell out of Ed LeBreton, whom I've always admired as a reporter and as a man. Bell slapped Ed's story down on his desk and snarled: "This is lousy!" This is scary in itself but even worse is the fact that he wants me to write absolutely screwy feature stories. I'm supposed to step into the shoes of a reporter who, by common consent, was the wittiest man on the staff. Furthermore, as a general practice, even some serious stories are burlesqued. I don't get it.

And—the *Times* city room is neat, clean, calm, quiet, orderly. The *Item* is disorderly, frenetic, loud, picturesque, and has trash on the floor. Here at the *Times* no piece of paper is allowed to fall to the floor. At the *Item* it is almost a sacred obligation to litter the floor. Here at the *Times* the managing editor has sent around a memo calling upon editors and reporters to keep their desks as neat as possible. It looks more like an insurance office than a newspaper office. I prefer the chaos of the *Item*.

SATURDAY, SEPTEMBER 5, 1936 ▪ This evening Ed and Barbara LeBreton took me to dinner with Beth Campbell, who is on the staff of the *Times*. I've heard from everyone that she's one helluva great reporter. She also is pretty and bright and, as I learned, a great dancer. I like her a lot. The state of Oklahoma is supposed to be a dry state, but everyone from state legislators on down manages to drink booze. This evening we all chipped in to buy gin, which was delivered by a bootlegger on a white motorcycle.

THURSDAY, SEPTEMBER 10, 1936 ▪ This afternoon Jack Bell sat down on a corner of my desk and drawled:

"Well, Ellis, I guess by now you know you're not the man I was looking for. You just can't write the sort of nut story I want. Tell you what to do: You go on back to New Orleans, back to your job, and keep in touch with me. After awhile I'll probably have an opening for you here. Right now I want a definite sort of man, one who can write freak stuff. I can't exactly define the thing I want, but I want it . . ."

He was smiling.

"The fact that you can't write this sort of thing doesn't mean that you're not a good feature writer, though. You've turned in some damned fine feature stories."

FRIDAY, SEPTEMBER 11, 1936   ■   Today I had seven stories in the *Times* and tonight I had a date with Beth Campbell.

SATURDAY, SEPTEMBER 12, 1936   ■   Since this is my last day at the *Times* I thought I had nothing to lose by pounding out a truly nutty story, and it made the front page under my by-line. I saw Jack Bell laugh over it. Here's the story:

HONK! HONK!
WHO'S DERE?
FEBER BOYS

De city editor called me ober to his desk. "You're a fide loogig specibum," he said. "Whud's a maddur?"

"Hey feber," I gasbbed. "Id god me, pal!"

"Hay feber—haw, haw, haw," he labbed.

"Yes, hay feber," I snordded. "Fuddy, isn't id? Too fuddy for words. You'b god de sense ob humor ob a grave-digger."

When he god through labbing, he said, "Wride me a story about hay feber. Whud's it lige? What causes id? Whud can you do for id? You know."

I starded bag to my desg, bud was blowd off my course three tibbes by udder guys here who god id, too. De noise dey made was worse'n a boiler fagdory. I hug ub de tweddy-sig haggerchiefs I brod to the office to dry, gathered ub all de papers I blew off my desg in sneezig, hed four of the cobby boys jerg by bagbone bag indo place, add here I ab!

Zero hour for hay feber subberers was 4 P.M. Thursday, mosd ob them agree. Then they led loose with a concerted sneeze that'd make de artillery barrage of the battle of the Marne loog sig. Seismiographig instruments in California pigged ub de tremor.

Droud dis year delayed de season. Pollen-bearing plands didn'd mature as fast as usual. Frub now udtil Ogtober 10 dey'll be in full swig. On an average year dey begin to ged bad aboud August 18. Aroud here we have ragweed, pigweed, Berbuda grass which do de dirdy worg. In de panhandle seggshun of Texas where dey habe Russian thistle, 10 percent of de people have hay feber. Aboud 2 percent suffer in Oglahoma.

For some reason de worst of id comes in de early morning just avder you get ub, add lade in de afderdood. Dis is unofficial, howeber, add no arrests are made to addyone foudd sneezing before of afder dese hours. Id's open season add a limitless bag.

Dogdors can heb some by desentizing dem, while some only ged temporary relief. Close your widdows at nide, as dis keebs out de pollen. Don'd sleep on feather pillows. Watch your diet.

As a victim of years stadding, I wish to propose dese rules:

1—In de fall of de year take an apartmund in a safety deposit vault.

2—When a sneeze begins to cub on, stard talking aboud your operation add the sneeze will be ashamed add go hide ids head.

3—Write your congressmad.

4—Stop breathing.

NEW ORLEANS, WEDNESDAY, SEPTEMBER 23, 1936 ■ In all the months I've covered the waterfront nothing happened that was so beautiful, so spiritual, as what happened tonight. To get a story about a river pilot, I met him at the Gulf of Mexico and we boarded a freighter, climbing up the Jacob's ladder to the deck, so that we might steam up the Mississippi River to New Orleans. It was a moonless star-lit night. I stood on the bridge of the ship, my arms on a railing, the pilot and quartermaster nearby but speaking softly whenever they had to speak at all. Peering toward the bow I saw the outline of the lookout man, and I saw the lantern on the forward mast, and then I turned aft and saw a second high lantern. Every quarter-hour a bell's clang split the air, the pure sweet-smelling air, and when I glanced from starboard to port I could not detect whether it was our ship that glided along, or the shoreline itself. The stars, like the eyes of celestial cats, were brighter and larger and closer than any I'd seen since crossing the Mojave Desert. I was conscious of my body only because I felt healthy and because my skin tingled pleasantly in the chill of the night. What surprised me was my mind. The littleness of life, the trivial worries, the humdrumness of existence—all had vanished. I felt high on beauty. I felt I floated in a bubble of serenity swinging heavenward, high and ever higher, and when part of my mind looked down it seemed to see other parts of my mind like diamonds sparkling with truths I'd never glimpsed before. I felt calm and clean and clear, at peace with myself and the world, in a soft mood like the sustained sound of a flute.

WEDNESDAY, SEPTEMBER 30, 1936 ■ Don Higgins, the city editor, called me over to his desk and told me to sit down. He said I'm being taken off the waterfront run, which I've had the past year and a half. At a conference held by him, the managing editor and the telegraph editor, it was decided to create a new position, that of rewrite man to the telegraph editor, George Coad. In fact, Don said, George specifically had asked for me.

This position was created so that the paper can give greater emphasis to national and international events.

When I left Don I walked over to talk to George. He is a man I like and respect. He is 34 years old, attended Princeton and Johns Hopkins, is the best-read man in the office, burns with the desire for more knowledge, has fiery eyes. I am aware that politically he leans toward the left.

"We're proceeding on two assumptions," he told me. "The first is that the average man who reads his newspaper on the streetcar is able to consume more words about national and international affairs than we've been giving him. The second assumption is that he's more interested in matters of this kind than we've given him credit for having. Now it will be up to us to inform him of vital matters—comprehensively, but in simple language.

"To be able to do this, you'll have to know a lot about the background of everything in the world. You'll have to be alert to every event taking place, wherever it happens. You'll spend about half your time in the city's two main libraries, reading up on whatever subject I assign to you. The other half of your time you'll be here in the office, rewriting Associated Press and United Press copy, interpolating background information when needed. Your hours will be from five in the morning until one in the afternoon. . . . Want the job?"

"Hell, yes!"

MONDAY, OCTOBER 5, 1936   ▣   Today I began my new job with George Coad. Arising at 4 A.M., I was in the office by five o'clock and no one else was there. George arrived about 6 A.M. He said he wanted me to research the life of Sir Oswald Mosley, the British fascist. I hied myself to a library and thoroughly enjoyed all I read.

TUESDAY, OCTOBER 6, 1936   ▣   George was not entirely pleased with the 1,000 words I wrote about Mosley this morning. He wanted less about the man's personality and more about the economic conditions that fertilized his bid for power. When I rewrote the piece I made it as simple as possible. Later I went to the library to learn all I could about Colonel Francois de la Rocque and his Croix de Feu movement in France. Having learned my lesson from George, I did not stop with him and his party but also examined current trends in French politics and economics.

WEDNESDAY, OCTOBER 7, 1936   ▣   George read my piece about Colonel de la Rocque and called it completely worthless. In a bit of a huff I said I could not be expected to learn everything about recent French history in a single afternoon. George smiled and agreed. He explained that he reads so fast and is so conversant with political trends that he is apt to expect too much of me too fast. Then he launched into a little lecture:

"Get this in your head: First, everybody lies. Second, discover the background and prejudices of the writer, and why he lies. Third, figure out the direction his lies are likely to follow. Then, and only then, make your own guess about the truth of the matter."

He said he would give me more time to research de la Rocque. On my way home I stopped in a dime store and bought a briefcase for only 50 cents. It's the first I ever owned and I suppose I wanted it because of the spurious importance given to anyone carrying a briefcase.

SATURDAY, OCTOBER 10, 1936 ▧ I went to the library again to read more about de la Rocque, then came to the office and rewrote my story about him. George liked the rewrite much better than the original copy, and made only a few changes. My next assignment is to learn all I can about lettuce so that I might write about the strike of lettuce pickers in the Salinas valley of California.

MONDAY, OCTOBER 12, 1936 ▧ From Sir Oswald Mosley to Colonel de la Rocque to lettuce to red blood cells. Such have been the subjects of my education under George Coad. Today he kept me hopping to get data and pictures of blood, since he plans to write a piece about the detection of criminals through blood analyses. I consulted several blood specialists at Tulane's medical school. One doctor is glad we are trying to verify our data before rushing into print. Another specialist knows George and said he has a high regard for his work.

THURSDAY, OCTOBER 15, 1936 ▧ Yesterday I wrote an article about lettuce. Today I spent 12 hours learning how oil wells are drilled. Only God and George know what I'll be studying tomorrow, but I'm not complaining. I enjoyed my day's work, lengthy though it was, and walking home I felt so righteous it seemed a halo hovered over my head.

MONDAY, OCTOBER 19, 1936 ▧ I'm learning so much! My social life has almost vanished, but I'm learning how to study, how to detect fraud in news. I'm learning there are so many things in this world about which I know nothing, about which I want to learn much. I'm learning the joy of hard work. Before I began working for George, I was more or less drifting along as the waterfront reporter, a picturesque assignment, to be sure, but I let life drift toward me instead of running out to meet it headlong. Now I want to know why, why, why? I am becoming aware of economic malad-justments, the suppression of civil liberties, the value of research, the importance of scientific principles, the selfishness of mankind, the spirit of imperialism, the drift toward another war.

FRIDAY, NOVEMBER 6, 1936 ▪ This morning I arrived at the *Item* at 5:20 and just before I stepped into the elevator our porter, keg-shaped Norman, handed me a letter. It was from the *Oklahoma City Times*. My guts were surprisingly quiet as I reached the city room, sauntered inside, put down my briefcase and book, sat down at my desk and casually slit the envelope. Yes, Jack Bell is offering me a job at $35 a week. I was calm. I arose and ambled into the men's room and there, all alone, I yowled in glee and danced a rigadoon. Moments later, back in the city room, I saw George Coad walk in. When I told him I'd been offered a job in Oklahoma City, he said: "By all means—take it! Don't pass up an opportunity like this. You may not get another offer as good as this in a long time, and you'll certainly never get anywhere on the *Item*. They'll never pay good salaries here."

Years later I heard that George Coad killed himself. I don't know why, and I'm sorry.

FRIDAY, NOVEMBER 27, 1936 ▪ Now that I'm about to leave New Orleans, after living here two years and three months, I want to record some impres-sions, especially about the French Quarter:

The faded blonde, with an old escort, lagging along Royal St. and sigh-ing: "I'm lonely . . . I'm always lonely . . . I think most people are lonely" . . . the sad little man who walks five feet in front of his gray-haired mother, scolding her for being slow . . . the beggar, a giant with an enormous Adam's apple and a voice so deep it scares everyone he approaches . . . the male homosexuals with dyed hair and plucked eyebrows, holding out ciga-rets and asking men for a light . . . the Nut Club, boiling with noise deep into the dark funnel of night . . . the green wooden fence around the ruins of the old French Opera House that burned down long ago . . . and across the street a whorehouse with a bar pretending to be a saloon . . . the legion of stray cats all over the Quarter . . . the retired naval officer now selling perfume from a dainty shop on Royal St., using his shoulders as punctua-tion marks . . . the Olde Curiosity Shoppe with the owner in a black skull cap studying coins through a magnifying glass . . . the singing waitresses and the ethnic mix of customers in the International restaurant at Chartres and Dauphine Sts. . . . the Filipino bars and pool halls . . . the bar called

Drop Your Anchor Here, and Popeye's and Mamma's Place . . . Decatur
St. at midnight with its harlots and pimps and peddlers . . . the French
Market with its stalls of fruit, fish, vegetables . . . the Morning Call coffee
shop with the funny tables where one can see himself in a mirror as he eats
and drinks . . . there, too, the drunks and debutantes, sitting side by side on
stools . . . the Martin Poor Boy shop on Rampart St. . . . the blind beggar,
the ugliest man I ever saw . . . morning fog enshrouding the spires of St.
Louis Cathedral . . . Jackson Square with its bronze statue of Andrew Jackson and its cannons and frisking dogs and afternoon forums and gawking
tourists . . . in a book shop on St. Peter St. the horse-faced woman wearing
a monocle and quoting Gilbert and Sullivan . . . the dreamily beautiful
Court of the Two Sisters, with its banana trees and flowered walls and iron
deer and lazy waiters and mint juleps and blue floodlights . . . the Orleans
Ballroom at 717 Orleans St., believed to have been the site of the long-ago
quadroon balls, elegant affairs attended by rich white men and quadroon
mistresses . . . Enrique Alvarez, the artist, with his beret and dusky face and
Bohemian swagger . . . the fat scowling priest who lets his shepherd dog
play in St. Anthony's garden . . . the old black women in red-checkered
dresses sitting near the Square, puffing on pipes and selling pralines . . .
Montalbano's delicatessen with its statues of saints and its candles and
wines and holy pictures and delicious sandwiches . . . the hot biscuits with
crisp bacon to be enjoyed at Core's . . . Maylie's restaurant, famous for its
turtle soup . . . the soul-soothing beauty of the river seen through lavender
twilight . . . the girl with a lover who visits me because I listen . . . recently
she had an abortion, and wistfully she said: "Sometimes at night I seem to
hear a baby crying . . ."

CHAPTER 5

OKLAHOMA CITY, MONDAY, NOVEMBER 16, 1936 ■ Today I began working for the *Oklahoma City Times*, an afternoon paper. Jack Bell, the city editor, greeted me this way: "Welcome home, Eddie!" Nothing could have been nicer.

TUESDAY, NOVEMBER 17, 1936 ■ I had hoped to see a lot of Beth Campbell, but today she told me she is leaving here to go to Washington to work for the Associated Press and cover Eleanor Roosevelt. I'm glad for her and sad for myself.

THURSDAY, NOVEMBER 19, 1936 ■ Today in the Biltmore Hotel I ate lunch with Christopher Morley, the novelist, essayist and editor who, years ago, was a Rhodes scholar at Oxford. A witty, pleasant man. He said the best advice he ever received was "to look at a thing until you see in it something no one else has ever seen." When I asked what he regarded as the best line he ever wrote, he grinned and said: "Well, I guess it would be: 'A human being is an ingenious assembly of portable plumbing.' "

THURSDAY, DECEMBER 3, 1936 ■ I'm still having trouble adjusting to the city room of the *Oklahoma City Times*. When I worked for the *New Orleans Item* the office was a happy Bedlam, while this office seems like Sunday School. Today the managing editor sent me a note requesting that I make sure my desk is neat before I leave. Nuts! A newspaper office should be the last refuge of non-conformists! "Scoop" Thompson even declares there should be a Constitutional amendment stating that it is the duty of every reporter to get drunk every Saturday night—at least.

TUESDAY, DECEMBER 8, 1936 ■ When I arrived at work Jack Bell told me to go to the Biltmore Hotel and interview General Pershing. I almost gasped. General John J. Pershing, who commanded the American Expeditionary Forces in France during the World War! And before that fought

Apache Indians, fought in Cuba in the Spanish-American War, served in the Philippines, studied modern warfare in Manchuria where Russians and Japanese were fighting.

I ran out of the office and down the street. At the hotel a clerk said he was not allowed to give me the number of the general's room, but Pershing had left a call for eight o'clock so he might be coming down for breakfast soon. I found his chauffeur, an army sergeant, who is driving him to Phoenix. He smiled but said little. I walked to the coffee shop and waited.

General Pershing walked in. He looked exactly like his pictures—handsome face, moustache, ramrod posture—but perhaps a little older, for now he is 76. He sat down alone at a table.

Walking over, I said: "Good morning, General Pershing. It's a shame to bother a man before breakfast but I'm a reporter from the *Times* and I'd like a few words with you, if you don't mind."

He glanced up. He did not smile, but his eyes were friendly.

I said: "Please go ahead and order, sir." His eyes questioned me. "Oh," I said, "I've already eaten, thank you."

With a waitress at his side, Pershing bent over his menu, ordered grapefruit, toast and honey and coffee. Then he turned to me.

"Now! What can I do for you?"

"Well, sir, I understand you're en route to Arizona. Do you plan to spend the winter there?"

His face froze. "Oh, ho! . . . So it's an interview you want. Well, I'm not going to answer any questions!"

Taken aback, I mumbled: "But, sir—just a few? After all, you know the interest people take in you."

"Young man! I've been interviewed at every damned town since I started out on this trip. This is supposed to be a pleasure trip for me, but with the press hounding me, as they have been doing, there's damned little pleasure in it for me! Now, if you'll promise not to print anything I say, we can have a little talk, but—"

"General!" I cried. "I can't bind myself to a promise of this sort. I don't intend to ask you much, just—"

The man simply would not talk, and I didn't blame him. When the waitress brought his breakfast he said: "Well, well! That's what I call prompt service!" But as she was leaving he called her back, shoving away a glass of milk disdainfully, "I said I wanted coffee! Who wants this weak white drink in the morning!"

As I got up to go, General Pershing said, not unpleasantly: "Good day, young man."

Years later in San Francisco I was strolling through Golden Gate Park and suddenly saw a statue of General Pershing. It felt odd to see in stone a face I had seen in the flesh across a table.

1937

SATURDAY, JANUARY 23, 1937 ▦ Today I tried to interview Dr. Alfred Adler, the Austrian psychiatrist. Although he was cordial, he didn't say much of interest. When I asked him about the school of Individual Psychology, which he founded, all I could get out of him was that he refused to consider any psychological problem except in its entirety.

The failure of this interview was my fault, not his. I was not qualified to interview him because I knew almost nothing about psychiatry. Of course, it is the fate of reporters to quiz specialists about their specialties. This explains my passion for encyclopedias—the hope of learning a little something about everything.

MONDAY, FEBRUARY 15, 1937 ▦ Today I lived through the first dust storm of my life. A wind is depositing Oklahoma real estate all over the landscape. All day long my mouth has been full of grit, and my face and hands are dry and dirty as I write this.

SATURDAY, MARCH 13, 1937 ▦ Mrs. Franklin D. Roosevelt came here on her lecture tour of the country and held a press conference in the Biltmore. I was just one of some 15 reporters, only three of whom I recognized, the others being young ladies from somewhere else. When the First Lady settled herself on a davenport, composed and ready to answer questions, no one said anything. The air seemed starchy with group embarrassment. Since I cover the New Deal agencies here, I broke the silence by asking how she first became interested in the National Youth Administration. I had not known that she is slightly hard of hearing. Bending forward and fixing me with a steady gaze, she politely asked me to repeat the question, which I did.

As she answered, I memorized her features. She is at least six feet tall. When in repose she appeared somewhat ugly, but once she began speaking her face came alive, her eyes sparkled and she became charming. She does have a well-shaped nose and soft brown hair and skin glowing with health. She wore a maroon dress trimmed in black, dangling from her neck was a pair of folding glasses, and on her long pointed fingers she wore five rings.

At the end of the press conference she arose and graciously escorted us to the door of the suite. I happened to be walking near her, so I asked about my friend Beth Campbell, who covers her on a daily basis in Washington for the Associated Press. The President's wife brightened at my question, quickly letting me know how much she likes Beth. Last Christmas Eve when all the other women reporters who follow her had faded away, there was Beth, said Mrs. Roosevelt, still doggedly on her trail, so the First Lady stopped her car, opened a door and invited Beth to ride with her.

"When you get back to Washington," I said, "please give Beth my best regards."

Smiling, Mrs. Roosevelt said: "I will. What is your name, please?"

I told her.

THURSDAY, APRIL 15, 1937   ▪   I'm very impressed by these lines from Virginia Woolf's novel *Orlando*:

"If one is a man, still the woman part of the brain must have some effect; and a woman must also have intercourse with the man in her. Coleridge perhaps meant this when he said that a great mind is androgynous. It is when this fusion takes place that the mind is fully fertilized and uses all its faculties. Perhaps a mind that is purely masculine cannot create, any more than a mind that is purely feminine. It is fatal to be a man or woman pure and simple; one must be woman-manly or man-womanly."

FRIDAY, APRIL 23, 1937   ▪   Today I witnessed another dust storm. When I left the office about 5 P.M. the air was so thick with dust that I could look at the sun without squinting. A little later as I walked out of a book store I saw that the sun looked like putty.

SUNDAY, APRIL 25, 1937   ▪   Margaret Redding drove me to a farm 15 miles east of the city to join her family in a Sunday picnic. Dust blurred the horizon. Again I was able to stare straight into the sun, and this time I thought I saw a sun spot. The dust thickened until it erased the sun from the sky. These dust storms are awesome to behold. My lungs still hurt from breathing that stuff.

THURSDAY, MAY 6, 1937   ▪   Mary was cooking dinner for the two of us in her apartment when we decided we needed some booze. Oklahoma is legally a dry state, of course, so I called a bootlegger I know. Soon he arrived with a pint of whiskey for which I paid two dollars. He is one of nine deliverymen working for a rich man named Fred, and today he was in such a talkative mood that he told us how they operate. Each runner owns his own car and every morning he loads it up with two cases of liquor, which he covers with blankets. At this season of the year each man grosses about $700 a day, although in cold weather it can reach $1,000. He gets a weekly salary of $45, plus 20 per cent of the gross after attaining a certain quota of sales.

SUNDAY, MAY 9, 1937 ■ Dale Clark sat with his eight-month-old son on his lap and said:

"Funny thing about his eyes . . . I took him up on my lap when he was still quite young and absently looked into his eyes. They held mine. He was staring at me with all that innocence of an infant. I couldn't help but stare into his eyes, and as I did so I seemed to see way beyond him, back, back, back, until I began to get frightened. I seemed to see things I'd never seen before and couldn't understand."

TUESDAY, MAY 18, 1937 ■ I would rather have written *Gone With the Wind* than be President of the United States.

SATURDAY, JUNE 26, 1937 ■ Here at the *Times* I've learned a new skill — dictating spot news stories and even feature articles, word for word, to a rewrite man in the office. This requires concentration of the highest order.

FRIDAY, JULY 2, 1937 ■ I have become friendly with an intelligent married woman who works in the book section of a department store. I am 26, years old and she is 36. I like older women and have told her so. Today our conversation drifted around to the subject of loneliness.

I said: "I don't think loneliness has been adequately analyzed in a great novel. Have you ever seen it treated thoroughly?"

"No," she said, "I don't believe I have — but I don't believe it can be expressed. What words can you use to tell of loneliness? There are many kinds of loneliness. The loneliness of sitting at home and wishing you had someone to take you to a party — that's just a small part of it. The greatest loneliness is intellectual loneliness. You are probably familiar with that fable which says at one time human beings were entirely round, with arms and legs sticking out on all sides, and because of the way they were formed they had no trouble getting to the top of Mount Olympus. Because of this, the gods divided them and made them as they are today, and ever since then the two halves have been trying to become whole."

FRIDAY, AUGUST 13, 1937   ■   Out at the airport a pilot offered me a stunt ride. He is Leslie Bowman of Dallas, an expert at aerial acrobatics. When I agreed, he told me to take everything out of my pockets because part of the time we would fly upside down—and that's when I became nervous.

He has a low-wing monoplane, a duplicate of the one that last month won the international stunt contest in St. Louis. He buckled a parachute on me and when I sat down in the cockpit he tightened a strap across my lap. Then we soared up into the blue, where my body denied gravity for the next 45 minutes.

Bowman put the plane through every maneuver known to aviators—rolling wing over wing, executing outside loops, etc. Twice he tried inside loops. This means the plane starts at the top, dives down and under and back up to the top again. Each time, however, the engine stalled when we were at the bottom of this stunt, so instead of trying to climb back he quickly pulled the plane horizontal.

We also flew upside down many times, and for many minutes each time, and I was delighted to discover that I was unafraid. Perhaps this is because I enjoy diving off high boards into swimming pools. Anyway, it was exciting to know there was nothing between my head and the earth. I saw a wrong-side-up perspective of fields and haystacks sailing past me.

When we landed I smiled at the pilot and thanked him and said I enjoyed it and would like to do it again some day. He looked a bit disappointed.

SUNDAY, AUGUST 29, 1937   ■   About a week ago Robert Taylor passed through here and the women of Oklahoma City went plumb off their noodles in hero worship. He is handsome yeah, and he is a movie star, yeah, and I tend to believe he's a nice guy. A girl reporter for the *Oklahoma City News* rode to Kansas City on the same plane with Taylor, and when he fell asleep she sneaked up and kissed his lips. The *News* splashed her story all over its front page under this headline: I KISSED ROBERT TAYLOR. Ugh!

THURSDAY, SEPTEMBER 9, 1937   ■   Today's assignment was the most dangerous of my life—gas escaping from the earth.

The pool of oil under Oklahoma City is amazingly productive. Sometimes 60,000 barrels of oil gush from a single well in one day. This is due to gas pressures so great they have caused spectacular fires here in the city.

Some poor people dig down three feet until they reach a gas pipe and then tap into it by attaching a valve that diverts some of the gas to their homes. Some pipes thus tapped are huge and carry so-called wet gas under pressure suitable only for running engines at oil wells.

The city editor sent me to the east side of town where one such illegal connection had been discovered. The valve had jostled loose, so now gas was escaping at the rate of 100,000 cubic feet per day, according to the fire captain on the scene. It was, in fact, the largest illegal tap ever found here. The hissing of the gas was so loud that we had to shout to be heard. With me was a *Times* photographer who took a shot of the hole in the ground and the disconnected valve. I was afraid the magnesium in his flash bulb might explode the gas and blow up the block.

What does fear feel like? Well, the scalp of my head felt prickly.

THURSDAY, OCTOBER 28, 1937 ■ The other day when I learned that Sinclair Lewis was coming to town I became excited and prayed I'd be assigned to interview him. He will go on to the University of Oklahoma in Norman to give a lecture entitled "The Novelist as a Prophet."

Sinclair Lewis has been a literary god to me ever since my college days when I twice read *Arrowsmith*, weeping each time. In 1926 he won the Pulitzer Prize for literature with *Arrowsmith*, but declined it—perhaps because he thought he should have received it sooner for *Main Street* or *Babbitt*. In 1930 he became the first American author to win the Nobel Prize for literature.

Well, the famous man arrived here today and I was lucky enough to be told to interview him. Lewis was staying in the home of Dr. Roy Rutherford, pastor of the First Christian Church. I arrived at the minister's home at 9:15 this morning with a *Times* photographer, Milt Mumblow. Two other reporters were there. When I said my photographer would like to take a picture, the minister fluttered like a bird in a bath and chirped:

"Oh, Sinclair, take this davenport over here—that's it!—and sprawl for these boys just as you did a moment ago. Boys, Sinclair is at his best when he is draped on the end of my davenport here. That's his real self—nonchalant, you know. That's it, Sinclair, right over here!"

Fighting the impulse to hold my nose, I wondered whether this candy-dandy minister was the model for Elmer Gantry, the hypocritical and unscrupulous evangelist in the writer's novel of that name. I also thought that his friends called him *Red*. He yanked himself out of a chair, walked over to the davenport and sat down at one end. I slipped into the seat at the other end because this placed me closer than the other reporters; he spoke toward me most of the time.

Lewis is taller than I had expected and has a belly like a basketball—

something I'd not seen in photographs of him. Fifty-two years old, a prolific author, a Nobel Laureate, world-famous, Sinclair Lewis is a very ugly man. His face looks like a skull.

"Well," he began, with a grin like a long crack, "and what can I tell you about the state of the nation?"

Dr. Rutherford slapped his knee, again and again, then roared:

"State of the nation! State of the nation! Did you get that? Best I ever heard! State of the nation, indeed!"

I wanted to vomit.

Ignoring the exuberant evangelist, Lewis began speaking.

"I am," he said, his tongue tucked into his cheek, "a reactionary. Or at least that's what they tell me—those who have read my latest book. It'll be out January 21. This book of mine tells about the revolt of the older generation against the revolt of the younger generation. I'm calling it *The Prodigal Parent*. My principal character, Fred Cornplow, is a middle-aged man who suddenly declares that he, too, might as well raise a little hell. He is just a shade more analytical than Babbitt was. Babbitt was introspective only when he had a hang-over. Then he might possibly bring himself to the point of asking himself, 'Why did I make such a damned fool of myself last night?' "

Sinclair Lewis chattered with the speed of a machine gun. It was obvious that he likes to hear himself talk and, having gotten in a plug for his next book, he skittered from one subject to another and strayed so far afield that I interrupted him a few times to put some pertinent questions. The other reporters couldn't get in a word sideways, whereupon I became as smug as the pastor. Talk about *him* being an ass! Nonetheless, when Lewis mentioned Charles MacArthur I told two anecdotes about him that I'd read in Woollcott's *While Rome Burns*, with Lewis keeping his eyes on me, and when I finished he guffawed in appreciation.

But he wanted to get back to his next novel, saying:

"The chief editorial writer of the *Daily Worker* has abused and even threatened me for becoming a reactionary because, he says, my book is against communism. This is stupid because it is not against communism. It is not even about communism. One of the characters just happens to be a communist for a time. She is a young girl who takes to communism temporarily as she might take to doing literary reviews for tea table women's clubs."

I asked how he gets the data he uses as the theme or background of his novels.

"I'm trying to get away from documentation," he replied. "I don't take voluminous notes. Notes don't serve any purpose but help one remember what he already knows. I over-did this documentation in *Arrowsmith*. There was too much bacteriology in the book. However, I guess I had more fun writing *Arrowsmith* than any other of my books because while getting the material I knocked around the Bahamas and down around there."

Aware that Lewis had been a reporter, I asked how he liked journalism.

With a grin he replied: "I was fired from a paper in Waterloo, Iowa, one in San Francisco and the Associated Press."

"Why?"

"Why? . . . I was just naturally incompetent! If I liked the man I happened to have interviewed, I'd go back and write a dandy story. But if I didn't like him, my story would be a flop."

Dr. Rutherford walked over and put his hand on the arm of the author, then turned to us reporters and said: "Well, Sinclair has to go up now and get his shave. He must get some rest, too, you know. He has a busy day ahead of him. Better come on now, Sinclair."

Sinclair Lewis kept on spouting words, gesturing with his free hand, eager to go on talking, but the minister tugged at his arm, so he arose and let himself be led out of the room, still chattering like a machine gun.

FRIDAY, NOVEMBER 5, 1937 ▇ For the second time within the past few weeks an attempt was made to recruit me into the communist party. This time the overture was made by the wife of the secretary of the communist party of Oklahoma. She is in charge of the party's Progressive Book Shop at 129 1/2 NW Grand Ave., and I've gone there several times to browse among the books, fully aware that it's a communist place. Ina, the woman who runs the shop, knows that I am a reporter and that I cover the Chamber of Commerce every working day. Because of my job, if she were able to enroll me in the party it might be something of a coup for her, I suppose. Although she did not make an overt political advance to me, I knew what she meant and she knew I knew. I was willing to debate her, for I know there are some things about capitalism I dislike, just as I know that people are suffering because of the Depression. When I declined to take Ina's bait, she said contemptuously: "—but, of course, you're middle class!" I? With maybe $30 in the bank? The man who made the first political pitch to me must have considered me a moron because he said that the communist party can change human nature. Really?

SUNDAY, NOVEMBER 7, 1937 ■ Zola defined literature as "a slice of life seen through a temperament." Yup, and so is this diary.

WEDNESDAY, NOVEMBER 10, 1937 ■ The Works Progress Administration is again certifying people for relief for the first time since November 1, 1935. This morning I walked to the WPA state headquarters at 431 W. Main St. and stood on the first floor studying the faces of the applicants. A young man whom I know handed me a candy bar and I had begun eating it when I was approached by a social worker I know.

"We don't allow any eating in here," she said to me.

Thinking she was joking, I uttered a wisecrack.

"We don't allow any eating in here!" she repeated sternly. "Some of these people haven't had any breakfast. We make it a rule among ourselves never to eat or drink Cokes before them."

Instantly ashamed, I mumbled something and slunk away. I wanted to throw away the candy but felt that that, too, would be a sin.

SATURDAY, NOVEMBER 27, 1937 ■ This afternoon I was in the press room of police headquarters when I saw a young woman with two daughters enter the office of the captain. Curious, I followed her inside, slipping into a chair, hoping the cops would not throw me out. This morning the woman's husband was jailed for drunkenness. She told the captain she had no money and needed her husband at home to chop wood to keep them warm. Agreeing, the captain said he would take her upstairs and set her husband free.

As they walked out of the office I slipped a dime into the hand of one daughter who looked about seven years old, and she handed it to her mother. In the lobby near the elevator a newly arrested prostitute was screaming, so the elevator operator insisted the officers keep her out as he carried the wife and her kids upstairs. I liked him for that.

The captain had the husband brought out from behind bars. He was in his late twenties. He was trembling all over, due to a hang-over, remorse and perhaps hunger. "I'm so nervous I can hardly stand up," he said to no one in particular. He was humble in the presence of the captain, who bawled him out and threatened to jail him for 90 days if he were caught drunk again. He thanked the captain, his wife thanked the captain, and she did not nag her husband. I wanted to give them money but didn't want the cops to see me doing this. At the rear entrance I caught up with them.

"I hope you won't be offended if I offer you one dollar," I said, holding out the bill.

Looking at me in amazement, the husband murmured: "I don't guess we have so much as a dollar . . . What is your name, mister? . . . I'll pay you double for this!"

I refused to tell him my name. When I walked back into headquarters my throat felt tight, my eyes moist. Those four people—wife and husband and two kids—they're starving! Actually starving! And to think that every so often I spend money on booze!

SUNDAY, NOVEMBER 28, 1937   ▦   Ernst gave a cocktail party this afternoon and I went there with Peg. Soon I began caricaturing everyone in the room, my host rewarding me with drink after drink until I became drunk. After the drawing, I told the story of the flying angels, replete with gestures, then sang some songs and told some jokes, thus becoming that abomination—*the life of the party*. Ugh!

MONDAY, DECEMBER 20, 1937   ▦   One week from today my diary will become ten years old. It's getting to be a fat little rascal and perhaps may be the only literature of any value I'll leave when I die. The other day it occurred to me that it might be a good idea for someone to get an advance from a publishing house and then travel around the country in search of men and women who keep diaries. The good diaries, the ones that are truthful and readable and revealing—these should be published. The ordinary lives of ordinary folks. Personal history, en masse, becomes national history.

If I remember correctly, Voltaire called footnotes in a book the sound of slippers sneaking up the back staircase—something like this. Anyway, this is the kind of history found in diaries—the slippers-under-the-bed, the Mrs. Grundy-just-told-me, the sure-crossed-up-that-guy-yesterday, the hope-that-I'll-get-it-tomorrow, the but-you-said-you-loved-me, the wail-of-a-lonely-frail, as the song says. The marginalia of civilization.

1938

WEDNESDAY, JANUARY 12, 1938   ▦   Willa Ann Harrison, 15-year-old daughter of Walter M. Harrison, the managing editor of the *Oklahoma City Times*, is on the verge of death in Oklahoma City General Hospital. A sty on her eye went inward instead of coming to a head on the outside, and the poison now runs throughout her circulatory system. This afternoon seven of us editors and reporters went to the hospital to have our blood typed. My blood, No. 4, cross-matched Willa's better than that of the other six.

THURSDAY, JANUARY 13, 1938   ■   Nearly a pint of blood was taken from me. The Skipper, Mr. Harrison, said that Monday Willa Ann told him good-bye and this morning she repeated the Lord's Prayer with him. However, he refused to repeat the words "forever and forever," even when she mumbled them repeatedly. This he told me with dry eyes, but I could have wept.

FRIDAY, JANUARY 14, 1938   ■   God, how depressed I felt today. I learned that as they were feeding my blood into Willa Ann's veins yesterday she suffered a relapse, one side of her heart stopped beating, and they gave her only five minutes to live. A clinical technician told me she had cross-matched my blood with Willa's not once but three times, and said it was free of any impurities. She explained that Willa was just so weak she couldn't take any more blood into her system, but I felt like hell.

SATURDAY, JANUARY 15, 1938   ■   The Skipper picked me up as I was walking home this afternoon. He said it was the doctors' fault that Willa suffered a relapse while being given my blood. He said they later learned she already had more blood in her than the normal adult. This made me feel a little better because I had been blaming myself for what happened.

FRIDAY, JANUARY 21, 1938   ■   Willa Ann Harrison died early this morning.

SATURDAY, JANUARY 22, 1938   ■   The newspaper men and women of Oklahoma City present an annual Gridiron show like the one staged by the press corps in Washington, D.C. We reporters and editors write skits lampooning politicians and sundry celebrities. Then, amateurs though we be, we perform on stage—talking, singing, dancing. Gridiron night has become a Social Event!

This year's Gridiron was presented this evening before an audience of 700 people. Among those attending were delegates to a state convention of the Oklahoma Press Club. One of their speakers had been President Roosevelt's second son, Elliott, now in charge of news at a radio station in Texas. After watching our show, he came to the party we held afterwards.

The party was in the main dining room of the Biltmore Hotel, with a bar so long that it stretched across the entire room. Despite the fact that Oklahoma is supposed to be a dry state, the head bartender was the chief of the city's fire department, while a man running for governor was careful not to be seen with a glass in his hand, but sipped from the highball glasses held by other people, including myself. He is General Smith, a man I like and one I have come to know because I have driven with him to various functions here and there in this state. During midnight rides the general and I harmonized together, so this evening I struck up a tune and he chimed in.

My date was Ethel. She is an executive secretary, so bright and cool and sharp that she is the very model of efficiency. My admiration for her is limitless. I know she also can be softly feminine. Somehow, she had become a friend of Elliott Roosevelt and this evening she took me upstairs to his suite not once but two or three times. There the three of us drank together and when she had to leave for a few minutes he and I conversed alone. I am 27 years old and he is 28, a man so large and friendly that I began thinking of him as a St. Bernard dog—although he carries the drinks *inside* himself!

The three of us came back downstairs to rejoin the party, leaning against the bar, our arms around one another, Ethel in the middle, I on her left and he on her right. We were in our cups. Ethel turned toward Elliott to kiss his cheek and when I brayed I was being left out, she kissed my lips. The room was noisy because of all the people and conversations, and suddenly I realized that Ethel had vanished.

The next thing I knew, she materialized at the far end of the room, wearing an enormous gun-belt with two holsters, brandishing a big gun in each hand. They were .45's. Later she told me that this gear had played a part in 27 bank robberies, and had been given to Elliott as souvenirs. She had donned the belt and picked up the revolvers in his suite, and now she laughed as she flourished the weapons left and right, up and down, playfully poking them into the faces of suddenly frozen folks. Another guy and I ran to her and disarmed her. We looked into the chambers of the guns and were relieved to find that neither had any rounds in them—but I was sweating bullets!

Years later, reading Time *magazine, I saw a photograph of Ethel in it. By that time she had become an executive officer of a huge corporation where, I'm sure, her intelligence and efficiency were put to full use. And years after that I learned she had married a millionaire who had been a member of a Presidential Cabinet. Good for her!*

SATURDAY, APRIL 2, 1938 ■ An escaped convict has been captured here and I watched him as he was finger-printed in the bureau of records. After the youth had been let away, the man in charge of the bureau told me never again to get in a corner with a criminal, as I had done momentarily.

When this fellow learned I was a reporter he begged to be let loose just one minute so he could bash in my head.

THURSDAY, MAY 5, 1938 ■ Herbert Hoover came to Oklahoma City today to make a major political address to the nation by radio from the Coliseum. At the age of 64 the former President travels alone across the country to speak against many New Deal policies. A suite was reserved for him in the Skirvin Hotel, built by William B. Skirvin, a rich oil and real estate man.

I was not assigned to interview him, that pleasant task being given to our editorial writer and also our chief political reporter, but I tagged along with them to the hotel and was in the suite when President Hoover walked in. He looked younger and fresher than I had anticipated. He has plump cheeks, soft flesh and gentle manners.

Bill Skirvin's daughter, Mrs. Perle Mesta, had placed a newly published book in the suite set aside for Hoover, *The Hoover Policies*, written by Ray Lyman Wilbur and Arthur M. Hyde. When it was shown to Hoover he said he would not have time to read it, so I turned to Mrs. Mesta and asked to buy it so that I might get it autographed by the former President. Nice lady that she is, she insisted upon giving it to me. When I handed it to the celebrated guest, willingly he wrote in it: "This is not my book but I am glad for you to have it . . . Herbert Hoover."

The rich Perle Mesta moved to Washington, where she was "the hostess with the mostest" and became the model for the 1950 musical Call Me Madam.

SATURDAY, MAY 28, 1938 ■ Tonight on the police run I covered a horrible tragedy. A man of 23, a junior at Oklahoma City University, was at home with his wife, 22, a former college beauty queen. She was pregnant. He was cleaning his shotgun, which fired accidentally, hitting her in the belly from a distance of only four feet.

When I heard the news I sped to St. Anthony Hospital. The dead beauty queen lay on a cot in the emergency room, and as I walked in an attendant pulled open the sheet to show her body to the coroner. I looked.

Suddenly I heard sobs from a room next door and walked there and saw the husband crouched against a rolling table, his shoulders heaving, his face in his hands, wailing "Oh, God! . . . Oh, God! . . . Oh, God! . . ."

I backed away, wishing I were not a reporter, and the rest of the night I smoked too many cigarets. I watched as cops and detectives gently led the husband to detective headquarters, where he made a statement. There was no question about this fatal shooting. It was an accident. When the youth left, curly head bowed, strong shoulders sagging, I felt tears in my eyes.

When I got back to the city room I spoke to the city editor of the *Oklahoman*, the morning edition of the *Times*. He asked whether I had obtained a picture of the young man. I said no.

"But he made a statement at the detective bureau, didn't he?"

"Yes."

"And you were there at the time, weren't you?"

"Yes."

"Well, why in the name of God didn't you call for a photographer?"

"Look," I said slowly, grinding out a cigaret in an ash tray, "this is absolutely the worst tragedy I've ever seen! I don't think a newspaper should run this boy's picture. It would only harm him. It was an accident—all the cops said so! There'd have been no use in calling a photog because as sure as I'm standing here, I know he wouldn't have posed, and I sure as hell wouldn't have tried to steal a picture of him as he wept his heart out!"

The editor's face flushed.

"Of course this is a tragedy!" he shouted. "But is that our fault? After all, we're just here to print what happens. If you don't like this work, you can get out of it!"

Sickened, I turned away. Then I heard a rewrite man holler: "Hey, here's a guy who's trying to make this an ethical paper!"

I walked out.

SUNDAY, MAY 29, 1938 ▓ I'm unhappy with myself. I started writing a novel called *Night Is My Sister* but haven't worked hard enough on it. I also have failed to keep this diary up to date. I haven't done anything constructive—dammit! Worst of all, I guess, is the fact that I want to get married. Now that I have arrived at the age of 27, I suppose this is natural. Another reason is that I waste time chasing women. With the approach of summer weather and long evenings, I'll find it even more difficult to stay alone in my apartment, regardless of the fact that I am fond of it. I don't love Helen enough to marry her, but at the same time I believe I will not become a success at anything until I am a happily married man. But where, oh where, is The Woman?

THURSDAY, JUNE 2, 1938 ▓ Last night I was walking home from a date with Helen when I came upon an auto accident that had happened only minutes earlier. I showed my press card to a cop who said that two cars had collided and the impact was so great that a girl had been catapulted through a windshield. She had been ambulanced to Oklahoma City General Hospital. Hailing a cab, I sped there.

In the emergency room I found the girl, who is 20 years old. A surgeon was sewing her face. Other doctors clustered around, helping him, but they parted when the girl's mother arrived. The mother looked, spun around, staggered into the hall, slumped into a chair and sobbed. I heard someone whisper that the surgeon had taken 75 stitches in the face of the poor girl.

Through a needle in her right arm they were feeding her glucose. Her face looked like a ball of putty slashed by a meat cleaver. She had bitten through her lower lip. She was out of her head and muttering incoherently when the mother walked back into the emergency room to hold the girl's left hand. I watched from the back of the room, staying out of the way.

Time passed. The surgeon kept on sewing and the room was hot and the mother's shoulders sagged and she looked around and saw me and asked whether I'd hold the hand of her daughter. I stepped up to her side and grasped her arm. The girl moaned that I was holding her too tightly, so I loosened my grip. Sighing her thanks, she reached up and clutched my coat with her bloody hand. Now I was standing too close to this surgery and frantically I felt I might faint. I'd never fainted in my entire life, but now the lights danced before my eyes and I felt sick at my stomach. I started to pull away.

"Don't go!" the girl gasped. She wasn't seeing me. Her eyes were empty.

I knew the trouble I'd become to everyone in the room if I vomited, so I signalled the mother with my eyes and she understood and came back to take the hand. I slipped out of the room and weaved into the street. The cool night air revived me until, a block away, my belly revolted. Walking home, I mourned that such pain exists in this world, and I vowed I'll become as gentle as possible.

WEDNESDAY, SEPTEMBER 14, 1938 ■ For several hours this evening I sat and read *The Importance of Living* by Lin Yutang. He advocates the art of living, as opposed to the busy business of earning a living. Slowly I realized that in the hurly-burly of my work as a reporter, and in the passionate pursuit of women, I have forgotten how to appreciate nature, simplicity, peace.

About one o'clock in the morning I decided to take a walk in the moonlight, heading north through a pleasant residential neighborhood. Remembering what Lin Yutang had said, I paid close attention to the trees and flowers and houses and grass and crickets and breeze and stars and everything else I could see, hear, smell, touch. I hugged the trunks of trees, plucked leaves from their branches, bent down to run my hand over grass. I listened to the silence. I admired the pearly glow of the moon on metal lamp posts, appreciated the dappled shadows of trees in moonlight, inhaled the night air, stood erect with shoulders straight. I moved amidst beauty and felt tinged with happiness. Happiness can be so commonplace, so close, so easy? Lin Yutang was correct, but as always, something was lacking. What? Oh, you know, Ellis! A woman at your side. Not just a woman, but The Woman . . .

MONDAY, SEPTEMBER 26, 1938   ■   Today I heard the voice of Adolf Hitler. Some other people and I sat on a balcony in the Black Hotel and listened on the radio to what is being called the Munich Crisis. Hitler spoke in German, of course, his words being translated into English as he spoke. He demanded that Czechoslovakia give Germany the Sudeten area of that country, which is inhabited by a German-speaking minority. Prime Minister Neville Chamberlain has flown from England to Germany to confer with Hitler. He has been called the Mad Dog of Europe, and now I understand why: His demands are extreme and his oratory so menacing that he chills one's blood.

The war scare is a reality here in Oklahoma City. People buy the latest editions of newspapers and talk about diplomacy and war. Young men ask one another how they feel about conscription. Young women tremble lest their men be thrust into battle. I, for one, am a coward and an isolationist. Not only do I not want to go to war, but I don't consider it necessary for the United States to enter the war that seems about to begin.

Late in 1937 the Oklahoma Federal Symphony Orchestra was created. It was part of the Federal Music Project, which was a part of the New Deal agency called the Works Progress Administration. As a reporter I covered all New Deal offices in Oklahoma City on a daily basis and because of this I met Dean Richardson, state director of the Oklahoma federal music project. He offered me a part-time job as press agent for the symphony and I checked with my city editor, who said it was okay.

The orchestra's 65 musicians, paid $75 each per month, rehearsed in the Shrine Temple. Their conductor was Ralph Rose, 26, a violin virtuoso, short and slender and dark, with a volcanic temper and a magnetic personality.

On February 17, 1938, I attended a rehearsal and that day I saw her for the first time. She was a first violinist, and as she bent her head over her fiddle I saw her hair, so golden it seemed to glow in the dim auditorium. I kept watching her, rather than listening to the music, until Rose gave a last flourish to his baton and ended the rehearsal.

Dean Richardson stood up.

"I want you to meet Eddie Ellis," he said. "Eddie, stand up. This is Eddie Ellis, folks, who is going to be our press agent. Eddie is a reporter on the Times.

For the first time ever I heard the curious applause of musicians who play stringed instruments—the wooden sides of bows slapped against metal music stands. A little later in another room the girl with the golden hair approached me so softly I was unaware of her presence until she spoke.

"I'm very glad," she said in a soft voice, "that you're going to be with us."

I thanked her, sensing she was a shy woman who had forced herself to welcome me. I asked her name. Leatha Sparlin.

A few days later, after an evening rehearsal, Richardson invited me to go to his apartment and I learned she would go with us. He called her Lee. The three of us got in his car. It was a cold night but she had no gloves because she had forgotten them. I took off my gloves and asked her to put them on. She smiled and declined. I insisted. She smiled and put on my gloves. She seemed to smile all the time. When we got to Richardson's home we had a drink and I caricatured them, and as we chatted I picked up the information that Lee was being dated by Ralph Rose.

Two days later a woman harpist from Tulsa came to town as guest soloist at the symphony's next concert, and as its press agent, I felt obliged to entertain her, so I suggested a movie. I also invited Lee, so the very first film that Lee and I saw together was Walt Disney's Snow White and the Seven Dwarfs, Hollywood's first full-length animated cartoon feature. Then we picked up Ralph Rose and went to Lee's apartment where we were served dinner by her sister Carmen. He turned on the radio to hear Albert Spaulding, the renowned violinist.

Lee suggested we ride in Ralph's car through the downtown area to see what posters had been put up to advertise the Monday concert. After that I invited all of them to my apartment, built over a double garage, a cozy place I called the Hermitage. We drank highballs and Ralph read aloud from Shakespeare and Lee sat on the edge of his chair, touching his cheek. I felt jealous, although I had no right to be.

Some months later I was home with a bad cold and feeling lonely, so I called Lee to explain my condition and say I'd appreciate company. Charmingly direct in accepting my invitation, she said she'd be right over. I combed my hair, slapped on after-shave lotion and resolved to remain a gentleman this evening.

She arrived. She sympathized with my ailment. She listened to me read the blithe philosophy of Lin Yutang. She and I sat on my green sofa, so deep one almost needs a ladder to get out of it. I was reading aloud, carried away by the saucy witticisms of the Chinese scholar, when I felt her hand caress my hair.

I kissed her.

"I couldn't help it!" she cried afterwards, after that first kiss. "Your hair looked so soft I just had to touch it."

In her caress there were sparks that lit a fire within me, so I did not remain the perfect gentleman, although I remained a gentleman. She was sweetly yielding, to a degree, then gently forbidding at that degree. I forgot my cold. I forgot everything but her because I realized I had fallen in love with her.

All my life I have been impulsive. Although Ellis is a Welsh name, and although my heritage is Welsh, English, Scotch and Irish, my temperament is such that I've always felt as though my mother was Spanish and my father Italian. I had dated so many women in my 27 years of life that I worried lest my diary leave the impression that I was nothing but a tin-horn Casanova.

Well, life is a long line of et ceteras, and Ralph had quit his job as conductor and moved away, so Lee and I began dating steadily—which explains why this diary fell behind events. I never really asked her to marry me because she also fell in love with me and so from the start it seemed we understood we would become husband and wife. Just a question of when. As we stood one evening on a street by a church I sought her moonpale lips, and as we huddled on a bench near her apartment I traced the warm geography of her dear figure with a respectful hand. Eddie Ellis, that rake, that scoundrel, that seducer of women, now became pacified by pure love.

Lee and I knew we were poor but wanted to get married and felt unable to wait until I had a big income. No, we'd go through poverty together. She was 21 and I was 27. I did pry from her a promise that we would not have a child for at least three years; I hoped that by then we'd be able to afford one. But what about her parents? Here we were, rushing into marriage before three weeks, so hadn't she better check with her mother and father? Yes.

Her father, Will Sparlin, was an auto salesman in Miami, Oklahoma. In addition to her elder sister Carmen, Lee had a younger sister called Billie. One day Lee and I rode a train to Tulsa, where we were met by the Sparlins. After a nervous lunch in a cafeteria, I went to a hotel while Lee drove with her parents and sister to a park. There they spread out a blanket and she said she planned to marry the man they had met. Just like that.

I sat alone in the hotel, wallowing in anxiety.

They picked me up and drove to a place where we ate hot dogs while Mr. Sparlin asked me a few gentle questions. Did it matter that Lee lacked a college degree, while I had one? No, I laughed. Lee's father and mother urged us to wait until we learned to know one another better, but Lee hemmed and I hawed, finally agreeing we would not marry until Thanksgiving.

That night, on the train back to Oklahoma City, Lee jotted down on an envelope what our income was and what our expenses might become. Yes, we agreed we could wait awhile—but then Ed LeBreton had to go and drop his hat!

Ed was my dear friend and fellow reporter from our days in New Orleans, and now we were together on the Oklahoma City Times. Ed and Barbara had been married only two years and considered wedlock the greatest thing since the First Cause. So! So they invited Lee and me to their home for an engagement party—with champagne, no less. The date was October 19, 1938.

That evening both Lee and I were tired, she from orchestral rehearsal, I from an iron day in the city room. We were so tired that our fatigue, in combination with champagne, caused us to behave in a silly way. I sat on a stool behind Lee, playing with her honey-colored hair as she leaned against me.

Suddenly I blurted: "I'd get married this evening at the drop of a hat!"

Ed LeBreton uncranked his lanky carcass, stood up, walked out of the room and when he returned he held a hat in his fingers.

"Hey!" I cried. "Wait a minute!"

Ed picked up the hat, struck a pose, dropped it again. And again.

"If you think," he said in a droll voice, "that I'm going to stand here dropping my hat all night until you two get married, you're nuts!"

Barbara yelled: "Hell! You two've got to get married before I leave. I want to be with you, and I'm going day after tomorrow!"

Lee looked at me. I looked at her. We were half-eager, half-afraid.

"Come here," I said. Taking her hand, I led her into a bedroom and closed the door.

"Now, look," I said, taking Lee into my arms. "This is fun. We're having a great time and this is a very romantic sort of way to get married, to be sure, but, darling, marriage itself is a very serious thing. I'm willing to go through with it this very night, but are you? Earnestly? Seriously? Among other things, you've got to decide whether you can tolerate the fact that night after night, the rest of our lives, I'll have my nose stuck in a book. Think you can stand that? For that's what I'm going to be doing. . . . Take your time about answering . . ."

She did. Snug in my arms, eyes looking inward, she thought and thought and, at last she exhaled and looked into my eyes and said: "Yes! That's just what I want, Eddie!"

Well, when we walked back into the front room and told Ed and Barbara, they took charge of everything. Barbara offered Lee her own white wedding gown but Lee preferred a blue evening gown she had just bought; it was in her apartment. Ed slipped off his wedding ring and handed it to me. Because he covers the courts and knows legal procedures and judges, he obtained a wedding certificate and even found a judge willing to marry us at any hour. Lee and I were bewildered by all this instant activity.

It was decided that Ed would drive Lee home to change clothes, and then he would buy flowers. Barbara took on the task of keeping me sane while I also changed in my apartment. Half an hour passed. Ed arrived at my place with Lee, who bounded up the stairs, holding out her hand to me. When I took my hand away I found she had given me money, for she knew all about the salaries paid to reporters. By phone we reached a few friends and told them where to meet us. Now it was almost eleven o'clock.

We drove to the home of a judge wearing pajamas. His parlor was decorated with orange and black Halloween figures; since Lee and I had been living in a world of our own making, we hadn't realized that Halloween was near. From the chandelier there dangled a cardboard skeleton. I asked Lee whether she wanted it taken down. Gaily, she said no.

Then the judge asked us to stand in front of him. Pulling out a book of some sort from some place, he asked: "Do you, Edward Robb Ellis, take this woman . . ." etc. Ah, yes!

Turning toward Lee, the judge asked: "Do you, Edward Robb Ellis, take . . ."

Confusedly, she began: "I, Edward Robb—"

Then the judge got it right and pronounced us husband and wife.

Ed Wallace, another reporter and friend, flashed a lightbulb in our faces as he took picture after picture, and then there was an awkward silence and Lee staggered back and sank upon the sofa. Barbara bounded toward me, hissing: "Here! You haven't given her your flowers!" As in a dream I took the flowers bought by Ed and handed them to the woman who now was my wife. Then, slowly, all of us began to recover our wit and the judge in this dry state broke out some wine and he and our friends toasted us.

We left in two cars, picking up a friend who had not been home when I called the first time. He is Billy Priakos, of Greek descent, a violinist in the symphony orchestra and its favorite clown. We drove to a roadhouse and ordered drinks and stared at one another and I told a naughty joke and then Billy recited his celebrated story called "Billy's Goat Gruff" but it somehow didn't seem funny tonight. Everyone seemed stunned by our impulsive marriage and soon all of them did the only proper thing to do, which was to drive the bride and groom to his apartment and then vanish. Vamoose! But not until they had thrown some rice at us. Leave it to Barbara to think of that detail.

I carried my wife upstairs and kissed her before setting her down in her new home. After I lit a gas grate we sat down on the green sofa, where she had stroked my hair three weeks ago, to the day.

Suddenly she sprang up and playfully beat her fists against me.

"Tell me!" she demanded. "Tell me the meaning of that joke you told this evening! I'm a married woman now! I have a right to know!"

CHAPTER 6

Now I was a new husband — and unemployed reporter. Many of us were fired in a third wave of retrenchment, leaving me frantic with worry. My bride and I went to my home state of Illinois and I was hired by the Journal-Transcript in Peoria, 50 miles south of Kewanee. I was glad to leave drab Oklahoma City for beautiful Peoria, lying at the foot of a broad basin of the Illinois river and called Peoria Lake. Lee and I rented an apartment on a bluff so high that we could see miles and miles. My starting salary at the paper was $32.50 a week, soon raised to $35. Peoria, famous for its whiskey and Caterpillar tractors, had a vigorous association of commerce. I replaced a reporter named Charles Pearson, who had covered this organization on a daily basis. Then one day he walked into the office of the executive secretary, carrying something under his trench-coat. Hollering "here's your mascot!", onto the desk he dumped a live skunk. Of course, he was fired within an hour. Charlie was a brilliant eccentric, with whom we soon became friendly. Lee began playing first violin in the Peoria Symphony Orchestra, but just as our personal life was settling down, the news from abroad became disturbing.

1939

PEORIA, ILLINOIS, SUNDAY, AUGUST 27, 1939 ■ The shadow of war creeps over Europe. Lee and I stay up late to listen to broadcasts from Washington, London and Paris about the gathering crisis. Hitler wants Poland. England and France are negotiating with him. There is diplomatic activity in all the capitals of Europe. What happens over there colors our thoughts here, thousands of miles from the potential conflict. I realize I am but one of millions of worried Americans living our daily lives amidst a rumbling, as though of an oncoming earthquake.

FRIDAY, SEPTEMBER 1, 1939 ■ WAR HAS BROKEN OUT IN EUROPE! Tonight Lee and I felt as though we sat on a pinwheel of history.

From midnight until now—I'm writing this at 4 A.M.—we listened to radio reports of rapid-fire events: . . . The Nazis invaded Poland without declaring war . . . the British and French demand that Hitler withdraw immediately . . . the Germans are overwhelming the Poles . . . the British army is mobilizing . . . children are being evacuated from London . . . Warsaw is being bombed . . .

We heard Hitler address members of the Reichstag in the Kroll opera House in Berlin. Earlier I had read aloud a short biography of Hitler in a book called *Men of Turmoil.* Then, my fingers touching the radio, I felt the vibrations of his voice invading my body.

At this moment, here in Peoria, I hear whistles blowing to signal the start of war.

This is it. This is—what?

England and France will fight. Will the United States? I think so— within a year. Will I be drafted? Probably. Then what will happen to Lee? I feel paralyzed by the scope and tempo of events in Europe. It is hard to think beyond the next second. Now I only *feel*—not reason. I'm so saturated with emotions I can't understand them.

SATURDAY, SEPTEMBER 2, 1939 ■ All last night I had nightmares about war, war, war!

SUNDAY, SEPTEMBER 3, 1939 ■ Early this Sunday afternoon Lee and I took a nap, but about 2:30 she nudged me and said: "Eddie, something's happening! They're selling extras!" I awakened instantly. I heard newsboys nearing our place yelling words I couldn't understand. I ran downstairs and bought a paper, an extra edition of the *Journal-Transcript,* with this headline:

BRITAIN FRANCE
MARCH TO WAR

I took the paper up to Lee and we stared at one another, dumb with horror. Chamberlain proclaims a state of war exists with the German Reich . . . President Roosevelt and his aides scan war situation . . . Berlin quickly accepts envoy from Moscow . . . giant German liner in peril at sea . . . text of fateful radio speech . . . Chamberlain message text . . . war bulletins . . .

I asked my wife: "If you could kill Hitler, would you?"

"Gladly!"

Then she added she is so afraid I might have to go to war that she may shoot off one of my toes.

FRIDAY, OCTOBER 20, 1939 ▪ Ever since the war began a reporter has remained in the office all night to watch the Associated Press teletype machines, ready to call an editor if something very important happens. Now and then I get this job and Lee goes to the city room to stay with me. Last night we sat at a desk, holding hands, when in walked our night watchman, Joe. He is a German, a handsome 64 year old, once the city's fire chief, moustached and sturdy.

When I said we are celebrating our first year of marriage, his eyes softened. He said that a year ago his wife died after 38 years of happiness together. He sat down to tell us about her, speaking haltingly. His grief seemed to dig a grave in my heart. When he began weeping, I looked away.

He muttered: "I'd better move away from our little house. Every time I walk home I expect to see Mom there waiting for me . . ."

Later he returned to give us fresh doughnuts.

THURSDAY, NOVEMBER 30, 1939 ▪ I'm hearing more and more jokes about President Roosevelt. Here's one of them: A man dies and his soul goes to the Pearly Gates. St. Peter asks what he did when alive on earth. The man says he was a psychiatrist. St. Peter cries: "Come in! Come in! You're just the man we need. God thinks he's Franklin D. Roosevelt!"

WEDNESDAY, DECEMBER 20, 1939 ▪ The river runs below a window of the office where an old man sits with fingers laced over his belly. He loves the river and wants to watch it, but put a piece of tin along the bottom of the window to block his view.

"The river's beautiful," he explained, "too beautiful, in fact. I had to put up that thing because otherwise I'd spend all my time just gazing out at the water."

This dreamer is a realist named Charles M. Putnam. He was born 85 years ago in Massachusetts, prospected for silver in Colorado, helped build a railroad in Texas. Now he owns two parking lots in Peoria, his own coal company, and has a part interest in a nearby coal mine. Although he earns a good living, he lives in a hotel room costing only four dollars a week. He is bald, has a stubby white moustache, eyes ending in laugh wrinkles, wears round spectacles and a bow tie. He is a capitalist who invests in human souls.

One day in 1932 he was sauntering along railroad tracks near his office when he saw a woman ahead of him. She was ill-clad, held a baby in one arm and led another child by the hand. She was weeping and walking toward the river. It looked as though she intended to drown her children and herself. Catching up, he asked what was troubling her. She said her husband had beaten her up, they had been dispossessed, she had no food and no money to buy food for her kids. Handing her some cash, he decided then and there to help the poor.

The next day in a shabby part of town he rented a building, converted it into a kitchen, and began giving food to hungry people. Later he opened his Blackhawk food kitchen at 1302 N. Adams St. and for the last seven years has spent most of his money on folks with withered hopes. He asks at two nearby schools for the names of children most in need of food and then his four amateur case workers visit their homes to gauge the needs of the families themselves. This year he is feeding 425 individuals representing 85 families.

Every day except Sunday a child from each family arrives at the kitchen with containers to carry the food home. On Saturdays they get enough to last over Sunday. Everything is free.

One evening near his office a rough-looking man stepped up and asked: "Are you Mr. Putnam?"

"Yes."

"I just got back to Peoria," said the man, removing his hat, "after bein' away a spell, an' my old lady told me about you. She said if it wasn't fer you, she and the kids would've starved to death. I ain't got no money, Mr. Putnam, and I ain't got no job, but I just wanted to tell yuh that if anyone ever causes yuh any trouble—you just git in touch with me!"

Putnam reminds me of Count Leo Tolstoy, Russia's immortal writer and social reformer. In his treatise called *What Is to Be Done?* Tolstoy used words that could have come from Putnam's heart: "What is it I really want? I want to do good. I want to so contrive that no humans should be hungry and cold, and that men may live as it is proper for them to live."

Putnam told me: "People sometimes ask me whether these people are worth this. Worth! There is no question of worth when a child is hungry."

I asked: "Are you religious?"

"No . . . quite the opposite, as a matter of fact."

"Agnostic?"

"No," he replied. "I'd just say I'm a free-thinker."

"Do you enjoy your welfare work?"

"Yes!" he cried, his laugh-wrinkles deepening. "It's fun. As a matter of fact, it's even romantic."

Beautiful river. Beautiful man.

1940

FRIDAY, JANUARY 19, 1940 ▨ Last night a fire broke out in the business section of East Peoria across the river. I took a cab over there and spent two and a half hours in weather 10 degrees below zero. With flames whipped by a wind of 20 miles an hour, the fire developed into the worst in the history of East Peoria. Water from the hoses of firemen quickly became icicles on walls, furniture, clothing and everything else. I already had a cold and was afraid it would turn into pneumonia. Some firemen had cheeks and fingers frozen. Ten below is a bit much.

FRIDAY, FEBRUARY 2, 1940 ▨ In *Life* magazine I was reading a long article about Eleanor Roosevelt when I saw this sub-head: WHO THE HELL WAS MR. ELLIS?

In paragraphs describing the way the First Lady conducts press conferences in Washington, I read further: "Returning from trips around the country, she brings the reporters messages from friends and relatives she has run into. 'Mr. Ellis in Kansas City sends you his best,' she told a member of the *Washington Post* staff one day, baffling the reporter completely. 'I don't know who the hell Mr. Ellis is,' the *Post* reporter said later."

Well, I understood, so I wrote a letter of explanation to *Life*. In March of 1937 when I was a reporter for the *Oklahoma City Times* I covered a press conference Mrs. Roosevelt held in the Biltmore Hotel. Beth Campbell of the *Times* had gone to Washington to cover the President's wife for the Associated Press. That day in Oklahoma I asked Mrs. Roosevelt to say hello to Beth for me, since she saw Beth almost every day. The First Lady had mistakenly thought she had met me in Kansas City and that I had given her a message for a woman working for the *Washington Post.* It was kind of her to try to do me a favor.

Life published my letter on February 26, but compounded the errors by calling Beth Campbell *Ruth* Campbell. Hurriedly I wrote Beth to assure her I remembered her correct name. Then I began getting letters from friends all over the country, twitting me for using the President's wife as a messenger girl, so I had to explain to them, too. A comedy of errors and sorta fun.

SUNDAY, FEBRUARY 25, 1940 ▨ Today in the Shrine Mosque I interviewed Allan Jones, 32, the tenor and movie star. He has made eight movies and soon will begin a ninth. Having seen him with the Marx Brothers in *A Night at the Opera*, I asked what it is like to work with them.

"They're always clowning," he said with a slight frown, "both on and off the set. After awhile, they begin to get on one's nerves . . ."

I noticed that he wore Cuban heels to make himself look taller. We were standing in a wing of the theater moments before he was to walk on stage to give a concert, and I said I was surprised to see him smoking just before singing.

"Yes," he said, "I endorse Chesterfields"—he was smoking a Pall Mall—"but I'd die if I thought I had to smoke Chesterfields the rest of my life!"

And people wonder why reporters are cynical.

SATURDAY, MARCH 23, 1940 ■ My sister Kay is a librarian at the Peoria Public Library and very helpful to me from time to time. When I learned that Archduke Otto of Austria was coming here, I asked her to give me background information about him. Today, thanks to her, when I walked into his suite in the Pere Marquette Hotel I was able to ask intelligent questions.

He is the son of an emperor. His father was Charles I, His Apostolic Majesty, the Emperor of Austria and King of Hungary, the last Hapsburg emperor of the Dual Monarchy of Austria-Hungary. The Hapsburg family took control of Austria as long ago as the year 1276. During the recent World War his father fought on the side of Germany, was defeated and overthrown in 1918, died in exile in 1922.

Otto von Hapsburg was born near Vienna in 1912, the son of Charles I and Zita, Princess of Bourbon and Parma. His first language was German. Educated in Spain and Belgium, he learned to speak English, French, Hungarian, Spanish, Czechoslovakian and Croatian. The name Hapsburg means "Hawk's Castle," which the family owned in Switzerland. Early this month Otto arrived in the United States and on March 8 he enjoyed tea in the White House with President Roosevelt. Today he came to Peoria with his younger brother, Felix, 23.

When I entered the suite the brothers were alone. Shaking hands with Otto, I said: "I'm afraid I don't know how to address you properly, sir."

Smiling, he said: "Oh, call me anything."

He is of medium height, has liquid brown eyes, eyebrows that meet on the bridge of his nose, a wide moustache. In *Time* magazine I had read he does not have much money, which may explain why his coat and trousers were poorly matched and somewhat rumpled. However, he was pleasant and obviously intelligent.

I pulled out a notebook and read aloud, asking: "Is it true, sir, that your full name is Franz Josef Otto Robert Maria Anton Karl Maximilian Heinrich Sixtus Xavier Felix Renatus Ludwig Gaetano Pius Ignaz?"

Amused, he replied in a soft voice and unaccented English: "Perhaps that is my full name. Maybe. Really, I'd have to look it up."

Then the emperor's son lit my cigaret.

He is touring this country to study our government, economic system and agricultural program. He told me he is confident that Nazi Germany will be defeated. He is a man with a price on his head, for Hitler has ordered his death if he's ever caught by any Nazi. His dream is to reunite the nations his father ruled, thus establishing a parliamentary monarchy. This means that he is the pretender to the throne of Austria-Hungary.

"If your dream is realized," I asked, "would you then become emperor?"

Flicking his black cigaret-holder, he said softly: "If I make a statement of this sort it would be interpreted here as propaganda, so I prefer not to say."

By this time we had been joined by a woman reporter and woman photographer from the *Peoria Star*, a rival newspaper.

The photographer pointed her camera at the son of the emperor and said: "Watch the birdie!"

I felt like resigning from the Fourth Estate.

WEDNESDAY, MAY 29, 1940 ▮ It's 11:45 P.M. Lee and I are again in the office watching the wire service teletype machines. In the past few days the Belgians have lost 100,000 men fighting the Nazis and now King Leopold of Belgium has surrendered. British and French soldiers are surrounded on the beaches of Dunkirk. I hover over the chattering teletypes, read words, wonder what they mean to me. Nothing really. Bullets kill soldiers; bulletins splash no blood on teletype machines. All I see are symbols.

This is history in the making, telescopic history; the details, microscopic history, may not be known for a decade or two. In *The Road to War*, a history of World War I by Walter Millis, when I read about the sinking of the *Lusitania* I felt more of an emotional jolt than I do now as I read daily dispatches from Europe. Why? Because Millis has collected all the facts, analyzed them, synthesized them, presented them in chronological sequence.

This present war is ever with us, with me. Behind my every utterance, my every act, my every thought, this monster called war slouches and grimaces and menaces me. We Americans still eat hamburgers, kiss our wives, play with our kids, gripe about our jobs, take baths, go window-shopping—do all those million-million things constituting normal living.

Meantime, we perch precariously on the fulcrum of history, worrying about which end is up, which down.

Why am I writing this? Because I want to preserve a record of the mood of the people at this period. And what do I succeed in doing? Merely demonstrating how vague is our comprehension of those horrific events beyond the horizon, how unsure we are of their relationship to us, how unstable seems the future and yet, how blithely we go our accustomed ways.

It's true that the first casualty of war is truth. Peoria is polluted with rumors. The best restaurant in town is the Reiss German Restaurant on a bluff one block from the river. Now we're hearing vicious rumors about its owner, Karl Reiss: "He dug a tunnel from his restaurant to the river so that he might provision Nazi submarines . . . He is broadcasting to Berlin from a radio in the basement of his restaurant . . . His body bears diagrams of American arsenals, written in invisible ink . . ."

On our staff we have an editor of monumental ignorance. When he heard these rumors, he ordered a reporter to go to the restaurant to *ask* Karl Reiss about them.

His eyes popping out, the reporter gasped, "*What?*"

Yes, the editor told him to go there right now and ask Reiss about the rumors. The reporter swore, balked, stamped around the city room, but at last did as he was told. Sheepishly.

What some people don't understand is this: Most newspapers are conservative because publishers are wealthy. Most reporters are liberal because they are underpaid.

We reporters were so outraged by the stupidity and arrogance of that editor that we made a point of eating in that restaurant as often as possible. Karl changed its name from the Reiss German Restaurant to the Reiss Cosmopolitan Restaurant.

MONDAY, JULY 15, 1940 ▪ Today, much to my astonishment, I was invited to lunch in the Peoria Room of the Pere Marquette Hotel by Mrs. B. L. Sommer, very rich, very Republican, very powerful.

Wendell Willkie has become the Republican candidate for President and now travels around the country attacking New Deal policies and his rival, President Roosevelt. Willkie has three brothers. One of them, Edward, came to town a week or so ago to visit a friend, bringing his wife and their teen-age daughter. Edward is an executive of a packing plant in Chicago, built like a fullback, weighing 245 pounds, full of fun, fond of laughing. As soon as I sat down to interview him, he began joking.

"If you want a statement—" he began, whipping out a pencil. "If you want a statement, I can state categorically that I deny all rumors to the effect that I expect to go into the movies, radio, or any kindred business."

His wife laughed, nodded understandingly and chirped: "James Roosevelt!" Her husband was mocking a son of President Roosevelt.

That was the tone of the entire interview: Fun and games. I liked the man and his wife, so obviously in love. Every so often she would cry, "Now, sweetheart, try to be good!"

Mrs. Peoria Republican said at our luncheon table that she disliked my story, that it harmed Edward Willkie, Wendell Willkie and, therefore, the entire Republican party. She was polite, but I saw the steel behind her smile. She asked whether I would accompany her to the office of my managing editor, E. E. Soules. I agreed. I like our M.E., but felt I would lose this battle because our paper is a Republican paper.

When we reached his office Mrs. Sommer told him what she had said to me, then suggested they call Edward Willkie in Chicago to get his reaction to my story. I felt tense. Soules called Willkie, spoke to him, then she spoke to him, while I sat and listened.

Willkie told both of them he'd never been interviewed before, that he just happened to be in a jocular mood that day, that he liked the story I'd written about him and ended with the remark: "I just made a damned fool out of myself!" Not in my opinion. I liked him. He was human, candid, honest.

Mrs. Peoria Republican: 0. Mr. Peoria Reporter: 1.

SUNDAY, OCTOBER 13, 1940 ■ Among the books I borrowed from the library the other day was *Why England Slept*, by John F. Kennedy.

THURSDAY, OCTOBER 24, 1940 ■ I can't recall any time when I was so sour and cynical as now. I walk gloom, talk gloom, dream gloom. Why, just the other night I dreamed I was being tortured in a Nazi concentration camp, perhaps the result of seeing an anti-Nazi film called *Pastor Hall*. I also face the draft.

That month our navy called up reserves to man new ships, the Balkans were tense as Nazis moved down the Danube River, Nazi troops poured into the capital of Rumania, Nazi aviators dropped a bomb on St. Paul's Cathedral in London, Hitler met with Franco of Spain, and on October 29 in Washington the first numbers were drawn to draft men into our armed forces.

1941

THURSDAY, MAY 1, 1941 ■ I've received my draft classification: 3-A. This means I'm safe from active service awhile—provided the U.S. doesn't plunge into war. I guess having a wife and a hernia helped me. I'm pessimistic about the future. It seems Roosevelt is doing all he can to drag us into the war.

THURSDAY, JUNE 5, 1941 ■ Tom is the first man from our staff to be drafted into the army. He did all he could to escape this fate and I had cheered him on. Tom is a brilliant and sensitive young man, educated by Jesuits, with a master's degree, an ardent Roman Catholic who tried in a pleasant way to talk me out of my atheism. We remained friends despite our debates.

Lee and I knew he was going to be taken away today so we drove to the armory. She had said good-bye to Tom previously, and hates good-byes, so she stayed in the car when I got out. I was looking for him when I heard him say; "Here I am, Eddie."

Unshaven, eyes dull, shoulders drooping, he leaned against a brick wall of the armory straddling a laundry bag with enough civilian clothes for three days. A red 29 was painted on the back of his right hand.

"Yeah," he muttered, "they numbered all of us when we came in today. Just another indignity."

He told me that earlier this morning, when he took the oath of allegiance to the President and Commander-in-Chief of the United States, he added under his breath "—the son-of-a-bitch!"

His face was woebegone. I noticed that he wasn't looking me in the eyes.

"Helluva funny rupture in one's life," he drawled.

Lee, despite what she had said, got out of the car and walked over and kissed his cheek. We smiled thin smiles. And then they took Tom away.

THURSDAY, JUNE 26, 1941 ■ Today I accompanied city officials and civic leaders to St. Louis to find out how that city overcame its smoke problem. Coming back I sat in the parlor car of the train across the aisle from the publisher of my paper. As we chatted, I showed him the copy of the story I had filed from St. Louis to the *Journal-Transcript*, and after he read it he came over and took a seat near me.

"I like it, Eddie. Good story, but—" He lowered his voice. "I wish you'd get in the name of P. A. Singer." (Singer was chairman of the smoke abatement committee of the association of commerce.) "But," I said, "we carried his name in four or five advance stories."

"Oh, you did? Well, try and get it in again some way, can you? You see, I'm trying to sell him my house."

MONDAY, NOVEMBER 3, 1941 ▪ A photographer and I drove to Kingston Mines, about 15 miles south of Peoria, to get a story about an elderly man who is a light-tender on the Illinois River. As we approached his little house we met his son, 19-year-old Allen. He hollered: "Pa, they's a couple-a men here to see yuh!"

Then I saw the old man, standing in front of a woodshed, a stick of firewood in his arthritic fingers. A half-hostile look on his face, he squinted through narrowed blue eyes. He spat.

"Well, yer-a seein' me," he rasped. "Start talkin'!"

I said: "We came down to see about your work taking care of the river lights. Thought maybe—"

"Ain't been any complaints, hev they?"

"No, no complaints," I told Lemuel Richardson. "You see, we're not government men. We're newspaper men."

The bantam-size figure straightened up a little. With the wood, Lem rubbed the side of his rubber boot. "Oh," he said vaguely.

"Ma" Richardson came out of the house, wiped her stout arms on her apron, smiled, then said to her husband, "Ask the gentlemen to come in."

"Okay," Lem grunted. "G'wan in. Wait'll I git rid of this dang firewood."

He stumped away, then reappeared in the front room without his hip boots and minced over the rug in red wool stockings.

"Now, young fellas, what wuz thet you was a-sayin' 'bout my work?"

President Roosevelt has never heard of Lemuel Richardson although both work for the same company, the United States of America. In fact, Lem holds seniority over F.D.R. because he's been on the federal payroll 15 years.

Lem's job is to keep aglow the kerosene lamps atop permanent light stations along the banks of the Illinois river in the vicinity of Kingston Mines. He works for the U.S. engineering corps, whose local headquarters are at the foot of Grant St. in Peoria, and the corps is a part of the war department. I asked him to show us what he does.

"Better git some high boots on yuh, young fella, if you want ta come down to the ole flat-boat with me. Tarnation, but it's slick-like an' muddy!"

Before leaving, Lem consulted a plug of tobacco, tested it with his knife, found it good, sliced off a hunk, popped it into his mouth, shifted it deftly to one side, then bent to the work of squeezing through the mud.

"Hed some pigs sent ta me t'other day. Six of 'em. S'ppose I gotta slop'em right smart from now on. Allen—" His cud stopped in mid-chew as he thought about his son. "Allen, now, he don't like pork eatin', no how. Well—"

By now we had reached the edge of the river. Lem cocked his eyes upstream. The sky was the color of an oyster, the air was moist, and the river dragged its weary length downstream, blurring into an invisible horizon.

Lem pointed. "See that there pole? That's where Ma an' me tied up fust time we laid up here. Ran out an 18-foot plank, we did." He was pointing to a spot about a city block from the edge of the river.

"Shore is low now . . . This's been the doggondest season uh yet seen. This here Illinois river ain't never been so gosh-awful low afore. I dunno—" He wagged a rueful head.

"Things ain't like they used to was, an' I oughta know, young fellas. I is the dangdest river rat around this here Illinois River yuh ever laid eyes to! Fished her fer years afore I took this gov'ment job. Ask Cap Spears 'bout me. He'll tell yuh! I is the dangdest guy!"

Lem plodded through the mud, muttering to himself, waggling his hunting cap from side to side. At last we reached one of the lights he tends. It consisted of a slim wooden pylon about 12 feet high with rude steps leading to its top. On it was a board with 145.5 painted on it. This meant that this light is 145.5 miles upriver from Grafton.

"Will you show us how it works?" I asked.

"Huh!" he snorted. "Simple as all get-out." At the top of the pylon there is a glass globe. Lem took it off and then fingered the wick.

My photographer yelled: "Hey, Dad!"

Lem jerked his head around as the camera's lightbulb whitened the scene.

"Tarnation!" he shrilled. "Whatcha all mean, a-flashin' and a-blinkin' that there contraption at me?"

"You're going to get your picture in the paper."

"Dang near knocked me offen this here—" His mind mulled what he'd just been told. "Oh!" he said tentatively. He thought some more, and then a slow grin lifted the salty stubble of his whiskers. "Oh!" he said knowingly.

Finding that the kerosene lamp was working properly, Lem backed down the steps and into the mud. I asked to see his boat, so he led us down to the edge of the water.

"Got any oars?" the photographer asked.

"Good gosh a-mighty, buddy!" Lem cried. "Had 'em at the house when we left. Whyunt yuh ask me while we's up there?"

Poking around beneath an overturned boat, he found a pair of oars.

He pulled them out, chuckling: "Jim see me a-takin' his oars an' he'd shore as heck git duck fever a-bellyachin' 'bout it!"

He squished through the mud to his own boat. "Here's my flat," he announced with pride. "Wear one out 'bout every three years, ice 'n stuff. Had one of my boys make this fer me. Used t'other one over there fer four years till Ma made me git this new one. She's tough as a turtle, though, an' I ain't a-skeered ta take her out, only Ma, yuh know—"

Lem's universe is the river and his world is his boat. He is as natural and essential a part of the river as its channel he guards. He takes care of six lights. He is paid $10 per light, or $60 a month, and the money is well-spent because it saves countless lives and thousands of dollars each year. He rows about 24 miles a day getting to and from his lights, and he has been doing this for 15 years. All by rowboat. Once Lem tried a motorboat, but the propeller got caught in his britches "—an danged near left me jay-naked!" No, Lem Richardson doesn't care for these new-fangled contraptions.

Now the photographer and I were in his boat with him as he maneuvered on water as flat as paper. He was showing off his skill—and skill he has. No water bug ever scooted more gracefully over the bosom of the water than Lem in his old flat. Flashing back to the bank, he rested on his oars and bestowed a tobacco-rimmed grin on the newspaper fellas.

"Ain't nothin' on this here river kin grab my oars and skunk me! Ain't nothin' ever growed or was made what could skunk ole Lemuel Richardson once he gits in his ole flat. Ask Cap Spears, if yuh wanna know. Jest ask ole Cap Spears, he'll tell yuh!"

When we got back to his home he pulled off his heavy boots and sat down in his favorite chair by the stove. Hanging in the air was the appetite-priming smell of good cooking. "Ma" Richardson walked into the room smiling a plump smile.

"Now, young men, how would a piece of mince pie sound to you . . . made it myself."

"I gotta have my mince pie," Lem said ponderously. "Don't tie into much-a anythin' else. Don't eat so much. Not that I ain't healthy, though. Weigh nigh onta 117 pounds."

"No, Pa," his wife said. "You know you don't even weigh no 100 pounds." She beamed at their visitors. "Only weighed 120 pounds when I married him, he did. I fattened him up to 135 onest, but that was the most."

"Ez I was sayin'," Lem continued elfishly, "I don't eat so dang much these days. Take our nine kids, though, every one of 'em—"

"Ten!" his wife interrupted.

"Oh, yeah ... Ten ... Well, now, they kin eat a hog whole, seems ta me. Course they ain't none of 'em home now, 'cept Allen here. And Allen. He's a good workin' boy, Allen is, but they jist ain't any work to be had 'round here. Two years now—"

"Here's the pie!" his wife cried, bursting in.

"I tell you," Lem declared, scratching his leg, "they ain't no better folks in the whole dang world'n we is! Ain't got much to offer folks in the way of grub, but we—"

"Now, Pa," said his wife, gently admonishing him.

"Good gosh a-mighty, woman!" he yelled. "I'm jist a-settin' here an' a-tellin' these young fellas we know how tiz ta be hungry, an' so thet's why we never lets anybody git away without they hev a bite with us—even if it's jist cold beans."

"Pa's right," she said with a smile, wiping her hands on her apron. "We like to do what we kin for deservin' folks."

Lemuel Richardson held the palms of his hands to the welcome heat of the stove.

"Way I look at it," he said solemnly," we like ta eat an' we lets live. Thet's about it, I guess."

SUNDAY, DECEMBER 7, 1941 ▪ Early this Sunday afternoon Lee and I sat in the front room listening to a news broadcast from WMBD by George Barrett, my boss, the editor of the *Journal-Transcript*. Suddenly he hesitated, paused, then said rapidly: "Ladies and gentlemen, we have a flash from the United Press: Japan has attacked Pearl Harbor!"

With a reporter's reflex, I looked at my watch. The time was 1:33 P.M. Lee, who had been chewing something, stopped chewing. Our eyes met. I remember gasping. Then I walked over and took my wife in my arms. She had a far-away look in her blue eyes but she had resumed chewing. She said: "I'm sorry, Eddie, but I don't feel it yet."

I ran to the phone to call the office. The boy on the switchboard said nobody was there. When I called the home of my city editor, his wife said he was out hunting. As I hung up, the enormity of this event hit me so hard that my profanity suffered. In astonishment I heard myself say "Pooh!"

Sort of a Gilbert and Sullivan reaction to a world crisis.

I pulled out an encyclopedia and maps to look up Pearl Harbor, then recent issues of *Time*, *Life* and *Newsweek*, cluttering up the floor with the stuff. While trying to absorb as much data as possible, I kept listening to the radio spew out one bulletin after another. Lee had to attend a rehearsal of the string section of the Peoria Philharmonic, so I decided to ride downtown with her to take some of my data to my office.

When I got there I found Vic Kaspar, who said an extra would be published and that other staffers were on their way to the building. Barrett, who had come from the studio, was in his office. I walked in and dumped an armload of information about Hawaii, Japan and the Philippines on his desk. Vic sent me to the composing room to read proof, the first time I've done this in years, and there I remained, the only proof-reader, until the paper was put to bed. Our managing editor is such a mild man that I was surprised when, for the first time, I heard him say *hell!*

As soon as I got my hands on a copy of the extra, I was sent into the streets to show it to pedestrians to get their reactions—which were varied. Some people were surprised, some not. Some were excited, some calm. Some made intelligent comments, most did not. But what all had in common was one idea: Kick the hell out of Japan! Two young women said they had come downtown for Cokes, but after hearing the war news they decided Scotch and soda were more in keeping with the crisis.

Back in the office I wrote my story, then telephoned around town to try to find a list of names of Peoria boys in the service in the Pacific. A woman who belongs to the Peoria Sailors and Marines Mothers' Club had such a list and offered to bring it to me. When she arrived she said her son is on an American gunboat that has just been captured. Her black eyes were moist. In our own office there is a young woman whose husband is at Pearl Harbor, and I saw her tremble.

At last I ran across the street to a Greek restaurant for a bowl of chili and its juke-box was playing symphonic music. As I began to relax I heard a newsboy racing past shouting: "War declared!" I sat there, bathed in the beauty of a masterpiece by Tschaikovsky, while beauty leaked out of this world.

In the office again I learned that Japan has declared war against the United States. Its attack on Pearl Harbor astonished me because I thought it was bluffing. For many months I have been an isolationist; now I know that we isolationists were wrong, dead wrong! Nothing could have unified the American people so much as that sneak attack. If I were single I might enlist. My sister Fran said on the phone that she's terrified because her boy friend plans to enlist. My sister Kay said the war news had brought on a fresh attack of ulcers. My friend Max Bosler said that when he heard the flash he thought it was just another radio stunt by Orson Welles. Worst of all was the reaction of seven-year-old Mickey Gearhart, the son of a friend, who screamed: "I'm going to kill myself! I don't want to get blown up by a bomb!"

WEDNESDAY, DECEMBER 10, 1941 ■ This evening one of my best friends brought his girl to our house. All the talk, of course, was about the war. I asked whether he plans to enlist. He replied: "No, sir! Not for me! I'll lie, I'll crawl, I'll sham, I'll do any damn thing to stay out of this war. I'll let the other fellow be a hero if he wants to. I don't want myself shot up! Not for me! No, sir!"

1942

MONDAY, MARCH 9, 1942 ■ Dr. Will Durant is a hero to me, so when I learned he was coming here to lecture for the Peoria Citizens Forum, I reread his autobiographical novel *Transition* and dug into data about his background. I'm fond of him because he writes about history and philosophy, and also because his style is simple. To borrow Schopenhauer's phrase, he uses common words to say uncommon things. Durant once said it is the curse of his life that some people "take it for granted that anything that is clearly expressed must be superficial."

He was born 56 years ago in Massachusetts, one of eleven children of French-Canadian immigrants. His father was illiterate. His mother wanted him to be a priest. Instead, he studied philosophy, earned a doctorate from Columbia University in 1917, published a book called *The Story of Philosophy* in 1927. It became an immediate best-seller. Then he settled down to write a history of civilization in several volumes. The first one, published in 1935, is called *Our Oriental Heritage*; the second, published in 1939, is *The Life of Greece*. I bought, read and underlined both volumes.

At 12:50 P.M. today Durant arrived in Peoria by train. I was one of seven persons who met him at the station and then I was lucky enough to ride beside him in a car that took us to the Pere Marquette Hotel for lunch. When I mentioned a couple of anecdotes in *Transition* he was so pleased to hear that I knew something about his life that he smiled and patted my arm.

When we assembled for lunch in a private room in the hotel, I had a chance to get a good look at Durant. He is diminutive, about the size and shape of Charles Chaplin. He has a small face, small eyes, small hands, white hair, black eyebrows, a salt-and-pepper moustache.

When he was 28 and teaching in New York City he married a pupil, 15-year-old Russian-born Ada Kaufman. She rollerskated from Harlem to lower Manhattan to marry him. Because she had a blithe personality he called her Ariel, the name of a spirit in Shakespeare's *The Tempest*; later she made this her legal first name.

Today at lunch, eyes twinkling, he said: "I'm a vegetarian, but I make one exception—women!"

There were two ladies at our table and I thought I saw their eyebrows lift a fraction of an inch. Our celebrity, it seemed, is a playful man. Voltaire was called the Laughing Philosopher; once he said: "I look upon solemnity as a disease." Durant can be called the Mischievous Philosopher.

Asked why he lectures, he replied: "It's simple. I indulge in talky-talk for three reasons: One is to make money. The second is because I like to hear people applauding me. And perhaps the third reason is because I might be able to start people thinking about something new."

As the luncheon ended I asked Durant whether he would autograph my copy of *The Life of Greece*. Taking my arm, he led me to a sofa where he pulled out a pen and wrote his name on a page opposite a picture of a bust of Hygieia, the Greek goddess of health.

"Isn't she a lovely girl!" he exclaimed. "I discovered her myself. I found her in a Greek museum and took this picture. The curator was pleased as the devil when I sent him a copy of the book with her picture in it."

Among those at lunch was Genevieve Alloy, a debutante who handles publicity for the Forum. She and I took a walk with Durant and during the next thirty minutes he spouted so many puns and profundities that I can't remember all of them. However, I do recall his remark that he has coined a new definition of war, so of course I asked what it is.

Eyes twinkling, he replied: "Competitive perforation."

As we neared the hotel he said the walk had caused him to perspire so much that he needed a bath.

"Genevieve," he said with a straight face, "perhaps you might care to bathe me."

"If she does," I cried, "I'm going to get one of our photographers to snap a picture of it, and then I'll blackmail you! How would you like to see in the paper DEBUTANTE DUNKS DR. DURANT?"

"Debutante dunks Dr. Durant," he repeated. "That's marvelous!"

This evening my wife and I were among the 1,500 persons in the Majestic Theater listening to him for almost two hours. It was the best lecture I ever heard in my life. Afterwards, backstage with him, I heard someone ask when he expects to publish the third volume of his *Story of Civilization*.

"Oh, about 1945, I guess—and by then I'll probably have to be speaking Japanese."

Genevieve had invited Lee and me to the party she was giving for Durant in her home. First, though, I went to my office to write a story about his lecture, so we arrived late. When we walked into the house I saw that so many people were crowding around, lionizing him, that he wore a sick smile. There were no empty chairs, so Lee and I sat down on the floor in the dining room. I saw Durant leave the cluster of admirers and walk to the buffet table to get a plate of potato salad. Turning, he saw me, saw my beautiful wife, headed toward us. I introduced them.

He sat down on the floor between us, quipping: "We can see the ladies' ankles better from here."

He asked me to help him eat the potato salad. Lee held a highball glass in her hand. Durant asked her whether he might take a sip. Smiling, she handed the glass to him and watched as he turned it around until he was drinking from the place her lips had touched. Then his merry eyes challenged me.

"I'm never jealous of my wife," I said.

Snorting, shrugging, staring at Lee, he sighed: "And to think I liked him this afternoon!" Then, turning to me: "Why should you be the only man since Christ to be without jealousy? Do you know what was wrong with Christ?" he added. "He said that whosoever looks upon a woman with desire has already committed adultery in his heart. Now, isn't that terrible? It doesn't leave you anything."

And he took another sip from Lee's glass.

In 1977 Simon and Schuster published A Dual Biography by Will and Ariel Durant, which explained his merry naughtiness. He really did like the ladies. His wife said: "He could never feel the depth of my loneliness when he was away, or the bitterness of my doubts as to the ability of his erotic and romantic nature to resist the charms of women after a week or two away from his wife." She helped him write eleven volumes of history covering 110 centuries, a monumental work that opened the way for a school of popularized history. In 1968 the two of them won a Pulitzer Prize for the volume called Rousseau and the Revolution. I was fortunate enough to interview him a second time in New York City. Both of them died in 1981. For years afterward, the Book-of-the-Month Club continued to use The Story of Civilization as a lure to enlist new members.

WEDNESDAY, MAY 6, 1942 ▪ The handsome 60-year-old woman with the gorgeous white hair emptied her glass, put it down on the table and nestled against the back of the booth in the cocktail lounge. Someone had fed a nickel to the juke box and suddenly Tommy Dorsey's trombone moaned through the place.

"Have another drink," I said, turning my neck to try to find a waiter.

"I really don't think I should have a second one, Eddie," she protested mildly. "What if our managing editor walked in here?"

Grinning at her, I said: "So what? In the first place, he doesn't drink booze, so he won't come in here. Anyway, a second drink won't hurt you."

The handsome woman broke the last of her wooden stirring rod into tiny pieces and touched the fingers of her left hand to her hair. "Well," she said.

Catching the eyes of the bartender, through Tommy Dorsey's trombone I said: "Two more."

"You know," she said, "I've been on the editorial side such a short time I really don't know what's expected of me and what isn't." She folded her fingers on the table. "I know you like me all right, but I'm not sure about the other fellows on the day side."

"Look," I said, lighting a cigaret, "you can take it from me that all the fellows like you. Granted, you have two strikes against you because you came from the society department. Generally, we guys have no respect for the dames who write the la-de-dah society notes, but you're different. Now you're just one of the fellows in the editorial department, and that's the best compliment I could give you."

The bartender brought the drinks. I smiled at Lillian and said, "This will do you good. They've worked you too damned hard since you made the change. Whenever there's a woman's angle—that mysterious non-entity—you always get shoved off onto the story, but you're taking it swell and all the guys like you."

"You're awfully nice to me, Eddie," she said. "And to think I'm old enough to be your grandmother!"

I said, "You're just a big blonde bombshell to me, baby!"

After taking another swig of my highball, I added: "And although they probably didn't speak in terms of bombshell babes when you were—when you dated, I'll bet you still set fire to many a heart."

"There you go again," she said, "trying, to probe into my past. I've had two husbands, don't forget, so how did I have time to have a past?"

"I still think you caused many explosions."

"Maybe I did," she murmured over the rim of her glass, "and maybe I didn't. Don't you wish you knew, smartie?"

"Yes," I said.

"Well," she said with a laugh, "I'm not going to tell you anything."

"So you didn't have a past," I sighed mockingly. "What a shame to have wasted your looks." I toyed with my glass. "Of course, no one ever told you you were beautiful."

The handsome 60-year-old woman took a long drink. "Have you ever heard of the actor Richard Bennett?" she asked. "Or are you too young?"

"I have," I said, "heard of Richard Bennett and I'll beg you to remember I'm 31. So Richard Bennett fell in love with you, you lived in sin for ten years, his three daughters, Barbara, Constance and Joan, are really your daughters, too, and now you're in disguise, living out the rest of your life in this burg."

Very slowly she put her glass down on the table. "Richard Bennett," she said softly, "was in love with me."

"Sure, sure! And he gave you gold bracelets and rings and everything."

"Richard Bennett," she said, and she seemed to be talking to herself, "did send me a bracelet, a gold bracelet, and I sent it back, but it was a bracelet and it came from Richard Bennett."

I knew when to back off and shut up.

"Eddie," she said, looking into my eyes, "I was on a newspaper before you were born. Oh, I never was very good. Just another reporter, that was all. But one day they sent me downstate to interview Richard Bennett. He was due to appear here in Peoria the next day, so they wanted some advance stuff on him. Somehow, they sent me.

"When I got there I went to his hotel and called his room. It was in the afternoon, after his matinee, and his manager answered the phone. He said, yes, it would be all right to interview Mr. Bennett and would I mind coming up to his room. Well, I was young then, remember, and so I hesitated, but the office wanted a story and Mr. Bennett wanted me to come up to his room to get the story, so I went.

"When I walked in," she said, her eyes unfocused, "Mr. Bennett was very pleasant. For some reason or other I took off my hat—I don't remember why. Maybe it was because I was proud of my hair. Even then—I was about 24, I guess—I had white hair. Runs in the family. Well, when I took off my hat Mr. Bennett gasped. I really think he did. It seems to me I remember him gasping."

Looking at her beautiful hair, I believed her.

"He asked me to sit down and it didn't seem as though I were interviewing him. Before I knew what was happening, he was asking me all the questions. He was big and broad-shouldered and even more handsome than I'd expected him to be, and before I knew what was happening he was holding one of my hands."

She stopped, took out a cigaret. I lit it for her and waited, but she seemed to have finished.

I was careful to keep my voice soft. "What did you do?"

Leaning back in the booth, she said: "I let him hold my hand. After all, I wasn't married—then—and here he was, America's great matinee idol. That's what we called them then, before the movies, you know. Yes, I guess I let him hold my hand. In no time he chased his manager out of the room on some fool errand or other. I didn't like that very well, but it would have looked silly for me to say anything, so I just sat there, although I did get my hand loose. Mr. Bennett was in a velvet dressing gown, I remember. It was toward evening then and what I could see of the sky through the window was getting orchid. Mr. Bennett saw it, too, watching my glance. Then he said some pretty things—"

She sat very still in the booth.

"He said—" I leaned slightly forward—"but I can't remember just how he said it. He was an actor, after all. I told myself to remember that. Don't forget he's just an actor, I said to myself. He knows how to put a face on things he doesn't really feel.

"Well, I kept saying that to myself while he was saying pretty things to me and all of a sudden I discovered that he was holding both my hands. You know, Shakespeare was all right. He wrote beautifully. It was something Shakespearean that Mr. Bennett was saying to me, but I don't remember just what.

"But the combination of Shakespeare and Mr. Bennett and the orchid sky and some cologne he was wearing—well, the combination almost got to me. But I remembered myself and straightened my hair and I put on my hat and I said I had to go.

"Mr. Bennett said he wouldn't have it, that I had to stay, but now I had to go, and just then I did become frightened. He followed me to the door and wanted to put his arm around me, but I smiled innocently at him and opened the door. He became very correct at that. He straightened and smiled and put his hands in the pockets of his dressing gown and asked me to have dinner with him that evening before the show.

"Well, because he was acting like such a gentleman and because he really hadn't insulted me and because I felt maybe I had had him wrong all the time, I felt I should be civil about it, so I said yes."

Keeping my eyes on the face of the handsome lady across the table, I motioned toward the bartender.

"And after that—?"

"After that," she said, "we had dinner and then he gave me a box seat to see his show, and afterwards we had supper and—Eddie, it was funny! Here was America's greatest actor sitting in a hotel in what to him was a small town, I suppose. He ordered the best of everything, but their best wasn't Rector's in New York and Mr. Bennett kept apologizing about it. In Rector's, he told me, he always mixed the salad himself, and when he called for the wine list they sent the wine chief—oh, what'd you call'em—the men who wear the keys to the wine cellar around their neck—he'd come up and Mr. Bennett would study the wine list very carefully before he made a choice. He told me that. I believed him, too, because—well, he was Richard Bennett, after all.

"When I took the train home late that night—and I did take it, you naughty boy!—I was in a whirl. Here I was, a girl reporter on a fairly small paper, and here was Mr. Bennett, of all people, raving about me! Eddie, he said he was in love with me. And when he said it he trembled. That trembling worried me a bit. I thought maybe it was just some more of his stage acting, done for my benefit, but—God!—how real he made it sound! It seems he fell in love with me first thing. I took off my hat and he thought my hair was the most beautiful he'd ever seen.

"Well . . . he did come on up here to Peoria the next day. I was covering a wedding when he called the office and left his number. He didn't tell the girl who took the message what his name was, but I knew, right away. I didn't know whether I should call him or not. I wanted to and didn't want to. But at last I did slip out to a telephone and call.

"Mr. Bennett said he wanted to see me after his show that evening. He'd been invited to a big party that was to be held at Mrs. Randolph's house in his honor, but he said he'd duck it if I'd meet him. He said he'd rush back to his hotel after the performance, throw off all the other people, take the freight elevator downstairs and then slip out a side door to meet me. He'd already hired a car, he said.

"I met him. We went driving all alone. You know how beautiful the bluff is here, and there was moonlight that night and, well, he was Richard Bennett. I had a hard time remembering I was just a young, small town girl, yes, a young, small town girl, even if I did have unusual hair, and . . .

"Mr. Bennett left the next day. He was, well, sort of huffy when he left for, well, obvious reasons. Two days later, though, I got a letter from Cleveland in which he repeated all the pretty things he had said to me. He wanted me to join him there."

With a dead match she drew a line on the spotted table.

"That wasn't the last letter I got from him, either. He continued to write—for about two years, I think it was. That was a long time ago, of course. The more he wrote the more ardent his letters became. I never did see him again. Once he came back to Peoria to find me, but it just happened that I was visiting upstate that day and he couldn't find out where I was. But even after that he continued to write awhile."

She leaned back against the booth.

"And then he stopped writing," she said abruptly.

The handsome 60-year-old woman picked up her glass.

"Think I will have another drink," she said.

MONDAY, NOVEMBER 2, 1942   ■   The draft is taking so many men from their jobs that Eddie Meier and I decided to drive to Chicago to see whether there are any openings in the big city. Eddie, whom I knew in high school, now is state editor of the *Peoria Journal-Transcript*. We know we won't get raises here, although the cost of living is increasing. One young reporter is paid only $25 a week, while the janitor gets $27.50. My salary is $45.

We left Peoria at 5 A.M. in Eddie's car. To save gasoline for the war effort, the speed limit has been reduced to 35 miles an hour, so it took us a long time to drive the 150 miles to Chicago. There we split up, each man going his own way. I applied for work at all the major newspapers and wire services. While they are losing staff members to the armed forces, none had an opening today.

My last stop was in the Chicago bureau of the United Press in Room 739 of the *Daily News* building on the Chicago River at 400 West Madison Avenue. There I spoke to Boyd Lewis, central division news editor; he has a moustache and looks like Alec Guinness, the British character actor.

"Last week," I told him, "I made a marvelous discovery; I found I have a hernia and the army won't have me, so I thought I'd come to Chicago to look for a job."

Lewis cried: "That's swell! Hernia's about the only thing that can keep a man out of the army these days . . . How long have you been on the *Journal-Transcript?*"

"Three and a half years. All told, I have 13 years' experience."

Lewis frowned. "Well, afraid I can't use you."

"What do you mean?"

"Well," he said, "we have a contract with the Newspaper Guild and we have to pay so much to men with more than five years of experience that we don't hire them. Whenever we need another reporter we get some inexperienced guy and pay him less."

"Oh, well, if that's the way it is—"

Lewis said: "Might as well fill out this application form."

Accepting it, I asked: "Would you like to see some of my work?"

"Yeah."

I handed him five feature stories. Then I took a chair at a distance and pretended to look through a window at the Chicago Opera House across the river; in reality, I was watching him from the corners of my eyes. He looked up and exhaled.

"Whew, man, you sure can write! Listen: Forget what I just told you. Go back to Peoria and in a week or so I'll call you."

"I don't understand."

Lewis grinned and said: "That's okay. Go back to Peoria, write me a letter telling me all about yourself and you'll hear from me."

"Okay," I said, and walked out.

Those few minutes changed the rest of my life. Boyd Lewis hired me at $60 a week, let me choose my own feature stories, studied them word for word, demanded that I simplify my style, moulded me into a prize-winning feature writer, became my friend. An amateur painter, Boyd later put my likeness on canvas in oils and made it possible for me to work on a newspaper in New York City. In turn, I influenced him a little. Although he never read my diary, its existence persuaded him to write his memoirs. Published in 1981, his book is called Not Always a Spectator: A Newsman's Story. *He asked me to write the foreword.*

CHICAGO, THURSDAY, DECEMBER 17, 1942   ■   So much has happened so fast I've been unable to keep up with events in this diary. I began working in the Chicago bureau of the United Press on November 23. Lee is pregnant, due to deliver this month, and her mother has come from Oklahoma to be with her.

We found a six-room apartment at 1059 W. Columbia Ave., just a few steps from the shore of Lake Michigan, and pay $62.50 a month. I ride the elevated 8.5 miles south to my new office. The United Press staff members are the most intelligent reporters and editors with whom I've ever worked.

The job itself is exacting, exciting, fascinating, stimulating. Now that I work for a wire service I'm learning to think of news in national and international terms. Already some of my stories have been published in newspapers in Los Angeles, Detroit and San Juan, Puerto Rico.

I've talked with Joseph Grew, former ambassador to Japan; Claude Wic-kard, federal food czar; the army colonel in charge of building the Alcan (Alaska-Canadian) Highway; lunched with the president of the America Chemical Society; enjoyed drinks with a top official of the Australian gov-ernment. This reporting is easy because it's what I've done for years; now I do it on a larger scale.

What I do find difficult is filing the wire. This means that from 3 to 5 P.M. I sit at a desk by a long row of teletype machines and select stories for the teletype operators to send to newspapers as far west as San Francisco and as far north as Minneapolis. This is a responsible job because I must decide, sometimes in seconds, which items will be read by hundreds of thousands of people in one-third of the nation. Noise fatigues me. The teletypes chatter like machine guns; I sit close to them, and by 5 P.M. I've sweated so much my shirt is sopping wet.

MONDAY, DECEMBER 28, 1942 ■ Our daughter was born at 12:07 P.M. today in the Frank Cuneo Hospital in Chicago. We named her Sandra Gail Ellis.

1943

MONDAY, FEBRUARY 1, 1943 ■ Long before Sandy was born I thought a lot about educating her. I intend to supplement her public school education with tutoring at home. Regarding tutoring, I was influenced by the auto-biography of John Stuart Mill, the 19th-century philosopher and reformer. His father, James Mill, was a scholar and historian who wrote a history of British India and also wrote many articles for the *Encyclopedia Britannica*. Instead of sending his son to school, the father kept him at home, at his elbow near the table where James did his research and writing. Although the father was irascible, he was patient with his son, answering his ques-tions, supervising his studies, giving him a perspective on history. As a result, John Stuart Mill became a scholar with the highest I.Q. of anyone ever known—according to some modern psychologists. I haven't the faint-est idea how they arrived at this conclusion.

THURSDAY, FEBRUARY 18, 1943 ■ I talked to Wendell Willkie today. For 20 minutes I chatted with him alone in his Blackstone Hotel room. That is, I talked to a man who may yet become President.

When I phoned him from my office he wouldn't say anything on the record. However, he did say he'd be glad to chat with me off the record. I called him a second time to get his reaction to a vicious story the *Chicago Tribune* published about him today, and he came forth with this quote: "I read the *Tribune* like I read the funny supplements. It's my comic relief." Shortly after 5 P.M. I called him a third time to say I'd like to take him up on his offer to chat, if he still had the time. Affably, he told me to come along, so I took a cab to his hotel.

Willkie himself opened the door when I knocked. After greeting me in a friendly fashion he turned and walked back into the room, and I began to feel guilty lest I were breaking in on something important. But as I followed Willkie, another man passed me on the way out. This left Willkie and me alone. He sank down into a big easy chair while I deposited my hat and overcoat on a davenport. Still standing I said:

"I really have no excuse for coming over to see you, Mr. Willkie, except that I wanted to talk to you." Then, spread-eagling my arms, I asked: "Is this okay?"

Willkie grinned broadly and leaned forward and took my hand in his big hand. "Sure," he drawled. "Sit down."

As I took a chair, he got in a question before I could ask him anything. "What," he asked, "do you hear?"

"Well," I said, "what I hear is pretty limited because I've been in Chicago only a short time and because I don't get out onto the street as much as I used to. However, I do believe that Roosevelt is losing his popularity." Then I elaborated a bit, explaining that lots of people thought the President's Casablanca trip good opera but little else.

Willkie nodded agreement. "Yes," he said, "his stock's gone down from where it used to be, but don't forget that he still holds a lot of tricks. It remains to be seen whether he can recapture his hold on the people entirely."

I said that the revolt in Congress seemed to signify a trend of sentiment against Roosevelt.

"Anything new on that today?" Willkie asked.

"No. Just more of the same. But I do believe the revolt will continue to grow."

Willkie said: "Well, that's true, but there's always the danger of the revolt going so far that a popular reaction will set in against it. Then the people will cry for a strong man again, as they did after Hoover's time. Hoover was all right in his own way, but he was on the scene at the wrong time—at a time when people were yearning for a strong man."

The conversation got back to President Roosevelt again, and after I had asked him three times, Willkie expressed his opinion of Roosevelt's motive in nominating Ed Flynn ambassador to Australia. "It was Roosevelt's first move in getting ready to run for a forth term. He couldn't run again with a man like Flynn at the head of the Democratic party, a man whose hands were dirty. So he nominated him to get him out of the way."

"Then you're convinced that Roosevelt *will* run again?" I asked.

"Oh, absolutely!"

After hesitating, I asked: "Would it be out of keeping for me to ask—this is entirely off the record, of course—what your plans are? Do you plan to run again?"

Willkie said reflectively: "That depends . . . I'm in a pretty bad spot right now. I want to wait and see how things shape up. If they fall right, I might—I don't know."

From the tone of his voice and the look on his face, Willkie left me with the strong impression that he will indeed run again. Throughout our chat, he solicited information from me about common talk regarding politics. No doubt he does this with everyone he meets. An intelligent individual, Willkie won't content himself with the opinions of practicing politicians. He wants to know about the little guy from the little guy. I admired him for this.

I asked Willkie: "Is there anything more you can add about Stalin that you didn't say in the article you had about him in *Life?*"

"Stalin," said Wendell Willkie, "is a brilliant man, a very brilliant man. He is the sort of a leader you would go to when in trouble. He inspires confidence. He knows how to lay down his premises and then, from them, arrive at a profound conclusion."

"He has a great sense of humor, hasn't he?"

"Yes, Stalin knows how to laugh. His is rough-and-tumble humor."

"That isn't true of Chiang Kai-shek, is it?"

"No," Willkie said. "He's more serious. He's all intellect."

All the time he sat speaking, Willkie was scrooched up in his chair, swinging his legs over one arm of it, crossing and uncrossing them, squirming this way and that way with no regard for his clothes, which were badly rumpled. When I held out a cigaret and then a light, he accepted these abstractedly, his eyes far off in thought, smoked fast, carelessly flicked ashes upon the rug, and then crushed the cigaret only partly out, with a vigorous lunge of his big hand. I seemed to see the man entire in that last gesture. He concerns himself with big problems. He charts trends and thus has no time for details. Let others fussily stub out their cigarets in tiny stabs, if they care to. He gives it one big squashing movement and if it isn't out, why, he already has galloped conversationally to other and more important things.

Willkie had pouches beneath his keen eyes, and near these pouches I saw several small wens I hadn't noticed in any of his pictures. His face doesn't photograph as it really looks. Instead of being beefy and round it is long and horsey. When he stood up again I saw how shaggily big he is. And as I told him an anecdote about his brother, Ed, and how Ed saved me from an over-zealous Peoria woman, he cocked one foot on his chair to listen, laughing heartily when I had finished. I liked Willkie. He is a man of strength and intelligence. I said:

"The one characteristic you have that the American people like—since they're individualists—is your readiness to speak your mind and let the political chips fall where they may."

Wendell Willkie said that he had thought for a long time that that's what Americans wanted, but he thanked me for telling him so.

CHICAGO, THURSDAY, MARCH 25, 1943   ■   On March 19, I met William Allen White, the great newspaper editor from Emporia, Kansas. He appeared in the Sherman Hotel to speak before members of the Executives Club of Chicago, his address being entitled "Between the Devil and the Deep Sea." As I approached him where he sat at the speakers' table, I saw how tottery old he is, but also how smilingly friendly. He extended his hand the moment I appeared, our hands slightly jostling his waterglass. Because there had been complications regarding the text of his speech, I had to remain to cover him directly—which certainly was no hardship. In fact, his was one of the thee or four great speeches I have ever heard. I don't care that his delivery was faltering, due to his age. It nonetheless marked him as an independent thinker, and a witty one. Furthermore, many of the things he said echoed conclusions I recently have acclaimed, conclusions regarding the dire fate that seemingly is before all of us human beings. He is so short and so all pink and white and smiles, he is like a delicious little billiken. I hope never to forget him as I first saw him, sitting, spoon in uncertain hand, carefully spilling two small tablets into his spoon and then lowering them gently into his coffee for what ailed him. In my book, nothing ails him mentally or spiritually. I affirmed that his speech was not so much a speech as it was a manifesto, a manifesto of the "Little Guy," as he put it. And—wouldn't you know—some stupid listeners, being, after all, only members of the Executives Club of Chicago, snickered at portions of his speech, thinking it funny instead of realizing that this great man was merely tempering his frightening predictions with the leavening agent of wit.

THURSDAY, APRIL 29, 1943   ■   Today I sat near a piano in a rehearsal hall in the Loop to listen to a young jazz pianist on the cusp of a great career. She is cocoa-colored Dorothy Donegan, only 19 years old, and day after tomorrow she will make her debut in a classical setting, Orchestra Hall, home of the Chicago Symphony Orchestra.

She was born in Chicago, the daughter of a Pullman chef, and she's never been far from here, except for her far-out music. At the age of three she was picking out tunes on the piano; at eight she began studying classical music; at 15 she began playing boogie-woogie in cocktail lounges, always escorted by a brother. Already she has made a few records.

She is so addicted to the 88 keys that after six hours at the keyboard in a bar, when it closes she stays at the piano, improvising, improvising, improvising. Other musicians, eager to hear this phenomenon, slip inside and dawdle in the dark while absorbing her riffs. She plays melodic variations over a constantly repeated bass pattern, never rendering any blues again in exactly the same way.

"I compose," she told me, "every time I play."

Her manager suggested she show me her style, so she turned to the keyboard. I sat where I could see her face. I'd heard that at her debut she would perform half-classical, half-jazz compositions, but this information failed to prepare me for what now followed.

Her long fingers spanning three keys more than an octave, she began playing Chopin in the traditional style, pouring honey into my ears with its beauty, meandering all over the keys with casual grace, and then—

Clump! That was Miss Donegan's right heel slamming into the floor. She crouched over the keyboard, eyes shut, lips curled, her right foot thumping the floor as she chopped Chopin into chaos, dragged him through a boogie-woogie swamp, and sent my blood pressure soaring into the danger zone. Gene Krupa, the great drummer, once told me that a solid socking rhythm, sustained a long time, increases one's heartbeat, and now I knew he told me the truth.

I was so astonished by her mannerisms that I scribbled notes as fast as possible. Miss Donegan sneered, snarled, whimpered, winced, pouted, puffed, panted, leered, smiled, brayed, twitched, bit, sucked, moaned, puckered, growled. Intentional or unintentional, her behavior was hypnotic and erotic. When she finished playing I asked about her grimaces.

"I can't help my face," she said. "Yes, I suppose it's good showmanship, but I do it even when I'm practicing at home." She added that she has worn out one of the two pianos in her home on the south side of the city.

"What is your ultimate ambition?" I asked.

"I want to be wealthy."

"Why?"

"Well, I won't be young all my life, and I want to put something by. And then I want to help youngsters."

"Meaning colored kids with musical talent?"

"Yes," she said. "Recently I found a 14-year-old boy who plays drums. What I mean is—he—plays—drums! I told my manager about him. That same week this little kid went from $5 a week to $56 a week. That's what I mean.

"And that made you happy?"

"Yes—and the fact that a saleslady in a music store told me that Marian Anderson bought one of my hottest records." Marian Anderson, that great contralto, that immortal.

Soon there will be more records, movie contracts, concert offers. I asked the *Saturday Evening Post* to let me write a long piece about Dorothy Donegan, but here was the response: "This leaves us cold. We hear rumors that the young lady can't play the piano very well, but can certainly make with the muscles."

Really? Gentlemen, I'm afraid you were wrong. Miss Dorothy Donegan became so famous that now she is enshrined in Who's Who in America. *And, just as she told me she would, she kept helping kids. She also became an "artist patron" of the Boy Scouts of America.*

THURSDAY, MAY 20, 1943 ▪ On my way home from work I stopped in a grocery for food. When I reached our apartment I found Lee cooking dinner with Sandy lying in a bassinet in the kitchen. Our five-month-old daughter is plump, pink and beautiful. I gave her a vanilla wafer to nibble, turned away a moment, and when I turned back I saw Sandy flailing her arms, her face red, no sound coming from her. She had tried to swallow the wafer whole!

Afterwards, Lee told me I screamed. I don't remember that. What I do remember is snatching her out of the crib, turning her upside down, and thumping her back. Then I heard Lee:

"She's all right now, Eddie!"

Turning the baby right side up, I looked at her. She was breathing again and her eyes were red-rimmed from choking. I held her toward her mother.

"Take her," I gasped. "I . . . I can't hold her! I can't . . . stand up."

As Lee took Sandy she exclaimed: "You're white!"

On legs like Jello I wobbled into the study and put my head on the desk and wept.

CHICAGO, SUNDAY, MAY 23, 1943   ■   This deserves more adequate treatment, but I'm lazy so I'll boil it down. It concerns John Barrymore. Boyd Lewis was telling me about it yesterday. During Barrymore's marathon run of *My Dear Children* in Chicago, he rented a home in suburban—Glencoe, I think it was. The wives of the neighborhood were thrilled spitless, as the saying goes, at his proximity. One fond matron living next door decided to throw a Watch-John Barrymore-Come-Home Evening. She invited a dozen or so equally enthralled wives out for bridge. They played at cards until the great man drove up in a taxi. Then, as had been pre-arranged, they switched off the lights and crowded to the darkened windows to peer out. Barrymore, with a flourish, paid off the cab driver, tugged his hat further aslant across his thespian head, and swaggered up his walk. Half-way to the house, as the women watched, he stopped short, peered around with dramatic seeking. Then, in full view of the assemblage, the great John Barrymore proceeded to unbutton his fly, limber himself and indulge in a hearty piss.

FRIDAY, JULY 23, 1943   ■   In the office today I was looking for ideas for feature stories by glancing at personal ads in the *Chicago Tribune*. My eyes locked on one line: "Missing—parakeet. Answers to the name of Socrates . . ." Reward, phone number, etc.

Socrates? What kind of person would give a bird that name? Calling the number, I reached a man named Leslie Evan Schlytter. He was no nut, I discovered, but very intelligent. Might I visit him? Yes. He lives near the campus of the University of Chicago.

When I reached his apartment I found a man older than myself, with a wife and daughter. He is of Scandinavian descent, formerly a school teacher in Minnesota, almost ugly, with one eye askew, tall and thin and very ill. Immediately I felt comfortable with him. He had caught Einstein in a small error, pointed this out in a letter he wrote in German, and in a reply Einstein confessed his mistake. Leslie, as I soon was calling him, had had a couple of novels published and then began writing a book of philosophy. He tore up the first four drafts, content only with the fifth one.

Yes, he had owned a parakeet, a small bird, had taught it to speak a few sentences, and then the other day it escaped. I asked what the bird could say.

"Well," he replied, smiling, "we have a woman who is a very good friend and one day when she walked in here Socrates flew over, perched on her shoulder and said something in her ear. She laughed so hard she had trouble explaining, but at last she said:

"First time I've been propositioned by a bird. It said: 'Wanna go to bed? Wanna go to bed?' "

Leslie was so amusing, so witty and intelligent and kind that I often visited him and began to regard him as a foster-father. Since my mother divorced my father when I was an infant, all my life I've been searching for a substitute father.

MONDAY, AUGUST 9, 1943   ▪   Today I met Joseph (Yellow Kid) Weil, perhaps the greatest con artist of this century. In one breath he told me he is reformed. In another, he said he owns a chicken farm and is developing a double-yolked egg he'll sell for the price of one egg. Maybe—but not to me.

At the age of 68 he is of medium height, slender, wears rimless glasses and sports a Van Dyke. When he was in the money, between prison sentences, he dressed in winged collars, colorful cravats held in place by a diamond stickpin, striped trousers, cutaway coat, spats and patent leather shoes. He picked ladies to match his cravats.

Born in Chicago in 1875, the son of a man who owned a saloon, he learned about swindling in his teens. He sold suckers an alleged cure-all patent medicine called "Meriweather's Elixir." His favorite comic strip was *Hogan's Alley*, drawn by Richard F. Outcault for the *New York World* and other papers. When the *World* made a color test in 1896, it put yellow on the nightshirt of the cartoon's principal character, an urchin known thereafter as "The Yellow Kid." Weil was so fond of that character that soon he was nicknamed "Yellow Kid."

Weil was so brilliant that had he gone straight he might have become a captain of industry; instead, he chose to match wits with people, using his imagination to swindle money from them. He had the manners of a dancing master, the rhetoric of a Senator, the wardrobe of a movie star and the morals of an oyster. He hated guns. His weapon was his tongue.

He doted on disguises and exotic identities. He posed as Dr. Joseph R. Warrington of Shanghai, Berlin, Paris and New York; Dr. Otto Kammerer, chief chemist for the Kaiser of Germany; General Goritz, Russian nobleman and military expert, exiled by the Bolsheviks; R. Joseph Warrington, eminent author; and Harry Pelham of the socialite Pelhams of New York State.

He had the Harvard Classics and other books rebound after inserting pages with his picture and fake stories about his philanthropies, such as his alleged gift of $15 million to the poor of China. He forged letters of recommendation from the Morgans and Vanderbilts. He was so fond of melodramatic schemes to bilk the rich that sometimes he spent more money on elaborate stage-sets than he got back in tainted profits. He would rent office suites, staff them with dozens of lesser con men, to entrap victims. He engaged in wire-tapping, faked bets on the horses, sold bogus stocks, and claimed he took suckers for $12 million.

He was so cocky he sent telegrams to Chicago's chief detective to announce where he was—and sometimes was caught. Always smooth-talking, in court he would cite Brutus, Judas and Benedict Arnold to try to prove he had been double-crossed by witnesses for the government. Some-times he attacked the press, orating: "The dastardly fabrications of the met-ropolitan newspapers, the reprehensible conduct of journalists to sur-round me with a nimbus—er, a nimbus of guilt, is astonishing! It is what has led me to this prosecution. I am an honest man—now."

He owned 1,500 books and once, being led to jail, he cried: "I am a broken man! What is a man like me without his Balzac?"

This colorful crook amused me so much that I wrote again to the Saturday Evening Post *to say I wanted to write about him for the magazine.*

This was the response: "Unfortunately, we thought he was a bit too old a number for us." But within months the magazine published a piece about Weil, written by someone else, of course. "The Yellow Kid" died in Chicago in 1976 at the age of 101. Penniless, he was buried in a potter's field.

Soon after my encounter with Weil, my editor gave me a choice assign-ment. Two other wire service reporters and I were selected to fly with Rear Admiral John Downs, commandant of the Ninth Naval District, which embraces 13 states. He was making an inspection of part of his command, so in five days we flew in his blue plane to Minneapolis, St. Louis, Indianapo-lis, Columbus, Cleveland, Detroit and then back to Chicago.

DEARBORN, MICHIGAN, FRIDAY, SEPTEMBER 17, 1943 ▇ I've been living a lux-urious life, flying in the admiral's plane, lodging in posh hotels, greeted by local big-shots, attending a dinner given by Indiana Governor Henry F. Schricker. Now we are in Dearborn, where Henry Ford has built a naval training school. We were ushered into its library and then in walked Ford himself. He has bad breath and blue hair. I suppose he washed his hair in a solution to enhance its whiteness, but got too much coloring in. I stood near him as we chatted, but he had nothing piquant to say and our ques-tions evoked little of interest. Still, it was a thrill to meet him.

In 1951 I read an Encyclopedia Britannica *article about Henry Ford that astounded me because it implied that he was nearly perfect. Having just finished reading an unauthorized biography that showed how petty, cruel and even stupid he was at times, I challenged the encyclopedia to revise the article. And they did. To have changed an article in this encyclopedia is one of my proudest achievements.*

That trip with the admiral was my last big assignment because Uncle Sam caught up with me. I did not have a hernia, as a Peoria doctor had said. Aware that I would be drafted, I sought a commission in the navy and took several tests. I passed an IQ test with a "very high grade," which flabbergasted me because only one-third of the test concerned language, while the other two-thirds were about mechanics and mathematics—subjects about which I am almost totally ignorant. However, I weighed seven pounds less than the required standard. When I reported to the induction station in Chicago on October 25, I was given my choice of army or navy. I chose navy in the hope that maybe, after all, I might get a commission. We were given one week to take care of personal matters.

In a flurry of activity I sent my wife and daughter to live with Lee's parents in Miami, Oklahoma, sold our furniture and got rid of our apartment, sold 500 books and stored another 500 in the basement of my father's apartment on the near north side of Chicago. On Tuesday, November 3, I reported to the recruiting station with one bag of clothes and The Brothers Karamazov *by Dostoyevsky.*

From there we were marched to the Illinois Central railway station and herded aboard a troop train. This consisted of nine cars filled with 225 recruits and two officers. We left on a journey of 2,130 miles to a naval boot camp in northern Idaho near the Canadian border. No one, I heard in dismay, was allowed to keep a diary. At first I panicked, then realized I could maintain my journal by writing my wife letters reporting all that was happening to me. I wrote Lee my first letter from "somewhere in Iowa." At the age of 32 I began experiencing a series of massive cultural shocks.

CHAPTER 7

CAMP WARD, UNITED STATES NAVAL TRAINING STATION, FARRAGUT, IDAHO, SUNDAY, NOVEMBER 7, 1943 ■ My darling:

I sigh as I write for I am lonesome and yearn for sight of you & Sandy. This way of life is so revolting I shake my head every now and then, half believing it is but a bad dream from which I shall awaken. But it is real, the most painfully real thing I've ever experienced.

You should see me now. I'm perched on the edge of a bunk with this pad on my lap. In this barracks room there are 130 men, all looking alike in coarse overalls, blue work shirts, black sweaters, work shoes and brown leggings called "boots." They cut off all my hair except a small patch on top that is 3/4 of an inch long. My moustache is gone, whacked off unceremoniously. I don't resemble the person I was. I look like a convict—and feel like one.

We are treated like children, told when to do this, that and the other thing. We are not permitted to exercise independent judgment about anything. Both my arms are sore because yesterday I was given three shots. However, I'll try to tell you what has happened to me.

Our special train backed into Farragut at 5:45 P.M., Pacific war time, last Friday. There actually are mountains on all sides of us, and at that twilight hour they were orchid-hued and dazzlingly beautiful. Since then I've learned that even such beauty can't compensate for life as a "boot," for unless one has freedom he is unable to appreciate anything else in life. We were marched to a receiving building and soon given chow. Then we took up formation in the main hall.

Up stood a baboon wearing the stripes of a petty officer. He had a southern accent, though he extended anything but southern hospitality. To the front of the room he called four youths who foolishly had chopped away some of their hair while en route here. Baboon made this sound like a capital crime. Baboon enjoyed his authority. Fists on hips, he snarled at them, asked their ages, sneered that they are "kindergarten kids!" He was a sadist masquerading as an officer. The longer Baboon babbled, the angrier

I became, but there was nothing I could do. With the other men I marched, when told, to a barracks in the outgoing units section of the Camp, known as O.G.U. There we were assigned temporary quarters.

Since none of us had had a chance to take a bath since last Tuesday, we ran joyfully into the showers, but there we were jolted by another ugly reality: There were only 10 showers for 225 men. We fought one another, elbows poking into eyes, feet thrashing at slippery thighs, wet buttocks sliding past soapy arms. It was a mad scene!

Next we were herded into a sleeping room 150 feet long and 50 feet wide. A Texan with a bloated face and squinty eyes bellowed ungrammatical orders to us, assigning men to bunks whose springs consisted of chicken wire. Lights went out at 9 P.M. but I had trouble falling asleep because a guard paced back and forth all night long.

Saturday morning we were awakened at five o'clock, dressed in our civilian clothes for the last time, then were marched to the mess hall for chow. The outdoors was pitch-dark except for the stars, which look three times larger than when I saw them in Illinois. We shivered in the chill air while hundreds upon hundreds of men ate before us, new sailors who would hail us with a sing-song *You'll be sorrrrry!* This cry is the most common one in the navy. When at last we reached the mess hall I gasped, for it looked as though it could seat 2,000 to 3,000 men simultaneously. I grabbed a metal tray with six depressions in it, a tray still wet from washing; a metal bowl the size of a large cereal bowl; a huge porcelain mug with no handle; and a fork, spoon & knife. I soon learned to hold the knife up at an angle so that two slices of bread could be slapped down onto its point. We had a copious breakfast which, curiously enough, included beans.

Back outside the mess hall we formed another line to march elsewhere for the induction process. Now a green tint of light behind the mountains silhouetted them so starkly I was reminded of the scenes we made from colored paper in the sixth grade of school. Tiny rectangles of orange served as windows for the blue-black long rectangles of barracks. As we shifted from foot to foot, trying to keep warm, the men asked one another where they were from. Finding a fellow from the same state was a beginning. Narrowing it down to the same city was better. Here we were, part of some 65,000 men in this camp 2,130 miles from Chicago, but some fellows found men from their own neighborhoods!

Marching again to the reception hall, we had our hair cut. This is a brutal process. Only electric clippers are used and no man emerged with hair longer than one inch. A young machinist almost wept when his long & curly locks were shorn. Of the 225 of us who came here together from

Chicago, I was the only guy with a moustache, so the others were boisterously curious about what would happen to me. Off with the moustache! Now I wouldn't recognize myself in a mirror.

The physical inspection here was even more rigorous than in the induction station in Chicago. I watched the men ahead of me and it really looked bad. A medical officer on my right side thrust a needle three inches into my right arm without even pinching the flesh while, at the same moment, an officer on the left jabbed a needle about half that depth into my left arm. However, it didn't hurt half so much as I had expected.

Next I was given my navy clothes, the number, variety and bulk of them surprising me. Of course everything is new. I was given the correct fit except for the shoes; the pair given me was size 8, but I take a 9 1/2. Toward the end of the line some regular sailors began talking with me, asking where I was from and what I did. For some reason, a couple of them were impressed when I said I had been a reporter. The more we talked the friendlier they became, so I complained about my shoes. One of the men took me back down the line and got me shoes the right size.

We were allowed to send home only one package—a small one. Most of all, I wanted to save my suit, so I abandoned other things to make room for it. The things we discarded were given to the Salvation Army. I had to send back *The Brothers Karamazov*—dammit!—because we aren't allowed to keep any reading matter other than the Bible and religious tracts. This angered me, since I am an atheist.

Now we have been assigned barracks that will be our permanent quarters during the six to eight weeks we'll be at Farragut. Last night I had a chill as a result of those shots and everyone has sore arms. Mass misery. Again we were warned not to keep a diary. I would be unable to endure this regimentation, this depersonalization, this indifference to love and truth and beauty were it not for the fact that conditions would be a hundredfold worse if we were conquered by the Nazis.

Please hug Sandy for me, I hope all is well with you.

Love, Eddie

SUNDAY, NOVEMBER 21, 1943 ▪ Dear Lee,

Here in boot camp there is so much to observe that I want to get down on paper as many details as possible. For one thing, men don't shake hands when they meet. This may be due to easy acceptance of one another because we share one thing—misery. In the smoking pit near the barracks few cigarets are lit by matches; instead, they are lit from the glowing end of a cigaret being smoked by someone else. A man will put a cigaret between his lips, then turn to the nearest man to get a light. I watched two men, both with their hands in their pockets, one giving a light transfusion to another, with no word of *thanks* requested or given.

I'm also surprised by the casual way in which strangers tell one another about their loved ones and family problems. I began chatting with one guy who, within five minutes, told me his wife has had *three* miscarriages and has been warned never to conceive again.

The food isn't bad and there always is an abundance of it. Sometimes we have no butter, but I suppose you civilians—how curious this sounds!—have less than we. What irks me is the lack of pepper! We're never served pepper, and sometimes do without salt. However, I suspect we are fed salt-peter to quell sexual desire; several times the chow has tasted suspiciously salty.

The other night I saw some boxing matches from a front row seat. In the last bout two heavyweights fought. One was squat and skilled. The other was rangy and awkward. The rangy boy was badly beaten and then knocked out. He fell on the canvas just a few feet from me, eyes clouded with pain, limbs twitching in agony. All the bluecoats laughed at his suffering. I thought: This is war in miniature. Man hurts man. Why? What satisfaction is there in inflicting pain on someone else? Are we human beings such beasts that we must glory in brutal strength?

Now that we are in the navy we are told again and again that our training "will make a man" of us. Oh, yeah? This phrase cloaks a variety of cruelties. We drill in cold gray drizzles without coats, work our muscles until they scream in pain, are told to obey commands unexplained and often illogical just because they are commands.

Each company is commanded by a chief petty officer. Many are former football coaches, bull-necked bullies who praise muscles and prattle platitudes about "clean living." I suspect that many are sadists given license by the navy to do evil in the name of the good.

Repeatedly we are told that the navy's chief concern is our health. *Sure it is!* Of the 130 men in our company, about 115 have colds. They are not due to bad weather but bad judgment. Besides drilling in rain, we have to sleep with the barracks' windows open to thus-and-such a height, and each week we get a succession of medical shots that sap our resistance. "Physical fitness" is a polite term for torture on a filthy gym floor. I am so muscle-weary and sleep-deprived that yesterday as I talked to the chaplain I damned near fell asleep.

I hope you and Sandy are well.

Love, Eddie

THURSDAY, DECEMBER 2, 1943 ■ Dear Lee,

Two days ago the rains came. We live in a valley that is a moist gray blanket strung between mountains. The word is that the rain will continue, and then the really cold weather will arrive. Now we wear foul weather clothing over our pea jackets and expect more and more men to report to sick bay.

I continue to feel enraged by the ban against any reading matter other than the Bible and religious tracts. Lacking newspapers and news magazines, we know less about the course of the war than civilians. As a reporter for the United Press, I kept abreast of most of what was happening in the world; now I am a prisoner of ignorance. This is one helluva way to motivate men to fight for their country!

I wish I were with you and Sandy.

Lovingly, Eddie

1944

TUESDAY, MAY 9, 1944 ■ Dear Lee,

Now I have completed boot camp and been moved to our naval hospital, also at Farragut, Idaho. This is a 5,000-bed hospital with wounded servicemen from battles in the Pacific. It is commanded by Captain H. S. Harding, who gives true meaning to the phrase "an officer and gentleman." Hearing about my newspaper experience, he sent for me, talked with me, appointed me editor of the hospital's newspaper. In taking this action, he demoted the enlisted man who had been editor because, so I've heard, the paper had become the laughingstock of the hospital. The defrocked editor had had but limited newspaper experience in private life.

It was on February 7 that I took charge of *The Bedside Examiner.* An unfortunate name, to be sure, especially since many sailors call it *The Bedpan Examiner,* but I can't change the name. What I can do, and am doing, is changing the paper itself.

When I arrived it consisted of four pages; now there are eight. It's circulation was 3,000 copies; now it's 4,000. It is a weekly paper and every Wednesday I travel the 18 miles to Coeur d'Alene to put it to bed at the *Coeur d'Alene Press,* which does our printing. My staff consists of two corpsmen and one WAVE. The four of us work in an office that had been a linen closet. I found a wounded but ambulatory sailor who is our cartoonist, although he does not work in our office.

I decided to use him to create a cartoon strip called "The Captain and the Little Sailor," with the two characters usually in conflict. Now, when

we need an idea for the strip, I call a meeting in which the five of us babble whatever comes to mind. I said I wanted them to articulate any idea,
however bad, that came to them, since it might set up a new association in
the mind of another staffer. This method works. In only 15 to 20 minutes
we knock out a new idea.

I write many news stories, feature articles and all the editorials. In one
editorial I discussed the nature of war, warning that it has been glamorized
down through the ages when, in fact, it is all about death. My cartoonist,
Dave Cunningham, drew an editorial cartoon for me. It is the figure of a
beautiful woman — except that her beautiful face is a mask. In the sketch
she has removed that mask and holds it lightly against a coyly tilted head,
which is — a *skull.* Powerful! It is called *The Face of War.*

As editor of the paper I have an identity that was lacking in boot camp,
and even power and prestige, although I'm not an officer. My rating is
Pharmacist's Mate, Third Class. Why? Because the day we were classified
all college graduates were given this rating, for reasons that defy logic.
Among the men the most common remark is this: "There are two ways to
do things — the right way and the navy way." I'm beginning to understand
that the larger the institution, the less is its efficiency.

An officer must have nominal charge of the paper, and this assignment
fell to a chaplain who is bright, admits he had no newspaper experience,
and so leaves everything up to me. But the officer who pays our bills
sought control of the paper, so a power struggle ensued. I won because our
commanding officer has confidence in me.

Most officers in this hospital are physicians who, until recently, were in
practice in their home towns. They're easy to get along with. It's the navy's
career officers who give us enlisted men a hard time. I wrote a long editorial critical of officers. Included in it is this paragraph: "We American sailors are now outside civil law; however, we still look to moral law. Just as in
civil law a man is considered innocent until proven guilty, so do we expect
to be considered as men until proven otherwise . . ."

All of my copy must be approved by the commanding officer, so the day
I handed this editorial to Captain Harding I wondered whether he would
approve of it. I watched his face as he read all the pages I handed him,
marked the top copy Okay and handed them back to me.

"Captain, did you see my editorial?"

"Yes," he said with a smile. "It's fine, Ellis."

Bless him! When the paper was published and the enlisted men read
what I had said about officers, they became so deliriously happy that they

almost wanted to carry me around on their shoulders. I really felt great about this, honey.

Lovingly, Eddie

1945

But . . . my wife's letters had become infrequent and chilly, which puzzled and scared me. I got a leave of absence and went by train from Idaho to Miami, Oklahoma, where Lee and our baby daughter were staying with Lee's parents. As soon as I was alone with my wife she said she wanted a divorce. Astonished, I asked why. Because she had fallen out of love with me. Why? She said she didn't want to talk about it. About to lose the woman I still loved and the daughter I adored, I wept. I liked Lee's parents, they liked me, and both tried to console me. At last I told Lee I thought I soon would be sent to Okinawa, and if I were killed there she would be free; if I survived and returned, I would grant her a divorce. It was not the best of times for me.

My guess about Okinawa was correct. When I got back to my base, an officer told me that morale was so poor among land-based sailors that I was being sent there to publish a paper for them. This meant that I left before the rest of the men in my company, that I was put aboard an overcrowded troop-ship without any of my friends. The ship was the USS Granville.

We sailed from San Francisco at 4:55 P.M., Wednesday, June 27, 1945. At that very moment President Harry Truman was speaking in San Francisco to the conference that was creating the United Nations. I jumped from a winch to the deck to get a last lingering look at America—and sprained my ankle. Now I wanted three things: To go below and take care of my ankle; to line up for chow, because I hadn't eaten since 10 A.M.; to live through this dramatic moment in my life.

Curiosity won. Balancing myself on one foot I saw a submarine slithering by, got a new perspective on wonderful San Francisco, heard the wind belching through the cables of the bridge above me, became hypnotized by the shadow of the bridge on the water. I became as rigid as a chicken with its beak on a chalk-line. To me the line in the water marked the end of my past life and the beginning of a new one. I stared and pondered and might have crossed myself, had I been a religious man. So what happened? The bow of the ship cut through the line as two girls on the bridge yelled down at us, and I laughed at myself for taking myself so seriously.

I floundered below deck, taped my ankle, filled my gut, and then the other men took over. Hundreds became sea-sick. Since I am a landlubber I didn't know whether the sea's roughness was usual or unusual that near shore;

soon I heard it was unusual. The ship was heeling over 35 degrees and two life rafts were torn off. Although I did not become sick, I had to be careful where I walked. One man became so sea-sick he was paralyzed from the hips down.

We had to eat standing up at long mess tables. My first meal was something like Alice's tea-party: I'd reach for my cup, only to see it sailing down the slanting table and crashing onto the deck, while in a corner a jukebox tumbled—jingle-jangle-jingle!—onto its side.

It took 40 days and 40 nights for us to travel the 6,200 statute miles from San Francisco to Okinawa. We were unable to take showers. The only place to sit down was on the deck, so oily in spots that my trousers became rigid with filth and, when removed, could stand by themselves. Here I was, sardined with strangers, most of them younger than myself, few of them able to converse. I felt totally alienated. I had brought along 10 books but, able to read all day, I soon consumed them. I began sneaking into the ship's library to steal paperback books issued by the Editions for the Armed Services, bless them!

In 40 days I read 35 books, many of them philosophical studies. One volume was written by Herbert Spencer, the British philosopher, and he taught me that one can neither prove nor disprove the existence of God. At the age of 16 I had become an atheist; now, at the age of 34, I became an agnostic.

One day as I stood at a swaying table I heard two youths opposite me arguing the ancient question of the irresistible force and the immovable object. Astonished by their topic, delighted by their intellectual playfulness, I asked whether theirs was a private argument, or could anybody play. They looked at me, smiled, welcomed me into their discussion. They were two bright Jewish boys from Brooklyn, and their company made the rest of the voyage less unpleasant for me. Sprawled on deck, we chewed on philosophical questions, swapped stories, invented brain-busting, time-eating games.

None of us had been told much about Okinawa. Here is what I later learned:

Okinawa is the largest island in the chain of Ryukyu Islands in the East China Sea, 350 miles south of the most southern Japanese home island. Politically, it was a prefecture of Japan. Militarily, the Allies wanted to capture it to use as a base for the invasion of Japan, scheduled for November of 1945.

Okinawa is 67 miles long and two to 16 miles wide. The northern end has jungles and mountains, while in the south there are low rocky hills. The climate is hot and humid. The island grows rice, sweet potatoes, pineapples and sugar cane. In the spring of 1945 Okinawa had a civilian population of 450,000 and a Japanese military force of 130,000.

On April 1, 1945, American forces invaded Okinawa, helped by the largest naval operation in the Pacific during the war. For three months the Americans and Japanese engaged in a bitter air, sea and land battle, the last major land battle of World War II. Japanese pilots made suicidal attacks on our ships, sinking many of them.

On June 22 the fighting stopped. American losses were 12,500 killed and 35,000 wounded. About 120,000 Japanese soldiers were killed, 10,000 surrendered, and 42,000 civilians lost their lives.

Before we left the states we were told that Okinawa had been secured. I wondered. Really? Finally, my superiors no longer seemed to care about the ban on diary-keeping. I was relieved that I could return to my preferred routine.

OKINAWA, SUNDAY, AUGUST 5, 1945 ▪ I could *smell* land, and what I was smelling was Okinawa. Laden with carbine, gas mask, back-pack, canteen, etc., I floundered over a railing about 5 P.M. and climbed down a swaying cargo net into a landing craft, timing myself perfectly so that I wouldn't break a leg. A smoke screen was whooshed around us, a thing that surprised me because we thought the island was secured. Salt spray blurred my vision as I stared toward the bloodiest battleground of the war in the Pacific. It looked like a country club. Its hills, sloping up almost from the surf itself, were green and neat. It had a look of cultivated precision. But despite its clipped greenery the boots of war had ground men to coral death.

When I stepped out of the landing craft onto the beach I muttered: "Okinawa!" Later I learned that many other men said the same thing. It is a word expressing surprise that a kid from Kewanee or Walla Walla actually has reached Asia. However, this tiny spot of the Orient which we had reached did not look exotic, was not dramatically different from the scenery at home. While it was a little strange, this strangeness was based upon a foundation of the ordinary. Okinawa has many beet fields, and beet fields are beet fields, be they in Illinois or Okinawa.

However, five minutes after landing I did see something that made me stare: a navy truck passed, filled with peasant women wearing cone-shaped hats. The natives of Okinawa are shorter and darker than the Japanese people, so short, in fact, that the tops of their heads rise only to our shoulders.

Since I was a one-man draft (Navy lingo meaning that I had travelled across the ocean ahead of my own echelon), I had to take care of myself. A hillbilly sailor drawled he knew of an empty bunk, so I trudged up a hill behind him, trying to balance my heavy gear on my shoulders. I found a bunk draped in mosquito-netting. Wearily, I sat down.

From high on a hill the view was spectacular. There, as in a Greek theater, stretched the panorama of Buckner Bay, freckled with ships. Their diamond-sparkling flashes of signal lights defied the approaching dusk. My reverie was interrupted by the entrance of men occupying the tent. After the exchange of awkward greetings, they told me what to expect at night.

They said that while Okinawa was secured in the sense that organized Japanese resistance had ended, there still were thousands of enemy soldiers here and there on the island. Whatever you do, they told me, don't leave the tent at night. We Americans had a string of fox holes along the rim of the hill only a few feet away, and in the fox holes were GI's who shoot at anything that moves. You'll hear them begin to shoot, I was told, as soon as it really gets dark.

I unpacked some of my gear. It really got dark. . . . Splatttt! . . . Whiiiinnng! "Well," said one of the guys, "there goes the first one . . ." Splaaaat! . . . Splaaaat! . . . Splaaaat! . . . On the hill and close. I stretched out on the bunk and for the first time in my life listened to the sounds of war.

The carbines began splatting to our right, then to the left, then behind us. In my tent one of the men stirred uneasily and said: "Damn Japs must of sneaked down to the pier. We gottem all around us."

Putting an arm through a fold of my netting, I reassured myself that my carbine was near at hand. Also my sheath knife. Then I lay back for a little session of analysis. For years I had wondered what fear feels like. At the naval hospital in Idaho I had asked wounded sailors about fear and most of them were unable to define it. The best answer I got was that fear was regret that a guy might never again see the people and things he loves. Now, here I was on Okinawa with shooting all—just then a siren snarled. A man in a bunk near me yelled "alert!" Another moaned: "Geez, are we gonna have to put up with them damn planes again tonight?" Being more of a reporter than sailor, I wanted to see what was happening, so I left the tent and stood on the hill and looked all around me. But as a matter of record, not one damned exciting thing happened after that. I was not given a chance to find out whether I was cowardly or courageous.

C. Monville Schwarz and I began publishing a daily mimeographed paper for all the naval personnel based on Okinawa. It was named the N.O.B. News, meaning Naval Operating Base. We were allowed to use Associated Press stories. The man nominally in charge of the paper was a welfare officer so corrupt that he gave baseball gear and other sporting equipment to men who had found samurai swords and other Japanese memorabilia. The heat was so intense that we wore only shoes, jungle shorts and sun helmets. Because of the heat and my depression about my wife and baby daughter, my weight fell to 100 pounds.

MONDAY, AUGUST 9, 1945 ▓ Today another sailor and I picked our way through the ruins of what once had been the town of Shuri in the southern part of Okinawa. Its former population was 16,000, the size of my home town in Illinois, but then American bombers obliterated it. This was the first time I ever saw a city levelled by war.

In mounting horror I climbed through the debris, through one shattered house after another, the odor of death in my nostrils, seeing here a broken vase, there a child's coloring book, and on the lawn a severed hand fingering black and white pebbles like piano keys. My mind reeled.

Nauseated, in need of fresh air, I stumbled out of that row of jagged dwellings and walked onto a coral road. There I stood and trembled, unable to comprehend the magnitude of the holocaust to which I was witness, and suddenly within my skull I heard the music of a famous symphony. What was it? I *had* to know the name of that composition, for otherwise I might never expel it from my mind. So I froze on the road by the ruins and thought and thought and thought, and at last remembered. The symphony I was hearing in my brain was written by Sibelius and is entitled *Valse Triste* — Sad Waltz.

THURSDAY, AUGUST 16, 1945 ▓ Last night I sat in my tent with an American sailor who says he is a communist. He tried to persuade me that the assassination of the Czar by the Russian Reds was an *ennobling* act. I contradicted him. I watched his face, a shadow among shadows.

"As a communist," I said slowly, "you would do anything to accomplish your goals, wouldn't you? Even murder?"

"Certainly!" he snapped.

"Torture? Even torture? Would you, for instance, torture me if, for argument's sake, I were the sole barrier to your communistic success?"

I like the man and know he likes me.

"That's not fair," he began. Pause. Then, in a gush to get it over with quickly, he said: "Yes. Since you ask me this. Yes, I would torture you, if you alone were blocking the worldwide realization of the communist program."

My brain went blank. What was there to think, to say? From outside the tent I heard men shouting. I stared into the shadows. The shouting became closer and louder. In my tent the men began to stir.

"Those guys from the radar station," someone suggested "Wonder if they heard something."

The communist and I walked our shadows outside the tent. It was 9:20 P.M. Two guards peered across the field at an approaching figure. The figure rumbled sounds. Closer and closer, and the words came into focus:

"War's over! . . . Goddam war's over! . . . Yeeeeaawowwww!"

I felt as though I had been hooked up to a huge dynamo. Splattering mud with each step, I jolted toward the figure. It was an American kid and he was slightly insane. I grabbed his blue shirt. Thinking and acting like a reporter, I machine-gunned questions at him. I had to know. I wanted facts. He knew, all right. Emperor Hirohito had gone on radio to tell the Japanese people that Japan was accepting the cease-fire demands made by the Allies. The emperor did not use the words *unconditional surrender*, but this is what he meant. It was the end of the war.

Something inside me began humming. The something just hummed there inside me for a few moments and then I saw sparks slashing through the dark of my brain and suddenly it was a Fourth of July celebration in my head. Nearby, a guard yipped and let go a burst of bullets into the sky. Yells flared from throats that all too long had been lumps of loneliness. I yelled. The next second I felt ashamed because this thing was too big to yell about. The fireworks inside me settled down again to a steady hum. I tried to think. I was unable to think. The idea of peace was a cathedral so huge that one had to stand miles away to see it, appreciate it.

The communist and I slowly walked back to my tent.

"Soon," he said softly, "I'll get to see my little boy again."

Human beings do not surprise me any more. They fascinate me, but they do not surprise me because I've learned to expect the unexpected from them. So this other human being and I found a firm foothold among the slippery vines of the sweet-potato field and looked at the stars. I prayed in the most violent oaths I knew. An agnostic, pious about peace, I muttered idiotically and don't remember what I muttered.

Then the fleet exploded. Lying offshore was an enormous flotilla, and it turned loose with everything—tracers, flares, big stuff. Red tracers etched V's for victory against the backdrop of night. The joyful barrage out-thundered individual yells. My feet were muddy, my heart was happy, and still I swore reverently.

My thoughts, like homing pigeons, soared past the longitudes to loved ones on the other side of the earth. Carefully, deliciously, I thought of one, then another, sharing my joy with theirs. And then I thought of a neat little apartment in Peoria and a dismal September morning and the radio and the guttural voice of Hitler boasting that the Nazi army had crossed the border into Poland. That night opened a parenthesis in my life; this night closed it.

"He's so easy to handle," the communist was saying, "and he learns so fast . . ."

Oh. Yes. Of course. His boy.

Now the communist and all other fathers and mothers could think and talk more freely about their children, about everything, for this was peace, was it not? Was it? Is it? Who says it is peace? Can my communist friend call this peace? No. To him it is an opportunity. Opportunity for what? A better opportunity to propagate his ideology, his faith, his crusade. How? Through strife, if necessary—for he confessed he would torture me, if necessary. And, in one sense, he is horribly, realistically correct, for life is strife. Turn over a leaf of grass and you will find insects battling one another to death. Or, to change the image, life has been defined as big fish eating little fish. Living things live by killing other living things. Clever men kill with lies. Stupid men kill with force. Is life itself worth the price? My communist friend has one answer. I have another answer.

November 10, 1945—I sailed homeward from Okinawa.

November 25, 1945—I landed at San Pedro, California.

December 3, 1945—I was discharged from the navy.

December 10, 1945—I let my wife divorce me in Santa Barbara, California.

To this day, I do not understand why she wanted to end our marriage. I suppose this happened to a lot of guys who went into the service.

CHAPTER 8

1946

CHICAGO, MONDAY, JANUARY 7, 1946 ■ Today I returned to my job in the Chicago office of the United Press. Boyd Lewis, who had hired me, is no longer here. He served as a war correspondent in Europe and watched the Nazis surrender May 7, 1945, in General Dwight Eisenhower's headquarters in a little red schoolhouse in Rheims, France. Then, instead of returning here, Boyd has settled in New York City as executive editor of a syndicate called Newspaper Enterprise Association.

Now the central division news editor in Chicago is Joe Morgan, who was second in command under Boyd before the war. After Joe greeted me and introduced me to other reporters and editors, I sat down at a desk and began reading newspapers, feeling unsure of myself. Soon, though, Joe called me over to his desk to say that a six-year-old girl named Susan Degnan had been kidnapped from her second-floor bedroom. He wanted fast coverage of the story, so I sailed out of the office and didn't get back for three days.

FRIDAY, JANUARY, 11, 1946 ■ This murder story has developed into one of the most celebrated crimes in the history of Chicago. It certainly is the most important spot news story that I have ever covered. This story is so dramatic that it has attracted correspondents from all over the world.

Later, we learned there was a University of Chicago sophomore named William Heirens, 17, who was mild of manner but in fact was a psychotic killer. He engaged in more than a score of robberies, burglaries and assaults. He stabbed two women to death. In the apartment of one of his victims he scrawled on her bathroom mirror: "For heaven's sake catch me before I kill more! I cannot control myself!"

But after that he snatched the little Degnan girl from her bedroom, carried her down a homemade ladder, took her to a nearby basement, killed her, then cut her body into pieces, shoving them down into several sewers. In her bedroom he left a note demanding a ransom of $20,000 for her return. I *watched her head being pulled out of a sewer. The child was only a little older than my daughter.*

Heirens was arrested for burglary and the police, to their satisfaction, found that his fingerprints matched the fingerprints found on the ransom note. He was pressured to confess; his own defense attorney said that the state had a solid case against him.

THURSDAY, APRIL 4, 1946 ■ Recently I interviewed James Roosevelt, the President's eldest son, in the Drake Hotel. He was frank, quick-minded, intelligent and likable. At the end of the mass interview I grabbed the nearest phone, which was at one end of the davenport between us. As I began phoning my story to a rewrite gal, Shirley Hutchinson, I was amazed to notice Jimmy edging closer, bending his angular form toward me so he could hear what I was saying about him. He's been interviewed so many times I'd have thought he was case-hardened by now. Maybe this was the first time he ever had a chance to actually hear a reporter phoning in a story about him.

FRIDAY, APRIL 5, 1946 ■ Paraphrasing Wordsworth, the city is too much with me. Early and late it clatters its insane dirge into my ears until I am bowed down by the fatigue of noise. The city is thousands of commuters streaming across the bridge at the *Daily News* building to let electricity and steam buoy them back to their cubicles called home. The city is the puffy-faced prostitute I saw at a police station, slyly stuffing $5 bills into her commercial bosom. The city is store clerks who take your money with the air of doing you a favor. The city is soot in the eye and cement under foot and your shoulder being bumped and hands that never stay clean. The city is a harlot in Max Factor makeup and patched ermine, grimacing at the highest bidder. It sells its golden beads supplicating Success and sneers at characters without a name. Yet I am half in love with this harlot. Because it asks much, it evokes the strength necessary to live. It teases the best out of a man, while bleeding him of his worst. It electrifies by a thousand contacts of person with person, and also soothes by honoring privacy. The city is a forum and a convent, a treadmill and a rainbow, a rotten log teeming with termites and a cool temple worshipped by esthetes. It is a purple paradox and I hate it with a tremendous love and love it with a passionate hatred.

THURSDAY, MAY 9, 1946 ■ Newspapers from coast to coast have published my United Press story about that horrible train wreck last month.

It happened on April 25 at Naperville, Illinois, 28 miles southwest of

Chicago. The Burlington Railroad's Exposition Flyer, streaking west from Chicago at a speed of more than 75 miles an hour, crashed into the rear of a stalled train.

When the first word of this accident reached our UP office in the *Chicago Daily News* building, our bureau manager, Joe Morgan, stuffed a wad of money into my hand and told me to get a cab and get the hell there as fast as possible.

When I charged out of the *News* building I found a taxi and told the driver I was a reporter and wanted to get to the site of a railway accident. I kept that cab for the next eight hours.

A disaster of this magnitude is, at first, total confusion. Splintered railroad cars were piled irregularly, like jackstraws, atop one another. White-faced cops and firemen and spectators milled around. I saw a dead woman dangling inside a shattered metal car, her long hair and one arm pointing toward the bloody earth. Someone's brains had become a red streak along a metal track. Forty-six persons had been killed and 100 others injured.

Until the arrival of Bobby Loughran, I was the only United Press reporter there. I saw two or three reporters from the Associated Press but, nonetheless, my by-line story landed on the front pages of newspapers from New York to Los Angeles.

Joe Morgan, reporting on the coverage to United Press headquarters in New York City, said, "Ellis did a fine job."

Yeah, I guess so, but that tragedy burned searing images into my mind.

MONDAY, MAY 20, 1946 ▪ Thomas Mann has been called "the heir of Goethe." I can't judge. I don't know enough about Goethe and I have read only part of one of Mann's works—*The Magic Mountain*. But I was excited today when Jess Bogue assigned me to interview Mann. The exiled German author, winner of the Nobel Prize in literature, had agreed to an interview as he left Billing Hospital on the campus of the University of Chicago. Because he's still weak, we had been warned that the interview would be brief.

Before Mann arrived in the board room of the hospital, his daughter, Erika Mann, showed up. Married to poet W. H. Auden, she is also a writer. In fact, in today's *Chicago Daily News* she had an article about present conditions in Germany. She claimed that American occupation officers are being seduced by lingering strains of Nazism. She is tall and spare with a pompadour haircut, vibrant brown eyes, the eyes of an intellectual. Her English was perfect.

Mann entered and took his place at one end of a table with eight chairs pulled up to it. Patiently he posed for five or six photographers. Full-face his features are imposing and dignified. However, he looks less dignified in profile. His head is small and his face is big. His club-like nose dominates even his sturdy brow, while the remaining half of his face reclines into insignificance. A deep cleft rims the top of his nose, as deep a cleft as ever I saw in the bridge of a man's nose. A wen bubbled out from his right temple, while a brown mole dotted the pouchiness under his left eye.

His thin hair was parted far to the left side of his head, otherwise streaking back pompadour fashion. It was so close-cropped about his ears that it gave him something of a Prussian look. This was enhanced by the barbed wire of his salty mustache. The expansiveness of his mouth was contradicted by its rigidity, although he can smile and does so easily when moved.

Somehow, his features didn't seem to hang together. They lack harmony. They seem to have been thrown about that column which is his nose. And aloof from all these physical features are his brook-cool eyes, half-blue, half-gray. They look in more than they look out. They appear to see life realistically and precisely, an impression heightened by the slash that is his mouth.

He wore a slate-blue suit—the first time he'd worn one since entering the hospital, Erika said. A two-button affair, it was buttoned at the top, hiding the tag-end of a blue-and-white-striped shirt. The cords of his neck looked like celery stalks—a stark reminder of the sickness he had endured.

I slipped into a chair to his left, only four feet away. When the photographers had finished shooting, I began the interview with a question about what he plans to do when he gets back to his home on the Pacific Palisades in California. (Never open an interview with a big question.)

Spreading wan fingers atop the polished board table, Mann said slowly: "Well, I hope to finish a novel I've been working on, a fictional biography of a German composer."

"Is it drawn from the life of any real person?" I asked.

Erika broke in: "No, it's purely fictional."

"It's connected with the destiny of Germany," Mann said. "Sort of a symbol."

I asked for his opinion of Germany's destiny.

"The future of Germany is very dark," Mann said softly. "I only hope that ten years from now Germany will be mentally and physically better than at present."

"Do you want to go back there to live?"

"No, I don't want to go back. I have always declared, privately and publicly, that I would never turn my back on America, and I'm going to stick to that promise. I'm an American citizen now. I have English-speaking grandchildren growing up around me. It would be nonsensical for me to go back. A new life is developing for me. For twelve years I have been far from Germany. We built our house on the Pacific Palisades—"

"—just about the time of Pearl Harbor," Erika interjected.

"Yes," Mann smiled. "We just got it under way before building restrictions went into effect. I'm very happy there. There's a beautiful view. It's quite the loveliest study I've ever had. There's the ocean on one side of it and on the other side the beautiful mountains."

Mann is 71 years old.

TUESDAY, JUNE 11, 1946   ■   Washington Square, in Chicago, is called Bughouse Square. This is so because crackpots hang out in it and radicals orate to their heart's content. Hoping I might find a feature story, I walked to the small park and sat down on a bench. I hadn't been there long before someone pointed and cried: "There's the Bird Woman!"

My eyes following the pointing finger, I saw an old woman sitting on another bench nearby. She was throwing pieces of bread to pigeons on the grass, mothering them with a smile. Suddenly, a stone arced out of the air and landed amidst the pigeons, who exploded in flight. From behind a bush three naughty girls smirked at the woman.

"Pity!" she shrieked. "Pity! There is no more pity in this world! Even the children are brutal!"

With an effort she arose and teetered on her heels while yipping; "Mrs. Hagan! Policewoman! Mrs. Hagan! Those bloody little kids are killing my pigeons!"

The policewoman, built like a tank, invaded the bush and scattered the girls. I walked over to the old lady, introduced myself and sat down beside her.

She murmured: "Other people don't screech at things like this, but I do. I figure we all have to do our part. It's up to us to keep our cities fine and wholesome."

She said her name is Sarah Duggan.

"I've been coming here every day for fifteen years to feed the birds. I'm getting old, though—I'm seventy-three—and can't walk far, begging bread for them. That's why I'm trying to spread the word. I am sick with poverty and want to do good works, but so many doors are closed to the poor of the earth, such as my birds and me." She massaged her thin coat up toward the cords of her ancient throat.

"My birds know me and love me like children. They're the only friends I have left. Trouble with the world is, there just isn't enough pity left in it. I feel that if I am gentle with the birds it will help teach human beings to be kinder to one another, and so the world will be a safer place in which to live."

She reached into a shopping bag for more bread to throw to the pigeons with an awkward over-hand pitch.

"Last winter," she said, "I had a little room off an alley. Kept the windows open so the birds could come in. My pet, my love, was a jet black pigeon I called Haile Selassie—the little king.

"He mated with Lady Jane Grey. You've read about Lady Jane Grey, haven't you? Well, Haile Selassie—I don't know what got into him! He flew into a pot of scalding water I had on the stove.

"I grabbed him fast, but he was horribly burned. I bought salves for him and gave him a little wine. Thought it would warm his little body. I kept him alive a month, but then he died."

Staring at the sky, she wept.

"The night the little king died," she quavered, "I stopped believing in God."

TUESDAY, JULY 30, 1946 ■ A mad day. A swirling day. A futile day. This is the day on which William Heirens was supposed to confess in full to State's Attorney William J. Touhy, and we heard that his confession would be so detailed that it might take eight hours just to telephone it to our office.

Touhy said yesterday that only one copy of the confession would be made available—to the City News Service, an intra-city press association. Well, the Associated Press got a copy, but not the United Press. Our veteran police reporter, a tough hombre, roared into the DA's office, pounded his desk for a half hour and came out with a promise that a second copy would be made available to the United Press.

Now, with our client newspapers yapping for more and more stories about Heirens, we made ready in our office to handle a huge volume of news. Joe Morgan said I was the fastest typist in the place, so I was told to receive the story. Although I am a hunt-and-peck typist, I can bat out 80 words a minute. I don't even know what fingers I use.

Bobby Loughrin, our cop shop man, was in the criminal court building. With him was one of our cub reporters, whose duty it was to open a phone to our office and keep it open until Bobby came running out to deliver. The cub reporter called at 9:50 A.M.

I put on earphones and sat down at a desk and took his call. In front of myself I spread the data I needed to refresh my memory about this case, then began sweating it out. The cub reporter across town and I kept the wire open, idly chatting about this and that. I sat. And sat. And sat. No one dared to leave the office, so a copy boy went down to get sandwiches for the staff. Joe sat down at a desk next to mine so that he might snatch my copy, take by take, as I ground it out. *When* I ground it out, because so far nothing had happened.

And so I sat. An hour passed. I began improvising singing telegrams to try to amuse the cub reporter at the other end of my line. Heirens was with Touhy? Yes. A second hour passed. Other staff members in the office sometimes jumped when I said something to the cub reporter. Nerves. A third hour crawled by. We chomped hamburgers and then began horsing around, the strain was so great. My ears were getting tired. I fidgeted.

Someone oiled my typewriter. When I finished a pack of cigarets, another guy tossed a second pack to me. Never had I seen so many people looking like bird dogs on the point. Every time I so much as grunted into the mouthpiece, I seemed to see ears standing erect.

Cub reporter to me: "Reporters gone into Touhy's office!"

I yelled, "Reporters with Touhy!"

End of horsing around. Thrice-sharpened pencils impatiently tapped desks. I glared into the mouthpiece as though it were the Evil Eye.

Bobby Loughrin on the line: "Heirens refuses to talk!"

I yelled, "Heirens refuses to talk!"

Joe Morgan was writing before I finished the last word.

Bobby, talking fast, began delivering: "Touhy says—"

Listened to Bobby. My fingers tumbled about the keyboard. Riiiipppp! Three and a half hours of tense idleness had become flaming seconds of searing concentration. More notes. More notes. Typewriter bell jangling. Other bells from teletype machines across the room. Blurred view of trousers swishing past my line of sight.

"—at the request of Heirens and his parents. There is nothing that—"

Hit the right keys, boy! Hit'em hard and hit'em right! Ten men crouching nearby, waiting for little ink spots on yellow sheets. Millions of readers believing they are the correct spots. Gotta be right! And fast, fast, fast!

My last sheet of paper is snatched away and it's all over.

I slump in the chair. I stare dully at other staffers, who now yell as they help one another to get the story on the wires. Seven minutes of dynamite action, and that's it, brother. For what? I continue to sit and crank out a thought or two of my own and gripe at a young schizophrenic for jangling my nerves and hurting my belly. What happened to the Degnan girl and the two women Heirens murdered is, of course, a tragedy. What happened to him is also a tragedy. What happened to me today was a farce, the most dramatic anti-climax of my life.

William Heirens finally did confess to all three murders, was convicted and then sentenced to three consecutive life terms.

TUESDAY, SEPTEMBER 3, 1946 ■ This story of mine about boys and their guns was reprinted in the *Reader's Digest* and ran in newspapers from coast to coast.

Eight little boys who live in Forest Park threw their toy guns into a bonfire today and signed a treaty which said: "Peace begins on our street."

A little old lady watched the ceremony with glistening eyes. She is Miss Anna Grace Sawyer, 68, an amateur student of foreign affairs and a child psychologist.

She organized the peace conference and demobilized the small army that had fought battles on the big lawn around her house. She liked to have the children play in her yard even if they did trample a flower, now and then. But there was one thing she didn't like.

"No guns, kiddies!" she would cry from a window. "No guns!"

But big brothers were home from the war with guns and talk of guns, so the boys on Elgin Ave. whittled and hewed until they had their own toy guns. One twilight as the little lady with the graying hair was tending her flowers, she heard something dreadful. "Bang, bang! You're dead! Bang!"

There was a rustling in the bushes.

"Boys!" Miss Sawyer called. "Why don't you come on out and we'll have a little talk and lots of fun. Different fun."

The dead came to life and the enemy became friendly and the little old lady talked softly as the twilight deepened. She explained that guns cause pain. She spoke excitedly of other adventures. She made peace sound thrilling.

"Now, would you like to put your guns in this bushel basket?"

They would. And did. Eight little boys disarmed themselves of 12 guns.

"I suggest," said the peace-maker, "that we have a nice big bonfire and burn them all up. Then I'll have a surprise for you."

It was fun burning the guns. It was fun when the little old lady led them to a little green table by the sand box. Lying on the table was a piece of brown paper with paper flowers at the corners. Scrawled on it in red crayon was:

"Peace begins on our street—Elgin Avenue. Boys' Peace Club. Our world would be better without guns and with more fairness and kindness . . . signed:

They signed—Jimmy, Jackey, Jerry and John, Milton, John, Ralph and Richard.

The little old lady cried; "Now for the surprise!"

She had bought eight soap wands and eight bottles of soap fluid. With flushed faces, eight little boys waved their wands and peaceful bubbles wafted away into a world awaiting peace.

Meantime, my private life had become a wasteland. Divorced from my wife, missing my daughter, longing for love, I began drinking and womanizing. On Okinawa I had picked up a tropical virus that now elevated my temperature every afternoon, exhausting me. Nonetheless, I abandoned myself to a wanton life, flitting from bar to bar, pursuing woman after woman, seeking love, finding only sex.

In Chicago after World War II the housing shortage was so acute that I had to take a room in a cheap hotel on the near north side, and from its window I saw no beauty, no sunsets. My father, who lived two blocks away, took me to museums and parks where he introduced me to people as his friend. This hurt so much that I complained to his wife, my step-mother, whom I loved. She said perhaps my father didn't want others to know he had a son my age—thirty-five. I stormed that I didn't care, that he was rejecting me. Fritzi agreed and must have told him the barbed-wire truth, because after that he introduced me as his son.

Nonetheless, rejected by wife and father, bereft of an emotional anchor, I became cynical and even suicidal. My epitaph, I decided, should be: "So what?" My work as a reporter was interesting, indeed fascinating, but at the end of the day I did not know what to do with myself. While I was overseas during the war my father had kept my books in the basement of his apartment building; now I hauled about 400 of them into my tiny room. I also gave myself a present—my first set of the Encyclopedia Britannica. *I went to extremes, leading a wild life awhile, then burying myself in books. I also set myself the task of writing a book about suicide.*

Compulsively, I felt I had to find love or die. Sometimes I thought I was going mad. Often I despised myself. Although I pursued pleasure, I found satisfaction in nothing but my work as a reporter. Covering the divorce of

Sonja Henie, the champion skater and movie star, I met a pretty woman who had won her own divorce that same day in that same court. After I phoned in my story, she accompanied me to a cocktail lounge and soon begged me to take her to bed within 24 hours of her divorce. I, of course, was an obliging fellow.

At the Chicago Art Institute I interviewed a model, an Arab woman who posed in the nude for life classes, and soon thereafter romance blossomed. Then there was the amusing press agent who wanted publicity for the lipstick he was promoting. To a hotel room he brought five professional models and had each of them put on a different shade of lipstick. After he hooked me up to a machine that records brain waves, he told each girl to kiss me on my lips. It was the red-headed model who sent the needle almost off the paper, so I got her phone number. Yeah, reporting is tough work, but somebody has to do it. I fell half in love with a brilliant woman reporter whose mind I respected and whose body I enjoyed.

Nonetheless, I continued to feel depressed.

FRIDAY, NOVEMBER 22, 1946   Today I was named the best feature writer in Chicago.

I belong to the Chicago Newspaper Guild, which annually picks the best journalist in the city. I was lucky enough to be among those chosen this year.

The award ceremony was scheduled for this evening in the Hotel Continental. Some United Press staffers gave a cocktail party before the Page One Ball, so I was a little drunk when I arrived at the hotel.

It had been announced that the ball would be attended by Jane Russell, the actress with the spectacular bosom. She had made her film debut as a hot-blooded halfbreed in a 1943 Howard Hughes picture called *The Outlaw,* but because he emphasized her breasts in both the movie and its billboard advertising, it was not released until this year. Here in Chicago I had spoken to her three times, seeking quotes about the banning of the film in San Francisco. In fact, once she posed as I caricatured her.

Bob Hope, to our surprise, also came to the ball. He and Miss Russell took charge of handing out the awards. Each prize was a stick of type, that is, one short paragraph of type that non-journalists can read only by holding a hand mirror to it. This is precisely what the comedian did as he held my award. Speaking into a microphone, he called:

"Edward Ellis! . . . Where's Edward Ellis? . . . Oh, Edwaaarrrd, come get your prize!"

I walked to the stage, climbed the steps, shook his hand. As he began to introduce me to Jane Russell, I said: "Oh, I know Miss Russell. I chased her around three times."

I wasn't trying to be funny, but Bob Hope took it that way.

"You chased—" he began, then did one of his double-takes. Everybody laughed.

Seeing a cameraman below us about to take a picture, he stepped off the stage and pretended to direct. In the photo Miss Russell stood to my right and Miss Page One to my left.

I still use the award as a paperweight. It says:

> CHICAGO, Nov. 22, 1946—
> Edward Ellis tonight was
> given a Page One Award by
> the Chicago Newspaper
> Guild for his feature stories
> for the United Press.

1947

FRIDAY, JANUARY 24, 1947 ■ Jack Hess is a Chicago press agent with an imagination and a sense of what makes a good feature story. Every so often he offers me an idea I can use. Today he called me in the United Press office to ask whether I'd like to interview Gertrude Lawrence, the great English actress and singer.

"Of course," I replied. "What's the angle?"

Jack said that one of his accounts is the Elaine Allen hat shop in the Congress Hotel on Michigan Avenue. The shop owner retains an artist to sketch the faces of her customers and then adds to the sketch a drawing of a hat that goes well with the face.

Gertrude Lawrence happens to be in Chicago right now, appearing in *Pygmalion*. Jack called her press agent to suggest that the actress visit the hat shop, be photographed wearing various hats, and thus get publicity for both the shop and the actress. Agreed.

Jack hired a long black limousine and picked me up, then told the chauffeur to drive to the theater where Miss Lawrence was appearing. She was pleasant and entirely natural, thus confirming what I had read about her "magnetic personality." Her real name is Alexandre Dagmar Lawrence-Klasen; she was born about the turn of the century; as a child she appeared on the musical stage; and one of her childhood friends was Noel Coward, the playwright, actor, director.

Miss Lawrence is so famous that when she entered the hat shop everyone inside became flustered. The artist bowed her into a chair near a window overlooking Michigan Avenue and soon passersby peered in, recognized her, gasped, clucked and pointed. With mischievous eyes, she looked back at them, as one monkey to other monkeys, and beckoned them to come on in and join the fun.

The artist politely asked her to sit still as he sketched her. She did as asked, but to break the monotony she softly sang a nauseating radio commercial about beer: "Atlas Prager—got it?" Atlas Prager—get it!"

Then the sophisticated lady smiled and glanced at me and said: "Love it! Simply love it!"

She had to wait while the artist added to his sketch the kind of hat that the designer thought she should have. To while away the time Miss Lawrence tried on one hat after another, then selected a very flouncy hat and stuck it on my head. The press agent had hired a photographer, who now snapped a picture with the actress behind me as I struck an arch pose while gazing at myself in a hand-held mirror. She was delightfully playful.

But her mood swiftly changed. The hat designed exclusively for her was brought out and placed on her head. As she looked at herself in a mirror, she asked how much it would cost.

"Oh," said the designer, "about thirty-five dollars."

"That's criminal!" Gertrude Lawrence cried. "In London thirty-five dollars would buy food for a family of nine for one week!"

The designer looked like a little girl caught stealing candy.

Turning to Jack Hess, Miss Lawrence said she did not want to ride in the limousine to the theater. Hesitantly, I asked whether I might escort her there in a taxi. She smiled and said yes.

In the cab she said to me: "You have no idea, you *simp-ly* have no idea what it was like in London during the war! That beastly rationing, you know! And the scarcity of foodstuffs. My deah, it was piteous! And even now—the poor dears just don't get enough of the right food yet. They have to queue up at the shops and wait for hours and then they aren't able to buy what they need. And to think that bloody hat back in that shop sells for thirty-five dollars. That's disgraceful! Do you know how I spend my time when I'm appearing in American theaters? Well, I go around to grocery stores for Crisco to send some to my friends back in London."

We arrived at the theater. I helped Gertrude Lawrence out of the cab. Then I tipped my hat to her, and never before had it felt so good to tip my hat to a lady.

WEDNESDAY, FEBRUARY 19, 1947   ■   Mae West's press agent gave me a ticket to a theater to see her on the stage in a comedy—alleged comedy, that is. This misbegotten soon-forgotten thing is called *Ring Twice Tonight*. I went, I saw, I yawned.

The plot, for want of a better word, concerns a female FBI agent posing as a nightclub singer. To avoid involvement in a murder, she holes up in an apartment. Her maid releases balloons inviting finders to come up and see her—don't ask me why—so she has to fight off one man after another. Mae West fight off men? Don't be ridiculous!

I had been lured into seeing this abomination with the promise that immediately after the performance an event of transcendental importance would occur on stage: Mae West would meet Mr. America. Could any reporter shun such a scoop? Does a horse run? Does a bell ring?

So after the final curtain I headed backstage, humming: *When a body, meets a body . . .* A wry note, perhaps. I'd always heard that Mae West could coin naughty wisecracks faster than a kid scrawling on a wall, "Jeeter does it to Agnes!" I wanted to find out how well Mae could do this when no censors were poking their blue noses into her pink business.

You remember her lines:

Too much of a good thing can be wonderful!

I'm not good and tired—just tired.

Between two evils, I always pick the one I never tried before.

When I arrived backstage I looked around. Saw no censors. However, there was a cluster of autograph hounds and hangers-on and press agents and reporters and photographers. And then—there was Mr. America of 1946. His name is Alan Stephens. His suit was so tight he looked like a steak too big for its platter. With him was his date, Miss Legionnaire.

Off to one side was Mae West signing her name for her fans. She was an S-curve in a white gown. As the autograph hounds melted away, her press agent angled over and whispered into her ear. Mae glanced around, almost getting her eyelashes tangled up, and mooed: Where's this beautiful hunk of a man, Mr. America?"

Mr. America's press agent led him forward and said: "Alan, this is Miss West . . . Miss West, this is Mr. America."

She held out a soft hand, then pouted: "He has clothes on!"

Everybody laughed. Good old Mae, right there with a wisecrack!

Mr. America's press agent cried: "Oh, Alan'll strip down! We'd like to get a picture of the two of you together, Miss West."

"Deee-lighted!" she purred.

Mr. America, carrying a gym bag, disappeared behind some curtains. Mae West just stood there. Nobody said anything. Must have been two dozen people, but none spoke. The silence became thunderous.

When Mr. America emerged from behind the curtains, everyone erupted in artificial excitement. He was naked except for a pair of white shorts. His skin glowed a healthy pink. He was a mass of muscles, with shoulders bigger than a meat loaf, hips leaner than a sandwich, and he winced in embarrassment.

Mae West filtered a look through her eyelashes and gasped "Whew!"

Everybody laughed. Hadn't Mae whewed "Whew!"?

Mr. America rippled over to Mae West. She put a white hand on a pink shoulder that was becoming red. She giggled. Keeping her hand where it was she wiggled her eyebrows. Mae West was trying to think, so everybody kept respectfully silent. She compromised on a second "Whew!"

Everybody laughed.

Mae tried again: "You're a big hunk of—" She knitted her brows.

Her press agent walked past, whispering into her ear.

"—a big hunk of romance!" Mae concluded. And smiled a triumphal smile.

Everybody laughed. That Mae! A killer-diller with the wisecrack!

Photographers began pointing their cameras. Mr. America's press agent suggested that she lean against him, so Miss West, age 54, leaned against Mr. America, age 23. Then she put her arms around him. Miss Legionnaire was watching. Mr. America fidgeted, but at last twined his arms around Mae West.

"My, my!" Mae wisecracked.

Everybody laughed.

So the cameramen shot picture after picture and then nobody seemed to know what to do and at last Mr. America vanished to change into his light blue suit and when he emerged he took the hand of Miss Legionnaire.

The last I saw of Mae West she stood in the center of the stage. Her press agent was still doing all the talking.

SATURDAY, APRIL 19, 1947 ■ Paul Robeson is on a concert tour. The bass-baritone, perhaps the most famous Negro in the world, arrived in St. Louis the other day and fell into a fight about segregated facilities in local theaters.

Angered by such bigotry, he announced that when his tour ends he will abandon the concert stage and the theater for two years in order to "talk up and down the nation against race hatred and prejudice."

The House Committee on Un-American Activities has said he is "invariably found supporting the Communist Party and its front organizations." He was just one among almost a thousand persons cited, among them former Vice President Henry Wallace and Harlow Shapely, the Harvard astronomer and Nobel Laureate.

Robeson's next scheduled concert was in Peoria, a city of about 105,000 people. When news of the House citation reached there the Peoria city council passed a resolution opposing the appearance of "any speaker or artist who is an avowed propagandist for Un-American ideology." A few brave citizens protested this blow to civil rights.

Peoria's mayor agreed to let some people hold a reception for Robeson in the assembly room of city hall. However, star-spangled patriots put so much pressure on him that a day later, he withdrew this permission. There were rumors of violence and talk of guns. Peoria had a reputation as a violent city and, as a former reporter there, I knew it deserved this reputation.

Eight detectives and six cops waited for Robeson at the railroad station, but he slipped into town in an auto. His concert having been cancelled, the singer wanted to tell his side of the story, but the local radio station would not let him speak on the air. All he could do was to meet a few people in the home of a union official.

He drove from Peoria to Chicago and checked into the Sherman Hotel. I called him there to ask for an interview and he told me to join him. When I walked into his suite we shook hands and he bowed me into a chair.

"You're pretty much in the news," I said, grinning.

Grinning back, he said: "Seems so."

He wore a gray suit and black knitted tie and his weight seemed to have increased considerably. Paul Robeson is a giant of a man—physically and intellectually. I had read about him in the *Chicago Sun*'s library, across the hall from the United Press. Now, I realized, I was in the presence of one of the most distinguished *and* controversial figures of the 20th century. *Who's Who in America* had much to say about him.

He was born in 1898 in Princeton, N. J., the son of a man who had escaped from slavery. Shortly before Paul graduated from high school in

1915, he made the highest score in an examination that won him a four-year scholarship to Rutgers College—later Rutgers University.

He was only the third black student in the history of the college but popular with classmates. Standing six feet three, weighing 240 pounds, he was described as "massive, beautiful in physique, muscular, strong and handsome." He won the freshman prize for oratory. He won the sophomore and junior prizes for extemporaneous speaking. He won 12 varsity letters in four sports—football, baseball, basketball and track. In 1917 and 1918 he was named an All-American football end. In his junior year he was elected to Phi Beta Kappa and when he graduated he gave the commencement address.

In 1920 he began studying law at Columbia University, paying his way by playing professional football on weekends. He met and married a brilliant chemistry student, Eslanda Cardozo Goode. She persuaded him to take the lead in a play that ran only briefly on Broadway but launched his theatrical career. His wife became his business manager.

After getting his law degree from Columbia he joined a law firm in Manhattan but, rather indifferent to the law and extremely resentful of the attitude of white law clerks to him, he quit. More to his liking were the legitimate stage, the movies, singing at concerts and making records. He became a star on the stage in London and enjoyed an enormously successful concert tour of Europe. He spoke more than a dozen different languages.

Now, lighting a cigaret, he began telling me what happened in Peoria.

"This is more than a personal issue, believe me! Peoria was like an armed camp. But you can't understand what happened to me without understanding the background. You've got to know what's happened in Peoria in the past two or three years. There've been three railroad workers murdered there—and a railroad president. They just got the railroad started again. Maybe you read about it?"

I nodded yes.

Robeson said: "I was going to Peoria as an avowed friend of labor. I was going to sing *Joe Hill*—"

"Did they know in advance," I asked, "that you'd sing *Joe Hill?*"

"I've sung *Joe Hill* on every one of my programs for the past six years!" Robeson stared at me with bulging eyes. "But who was I going to sing for? There was a top ticket price of three dollars and thirty cents. The working man can't afford that. Who can? The men who hate labor. They knew I was going to sing about Joe Hill, and they're the guys who try to beat down labor, just as Joe Hill was framed and murdered by the copper mine guys!"

"Mr. Robeson," I said, "there are a lot of people who will want to know why, if you're such a friend of labor, you sing at a top of three dollars and thirty cents. Why not sing for one ten, so the working man can hear you?"

Leaning forward in his chair, Robeson boomed: "I do better than that! I sing for the working man for nothing. I sang here at the Henry Wallace rally, and I sing plenty of times for the working man for nothing. They know what I do for them."

"Getting back to the Peoria situation—"

"Christ, yes," Robeson exclaimed. "That! Well, labor would have taken over my concert, but my management cancelled it. I don't mean that my management was wrong, but the concert was cancelled. I want you to get one thing straight: The papers quoted me as saying, I was going into Peoria 'amply protected.' I never did say that."

"You had heard there were some threats made against you?"

"Hell, yes!"

"How did you know this, Mr. Robeson? Actually, what evidence did you have that threats had been made against you?"

"You know how it is," Robeson said. "Word of mouth."

"And, believing this, you didn't take the precaution of having any protection?"

"Well," he said with a sly smile, "I wasn't absolutely without an awareness of the situation." He threw up a huge hand to help him say the thing. "However, I wasn't, as the papers said, 'amply protected.' Maybe someone on my side in Peoria did say, 'Well, we'll see that Paul's amply protected.'"

My notebook slid off the arm of my chair. I picked it up.

Robeson said; "There's a lesson that must be learned from this Peoria affair." His eyes, so wide before, now were narrowed. "Americans seem to be on the go here regarding a Red Hysteria, but they don't understand the nature and the danger of fascism. I can't understand it. . . . For Christ's sake, look! Who besides myself was named by that House committee? Who? Who were they? Well, I'll tell you: Joseph E. Davies, former American ambassador to Russia, and Edward G. Robinson, the movie star. That's the company they put me in!

"The charges were completely unsubstantiated. I haven't been convicted of anything. There's been no jury trial. Well, where do I go from here?" He spread out his arms. "It was obviously unconstitutional!"

I said: "I want to make sure I understand you . . . You mean that the resolution of the House committee was unconstitutional?"

"No, no! Get me straight. I mean that the resolution passed by the city council of Peoria was unconstitutional."

Sometimes reporting is a dangerous trade. Even with the best of intentions, a reporter can misquote someone.

Robeson continued: "What if Senator Pepper wanted to go to Peoria to speak? Or Wallace? Or Eddie Robinson? And what if they were refused the right to speak? Then what if they came to Chicago, and what if they were refused the right to speak here, too. Where would we go from there?"

Robeson shrugged mountainously.

"What Americans must understand is that the police in Peoria were there to back vigilante bands of Legionnaires. And these vigilantes had lanterns, I was told. *Lanterns!*"

"You mean lanterns indicated a lynching?"

"What else could it mean?" he asked rhetorically. "And, you know, no minister, white or colored, had the courage to let me use his pulpit to speak!"

"How do you know? Were they asked?"

"Yes, they were asked. The whole city was in a reign of terror! The whole city was afraid to move. I've never seen anything like it since Franco's Spain. And who organized this reign of terror? The guys who own Caterpillar and the other industries in Peoria. They're the guys who are trying to beat the brains out of labor! It was the complete fascist technique. I've seen it used in other parts of the world. As far as Peoria is concerned, fascism has moved in there.

"The communists weren't in the streets. The police were out to protect the guys who own Caterpillar, the guys who own the industry and the wealth. There were threats against the laboring men and Negroes. If anything is going to take over America, it is the fascists!"

"Mr. Robeson," I said, "there's one question that must be asked. It's the sixty-four dollar question: Are you a communist?"

"I'll answer that," Robeson said. "I'm not afraid to answer it. But first you've got to see the thing against the big background. I project it against the background of the last war. There was danger of fascism then. We were fighting the fascists like Hitler and Mussolini. Russians were dying by the millions so that British and American soldiers wouldn't have to die. We got along with the communists then and we were thankful for them. Yeah, and we were thankful for the communists in France, who were fighting and dying in the underground movement against Hitler. And we were thankful for Tito of Yugoslavia, too.

"I label myself anti-fascist. I divide the world into only two groups— fascists and anti-fascists. The communists belong to the anti-fascist group. They're the only ones who have any claim to belong to this group in America. Now, when I say I am an anti-fascist, it could mean that I belong to any one of the anti-fascist groups.

"So far as I know," Robeson continued, "the communist party is a legal party like the Republican or Democratic party. The communists control a lot of the world today, and we have to get along with them. Either that or fight a war nobody could win. We've just got to get along with them."

"Mr. Robeson," I said, grinning at him, "this question may get us into casuistry, but will you *tell* me why you *won't tell me* directly whether or not you're a communist?"

Returning a grin, he said: "That's as far as you'll get in any definition from me. I've seen all too often what happens when someone labels you this or that—"

The phone rang. He answered it.

When he beamed his attention back to me, I said: "Mr. Robeson, I can understand in part how you feel. There's plenty that's damned wrong, and even I get sore about it. But after all, you, a Negro, have been able to climb high in the United States. You've made money and you've achieved fame. You're a Negro, and yet you'be been able to do this here."

"Sure," he said, "but it's not important to me. It's not important that I am staying in this hotel. My success isn't important to me. My responsibility is greater than anything like that. Because of my success I'm in a position to do something about conditions, and I'll do all I can about them.

"I'm much more dangerous than other Negroes. Why? Because I'm educated. You tell us to get educated, and then you stop us on every hand. Why, I can't walk into a restaurant in Chicago! My dad was a slave and I have some cousins who are sharecroppers in Carolina, living off the soil. I feel for people like that. I'm interested not in myself but in the great mass of Negro people.

"Hell, why should I choose to live in America at all unless I were interested in doing something about it? Unless I were interested in the Negro people? I could make my living in any part of the world. It's absurd that anyone thinks he can pressure me into silence by cancelling a few concerts of mine. Why, I could play *Othello* in London next week, if I wanted to, and I could live for five years in the Scandinavian countries, just singing, and make a damned good living without even moving."

Closing my notebook, I said: "Well, I've taken up enough of your time. Thank you. I'd better get along." Robeson stood up as I arose.

"But," I said, "there's something I've been wondering about for a long time. Something I read about you in Alexander Woollcott's book *While Rome Burns*. Remember?"

"Sure," he chuckled, "I remember."

I said: "It was about your wife. Woollcott said she was of mixed Negro and Jewish blood. Jerome Kern had just composed *Old Man River* and had gone to your apartment in Harlem to show it to you. Then he wanted you to go downtown with him to sing it for Oscar Hammerstein, who had written the words. According to Woollcott, you turned to your wife to ask for two dollars for cab fare back home, but she gave you only one buck. You said: 'Aw, go on! Be all nigger and give me two!'"

"That's right!" he roared. "Aleck got it right! That's what I said!"

His huge body shook with laughter as we parted.

Joe Morgan, my new boss, and I had become increasingly unhappy with one another. When I won the Page One Award in 1946, Joe didn't mention it or congratulate me. Here is a letter I wrote to Boyd Lewis, my former boss.

TUESDAY, MAY 6, 1947   ■   Dear Boyd:

Jess Bogue hunched over my desk and said: "Joe wants to see you in the front office, Eddie."

I thought of Amy Lowell: *I stood upright too. / Held rigid to the pattern . . .*

Because I tried to break a pattern, last Saturday I walked a patterned path to a door leading to a patterned decision.

"Eddie," said Joe, "you're a square peg in a round hole."

Oh, he said I'm a nice guy, enterprising, polite, hard-working, pleasant, imaginative. But slivers stick out when I'm forced into a round hole. And, of course, Joe was right.

I could have fitted into the pattern. I could have become a hack. I could have written the style Joe likes: "An atomic scientist said today that—. . . A plumber said today that—. . . A wig-maker said today that—"

But I was trying to slice through a vicious circle: You can't write a sparkling feature story unless you're given a free rein, and you're not given free rein unless you write a sparkling feature story. No reporter can be better than his editor will let him be.

The past several months here I was being nailed into a coffin of conformity. I don't want to become a hack, will not become a hack! After Joe fired me I reread some feature stories I wrote for you. Some other guy must have written them. They had the bread of facts salted with the tang of imagination.

A reporter must never ignore facts. True. But I believe it is okay for him to find in facts a meaning beyond the obvious one. You and I used to discuss "the judicious juxtaposition of seemingly irrelevant details." Take fact (A) and team it up with fact (M) and you create an effect far more fascinating than yoking fact (A) to fact (B).

This is a race between a hole in the head and a hole in the wall of conformity; I've been butting against it again and again. So now I've been fired. So now I need a job.

Sincerely,
Eddie

Boyd Lewis helped me get an interview for work on the New York World-Telegram.

CHAPTER 9

NEW YORK CITY, THURSDAY, MAY 22, 1947 ■ Today I arrived by train in New York City, which I'd never seen before, walked through the grandeur of Grand Central Terminal, stepped outside, got my first look at the city and instantly fell in love with it. Silently, inside myself, I yelled: *I should have been born here!*

At the *World-Telegram* building I was interviewed by Lee Wood, executive editor, and B. O. McAnney, city editor. They hired me, told me to go back to Chicago to wind up my affairs there, then report for work here on June 2. I walked up Barclay Street toward Broadway and near City Hall saw something that astonished me: Crossing Broadway at Chambers Street was a horse-drawn wagon full of manure.

MONDAY, JUNE 2, 1947 ■ Today I began working for the *New York World-Telegram*. It occupies a ten-story building on the west side of lower Manhattan at 125 Barclay St., corner of West St. The *World-Telegram* is an afternoon paper with a circulation of about 400,000 and is known as the flagship of all the Scripps-Howard newspapers. Its editor and president, Roy W. Howard, does not have his office in this downtown building, but in mid-Manhattan at 230 Park Ave. I'm told that from time to time he drops down here to keep an eye on his pet property.

The city room is enormous. On the third floor of the building, it stretches almost the width of the block between Barclay St. and Park Place, its western windows on a level with the tops of the piers along the Hudson River. The editorial staff consists of 125 men and women who work a five-day forty-hour week. Experienced reporters, such as myself, are paid a minimum of $110 per week. Monday through Friday the paper prints six editions—fewer on Saturday. The paper costs five cents.

In all of New York City there is just one person I knew before arriving here. He is Edward Tatum Wallace, my friendly rival in Oklahoma City, and he is one of the best feature writers in the world, much better than myself. He has a quiet, pastoral, understated style unlike anything I've ever seen. When I asked Ed how much freedom is given feature writers here, he said that if a story is accurate and not obscene, almost anything goes. The *World-Telegram* specializes in light, human-interest stories. In fact, the *Saturday Evening Post* calls it "the city's most ebullient newspaper."

I'll work from 9 A.M. to 5 P.M., with one hour for lunch. Reporters write on so-called books, made by copyboys. These consist of one top copy and three duplicate copies. So far I like the reporters I've met here.

SUNDAY, JUNE 29, 1947 ■ This sunny afternoon in Central Park I caught a runaway horse. In my home town I lived two blocks from the country, but this sort of thing did not happen to me there. Fate has screwed up my chronology.

MONDAY, JUNE 30, 1947 ■ A New Yorker is a person who runs *up* an *up*-escalator.

MONDAY, JULY 7, 1947 ■ Times Square is a parrot pretending to be a peacock.

WEDNESDAY, JULY 9, 1947 ■ The Manhattan skyline, seen from Queens, looks like blocks with which children play . . . the skyscrapers are not clumped into just one site, as I had anticipated, but in two piles—mid-Manhattan and downtown Manhattan . . . it is at these sites that the thick bedrock rises close enough to the surface to shoulder the enormous weight of the buildings . . . I am surprised by the politeness of New Yorkers . . . Whenever I ask a passer-by for directions, I always get help, and some people even walk a block or two out of their way to point me in the correct direction . . . the woman artist on a canvas chair in Greenwich Village has *the Answer:* The trouble with the world is that geniuses won't get together!" . . . near City Hall there is a statue of Benjamin Franklin, and beneath it is a demented evangelist who chalks two parallel lines on the sidewalk, writes the name *River Jordan* between them, then steps in and crouches down to show how Jesus was baptized . . . during a rain storm a shoeless bewhiskered drunk stands in the entrance of a clothing store and mutters the manual of arms to himself . . . a man in a cafeteria eating nothing but horse radish . . . NYC's transportation system is much better than the one in Chicago . . . in mid-Manhattan a huge blind musician, called Moondog, wears a brown monk-like robe and stands motionless hour after hour . . . I thought Grant's Tomb was at the Battery, but instead it is far up Riverside Drive . . . I've bought the 700-page WPA *Guide to New*

York City, compiled by the Federal Writers' Project, to learn as much about this city as fast as I can . . . I've never seen a building as skinny as the front of the Flatiron Building . . . the secondhand book stores on Fourth Avenue are my El Dorado . . . on nights and weekends Wall Street is so empty that my shoes churn up echoes . . . in City Hall park the pigeons are so numerous they almost knock down pedestrians when they wheel into the air . . . in this Metropolis there are remote corners where people hunt ducks in autumn . . . New Yorkers pronounce Canada as *Cana-der* . . . and law as *lore* . . . however, we Midwesterners put an "r" in the middle of the word Washington . . . introduced to a woman, said I was pleased to meet her and she said "Likewise" and at first I thought she was being a smart aleck . . . work is so specialized here that one man makes a living just making G-strings for strip-tease girls . . . standing in Times Square and staring up Broadway is like peering into a kaleidoscope . . . the ebb and flow of pedestrians create an infinity of patterns . . . the only constant is change, and here in New York City everything changes faster than anywhere else on earth . . .

WEDNESDAY, AUGUST 6, 1947   ■   Murray Davis sits at the desk behind me. He is 46 years old, a huge and friendly man, on the staff here since 1933. For a few years he covered City Hall when Fiorello H. La Guardia was mayor and the two of them had a man-to-man love-hate relationship. Murray told me some anecdotes about La Guardia's volatile temperament.

At one press conference La Guardia screamed at Murray: "I'll tell Roy Howard on you!"

Murray barked: "And I'll tell my mamma on you!"

LaGuardia shrieked: "Get the hell out of here!" End of press conference.

At the opening of the airport called La Guardia Field, the mayor prowled around as though looking for something, trailed by puzzled reporters and photographers. At last he found a shallow hole in the ground. La Guardia is five feet two inches tall, Murray is six feet three. Pointing at the hole, the mayor said: "You stand in there, Murray!" Amused, Murray did so, letting LaGuardia cut him down to size as photographers took pictures of them.

A couple of years later, with the approach of Groundhog Day, a parks department worker put a live groundhog in a hole in the park in front of City Hall. Boy Scouts were to watch what the animal did. They did not know that the city worker had arranged to give the groundhog an electric shock to make sure he came out—but Murray knew.

Pretending to be a horrified businessman, he telephoned the American Society for the Prevention of Cruelty to Animals and protested the cruelty of giving a shock to a harmless beast. Just as the ceremony began, an ASPCA agent arrived, displayed his badge, disrupted the affair, while Murray and other reporters roared with laughter. When La Guardia learned of Murray's trick he sputtered in anger, but the next day admitted it was funny.

Much later, when Murray was taken off the City Hall beat, La Guardia phoned Lee Wood, the executive editor of the *World-Telegram*, to ask that Murray be kept there.

MONDAY, DECEMBER 29, 1947   ■   I have been asked to write a series of articles about New York State's mental health system. This is a monumental job because there are 94,000 patients in the state's 24 mental institutions. I began by visiting Creedmore State Hospital in Queens Village in Queens.

Its director is an affable psychiatrist who opened all doors to let me see whatever there was to be seen. In some locked wards I was surrounded by men certified as insane. At noon the doctor and a couple of staff members took me to lunch.

"Mr. Ellis," said the head doctor, with a smile, "you didn't seem to be afraid of our patients."

I said: "No. Mentally ill people don't frighten me. They do arouse my curiosity and, come to think of it, do you have any 'Napoleons' here?"

"No," the doctor replied, "but we do have a couple of men who believe they are God."

"Will you please let me talk to them?"

"Sure . . . Tell you what: You can sit at my desk in my office and I'll have them brought to you, one after another."

Lunch finished, we walked to his office and I sat down at his desk and he left. A knock on the door and an attendant ushered in the first patient. Shaking hands with him, I invited him to sit down. I looked into the eyes of a certified madman but detected nothing unusual. Then I asked whether it was true, as I had heard, that he was God. Oh, yes, he assured me in a quiet voice. I said I was glad to hear this because perhaps he could explain the solar system for me. He launched into a crazyquilt of words about stars and planets and galaxies, all too bizarre for me to be able to remember. Thanking him, I rang for the attendant, who led him out.

Then the second patient came in. He was huge and had the face of a hungry hawk. A long time ago he was found kneeling on a sidewalk, praying and proclaiming himself the Son of God.

"How are you feeling?"

"Fine!" he rumbled in a basso profundo voice. "Fine, and I'm glad you asked me because twenty years from now I'll be different because I'm the Son of God and twenty years from now I'll be God and do you want to hear God speaking through me just listen!"

His face froze as he focused on something inside himself . . . Silence . . . Then his voice exploded like a bomb.

This is God!

His eyes pinned me against the back of my chair.

"This is the Lord Jehovah and I'm speakin' through my Son and I want-cha all to know you better be good to Him else there'll be scabs on you and I can do anything and you should know this is God because it *is* God so watch the environment 'cause angles are that way!"

I said softly: "A few minutes ago I had another gentleman in here and he said he was God."

The big man thundered: "Naaaaaww! He's a phoney!"

Afterwards I thanked the director and later in the afternoon visited a women's ward. An old woman shuffled up to me and said; "You look nice." Her face was like a crumpled dishrag. Her eyes and her voice did not match. Her eyes were as gray and soft as pussywillows but her voice screeched like a nail pulled down a windowpane.

"Thank you," I said. "You look pretty in that red dress. Are you feeling all right?"

"Heee, heee, heee! . . . Yes, I'm fine, I am!"

The wrinkles tightened on her face. "I want to get out of here!" she shrieked. "Let me get out of here! I don't like it here!"

"Do you know where you are?"

She looked past me, looked through the walls, looked over the horizon into infinity. And just stood there.

"Do you know where you are?"

Her hands fluttered up and trembled in the air.

"Know . . . know where . . ." She turned to a patient in a chair near her. "Where am I?" she asked plaintively.

The other woman glared at her with crossed eyes. She was a tub of flesh, her gray hair hanging down in ragged bangs. Wobbling her chins, she bellowed:

"Creedmore State Hospital!"

My new little friend seemed not to hear. She smiled to herself as at some cosmic joke. The fat woman looked away in disgust, then looked back.

"Queens Village! New York City!"

"Oh!"

The pussywillow woman quavered: "Creed—Creedmore State Hospital . . . Queens . . . Ah! . . . New York City."

Then came belated understanding.

"State hosp—! Oh, no! I want to get out! Let me out, please! Let me out! Let—"

A female attendant gently took an elbow of the little old lady with the pussywillow eyes who suddenly remembered she was in an insane asylum, led her into another room and the door closed behind her and the lock went *click*.

1948

THURSDAY, JULY 1, 1948   ■   Today the subway fare was increased from five to ten cents. This was the first time the fare has been raised since the subway system began operating in 1904.

TUESDAY, OCTOBER 12, 1948   ■   This afternoon I saw General Dwight D. Eisenhower inaugurated as president of Columbia University.

The ceremony was scheduled to begin at 2 P.M. on the campus at Broadway and 116th Street, but I arrived early. Some 20,000 spectators were assembling on the south court, sitting in wooden chairs. Not since Nicholas Murray Butler became president in 1902 had there been such a gathering of notables at Columbia. A total of 223 college presidents attended, probably the most impressive collection of educators in the history of this nation, even surpassing the celebration of Harvard's 300th anniversary a few years ago.

Also present were Admirals Stark, Halsey and Leahy; Generals Doolittle, Spaatz, Bradley and Vanderberg; Secretary of Air Symington. I also saw Bernard Baruch, Robert Hutchins and Harold Stassen, along with hundreds of faces vaguely familiar to me from having seen them in the pages of newspapers and magazines. If a bomb had been dropped on the campus it would have destroyed most of America's elite class.

And Mrs. Mamie Eisenhower. She wore a mink stole, pearl earrings, pearl necklace, electric blue hat with a black veil, a black coat with velvet blue trimmings. To her right sat their son, Captain John Eisenhower, clad in a long green coat with brass buttons, his wife at his side. Near them sat brother Arthur Eisenhower from Kansas City and brother Earl from Charleroi, Pennsylvania. Arthur told me that their other two brothers, Milton and Edgar, would march in the processional. Arthur joked that Earl, beside him, was the black sheep of the family, and he almost looked the part because his left eye had been marred and his face was beefy red.

The ceremony began with the ringing of bells in St. Paul's Episcopal Chapel. I had a front-row seat in the press section and, turning around, I saw Ike following a mace-bearer up an aisle, past his wife, on up to a position on a platform in front of the statue of Alma Mater on the steps leading to the Low Memorial Library. Looking back at Mamie, I noted that her mouth was twitching and tears stood in her blue eyes.

Ike sat down on a chair on the platform, then arose to participate in singing *The Star-Spangled Banner.* Only then did he see his wife. His eyes moistened and his lips lifted into a limp grin. He looked very emotional.

The sky was overcast until he was handed five huge silver keys symbolizing his presidency, and at that very moment the sun burst through a cloud to engolden the scene. I had read about this sort of thing happening to other people in history so now, seeing it actually happen, I almost gasped. Then, so absurd is life, Ike had to sniff his way through his speech because he had a bad cold. Once he had to stop to blow his nose in front of 20,000 people.

In this era of mindless Red-hunting, I was gratified to hear Eisenhower say that "the facts of communism . . . shall be taught here—its ideological development, its political methods, its economic effects, its probable course in the future. The truth about communism is, today, an indispensable requirement if the true values of our democratic system are to be properly assessed . . ."

When the ceremony ended I walked the few steps to Mrs. Eisenhower and offered congratulations and she smiled and thanked me. Arthur and Earl were pounding one another on their backs, apparently as proud as though they had sired the universe. A Columbia professor in cap and gown fingered a copy of the poetry of William Blake. A male student climbed into the lap of Alma Mater, sculpted by Daniel Chester French, to have his picture taken. I wondered whether he knew that deep within her robes on her left side is a small stone owl.

Suddenly I saw a somewhat familiar figure jigging up the steps near me. He was old, his hair white, his face seamed. I said to myself: By God, that's John Dewey! Turning to another cap-and-gowned professor, I asked, and he said, yes, John Dewey. I thought: The great educator and philosopher!! He stopped near the economics building and I approached him, identifying myself as a reporter and asking whether in his long career at Columbia he had witnessed any spectacle comparable in prestige and scope to this one. Chewing his gums (later I learned he'd just had his teeth and tonsils removed) he said that, no, this probably was the greatest gathering of brains in our history.

Thanking him, I walked south on the campus toward Butler Library and saw Ike emerge from it. He wore a blue business suit, was bareheaded, held a cigaret in the fingers of his left hand. His appearance triggered applause from the people lingering nearby. He grinned his trademark grin, waved, shook a few hands, began walking at a brisk pace. I followed him. A woman held out her hand and he smiled and shook it, and after he passed she walked on unsteadily, still holding her hand out in front of her. I watched her hero enter 60 Morningside Drive, the president's residence, a three-story red-brick building with a balcony overlooking grass and shrubbery.

When I got back to Broadway I again found John Dewey, this time trying to get a cab. With him was a woman I assumed was his wife. Traffic was thick. I walked over to the couple.

"Let me get you a cab," I said to her.

She said: "Why, that's very kind of you." Turning to her husband, she said; "This gentleman is going to help us."

Looking up through his tangle of white hair, Dewey said: "Ah, yes, I know him. He's the young gentleman who spoke to me earlier this afternoon."

I said: "I didn't expect you to remember me."

Rubbing his face, bouncing up and down on his old rubbery legs, he cried: "Never forget a face! . . . Never forget a face!"

While keeping my eyes open for an empty cab, I said to her: "I'm a great admirer of Professor Dewey."

"Well, that's nice," she said."Why don't you come up to our place and we can all have a drink.

Then she grabbed her husband's arm as he teetered dangerously near the curb.

"John! . . . John! . . . This young man says he is an ardent admirer of yours, so we're going to have him come up for a drink."

She spoke slowly because the old boy is hard of hearing. Glancing up, he nodded agreement.

I saw a cab and let out a piercing whistle. It stopped. Dewey bounced off the curb into the street, frightening me, so I took his arm and helped him into the taxi, then helped his wife. I stood on the pavement and asked: "Are you really sure you meant it? I don't wish to intrude."

"I never say what I don't mean," she said firmly. "C'mon and get in."

I got in. The cabbie asked where to. America's greatest living philosopher tried to tell him, but his wounded mouth made his words mushy. Mrs. Dewey said: "Fifth Avenue at 97th Street." As the taxi pulled away, she patted her husband's hair over his right ear.

"The other way, my dear," he said, smiling like a pixie.

"Dear me, yes!" she cried. "I've known Mr. Dewey since I was five years old, and I've smoothed out his hair thousands of times. You'd think I'd know which way it goes."

She put her hand on his knee while he pulled thoughtfully at his moustache. Then she said she is his second wife and formerly was his secretary.

In the back of my mind I heard the name William James. He was a great thinker, a psychologist and philosopher, taught at Harvard, believed in pragmatism—namely, that truth is tested by its practical consequences.

"Professor Dewey," I said, "you knew William James, didn't you?"

"Oh, yes," said the old man. "Remarkable man, Bill!"

Bill? My God, I was with a man who knew the celebrated William James so well that he calls him *Bill!* Time seemed telescoped.

The cab drew up in front of 1158 Fifth Avenue. I watched the gentle manner in which the philosopher was greeted by the doorman and elevator operator. A note had been stuck on the door of the Dewey apartment. Neither could read it without getting out their glasses, so I read it aloud. It was scrawled by their six-year-old adopted son, informing them that he had gone to a movie with someone and would be back at thus and such a time.

Amused, the professor grunted: "Wonder who he dictated this to? Can't read yet, you know."

We walked inside, landing smack-dab in a domestic crisis. Their male Chinese cook had quit because the Irish washerwoman had dirtied his kitchen. Mrs. Dewey hustled to a phone and talked the cook into returning, while the professor disappeared into a room. The apartment was big and filled with books.

For a few minutes I sat alone in the living room, which is decorated in a Chinese motif, reminding me that Dewey once taught in China. Two large Chinese scrolls hung on walls, two wooden chairs were carved in Oriental style, and small Chinese statues stood here and there in the room.

When the professor appeared he wore a hearing aid in his left ear, its microphone dangling into the pocket of his jacket. Then Mrs. Dewey appeared, carrying a tray with a bottle of rum and three huge glasses. She poured drinks big enough to drown Paul Bunyan.

"I'll go out in the kitchen and get a puddler," she said.

"Be sure to get a puddler," he said, not having heard her.

While she was gone I told the professor that I plan to write a study of suicide, then asked whether he thought there is need for such a book. Yes, he thought so.

Mrs. Dewey returned with the puddlers, stirred his drink, handed it to him. Through a western window overlooking Central Park I saw an orange sun extinguish itself. The professor slurped his drink. His wife grabbed a paper napkin and blotted his lips.

"His tonsils," she said apologetically, "and then his teeth, you know."

Dewey slurped again. She wiped the lapel of his jacket.

Leaning forward, I said: "Sir, I'd like to ask you a question. It may be a silly question, but I know from experience that this kind of question sometimes elicits interesting reactions."

Professor Dewey fixed his weak eyes on me.

"Do you consider yourself the greatest living American philosopher?"

He didn't hear me. I repeated the question. When he understood, he leaned back and laughed pianissimo, then turned to his wife.

"Did you hear that? Am I the greatest American philosopher? I don't believe in grading things. How could I possibly answer that? What I always say is that I'm so egotistical I can afford to be modest."

I remembered something I'd read about Thomas Mann, whom I interviewed in Chicago. When the German novelist and Nobel Laureate visited Hollywood, a scenario writer almost licked his shoes in adulation, whereupon Mann said to him: "You're not big enough to be able to make yourself so small."

TUESDAY, OCTOBER 26, 1948 ■ Today the *World-Telegram* began publishing one full page of news about civil service employees. New York City itself has 160,000 workers on its payrolls; there also are thousands of state and federal employees here, too. This is the audience we seek. I have been assigned to write one feature a day about these people. Walt MacDonald, the editor of the new page, laughingly said my job is to make dull people sound interesting. His remark made me feel apprehensive, but I'll have the freedom to choose my own subjects.

1949

FRIDAY, JANUARY 21, 1949 ■ By subway, bus, cab and ferry I reached Riker's Island in the East River north of La Guardia Airport. In 1664 the island was bought by Abraham Rycken, and it remained in his family until the city bought it in 1884. Now it is the site of the city penitentiary.

The warden, Milton Klein, showed me around the $12 million facility with its 2,198 prisoners and 344 city employees. In one wing of a building I saw more than 100 homosexuals segregated from the other inmates.

I decided to write about the mail-room clerks who censor the 1,000 daily outgoing letters and 500 incoming letters. One of their problems is love letters written by homosexual prisoners to their lovers on the outside. A larger problem is mail from heterosexual sex-starved inmates who write to women describing in clinical detail what they want to do with them after they get out of the penitentiary.

THURSDAY, JANUARY 27, 1949 ■ Today I interviewed a blacksmith. Here in Manhattan, imagine. He is Patty Scannell, 48, from County Cork, Ireland, and he nails iron shoes on horses of the mounted patrol of the police department. A jolly fellow, he works in the armory at Madison Ave. and 94th St.

At noon he walked me to an Irish bar on Madison at 97th St. A close friend of the owner, he went into the kitchen to cook hamburgers for us. In a corner of the bar I found a green stovepipe hat, the kind worn in the parade on St. Patrick's Day, and just for the hell of it stuck it on my head, to Patty's boisterous approval.

Some people say I'm an intellectual snob, and I confess I have trouble communicating with ignorant people—but who doesn't? However, lack of a formal education is one thing, while native intelligence is a horseshoer of a different color. You can imagine, then, the pride I felt when Patty asked:

"Work on Saturday? . . . No? . . . Well, then, why don't you come around next Saturday? We might have a drink together."

WEDNESDAY, MARCH 23, 1949 ■ Once upon a time there was a man who was in love with a bridge. The time is now, the man is Fred Bronnenkant, and the bridge is the Brooklyn Bridge.

He waits on her hand and foot, for Fred is a bridgeman and riveter employed by New York City. She is a queen—perhaps the most photographed, most painted, most sketched, most etched, most written-about, most movie-filmed bridge in the world.

Fred, now 74 years old, has been in love with the Brooklyn Bridge ever since he was assigned to her 30 years ago. It's not that he's in love with bridges—any old bridge. Not at all. Fred drove rivets into the Williamsburg Bridge, further up the East River, and he bossed a steel gang on the Queensborough Bridge, still further north.

As he and I stood beneath the Brooklyn end, he gazed up at the gray

Gothic pylon and mused aloud: "Never has been a bridge like this one, never will be."

A tall sturdy man, he stropped his hands against his overalls as he spoke. A shadow of embarrassment filled his deep-set blue eyes, embarrassment such as many men feel when talking about the women they love, for Fred regards the Brooklyn Bridge as his woman, his mistress.

At home he has a wife who knows all about this love affair because the bridge is all he ever talks about. She's jealous, too. From time to time she will wail: "You think more of that bridge than you do of me!"

A man who quit school after the sixth grade, Fred paws for words as he tries to explain the great passion of his life. "I guess," he mumbles, looking down at his shoes, "I guess I just love this here bridge more than any man ever has."

He tends her lovingly. With the help of seven other bridgemen and riveters, Fred sees to it that she is properly maintained. Rusty rivets to be gouged out. New steel spangles to be studded along the hem of her skirt. Corroded roadway beams, like the stays in a corset, to be replaced.

Fred goes to bed about seven every evening so that he may be at his best when he greets her the following morning. By 4:30 A.M. he is up and dressed, while his wife still sleeps. By 6 A.M. he is at the side of his mistress.

This is two hours earlier than the hour in which his work is supposed to begin, but this gives him time to be alone with his darling before she consorts with the thousands attracted to her every day. He likes to view her from many angles, as another man might ogle the curves of a bathing beauty.

Squatting on the riverfront, Fred stares up at her majestic height, then down to the river to see her reflection shattered by sequined waves, looks again at the proud up-thrusting of her twin towers and finds, as usual, his heart caught in the web of her cables.

Although he is entitled to three-week vacations, he never has been able to stay away from his beloved for more than one week. After he has prowled restlessly around the house six or seven days, his wife is glad to send him back to his mistress.

Years ago other men who worked on the bridge made fun of Fred Bronnenkant and his lovelorn ways, but now they take it for granted. The gossip has worn thin. Time has sanctified the scandal. To the others a bridge is a bridge is a bridge. To Fred, the Brooklyn Bridge has a personality.

"Why, she's alive!" he'll exclaim, forgetting to be embarrassed. "She has more life in her than anybody."

He looks lovingly along the arch of her roadbed.

"The way she snakes up and down when traffic passes over her! The give to her! And in winter she contracts like—" He pauses. Pulling a toothpick from the band of his hat, he stabs the air trying to pinpoint his meaning.

"It's like—well, in the winter she contracts like a woman sort of shrugging into her fur. Know what I mean? Then, in the summer—"

His eyes roam his upper eyelids. Finding the proper phrase, he lowers his gaze. "You might say, well, like in the summer she expands and it's like a beautiful girl throwing her clothes open to the sun and air."

Aware of her own charm, in winter she can become churlish—even dangerous. When ice spangles her figure she is a menace to people below, for a single icicle can kill. Whenever she is in this mood, Fred picks up a club, winds its thong around his right wrist and climbs high into her glistening tresses of cables. Hanging by one hand, high above the river, he beats the frigidity out of her. After all, did not Slavic fathers give their new sons-in-law leather whips with which to tame their brides?

At present the Brooklyn Bridge is having her face lifted—a modernization program to rip out the streetcar and elevated tracks and expand her traffic lanes from two to six.

Fred mutters: "She doesn't look like the same old girl."

All things changeth, so Fred knows he must retire. Other workmen ask what's he gonna do when he's gotta leave.

"I'll take her with me!" he cries.

He's spoken to his wife about this matter. "When I die, there's just one thing: I want my hearse to drive across the bridge. The last time. You'll see to this, won't you? Please?"

FRIDAY, OCTOBER 14, 1949 ■ I rode the subway to Harlem and then walked to the Harlem Welfare Center at 2 West 140th St. There I interviewed Romare Bearden, an artist who supports himself by working as a case-worker. Although he says he is black, his complexion is so light he could pass as a white person if he wanted to. He doesn't want to do so.

Heavy-set, with a round face, balding at the age of 36, he is a man who smiles a lot. He is obviously intelligent, very articulate, and has a charming personality. I liked him the moment I met him.

He was born in Charlotte, N.C., the only child of Richard and Bessye Johnson Bearden. When he was small his parents moved here. His artistic talent comes from the paternal side of his family, for his father plays the piano and is related to the Negro artist Charles Alston. His mother is a newspaper woman and political activist.

Romare played professional baseball, majored in mathematics at New York University, was art editor of the campus humor magazine. He graduated in 1935, in the depth of the Depression, and when he was unable to get a job as a mathematician, enrolled in the Art Students League. In 1938 he was hired by the city department of social services and kept on painting. In 1940 he held his first one-man show. It's a pity that such a talented man has to work a nine-to-five job.

Romare and I became friends. I visited him in his studio at 243 West 125th St., in the heart of Harlem, and he visited my apartment. I missed him when he left in 1950 to study philosophy at the Sorbonne in Paris, welcomed him when he returned. He introduced me to many bright and talented black people, with whom I also became friendly. Romare was a raconteur whose amusing anecdotes often had me on the floor laughing. My diary contains page after page of the funny stories he told me. In 1954 he married a dancer, Nanette Rohan, and after he died in 1988 she came to my home to tape-record me as I read aloud from my diary some of his most colorful anecdotes. By the time of his death Romare had become famous, and his reputation continued to grow, with new books being written about him, and his name appearing in encyclopedias.

MONDAY, NOVEMBER 21, 1949   ■   Today I climbed up inside the Statue of Liberty to get a story about the man who changes the light bulbs in the torch. The arm and torch have been closed to the public since 1917, during the World War, but the man let me climb to the very top with him. Each light bulb is about twice as large as a basketball. Inside the torch I saw a dead bird. Attracted by the light, it had flown toward the torch and crashed through a glass plate.

THURSDAY, DECEMBER 29, 1949   ■   I had been invited to a Christmas party given by Selma Fried and Janice Griffiths in their Greenwich Village apartment at 137 West 13th St., but I almost did not attend. A cold had settled in my neck and shoulders and, besides, I felt in a melancholy mood due to the dreary drip drip drip of days. Early in the evening I sat in the dark on a bench in Washington Square, feeling sorry for myself, but at last I forced my feet to take me to the party at about nine o'clock. The apartment was filled with well-dressed women and men.

Selma introduced me to one woman: "Eddie, this is Ruth Kraus. She works at the *Herald Tribune* . . . Ruthie, this is Eddie Ellis. He's a reporter with the *World-Telegram.*"

We shook hands, she had a firm grip, and I asked her to sit down on a nearby sofa. I thought she also was a reporter, but she said she is private secretary to the executive vice-president of the *Herald Tribune.* Sweet smile. Hazel eyes behind glasses. About five three, with brown hair, good figure, beautiful hands, immaculate nails. Natural, at ease with herself, articulate, friendly. I rubbed my neck.

"What's the matter?" she asked.

"Oh, I've got a cold and it's settled in my neck and shoulders."

"Well," she said, and she smiled again, "I'm pretty good at massaging muscles. Let me try to give you some relief."

I turned my back so she could get at my neck, but she urged me to take off my jacket. I liked her informality. The jacket off, again I presented my back to her. and she placed both hands on my neck. Instant chemistry! She massaged my neck and eased my pain and I thanked her and I liked her.

One of the guests was an electrical engineer who works for Douglas Leigh, the man who has designed many of the spectacular signs in Times Square. He announced that at midnight a new vertical beacon would be switched on, and he invited us to accompany him to watch this happen. I turned to Ruth. She said yes. We went to Times Square and saw a new light illuminate the sky.

1950

FRIDAY, JANUARY 6, 1950 ▥ This evening I went by train to Ossining, New York, to watch an electrocution in the state prison named Sing Sing. There I was led into the office of the warden, William E. Snyder, who has presided over 56 executions. After we shook hands he sat down at his desk and opened and closed, opened and closed a book of paper matches.

"Off the record," I asked, "what's your attitude toward capital punishment?"

He replied; "Doesn't stop murder, does it? Did you know that only one per cent of all persons indicted for murder in the first degree are ever convicted? One per cent."

When he stopped talking I asked the location of the men's room and he said out in the hall, so I excused myself. When I got there I stared at my face in a mirror and didn't look like a man about to see another man die tonight—whatever the hell this means. But I did need to drink some water. My throat was dry. I walked back into the warden's office, where I met Maxwell Felson, 26, a reporter on the *Tarrytown Daily News.* The warden was in the middle of a sentence when in walked Clement J. Ferling, his administrative assistant, short, gray-haired, wearing a gray suit. Standing just inside the door he looked at his watch and then at a clock on the wall. The time was 10:54 P.M. "All right," the warden said softly. Ferling stepped out and then came back at the head of a group of 10 men. We were to be the 12 witnesses. The other reporter and I stood up and took places in an irregular line in front of the warden's desk. He arose and began speaking.

"Gentlemen, you have been invited here tonight . . ."

Short. Neat. Then we filed out of the office and picked up our coats. Mac was behind me.

"How do you feel?" I asked.

"I got butterflies in my belly," he replied.

Walking toward a stairway, I analyzed myself, then said: "I don't."

Down some stairs, through a door of bars. A guard in a blue uniform felt my coat as it lay across my left arm, patted my sides and hips. He was chubby, polite, cool.

Then we stepped out into the night and from the nearby Hudson River a breeze stroked the backs of our necks. Two vans were waiting. Stooping, we stepped into them and sat down on benches along its sides. Two guards swung in behind us. The warden was in my van and he said a few words to the man beside him, but otherwise we moved in silence.

In two minutes we stopped at an open door with light pouring out. We climbed down to the ground. The guards led us through the door. This entrance to the death chamber was different from the one I'd used a couple of months ago when I first visited Sing Sing. That day I had sat in The Chair. Now I was seeing it a second time. Somehow, the lights seemed too bright. In Warner Brothers movies about gangsters walking to the chamber the corridor looked shadowy, mysterious. In reality, it is starkly lit.

Inside, on the right, were three benches. The first row was filled. I slipped into the second row and sat down by a Yonkers detective who started to whisper something to me. I ignored his words because the warden had told us not to talk in the execution chamber. Additionally, I wanted to imprint the scene in my mind. Before I could do so, the door to our right opened and in surged a group of men.

In the center of this blue blur I saw Frank Bruno, the condemned man. He was short, dark, lean. He had a hooked nose and his black eyes blazed brighter than the overhead lights. Not a hand was on him as he entered, which he did in a rush, striding halfway inside before being stopped. Gesturing with his left hand, he bent his head to say something to the guards clustered around The Chair. One of them gave a short reply. Bruno straightened up, stepped over to The Chair, sat down.

He wore a blue shirt open at the neck, black trousers split up the right leg, white wool socks and brown slippers. He did not look toward the witnesses. Instead, he watched the guards as they strapped him in, adjusted the metallic cap on his head. Bruno grinned on and off, like the flickering of heat lightning. His grin never left his living face. His left hand, on the arm of The Chair, did not quiver. Only when a guard tightened the strap over his right arm did the fingers of his right hand tremble.

Frank Bruno, one minute from eternity, sat and grinned. A long time ago the district attorney said he'd laughed and slapped his thigh as he confessed killing his gangster pal. Shot Zarcone through the back of the head! Sure, Zarcone was a rat, according to Bruno, a 32-year-old Brooklyn mobster who believed rats had to be bumped off.

His explanation then was different from the answer recorded on a form I'd seen in the warden's office. Asked why he murdered the man, Bruno answered: "Ignorance." Correct! Ignorance. He quit school after the seventh grade and drank a lot of booze and became a tough guy because life is tough. Frank Bruno met his match in life, and life met its match in Frank Bruno.

The day the judge sentenced him and asked whether he had any last words, Bruno said: "Judge, when you get to that part about '—and may God have mercy on your soul—' just skip it, will you?" Yet the padre was here tonight. Earlier the warden had said he gave the prison chaplains credit for steeling men to meet death bravely. Now the Catholic chaplain stood in front of me and I could tell, by the movement of his elbows, that he was saying the rosary.

The warden, hat in hand, leaned against a wall. This was his 57th execution. This was the 550th electrocution in the history of Sing Sing. A guard pulled a strap under Bruno's chin.

"It's too tight," he said, and that was the last thing he ever said.

A man left his seat and walked to a niche in the wall behind The Chair. Suddenly, so suddenly it took me by surprise, Bruno stiffened in The Chair. His back arched. His throat muscles froze into marble cords. His fingers snapped into tight fists. He had been hit by 2,000 volts of electricity.

Frank Bruno was a wiser man than I. He knew the last answer.

He sagged. The man at the panel turned down a rheostat. Bruno stiffened again, his body held in that position by the current flowing through him. A crackling sound zittered through the death chamber. Did this really sound like steak frying?

Now his body sagged again. His eyes and mouth were hidden behind black leather straps. Again he stiffened, and this time a plume of gray-blue smoke curled up from his right leg. I wondered whether I would vomit. The plume disappeared and then Bruno sagged for the last time.

Guards swarmed over him. One tore his shirt open, down to the navel. A broad white stripe crisscrossing his pink torso showed where a strap had been when the current was turned on. The prison doctor held a stethoscope to Bruno's chest.

Softly he said: "This man is dead."

"This way out," said a guard.

A shuffling of feet as we edged along the benches. Keeping my eyes on Bruno, I saw two guards remove the straps that had hidden his eyes and mouth. His eyes were open, windows revealing—nothing. His mouth was open, a strand of spittle connecting the lips. When the guards took off all the straps, Frank Bruno, non-mortal, slumped in The Chair, his head flopped onto his right shoulder. Two guards picked up all that was left of what once had been a curly-headed, little Italian boy, and dumped him onto a rolling table.

When I got outside I took a deep breath of air. The river breeze chilled me. I think it was the breeze. Shoes scuffed on gravel and then I heard the plunking of big behinds on the benches in the lorries. Otherwise, silence. And the lorries whirred away.

Now I feel guilty about watching a man die. Charles Dickens saw a man hanged in London and another guillotined in Paris, while the British diarist, Samuel Pepys, watched a hanging in London. These facts do not relieve my guilt. My father lived in Wisconsin, and when he learned that I had seen an execution he refused to write to me for a year. However, he continued to hunt deer.

MONDAY, APRIL 17, 1950 ■ At work today I drafted a memo to one of my editors:

Memo to Walt MacDonald
Editor Civil Service Page
Seems we have a chance to get a flock of civil service features with something of a new slant. Here's how:
An arm of the navy, called the Military Sea Transportation Service, transports federal civil service employees to jobs in foreign countries and U.S. occupied territories. A fleet of naval vessels plies between New York and Europe, carrying them and also military personnel.

These ships are not manned by sailors but by civil service workers. We've been invited to interview both passengers and crew members en route to Europe. Here's the way it would work:

Elmer (Al) Borsuk, public relations officer at the N.Y. Port of Embarkation, and his co-worker, Capt. Lawrence Phelan, suggested this to me one day—and at first I thought they were kidding. However, they meant it. They said they've studied our civil service page and believe they know what we want.

They want to put me on one of these ships and give me the run of the vessel. If I were to interview crew members and federal passengers, we'd get a lot of civil service features. What the press agents would get out of it is publicity for this huge operation.

Borsuk and his wife will sail from New York May 23 aboard the General Alexander M. Patch. He suggests that I go with him at that time so that he might help me. Afraid of supervision, or censorship, I made him promise to let me pick my subjects and write as I please. Every day one of my stories can be wirelessed from the ship back here. Borsuk vowed he wouldn't even ask to see my copy.

There'll be an army photographer aboard ship to take pictures of the people I interview.

As you know, I'm now about one week ahead on features. These would provide a cushion if there is some slip-up. Sailing time across the Atlantic one-way is nine days. Ports of call, from which photographs could be sent to you, are Southampton, England, and Bremerhaven, West Germany. Aboard ship my expenses will be $1.50 a day for food. In port I'll have to pay for my own meals.

I think this thing makes sense. It will do two things for our civil service page: 1) Provide us with refreshingly new stories about civil service workers; 2) demonstrate to our readers that we have enterprise.

—ellis 5:13 P.M.

Walt approved of this idea, as did our senior editors. I managed to fold my vacation into this trip and so did Ruthie, at the Herald Tribune. *We agreed to meet in Amsterdam; she had friends living there.*

Delighted to get a free trip to Europe, I nonetheless paid my way in hard work, sometimes laboring 12 hours a day. I interviewed crew members, one after another, two a day, but some men were too dull to merit a story so I'd have to hunt some more until I found an interesting personality.

On the New York-to-Germany run in 1950 there still was danger of hitting a mine sown at sea in World War II, so our ship had to be degaussed. This meant that the ship's engineer threw a switch and turned a rheostat to let electricity pulse into three copper coils encircling the vessel. This neutralized its magnetic field.

Just before we landed in Bremerhaven in the American Zone of Occupation, I was amused to discover I had been classified as a VIP—Very Important Person. At the dock I was met by an army colonel and a navy commander. As the captain drove me the 38 miles to Bremen, I looked in horror at the rubble that once had been German mansions and homes.

In Bremen I was welcomed to a luxurious German hotel that had been commandeered by the American military. There I was given a suite. I mean, I had six rooms: a living room 33 feet long, two baths, a balcony, two huge oil paintings, five full-length mirrors, four beds, a long bar stocked with brandy and whiskey, plus a few other opulent trappings. But—no soap. Literally. In Germany soap was so scarce that my elegant quarters lacked even one teensy-weensy bar of soap. But—what the hell! Now that I was living in baronial splendor, I was getting revenge upon the military that had heaped indignities upon me during the war.

The next day I left and had to pay my hotel bill—75 cents!

CHAPTER 10

EUROPE, JUNE, 1950 ▩ Europe! How can I possibly tell all that I did and saw in Bremerhaven, Bremen, Amsterdam, Paris, London and Hamburg? I grew a Van Dyck and wore a beret and most people mistook me for an Englishman. In Germany I had my hair cut by an obsequious German barber, and the moment his fingers touched my neck I stiffened. Churchill, I recalled, said the Germans are either at your knees or throat. I heard a true story about an American sailor who became friendly with a German girl. One night she got drunk and bragged about having tortured men. I'd have throttled her, then and there, but the sailor kept on dating her!

As I crossed the border from one country to another, I was surprised by the lax way customs men inspected baggage. I could have smuggled 100 pounds of drugs here and there. But that wasn't my problem. Since I am stupid about even simple arithmetic, I realized my problem was converting the deutschmark into the guilder and then the franc and then the pound sterling. Next time I go to Europe I'll take along a certified public accountant. This time, thank God, I had Ruthie to help me.

We had a glorious and somewhat bibulous reunion in Amsterdam. I recall riding with her, and a husband and wife, in an open horse-drawn carriage along a boulevard. Wine-soaked, instantly fond of the Dutch people, I stood up in the carriage and serenaded them at the top of my voice. Passersby smiled, laughed, applauded.

In the Dutch countryside I saw peasants wearing wooden shoes and I saw real windmills, but never did I see any windmill in motion. At little railway stations, ice cream men wear white ties and tails. The most polite and efficient waiter of my entire trip was the swallow-tailed Dutch waiter in my hotel in Amsterdam. He was much superior to any waiter I met in Paris.

I like the fact that the Dutch are fond of flowers. On the sleek, low, clean sight-seeing launches of Amsterdam a vase of flowers was fixed onto the dashboard of the pilot. Other flowers bobbed from vases over the heads of the passengers. We visited Rembrandt's home, saw his studio, the press he used to make etchings. We also saw the museum hung with his most famous paintings, particularly *The Night Watch*. One thing that struck me in Amsterdam was that nearly every Dutch person spoke some English.

In Paris, on the other hand, we found few who know our language. But of course I don't know French currency. As we got out of a cab Ruthie laughed and asked whether I knew how much I tipped the driver. I said no. Said she: Seven cents.

Dutch police, I'd noted, wear swords, even riding bicycles, their scabbards dangling dangerously near the spokes of the rear wheel. The French gendarmes use white batons to direct traffic, looking romantic in their blue capes. I learned, however, that they weigh the bottoms of their capes with lead and during a riot they remove their capes to use them as weapons, slashing people with the heavy pleats.

At the palace of Versailles I saw the Hall of Mirrors, where the peace treaty of 1919 was signed. I also saw Marie Antoinette's so-called jewel box—actually, a cabinet seven feet long and six feet high. In the Louvre I gazed upon the Mona Lisa, the Winged Victory of Samothrace and Venus de Milo, but found many other works of art I liked even better.

On the Left Bank of the Seine we accidentally found the house in which Voltaire died; instantly I remembered reading about his death scene. A priest arrived to shrive the great skeptic. Voltaire looked up from his bed and asked: "Who sent you?"

The priest replied: "God."

Voltaire said: "Show me your credentials." And turned his face to the wall.

Ruthie knew an Englishwoman who worked on the Paris edition of the *Herald Tribune*. This lady, Muriel King, shared a country home with a Frenchwoman 60 miles northwest of Paris on the road to Dieppe, and we spent a weekend there. I watched the women use ropes to lower bottles of wine into the well to keep them cool. I've never really liked asparagus, but our French hostess soaked our servings in heaps of butter that converted it into a delicacy to me.

In London, though, I ate only one decent meal—and that was fried eggs for breakfast. In an English pub the pork pie was downright repulsive to me, and I couldn't even like their beer. The fact is that I found all British cuisine lacking in taste, although I confess I am no connoisseur of food.

What did thrill me in London was sitting in Samuel Johnson's favorite chair in Ye Olde Cheshire Cheese, and gazing at the crypts containing the corpses of Charles Dickens and Thomas Babington Macaulay. I found the

London subway, called the Underground, much more comfortable than our subway in New York; the seats are upholstered and smoking is permitted. I walked across Westminster Bridge to get a long view of the Houses of Parliament, later stood in a drizzle at the foot of the statue of Lord Nelson in Trafalgar Square, got caught in the rain and took shelter under Waterloo Bridge.

My European trip produced 32 feature stories for the World-Telegram. *The 28th piece seems to have been the best. It elicited praise from the news editor and was declared the best of the month among all the Scripps-Howard newspapers. This is what I wrote:*

AT SEA RETURNING FROM EUROPE—The master-at-arms is handsome, dignified, Russian-born. Handsome, don't forget. That's probably the key to this story.

He wears a blue uniform. On it are the U.S. Silver Star with a cross, the French Croix de Guerre with a palm, a medal of the Canadian Royal Mounted Police.

Michael Charitonowitz is 54. He has electric blue eyes and a moustache that angles down like the downward beat of the wings of a seagull. Muscular, standing very erect, his bearing fits his job on this ship. He is the police officer aboard the General R. E. Callan. In his cabin there are pictures of his wife.

He says she is a Russian princess. He claims he saw a picture of her as a child, posing with the late Czar Nicholas and the royal family. An aristocrat, she said she always gets what she wants, and she wanted him.

His first wife had died after 27 happy years together. Grieving, he slumped in his New York apartment, drinking bourbon. Born in Minsk, he says he loathes vodka made in the United States. To his landlady, also a Russian, he grumbled: "Why don't you find someone I can marry?" He emphasizes that he was drunk when he said this.

"Very well," replied his landlady.

A little later she invited him to a party in her apartment. There she introduced him to a Russian-born woman, the widow of an Italian-American restaurant owner. The guests played poker until 3 A.M. and then the Russian lady asked him: "Will you please take me home?" He took her home, leaving her at the door.

However, the next Sunday he took her to dinner, and after that, on more and more dates. She never let him forget that she was a princess, that she had escaped from the Revolution, that her blood was blue.

"So, Princess Xenia," he would jeer, "if you cut your finger what color would your blood be? Red. Like mine."

Before long, she asked his intentions. None, he told her. Sober, marriage was the last thing he wanted.

She pleaded loneliness. Male members of her late husband's family kept pestering her to marry one of them, but she wanted none of them. She wanted him—Michael Charitonowitz.

"You're a princess," he would say, "while I'm only a peasant."

"That's not true," she would argue. "Here we are Russians together. We have so much in common."

"In common? I'm only a sailor. You came to America with $100,000. Your husband left you rich."

Then he arose, saying: "Excuse me. I have to catch my ship."

On that voyage he got a letter from her when the British pilot came aboard at Dover. Everything's all arranged, she told him. When you get back we'll have our blood tests and get married.

Back in New York, he stalled for time. He argued that it would be easier for him to get his blood test aboard ship. On the next voyage, though, the ship's doctor lacked the necessary equipment. And at the army hospital in Bremerhaven, Germany, he learned that a blood test taken there would not be valid in New York.

The next time he returned to New York he tip-toed into his apartment. After stowing his things, he headed for the nearest bar. She was waiting at the door.

Again they talked it over.

"Why hurry?" he asked. "The world wasn't built in a day."

But she coaxed him. His own sister coaxed him. At last, he says, he thought: What the hell! What have I got to lose?

After the wedding they went to his mother's home. She met them at the door with the traditional Russian gifts of a loaf of bread, a candle and a cup of wine.

Now the princess and the peasant live at 31-28 Crescent Street, Astoria, Queens.

And aboard his ship, in the long hours of the night-watch, crew members sometimes talk about him.

"Hear he married a Russian princess. Wonder how he landed her?"

1951

THURSDAY, FEBRUARY 22, 1951   ▓   Today I became 40 years old. When people ask what I want, I reply: "To become a wise old man." I don't exactly know what I mean by this. I cram facts into my cranium, but am not at all wise.

WEDNESDAY, APRIL 11, 1951   ▓

As I ate breakfast I heard on the radio that President Truman has relieved General Douglas MacArthur of his command in the Korean theater of war. I believe he did the correct thing. It is obvious that MacArthur disobeyed his commander-in-chief. It is probable that MacArthur's frequent political statements might have triggered World War III.

United Press editors later called this the biggest news story of 1951. On February 20 MacArthur had ordered a counterattack by United Nations forces on a 60-mile front in Korea. On March 24 he said he was ready to meet the commander of the Chinese and North Koreans to discuss a truce, then warned the Chinese communists that their regime might fall if the U.N. let him lead an attack on China. On April 17 MacArthur landed in San Francisco after an absence of 14 years from the continental U.S. On April 20 his reception in New York City was seen by 7.5 million people.

FRIDAY, APRIL 20, 1951   ▓   General MacArthur was due at City Hall at noon, so I made sure I got there early, but ran into a wall of human flesh that kept me about 150 feet west of the building. From there I could see the lectern, brambled with microphones, on the front steps.

The sun shone. A breeze stirred the confetti thrown down from the windows of nearby skyscrapers. This paper snow storm evoked a mood of unreality within me, and I wondered why. Soon I understood: I had seen a vaudeville act in which a spotlight had blinked on and off, on and off. An actor crossing the stage is seen only now and then, now and then, half his movements being blotted out. This interruption of continuity creates a weird mood. And so it was today as I peered between the gaps between the tiny pieces of paper.

Despite this illusion and flags and other trappings common to an event such as this, I did not succumb to mob hysteria. All of us were waiting because the tickertape parade for MacArthur began at the Battery and moved slowly northward up the slight incline of Broadway to City Hall.

He rode in an open car and when it reached the back door of the building he got out, walked through, and emerged on the front steps.

There he was introduced by Mayor Vincent R. Impellitteri, who never once has been accused of being a great speaker. The way the mayor spoke reminded me of the way a boy blushes. His pauses were long, awkward and painful. Barely was he listened to by the crowd.

Now, a crowd or mob is a strange animal. It can wait endlessly if it is to be rewarded by a view of the hero, and during the wait a kind of collective consciousness is created. Individuality melts into commonality, differences blend into conformity, and as hearts begin to beat in unison the many become the one.

All await the supreme moment—the appearance of the hero. But when that happens he becomes clearly visible only to the privileged few who stand nearby, while those at a distance find hats and heads in their line of vision. Then the great man speaks.

General MacArthur said, "New York is the greatest city in the world!"

Hurray! Hurray, but—? Well, every New Yorker believes New York is the greatest city in the world, but it's great to have one's opinion seconded by the opinion of the hero. Now that MacArthur had voiced this idea, what else fell from his lips? Platitudes. Nothing else. Platitudes delivered in a slow and sonorous voice. Still, it is more important to the crowd to hear the hero's voice than to understand his meaning. So the great man was cheered.

Later, when the cheering stops, one feels cheated. One has waited and waited, tolerated elbows in the belly, smelled bad breath in the nostrils, and then this moment, anticipated as the supreme moment in one's life, one that will transport the listener to the apex of the American Dream—the moment somehow still feels ordinary. Anticipation: 2; realization: 1. The rapture leaks out of the biggest reception in the history of the biggest city in the nation.

WEDNESDAY, MAY 16, 1951 ■ Last night I dreamed Ruthie and I were caught in an atomic bomb attack on New York City. In one scene we were descending in an elevator, eager to get to ground level so we could run out of the building. In a second scene we picked our way to safety over the twisted girders of a blasted bridge. We seemed surrounded by a twilight haze.

SUNDAY, JUNE 10, 1951 ■ After dinner this evening I sat down and read from 7:30 o'clock until one in the morning. When I put down the book my mind seemed to take off from it, as though from a springboard, to dive into a pool of meditation. For another hour I sat in the chair and sipped some wine and felt totally peaceful.

There was nothing I desired, and to want nothing is to be happy. My mind had wings that sent me soaring over a wonderland of ideas, symbols and sensations. I seemed to exist in the very core of my being, a condition superior to a sexual orgasm, the light of the setting sun, the hush of moonlight on grass, the ripple of waves seen from shipboard, the praise of a friend, the touch of a child's hand. Now I understand that the deepest awareness of life is known alone, always alone. Nonetheless, one's connection with all humanity is intensified, becomes more direct, more immediate. This is perhaps the sixth time in my life that I have felt this way, and now I begin to understand the ecstasy of the mystics. It was not so much the feeling that I knew the world better, but rather that the world was inside of me.

THURSDAY, JULY 19, 1951   A press agent called to say that Eleanor Roosevelt's secretary had telephoned him about an article I wrote. The piece concerned a man who checks on the security risk of certain federal employees. Mrs. Roosevelt wanted him on her television program. It's a pleasure to know that Mrs. Roosevelt has read my stuff.

WEDNESDAY, AUGUST 18, 1951   Today I wrote this letter to Walter Yust of the *Encyclopedia Brittanica*:

Mr. Walter Yust
Editor-in-Chief
Encyclopedia Britannica
20 North Wacker Drive
Chicago, Illinois

Dear Mr. Yust:
    Because I own a set of the *Encyclopedia Britannica* and admire this mighty work, I want to help improve it by pointing out that one of its articles badly needs revision. I speak of the article about Henry Ford.
    This begins on page 490 of volume 9 in my 1945 edition of the *Britannica*. Seldom have I read any article in the *Britannica* so rife with inaccuracies. In the first place, you retained the wrong men to write it. Both Samuel Crowther and W. J. Cameron were special

pleaders—Ford's kept men. How, in the name of human nature, could you expect them to furnish the *Britannica* with an objective report on Henry Ford?

Why do I tell you this? Is it because I am a special pleader of some breed? Not at all. I am a feature writer for the *New York World-Telegram & Sun*, and I happen to read rather widely.

How do I know what I am talking about? Well, I have just finished reading a book which must present the real truth about Henry Ford because it is closely documented from a diversity of sources. This book is *The Legend of Henry Ford*, written by Keith Sward, published by Rinehart & Co., in 1948. Mr. Sward, whom I do not know, devoted ten years of research to this project.

Your article about Henry Ford is raising a generation of Americans on myths, not facts. Line after line of your piece consists of bald lies. Why? Consider, I pray you, the kept men who wrote it. But, this propaganda apart, the article also is at variance with common sense. Listen: ". . . The difficulties attending the putting of the new model into production were largely those of detail . . . The cost of this ran into about $200,000,000 . . ." Is this staggering sum of money a mere *detail?*

I suggest that your article on Henry Ford needs to be completely rewritten so that the high standards of the *Britannica* might be maintained.

Yours truly,
Edward R. Ellis

SATURDAY, SEPTEMBER 1, 1951   ■   Today I received this reply from Walter Yust:

AUGUST 28, 1951, OFFICE OF THE EDITOR, ENCYCLOPEDIA BRITANNICA, 425 NORTH MICHIGAN AVENUE, CHICAGO, ILLINOIS

Mr. Edward R. Ellis
New York World-Telegram
Corner of West and Barclay Sts.
New York 15, New York

Dear Mr. Ellis:
I have your interesting letter of August 18. Your criticism is, in

large part, valid and the article will be rewritten immediately.
Thank you very much for your interest.

Sincerely yours,
Walter Yust
Editor

This is the caricature I did of Ford shortly after we first met in 1943.

1952

*In 1950 the National Broadcasting Company and the Columbia Broad-
casting System fought a war over radio ratings. CBS had lured away many
NBC entertainers by paying them enormous salaries and giving them long-
term contracts. NBC executives decided to retaliate by staging a spectacular
radio show crammed with stars, called* The Big Show. *For mistress of ceremonies they chose a dramatic actress with a flamboyant personality—Tallulah Bankhead.*

*Tallulah was her real first name. Radio was a new medium to her, but she
rose to the challenge, helped by headliners such as Ethel Merman, Jimmy
Durante, Fred Allen.* The Big Show *premiered in November of 1950 and
was an instant hit with critics and public alike. It was broadcast every Sun-*

day evening from 6:30 to 8 o'clock from the stage of the Center Theater, then
a part of Rockefeller Center. I had become friendly with Don Bishop, an
NBC press agent. Tallulah liked him so much she insisted he go with her to
Paris and London, when the show was aired from there in 1951.

Don told me this story: Tallulah knew Beatrice Lillie, the Canadian-born
comedienne and revue singer, who married Sir Robert Peel, thus becoming
Lady Peel. The two women made the rounds of London pubs and were
drunk when they returned to Bea Lillie's hotel. After staggering through the
lobby, Bea reached the desk clerk and said: "Lady Keel's pee, please!"

SUNDAY, FEBRUARY 17, 1952 ▪ Don Bishop gave me two tickets to *The Big Show* — excellent seats, as Ruthie and I found out. On Tallulah's show this evening she had Fred Allen, his wife Portland Hoffa, an English singer named Vera Lynn, and Meredith Willson and his orchestra.

When the show was over Don led us onto the stage. Grabbing a sleeve of her mink coat, he said: "Doll—" I'd never heard Don talk this way before, then realized he was playing Tallulah's game. "Doll, I want you to meet two good friends of mine—Ruth Kraus of the *Herald Tribune* and Eddie Ellis of the *World-Telegram.*"

Tallulah turned around, hugged Ruthie and then approached me with open arms.

"The *Herald Trib*—well, really, dah-ling!—I mean, the *Trib!*—and the *World-Telegram*—the only papers in town worth a real good God, I mean, take the *Times*, a stuffy, nauseating old sheet, if ever, so you're really from the—you must say hello to Morton [Norton] Mockridge and Jim [Bob] Prall for me, those dah-lings—and—"

I managed to slip in a few words: "Miss Bankhead, when you appeared in *The Little Foxes* in Peoria in 1940, I reviewed the play and compared you to Modjeska, mentioning the time she recited the Greek alphabet and—"

By now Tallulah had a grip on my right sleeve. She swayed as she talked, her pelvis thrust forward, and she looked shorter than I had remembered her—about five three, I'd guess. She looks taller on stage. Her most attractive feature is her hair, thick, shoulder-length, shiny, tawny. Hearing her deep husky voice, I recalled reading that when she was a baby she had whooping cough.

"Well, really, dah-ling, I never, I mean, after all, I'm not old enough to have seen Modjeska—but nevah, nevah, nevah be afraid to admit how old you are, dah-ling!—I just had my forty-ninth birthday, just the other day, really, and—"

As she confessed her age she threw both arms around me and pressed her cheek to mine, so that the words "forty-ninth birthday" were spoken huskily into my left ear. Even when she broke this embrace she still clung to my sleeves holding it throughout the rest of her rambling.

"—while I did see Bernhardt and many of the other greats, but—God!—*The Little Foxes!*—I mean—what a ghastly—one of the members of the cast asked me how a certain line should be spoken, and I said, really, dah-ling, how the shit should I know—I mean, I can't even get my own—that show, I mean it was a son-of-a-bitch—oh, my language, aren't I really awful, but really? So you're from the *Trib* and *Telly*—well, I must—Fred, oh, Fred! I want you to know these charming people from the *Telly*, the *World-Telegram*, and the *Trib*—wait a—"

Convulsively she led Ruth and me toward Fred Allen, the famous comedian, and his wife. He was unsmiling as we shook hands—not hostile but slightly indifferent. I felt guilty about taking up his time when he probably wanted to go home. Searching for common ground, I mentioned the name of H. Allen Smith, formerly of the *World-Telegram*. Fred Allen wrote the foreword in Smith's first book, *Low Man on a Totem Pole*. The comedian's face brightened, and we chatted awhile about Smith, another humorist.

By this time the people on the stage had begun to drift toward an exit, and for every step that Tallulah took toward the door she uttered a thousand words. She patted and petted and kissed every man in her path, and when she reached the stage door and found two cops, she snatched a cap off one of them, stuck it onto her hair, leaned back for general approval.

When someone said something about politics, Ruthie said: "I almost wore my *I like Ike* button tonight."

Tallulah twisted her face into an expression of horror, but the next moment said: "Actually, dah-ling, I do like Ike myself, I really do—"

Still chattering, she was swept out the door and into a snowstorm that had begun while we were in the theater. Squinting through the light storm I watched Tallulah being wafted toward a waiting limousine, babbling, babbling, babbling . . .

TUESDAY, MARCH 18, 1952   ■   Willie Sutton, the nation's most notorious bank robber, went on trial today and Joe Alvarez, Bill Longgood and I were assigned to cover it.

The Willie Sutton case has special meaning to me. He was on the FBI's list of the 10 most wanted criminals, and last month he was captured by two cops within four blocks of police headquarters in Brooklyn. For almost two years he had lived in the neighborhood in obscurity.

When news of his capture reached our city room I was working the night shift. The night city editor was John (Mickey) McGuire, who is a friend as well as a colleague. He walked to my desk with a batch of clippings about Sutton, who is known as "The Actor" because he is a master of disguises. The cops who took him to headquarters made several mistakes. For one thing, they waited an hour before searching him, and when they did they found a .38 tucked in his pants.

Mickey said: "Write me a story about all the mistakes the cops made, Eddie—and make it funny!"

Make it funny? This alarmed me. I have enough sense to realize I am not a humorist. However, I do know the nature of satire, which is to praise that which one dislikes, so I batted out a story singing the praises of the arresting officers. My feature was prominently displayed in every edition of the paper. Here is what I wrote:

By Edward Ellis
Staff Writer

Every little boy who likes to play cops-and-robbers will do well to memorize the following rules for the apprehension of criminals.

These precepts, as gleaned from the police work in the arrest of Willie (The Actor) Sutton, should help every fledgling Hawkshaw nab his prey with ease.

1) Don't memorize the features of the most wanted bank robber in America.

This will get you nowhere. Patrolmen James J. McClellan and Donald P. Shea talked to Sutton near his home for five or ten minutes. They failed to recognize him. Such alertness is encouraged by the FBI, which enjoys distributing photos of wanted criminals.

2) Believe everything a suspect tells you and every printed card he shows you.

This way, you prove your goodwill toward mankind. Willie told the cops his name was Gordon. The name Gordon was on his driver's license and auto registration card, which he showed them. Naturally, all this proved he wasn't Willie Sutton.

3) Drive away and leave your suspect.

Calm reflection, that's the thing. Talk it over. Drive back to the station house, as the two patrolmen did, musing over the ways of fate. If your absence gives the crook time to get away—well, every noble hunter shoots only at a bird on the wing.

4) Be unsure of the testimony of your eyes.

After all, who's perfect? You get back to the station house, as did the brace of cops, and you announce knowingly that you knew you almost knew the man was Willie. Then, when a detective suggests looking into the matter, firmly falter that, yeah, maybe you'd better go back for a second peek.

5) Never frisk a suspect.

It just wouldn't do to incur anyone's ill-will. Let your man sit around the station for an hour with a loaded gun under his coat. Since you want to be a cop, you want excitement. This is one way to get it. Of course, somebody might get shot, but that would be thrilling.

Now, kiddies, let's say the shoe is on the other sleuth's foot. Let's say you're a robber, instead of a cop. Here are the things you must do:

A) Ignore your chance to get away.

Remember, you're cleverer than all the cops in the world. This is being pretty clever. The cops talk to you, they question you—maybe they just like to pass the time of day. Willie had 10 to 15 minutes to take it on the lam, but he stuck around. A guy gets curious, you know.

B) Always carry your ill-gotten gains.

This proves you're a man of the world. Underworld—world—who cares? Willie had almost 8,000 bucks on him when he was arrested. If a cop asks where you got all this loot, smile and say a rich uncle in Pago-Pago just died.

C) Live as close as possible to a police station.

A man is known by the company he keeps. Besides, having a flock of cops so close gives one a sense of security. Willie took up his abode only two blocks from the Bergen St. station in Brooklyn. In case he got the hiccups in the dead of night, there always was a patrolman handy.

If all you kiddies will cut out this list and paste it inside your deer-stalking hat, you're a cinch to turn into Sherlock Holmes.

And remember—each and every rule as set forth here is bona fide, guaranteed, sure-fire procedure, since it was put to the test by real cops and a real robber.

The day this story was published the secretary of the police department called the city desk. He said the police commissioner took one look at my article and bellowed: "Who the hell is this bastard Ellis?" As Mickey went home on the subway he sat by passengers who were reading my piece and guffawing in delight. I heard that an FBI agent showed the story to the agent in charge of the New York bureau, and both men laughed gleefully. One of our police reporters said some cops are grinding their teeth in rage and praying they might have a chance to get their hands on me.

The next time I went to work I was surrounded by staff members who praised my story, but the accolade that meant the most came from reporter Allan Keller. Allan is older and more experienced than I; he also teaches journalism at Columbia University. I've always looked up to him. Well, Allan said he considers my piece the best feature we have published in the *Telegram* in many years, and he plans to use it in his class as an example of how a brilliant story should be written.

It turns out that the cops had been tipped off to the whereabouts of Willie Sutton by Arnold Schuster, a young clothing salesman, and the night of March 8 the youth was found murdered on a Brooklyn street. Because of this, there were tight security measures taken today in the third-floor courtroom of the Queens County courthouse in Long Island City.

Besides our police cards, we reporters had to have special blue cards issued by the chief clerk of the court. Part of the basement had been outfitted into a press room with pay phones along one wall and a battery of special phones directly connected to the city rooms of various newspapers in town. Covering the start of the trial was a pack of 16 photographers and some of the best reporters in the nation—among them, Meyer (Mike) Berger of the *Times* and Jimmy Kilgallen of International News Service.

We reporters took our places at the press table in the rectangular courtroom. This room is two-and-a-half stories high, with cream-colored walls interrupted by gilt flourishes at the tops of cream-colored columns. Overhead was a skylight. Four huge electric light globes were suspended near the judge's chair, while behind the chair was an American flag about twelve by eight feet. I sat at table No. 4. Scotch-taped on its surface was a slip of paper with my name and W-T-S for *World-Telegram & Sun*. In 1950 Roy Howard bought the *New York Sun* and merged it with the *World-Telegram*.

It was in this same courtroom in 1927 that the state tried Mrs. Ruth Brown Snyder and her lover, Henry Judd Gray, for the murder of her husband, Albert Snyder. That sensational trial was covered by a galaxy of correspondents, along with special writers such as Will Durant, Billy Sunday and Peggy Joyce. Both defendants were found guilty and hanged.

I was thinking so hard about that previous trial that I almost failed to notice Willie Sutton when he entered the courtroom. He is a skinny little man with a scrawny neck and the face of a weasel. Although his hair is dark, he has a thin blond moustache. All his facial features are pinched, while his nose is outlined by wrinkles like parentheses. He wore a blue pin-stripe suit and brown tie. He was guarded by only one man—nearly twice his size. As Willie sat down between his two attorneys, this gigantic guard shoved the chair under him with more force than courtesy.

Willie was charged with holding up the Sunnyside, Queens, branch of the Manufacturers Trust Company on March 9, 1950, and escaping with $63,942.

Naturally, he said he was innocent.

He was found guilty and given a sentence of 60 years to life. However he was released from prison in 1969 and became a consultant to banks on security matters. He died in 1980 in Spring Hill, Florida.

THURSDAY, MARCH 20, 1952   ▓   I'm a little tardy recording this, but I want to be sure it gets into the diary. Last Sunday night in Carnegie Hall I watched Toscanini conduct the National Broadcasting Company Symphony Orchestra.

All my life I've heard my mother say that on her honeymoon in New York City, she heard Enrico Caruso, the great Italian tenor. Perhaps in years to come I may regale my grandchildren with my description of Arturo Toscanini, the most famous musician of his time and the world's greatest living conductor.

My friend Don Bishop, the NBC press agent, got tickets for Ruthie and me in the center of the very first row of seats in the orchestra of Carnegie Hall. This hallowed hall is a bell-shaped chamber, its curving walls the color of Dubonnet wine. The facades of the four balconies may once have been cream-colored, but time has aged them to the color of sour milk. Since this concert was to be televised, four TV cameras were stationed here and there. One had been put within a hooded booth in the center of the back of the stage so that it might register every expression on the face of the maestro.

From my seat, No. 12, I could see every detail of the conductor's podium. It consists of a low platform about six by four feet, made of wood, painted black and looking very battered. Its three-sided railing was bound in scuffed maroon cloth. Don told us that in Toscanini's dressing room in an NBC studio he keeps a similar dais to practice springing up onto it. Don theorized that he wants to prove he still is vigorous, because five days from now he will become 85 years old. Ruthie, aware that Toscanini is near-sighted, said perhaps he just wants to be sure of his footing as he begins a concert.

At 6:27 P.M. NBC announcer Ben Grauer walked onto the stage to welcome the audience. It has been said he has the best-known voice in radio, and certainly I admired it. After he walked back into the wings, there settled over the packed house a silence like the hush of nature before a storm . . . silence . . . a spatter of applause, like the sputtering of a fuse, and then an explosion as the maestro came into full view. He bounded onto his podium, turned and faced the audience.

Toscanini is a man of three colors—pink, white and black. The pinkness of his cheeks and neck may be due to massages and extraordinary health in a man his age. His skin is clear and, except for a slight sag under his chin, it is drawn tightly across his face. He has a mole on his right temple. The whiteness consists of the whiteness of his hair. Two long plumes, like the folded wings of doves, swoop back from his lean temples to meet at the base of his skull and then project even further, like a short tail. His blackness—a heavy bass note vibrating beneath the treble of his pink skin and white hair—consists of a coat buttoned to his throat à la Nehru.

As the great man turned around to face his orchestra he smiled in our direction, although I doubt whether he saw us, due to weak eyes, and anyway it doesn't matter. What did matter was the surprising sweetness of his smile. Among musicians he has the reputation of a tyrant. Recently I was reading an article about his temper. He raged in Italian at a cellist who had made a mistake, when suddenly he realized the man had not understood a word. Trying to express his fury in English, he screamed: "You bad, bad, bad man!"

Now, from a distance of less than 20 feet, I was about to watch genius at work. He raised his baton in a commanding position. The first selection was "Symphonic Interlude" from *The Redemption* by the French composer Cesar Franck. Since I can hear a Toscanini concert on records or on radio at almost any time, this evening I chose to pay attention to the conductor more than the music. He used no score. Because of his weak eyes he has committed to memory hundreds of scores of symphonies and operas.

I was fascinated by the way he used the baton. He held it with all four fingers of his right hand in a straight line, down at its base. No dainty, pinched hold, no artistic lift of the little finger like a lady drinking tea. No, his grip was instead a solid workmanlike hold of the object, a rude clutch such as a lumberjack has on the handle of his ax. But what he did with it is beyond my powers to describe.

Winthrop Sergeant, in his essay on Toscanini, calls it a paddling movement. It is this—but it is also something more. At times he sawed the baton back and forth, like the cellist he once was. In fast passages of music his baton wove through patterns too complex for my eye to follow. Too complex for *me*, yes, but at every moment every one of his musicians understood that his every little movement had a meaning of its own. Toscanini's wand was like the tail of a spider weaving silky strands that began at the edges and then gathered in the center like glistening cobwebs of enchantment, of music. Wherever in space his baton was at any split-second, there and there alone was the center of the magical pattern, the vortex into which all of us were drawn.

This is the caricature I drew that night. Toscanini died in 1957.

TUESDAY, NOVEMBER 11, 1952   ■   "Did I ever tell you the story about Eugene?" Romare asked.

"No," I replied, "but I'd like to hear it."

This happened late last Saturday night in my apartment on Riverside Drive. A few of my friends and I were drinking and chatting and listening to Romare Bearden, a masterful raconteur. Recently he returned from Paris, where he studied philosophy at the Sorbonne.

Romare began: "I was a bad boy . . ."

When he was 12 years old he lived awhile in Pittsburgh, where his grandmother ran a rooming house. One day when he was playing with some boys they saw a strange kid watching them. He was skinny and weak and wore shoes much too big for him. Romare later learned the shoes were made to support his rickety legs.

One of Romare's playmates asked: "What's your name?"

"Eugene."

Romare's friend walked over and hit Eugene in the face. Eugene tottered but did not fall. He didn't even whimper.

The bully cried: "Hey! He didn't go down! You hit him, Romey!"

Romare sauntered over and struck Eugene. Again the frail lad wavered but remained erect, and he made no sound whatsoever.

His stoicism won over the other little black boys. They tolerated him, let him hang around, and at last liked him enough to protect him from other bullies. Romare learned that Eugene knew how to draw. He became fascinated with Eugene's sketch of the famous Victrola advertisement that showed a dog listening to "His Master's Voice." Streaming out of the bell-shaped loudspeaker were the figures of naked women.

Romare asked Eugene to teach him how to draw. They would get together in the basement of the rooming house. Romare's grandmother, seeing them huddled over sheets of paper would say it was so nice that they were spending their time in such a harmless manner. She was unaware that the only subjects Eugene knew how to draw were the naked bodies of men and women. All naked, all carnally connected, they twisted and sprawled in lascivious combinations all over the paper.

"That boy," Romare told us, shaking his head in admiration, "was a second Toulouse-Lautrec."

By this time his compassionate grandmother was feeding Eugene. One day when the two boys were together she stopped to look at their drawings and with one glance she drew herself up indignantly.

"Boy!" she boomed. "Where you learn all that? Where you live, boy?"

"Down to Mamie's," said Eugene.

Romare took another drag from his cigaret. "Mamie's," he explained softly, "was a whorehouse just down the street."

It turned out that Eugene was a son of one of the women doing business in Mamie's. Neither she nor anyone else took care of him, despite his obvious bad health, his rickety figure. He slept in a tiny room on an upper floor of the whorehouse and, to while away his time, he bored holes in the floor. Peering through the holes in the house of ill-fame he saw fleshly mysteries enacted night after night. This was the only world Eugene knew, the only subject matter for his artistic talent. It was his sketches that launched Romare into the field of art and led him toward his growing fame.

To his grandmother, however, Eugene's pictures were only filth. She burned all of his originals and Romare's crude copies of them. Then, taking Eugene by the hand, she marched him down the street and into the whorehouse.

Seeing her approach, one of the prostitutes warned: "A woman of God!"

"Where's this boy's mother?" the grandmother demanded.

Scurrying sounds in a back room, and then out came the mother, a cigaret in her lips. Romare told us he remembers her curves.

"This your boy?"

"Yesss . . . an he's a mistake, lady."

"Mistake or not," snapped the grandmother, "he's comin' to live with me! He got no right here. It ain't fittin' fer a little boy to live in such a place!"

Eugene's mother drawled: "All right . . ."

And so it was that Pittsburgh's little twisted Toulouse-Lautrec went to live with Romare and his grandmother. But Eugene didn't live long. His soft bones got softer despite all the milk and eggs and bread and carrots stuffed into him.

"The point to this story," Romare said, "is that my grandmother's charity was personal and total. This is the only kind of charity worth talking about, and the fact that Eugene died does not disprove the moral. But that wasn't the end of the story—"

A funeral service for little Eugene was held in a church. On one side of the aisle sat the saintly friends of the grandmother, while on the other side sat Mamie and her sisters. Then came the drive to the cemetery and the final rites.

Romare and his brother were among the pallbearers. Now, his brother was a good kid but clumsy. If there were a brick within a block, his brother's toe was sure to seek it out. There in the graveyard some planks lay across the newly dug grave. As a part of the ceremony, each pallbearer had to walk across the planks to drop rose petals into the hole. The inevitable happened: Brother lost his footing and fell into the grave.

The delegation of sinners, seeing the kid flop down, erupted in laughter. They screamed. They yelped. They hooted for joy. Some threw themselves onto the grass to roll back and forth, yowling in glee. They actually had brought a band with them and the musicians, bemused and amused, burst into a barrelhouse blues. As a funeral, it was some carnival.

1953

SATURDAY, JANUARY 24, 1953 ■ At noon this gray day about 150 people began demonstrating around the Soviet mansion on Park Avenue. The handsome five-story building, made of white stone and red brick, is at the northwest corner of East 68th Street. It houses the Soviet delegation to the United Nations.

The demonstration was sponsored by the Committee to Combat Soviet Religious Persecution and Genocide. The committee was organized last Friday at headquarters of the Jewish Labor Committee, 25 East 78th Street, because of recent events in the Soviet Union.

On January 13 the Soviet press reported that nine Kremlin doctors— six of them Jewish—had been arrested. The government accused them of assassinating two Soviet leaders and plotting the assassination of oth- ers. It said they acted at the direction of Zionist organizations and Amer- ican and British intelligence agencies. This new Russian manifestation of anti-Semitism agitated Jews around the world.

Here in New York one of the five members of this new ad hoc commit- tee is Norman Thomas, the former Presbyterian minister, the socialist who ran six times for the Presidency, a civil rights leader called "the conscience of America."

The pickets represented some 23 groups—religious, political, labor, vet- erans, refugees from behind the Iron Curtain. Most were well-dressed and mannerly, although a few of them hissed and booed a couple of Russians leaving the mansion. There were three groups of pickets, two in front and one on the 68th Street side. Blue-coated cops formed a wall between the pickets and the building. Mink-clad Park Avenue matrons had to walk in the gutter to pass the place. The pickets carried printed signs saying:

COMMUNISM IS DEATH TO FREEDOM
STOP IRON CURTAIN RELIGIOUS PERSECUTIONS
STALIN FOLLOWS IN HITLER'S BLOODY PATH
MURDEROUS RUSSIA STOP MASS MURDERS

Men and women passed out leaflets saying: "You are witnessing a spon- taneous demonstration by men and women of all faiths against the tyranni- cal Soviet regime. By their ruthless purges and brutal treatment of Jews and Catholics, Soviet Russia and its satellite nations have revealed the total ugliness and godlessness of totalitarianism . . ."

Some pickets tried to jam leaflets into the hands of the few men enter- ing and leaving the mansion. Most Russians kept their faces blank as they ignored them but one Russian took a leaflet, stepped into his chauffeur-driven limousine, glanced at the paper and began swearing.

The chief Soviet delegate to the U.N. is Valerian A. Zorin. Although I did not know whether he was in the building, I decided to try to find out and perhaps elicit some reaction from him. Wearing my press card, walking past the cops, I stepped up to the stately front door and rang the bell. Seeing me, some pickets speculated in high humor about my chances of getting inside. In a few moments a man emerged from an inner door and then opened the front door about two inches.

"I'd like to see Mr. Zorin," I said.

A shadow of annoyance passed over the man's face. A black cigaret-holder was clenched between his teeth. Without saying a word, he closed the door—but did not bang it shut.

Turning around and starting to leave, I saw Norman Thomas a few feet away.

"Hey!" I cried. "Mr. Thomas! . . . Why don't you and I go to the door together to try to get inside?" He saw the press card dangling from my coat. "Then you present this case to Zorin, if he's in. How about trying it?"

"Sure!"

Not a moment's hesitation. I admire Norman Thomas so much. His blue eyes seemed to glint like the eyes of an eagle. He certainly is one of the most intelligent men in America, and had he run for President on any ticket but that of the socialist party, he might have won. Nonetheless, I respect him all the more for remaining true to his ideals in the face of defeat after defeat.

A man of lanky build, standing perhaps six feet two, Mr. Thomas has a high cliff-like forehead; white hair, pouches under his eyes and thin lips that have uttered millions of wise words. I turned back to the door and he followed me, and a TV cameraman saw him and pointed a camera in our direction. Mr. Thomas and I took turns pressing the buzzer. No response.

I asked: "If you could get inside, sir, what would you say?"

The old orator fired off words as fast as a machine gun:

"I'd tell Mr. Zorin that the presence of these pickets shows that Americans have an abhorrence of the kind of thing for which they fought Hitler! This is not a war-mongering demonstration. This is the people speaking—no government, but the people alone, people from all parts of Europe whom Stalin displaced, yes, including the relatives of the folks you are keeping in your horrible police camps. And—I want you to tell Pravda about this and I hope that Pravda will print it in full—that's what I'd tell Mr. Zorin!"

Stalin died March 5, 1953, and then came a power struggle that reorga-

nized both the Soviet government and the communist party of Russia. Anti-Semitism became less blatant. On April 3 all the doctors were exonerated.

FRIDAY, JANUARY 30, 1953   ■   In the office today I had the sad task of telling a father on the phone that his son had been wounded in Korea.

McCarthyism began on Thursday, February 9, 1950.

The Republican Senator from Wisconsin, Joseph R. McCarthy, 41, had been rated by the Washington press corps as the worst Senator in town, so he sought an issue to help him win re-election in the fall. He decided to try out anti-communism.

That evening he spoke at a Lincoln Day celebration held by the Ohio County Republican Women's Group in the Colonnade Room of the McCrure Hotel in Wheeling, West Virginia. There he said in part:

"While I cannot take the time to name all the men in the state department who have been named as members of the communist party and members of a spy ring, I have here in my hand a list of 205 that were known to the secretary of state as being members of the communist party and are still working and shaping the policy of the State Department."

These hot words sizzled over the wires of the Associated Press and set off an explosion that surprised McCarthy himself. Later he said he wrote the speech, but that was a lie. It had been cobbled together by three conservative journalists.

In the next few days other reporters asked McCarthy for proof of this charge, but he evaded their questions and juggled his figures—maybe the number was not 205, but perhaps 81 or 57. A Senate committee investigated, then declared his charges were fraudulent.

This conclusion, however, did not deter McCarthy. Having found a burning issue, he poured gasoline on it. Many Americans were worried about communists. Whittaker Chambers had named Alger Hiss as a communist spy, the communists of North Korea threatened South Korea, for awhile Soviet Russia had blockaded Berlin, and the Soviets now had an atomic bomb. Here in the United States the communist party was a legal political party. Although its members had stopped carrying cards, McCarthy yammered about "card-carrying commies." His lies became wilder, newspaper headlines grew bigger, and soon McCarthy was elevated to the status of a mythical hero. Some people put in their windows photographs of McCarthy framed by religious trappings such as usually adorn pictures of Christ.

Eric Hoffer, the longshoreman and philosopher, once said of the hysteria of mass movements: "When hopes and dreams are loose in the streets it is

well for the timid to lock doors, shutter windows and lie low until the wrath
has passed. For there is often a monstrous incongruity between the hopes,
however noble and tender, and the actions which follow them. It is as if the
ivied maidens and garlanded youths were to herald the Four Horsemen of
the Apocalypse."

Max Lerner, a columnist, wrote: "Nothing quite like McCarthy has
crawled out of the dark and maggoty crevices of America's Cro-Magnon
period into public life. . . . He is the expression of the deep impulses of violence in our time. In Eastern Europe he would have been a communist commissar, in Germany a gauleiter, in a Latin American dictatorship he would
have been a putsch-making colonel."

Many books have been written about McCarthy's assaults upon civil liberties and I have studied most of them. Here are a few well-researched
generalities:

Joe McCarthy was a liar, a bully, a drunkard and a provocateur. Panting
for power, but lacking a program, he was anarchic. He defied two Presidents,
insulted the Senate, threatened Senators, paralyzed the State Department,
agitated the army, libelled Protestant ministers, defamed other honorable
folks, brutalized generals, beat up a newspaper columnist, insulted Cabinet
members, carried a gun and a bottle in his briefcase, broke laws, robbed
words of their meaning, manipulated the press, accused the Democratic
party of "twenty years of treason," expanded this to 21 years to include President Eisenhower, had a genius for creating chaos and finally became the
most feared man in the free world.

Almost everyone was afraid to criticize him lest he call them "soft on communism," but at last Edward R. Murrow of CBS aired a three-hour TV documentary about him. McCarthy reacted by snarling, "Murrow is a symbol,
the leader and the cleverest of the jackal pack which is always found at the
throat of anyone who dares to expose individual communists and traitors!"

On June 1, 1953, President Eisenhower wrote in his diary: "I very recently
read part of a German broadcast, in which the German Von Club stated in
effect, 'McCarthy makes it so easy to hate Americans.' " In his memoirs he
said: "No one was safe from charges recklessly made inside the walls of congressional immunity. . . . The cost was often tragic."

Nonetheless, Eisenhower failed to provide the leadership to defuse
McCarthy. Walter Lippmann, a columnist, said that Ike had abdicated his
responsibilities. Norman Thomas characterized the President as a "pillar of
jelly."

Joe McCarthy split this nation asunder. In 1954 polls showed that 50 percent of the people liked McCarthy, while only 29 percent disliked him. I

know about this personally: My half brother Jack said that his mother, my stepmother, whom I loved and respected, told her son to his face that anyone who is against McCarthy is a communist.

In Madison, Wisconsin, the Capitol-Times *asked people: "What is a communist?" Of the 241 men and women interviewed, 97 said they did not know. One citizen said: "I really don't know what a communist is. I think they should throw them out of the White House."*

Secretary of State John Foster Dulles *said European leaders felt the United States was moving into fascism under McCarthy.*

Walter Lippmann *said that in McCarthyism he saw the "seeds of totalitarianism."*

Adlai E. Stevenson, *twice the Democratic candidate for President, said McCarthyism was "sowing the seeds of dissention among Americans."*

Norman Thomas *called McCarthy "our Inquisitor General and Thought Controller."*

Supreme Court Justice William O. Douglas *said: "There is an ominous trend in this nation. We are developing tolerance only for the orthodox point of view."*

Former Secretary of State Dean Acheson *described McCarthy as "one of the most unlovely characters in our political history since Aaron Burr."*

Senator Richard M. Nixon, *who later became President, said: "I think McCarthyism has been created by [President Harry] Truman. I believe it is the creature of Truman."*

On December 2, 1954, *by a vote of 67 to 22, the Senate censured McCarthy for conduct "contrary to senatorial traditions" that brought the Senate "into dishonor and disrepute."*

Having lost power and prestige, Joe McCarthy *began drinking even more heavily, had to be hospitalized, suffering from delirium tremens. He died May 2, 1957, at the age of 49.*

The Annals of America *is a set of 18 volumes published in 1968 by the Encyclopedia Britannica. On page 16 of volume 17 there is this flat statement about McCarthyism:*

"No communists were actually ever discovered as a direct result of his charges."

THURSDAY, APRIL 16, 1953 ■ At a recent party I met a divorcée named Nancy. She and I were in the kitchen drinking when someone said something about McCarthy's investigation of the Voice of America.

Turning to me, Nancy said: "You're a newspaperman. Why don't you print what's going on?"

"Print—what?"

"You know . . . Everybody knows what's going on."

"Exactly what do you mean? Much has been printed about the McCarthy probe."

"Aw," she sneered, "the newspapers are afraid to tell the truth about it."

I said: "Well, just give me some hard facts and if they're valid I'll see that they get into the paper."

"I've got a friend who works for the Voice of America," she said. "The things that are going on!"

"Like what?"

"You know!" she cried. "You know all about it! Only you're afraid to print it!"

"Look! Just give me something to go on. Tell me what it is you know!"

"Aw, you damned well know all about it!"

I lost my temper.

"Just because I'm a reporter doesn't mean that I know everything about everything! After all, even a reporter can get news only by listening to what other people have to say. Give me a fact, just one little fact!"

"Why tell you, when you know all about it," she jeered.

"I challenge you: One fact! Just one fact, to begin with!"

"Everybody knows all about Senator McCarthy!"

"Quit talking generalities!" I yelled. "Be specific! Just give me one fact, something substantial!"

"And you know all about it!" she burbled.

I imagine that much of this kind of thing has been happening to other reporters, too.

TUESDAY, APRIL 28, 1953 ■ As I do fairly often, today I dropped into the Washington Market a block south of the *Telly*. I am fascinated by the wide variety of seafood sold there and the manner in which it is displayed. One part of this one-story block-square building is taken up by a firm called Petrosino's, which has the slogan: "If it swims, we sell it." Today I gaped at huge green lobsters heaped on ice, some still alive as I could see by the occasional twitch of a claw or antenna.

Petrosino's also displayed neat rows of shad, shad roe, weakfish, porgies, etc. I saw a counterman nonchalantly dip his bare hand into a bushel basket of live crabs to transfer them to a wooden box. A wonder he doesn't get nipped—but maybe he does. One counter had a montage made of photostats of old newspapers with stories about whale meat—for whale meat was sold here. One story said that the Vatican had ruled that whale meat is fish and may be eaten by Catholics on Friday. How blithely the Roman Catholic Church defies natural laws, dismissing a mammal from its proper genus in the interests of the faith!

Besides the exotic fish in Washington Market there also were displayed many kinds of animals and fowl uncommon to most dining tables. I saw Belgian hares, pheasant, caponettes (whatever the hell they are), buffalo, partridge, etc. There also were cheeses in shapes and sizes of kinds I never saw anywhere else. While I am no gourmet, I delight in looking at these delicacies.

THURSDAY, APRIL 30, 1953   ■   It is 1:35 P.M. and I'm here in the city room, having just returned from the Roosevelt Hotel where I had a drink with Edward R. Murrow. I'd been sent there to cover a luncheon at which the George Polk Memorial Awards were to be given by the journalism department of Long Island University. My paper's prime interest was in one of our reporters, Edward J. Mowrey, who received a plaque "for outstanding metropolitan reporting." Ed had crusaded a long time to obtain the release from Sing Sing of Louis Hoffner, an innocent prisoner.

I arrived early. In the reception room on the mezzanine floor I was looking at a display of Ed Mowrey's work when I glanced up and saw Ed Murrow. He, too, was about to receive a Polk Award for his CBS show called *See It Now.*

"Mr. Murrow," I said, extending my hand, "let me congratulate you. I'm Ellis of the *World-Telegram.*"

"Oh, thanks," he replied, shaking hands. "We've met before."

We hadn't.

For a few moments we chatted about Mowrey and then Murrow said: "Let's get a drink."

We walked over to a temporary bar. "Sorry, gentlemen," said the bartender. "We don't open for 15 minutes."

"Well, then," said Murrow, "let's go down to the Rough Rider Room."

We took a seat at a shaded table. He ordered a Scotch sour—without sugar—and it sounded good to me, so I ordered the same.

Murrow is tall and lean, dark and serious. He seldom smiles, but when he does it is a sincere smile. His voice, known to millions of people around the world, is rich and vibrant. We talked about a strange illness that has struck down staff members at both CBS and the *Telly.*

"It's a wonder," said Murrow, "that we don't all come down with ulcers in this business."

I asked where he was going on vacation. He said he didn't know yet, but he planned to take off for three months. Said he has a log cabin in Duchess County about 70 miles north of town, but he hasn't been able to visit it much lately. From the air, he continued, it's lovely. Recently, when he was flying over his place, the weather closed in.

"Speaking of weather closing in," I said, "I had a heartrending experience during the war. I was based on Okinawa. One day—I was editor of a navy paper—one day I thumbed a ride on a plane flying to Korea—over Seoul and back. On the return trip it occurred to me that we weren't far from Nagasaki. That was only about three days after it was bombed. Over the intercom I suggested to the pilot that we make a side-trip to see it. 'Good idea,' he said, and we swerved off our course. We couldn't have been more than 110 miles from the city. Then—when we were within 40 miles of Nagasaki—the weather socked in. Boy, was I one disappointed reporter! I don't think there'd been a plane over the city since we bombed it."

Murrow sipped his drink, his dark eyes on my face.

"I had a somewhat similar experience," he began, "only it turned out better. About five years after the end of the war I was over there in Japan. Friend of mine had a beat-up plane. We were out one day and I was flying it. We came near Hiroshima and just as we started to fly over that God-forsaken place, there was a sudden down-draft—the sort of thing you get where sea meets land. We must have dropped—oh, I'd guess a hundred feet. Darndest feeling! It was like an invisible hand had reached up to snatch us from the sky."

Lifting his right arm, he gave an abrupt downward jerk.

"My God!" I cried. "How eerie! . . . You know, I think John Hersey's book on Hiroshima was about the best bit of reporting I've ever read."

"Magnificent," Murrow agreed.

"And not a single opinion in it," I said. "All facts—one fact after another."

"And the details," Murrow murmured. "Jammed with details." He took a drink and then resumed talking.

"That's what makes good reporting. Attention to details. It took me years as a reporter to learn this but, once I did, I never forgot it. That's what made Ernie Pyle so great. But, you know, there are some reporters, some big-name reporters, who still don't seem to know this. Of course, when there are too many details they can sink you . . . I remember . . . I was the first uniformed man to get into Buchenwald. Just outside one of the crematoriums there were some children's shoes stacked—hundreds and hundreds of them. I remember thinking, If there was only one pair of shoes, I could get it, I could understand, but that entire stack of shoes—it was too big for me to grasp."

"I know," I said. "When you pile horror on horror, it seems that the human brain regurgitates—can accept only so much."

Murrow said: "That's right. And while I was over there I came across a diary kept by a Czech—a man who made that terrible death march from Auschwitz to Buchenwald. He kept his diary on toilet paper and the like. Plenty of details. Tremendous thing. Well, when I got back here I tried to interest various publishers in it."

"Too ghastly?"

"They said people were fed up with atrocity stories. Anyway, I think people should remember, so about next Christmas I'm going to have that diary privately printed, and I'm going to send around some copies—couple of hundred or so."

"I'd sure like to get one, if you don't mind."

"Of course," he said, "I'd be delighted to send you one."

I got out my notebook, wrote my name and the newspaper on one page, tore it off and handed it to Murrow.

"Thanks," I said. "Did you ever read *Warsaw Ghetto?*"

"I sure did," Murrow replied.

"Details in that," I said, "and you know—that little girl could write! . . . By the way, did you ever come across *The Jewish Black Book*—a book compiled by some Jewish committee about the atrocities suffered by the Jews under Hitler."

"No, I don't think so."

"Tremendous book," I said.

"Well," he said, "I guess we'd better get back."

We walked out of the cocktail lounge and up the stairs to the mezzanine. I asked: "Didn't you win the Polk Award last year?"

His forehead crinkled in thought. "Year before, I believe—oh, no! Last year . . . That's right, but—"

"Yes?"

"But this television work," said Edward R. Murrow, "it's not real newspaper work. It's not truly satisfying, either. Television is just a pictorial supplement to newspapers. There are some things you can tell in pictures, and then there are some things you can't."

On the next page is the caricature I drew of Murrow sometime after our meeting.

TUESDAY, MAY 12, 1953   ■   I went to Harlem to cover the funeral of a Negro cop who had been shot to death in the line of duty. Yesterday his body lay

in state in a Harlem mortuary. Today the police department was giving him a hero's funeral. As the police band started playing I looked up the stairs to the mortuary and saw something touching. Standing near the top of the stairs was a black woman of uncertain age. She may have been beaten up recently because her head was bandaged, her eyes were swollen and her lips were cut. The very picture of misery. However, upon hearing the music, she pulled herself erect, lifted a trembling hand to her eyes in a wobbly salute. The very picture of dignity. My eyes misted over.

FRIDAY, MAY 15, 1953 ■ Ruth belongs to the Seraphic Secretaries of America. Its members are executive secretaries to board chairmen of powerful corporations. It holds banquets, which I attend only to please Ruthie, since I have nothing in common with rich businessmen. My attitude toward them has been honed by one of the most important books I ever read—*History of the Great American Fortunes,* by Gustavus Myers. After researching court records eight years, he proved most fortunes are acquired by theft. His book was so accurate he never was sued.

Last night the Seraphics held a banquet in the elite River Club on the East River at 52nd St. The speaker of the evening was Barnard M. Baruch, 82. He has a towering reputation. He is an elder statesman, Wall Street

tycoon, philanthropist, prophet, park-bench philosopher, lifelong friend of
Sir Winston Churchill and adviser to every President since Woodrow Wilson. During World War I he mobilized American industry and helped win
the war. He holds so many honors that some people call him "the greatest
living American."

During the cocktail hour I found myself standing near Baruch. A tall
white-haired man, he wore white tie and tails, had a flower in his lapel,
was chatting with a couple of women and radiating Southern charm. He
was born in South Carolina and now owns a plantation there.

Later, after everyone had dined, up rose the master of ceremonies, Roy
Howard. He is my ultimate boss, head of the Scripps-Howard newspaper
chain, a little man who struts like a rooster, an egomaniac who thinks he's
witty, but isn't. He introduced Miss Elizabeth Navarro, Baruch's secretary,
who introduced Baruch. I wanted to ask him a question, so I handed my
pen and notebook to Ruthie and asked her to record in shorthand whatever reply he gave me.

A charmer, Baruch poked fun at himself, saying that Arthur Krock of
the New York Times once remarked: "Baruch gives lousy advice, and
nobody takes it." During World War II, when he again helped the government, one woman prayed: "May Jesus prop him up." This is especially
amusing because Baruch is Jewish.

When he said he would take questions, a secretary asked about the
national airplane program. After he answered, I arose.

"Mr. Baruch," I said, "do you care to express an opinion about Senator
McCarthy?"

In the banquet hall I heard a buzzing like the warning of a rattlesnake.
These secretaries of influential bosses hated my question.

Holding up his hand to quiet them, Baruch said:

"That's a fair question. I'll give you an answer that many people won't
like. I think McCarthy has done a good job. It is highly necessary for someone to do that job, and it took a man with intestinal fortitude. I don't like
what he said about General Marshall, and I think he was wrong. I've been
under severe criticism and accused of many severe crimes. I say, if a man is
not guilty and is on the level with his country, he doesn't have anything to
fear.

"I have never seen any man who has attempted to change the order of
things that hasn't been abused. I remember it happened to Teddy Roosevelt. I have read every word of the examinations and cross-examinations
that have been said before the congressional committee. If you read what's

been said before the Jenner committee, those people [the witnesses] won't say yes or no."

The room exploded in applause. I sank back, stunned.

As a reporter I covered Baruch several times over the years and was surprised one day when he sent me a note of thanks for an article I wrote about him.

SATURDAY, MAY 16, 1953   ▩   When I was living in Chicago after the war I interviewed a giant who was appearing on the stage of the Chicago Theater. The guy was more than eight feet tall. After he came off-stage I went with him to his dressing room, where he began changing out of his costume into street clothes. I was curious as hell to know whether a giant is big in every way, but I just didn't have enough guts to look directly at him when he stripped off his shorts.

Dave Snell, Bill Michelfelder and I are among those in the city room who take serious things lightly and light things seriously. I was reading Harry Butcher's book about Ike and about the time Butcher went to Hyde Park in London to listen to the crackpots. Finding a line I liked, I typed it out and showed it to Dave and Bill. I had written:

"Gentlemen, this is our problem: Is rhubarb bloodshot celery, or is celery anemic rhubarb?"

As I knew they would, Dave and Bill immediately began debating this profundity with serious faces.

MONDAY, NOVEMBER 9, 1953   ▩   Joe Williams, the noted sports columnist, sometimes comes into the office to write a story. He always chews gum, chomping at it with the rhythm of a beating heart. Although he has a face like a football coach, his hands are slim, delicate and shapely. They flutter about his face as he bends over his typewriter deep in thought, they stroke his chin and then his forehead. For many years I have believed in a theory which is my own, so far as I know. I theorize that all reflective people often touch their face in one way or another. After I first thought of this idea I began watching people, discovering that those who truly are contemplative sit with fingers to their cheeks, prop their chins on their fists, or hold their foreheads. Rodin knew all about this, as witness his statue called *The Thinker*.

THURSDAY, DECEMBER 17, 1953   ▩   I saw Joe McCarthy in person today, and he scared the hell out of me! He held a one-member hearing of the Senate permanent investigating committee in the stately courtroom on the first floor, north wing, of the federal courthouse of Foley Square in lower Manhattan.

I sat down in a red leather swivel chair in the jury box. A young woman in a red dress sat down beside me. She said she worked for the *Newark Star-Ledger*.

She asked: "Is this your first time here?"

"Yes. I want to see how this bastard operates."

"You don't like McCarthy?"

"Hell, no! Do you?"

"Well," she said, "I sort of like him because he arranged for me to get an exclusive interview with his wife. You know, she's the only one who really has him under control. . . . Tell me, why don't you like him?"

Two men took seats to my right. They didn't look like reporters. The man near me smelled of booze. He was well-dressed, medium height, about sixty.

I began reeling off my reasons for hating McCarthy. My new neighbor interrupted me.

"Excuse me," he said, "but I couldn't help hear what you were saying. Let me tell you, sir, this is the greatest thing that ever happened to America!"

"Nuts!" I sneered.

"Only the Republicans have done anything about the commies—"

"Like hell!" I blurted. "For your information, it was under the administration of President Harry Truman, a Democrat, that 84 commies were prosecuted under the Smith Act, that—"

"Political bilgewater!" the man snorted. "It wasn't until McCarthy began going after them that anything really was done!"

"You mean you like McCarthy—a jerk who stood up on the floor of the Senate to call General George C. Marshall a traitor?"

"He is!"

"What?" I twisted around to look the man in the eye. "You mean to sit there and tell me that General Marshall is a traitor to the United States?"

"Yes!"

"Well," I growled, "did he try to sell us out to the Nazis when he was chief of staff. Did he—"

"He lost China for us!"

I groaned: "I'm sick of that line. No American ever lost China because China never belonged to the United States. Just the other day I read about the China deal, the China lobby, in yearbooks of the *Encyclopedia Britannica*, and—I suppose you'll take the *Britannica* as an authority?"

"No," the man said. "I'm from Chicago and I know the editor of the *Britannica* and, no, I won't."

"Why, for God's sake?"

"Because he doesn't."

"Who doesn't what?" I asked, feeling like Ellis in Wonderland.

"The editor of the *Britannica!*"

I didn't understand what the guy meant. I asked what he did for a living. He said he is a lawyer. I asked what kind.

"Every kind, any kind. General practice . . . I'm Irish!"

"Jesus! " I cried. "What the hell does that have to do with anything? I'm English, mostly, but I don't go around hollering about it. What—"

"And the English persecuted the Irish!"

"Okay," I said, throwing up my hands. "You're Irish and McCarthy's Irish. Is that why you like him?"

"Just came from having lunch with him," the man gloated, blowing his whiskey breath into my face.

So! There I sat, cheek by jowl with a worshipper of McCarthy. I remembered reading that Hermann Goering had a weak joke: "I hope you will not tell Himmler." Himmler was the head of the SS.

"Next time you see McCarthy," I said, "tell him for me I think he stinks!"

Just then McCarthy walked into the courtroom. Although I'd seen him several times on TV, this was the first time I'd seen him in person. Suddenly my mind flashed back several years. When I worked for the United Press in Chicago, the newly elected Senator from Wisconsin went to Chicago to try to get some publicity. He invited reporters to a hotel suite for drinks and a buffet luncheon. I attended. There I met McCarthy, who was so dull I wrote nothing about him and soon forgot him.

Now I was seeing the same man, who had become famous in headlines but infamous in deeds. He sat down at a table in front of the judge's bench. He wore a gray suit and blue tie. In the tie's pattern were two tiny crosses like the double-cross symbol worn by Charles Chaplin as he impersonated Hitler in *The Great Dictator*. McCarthy has the slim hips of an athlete, a thick trunk and shoulders like a buffalo. Almost lacking a neck, his huge head seems perched on his shoulders. His mouth is long and thin, like a knife-gash in a melon.

I couldn't see the color of his eyes, which are edged by black eyelashes as vivid as stage make-up worn by an actor. His eyes are deep-set and hooded, with almost purple pouches under them. Above his nose two vertical clefts rose to meet the horizontal wrinkles of his brow, giving him a kind of perpetual frown.

To his left sat Roy Cohn, his counsel. Cohn is 26 years old while McCarthy is 44. Cohn wore a brown suit with a brown and yellow tie tucked into his white shirt. His thick black hair is worn in a pompadour style and slick with hair oil. He has a broad nose disfigured with scars, puffy cheeks and pouty red lips. On the desk between them stood a microphone, and as they conferred in whispers they would cover the mike with a hand.

The first witness was Sidney Glassman of New York City. As he took the witness chair he asked that the lights be turned off. A TV cameraman near the east wall had switched on twin floodlights. "Turn them off," McCarthy said nonchalantly.

He stood up to swear in Glassman, idly using his left hand to turn the pages of documents on the table, never once looking at the witness. Glassman said he wanted to make a statement. McCarthy nodded curt assent. Glassman read aloud a statement denying the authority of the committee to question him. McCarthy paid no attention, toying again with papers and conferring with Cohn.

Then the questioning began. Glassman was so afraid that his voice shook as he answered.

"Would you mind speaking a little louder, sir," McCarthy asked. I was surprised to hear that *sir*.

Glassman twisted nervously in his chair but failed to raise his voice.

"I can't hear a thing you're saying," McCarthy said gently.

When Glassman declined to say whether he was a member of the communist party, citing the Fifth Amendment, the McCarthy-loving lawyer on my right stared at me in triumph. I felt uneasy. I fantasized about how I'd behave were I the witness. *Member? No. Ever been? No. Fellow traveller? No. Espionage? No. Conspiracy to commit espionage? No.* Why was Glassman dodging the question? After all, the communist party still is a legal entity in the United States. Irrationally, I felt that Glassman was letting me down.

The next witness was Sidney Stolberg of Roosevelt, N.J., manager of the New Jersey Federated Egg Producers Co-operative. He was big, well-dressed, wore glasses, exuded self-confidence—at first. Later he wilted.

"My attorney," Stolberg began, "wants to make a motion."

McCarthy shrugged and said, "Make it."

As the witness read a statement written by his lawyer, McCarthy doodled with a yellow pencil. His air was that of a persecuted man forced to submit to trivia while in pursuit of monumental evil.

Stolberg also objected to the hearing.

McCarthy said: "When we examined you in closed hearings, Mr. Stolberg, you said you objected to Star Chamber sessions. Now you're being heard in open sessions, and you say you object to this."

Stiffening, Stolberg challenged: "Read me the testimony in which I ever said anything like that!"

"You want me to read it?" McCarthy bluffed.

"Yes!"

"Well," McCarthy drawled, "I may say, so many communists who come before me in closed sessions object to it—to closed or open sessions—that I may have confused you with one of them."

Although his bluff had been called, McCarthy was not embarrassed; he remained as bland as before.

His voice has a curious defect. Every so often he sounds as though he is about to belch, so he sucks in his breath to avoid being impolite. Then when he speaks the next couple of phrases, his voice sounds hollow. I'm sure this is an involuntary habit.

Hardly involuntary, though, is his behavior. At cocktail parties I have met actors who worked hard at being sincere, instead of just being themselves. McCarthy, like other politicians and demagogues, is an actor. He cultivates a mannerism he feels is suited to his work, his nefarious work. Sometimes he seems apologetic about bothering witnesses. Then he becomes patronizing, indulgent, paternal. He plays the role of father confessor who only wants to help you rid yourself of your sins and thenceforth walk in peace.

He hypnotizes people by speaking so softly they must strain to hear him, thus giving him total attention. He also uses a theatrical trick—casually throwing away a line. Because of his nonchalance, whatever he says, however banal, seems laced with overtones and undertones of meaning.

I thought of the common octopus (*Octopus vulgaris*). It exists in holes at the bottom of the sea. It is secretive. It ejects ink to screen itself. It paralyzes other creatures. It changes color fast. It tightens its tentacles around an object and then devours it.

1954

WEDNESDAY, MARCH 3, 1954   ▨   Last night I had a nightmare in a place that may have been my home town in Illinois. I was walking uphill when suddenly I saw some men heading for a house where they planned to hold a meeting. There were about a dozen of them and they all looked exactly alike—medium height, unshaven, wearing working clothes. When they saw me they stopped and turned around, blocking my path, cursing me, threatening me. I felt terrified. I feared they would beat me up if I said one wrong word. Forcing myself to be calm, I tried to figure out what would pacify them, then realized nothing would help because they had coalesced into a mindless mob seething with fury. And they did attack me and my fright became so intense that I snapped awake. I believe this nightmare was a metaphor expressing my anxiety about McCarthyism. I'll bet I'm not the only American plagued with nightmares about Joe McCarthy and his fanatical followers.

FRIDAY, NOVEMBER 19, 1954 ■ A so-called Committee for Ten Million is collecting signatures on a petition to try to keep McCarthy from being censured by the Senate.

Day before yesterday I ate lunch at a stand-up counter in Washington Market in lower Manhattan. Another man who eats there regularly is Hank—I don't know his last name. About 36, he is a fanatical follower of McCarthy and totally ignorant. Once, with sharp questions, I forced him to admit that all he reads is comic strips.

Hank was eating with another man, so I stood some distance away. Then Joe, the handsome Bohemian counterman, cried: "Eddie! See what Hank's got!"

When I turned toward Hank I saw he held a McCarthy petition. Picking up my plate, I walked over to him. Grinning, Hank asked: "Wanna see?"

Grinning back, I took the petition from him.

"Gonna sign it?" asked Hank, his eyes glittering.

"Sure!"

Spreading the petition on the counter, whipping out a thick editorial pencil, I scrawled in huge letters: ADOLF HITLER . . . BERLIN, GERMANY.

Hank looked, did a double-take, and without a word carried the document to a man behind a meat counter, apparently the guy who is circulating it here in the market. The butcher did not see what I wrote—at first. I resumed eating. Then—

"What jerky son-of-a-bitch wrote this!"

Wheeling around, I extended my right arm and pointed with my index finger at the butch, snapping: "I did!"

I expected that burly butcher to climb over his counter and have at me with a cleaver, but my instant reply may have taken him off balance.

"Well," he mumbled, surprisingly meek, "you sure messed it up!"

I went on eating. Then the butcher snarled: "Be a good idea if Hitler was alive!"

TUESDAY, NOVEMBER 23, 1954 ■ Today I learned that my father sent Joe McCarthy a telegram praising him.

TUESDAY, NOVEMBER 30, 1954 ■ Last night's rally for Joe McCarthy in Madison Square Garden was a cocked gun that failed to fire because the triggerman was in Washington with a bum elbow. The explosive charge was packed tight and dry: the "martyrdom" of McCarthy, the jiggled and juggled signatures of the boobocracy on the anti-censure petition, the 13 Americans jailed by the Chinese Reds, the vest-pocket war off the China coast, the issue of co-existence, the GOP defeat in the election and Joe's subsequent loss of his chairmanship, the renewed public snufflings of the Christian Fronters and America Firsters.

All the necessary ingredients, primed for a big BANG! Instead, the rally went pfff—f-f-f—ttt.

Hitler would have sneered, Huey Long would have guffawed. The three witches in *Macbeth* would have slunk away, disconsolate at the plot that misfired. No Guy Fawkes Day this, although it could have been the Night Fascism Came to Flower. "Fascism," Huey once said, "will come to America in the guise of anti-fascism." And black shall be white, and white shall be black, and never the twain shall meet.

Last night the tin-headed admirals and generals and majors turned truth inside out. Unwittingly revealing their own lust for power, they wailed that they had been brainwashed, that we are advancing toward a totalitarian state, that there is danger of a man on horseback—in those very words. *Their* man on horseback, of course. St. McCarthy.

To frenetically shrieking people they declared that everything they said was cold rationalism. We believe in law and order, they shouted, even as they ejected a girl photographer who had broken no law, committed no disorder. This is a government of laws and not of men, they shrilled, ignoring the fact that McCarthy had appealed on television for all federal employees to break the law and give secret information to him, a single man, not the whole government. They said more, much more, but they failed to spew the words that could have unleashed the beasts. The mob wanted to hear about mob-given laws. It wanted to be told that it had ascended the throne. The mob wanted a mirror held before its face. "Mirror, mirror on the wall, am I not fairest of them all?"

For a few suspenseful minutes it seemed that Roy Cohn might help the mob make love to itself. "Discovered" in a box seat on the south side of the arena, a would-be Caligula with a thumb ready to point down, a flayer of all enemies of McCarthy, Roy was photographed repeatedly by newspaper and television cameramen whose lights enabled the mob to realize that their champion was in their midst, and so there arose a throaty chant: "We want Roy, we want Roy, we want Roy!" On the speakers' platform ape-browed Major Racey Jordan boomed into his microphones: "C'mon, Roy!"

And Cohn, the violet who shrinks toward the sun, the bear-trap mind beneath gleaming patent-leather hair, humbly bowed to fate and arose and began striding along a balcony toward the speakers' platform. Two Garden guards, sudden bearers of a sacred treasure, marched self-importantly ahead of him to clear his path to the platform. Like a low-lying cloud bristling with electricity on a sullen summer night, the audience rumbled expectantly. Roy would tell everyone! Roy had all the answers! He stepped in front of the snake-slim microphones and pursed his fat red lips and then began to speak. This was the moment! But—he fizzled out.

A lawyer by trade, he unreeled long and involved sentences, spun out clauses and phrases, served pap when the mob wanted red meat. However, into the mob he did shoot one dose of hyperbole: "If the Senate," said Roy sonorously, "votes to censure, it will be committing the blackest act in our whole history!"

From near and far there came applause, but it merely pattered like an April rain, rather than booming like a cannonade. Had he machine-gunned bursts of short emotional words into that audience, he would have carried the night—and maybe the entire history of the nation. Greased with the poison of lies, they would have found their mark and killed the soul of an entire people. Instead, he shot over their heads. He should have aimed at their bellies. Surprise! Surprise! The golden moment gone.

The rally fizzled in other ways, too. Missing were those spectacular trappings that Hitler knew how to use so well at Nuremberg. Tonight the beasts in the arena sat amidst a bit of bunting, state flags at the rear of the speakers' platform, a sprinkling of hate signs, one piano, two singers and a band. But what a band! Apple-cheeked boys and girls flown here from Wisconsin, dazzled at finding themselves in the Big Apple, in Manhattan, in the hallowed Madison Square Garden, and they felt so awed that they floundered and fluted off-key and behind the beat and almost in panic.

Just as tom-toms are needed to drown out the screams of voodoo sacrificial victims, so was a proud and blaring band needed to camouflage the fracas that developed when the girl photographer was thrown out. Major

Jordan sensed what was needed, and he bent down and beseeched the band director to play, to play anything, but—no director. He had wandered off somewhere. The major beckoned forward, as a substitute, a Brunhilde-shaped black-gowned female who obligingly, but without musical accompaniment, began bellowing: "My country, 'tis of thee, sweet land of liberty—" Sweet land of *liberty?*

No one really listened to the singer. Few heard her. As the figures of men swirled and dissolved around the unhappy girl photographer, out of throats there ripped screams: "Throw her out! . . . Commie! . . . Commie, Commie, Commie!"

H. L. Mencken, when chided for his sarcasm, used to retort that he liked to "stir up the animals." Last night they wanted to be stirred.

Referring to communists, one orator asked rhetorically: "Who wants to shake those bloody hands?"

"Flanders!"

"And?"

"Lehman!"

"Flanders . . . Flanders . . . Lehman . . . Lehman . . . Flanders . . . Lehman!"

I saw a housewife touch her husband's arm to quiet him, and suddenly he subsided, a guilty look in his eyes. But most mob members declared at the top of their voices that Senator Flanders and Senator Lehman love to consort with murderers. A blood lust wracked the mob. The animals were stirring, tails flicking menacingly, crouched for the kill. Dazed with horror, I thought of the Colosseum in Rome and unfair gladiatorial combats between unarmed men and savage tigers. A coatless, spectacled youth screamed: "Pull out of the United Nations!"

Major Al Williams spoke about Senator Fulbright, adding sarcastically—"a typical Rhodes scholar!" Why, it is downright un-American to be an intellectual! At the Major's remark a titter tiptoed through the mob, came down flat-footed in a roar of laughter, and boos bounced off the walls. A Rhodes scholar! A scholar! An egg-head! Imagine! And in the United States Senate, too! What's this country coming to?

After one reporter got back to his office he drew up parallel lists of these persons, institutions and ideas that were: (1) booed; (2) cheered.

The boos were for: Senators Fulbright, Flanders and Lehman, Dean Acheson, General George C. Marshall, Eleanor Roosevelt, former President Truman, President Eisenhower, co-existence, the Civil Liberties Union, the Committee for an Effective Congress, the *New York Times*, the "leftist press," "trumped-up charges" against McCarthy.

The cheers were for: Senator Knowland, the late Senator Pat McCarran, George Sokolsky, Martin Dies, General Douglas MacArthur, Senator Bricker, Catholics, red-blooded Americans, just plain Americans, the right of Congress to impeach a President, and God.

The mob was delighted when it was informed that "God made our souls out of nothing." Theology and metaphysics in the Garden, yet!

The invocation—seven to eight minutes long—had been delivered by Bishop Cuthbert O'Gara (cq), a Roman Catholic imprisoned two years by Chinese communists.

"The loyal defenders of our cherished traditions," he intoned, while the mob stood with bowed heads but burning eyes, are arrayed against "powerful influences operating in subtle and devious ways—the slanted press, the slanted radio, the slanted television!"

Throughout the entire evening, as I sat in the press section at the front of the hall, I saw a gray-haired man glowering at us reporters. And moments before the end of the rally four reporters began walking out and were hissed.

"What an experience!" one reporter said as he neared an exit. "First time I've ever been hissed."

"Aw," jeered the other reporter. "It should have happened to you years ago."

1955

TUESDAY, MARCH 1, 1955   ■   Frank Kappler, assistant city editor, is the wittiest man I know. In the city room today some of us were discussing a report that the New Testament has been published in Braille. Frank said: "Yeah—but did you know that Lazarus was the original raised character?"

MONDAY, MARCH 28, 1955   ■   Last Saturday Ruthie and I visited David and Jacqueline Ellis in their apartment in Harlem River Houses. They are black friends whom we met through Romare Bearden. David is a kind of super-truant officer for the board of education. Jackie is pert and brilliant.

During World War II, in the summer of 1943, she was returning to New York after visiting Dave, who was stationed at Fort Knox, Kentucky. Her train stopped in Louisville. It was a hot day. Jackie walked into the station to get a Coke. No one waited on her. It became obvious that she was being ignored. Jackie decided to stick it out. After about 20 minutes a countergirl rasped: "Whaddya want?"

"I want a Coke."

The girl gave it to her in the standard Coke glass. Jackie drank it. The moment she finished, the girl glared at her and broke the glass on the edge of the counter.

Appalled, I asked: "So what did you do, Jackie?"

"I didn't do anything," she replied. "I didn't say anything. Unfortunately, I didn't have much money with me, but if I had had enough cash I would have stood there and drunk one Coke after another and made that damned white trash break all the Goddamn glassware in the place!"

FRIDAY, APRIL 29, 1955 ■ Ruth and I were married today.

Ruth was the kindest person I ever knew. The Torah says "the highest wisdom is kindness," and since this is true, she also was the wisest person I ever knew.

Once she startled me by declaring that I had more talent in my little finger than she had in her entire body. Hotly I denied her statement, crying: "Hell no, dear! I may have a little talent, but you are a genius. You're a genius at making friends and keeping friends!"

That was the truth. To her many friends she gave her time and attention, her laughter and tears. She kept a drawer full of cards of all kinds, mailing hundreds of them. Belatedly I would learn of her total generosity. We socialized with a husband and wife. He had surgery that almost cut him in half and kept him hospitalized three months. Ruthie sent him a card every day for three months. When at last he was able to phone her, he said he often thought he would die unless he received another card from her the following day.

Soon after I met Ruthie we were eating chili in a small restaurant. I like lots of crackers with chili, but the waitress would give me only a few. Ruthie jumped up. She said she was going to the grocery store next door to buy a box of soda crackers. She darted out and back again before I could stop her. To myself I said: Hey, wait a minute! Is this gal just trying to impress me? Having been divorced by my wife for no valid reason, I was suspicious of women.

It took about a year before I realized that Ruth was absolutely sincere. In that moment of insight I fell in love with her and have continued to love her to this very moment.

Ruth Kraus was born on July 4, 1909, on the east side of Manhattan. Her Jewish parents were immigrants from Austria, which meant that they were Galitzianers, not Litvaks, a distinction I soon learned. She had no accent of any kind—not even a New York accent. Born into Judaism, she became an atheist and died an atheist.

Her father was a tailor who died in the flu pandemic of 1918 when Ruth was nine years old. Her mother was left with four daughters and two sons to raise, so she opened a tiny needle shop in Yorkville, saved her money, gave her children food and love. Other people called her "Aunt Sadie." I never met her because she died before Ruthie and I met, but relatives and friends declared she had a sweet disposition. I believe it.

Ruth knew her parents loved her, so she enjoyed the emotional security I sought. A brilliant girl, she was first in her class in grammar school, Hebrew school, high school, and skipped a couple of grades, graduating from high school at sixteen. What she wanted, more than anything in the world, was to go to college, but instead she had to go to work to help support the family. She became a secretary—in my opinion, the greatest secretary in the world. One day, just for fun, we tested one another's typing speed. Ruthie batted out 120 words a minute!

From secretary she developed into an executive secretary. Early on, she was hired by William E. Robinson, an advertising salesman for the New York World-Telegram, and they began working there the day the building opened. She went with him to the Journal-American and then the Herald Tribune, where her boss became publisher. He knew Steve Hannagan, called the "Prince of Press Agents," and after Hannagan died, Robinson bought controlling interest in that public relations firm. Mrs. Helen Rogers Reid, who owned the Herald Tribune, had grown so fond of Ruth that she offered her an executive position if she would stay at the Trib, but loyal Ruth chose to go with Robinson to what became Robinson-Hannagan. She accompanied him again when he became board chairman of Coca-Cola.

Robinson was a close friend of President Eisenhower, so from time to time the White House would call Ruthie to ask where her boss was. Once when the White House operator said the President was ready to pick up the phone, Ruthie said: "Please put him on the line." She was fearless. Eisenhower gave her an autographed copy of his book called Crusade in Europe. A few times she and I socialized with Eisenhower's secretary and Richard Nixon's secretary. Because of all the years she worked for Robinson, a businessman and Republican, she was politically more conservative than I.

Apart from politics and business, Ruthie and I shared almost identical tastes. We liked or disliked the same people and books and plays and music and movies. She liked Ethel Merman a little better than I, but that's about the measure of our differences. She longed to read more and more books, but worked such long hours she had little time for them. In fact, she worked too hard—and had her first heart attack ten months after we met.

That was when she worked at the Herald Tribune. Her friends took up a collection and bought a huge fish tank they wanted placed by her bed in the *hospital.* When the head of the hospital said that such a thing was not allowed, Robinson called him and vowed to dismantle his building, brick by brick, unless Ruth got her fish tank. She got it.

Long before *Women's Lib* became popular, I often made the fatuous remark that "Ruthie has a man's mind in a woman's body." Okay, I'm sorry about that. She was, in fact, more logical than most human beings. She was a realist. At a party none of us could coin an acceptable definition of an intellectual until Ruthie spoke up. Said she: "An intellectual is a person who becomes excited by ideas." Ah, so!

While she made few mistakes, she did make an enormous one after getting out of the hospital: She resumed smoking. Every time I lit her cigaret she thanked me. She was as addicted to nicotine as I, and she also drank a little, while I was a spree drinker and would get drunk once every two or three weeks. Although my inebriation became a problem to her, she never nagged me. She was, however, very glad when I said I wanted to enter therapy to try to stop drinking.

Ruthie was mature; I was immature. She was at peace with herself; I was at war with myself. She gave me everything she was and had. Just passing me in the apartment, she would smile and say she loved me, and sometimes she even said she worshipped me. She did all she could to try to compensate me for the love I needed when I was growing up. She declared I had created myself and she predicted that I would become famous.

Awed by her love and compassion and enthusiasm and curiosity and sparkling personality, I sometimes asked her, in all seriousness, what made her so wonderful. She would smile a shy smile and softly say: "I'm a good kid." That was all; I'm a good kid.

At a cocktail party she met a man who failed to catch her name, so merrily she said: "Oh, just call me Stinky!" I, an immature guy, later berated her for putting herself down. Much later I read something about Daisetz T. Suzuki, who helped popularize Zen Buddhism in the United States. He had the playful habit of walking around wearing a sign saying: "I'm a nobody." He knew, and she knew, more than I knew at the time. Now I appreciate the gentle strength of my wife's ego.

I always told her that she soothed me, and she would say that I stimulated her. Each statement was true. We complemented one another so well that some friends said they didn't know where Ruthie ended and Eddie began. We agreed that the only things that made life bearable were love and work — only later learning that Freud had said the same thing. Ruth was a workaholic. I was a workaholic, bookaholic, alcoholic.

She was five feet three inches tall, had hazel eyes like mine, wore almost no makeup, was so near-sighted she always wore glasses, had brown hair that she let grow to her waist when I said I like long hair. Feature by facial feature, she was not pretty in the conventional sense, but because of her sunny personality and radiant face she was beautiful. Her body was lithe, her legs lovely, and she had the most beautiful hands I ever saw. She kept her fingernails in perfect condition with a shade of red nail polish I liked. Her skin had an electric quality.

She liked men but never flirted. Instead, she learned the language of sports so that she might share their interests. All her knowledge was wasted on me for I have little interest in any sport. Years earlier she fell in love with a man and hoped he would marry her. He rejected her because her toes were not perfectly aligned. When I met Ruth she lived with a sister and brother-in-law and saved her salary. I still don't know how she managed, but she handled money well, while at the same time she would spend freely during a spree. Early on, she persuaded me to let her pay my debts.

Ruth's voice was deeper than the voices of most women; on the phone she sounded like a man. She couldn't sing a note, but when my daughter visited us she croaked Yiddish songs, which Sandy was eager to learn. Sandy adored her step-mother. And just as my daughter welcomed Ruthie into our family, so did Ruthie's family welcome me into theirs, despite the fact that I am a goy. Now I had a family here in New York.

I dearly loved her elder sister Ann and Ann's husband, Dr. Sol Goldschmidt. Ann, a bluntly honest woman, once told me she was puzzled about the fact that Ruthie was so—well, noble. Ann added that she was unable to say this about anyone else in her family. A long time later I read Carl Jung, who said that the whole is holy. Although Ruthie was not perfect, she surely was whole.

My parents were divorced, my mother living in Kewanee, Illinois, my father in Chicago. When I realized I was in love with Ruth I called each to describe her, praise her, mentioned that she was Jewish. Each parent exclaimed: "Jewish!" I felt like strangling them.

At long last my mother agreed to meet Ruth, and one day I walked into a room where they sat and said: "Mother—" Looking up, she rebuked me, saying: "Edward! Can't you see that Ruthie and I are talking?" Bingo! Later I presented Ruth to my eccentric father, wary of his attitude toward her. He behaved courteously, led us to his apartment, chatted amiably, then said he wanted to show her something. He walked to a closet, brought out an elephant gun, cradled it in his arms, walked toward her and asked: "Ruth, would you like to hold my elephant gun?"

She and I lived in the Hotel Master on Riverside Drive at West 103rd St.

Occupying most of the 26th floor, we had three terraces overlooking the entire horizon. Ruthie liked to use them to sun-bathe in the nude. One evening we entertained a woman who lived in Paris. Just as lights began glowing in Manhattan, we led her onto the southwest terrace, where she stood and stared and then said our view was better than the view from Montmartre. Ruth and I would sit in chairs in the living room near two windows to gaze out over the Hudson River and miles into New Jersey. When we saw an especially beautiful sunset suggesting a painting by El Greco, we'd call it a religious sunset.

We enjoyed walking in Riverside Park—always hand-in-hand. Ruthie, a city-born gal, was fascinated by trees, so I bought her books about them and as we walked she would tug me over to some tree, identify it and exclaim over its beauty. I liked that. Each spring we watched the yellowing of forsythia, which Ruthie mischievously called fivesythia. When I spied the season's first dandelion, I would pick it and make a ceremony of presenting it to my wife, who would place the golden gift in her hair.

Whenever we reached Riverside Church we paused to stare again at the statue of Albert Einstein in the sculpture over the entrance. I've read that when the great man saw it himself he teetered back and forth on his heels, laughing, declaring he never intended to become a Hebrew saint, let alone a Christian saint. Then my wife and I would continue to Grant's Tomb and stroll behind it onto a knoll with a commanding view of the Hudson River, a pleasant place where people flew kites. One winter day when snow was deep on a football field under our windows, I tramped out the letters R U T H. She wept for joy.

One of the many reasons I cherished her was that she accepted me with all my sins and shortcomings, did not try to change me, urged me instead to be myself.

One afternoon we left a cocktail party with a woman friend. Walking toward the elevator, I put on my hat, which I wore at an angle. Ruth's friend snatched the hat off my head, making a sarcastic remark about the way I wore it. Ruthie grabbed the hat from her, gently handed it to me, turned toward her friend and snapped: "Eddie can wear his hat any damned way he wishes!" Well, hurrah for you, baby!

The World-Telegram often bought radio time for commercials advertising articles written by various reporters. Whenever Ruthie's friends heard my name on the air they would tell her, saying they regarded me as a romantic figure. I would explain to her that, yes, a reporter's life is interesting—which is why we were underpaid. I never resented the fact that her salary was bigger than mine.

She was proud of me. I was proud of her. Let the name of Ruthie be uttered and faces would light up. All my male friends, white and black alike, adored her. Romare Bearden swore that the sun rose and set on Ruthie. Along with my daughter, Ruth was the most important person in my entire life, the one who gave me the most, helped me the most. Many a night we would lie side by side in bed, silent and serene, her dear head on my shoulders and again and again I would whisper: "Darling, this is It! In all the world, in all of life, there is no greater bliss than this very moment."

On May 11, 1955, my wife and I sailed from Weehawken, New Jersey, aboard a United Fruit Company banana ship called the Antigua for a round-trip voyage to Ecuador. After a trip through the Panama Canal, we reached Guayaquil, the largest city and chief port of Ecuador. This low-lying city, only about two degrees south of the equator, lies on the west bank of the Rio Guayas.

MONDAY, MAY 16, 1955 ■ The harbor at Guayaquil is 2 1/2 miles long and has 1 1/2 miles of quays. Because of a strong current, big ships can't tie up at shore. Our ship anchored in the river about a half mile from the shore and right in front of the new Hotel Humboldt.

From dinner-time until we went to bed, Ruthie and I watched bananas being loaded aboard our ship. This is a colorful pageant. Clustered around the Antigua were banana-loading barges, together with the tugs that ease them up close to our white-painted vessel. In the forward part of the ship the loading was done by three conveyors. Back aft, all the work was done by manpower.

There were some 300 to 400 native stevedores at work. Most were scantily clad, wearing only shorts and no shoes. Some had draped cloths over their heads and shoulders to protect them from their loads, and this drapery gave them an Egyptian look. In fact, their rhythmic scuttling back and forth, together with the hard manual labor in which they were engaging, reminded me of the ancient Egyptians who built pyramids.

Aboard each barge were rich green banana stems, covered with the fronds of banana trees. When the fronds were stripped off and cast into the river, which swiftly bore them away, we could see that the stems were covered with cellophane—a recent development. Two men stood face-to-face on each barge, their feet planted widely apart. Bending over, they would pick up a heavy stem and deposit it on the shoulder of a third man, who would appear at just the right moment. With his burden in place, the man would walk across the matting of fronds covering the next layer of bananas, inch his way up an inclined board, then step down onto a work barge close to our ship.

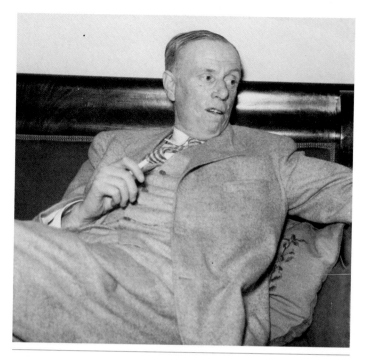

■ *I interviewed Sinclair Lewis, the first American to win the
Nobel Prize in literature, in Oklahoma City on October 28,
1937. He was a homely man with a face like a skull and a belly
like a basketball.*

■ *I met Herbert Hoover for
the first time in Oklahoma
City in 1938. I was astonished
when I learned that the former
President traveled by himself,
without any security men. In
my left arm I'm carrying a book
he autographed for me. Twenty
years later, on August 9, 1958,
the day before Hoover's eighty-
fourth birthday, I interviewed
him in his suite in the Waldorf
Towers in Manhattan and
wrote about it in my diary.*

■ I met Eleanor Roosevelt for the second time near Peoria in the early 1940s. She was warm, curious and generous, and much more attractive in person than in photographs. The man in the black suit is Clarence Chamberlin, the famous aviator. I wore a jacket so loud, it seemed to blind everyone except Mrs. Roosevelt.

Here I am in a hotel ball-room in Peoria with my first wife, Leatha Sparlin, called Lee. She was blonde, beautiful, a symphony violinist and the mother of my daughter, Sandra Gail Ellis.

Young hotshot reporter at work in city room of the Peoria Journal-Transcript in the early 1940s.

I met Will Durant, the famous historian, for the first time in Peoria on March 9, 1942. He and his wife, Ariel, wrote the eleven volumes of The Story of Civilization. I liked him because he was witty, playful and irreverent.

I met Paris-born actress Claudette Colbert at Dearborn Station in Chicago in June of 1943. In 1934, she had won an Oscar for her performance with Clark Gable in the film It Happened One Night. She was natural and pleasant.

■ On September 17, 1943, in Dearborn, Michigan, I met Henry Ford while I was working for the United Press. He and I are looking at one another. He was boring, he had bad breath and his hair was tinted.

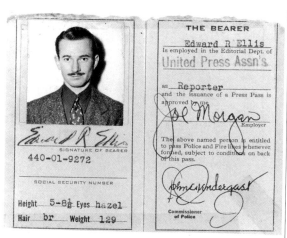

THE BEARER

Edward R Ellis
Is employed in the Editorial Dept. of

United Press Assn's.

as Reporter
and the issuance of a Press Pass is approved by me

Joe Morgan
Employer

The above named person is entitled to pass Police and Fire lines whenever formed, subject to conditions on back of this pass.

John Prendergast
Commissioner of Police

SIGNATURE OF BEARER
440-01-9272

SOCIAL SECURITY NUMBER

Height 5-8½ Eyes hazel
Hair br Weight 129

■ Back from Okinawa in 1946 and weighing only 129 pounds, I got a new police press card in Chicago, where I worked for the United Press.

■ *This portrait was taken by a girlfriend who was an artists' model at the Chicago Art Institute. She had learned photography from her former husband. She posed me in Lincoln Park in Chicago in 1946.*

■ On November 22, 1946, the Chicago Newspaper Guild named me the best feature writer in Chicago. To my right is actress Jane Russell; on my left is Miss Page One, who has just handed me the stick of type, which is printed on page 152 of this book.

■ In 1947, British actress-singer Gertrude Lawrence appeared on the stage in Chicago. I was touched by her compassion for the war-weary, hungry people in the U.K. and wrote about her in my diary. On January 24, a press agent persuaded her to meet a man who designed hats. She clowned around and stuck this hat on me.

■ Now a reporter for the New York World-Telegram, I sailed for Europe aboard the Gen. Alexander M. Patch *on* May 23, 1950, *to interview the ship's crew members, who worked for the federal civil service. Ruthie joined me in Amsterdam.*

■ *Here I am interviewing a sailor in oilskins aboard ship. Although the trip cost me nothing, I worked hard on this assignment.*

He would pass in front of a man with a machete, and two out of every three times the man would slash down with his ugly knife, slicing off the end of a stem. *Swish*, pause. *Swish*, pause. The blade rose and fell, and if a banana carrier got too close to the man with the machete, that man would place his left hand on a shoulder of the stevedore, turn him around a bit, then use the knife. The timing had to be perfect, for otherwise some worker would get an arm sliced off, or lose a piece of his buttocks. I marvelled at the rhythm of the performance and the unerring eye of the knife-wielder. The butt of each stem was about four inches in diameter, but the blade cut through it easily and neatly, the sliced-off bit flying onto the deck of the barge.

Also on each barge were three men counting the number of stems. One represented the farmer who had raised the bananas; the second, a government official; the third, an official of the United Fruit Company. I was surprised at the great number of stems they rejected. These rejects were stacked on corners of the barge for later sale in Guayaquil. Tape covered some of the butts that had begun to splay. I heard at least three explanations about why a machete was used to cut off the stems. Perhaps the true version is that it freshens the fruit, just as cutting flowers in the home tends to keep them fresh.

Once the stevedore was past the man with the knife he would approach two men who stood on either side of the foot of a conveyor at the forward end of the ship. They would lift the stem off the shoulder of the workman, gently heave it into the loop of the endless rubber belt riding vertically up the side of the ship, then horizontally across the railing, then downward into the hold, where other men took it off the conveyor and stood it on its end in a refrigerated compartment.

This operation, this entire trip of each banana stem from its resting place in a barge to its resting place in the ship, was a beautiful ballet of precision and grace, broken only by the occasional clanging of a bell in the hold, meaning a short interruption was needed. Hour after hour it went on and on and on, with flood-lights yellowing the scene. The greater the number of banana stems loaded into our ship, the deeper she sank into the mushy-brown and fast-running waters of the river. With fascination I watched the lithe figures of the stevedores, their serpentine-twisting biceps, the high-lighted ridges and valleys of the muscles in their backs.

As time wore on, some became frolicsome, beginning to tear to tatters the ragged shirts of the men in front of them. This became a game, carried on in the best of spirits. When a shirt had been reduced to shreds, its owner would tear it off his shoulder to wipe his brow and chest.

In the distance, on the terrace of the Hotel Humbolt, I saw starched businessmen taking their ease beneath beach umbrellas, sipping drinks. When it was time for the stevedores to eat, they would pick up bowls from the barges and precariously edge their way onto a floating mess hall tied up to our ship. This was a rude and dirty craft with a few cooks bent over a fire on the deck and some huge vats. I was unable to see what food was scooped out of the vats and splashed into the out-thrust bowls. When his bowl was full, a man would inch his way to some vacant place on the barge and squat down to spoon the food into his mouth. Soon another barge would be lashed to the unloading barge nearest our ship, and back to work went the men.

Today, I was told, 54,300 stems were loaded into the *Antigua*. Still green, they will be kept at a temperature of 52.6 degrees—a temperature that cannot be changed without a radioed order from company headquarters in New York.

The conveyors clanked on and on. At the base of each conveyor there stood a man whose sole job it was to pull free the endless rubber belt so that a proper loop would be formed to hold the next stem. Ruthie and I were grateful that we don't have such a brainless, monotonous job. On deck stood a man with a paint brush who slapped blue paint onto each freshly cut butt.

In the distance down the dark river another ship turned on its lights, and the river-borne fronds flowed silently by, and the night air took on an edge, and the tired stevedores threw themselves down wherever they could to catch a few moments of sleep, some wrapping themselves in cellophane from the stems, and then it was back to work again and clank, clank, clank, and higher and ever higher rose the green gold of the bananas into this glistening vessel, and I knew that henceforth whenever I eat a banana I'll think of Guayaquil, Ecuador, and the spectacle of brown men with green fruit on their shoulders.

CHAPTER 11

1956

WEDNESDAY, JANUARY 11, 1956 ■ Last Friday morning at 4:30 o'clock I was awakened by a call from the night city editor, Mel Snyder, who wanted a stake-out on Grace Kelly's apartment.

The previous day it was announced in her home town of Philadelphia that she had become engaged to Prince Rainier III of Monaco, a tiny principality on the French Riviera. Since then there has been a drum-beat of publicity about the two of them, and I don't know what the hell Mel thought I could get her to say early this morning. I felt surly.

But I left home, grabbed a bite to eat, bought all the newspapers I could, hailed a cab and at 6:15 A.M. arrived at 988 Fifth Avenue, where the actress has an apartment. Walking into the lobby I found a doorman named Otto mopping the floor. When I explained I was a reporter, plaintively he said: "Your job is so much more interesting than mine—"

He told me Miss Kelly has lived there since last February, that her 11-room apartment covers the entire seventh floor, that her rental is about $8,000 a year, that she lives alone but has two maids. He also declared she is pleasant—"no up-nosiness about her!" And the prince, he added, is equally pleasant and polite. Miss Kelly had arrived home just before Otto began work at midnight. She usually sleeps until noon. Hearing this, I sighed and resumed reading the papers. No point in calling her. I'd just get the brush-off. From time to time I used a lobby phone to call Mel.

The hours passed. At last I was joined by an Associated Press photographer, one from the *Post*, and a *Post* reporter named Carl Pelleck.

At 7:45 A.M. Otto was relieved by George, who was much less communicative. From time to time an elevator operator would call out the number of a floor when someone on that floor pressed the elevator button. This alerted the doorman, who then would summon a cab or limousine. At 9:22 I heard him call: "Number seven!"

We of the press corps jumped up, whipped out pencils and pads and camera plates, faced the elevator shaft.

The doors opened. Huddled against the back wall of the elevator was the glamorous Grace Kelly, winner of an Oscar, recently voted the best-dressed woman in America, renowned for her beauty, soon to become a princess. She hesitated before emerging, surprised and annoyed at seeing us at that hour. Unsteadily she walked out of the elevator and stood shyly in front of it.

I was astounded to hear Carl introduce me: "Miss Kelly, this is Mr. Ellis of the *World-Telegram* and—"

"What?" She blinked. "I beg your pardon—?"

Carl said: "We just want to ask you a few questions."

Grace Kelly wore tinted glasses through which I could see eyes wide with apprehension. Her champagne-colored hair was pulled back and tied with a black ribbon. She wore an orange and black checkered coat and a scarf barely visible at her throat. She is, indeed, beautiful.

"Miss Kelly," I began—and at that moment both photographers popped their lights—"will you please tell us your plans for today?"

I felt like an idiot and inside myself I was cursing my editor.

"Why . . . yes, well . . . I'm just going out this morning . . ."

"Can you tell us where?"

"Oh, just out. But I'll be back by noon."

"Will you see the prince today?"

"Mmmmm . . . yes."

"Can you tell us where? For lunch?"

"Yes, we'll lunch together."

"And then you'll attend the ball in the Waldorf this evening?"

"Uh, yes. We'll start for there, I guess, at 8:30."

As she spoke she had edged toward the front door, eager to be rid of us but too polite to snub us. Waiting in the street was a cab. The doorman held its door open for her. As she stepped inside, Carl and I spoke at the same time:

"Is the date set for the wedding?"

"When will it be?"

Grace Kelly said: "Uh . . . after Easter . . . I really must . . ."

"All right, Miss Kelly. Thank you!"

She closed the door. The cab glided away.

Carl and I ran east on 80th Street, scribbling the last of our notes. At Madison Avenue we found a drugstore with two empty booths, so we had no moral problem about which would call his office first.

I called Mel, who gave me Jack Ferris on rewrite.

"Did the prince come out?" Jack asked.

"No. He wasn't there, Jack."

"I thought he spent the night in her apartment."

"Good god, no! With reporters on their trail? Of course not."

So I had talked to Grace Kelly, but was not proud of myself.

Grace Kelly and Prince Rainier III were married April 19, 1956, in Monaco. This event, seen by a press corps numbering almost 2,000, was one of the top ten news stories of the year. In 1982 Princess Grace died after an auto accident. Later the U.S. government issued a stamp with her picture on it. To see a stamp with the face of someone you've met — an odd feeling.

FRIDAY, FEBRUARY 3, 1956 ■ For the second time within recent weeks I took a morning walk with Harry S. Truman. Whenever the former President comes to town he stays at the Hotel Carlyle at 35 East 76th Street, and as he leaves for a stroll he is surrounded by reporters.

At 7:27 A.M. today I was waiting in the hotel's white-walled lobby when Truman stepped out of an elevator looking pink-cheeked and hearty. When he saw us reporters he grinned and said: "Well! I didn't expect to see you folks again!"

Removing my hat, I smiled and said: "Good morning, Mr. President. Did you sleep well last night?"

He beamed at me. "Oh, sure! I always do. Anyone with a clear conscience sleeps well."

After giving autographs to a couple of schoolboys and signing his name on the flyleaf of the first volume of his memoirs for a woman reporter for the United Press, Truman pushed through the revolving door, emerged on East 76th Street and turned east. I took up a position at his left shoulder. At an intersection he glanced at a traffic signal and cried; "Wait, boys! Wait for the green light." The UP girl was asking a question as we rounded a corner and a pole came between her and Truman. After she was able to close in, he leaned toward her and in a sweet voice asked: "What was that you asked, dear?"

He has been out of the White House three years. Trudging along with us at his heels, he said almost to himself: "You know, after three years I thought all of this would wear off. I mean, being surrounded by reporters when I want to take a walk . . . Oh, I'm not complaining! I like you fellows, but everywhere I go I'm surrounded by reporters and others."

Joe Schroeder of the AP asked: "Do you have any trouble with crackpots?"

"Not much," replied the former President. "A little . . . I have to have an iron fence around my place in Independence, and I can't say I like that.

But then there was one fellow—they grabbed him as he was climbing over the fence. When they asked him why he did it, he said he wanted to interview the old so-and-so." With a sly grin at us, Truman added: "I don't know whether he was a member of the press or not." We laughed.

"Mr. President," I said, "you really crave privacy?"

Fixing his blue-gray bespectacled eyes on my eyes, a wistful hunger in his face, he exhaled and said: "Oh, yes!"

I felt guilty for being among those invading his privacy.

A reporter mentioned a speech Truman gave last night at the Sheraton-Astor Hotel for the annual dinner of the New York State Democratic Committee. I had watched it on television. Reading from his text, he said that the Republican party had gone so far as to "call General Marshall and myself traitors." Then he lifted his head and ad-libbed: "If we *are* traitors, all I have to say is that this country is in a hell of a fix!"

Now, responding to the reporter, Truman grinned and said: "I got a wigging from Mrs. Truman and Margaret about that! They said I should be cut off the air before I swear. I told them to blame Charlie Murphy. He helped me write that speech, and he's teaching me bad habits."

Suddenly Truman turned serious.

"After having served my country 30 years in the military and in government, to be called a traitor by the Vice President of the United States is pretty hard to take—"

Nixon, of course, is Vice President.

"—and it makes me not only want to swear, but to punch somebody!"

Wow! Had I heard Truman correctly? Was a former President declaring he would like to belt the current Vice President? I asked: "Mr. President, what was the last part of what you said?"

Staring into my face, Truman repeated clearly and firmly: "—punch somebody!"

"Have you seen Mr. Nixon since he made that remark?" I asked.

"No! . . . And I don't want to!"

Truman went on to say he had discussed Nixon's charge with Marshall. "The general just grins and doesn't say anything. He feels that if you can't nail a lie, you just build it up by discussing it."

"Mr. President," I said, "in the second volume of your memoirs will you discuss Senator McCarthy much?"

"No . . . I didn't write about McCarthy. He's a demagogue who's been laughed out of court and, like every demagogue, he can't stand the ridicule."

I asked: "Don't you think that President Eisenhower should have stepped in and stopped McCarthy before he did?"

His face hard, his eyes stern, Harry Truman said: "Yes . . . Ike should have moved faster."

SATURDAY, APRIL 7, 1956 ▪ Roy Howard, lord and master of all who work for the *World-Telegram*, spends most of his time in his office at 230 Park Avenue. Only rarely does he visit the city room. He appeared here yesterday. Yesterday was Holy Friday. Ed Wallace glanced up, saw Roy, murmured: "He is risen."

WEDNESDAY, JUNE 13, 1956 ▪ This afternoon I was walking along Park Avenue when I saw—*Greta Garbo!* With the reflex of a reporter, I checked my watch and saw that the exact time was 3:50 o'clock.

Greta Garbo was striding south on the west side of the avenue between 52nd and 53rd Sts. With her was a distinguished-looking man with silver hair in a brown suit. He was hatless and so was she. Friends of mine who have seen Garbo on the street say she usually wears a huge hat with a floppy brim that hides her face, but today she was not even wearing sun glasses. She wore a black blouse, a tan skirt decorated with black patterns, and on her feet were shoes that looked like moccasins. Contrary to what I have read, her feet are *not* big. I know, because I turned around and followed her at a distance. Slung over her left shoulder was a big bag, and in her right hand she carried a white package by its string.

As she and her companion passed before me, I wheeled around to follow them, I had heard her voice, with those throaty guttural tones so familiar to all of us. Her speech and gestures were animated. Her sunken thick-lidded eyes had a hint of mascara, but otherwise she seemed innocent of make-up. Because of her age her skin has begun to look like crinkled silk. Nonetheless, Greta Garbo still radiates a haunting, other-worldly beauty, a vision of a goddess half-remembered from some golden dream.

The moment passed. She walked on. Only then did I emerge from my trance and remember that in my briefcase there was a caricature of Garbo I recently had drawn. Paralyzed by her presence, I had failed to whisk out my caricature and ask her to autograph it. Stupidity, thy name is Ellis!

Here is the caricature of Garbo.

TUESDAY, SEPTEMBER 25, 1956 ■ President Eisenhower, despite his recent illnesses, is running for re-election. A political poll is being taken for the *World-Telegram* by Samuel Lubell, the professional pollster, with the help of our reporters. I consider some of Lubell's questions loaded questions. Today I was sent to Long Island City in Queens, where I interviewed 26 people.

My most revealing interview was with a 35-year-old railroad worker. He was drinking a can of beer as he sat on a clean garbage pail behind an apartment house. He was clean and neat and handsome, wearing a sports shirt and slacks, his yellow hair crew-cut, his face flushed, his eyes blue. Of Irish and German descent, he is a Catholic, the father of two little girls.

One Lubell question I had to ask him was: "What do you like most that Eisenhower has done as President?"

"Given arms to Arabia," the man said.

Glancing up from my notebook, I smiled and said: "That has implications."

"It sure has."

"You mean, there might be war between the Arabs and Israel, and that you'd like to see the Arabs win?"

"That's just what I mean, buddy." He was a little high on beer.

"Oh?"

"Want me to say it? Okay, I'm anti-Semitic."

"You're kidding, of course?"

He grinned and looked at his sister-in-law, sitting on another garbage can near him.

"He's not kidding," she said. "What he says—he means."

"You're really anti-Semitic?"

"Sure—80 per cent, 90 per cent. What's your name?"

I told him.

"Well, let me tell you: Some of my greatest friends are Jewish, but in the synagogue they teach that we're scum under their feet."

"Your Jewish friends teach this?"

"No! You're trying to put words into my mouth. In the *synagogue* they teach it."

"That who's scum under their feet? Gentiles?"

"That's right."

I said: "I'm afraid you don't know much about Jewish teaching. What's your evidence that they teach this?"

"Evidence! Ha! Whaddya want—evidence, like a prosecuting attorney?"

"Sure. Proof is based upon evidence."

The man laughed dryly. "Look! I know about Jews. I just don't like them."

Sister-in-law said: "He sure doesn't! Maybe when he was a kid, like, say something happened to him he don't like Jews."

"And," the man continued, "I'll tell you something, yuh wanna know? Hitler was right!"

"What do you mean Hitler was right?"

"Oh, maybe he went a little too far, but in the beginning, all Hitler wanted was to get back what had been lost."

"What do you mean—lost? I don't get you."

Holding out his right arm, he clenched his fist. "The Jews! They had everything in Germany."

"Oh? Really? Again I ask—what's your evidence?"

He just snorted.

"Hitler killed six million Jews. Was that right?"

He tossed his head contemptuously.

"Well?" I demanded. "Was that a nice thing to do? Look: If I pulled out a knife and killed this woman here, would that be a nice thing to do?"

I was beginning to sound sophomoric to myself, because my anger had begun boiling over.

He smiled a superior smile.

"Well! How about it?"

"Kill!" he snorted.

"Yes! Kill! Hitler killed! He killed six million Jews, and that's murder."

"What you got against the Germans?"

"I didn't say a thing about the Germans. I'm talking about Hitler."

"Hitler was a good German."

"Hitler wasn't even German. He was an Austrian—born in Austria."

By this time a small group of women had gathered around the man.

He said: "Hitler was a German Jew, if yuh wanna know!"

The man's ignorance was so monumental I felt dazed.

"He was not," I said. "Hitler was Catholic!"

The women murmured.

"He was *Catholic?*" one asked in a quavering voice.

"Yes."

The man sneered: "So he killed six hundred million Jews! So what?"

Glaring at him, slowly I said: "Six million . . . human beings."

"I better not say anything more," the man remarked with a crafty look.

"You mean—he should have killed more?"

He looked right into my eyes. "That's what I mean, buddy!"

"You know," I said, "You're the first person I ever met who *admitted* that he's anti-Semitic. Who else don't you like?"

Sister-in-law said: "Better ask him who he does like. The other way—it would take you too long to write it."

The man grinned and said: "The only good ones are Germans—and don't forget I fought in the war for four years!"

"But I thought you were part Irish. How about the Irish?"

"Yeah, I like the Irish and—maybe—the Scotch. Most of all, I hate the English."

"Because you're part Irish?"

"First," the man said, "I'm against the English, then I'm against the Jews, and then I'm against the niggers."

Sister-in-law said: "Something musta happened when he was a kid, the way he don't like Jews."

By now I felt so enraged I was afraid of losing control of myself. With forced irony I said: "Maybe you think all Jews should be killed?"

He said nothing.

"I'm married to a Jew," I said. I expected to get a big reaction from him, but didn't.

Mildly, he said: "Yuh lied to me."

"No I didn't . . . How?"

"When you said your name was—what was it?"

"Ellis . . . Edward Ellis."

"And what's that?"

"Ellis is Welsh. I'm also part Irish, part English, part Scotch."

"Scotch?"

"My middle name is Robb. That's a Scots clan name."

"What was your religion before you got married?"

"Protestant . . . Say, do you think I ought to go home tonight and kill my wife?"

He didn't reply.

Sister-in-law said: "Funny, ain't it, the way he don't like Jews? Like I said, maybe something happened when he was a kid."

FRIDAY, NOVEMBER 9, 1956 ■ Reporters hear many stories that never get into print. Here is one example:

MEMO TO CITY DESK

—ellis, nov. 8, 9:21a

A rare and delicate medical problem has come to my attention.

At Doctors Hospital in Freeport, Long Island, there is a man suffering from priapism. This is a permanent erection. This condition is so rare that urologists see but one or two such cases in a lifetime.

According to the hospital's medical director—who asked me not to use his name—this particular case is the worst ever seen by any of the doctors at that institution. A total of eight physicians have been consulted, some by long-distance telephone.

The patient is a married man 38 years old. He endured this condition 36 hours before checking into the hospital, and now he has been there two and a half weeks. The pain is so intense that he is kept under sedation.

The doctors have tried various therapies—all without success. For one thing, they shot a drug into his spine in the hope of blocking off a nerve leading to his penis. The apparent cause of his condition is a blood clot.

If nothing else works, he may have to have surgery, but unfortunately this would leave the patient impotent.

The hospital has 115 patients, so if we published a story we would not be identifying the poor man. Maybe we could write a piece using the correct word *priapism*, and leave it to our readers to consult their dictionaries.

1957

THURSDAY, JULY 11, 1957   ■   In the office today I received an amusing form letter from someone named Irving Hoffman. It bore this headline:

HANDY-DANDY LITTLE GIANT NERVOUS BREAKDOWN AVOIDER AND MAIL ANSWERING FORM

Here and there on the page were tiny squares to be checked by pencil to indicate agreement with this or that statement. One said: "Mr. Hoffman has been declared a mental incompetent. Your communication has been forwarded to his attorney."

Near one square was the word *Congratulations!* Pasted on this square was a small red star. To the right of the square there was this typed message: "Excellent story." Enclosed was a clipping of a recent story of mine about Bessie Wynn, once a famous singer who worked for Flo Ziegfeld. Now she is old and senile and a patient in a nursing home.

Chuckling, I phoned Hoffman to thank him for his whimsical form. He said he is a press agent. Okay. Some press agents annoy me, but Hoffman is witty and creative. We had a long talk and he mentioned that he works for Irving Berlin. He said this so casually I did not think he was trying to impress me but, nonetheless, I *was* impressed. After all, Irving Berlin is America's greatest composer.

Hoffman said his own father, Sam Hoffman, had been a friend of Irving Berlin for many years. Next Sunday, Sam celebrates his 81st birthday and Berlin has written a birthday song for him. Only one copy of the sheet music has been printed and only one record has been waxed.

If the press agent was dangling bait before me, I pounced. I said I'd like to write a story about this unique composition. Well, said Hoffman, he was talking from Irving Berlin's office and maybe I'd like to join him there to hear the record and then accompany him to his father's apartment on Riverside Drive. However, Irving Berlin feels uncomfortable near reporters, so when I arrived he, the press agent, would say I am a representative of a record company.

"Okay—but what if I bring along a photographer?"

Hoffman: "That's okay."

"All right," I said. "When?"

"How about now?"

It was early afternoon. It is common knowledge that Irving Berlin seldom talks to reporters, so when I told the city desk I have a chance to get to him, I was told to take off whenever I chose. Photographer Freddie Palumbo was to go with me.

It was 3:30 P.M. when we reached Berlin's office at 1650 Broadway in mid-Manhattan. Irving Hoffman is a thin, rumpled, nervous, breathless, entertaining eccentric. Before the end of the afternoon I realized he is a major theatrical press agent whose name I should have known.

When Hoffman introduced me to Irving Berlin, I gasped because he looks like my father—small, taut, energetic, all his movements quick and darting. Berlin is 69 years old. When I mentioned this resemblance, Berlin grinned and chirped: "That's good!" His dark eyes gleam behind horn-rimmed glasses straddling a sun-tanned nose. Eyebrows heavy, chin small. His flat black hair is streaked with gray. He wore a tailor-made checkered suit, light blue shirt and dark four-in-hand tie.

Hoffman lied, saying Freddie was his own photographer, hired to immortalize the song composed for his father. Berlin sat down at his piano and posed for pictures. After Freddie left, Hoffman suggested that the three of us sit in Berlin's corner office to listen to the record. It was obvious that Hoffman and Berlin are not just press agent and boss, but close friends.

Making the record, Berlin had sung with a bass fiddler, guitarist and accordion player backing him up. It sounded more like croaking than singing, but the affection Berlin feels for the elder Hoffman came through strong and clear. Listening to his own voice, Berlin stood with fists cocked on hips, head to one side.

When the song was finished he said he'd had no lunch and suddenly sang out: "Hilda!" In came his secretary, a smile on her lips. He said he wanted a pastrami sandwich and all of us needed Scotch. She brought a bottle, glasses and ice, then left to order his sandwich.

Sitting across the desk from Irving Berlin, truly a living legend, I smiled and said I had read of the stir made when he, a Russian-born Jew from the Lower East Side, had wed Ellin Mackay, of high society, daughter of Clarence Mackay, a leading Catholic layman and president of the Postal Telegraph Co. They left on their honeymoon without his blessing. Berlin grinned at me and said well, then, surely I also know that his father had been a rabbi. I told the story of the rabbi who mistook me for a Jew because of my Jewish wife, and Berlin laughed.

By now we were getting along so well that Hoffman confessed I was not with a record company but was, in fact, a reporter for the World-Telegram. Laughing again, Berlin said he didn't care. Nonetheless, I did not want to wear out my welcome, so I said I'd better leave, but the composer waved me back into my chair and poured a second Scotch for the three of us.

I said I knew I was asking a corny question, but which of his hundreds of songs did Berlin like best. With a nod and a smile, he agreed he hears this question all the time. He said he likes the songs the public likes best— *White Christmas, God Bless America, Remember* and *Always.*

I said that when I was in high school I romanced girls by singing *Always* to them. Looking pleased, Berlin said he wooed his wife with *Always.* Soon, he told me with pride in his voice, they will celebrate their 32nd wedding anniversary.

The Scotch must have been working its magic within me, for suddenly I felt bold enough to sing a couple of bars of *Always.* Berlin listened, chin propped on steeple-tipped fingers. "You have a good voice," he said.

Embarrassed, I tried to hide my feelings by saying I've been fascinated by reports about Berlin's special piano.

"Do you want to see it?"

Arising, he led me into another room and up to the piano where he sat when Freddie photographed him. I had read that Berlin can compose only in the key of F sharp. A piano manufacturer made him a special piano with a lever under the keyboard. Sitting down on the piano bench, Berlin pushed this lever to demonstrate how the entire keyboard shifts to the left, some keys on the extreme left-hand side actually disappearing.

I asked: "Does your piano have the standard 88 keys?"

Berlin said: "I don't know."

He may have been teasing me, but his eyes were serious. Then he began playing *Always.* I crouched at his right. His eyes were on mine—expectantly, I thought, so I began singing softly, while the genius who composed the tune played and watched and listened. I was afraid I'd forget the lyrics, but remembered all of them and stumbled through to the end. Then I thought: *Jesus Christ! Ellis! You really have some nerve! How dare YOU sing an Irving Berlin song to Irving Berlin? Well, sir, best I can figure it out, sir, is that I got a little high and Irving Berlin is a helluva nice guy.*

When we got back to his office Hoffman told Berlin that I'd written a great piece about Bessie Wynn. Berlin said he remembered her well, for her picture had appeared on some of his sheet music. Tomorrow he and his wife leave for the Catskills, but when they get back he wants me to take him to the nursing home to visit Bessie. Except—! He held up one finger.

"No publicity!"

Charmed by his modesty, I agreed.

Hoffman said he and I had better leave to go see his father. Berlin suddenly asked whether he might go with us. Grinning, he said he wanted to see the look in Sam's eyes when Sam realized he was getting a song written just for him. Hoffman dived for the phone and ordered a limousine sent to Berlin's building.

It was an air-conditioned Cadillac and I sat between the composer and press agent as it purred north to 190 Riverside Drive. As Berlin stepped out, a man on the sidewalk recognized him and called out his name. Inside the lobby, waiting for the elevator, Berlin paced back and forth and blabbed: "You know, I'm nervous! Do you really think Sam will like it?"

I stared at him. Was this genius staging an act in front of a reporter? No, I decided, he's just a Nervous Nellie.

Then he joked: "Think I could get Sam to push it for me?"

Before we left the office Hoffman had called his father to say that he and Berlin were bringing a demonstration record they wanted him to hear. When we reached the apartment, Berlin and the old man hugged one another and then Sam sat on the sofa, a smile on his lips. Berlin stood across the room, fists on hips, eyes on Sam. Young Hoffman put the record on the phonograph. The old man listened, and when he realized that Berlin had written a song just for him, down his cheeks dripped two tears like diamonds.

FRIDAY, JULY 12, 1957   ■   My story about Irving Berlin was published today. This afternoon my desk phone rang. When I picked up the receiver I heard: "This is Irving Berlin." Apparently he did not have his secretary make the call, but placed it himself. He declared I had written such a great article that he just had to call to thank me. Well! I've written hundreds of stories about people who never called to thank me. To have Irving Berlin behave so graciously—I felt overwhelmed.

THURSDAY, AUGUST 29, 1957   ■   I was summoned to the city desk and told to go to the Hotel New Yorker to cover a Billy Graham press conference. Since May 15 the evangelist has been conducting a "crusade" in Madison Square Garden. I covered the opening session, taking my wife with me. We were irked by much of what we saw and heard. I was born a Protestant and now am an agnostic. Ruthie was born a Jew and now is an atheist.

The editor who gave me this assignment handed me a long article Billy Graham wrote for the United Press, for release tomorrow. It ended with this sentence: "It's Christ or chaos." The phrase haunted my mind as I rode a subway train to the hotel.

The press had been invited to come for coffee and Danish at 10 A.M. in a basement room of the Hotel New Yorker. When I arrived I was surprised to find I knew almost none of the other reporters. Chatting with the strangers, I learned that they were editors and reporter for various religious papers. Wooden chairs had been lined up in rows in front of a dais that held a table covered with green felt. At 10:32 A.M. the great Billy Graham walked out carrying a cup of coffee, put it on a table and began talking.

Some time ago, while caricaturing Graham from a photograph taken in profile, I realized he has the face of an eagle. Hypnotic eyes. Jutting nose. It is a handsome face much like that of a man I knew who was national president of the Junior Chamber of Commerce. The evangelist looks like a successful young executive—well-pressed gray suit, blue shirt, red-and-gray striped tie. His hands in his pockets, he began speaking in a baritone voice.

"I want to thank the press, television and radio for their wonderful and splendid coverage while we've been here. It was more coverage than we expected. We did expect to get a few lines in the papers, but nothing like the headlines we received. After all, our story is somewhat the same, day after day. We're very grateful to you members of the press for the great contributions you have made . . ."

I thought: Billy, old boy, what you don't know is how much I resent all that free publicity we gave you, how often I groaned when I opened the *Herald Tribune* and saw its standing head: BILLY GRAHAM SAYS . . .

Now, totally self-assured, he took his hands out of his pockets every now and then to emphasize a point with abrupt, controlled gestures at the level of his waist. Whenever he held up his right arm, his index finger extended, cameramen crowded closer to get a shot of that pose. Graham also would cross his arms over his chest and sway from side to side. In a voice so rich it sounded the way claret wine looks, he said: "We are standing on the edge of a volcano in this country. Just yesterday I was speaking to the editor of one of the great papers in this city, talking about the shift in the balance of power . . ."

I thought: Here we go again! Billy's going to give a political tinge to his standard pitch—*fear.*

". . . and this editor said he had just talked to one of the men in the Pentagon, and they were deeply concerned about the news that has come out of Russia . . ."

I knew what he meant: Intercontinental ballistic missiles.

". . . There are forces moving in all around us. The penetration of the communists goes on all the time, seemingly without halt. Forty-eight square miles an hour are being taken over by the communists and with this shifting balance of power, some of the little nations of the world are wondering whether they hadn't better side with the biggest power.

"But—more than the communists—I am more concerned with moral conditions in this country. My prayer is for a spiritual revival here. We receive eight thousand letters a day from all parts of the United States—have, for 14 weeks. All of them say they now recognize Christ. This shows a concern, a hunger on the part of millions of Americans for God . . ."

I thought: Okay, Billy, so we agree that this nation is in spiritual crisis, but your suggested solutions are too simplistic.

". . . it is a paradox that crime and moral laxity are at low ebb, while on the other hand there's a spiritual revival. Why do we have this revival on one hand, and low morals on the other? Well, here are a couple of answers: If there are two gangs in Brooklyn, and one wants peace but fears that the other one is arming for street-war, then the peace-loving gang is going to arm, too. When God moves, the forces of evil move, too. The Devil also moves. So in the headlines we read about a spiritual renaissance and about crime. This is spiritual warfare. However, it is not a paradox, if you'll study the Scriptures. Satan is fighting for the soul of America! I believe this with all my heart!"

I thought, Ohh, please, Not that crap!

Billy Graham went on talking and at last he said: "I didn't mean to get into all of this." He grinned a boyish grin. The people in the room relaxed and smiled at him. "It just came to mind while I was speaking . . . Now . . . Are there any questions?"

I asked whether he cared to compare his methods with those of another well-known evangelist, Billy Sunday. I sat in the front row only a few feet from Graham. Like a radar beam, his gaze swept down and locked on my eyes. After making a few comments about Billy Sunday, who died in the thirties, Billy Graham concluded: "In many ways, I am unworthy to loosen his shoe laces. He was a great man. I don't care to compare myself with him."

I thought: Billy Sunday a great man? He was a vulgar, ignorant egomaniac!

As other reporters picked up the questioning, I sat and brooded about the copy Billy Graham had written for the United Press—especially his last line. It so happens that New York City contains more Jews than any other city in the world. Among the other reporters present there may have been one or two who are Jewish, but they might not care to put the question I intended to ask. I was hearing nothing but mushy questions. No one present dared to challenge the evangelist. Again I spoke up.

"Dr. Graham . . ."

The eagle face turned toward me. The eagle eyes bored into my eyes.

". . . this morning I read the article you wrote for the United Press—the one to be released tomorrow. You conclude it with this sentence: 'It is Christ or chaos.' "

Billy Graham nodded to indicate I had quoted him correctly.

"Well . . . in speaking of 'Christ or chaos,' did you mean to exclude the God of the Jews?"

A gasp arose from the other members of the press. For a moment the evangelist let his face show the shock he felt. Now his eyes seemed like the headlights of a speeding car about to run me down on a rainy road in the dark of night.

Then he said firmly: "The person I have given my life to was—racially— a Jew. I have dedicated my life to a Jew."

I thought: No! You can't get away with that! The word *Jew* has to do with religion, not race. Billy, you bastard, you evaded the issue!

When I left the room no one spoke to me.

This is the caricature I did of Graham sometime later.

FRIDAY, OCTOBER 4, 1957 ■ A couple of months ago an editor gave me a one-paragraph item and asked me to read it. The article said that Charles Corr, 64, an alcoholic and disbarred attorney, had been arrested for the 41st time for the *same* crime—breaking a window of a liquor store to steal one bottle of booze. And—always on Sunday.

"Sounds like a strange guy," said the editor with a smile. "A former lawyer, no less. Right now he's in prison in the Bronx, but here's what I want you to do: Write to him at the prison to say that when he gets out you'd like to have a chat with him. If he'll go along with the idea, maybe you can find out what makes him tick."

I began by enlisting the help of Anna Kross, the corrections commissioner, and Pascal Marsico, who is in charge of the legal department of the corrections department. When I wrote Corr, they made sure my letter reached him. He replied in a note saying he would be pleased to see me when he was released.

This morning I went to the Bronx and met him as he left the Bronx County Courthouse. Although he has often been in and out of jail the last 22 years, there was no prison pallor on his beefy Irish face. His scrubbed cheeks bloomed with health. His cheap suit was taut on his torso, his blue eyes alert, his bearing self-assured, and he spoke with the fluency of a man who had just kissed the Blarney Stone. I suggested we go to the Bowery and the restaurant of his choice.

When we reached the Bowery he led me into a cafeteria. A friend hollered: "Where yuh been, Corr?"

Corr smiled, waved the man away with a regal gesture, and said: "See you later, Steve."

I bought us coffee and Danish and we sat down at a table and he began telling me the story of his life, his fingers toying with crumbs on the table, pushing them back and forth, weaving a tapestry of his gaudy goings-on.

He said he was the youngest of 11 children and the seventh son of a seventh son, born and raised in Waterbury, Connecticut. His father was an Irish immigrant who earned, according to Corr, a quarter million dollars. One day when he was a boy he walked into a bank, holding his father's hand, as a hush fell over the place. When he looked up quizzically, his father said: "It's because they're afraid of me, son."

His mother died when he was three. His father spoiled him. The year he got long pants he was taken on a trip to Europe. In high school he was a football star, and after he entered Niaraga College he toyed with the idea of becoming a priest, changed his mind, got a law degree from the University of Pennsylvania.

During World War I he served in the army in France and still gets $66 a month in benefits from the federal government. After his discharge he practiced law in Waterbury and then moved here. His law office was in the financial area of downtown Manhattan. Soon he had many clients, some politicians, some theatrical people. Fond of the stage, he became, as he expressed it, an inveterate second-nighter, saw every show on Broadway, hung out with actors in the Hotel Astor on Times Square.

Then he married. As he talked about his wife he became evasive for the first time. They had no children. They quarrelled. One day she had him arrested for disorderly conduct, and although she withdrew this charge before it came to trial, they separated. Now she lives in Florida and is well fixed, he said.

Until the failure of his marriage he had drunk like a convivial Irishman, but soon thereafter he became a bottle-baby. He drank and drank and drank, finally running through the small fortune left to him by his father. When his nightly bouts with the bottle stretched out into two-week binges, his law practice suffered, and in 1938 he was disbarred for repeated failures to appear in court with his clients. He didn't even attend his disbarment hearing; he was drunk and holed up in a hotel in Atlantic City.

Faster and faster he swirled down into the maelstrom of alcoholism and came the day he returned to consciousness, parched and pained, to find himself on the Bowery. Penniless. Charles Corr had joined the brotherhood of bums. He got his federal check regularly, but couldn't stretch $66 over an entire month. When he was sober he would take a job, any kind of job—dishwasher, hotel clerk, hospital attendant.

With a mirthless laugh, he said: "You know, I was fired from a dishwashing job after they found out I was a disbarred attorney. Guess I wasn't good enough for them."

He would get drunk, get fired; get drunk, get fired. Nonetheless, he said he never was a fall-down drunk and insisted he dislikes the taste of all liquor except wine.

"I drink," he said, "because of the euphoria of intoxication. I become exhilarated. Liquor stimulates the imagination. I won't say I found any deep truths in the bottom of a bottle, but there actually were drunken moments when I saw life a little more clearly."

When broke, he could borrow drinks from a couple of bartenders on the Bowery because they knew he would pay his debt when he got his federal check. Sunday was a horror to him, for on Sunday, all bars are closed.

On Sunday he would wander onto any street and pick some liquor store at random. His method of operation was always the same: From a distance of four feet he would throw a brick through the lower part of the window, reach inside, grab a bottle. As he told me this, his fingers still played with the crumbs on the table.

He asked me: "Are you familiar with the legal concept of an attractive nuisance? . . . No? . . . Well, this means the unguarded display of some highly desirable object. Legally—now I speak as an attorney—I feel I could make a sound case against liquor store owners for displaying bottles in their windows."

I asked why a couple of times the cops found him carrying burglar tools.

"Simple. Any object that might be used as a device for burglarizing may be considered a burglar tool—a can-opener to break into a car, a rock to—well, you get the point."

He is sorry for giving liquor dealers the trouble of replacing shattered windows, but does not feel guilty about the cost of a new pane of glass—about $200. Nodding knowingly, he said: "The liquor dealer doesn't pay for it. His insurance company pays for it, and you can't rob an insurance company—their profits are too high."

Time after time Corr was caught at his little game. Some cops came to know him well. After he was locked up a friendly cop might ask: "Charlie—need a drink?" And then go out and buy him a bottle.

One day a cop said: "Charlie, I don't get it! You want money for booze, so why don't you heave a rock through Tiffany's window and be done with it?"

Making straight lines on the table, Corr told me: "I would explain that I am not a thief. All I want is a little liquor. I have no grudge against society and I'm at peace with myself. Only a man who has been up, and then down, can learn a true sense of values. I know—for I've been both places. And let me tell you, my friend, those who are up, the ones we choose to call successes, how little they know what life is all about!

"I happen to have a keen mind, sir. I believe I see deeply into life. Sometimes—true—it's a bit frightening to strip life bare to the bone, to get to its essence. Sure . . . maybe I try to blank out my consciousness with liquor at times, but I don't consider my life a tragedy. Oh, some prison psychiatrists have tried to make me believe this, but I don't. They don't even believe that sometimes I like to get drunk just to sit and think.

"Think—or talk, if you will. Oh, the conversations I've had, the times on the Bowery when there were three or four of us sitting and discussing things—attorneys and one physician. And what's so fearful about a prison? Take the one time I was at Sing Sing: I taught school there. Another member of the faculty was a Harvard graduate. We had discussions there—well, better than any held in the Union League Club.

"Four walls don't press in on me if I can get my hands on books. This last time I read Joseph Wood Krutch—some of his essays on T. S. Eliot and Eugene O'Neill. Although I have no favorite philosopher, I must admit I am very fond of Santayana. . . . Suicide, sir? Not for me! Never! I love life too much. Do I look like an embittered man? Once I fell into the East River—drunk, of course—and I swam to safety like anybody else. I tell you, I love life!"

He said one of his sisters died last January. Her estate will be divided among him and two remaining sisters; he estimates his share at $20,000 to $25,000. In probate court a sister was asked his address but said she didn't know. She was ashamed to admit that her brother lives on the Bowery.

Now that he is out of jail, Corr told me, he plans to collect three federal checks due him, buy a new suit and go to Waterbury to claim his portion of the estate. But—well, as of the moment, he found himself a little short. I handed him a ten dollar bill. After thanking me, he said:

"I think I might manage my sister's property and then—who knows? I might even practice a little law. After all, I'm not disbarred in Connecticut."

I asked: "But won't you do the same thing all over again—get a thirst, break a window, go to jail?"

His Irish eyes smiled at me.

"Oh, no. . . . With all this money coming to me, I'll have a feeling of security. I'm through with the other."

As we arose, I glanced down at the table. He had pushed the crumbs into a pattern.

A couple of weeks later I read in a newspaper that Charles Corr, 64, a disbarred attorney, had been arrested for the 42nd time for . . .

1958

THURSDAY, JANUARY 9, 1958   ■   Jim Egan began at the *World-Telegram* as a messenger boy and now works in our production department. Today he told me an amusing story. In 1940, when Franklin Roosevelt and Wendell Willkie were vying for the Presidency, Jim was sent on an errand to the *Herald Tribune*. He wore a huge Roosevelt button on his shirt. Going up in the elevator he was seen by Mrs. Helen Rogers Reid, who owned the *Trib*. Glaring at the Roosevelt button she snapped: "Why are you wearing that thing?"

"Why not?"

"Well, don't you know this is a Republican newspaper?"

"So what?"

"You're fired!"

"You can't fire me."

"Why not?"

"Because I don't work here."

FRIDAY, MARCH 21, 1958   ■   At 9:15 o'clock night before last I got a call from the office. There had been a loft fire at 623 Broadway and many persons had been killed. Only later did I learn what had happened: At 3:55 P.M. Wednesday a textile-drying oven exploded on the third floor of the five-story building just north of Houston St. On the fourth floor many employ-ees of the Monarch Underwear Co. were at work. They took the brunt of the flames and smoke. Some jumped to their death. The death toll hit 24—the greatest in the city in the past dozen years.

I was asked to go to the morgue at Bellevue Hospital to do a color piece about the relatives of the dead who might show up there. Not knowing what the night would bring, I took $16 from Ruthie's wallet, subwayed to 42nd st., then caught a cab to Bellevue. A wet snow was falling.

The first official I met at the morgue was Police Captain John Cronin of the missing persons bureau. He and one of his assistants gave me the names of five of the dead who had been positively identified. That was about 10:15 P.M. Fewer relatives and friends were there than I'd expected. No wailing or hysteria on a mass scale, as I'd thought there'd be. Soon I met Morgue Superintendent Michael J. Ambrose, who told me he'd dou-bled his staff from five to ten. Then I found Dr. Milton Helpern, chief medical examiner for the city. I recalled having met him the first time, shortly after his appointment, in Central Park where the body of a GI sui-cide had been found. He is gray-haired, with a fleshy face, half-glasses, and a kindly air. When I asked these three officials if I might see the bodies, they agreed and led me to the basement.

I found myself in a large room where seven bodies lay on rolling stretch-ers. Most of the corpses were uncovered. Affixed to their left wrists were tags reading: "Body #7." Or whatever the number might be. Dr. Helpern led me straight to the body of a woman. Although her limbs were charred, her face was beet-red. As though he were in a lecture room, the medical examiner explained to me that the color of her face was due to the carbon monoxide she had inhaled when she breathed smoke. All about me in that shipping room—as I learned it was called—were carcasses with arms and legs as black as burned bacon. Some legs had broken off at the thigh. Blackened bones protruded. Fire-scorched faces leered, as dark and gro-tesquely shrivelled as those of monkeys. I was surprised to note that I did not feel sick—not at first, at least. As a reporter I had seen the bodies of the burned, but nowhere near so many at once.

Dr. Helpern led me over to another rolling stretcher. On it lay the re-mains of a woman, her right fist doubled and frozen in front of her face, her left fist likewise doubled and thrust out at an angle from her body.

"This," said the doctor, "is the classic pugilistic attitude of a person who died in a fire. Notice how she looks as though she's fighting off something. People seeing this believe it's the result of an attempt to fight off the flames. This isn't so. No, it's a matter of the heat contracting the muscles of the arms, which then pull the arms up into this posture.

"Maybe it might help the relatives if you'd stress that most of these people didn't suffer too much. You see, they inhale carbon monoxide, which makes them pass out quickly. Most of them were unconscious or dead before the flames got to them. Their bodies are filled with soot, too. You can see soot in their nostrils. See the soot inside this woman's nostril?" he asked.

I saw the soot inside her nostril.

Across the room, under the bright ceiling lights, lay the body of an older woman, her naked belly whale-big, so it seemed. Pointing, I asked: "Is she pregnant?"

Dr. Helpern glanced that way.

"No . . . Just an obese woman."

Together we walked over to her. The doctor thumbed her belly. This made at least the second person—that is, corpse—he had touched. I wondered when he would be able to wash his hands. Fragments of hose clung to the woman's stumps of legs. Otherwise, she was almost practically naked. Her left foot seemed broken at the ankle, for it bent unnaturally toward her right foot. Dr. Helpern explained that when the flesh burns away, when the ligaments are eaten by flames, then there's nothing left to hold joints together properly. We started to stroll away. The doctor turned, went back, and threw a flimsy, scorched garment at her feet over her crotch. I liked him.

At the other end of the room lay the body of a tall Negro man of excellent build. His wrists and ankles were tied together, and a bit of gauze was bound around his ebony penis. The doctor said that this man had died after reaching the hospital.

Standing to the right side of the Negro, Dr. Helpern again used his fingers to pull back the gauze covering his face, and then pull down the lower lip, exposing the teeth.

"No problem of identification here," the doctor said. "We happen to know his name, but even if we didn't, it wouldn't be any trick to identify him. Teeth: excellent."

Unlike the other corpses, the flesh of the Negro was so soft it gave easily. He was but recently dead. As the doctor pulled open his mouth I had the sensation that the man still was alive and submitting meekly to a necessary examination.

Going from body to body, the doctor showed me how the blood was seeping down to the lower part of the bodies, due to gravitation alone. All corpses were lying on their backs, and so the lower third of their frames showed a pink flush—those, at least, which were not too badly charred. I was surprised at the lack of stench, for I had thought the odor would be overpowering. Still, after 15 or 20 minutes down there with those fire victims, I felt a little light-headed. I asked myself whether I was about to faint, decided I wasn't, wouldn't.

Captain Cronin—of medium height and slim build—began talking to me.

"Upstairs," he said, "there are some poor people hollering to come down here and identify their dead, to find them. Some of them are asking what the hell is wrong with the police department that we won't let them come down here. But—" and he waved his hand over the grisly scene— "could we let them see this?"

I asked how the matter was handled. He told me that each relative is asked the following questions about a victim: Sex? Age? Height? Weight? Jewelry? Distinguishing facial features? Condition of teeth? Any bodily defects or scars? Operations?

Earlier, Dr. Helpern had told me that many identifications are made from the inside. That is, post-mortems disclose heart conditions and tissue scars from old operation. Out of 10 women, he said, at least five are found to have had hysterectomies.

An attendant approached with a cardboard box containing valuables taken from one victim. The captain said that women are harder to identify than man because most of their possessions are carried in purses, which tend to get lost, rather than in their pockets. He said, though, that in at least the last 20 years not a single victim of any local disaster has failed to be identified.

The morgue superintendent came up to me. He said that other reporters, upon learning that I was downstairs, had asked to come down, too. He said he hoped I wouldn't mind, but that he didn't want to play favorites. Naturally, I agreed readily. I had seen enough. Shortly after three other newspapermen showed up, I walked upstairs.

Now it was after midnight. Still there were few relatives and friends on hand. I began to wonder whether I could get the kind of story I'd been sent to get. With some of the other reporters, I went over the list of the dead again. Ten positively identified. Ten reported missing and presumably dead. Four bodies unaccounted for.

A *Post* reporter named Fox chatted with me about the difficulty of getting stories from the bereaved. Many speak Spanish. Most are too numbed to talk. They tended to talk in monosyllables. As the minutes clicked by, here and there a man or woman suddenly would break into a wail upon learning of the death of a wife or sister. I just couldn't bring myself to intrude upon their sorrow with any questions.

Pacing the corridor near the entrance to the morgue were two men. Slowly I fell into a conversation with them. Under normal circumstances I would have described them as tough. They came from the Mulberry section of Manhattan and appeared of Italian ancestry. One was a truck driver.

Said the bigger of the two: "How can I tell them? Her folks are waiting up to hear if she's alive. How can I tell them? Slug down a half a fifth— that's the only way I can tell them!

I offered the smaller man a cigaret.

"Thanks anyway," he grunted. "Got two packs right here. And, lemme tell you—before the night's over I'll have smoked both of 'em!"

The two men, I learned, were waiting to identify a 38-year-old unmarried woman whom they knew.

"You can't know," said the bigger man, "how good she was! She was so good! Whatta sweet gal! And now . . ."

"I'm only a truck driver," said the shorter one, "so you mebbe think I'm off my rockers or somethin', but lemme tell you—I drive in that district, and I know the flammables they leave in the halls like. I tell you, somethin' oughtta be done! I could take you down and show you, Mac . . ."

An attendant walked up with something in the palm of his right hand. He opened his hand and held it out to the two men. There lay a ring.

"This her ring?"

Both men nodded. Then the chin of the big man sunk onto his chest. His face went fierce with the work of keeping from crying. Up came his chin.

"The rings! The jewelry! Throw 'em all away. Throw 'em far away! Who needs souvenirs about a thing like this!"

Since some relative, rather than any friend, is preferred for identification, a phone call was placed to the woman's home. Her brother would come to the morgue. In no time at all, it seemed, he appeared, snow melting on his dark, short coat. I followed him into a side room where he was asked the usual questions about his sister. With him was a male friend. Both men were in their early thirties. The brother answered all questions in a flat, calm tone, his friend supplying additional information. I was surprised to note how composed both were. Then they were led to still another room where the woman's body had been brought by elevator from the basement. Again I followed.

I stood just outside the door. The attendant lifted one corner of a blanket to reveal the woman's face. It was black and monkey-like.

Then, as though from a distant horizon, there arose a high thin wail, an animal-like cry such as that of some beast wounded unto death. For a second I couldn't located the source of this eerie screech. It was the brother, his reserve broken. He crouched against the door near me, his arms flung over his face. The friend jerked out a handkerchief and held it before his own eyes, averting his face. The friend's mouth was working, and it appeared he would vomit.

"Is this Josephine?" the attendant asked gently.

The friend tried to speak. For a second no sound came, although the brother was keening like a tortured violin. The friend's mouth slobbered and worked, and then he stammered: "Y—yeah . . ."

The brother wheeled about. He threw himself out of the room, tottered a few steps to a nearby door. Raising his arms high, he crashed both fists into the wood.

"What they done to her!" he whimpered. Then, roaringly: "Them dirty bastards!"

The friend threw his arms about the brother's shoulders. They stood there a split second, a tableau of tragedy. Then they pushed open the door and walked blindly down a corridor.

It was about 1:45 A.M. when I left the morgue. The snow was coming down more heavily. After getting a north-bound cab for a girl reporter, I found one of my own, which took me down the East Side Drive, around the Battery, and up to the *World-Telegram.*

The writing came hard. I smoked cigaret after cigaret and thought and thought, and rejiggered the lead about eight or nine times. What I finally came up with started like this:

"The dead were taken to the Bellevue morgue. Then came the living, the relatives and friends, stumbling snow-spangled out of the dark of night into this house of darkness.

"In couples, in family groups, they came to identify their beloved. They were wet with snow and tears. They were heavy with grief. They walked clumsily, carefully, as though they brimmed with some sacred secret that might spill out of them . . ."

THURSDAY, MAY 15, 1958 ▦ Steve Seskin and I were alone in his book shop at 91 Chambers St. The front door was open invitingly, almost beseechingly, so I kept within my trenchcoat against the chill gusts prowling this gray day. A moment after I entered, Ruthie phoned Steve to order a book for her boss, and my eyes met his laughingly. After hanging up the phone, Steve turned to me. The laughter had drained from his brown eyes and his face became cloud-gathered.

"Eddie," said Steve, "I've come to a decision."

I waited, my eyes on his.

"I've decided to sell out. I'm putting an ad in the Sunday paper."

The moment I had dreaded was upon me. Turning on my heel, I muttered "Jesus Christ!" and strode away, walked several paces away with my face averted, snorted "Jesus Christ!" and stalked back, wheeled again to pace and pace and heavily breathe. "Jesus Christ!"

Finally, drawing up in front of Steve, I stopped and faced him. Steve fumbled with lean fingers in his tobacco pouch.

"I'm defeated," he said. "I've had it. I've come to the end of my tether."

The words I spoke seemed forced through my pores: "What do you plan to do, Steve?"

"Oh, teach school, I guess." I knew that he has a master's degree. "Guess I'll get a job as a high school teacher—that is, if they'll have me now.

"You know, Eddie, everything I've done seems wrong. This business is a failure. I'm a failure—"

"Goddamnit!" I interrupted. "Now, none of that! You're not a failure Steve. Don't ever let yourself think that."

"And why the hell not?"

I said: "Look: So you've been in the book business 25 years and so you haven't made any money. This doesn't mean there's anything wrong with you. It's just that your values don't happen to be the standard values of this particular civilization—the Goddamn businessman's civilization!"

As though not hearing me, Steve spoke, his saddle-brown eyes vacant: "The truth of the matter is, Eddie, I'm suffering from a deep malaise. You know what this means. Here in this shop I tried to create a little cultural center, you might say. I threw out all the Goddamn cheap paperback novels of crime and lust so that I might give the public the worthwhile books. I didn't want to cheapen myself by handling that kind of trash. Culture? There is no culture in America! I don't know why I should be so proud as to try to sell the books I have here. The hell with it. Better yet I should turn this into a schlock house and sell whatever Goddamn trash the people want."

"You couldn't," I said.

"I know I couldn't," he said hopelessly. "But the fact remains, Eddie, that I'm a failure."

"Like hell you're a failure!" I snorted, glaring at him. "Now, I know this won't solve your problems or put any money in your pockets, but some day you may remember this: You may remember that one day a guy named Eddie Ellis looked you in the eye to say: Steve Seskin, you're one helluva nice guy!"

From a pocket, Steve extracted a Kleenex and put it to his nose.

"So I'm a nice guy," he said in a hollow voice, and his cheeks appeared even more sunken.

"*Yes* you're a nice guy," I repeated.

"This malaise . . ." Steve mumbled.

"You tried," I said, and the words sounded like mockery in my own ears.

By this time, to get off my broken foot, I had taken that chair I often use in Steve's store. He stood behind his counter, a man of 46, middling height, lean, his hair whitening, dapper moustache, neat in appearance, a victim of America's bitch goddess Success, his heart laid open on her altar, the red oozing out in a meaningless sacrifice.

"I wish I had words of wisdom," I tried again. "But I haven't. I can't be a Pollyanna." I sighed. "After all, Steve—it's all a lot of shit!"

He knew that by this I meant—Everything. "Yes," he nodded, animated for the first time, "it sure is all a lot of shit! You work and you plan—why, how long can I go without a vacation? In a one-man operation like this, I get up in the morning and I don't feel too well and then I worry about what happens if I can't get to the store, because there's only me. It's— Look: Twenty-five years in the book business, and now I come to this!"

The phone rang. As I later learned, it was Steve's sister, Selma. "Yes," he was saying, "I've decided to sell out. . . . Yes, I've talked it over with Helen . . ." He meant his wife.

I walked and cursed and cursed and walked, and with curses on my lips there was very little in my brain. After Steve got off the phone we spoke mostly in silences.

"Did I mention how much I'm asking?" Steve said.

"No. No, you didn't say."

"Well, I'm asking for only $15,000—although my stock alone is worth at least $20,000."

"What happens if you don't find a buyer?"

"Well, my lease has a year or so to go. Way I feel, maybe I'd do something unethical, really compromise. Such as, for instance, stop buying any more books, just sell what I have here, then get out."

"What's unethical about that?"

Steve hesitated. "There might be some creditors left."

"You owe some money, Steve?"

"Every businessman owes money."

Then he said: "If I can't win fighting fair, maybe I'll fight some other way."

"Hell!" I snorted, "and have ulcers again in six months!"

"A man has to compromise."

"Sure," I agreed, "sure a man has to compromise—but within limits. I compromise every day and I hate it. But life is compromise. As I said though—within limits."

"I'm tired," Steve said. "I'm tired of fighting. I can tell you, Eddie, but I couldn't even tell Helen or Selma: This malaise of mine . . . truly, it's a deep-seated thing."

"I know," I said, and I really did know. "I'm like you, Steve. I'm a confirmed pessimist. That's why we agree it's all shit."

For awhile we didn't talk. Steve tamped his pipe and struck another match. Trenchcoated, I leaned my elbows on the counter. After long thought I raised my chin.

"Steve, if you're really going to sell out—all at once, to one man—which way would it help you more: If I bought some books from you, I mean if I came in with a check for $200 or $300 and bought some titles I've been wanting, or if this man, whoever he is, if he came in and bought it lock, stock and barrel?"

"Why, by selling to you."

"It would be only a drop in the bucket."

Steve's cheeks seemed to flatten. "Now if you're doing this just to help me—" he began.

"Nuts! I buy books. If I can get a bit of a bargain from you, I'm helping little old Eddie Ellis. But if I can help you a little bit at the same time—well, Steve, it's a mutual sort of thing."

Steve thought a moment. "I'd sell 'em for what they cost me and just a little bit more."

"Naturally! You have to take a profit! But, Steve, I'm thinking of myself now—really. Still, I sort of feel like a vulture picking over bones."

"You don't have to feel that way."

"No, Steve, I guess I really don't. Of course, I'd have to get Ruthie's approval."

"Of course."

"What if I came in after work some day and picked out what I want?"

"Well . . . How about Saturday? That way, I could sell some things to you before I put in the ad, and so my conscience will be clear. Besides, I could bring the car down, and then I could tote the books up to your place."

"Ruthie will scream," I laughed. " 'Where'll we put them?' she'll ask." Steve laughed, too. "Yeah, I know."

"If it's okay with you then—"

"Sure," said Steve. "Saturday?"

"I'll check with Ruthie."

When I got back to the office, I called Ruthie. She gave her approval instantly.

"I'll stop buying dresses," she said.

"Like hell," I said.

"Oh," she said, "I can buy dresses any old time. But this—well, this is the chance of a lifetime!"

I agreed.

"Poor Steve," she said.

Perhaps the biggest political scandal in the United States in 1958 concerned Sherman Adams, assistant to President Eisenhower. Early in the year a special House subcommittee on legislative oversight began to investigate alleged attempts by high government officials to influence decisions of federal regulatory agencies.

On February 11 Bernard Schwartz, chief counsel to the subcommittee, named Adams as one of the "White House clique . . . controlling decisions" of various independent agencies. On June 10 it was revealed that Adams had make telephone calls to the Federal Trade Commission and the Securities and Exchange Commission in behalf of an old friend, a Boston industrialist named Bernard Goldfine. It also was proved that Goldfine had paid $2,000 in hotel bills for Adams, given him a vicuna coat and lent him an Oriental rug.

On June 18 Eisenhower expressed confidence in Adams' integrity, stating "I need him." Many Republicans began calling for Adams' resignation.

WEDNESDAY, JULY 9, 1958 ■ This morning I awakened at five-thirty and rode a cab to Pier 84 on the Hudson River at the foot of West 44th Street, where I boarded the SS *Constitution* to interview Harry Truman. He and his wife, together with Judge and Mrs. Samuel Rosenman, were returning from a cruise on the Mediterranean. I had chatted with the former President on May 26 just before his ship sailed. That day he had declined to say anything newsworthy.

I was aware that 7:45 A.M. is the deadline for the first edition of the *Telegram*. About 7 A.M. I found Truman in a chair on the sun deck behind a lectern thick with microphones. His face was tanned and he looked vigorous. He wore a tan suit, white shirt, and blue tie with little white diamond patterns worked into it. He was chatting with some friends as he waited for us reporters to gather. Happening to glance up and see me, he interrupted his conversation and sang out: "Hello there! . . . Good to see you again!"

I felt delighted to have a former President remember my face. This made the fourth time I had covered him. Smiling and bowing, I said: "Welcome back, Mr. President."

Grinning at me, Truman said: "You'll never know how good it feels to be back!"

Moments later he arose and walked to the lectern and peered at the press and grinned again and said: "Let's go!"

With the Sherman Adams case very much in mind, I began: "Mr. President, do you mind if I start off with a big fat question?"

"Ask me anything."

"Well, sir, do you think Sherman Adams should resign?"

He replied that on July 1 while in Cannes he had made a statement about this matter, and now he would have to refer us to it. Out of a pocket he drew a clipping from the *New York Times* of July 2. Other reporters and I stepped forward to look at it. I realized I had not seen this *Times* story because I had been vacationing in California.

Quickly explaining this to Truman, I asked whether I might borrow the clip. He said he had some press releases including his statement and— well, he'd go to his cabin to get them. To my surprise, the former President did not ask Rosenman or anyone else to run this errand for him, but went himself and soon returned. A man I was unable to identify handed out those copies of Truman's mimeographed release.

Several of us reporters asked him a few more questions about the Adams-Goldfine case, but he kept repeating that he wanted to confine his remarks to his previous statement. This did not satisfy me. After listening to other newspapermen put soft questions to Truman, I said:

"Mr. President—do you mind if I try to draw you out on this thing a little more?"

Grinning at me, he replied: "You can try . . . Ask me anything."

I broached a series of questions about Adams. Truman disappointed me by making indifferent replies and then turning to other reporters, who got off on other matters. I decided to try a little shock therapy.

"Mr. President," I said, "do you feel that General Vaughan was unjustly abused while you were President?"

His eyes came back to mine. Quickly he answered: "Yes, I do! . . . There was nothing crooked about Harry Vaughan, and he was viciously abused—but not on his own account. They were trying to get at the man in the White House, but they didn't succeed. Vaughan was only my military aide. He had nothing to do with running the government."

My eyes on the pad on which I was writing, I faintly saw Truman's face swing away toward the other journalists and then swing back toward me again, sunlight sparkling on his glasses. Like an actor throwing away a line, he added:

"The government would be in a bad fix if it lost Adams . . . He's running it, you know!"

Truman was grinning at me. Great! Well aware of what he was doing, he had taken the bait I had thrown toward him. Now I had the kind of quote I wanted: Former President Harry S. Truman said today that the United States Government was not being run by President Dwight D. Eisenhower, but by his assistant, Sherman Adams. . . .

Last May, aboard the *Constitution*, at the end of that unproductive press conference, Truman had twitted us reporters because none of us had cried out: "Thank you, Mr. President!" This is the phrase spoken by the senior wire service White House correspondent that ends Presidential press conferences held in the executive mansion.

Well, this was a different stamping ground, and now that I had what I wanted, I sang out: "Thank you, Mr. President!"

End of press conference.

Worried about making my deadline, I scurried off the ship onto the deck and found a phone and called the office. Jack Ferris, who took me on rewrite, liked what I had to tell him. My story about Truman and his comments about Adams appeared on the front page of every edition the rest of the day.

During the political campaign in the fall, several Republican candidates demanded that Sherman Adams step down. On September 22 President Eisenhower accepted Adams' resignation, but declared that his former assistant still had his "complete trust, confidence and respect."

WEDNESDAY, JULY 23, 1958 ■ This morning on the subway I sat beside a woman in a short-sleeved dress who had a number tattooed in blue ink on the inside of her left forearm. My stomach soured with the realization that years ago she had been an inmate of a Nazi concentration camp. Eager to search her face for signs of the suffering she endured, I managed to get a peek at it and saw that her lips were outlined with deep lines looking as though they had been drawn with an ice pick. But when I looked at the faces of other passengers on the car I saw that they, too, had harsh lines in their flesh—and none had suffered a hundredth as much as she.

SATURDAY, AUGUST 9, 1958 ▪ Herbert Hoover becomes 84 years old tomorrow. An editor had asked me to write a story about him, and I did so. The standard story about the former President is *here's-a-really-great-man,* which may be true but can become boring. I cranked out a piece detailing the trivia in his life. It turned out rather well and won praise from a couple of editors.

Hoover had scheduled a press conference for 3 P.M. yesterday in his suite on the 31st floor of the Waldorf Towers. I was assigned to cover it. This pleased me because the very first newspaper story I ever had published was about Hoover's election to the Presidency on November 6, 1928. Later, when I was a reporter in Oklahoma City, I spent a little time with him.

Now, 26 years after Franklin D. Roosevelt defeated him, Hoover has four secretaries. His executive secretary is Miss Bernice (Bunny) Miller, whom I had met through Ruthie at a banquet held by the Seraphic Secretaries of America. I sat beside her. That was at the height of the uproar about Joe McCarthy and to my surprise she was pro-McCarthy. Was Hoover?

Yesterday, when Bunny admitted the press into Hoover's living room, I took a long look. It has four tall windows framed by tan drapes. In the center of the south wall there is a fake fireplace with a mirror above the mantle. The corners of the room have recesses containing four shelves, and mounted on them were pieces of blue and white porcelain. I asked Bunny whether they were Ming china that Hoover had bought in China when working there as an engineer. She said yes—Ming, and something else I didn't hear.

The former President sat behind a huge desk in the southeast corner of the room. Sunshine buttered the rug. Bunny said that since she was unable to remember the names of all the reporters and photographers, we could walk up and identify ourselves. The second before I shook hands with Hoover I got three fast impressions: the pinkness of his face, the blueness of his eyes and the whiteness of his hair. Then our hands met. His grip was mushy, he did not look into my eyes, he murmured something I did not understand. He looked old, very old.

Introductions finished, Hoover sat down again, beneath a picture of his dead wife. The cameramen sprang into action. Hoover, wearing a wisp of a smile, sat as still as a statue. Wanting some action, one photographer asked him to hold his pipe, so he reached into a pocket and brought it out. He wore a doublebreasted brown suit, a white shirt with a collar too big for his neck, a brown and white tie. Flash bulbs flickered. I wondered how many million flash bulbs had gone off in his face during his life.

Bunny, trying to tease her boss into a big smile, hollered at him: "Cheese!"

He didn't hear her because he is a little deaf.

"Chief!" she cried again. "Cheese!"

More flashes, like a firefly convention, until Bunny complained: "You're shooting him so much! Poor man he must be full of holes!" She liked this line so much that she repeated it. "Now, just one more, and that'll be all!"

"Two more," said a photographer.

She shooed them out and then led Hoover from the chair at his desk to one end of a sofa. When he loaded his pipe with tobacco, I handed him a book of matches.

I said: "Happy birthday, Mr. President!"

Other reporters wished him well, and he thanked us. Then he asked Bunny to sit beside him to "interpret" for him referring to his deafness. Someone once said that if Shakespeare and Goethe had been able to meet they probably would have begun conversing by chatting about the weather. As a reporter I had learned not to begin an interview with a hard question, but to warm up the subject with a couple of easy ones.

"To begin with," I said, "how is your health these days?"

He beamed his blue eyes to my face.

"My health," he replied, "has been a little short since I had an operation, but I'll get over it. After all, I did go to Brussels and back, then to California and back here again. My throat clouds up because of my vocal cords, but that's about all, and—"

He kept on talking, much to my surprise. I had thought he'd wait for more questions from us. Instead, he asked himself questions and then answered them.

"—the question generally propounded to me is: 'What does a former President do with his time?' Well, I have many occupations. My secretaries, I think, have given you a list of the things I've done—"

Indeed they had: Last year they wrote 55,952 letters for him. Between June of 1957 and now he received 1,620 invitations to speak; Actually, he delivered nine major addresses and gave 21 minor talks. He took part in several dedications—the Truman Library, seven new Boy's Clubs, and one Herbert Hoover public school. He is a member or trustee of 12 business, educational and scientific organizations. Last year he was awarded his 86th honorary college degree; he also got six other awards and two gold medals. He published another book, *The Ordeal of Woodrow Wilson*. He fished for trout in Oregon and angled for bonefish in Florida, visited the St. Lawrence Seaway, served as President Eisenhower's representative to the Brussels World's Fair, travelled 19,952 miles in airplanes and 3,000 miles in automobiles.

Here was a man who never *lollygags*. Never wastes time. Never dawdles.

Hoover continued: "I labor on the Commission for the Reorganization of the Executive Branch of the Federal Government. That's the full title."

He played at being pompous, although he is pompous without playing. He spoke each word with exaggerated solemnity, and while it wasn't really funny, at least it was an attempt to be humorous and, after all, this was Herbert Hoover.

On March 4, 1933, the day when Franklin D. Roosevelt succeeded Hoover as President, the two men sat side by side in an open limousine as they were driven from the White House to the Capitol. Hoover was glum and silent. F.D.R. tried so hard to make conversation that as they passed the new commerce department building, under construction, he heard himself mouthing some inanity about "the lovely steel."

Now, years later, sitting with reporters, instead of answering their questions and behaving naturally, Hoover was glancing at typed notes. Some of his friends may have urged him to lighten up. He said:

"People always ask why all Presidents of the United States go fishing. Well, it's the only way they can escape from a constant rain of visitors. They can keep away from visitors by praying and fishing, but they can't pray all the time."

He chuckled at his own words. It was pathetic.

Somehow I thought of that radio announcer who mistakenly called him "Hoobert Heever."

The interview dragged on. At last Bunny said some television people wanted the Chief in the next room, so he arose and left the living room, walking slowly, uncertainly. I said I hoped that next year at this same time we would be with him under the same circumstances. He thanked me and shuffled out.

As I departed I glanced into the room bright with lights as TV cameras ground away. Hoover was telling the television reporters the things he had told us. He looked hot and tired. He was an old man, ankles swollen, shoelaces untied.

Herbert Hoover died October 20, 1964, at the age of 90.

THURSDAY, SEPTEMBER 18, 1958 ■ An editor told me that a theatrical press agent had arranged for me to interview Jason Robards, Jr., and his father this afternoon. The elder Robards has been an actor all his adult life except for the past eight years when he was blind. Now he seems to have recovered most of his eyesight. What the editor wanted was a feature story about how Robards, Sr., felt and what he did during those years when he was unable to see.

I was eager to meet the younger Robards because I twice saw him in *Long Day's Journey into Night* and consider him one of the most gifted actors in America. I also wondered whether he had read a letter I sent to Mr. and Mrs. Frederic March, which she posted backstage.

Photographer Al Ravenna and I went to the Hotel Van Rensselaer at 17 West 11th Street and found the Robardses in the lobby. Moments later their press agent joined me, and we walked into the cocktail lounge.

When I expressed surprise at the Vandyke worn by the younger man, he explained he grew it for the Shakespearean roles he recently has been playing. Robards, Sr., will return to the stage for the first time since his illness when he appears next December 3 in a play called *The Disenchanted*. Moreover, this will mark the first time that father and son ever appeared on the same boards at the same time, so they felt excited. Ravenna took pictures of the two actors drinking ale, their arms entwined ceremonially.

The 66-year-old Robards, Sr., wore no glasses, explaining that he had been fitted with contact lenses. When I began asking questions about his blindness, he said an operation had restored his sight and thus his life—which is the theater—then switched the subject, indicating he did not care to talk about that painful period of his life. What he preferred to discuss were those days in the 1920's when he was a well-known Broadway and Hollywood actor.

The still-handsome elderly man clinked glasses with his son and chuckled: "Remember, Jason? . . . We were living in Hollywood and there was this picture called *We the People*. I played Gouverneur Morris, who had a wooden leg. Well, the studio called me and said to come pick up the wooden leg Wallace Beery had used in another picture, so I—"

Having heard the story before, the son choked on his drink in remembered amusement and gleefully slapped the arm of his chair.

". . . So I got Wallace Beery's leg and I stumped around the house practicing, the darned thing on my right leg . . . Remember? . . . After ten days of this, you know, they called me again to say—no! Gouverneur Morris wore a wooden leg on the left leg, not the right, so I had to start practicing all over again—eh?"

Gasping with laughter, the son put down his glass and began teasing his father: "Yeah, I remember! . . . But tell about Tim Holt . . . You were big in Tim Holt cowboy movies."

Arrr-rrruh! Growling, the father slammed his glass onto the table and turned to me and said:

"These days friends call me late at night on the telephone and—"

Becoming playful, an actor turning on his talent, his voice thinning into a whine, he continued: "—and they tell me they're watching Channel 9 and want me to tune in because they're seeing me in an old Tim Holt movie. Why can't they remember that I played opposite Dolores Costello? My God—what a beauty! And of course John Barrymore was always on the set watching my every move, since he was in love with her."

With a chuckle, he went on: "I used to be a pretty boy, which quality—" he bowed to his son and held up his glass in a toast, "—I passed along to Jason."

Amused, Jason Robards, Jr., snorted a veto through his beard.

I asked the father whether he had seen his son in *Long Day's Journey* last year? Yes, he had. Did he detect any of his own mannerisms in his son's technique? No—but maybe there is a certain similarity in the tenor of their voices.

"Watching him, I didn't see him as my son. Only as Jamie—the role he played. I think that's a tribute in itself."

Now that they will appear in the same play will there be any competition between them?

The father grinned and said: "Well, I'll up-stage him one night, and he can up-stage me the next night . . . How about it, Jason?"

Jason Robards, Jr., held up his glass, smiled at his father across the rim and then chuckled in a chuckle remarkably like that of his father: "You're on!"

My story about the Robardses was never printed in the World-Telegram. *The editor was angry with me because I had not written in depth about the father's eight-year blindness. I explained that it was obvious he did not care to discuss that traumatic episode, so I was reluctant to pry. I felt sorry for having wasted the time of two pleasant and talented actors, who felt free to show how much they cared for one another.*

1959

FRIDAY, APRIL 10, 1959 ▩ This morning Frank Kappler showed me a story written for the first edition. It said that at 3:30 P.M. today the United States Court of Appeals would hold a special session in the federal courthouse on Foley Square in lower Manhattan to honor 87-year-old Judge Learned Hand, who has served on the federal bench longer than any other judge in our history. Frank asked me to leave immediately to get advance details of this ceremony to telephone to the city desk.

I had known about Judge Hand in a general way, but not until I got home this evening and consulted my library did I learn the fascinating facts of his life.

In 1909—two years before I was born—President Taft appointed Hand to the United States District Court for Southern New York. In 1912, Hand campaigned for Theodore Roosevelt when Teddy ran for President on the Bull Moose ticket. In 1924, President Coolidge gave Hand a lifetime appointment to the United States Circuit Court of Appeals for the Second Judicial District.

Judge Hand's legal philosophy had two principles: judicial restraint and the preservation of liberty. He tolerated no threat to freedom from either the extreme left or the extreme right. He wrote more than 2,000 opinions which won praise for their clarity and wisdom. He is said to be the equal of such legal giants as Oliver Wendell Holmes, Jr., Louis D. Brandeis and Benjamin N. Cardozo. Although he never was elevated to the Supreme Court, he was called its "tenth justice."

In 1951 he wrote President Truman a letter saying he planned to retire from active service while retaining his position, as was his privilege. Replying, Truman said, in part: "There never has been any question about your pre-eminence among American jurists—indeed among the nations of the world."

This afternoon when I reached the courthouse I went to the 17th floor to see A. Daniel Fusaro, clerk of the Court of Appeals. He said: "Things are a little hectic around here today. Here we are, a bunch of amateurs, putting on a production, a party!" He turned me over to his chief deputy, David Jordan.

I asked whether photographers would be allowed in the court room. No. Well, then, had they hired an artist to sketch this historic moment? No. Nobody thought of it. Who would speak? Well, among others, Chief

Justice Earl Warren and Justice Felix Frankfurter, who had come up from Washington. Can I get an advance copy of their remarks? There might be some in Room 2403, where I could speak to James Ackell, secretary to Judge J. Edward Lumbard.

Ackell gave me copies. Did he have biographical data about Judge Hand? No, well, then, may I speak to his secretary to try to get some anecdotes? Ackell led me into the outer office of Suite 2402, Judge Hand's chambers, consisting of four rooms.

There I met Miss Lucille Mundy, the judge's secretary. Since she and Ruth belong to the Seraphic Secretaries of America, I thought she might remember meeting me from one of their banquets.

I said: "I'm the husband of Ruth Kraus—Eddie Ellis."

"Oh, yes, Eddie! Are you still with the *Herald Tribune?*"

World-Telegram, I corrected her. When I told her what I wanted, she introduced me to Paul Bender, the judge's law clerk, a tall man wearing glasses. Bender was helpful. He led me into his office and let me ask anything.

Although the judge retired from active duty on June 1, 1951, he still works five days a week in his office. He and his wife live in a four-story brownstone at 142 East 65th Street. Every morning a young judge drives Learned Hand to his office, arriving promptly at 9:30 o'clock. At noon the judge takes 30 minutes for lunch and then rests an hour, although he doesn't sleep but lies down, thinking. At 6 P.M. he is driven home. Saturdays he works in his home or in the library of the New York City Bar Association.

From the outer office came sounds of heavy footsteps and grunting. Glancing through the open door I saw the squat figure of the legendary Learned Hand. Swiftly I asked Bender whether the judge might see me a moment. When the law clerk asked, I heard the old man rasp:

"Well, I might as well be killed for a goat as a sheep! Yes, let him come in!"

Thanking Bender with my eyes as I slid past him, I entered the judge's inner chamber. Still standing, he turned awkwardly and held out his hand. As we shook, and later, I took mental notes: . . . short and thick . . . big head . . . almost no neck . . . looks like a bullfrog . . . gray hair flat on huge dome . . . ashen cheeks . . . sagging jowls . . . brown plastic glasses . . . blue eyes peering intensely from beneath the most luxurious salt-and-pepper eyebrows I had seen since the day I met John L. Lewis, the great labor leader.

Awed by the judge, I said: "I'll take only one minute of your time, sir."

"You're damned right you will!"

Clumping over to a chair, he plunked down and looked at me. His clerk had said he has a bad back and cannot stand very long without a cane.

"I have heard, sir, that you are not especially pleased about this ceremony to be held later this afternoon in your honor. Is this true?"

"You're damned right I don't like it! Why should an old man have it rubbed into him in public how old he is?"

My pen skimmed over my notebook.

"And you newspaper fellows—! You get ahold of things like this and spread it all around. This damned thing has got me all worn out!"

He was thundering at me, but I sensed he was not so ferocious as he pretended to be.

Trying to turn him in a new direction, I said: "Sir, I've just finished reading the Holmes-Laski correspondence . . . Fascinating. I suppose you've read the book?"

Supreme Court Justice Oliver Wendell Holmes, Jr., had exchanged many letters with Harold J. Laski, a British political scientist and a socialist.

The judge, replying to my question, said: "No, I haven't read it—and I don't plan to, either!"

He saw my mouth gape in surprise.

"What's more, I'm not going to tell you why I'm not going to read it. Laski, well, there was a clever fellow. Holmes liked to have clever fellows around him. I don't have to read anything about Holmes. I knew the man."

Again, time seemed telescoped: John Dewey told me he had known William James. Learned Hand was telling me he had known the great Justice Holmes, another of my heroes. My God!

Pocketing my pen and notebook, I arose and began walking out. From beneath grizzled eyebrows the judge shot an astonished look at me and asked:

"You're going? You're actually going?"

"Yes, sir, I said I'd take only one minute of your time."

I saw a glint of amusement in his eyes. He waved me back into my chair and grunted:

"Mmmrrmmfff! . . . Yesterday there was a fellow here from *Life* magazine. He took—must have been a thousand pictures. Damned if I know why they have to take so many pictures. Do you?"

This judge of 2,000 opinions now really wanted my opinion about something. I said that since I am a reporter and not a photographer, I honestly do not know why they take such an abundance of pictures. I'd sometimes wondered about this.

Peering at me through his glasses, Judge Hand asked: "Am I keeping you from doing something?" His voice was sincere, not sarcastic.

"No, sir! . . . I just—Judge Hand, would you mind if I were to ask for your autograph?"

"Ahhhww! . . . I'm not such an old crab as all that, of course I'll give you my autograph. You're damned sure I'm not taking up your time? Okay, then, what kind of paper do you want it on?"

His hands prowled the desk until he found a scrap of paper. Using a pen with green ink, he wrote: "To Edward Ellis with my best wishes, Learned Hand, April 10, 1959."

I thanked him. As I arose to leave, I saw the young eyes in the old face staring at me in puzzled curiosity. There's one thing about growing old: In intelligent people the eyes never grow old.

Leaving his chamber, I thought: *What a wonderful old man!*

I found a phone and called my office to dictate the texts of the speeches to be made, together with my impressions of the judge. Then I rode the elevator to the fifth floor. Since photographers would not be allowed to take pictures during the actual ceremony, the judge had been brought to room 512 to pose. Sitting on the edge of a desk, he looked like an angry bullfrog. Cameramen swarmed around him like mosquitoes—buzzing, buzzing, buzzing.

One yelled: "Hey, Judge! Smile! Let me see you smile!"

Swelling up, the old man croaked: "I'll be Goddamned if I'll smile."

"Then look at the top of my head!"

"Not even that will make me smile," the judge retorted—but then he ducked his head and swallowed his lips to hide a hint of a smile.

Freddie Palumbo, the *World-Telegram's* sweet-faced, gray-haired photographer, cried: "Hey, judge! Take off your glasses and wave 'em!"

"No! I won't do one Goddamned thing!"

Judge Harold Medina, in his black judicial robe, said to me: "Those guys are really working him over."

They yelled and yelled, and he swelled and swelled until it seemed he might burst in fury. Then the old bullfrog got off his log and padded through the cluster of cameramen, roaring: "Gawd damn! If this isn't the most disgusting exhibition I've ever seen!"

Judge Learned Hand died August 18, 1961, at the age of 89.

TUESDAY, AUGUST 4, 1959   ■   I am annoyed by most of the graffiti I see on walls of subway stations and elsewhere, but now and then I find something amusing. Today in the South Ferry station I saw this scribble:

GOD IS DEAD.
—Nietzsche

Beneath this, someone else wrote:

NIETZSCHE IS DEAD.
—God

THURSDAY, SEPTEMBER 17, 1959 ■ Khrushchev arrived in New York City today.

Anticipating his visit, hoping to be assigned to report some part of it, I've been reading books and magazines about the premier of the Soviet Union. This is the first time any Russian head of state has set foot on American soil. In 1871 the Grand Duke Alexis visited New York, but he was only a son of Czar Alexander II.

President Eisenhower had invited Khrushchev to make an official visit to the United States. Day before yesterday the Russian leader landed at Andrews Field near Washington in a giant silver Soviet airliner. That evening Ike gave a state dinner for him in the White House. Yesterday Khrushchev spoke at the National Press Club and then met with members of the Senate Foreign Relations Committee. This morning he came by train to New York.

From Penn Station he was to be driven to the Soviet's U.N. embassy on Park Avenue, and I was pleased when Frank Kappler told Woody Klein and me to go to Herald Square to see the cavalcade and watch the crowd for interesting reactions. I had my police press card. Now I was given a card that said:

September 1959
Visit of the Chairman of the Council of Ministers of USSR
Nikita S. Khrushchev
Edward Ellis
New York World-Telegram
PRESS

The sun shone. The air was chilly at first. When I reached Herald Square on 34th St. I found that all east-west vehicular traffic had been stopped, and 10 minutes later the cops halted all north-south movement of cars. The police had put wooden horses along curbs to keep people on sidewalks; there were thousands of people, all jammed together. As I walked in the middle of empty 34th St. I sensed that today something about the city was different. What was it? . . . Ah, yes, the silence, the absolute silence. Here stood thousands and thousands of people, but barely a sound was heard. Except for Wall Street on a Sunday morning in summer, never before had I heard in this city such an ocean of silence.

At 12:27 P.M., from a block west of the square, I heard a murmur. Glancing that way, I saw a blue-helmeted motorcycle cop, the first sign of the Khrushchev cavalcade. The lead cop was followed by other motorcycle policemen, some riding alone, others advancing in chevron-shaped formations. Behind them came a limousine, then another and another. They tooled along at about 30 miles an hour. I stood 20 feet from them as they passed. The fourth limo. This must be the one. A black Cadillac hard-top. Sitting on the right side of the rear seat was a moon-faced man. Khrushchev! Fast . . . too fast. Studying the faces of the people in the crowd, I saw that they felt cheated. They barely could see Khrushchev.

I ran to phone my office and deliver an impressionistic report to a rewrite man. Then I rode a subway back there and the moment I entered the city room I was beckoned to the city desk, where an editor leaned forward and asked: "Would you like to go to the Khrushchev banquet this evening?"

"Hell, yes!"

I was handed a memo written by Bob Herb, who had taken the data on the phone. It said:

"Economic Club invites us to send reporter to dinner for K. tonight at 8 P.M. in the Waldorf East Foyer. These are the regulations: Black tie. Must have State Department accreditation. Must not have camera—no photos allowed. No drinking. May not leave until entire program is over. If we decide to send, we should notify Mrs. Groper at Economic Club (MU 2-0830) as early as possible. If yes, we must pick up ticket from her as early as possible. The Waldorf is providing a general press room in the hotel for other reporters. The speeches will be piped into this room."

Thanking the editor, I walked back to my desk. I felt bothered by two things: 1) I have not owned a tuxedo since my college days; 2) What is the procedure for getting clearance from the State Department? I began working the phones in such excitement that I became self-conscious and turned to our travel editor, John (Mickey) McGuire, who sits to my left.

"Mickey, am I shouting?"

"Yeah," he said. "You sound excited."

"Well, I am excited! Jesus! To be able to cover Khrushchev—!"

Mickey said: "I don't blame you for being excited."

After many phone calls I learned that the special press card given me this morning is, in fact, the very State Department accreditation required.

I went to the office of the Economic Club of New York. On a bulletin board was a memo saying that so many club members wanted tickets that "there's been nothing like it since the California Gold Rush." I was handed my free ticket.

Then I walked to the Bond clothing store on Times Square to buy a tux and accessories. On a reporter's salary I can't afford to patronize a quality men's store. When I told the salesman and tailor that the tux I chose would appear tonight in the Waldorf at the Khrushchev banquet, they rushed through alterations in 15 minutes.

This evening, dressed to the nines—whatever the hell that means!—I left home early. I thought that when I neared the Waldorf I'd have to endure a slow security check. As my cab approached the hotel I saw that traffic islands in the center of Park Avenue had been planted with new shrubbery and then floodlit—a luminous spectacle I hoped would be appreciated by the Russian leader.

The hotel was surrounded by a wall of cops. Years ago when I was a reporter in Oklahoma City I covered a speech given by President Franklin D. Roosevelt, but neither then nor later had I seen so many policemen in one place at one time. Walking up to one cop, I showed him my three credentials—the State Department press card, my police press card, and my dinner invitation. He waved me through a gap in the line of wooden horses ringing the hotel, then laughed: "You sure got everything you need there, Buddy." I doubted whether I looked like anyone's *buddy*, because I was wearing a Homburg hat for the first time in my life—and feeling silly about it.

Entering the Waldorf, I walked through the lobby to an elevator that took me to the grand ballroom on the third floor.

The Economic Club had invited 2,000 guests to the Khrushchev banquet. No women. All men. Each paid $17. My table was #171 in a room opening to the east off the ballroom but within view of the dais. As I sat down by other reporters I was surprised to see that I was the only one in black tie. How come? My instructions on this point had been precise. Because of my tux a reporter for the *Journal of Commerce* mistook me for a businessman and then expressed disappointment, for he had hoped to solicit my reactions to this event.

Our red-jacketed waiter was so nervous his fingers trembled, and because we were only reporters he behaved boorishly, telling us to keep out of his way, and because we were nervous we failed to tell him to go to hell. It was neither his fault, nor ours, that we had been jammed so closely together at the table that he had trouble serving us.

This was the menu: *Supreme of Fruit Lucullus . . . Roast Prime Ribs of Beef . . . Chasseur Sauce . . . Baby Beets au Beurre . . . Tiny Stringbeans Saute . . . Crown Martinique . . . Sauce Fraisette . . . Petits Fours . . . Large Coffee.*

At our table one man sat in silence. He wore a business suit with a tiny red-and-yellow emblem in the notch of his lapel. I asked him whether he was a security officer. He said he works in the White House recording in shorthand President Eisenhower's press conferences. These days, he told me, people speak faster than in the past. Why? Because modern communications technology makes it easier for speakers to be heard. Sure! When William Jennings Bryan spoke at outdoor rallies without microphones or loudspeakers, he had to indulge in long pauses.

I left our table several times to walk into the ballroom and look around. When I saw that other men who had dined in adjoining rooms were bringing their chairs into the ballroom, I suggested to Don Ross of the *Herald Tribune* that we do the same. By making this shift we missed dessert but now sat closer to Khrushchev.

A long stage stretched along the south side of the ballroom. About 60 dignitaries sat there at tables rising in three tiers. Suspended behind and above them were two enormous flags. The one on the left was an American flag—with only 48 stars. The flag on the right, of course, was the Soviet banner, its red field emblazoned with a yellow hammer and sickle. Six overhead lights shone down upon the tables in the front row and in the center sat Khrushchev.

He is 65 years old. Short and broad and bald, he was born the son of a peasant in the Ukraine. In his youth he worked as a shepherd, steam fitter and coal miner. In 1918 he joined the Red Army and soon became a political commissar. After years of study at Moscow's industrial academy, he rose rapidly within the ranks of the party, became the party leader of Moscow, survived the Stalinist purges, became premier in March of last year.

After staring at him, I gazed around the ballroom. Although the press was under orders not to drink, I saw many club members at tables holding whiskey bottles. Many bottles were almost empty—which helps explain what happened later.

The club president is Herbert Woodman of Park Avenue; he also is president of the Interchemical Corporation. Arising to open the proceedings, he said everyone recognized the significance of the visit Chairman Khrushchev was making to the United States. Then he introduced Henry

Cabot Lodge, whom President Eisenhower had chosen to escort the Chairman across the United States.

Lodge is so tall that when he stood up he looked like a skyscraper next to Khrushchev. The Boston patrician and politician ad-libbed a few remarks, then stopped, grinned and said: "—but I'm sure Chairman Khrushchev will correct me if I'm wrong."

Khrushchev's aide interpreted.

To everyone's surprise the Chairman—who had not yet been introduced—stepped to the microphone in front of Lodge. Grinning broadly, he seemed playful. He spoke only a few words in Russian. His aide repeated them in English: "Only the grave will correct the hunchback!" Or was the word *great?* Was this an old Russian proverb? What did it mean? Did it mean that death is the final answer? Khrushchev was laughing. A couple of club members yelled, "Sit down!"

Sit down? The guest of honor? The man invited to the United States by the President of the United States? The head of a sovereign nation, the man whom Ike had asked all of us to receive with every courtesy? The Economic Club had invited Khrushchev to speak to its members and on the banquet program he was addressed as His Excellency—but now some members were yelling at him. *Sit down?*

I thought: You stupid bastards!

After Khrushchev returned to his seat, Lodge began reading from a text, defining capitalism as *economic humanism*—which is news to me. When Lodge cited the taxes paid by our citizens, the audience groaned. With the Communist leader hearing these groans, did he believe we are as fond of capitalism as we say we are? I recalled that Justice Oliver Wendell Holmes, Jr., once said he was glad to pay taxes because they are the price of civilization.

When Lodge finished, Khrushchev arose and mounted a low stool behind the lectern. His interpreter stood to his right. Khrushchev's round face was ruddy with health; his keg-shaped body radiated energy. Unlike the Americans in elegant attire, he wore a black business suit and a gray tie. Pinned on his jacket were three medals, two shaped like stars, one of them round. Before beginning his speech he made a few remarks in a soft voice about Lodge's comments:

"Why did Mr. Lodge so zealously defend capitalism here? He did it so zealously—and that is only natural. If he did not defend capitalism so fervently, he would not hold such an important post in your country . . ."

Khrushchev was smiling. Club members laughed and applauded.

". . . The only question is—what made Mr. Lodge plead the benefits of capitalism with such ardor today? Is it possible that he wished to talk me into adopting the capitalistic faith? Or perhaps Mr. Lodge is afraid that if a Bolshevik addresses capitalists he will convert them, and they will espouse the Communist faith? I want to reassure you: I have no such intentions. I know with whom I am dealing."

I was struck by his repetition of one word: Capitalistic *faith* . . . Communist *faith* . . . These sounded more like religions than economic systems.

Khrushchev put on his glasses and began reading his speech. In my hands I held an English translation on five sheets of legal paper, and because his speech was single-spaced, I knew it was a long one. His aide interpreted paragraph by paragraph, and as the Chairman waited he looked around the room with an air that seemed to say: Hey, I sure know what I'm doing, don't I, kid? Total self-assurance.

He talked about "the stagnation that has persisted in Soviet-American economic relations for almost ten years. The continuation by the United States of the policy of trade discrimination against the Soviet Union is simply a piece of senseless obstinacy. You are all informed of the fact that we are offering you economic competition. Some describe this as our challenge to the United States. But speaking of challenges, one might say perhaps—and it would be even more precise—that it was the United States that first challenged the whole world. The USA developed its economy to a higher level than in any other country. For a long time nobody ventured to dispute your supremacy—"

The rich Americans applauded themselves.

His face becoming grim, Khrushchev continued:

"—but the time has now come when a country has appeared which accepts your challenge, which takes into account the development of the United States, and in turn challenges you. You may rest assured that the Soviet Union will hold its own in this economic development. It will overtake you and leave you behind—"

The rich Americans yelled in derision.

At this moment the event began to disintegrate. Khrushchev, known to speak as long as six hours, was orating at wearisome length. Club members glanced at their wristwatches. When the speaker said that "excellent prospects are opening up for our gas industry," some club members snickered. Khrushchev probably did not know that in American slang *to gas* means to talk too long.

As he talked on and on, there were groans and hisses. The Chairman, who had begun speaking in high humor, clearly understood he was being heckled. Bristling, he cried:

"He who wants to have eggs must put up with the hen's cackle!"

I sat in a state of shock, muscles tense. These rich Americans, some high on booze, were heckling a man so powerful that he could turn the cold war into a hot war.

Near the end of his speech Khrushchev said: "I had no intention of offending and, still less, of insulting anyone. I just wanted to express my thoughts about the future as I saw it. In conclusion, allow me to wish that each of you make his contribution to improving the relations between our countries and bettering the international situation. Thank you."

Now came questions—from club members, not reporters. First, the president of Dun & Bradstreet, and then the retired president of the Bell Telephone Laboratories, asked questions that were long and rambling, complex and confusing. The third man to rise was Gardner Cowles, president and editor of *Cowles Magazines*. He said he would ask a simple question, but he didn't.

Every good reporter asks questions that are brief and to the point. While I had been irked by the mushy questions from the two first businessmen, I had not expected much from them in the first place. Cowles, however, is in communications, so I expected better from him—vainly. He too made a speech and then put a cloudy question to Khrushchev. What he wanted to know could have been asked this way: 1) Why do you jam the Voice of America? 2) Why do you censor dispatches from American correspondents in Russia? It took so long for Cowles to unwind his tangled questions and so long for Khrushchev's aide to interpret them that the audience became restless and some men even laughed.

Stiffening, Khrushchev said: "The fact that you ask such questions and the fact that some gentlemen are laughing before hearing my reply show how little they know about the substance of the matter—"

Stung by laughter and Cowles' questions, the Chairman launched into a meandering analysis of the history of the Soviet Union and the United States and their relative economic development.

From a balcony a man shouted: "That does not answer the question!"

I agreed. Regardless of the muddy language used by Cowles, his questions were legitimate—but Khrushchev was avoiding a direct answer.

Now the room erupted in a hubbub of hoots and howls and jeers! Khrushchev lost his temper.

"Gentlemen! . . . Since you have invited me, I would ask that you hear me out attentively. If you do not want to, I can stop talking. I am an old sparrow. You cannot muddle me by your cries. If there is no desire to listen to what I have to say, I can go! I did not come to the USA to beg. I represent the great Soviet state, a great people who have made the great October Revolution. And no sallies, gentlemen, can drown out what has been achieved and done by our great people, and what it is planning to do!"

I stiffened in fear. The leader of the communist world was threatening to walk out on the cream of American capitalists because they were badgering him, mocking him, insulting him. Good God! Hadn't President Eisenhower made it plain that he wanted Khrushchev to be received courteously? Didn't these rich idiots realize that to insult a powerful man is to invite aggression? Didn't they stop to consider that their boorish behavior might turn the cold war into a hot one? Or were some too drunk to think clearly about anything?

By the time the banquet ended at 11:15 P.M., Khrushchev had his temper under control. Smiling, he sang out in Russian: "Good-bye!"

As the applause began I checked my watch. It lasted—10 seconds.

The Economic Club apologized to Khrushchev. The next day its president wrote a letter saying in part:

"I sincerely hope that there was no real misunderstanding as a result of the apparent discourtesy on the part of a few members of the audience during the question period. In so large a group it seems almost inevitable that there will be a few people who are forgetful of their manners. I feel sure you realized how very few they were."

The day after that Khrushchev replied in a gracious letter:

"Like you, I am well aware that the individuals who tried to cast a shadow on our meeting with their unfriendly cries do not represent the opinion of either the businessmen who gathered at the Economic Club or the American people."

I had written a story for the World-Telegram *about the discourtesy shown to a visiting head of state, couching my public observations in language much more mild than my personal feelings. An editor said my piece may have been partly responsible for the apology the club offered to the Chairman, but I doubt it.*

In 1973 Henry Cabot Lodge published a memoir called The Storm Has Many Eyes. *One long chapter was called "With Khrushchev in America"— but it did not even mention the disaster at the Waldorf.*

In 1970 Little, Brown and Company published a book entitled Khrushchev Remembers. *The publisher declared that it "is an authentic record of Nikita Khrushchev's words." On page 513 there are these words:*

"The main thing that I noticed about the capitalistic West when I was in New York, which Gorky called the City of the Yellow Devil, is that it's not the man that counts but the dollar. Everyone thinks of how to make money, how to get more dollars. Profits, the quest for capital, and not people are the center of attention there."

I wonder how he got that impression.

CHAPTER 12

1960

■ Yesterday I sent this memo to one of my editors:

TO: Wes First
FROM: Eddie Ellis
RE: Christmas feature
Date: February 11, 1960
Although Christmas is far away, I'd like to suggest a one-page layout that might attract considerable attention.

At Yuletide, of course, all is "Peace on earth, good will toward men." Well, why not dramatize this?

A day or two before Christmas, we could devote a special front page to the ordinary, daily doings of average nice people.

That is, Joe Blow, auto salesman, gets up, showers, dresses, eats breakfast, kisses his wife, and heads out to work. Jane Smith, 8, takes to school that day a Christmas drawing she has made for teacher.

Such pleasant stories, showing what the vast majority of folks are doing on a given day, could easily be obtained if each reporter were, say, to interview a relative. With real names used, of course.

Beneath this special front page we could have our usual front page with its usual quota of unusual happenings. But—just one day a year—it might be a relief to learn what kind, considerate, good people are doing.

Chances are that this would attract comment from subscribers and trade publications. A real promotion job could be done on it.

This being February, such a page might be difficult to visualize. Near Christmas, however, as the holiday spirit takes hold, its feasibility would, I believe, become apparent.

Are youse wit me?

I still consider this a great idea. Unfortunately, no one at the Telegram *did anything about it.*

TUESDAY, APRIL 12, 1960. ■ The following story was published today in the *New York World-Telegram*.

By Edward Ellis
Staff Writer

Fifteen years ago today the sun spilled its liquid gold upon the white cottage at Warm Springs, Ga., which Franklin D. Roosevelt called his second home.

New York City was warm and humid. Lilacs bloomed in Washington, D.C. The U.S. Ninth Army trundled to within 60 miles of Berlin, where a black-forelocked madman cowered within his underground bunker, and his ferret-faced propaganda minister whined that "the war cannot last much longer."

That day of April 12, 1945, war correspondent Ernie Pyle stood on Okinawa to watch with sad elfin eyes as the Japanese lost 118 planes. San Francisco was grooming herself for the first United Nations conference. A note rebuking Stalin for mistrusting his allies had just been delivered from President Roosevelt.

There in his Georgia cottage the President was happy. He had regained eight of the 15 pounds he had lost at Yalta. That bright morning his blood pressure had tested normal for a 63-year-old man.

That afternoon he planned to attend an old-fashioned Georgia barbecue to ladle in some of his favorite Brunswick stew. The evening promised a minstrel show featuring a hoe-down fiddler he enjoyed.

A special plane had been late in getting his White House mail to him. Secretary William Hassett asked whether the President cared to wait until after lunch to work on them. The Negro cook, Daisy Bonner, was bustling about in the kitchen preparing chocolate souffle.

Mr. Roosevelt said, no, he'd have at it right away. The bull-shouldered, cigaret-puffing man sat in a brown leather chair near the fireplace. His pipe-thin legs were free of the 10 pounds of steel he usually wore.

Russian-born Mme. Elizabeth Shoumatoff of Locust Valley, L.I., was painting his portrait. For her benefit he had donned a dark blue suit and a Harvard-red tie. In the back of the living room the President's cousin, Miss Laura Delano, sat and knitted.

Mr. Roosevelt had been President of the U.S. for 12 years, one month and eight days. He knew the routine. As documents were placed on the small table before him, though, he did an unusual thing. He took his draft card out of his wallet and tossed it into a nearby basket.

Then the brown-blotched hands began moving swiftly over the papers. He signed State Department appointments, citations for the Legion of Merit, a long list of nominations for postmasterships in small towns. And—his last official act—he put his name to legislation extending the life of the Commodity Credit Corporation.

All this with chuckles and quips for the benefit of the women near him. The time: 1:20 o'clock. Suddenly, the laugh on his lips curdled into a moan. One hand quivered up to massage the temples of his massive head.

"I have a terrific headache," he said.

Those were the last words ever spoken by Franklin Delano Roosevelt.

He died at 3:35 P.M. Central War Time.

In Washington, an ashen-faced Harry S. Truman mumbled to reporters that "the whole weight of the moon and stars fell on me." In a Rochester, Minn., hospital tears scalded the eyes of Presidential favorite Harry Hopkins. On Leyte Island, a Navy orderly dropped a message on the cot of James Roosevelt, then fled in tears.

To all four uniformed Roosevelt boys in various parts of the world went this cablegram from a woman who now was a widow:

"Darlings: Pa slept (slipped) away this afternoon. He did his job to the end as he would want you to do. Bless you. All our love. Mother."

A Bronx woman heard the news on the radio and died of shock. A 13-year-old boy sobbed: "I love him so much!" A New York cab driver had to be pinned down lest he maim his passenger who had called the President a dirty name.

Servicemen back from overseas wept openly in Times Square. The New York Telephone Co. handled 947,017 more calls than usual. Movie houses and department stores planned to close. At the Winter Garden comedians Olsen and Johnson nervously removed a skit about Eleanor Roosevelt from their musical, "Laffing Room Only."

The tributes began pouring over press association wires. Herbert Hoover: ". . . magnificent leadership." Gov. Thomas E. Dewey: ". . . one of the great Presidents." Archbishop Francis J. Spellman compared him to Washington and Lincoln.

The sun shone, the earth whirled, the robins chirped, but sorrow shuffled into many hearts and whimpered wordlessly. Franklin Delano Roosevelt was no more.

My story on the day FDR died struck a chord with many friends and strangers. Here's one letter I received:

APRIL 15, 1960

Mr. Edward Ellis
World Telegram Staff Writer
World Telegram
125 Barclay St.,
New York, N.Y.

Dear Mr. Ellis:

I do so want to thank you for that perfectly wonderful article which appeared in the April 12th edition of the World Telegram regarding President Roosevelt.

As a great admirer of President Roosevelt I cherished every line of your article, it was done so exquisitely. Truly a fitting memorium to a great man, a truly great man, who made every person feel that he was their friend. As he so aptly put it on his fireside chats, when he said MY FRIENDS—you felt like he was speaking expressly to you.

Fifteen years ago at his passing I shall never forget the hush that fell upon this city. The prayers that were offered up. And I remember my son who was just 7 saying "what will we do we have no President." All his life he had known only PRES. ROOSEVELT. He could not understand how we could have another.

True, he has left many enemies behind him, people who detest his memory and think that he caused us many troubles we have today. But alas no man can be perfect and not make some errors in judgment.

It would seem to me reading between the lines that you too admired the man or you could not have written the way you did.

I clipped it and sent the article to my son who is stationed in Germany, so he too could enjoy the beautiful sentiment expressed in your article.

Thank you for writing it, it touched me deeply.

Sincerely yours,
(Mrs.) Esther K. Austin

Anne Cronin was executive assistant to William Benton, publisher of the Encyclopedia Britannica and the Britannica yearbooks. I had fun writing her this thank you letter in the style of Don Marquis's famous Archie and Mehitabel columns, which began running in the New York Sun in 1916.

SUNDAY, APRIL 17, 1960   ■   dear anne

my friend mehitabel was saying the other day archie why is it that you walk around with your head bent forward looking as though you are going to topple over forwards and i said mehitabel i said its all because of that anne cronin why whatever can you mean asked mehitabel then i explained i told her that this anne cronin has the bad habit of sending me yearbooks of the encyclopedia britannica is this bad asked mehitabel oh very quoth i how so asked mehitabel well i told her i read the darned things this means that i cram my skull with facts and i said to mehitabel whether you know it or not facts weigh a great deal hence i have become top heavy these days i just totter along ready to fall over at any minute but mehitabel protested isnt that the price all you intellectuals pay for your brains mehitabel i gasped me an intellectual her remark filled me with pride that i was able to hold my head up now im no longer in danger from the nefarious habits of one anne cronin and its all thanks to mehitabel

yers

archie ellis

I wrote a series of articles about small buildings on valuable land whose owners refused to sell to rich real estate firms even at enormous prices. One such holdout was on West 42nd Street; the ground floor was a bar and grill. The bar was run by the man who owned the building, a tough guy named Jimmy. After publication of my story about his place, he called excitedly and urged me to visit him again. When I got there I saw the two front windows filled with huge blow-ups of my story. Jimmy overwhelmed me with hospitality, declaring this was the first time in his life anyone had paid attention to him.

TUESDAY, MAY 3, 1960   ■   I got another call from Jimmy, asking me to stop in his bar and grill on my way home from work. In a vague way he said he had a proposition that would pay me a lot of money. Wary, but curious, I said I'd drop by.

When I arrived he led me to a table in the rear and ordered me a drink. Jimmy has a broken nose and ice-blue eyes. I asked what he had in mind. He opened the *Wall Street Journal* to a page of stock market returns.

"Numbers?" I asked, a light dawning.

I know nothing about the stock market or gambling, but have heard that men who run the numbers racket use certain figures on stock market pages to get the jump on people who play the policy game. The scheme was fuzzy in my mind.

Eyeing me, Jimmy said: "This is somethin' yuh go for, or yuh don't . . . Yuh familiar with this?"

"Not really. . . . I don't know anything about the stock market."

"Well, yuh got the same thing in the *World-Telegram.*"

"Sure."

"Comes out about three-fifteen."

"I suppose so. . . . So?"

Jimmy leaned toward me.

"Al' yuh gotta do is to get this table first thing off the press and phone me here. That's all. What I do after that, yuh don't have to know. Oh, it's legitimate. Yuh know me, Eddie! Yuh know I wouldn't get you involved in anything that's wrong. I never been wrong-o in my life! On my children's head, Eddie, I never been in jail in my life!"

Reaching under the table, he knocked its wood with his knuckles.

Slowly I said, "I . . . don't . . . know." Actually, I knew what my answer would be, but wanted to hear the whole pitch.

"You just get that three-fifteen edition of your paper every afternoon and call me and then I let some guys know—guys who, yeah, run policy in California. Then they do what they gotta do. Remember—every afternoon at three-fifteen."

"For how long?"

"Just one week, at 500 bucks a day for a week. There ain't nuthin' dishonest about it."

"If not, why is somebody willing to pay me $500 a day for this information?"

"It's business," said Jimmy. "They'll get a profit, like in business, an' that's why they're willin' to pay yuh this money. You don't have to go into it deep. Me, I got this bar it's worth $50,000 an' I got a wife an' two kids! You don't think I'd steer yuh to anything that's wrong, Eddie? I got everything to lose. Besides, I like yuh an' I wouldn't want yuh to lose anything."

So that was it! Jimmy wanted me to become a tip-off man, or whatever they call it, for the mob. I felt my face freeze into the holier-than-thou expression I sometimes saw on the face of my Puritanical grandmother.

"No, Jimmy! I don't want any part of it, and I'll tell you why: I think it's wrong!"

"But nobody gets hurt."

"The hell you say! With somebody paying me $500 a day, somebody has to get hurt—the little guys, probably."

"Aw! Let 'em look out for themselves! If they ain't got what we got, they ain't got the brains to protect themselves—so we gotta care?"

I felt both angry and amused. I had been born on the prairie in a small town of a WASP family with starchy Puritanical ethics, and although I have boozed and wenched and broken many of the Ten Commandments, I still have not forsaken the work ethic nor a sense of honesty, but now I sat in a second-rate restaurant on 42nd Street across a table from a tough guy with mob connections who wanted me to break the law and thereby put myself at the mercy of gangsters. If I were a scenario writer plotting a movie, I would not dare draw such a stark contrast between two men.

I yipped, "Yes, Jimmy! I care!"

"Well." He folded the *Wall Street Journal.* "Like I said on the phone, Eddie, if I put it to yuh, yuh either sez yes or yuh sez no. So that's the way it is. I ain't gonna try to pressure yuh. Have another drink."

He gestured toward a waitress, who brought me another drink, and then another, and slowly the booze began relaxing me. At first I told myself that never again would I come to Jimmy's place because I do not wish to associate with such a person. Then I said to myself I was being too goddam rigid. It was obvious that Jimmy liked me, respected me, and now perhaps he respected me even more. Why should I remain aloof from a man who came from such a different background?

We began talking family. Jimmy told me with pride that his son gets an A-plus in most subjects at school, while his daughter receives straight A's. He praised his wife, whom he fondly called a *Hebe*. I told him I had married a Jewish girl.

Jimmy's parents came from Italy. He was born in Hell's Kitchen on the west side of mid-Manhattan, the family desperately poor, so he stole a little here and there just to keep alive, and he only went through the sixth grade. I reflected that I might have become another Jimmy had I been as disadvantaged as he.

The other day, he told me, he dropped into a Bickford restaurant for a cup of coffee and ran into four men with whom he had grown up. Collectively, they had served 154 years in jail. After telling me stories about their experiences, he came back to the subject of his own children, lamenting the fact that they do not go to church, berating himself for not being a good father. What a bundle of contradictions are all of us human beings! From petty gangster to fond father in a half-hour. That was Jimmy. I liked the man.

As I started to leave, Jimmy said: "Yuh gotta come back often, Eddie!"

"But, Jimmy," I protested, "I'm not a freeloader and every time I come here you throw drinks and dinners at me!"

"Eddie, if yuh think I do this because of that piece yuh wrote about me—yer nuts! I just like you. So what's wrong with one guy what likes another guy buying him an occasional drink, maybe? Huh?" We shook hands. I said, okay, I'd drop in now and then.

Today I rejected a bribe of $2,500. That's hardly the $10,000 I once was offered, but I guess as far as the bribe business is concerned, I'm still in the running.

FRIDAY, MAY 13, 1960 ■ Today I went to the Madison Hotel to interview Ted Geisel, better known as Dr. Seuss. This is the story I wrote.

By Edward Ellis
Staff Writer

The tragedy of Dr. Seuss is that Dr. Seuss doesn't look like Dr. Seuss.

As any kid can tell you, he is a funny, funny man. Many parents agree he is the creator of some of the best children's books this side of *Alice in Wonderland*. And publishers point out that five of the sixteen current best-selling kids' books are by him.

He draws ten-footed lions and cows with 98 faucets. He writes of the Bustard, who only eats custard with sauce made of mustard. Some of his best friends are the Ooblecks, the Mop-Noodled Finch, the Salamagoox and Thidwick, the Big-Hearted Moose. He is the papa of Gerald McBoing-Boing.

Well, then, it's a bit of a shock to learn that his real name is Ted Geisel and that he looks, in his own words, "like the vice president of a bank." He came here from his home in La Jolla, Calif., to deliver the manuscript of his 19th book, *Green Eggs and Ham*.

Nineteenth? In his Hotel Madison suite, Dr. Seuss had to count to make sure. Yes, nineteen.

"It would simplify things," said Dr. Seuss, "if I looked like Bert Lahr. That way, I wouldn't disappoint the kids."

Once in awhile he has to appear at autograph parties. In Detroit, for example, a department store flew him by helicopter from the home store to its suburban branches, landing him on their roofs. Some schools had been shut for the occasion, and the kids were told they'd have a fantastic experience.

Dr. Seuss stepped out of the helicopter wearing a business suit and raincoat. A sigh went up from 3000 children. Dr. Seuss didn't have antlers, nor even a tail.

"They had a microphone," he recalled, "but I didn't know what to say. It was the lowest point of my life."

How about designing and wearing a fantastic costume, this interviewer asked.

"I tried that just once," Dr. Seuss said glumly, "but it didn't come off well. You have to be an actor to be convincing, and I'm no actor. That's why I say it would be better if I looked like Bert Lahr."

Once Dr. Seuss did draw a self-portrait that's properly fantabulous. He wears an orange hat that looks like a damaged periscope. His ears are pointed and sit near the top of his skull. His head resembles a hairy egg, while his eyebrows could pass for hedges.

At another appearance, in Cleveland, Dr. Seuss began drawing for a second-grade class. He admits he laid an egg. The kids sat on their hands and glowered at him. Finally, one tot piped up: "Gus can draw better than you!"

Gus, also a second-grader, turned out to be a mentally retarded boy who stood five feet nine. Dr. Seuss surrendered his crayons and drawing paper to the lad. "And, by golly, Gus *could* draw better than me!" Dr. Seuss confessed.

Thankfully, Dr. Seuss never learned to draw. When he tries to sketch a bird as faithfully as he can, it comes out funny. In his only adult book, *The Seven Lady Godivas,* he meant to draw "the sexiest seven naked ladies you ever saw, but they came out funny, too."

"I guess," Dr. Seuss sighs, "I have a very strong child's mind."

On May 1, 1960, an American spy plane was shot down in Russia. It was a supersonic U-2 plane piloted by Francis Gary Powers, a CIA agent. Captured alive, he confessed he had been on a photo-reconnaissance mission. A Big Four summit conference had been scheduled to be held in Paris on May 16. Gathered there were Khrushchev of the Soviet Union, Eisenhower of the United States, Macmillan of the United Kingdom and De Gaulle of France. However, Khrushchev refused to meet with the Western leaders unless Eisenhower apologized for the American reconnaissance flights over Russia, which had been in progress for four years. Eisenhower agreed to cancel future U-2 flights but refused to apologize. The summit collapsed. Khrushchev warned that Soviet rockets might be used to retaliate against American military bases.

TUESDAY, MAY 17, 1960   ■   Khrushchev's blasts at Ike and the disintegration of the summit conference swamped my thinking all day. I grabbed each new edition brought up from the press room. To another reporter I said: "This seems like September of 1939 all over again."

However, I can't bring myself to believe that Russia will launch an atomic war. Why? For reasons of self-interest. If they bomb us, we'll bomb them. Nonetheless, all day long I felt tense.

This afternoon I went to Lincoln Center, where I chatted with an attractive young woman who handles public relations for the center. We began talking about the possibility of war. She said she has nightmares.

"It's not so much that I mind it happening," she said slowly, "mind the end of everything while I stand here in the sunshine. It's just that I'm afraid, for some reason, to think of a bomb falling on New York while I'm alone in the dark in my bedroom."

SATURDAY, MAY 28, 1960   ■   I arrived too early at my therapist's apartment building last evening, so I tarried at the corner of West End Avenue and 101st Street. A little girl was blowing bubbles as her father stood nearby. She blew one bubble about a foot in diameter. Impelled by her soft breath, it peeled off her tiny pipe and soared into the air, higher and ever higher, a glistening round rainbow, it seemed, seen against the pumpkin-colored sunset. I felt hypnotized by its beauty and fragility, afraid that it might dash itself to destruction upon the corner of a building but, still higher it wafted, then floated westward toward the dying of the day, beyond the Hudson River. It glanced against a brick wall but veered safely away, mounting westward and skyward in majestic isolation on a journey toward infinity and then—! Then it burst and twinkled to eternity before my eyes.

MONDAY, JUNE 6, 1960   ■   In the city room of the *World-Telegram* an editor sends a copyboy to a reporter to say he is wanted at the city desk. Today this custom changed. A public address system has been installed in the city room. It began operating today at 10:35 A.M. and I was the first reporter summoned by this new technology.

"Ellis to city desk!"

This new sound was so strange that everyone stopped working and looked up. I jumped to my feet, snatched off my green eyeshade and my glasses, waved them aloft, bowed left and right while others applauded.

MONDAY, JULY 4, 1960   ■   This is Ruthie's 51st birthday, so I wrote her this letter:

My Beloved Ruthie,

Happy birthday!

This is a glorious Fourth of July. It is glorious because you are alive, because you have graced this earth a half-century. The world is a better place because you were born. Down through the decades Fourth of July orators unwittingly described you in their speeches. They talked about true democracy while you, in your quiet way, have fleshed out their words by practicing what they preached. They prattled of a higher civilization, while you evolved into a one-woman culture consisting of the good, the true and the beautiful. They hollered about a higher destiny, but there can be no higher destiny than your existence. You are, here and now and forever—a Golden Age.

This is a sane Fourth of July. No longer do hot-eyed little boys burn themselves with fireworks. Like them, I have ceased to singe myself, preferring to sit back and watch you light up the sky. Gently you took from my neurotic hands those explosives with which I used to tamper. Now I watch you illuminate life with your muted meanings, paint the world with your profundity, glow as a goal toward which I aspire.

My darling, I am glad you were born. I am grateful that you married me. And, sweetheart, with every passing year you burn brighter in my heart. You are my glorious Ruthie, and nothing can extinguish our mutual love.

> With humble gratitude,
> Your husband—
> Eddie

TUESDAY, JULY 5, 1960 ▪ I'm on vacation but Ruthie had to work, so I'm alone. The weather is so beautiful that I decided to walk from Riverside Drive to Central Park.

Two boys were fishing in a brown pool studded with the green pads of water lilies. They caught a three-inch carp, but I heard one boy say that what he really wanted were *goldies*—meaning goldfish. I like children. Slowly, I began talking with the boys.

Both are 12 years old. One is a Negro named Ricky. The other is a Puerto Rican called Junior. Suddenly I remembered that there are boats for hire on a pond at 81st St.; I asked whether they'd like to go out with me in a rowboat. Their eyes lit up with joy. Ricky suggested that we go instead to Harlem Lake near 110th St. In the lake Junior saw a goldfish, waded into the water and caught it in his hands. From the shore a tall man joked that the fish was pregnant, so Junior threw it back. At the NE corner of Harlem Lake I hired a rowboat for 75 cents an hour, leaving a $2 deposit.

After I paid, as we walked toward the boathouse, Ricky surprised me by asking: "Who was Dwight Morrow?"

Recognizing this as a challenge, I said: "I believe you mean the American ambassador to Mexico."

"Y-e-a-h!" Astonished black eyes on my face, he said: "Yuh know, man, I asked my teacher that—and she didn't know the answer."

"Dwight Morrow's daughter married Lindbergh," I said. "The flier."

"No kiddin'? . . . Now, this guy Richelieu—was he minister to Louis XIII or Louis XIV?"

Now I felt astonished. Unsure of the answer, but unwilling to undermine his confidence in me, I said "Louis XIV." Then I corrected his pronunciation of Richelieu, and he repeated it properly.

"I like history," he said.

The three of us got into the boat and I rowed into the small lake. Watching me in admiration, Ricky asked: "Where did you learn to row, man?"

"Oh, during summer vacations on a lake in Wisconsin. One never forgets how to row."

Both boys wanted to row, so I gave them the oars. Part of the time they tried rowing together, part of the time alone. The oars were too big for them and they knew nothing about rowing. I felt sorry for these city lads.

Ricky, the taller of the two, did the better job of rowing. Junior tugged at his oar awkwardly. They pulled so unevenly that most of the time our boat went around in circles.

"Mannnnn!" Rickey sang out. "Man, I never had so much fun in my life! I mean—man!—this is the greatest!"

Junior kept searching for goldies. When he saw four homosexuals walking along the edge of the lake, he whistled at them. Ricky stopped rowing. He sat still. He was thinking.

"Who was the richest President?"

"Oh, Franklin D. Roosevelt, I suppose."

"Yeah! Roosevelt. . . . Who was the most athletic?"

"Teddy Roosevelt—by far."

Looking puzzled, Ricky said; "I thought he was crippled."

"Oh, no, I said *Teddy* Roosevelt. You're thinking of Franklin Roosevelt."

"Y-e-a-h!" Pause. "Who was the poorest President?"

"You tell me."

"Johnson!"

"That's right," I said. "Andy Johnson."

"Which President didn't have no education?"

"That was Andy Johnson, too. His wife taught him to read and write."

Rickey looked at me with awe in his eyes. Apparently I know a little more than his history teacher. Earlier he had mentioned getting into trouble in school and being sent to some camp. How tragic that a boy of such a high potential was being mishandled!

"Andrew Jackson," said Ricky. "He didn't have much money, neither."

"No, he, too, was a frontiersman."

"Who was the crabbiest President?"

There he had me. I said, "I really don't know."

Junior was paying no attention to us. He was leaning out of the boat, looking for goldies.

Ricky sat still, eyes out of focus, searching for something inside himself. Then a flood of words gushed from his lips. He said he hates his brothers because they are so lazy they won't even look for jobs although their mother works very hard at keeping their home clean, that he wants to amount to something, that maybe he'd like to be a history teacher, that he could hardly wait until he became 16 so he might get a job, that his father earns $190 by holding down two full-time jobs. Then he mumbled something about his father I didn't quite hear. Now, speaking more to himself than to me, he said: "Naw, man, I *hate* him! Yuh know, I doan even believe he *is* my father. My hair ain't like his, or my—whaddya call'em— my features, my face."

Poor kid. Will he be able to overcome handicaps and become a history teacher, or will he be broken in the process? If he happens to go wrong, who will understand why he went astray? How many people would realize that this rich potential was lost to society?

I rowed us back ashore and we walked to an outdoor stand where I bought the boys something to eat and drink. Ricky asked whether I had gone to college, and when I said yes he slapped his leg and cried, "I thought so!"

As we parted we shook hands. Both boys clamored to know whether I'd show up again tomorrow. I said I'd like to see them again but was unable to promise to return. As I left I felt like a king.

MONDAY, DECEMBER 5, 1960 ■ There have been newspaper stories from New Orleans about a white mother who takes her child to an integrated school despite threats from other white mothers. Said she, "I'd rather take a beating from a mob than from my own conscience." A genuine heroine!

MONDAY, DECEMBER 12, 1960 ■ I walked through the snow in City Hall Park and entered the municipal building to see Jimmy Durante get a wedding licence. It was shortly after 12 noon when I reached the marriage license bureau on the second floor. The famous comedian had not yet arrived. Waiting for him, chatting with other reporters, I heard he is so generous he hands out money to the press. That made me feel squeamish.

About 1 P.M. I heard a commotion in the room and turned around. Jimmy Durante had swept inside—and then thrown up his hands in mock horror at the sight of reporters and photographers. The Schnoz wore a battered hat, dark blue overcoat, gray wool shirt with yellow trimmings. Spectacles straddled his enormous nose—supposedly insured by Lloyd's of London. Although he had a stubble of beard on his pinched cheek, his fingernails were immaculate.

His first wife, Jeanne Olsen, died in 1943. Thereafter, supposedly in tribute to her, he ended his radio and TV shows with the words: "Here's to yuh, Mrs. Calabash—wherever you are!"

The past few years he has dated Margaret (Margie) Little, formerly a hat-check girl in the famous Copa nightclub, and now he intends to marry her. Today she was with him. She wore a white camel's hair coat with a hood over her red hair, brown eyes twinkling, long fingernails painted garish green. I liked her because she laughed a lot and seemed to regard Jimmy as the funniest man in the world.

The press swarmed around them. Jimmy didn't mind. This little beat-up comedian is one of the most gentle persons I ever met. He walked over to a woman who sat behind a grilled window and asked, in a voice like a nail scraped along a file: "Whadda we do?"

Well, for one thing, they had to have blood test certificates. Pain registered in Jimmy's squinty blue eyes. They had left their certificate at the St. Moritz Hotel. No certificates, no marriage.

Jimmy told a member of his entourage to take their limousine back to the hotel, get the papers and bring them back. Then he and Margie posed for photographers, assuming attitudes of dismay because of their forgetfulness. Jimmy, the old pro, sweetly coached her how to look, where to stand.

I asked her how she landed Jimmy. Flashing a smile, she said: "It was a tough fight! It took me 16 years."

His personal representative, Bob Braun, told me that Jimmy is almost 68 years old, while Margie is 39. The wedding will be held next Wednesday at 4 P.M. in St. Malachy's Roman Catholic Church in mid-Manhattan, with only relatives and friends present. Then the newlyweds will leave for Jimmy's home in Beverly Hills. On January 16 he will begin work on a pilot film for a new TV series, and then come back here to open on February 2 at the Copacabana.

By now Jimmy and Margie sat at a desk filling out forms. I walked over. Suddenly he looked up at me and said: "My father's name was Bartholomew. How do you spell Bartholomew?"

Leaning over his shoulder, I spelled it for him. I recalled having read that Jimmy hadn't even finished grammar school. Using a ballpoint pen, he scrawled his father's name.

Then, lifting his face, quizzically he peered through his glasses at me. "An' he was born in Salerno, Italy. . . . How do you spell Salerno?" I told him and he thanked me.

It was nearly time for the next edition of my paper, so I ran out into the hall to call my office and report what was happening. When I returned I found everyone still waiting for Durante's man to return with the blood certificates.

To kill time, Jimmy reminisced about his childhood on the east side of Manhattan in an area now occupied by the Alfred E. Smith housing project, only a couple of blocks from where he now sat. With a grin, he said: "I was trown outta duh window in the second grade an' never went back." He was simple, sincere, sweet. Although he has been in show business most of his life, there was nothing theatrical about him, except when he hammed it up for the photographers. He was so charming I almost forgot that he is ugly—beady eyes, pinched mouth, banana nose.

He was pulling money out of a pocket when a clerk walked over and whinnied: "Jimmy, you're making my office important!" Then the clerk lowered his voice and the two men held a whispered conversation. At last Jimmy laughed, turned away and walked out, followed by Margie and his entourage.

After they left I asked a reporter whether Jimmy had given money to anyone.

A stunned look on his face, the reporter said: "Yeah! He handed me a $20 bill and told me to buy drinks for all of us, but I gave it back to him."

Relieved, I ran down one flight of stairs to the lobby. There I saw Jimmy hand a folded bill to a photographer—who kept it! I thought: Oh, Gawwd! This is all we need. Like Caesar's wife, the press should be above suspicion, but here were some of its members accepting cash from a celebrity! Bystanders in the lobby saw what was happening. Now they are sure to believe that the press is corrupt.

However, judging from what I have read about Jimmy Durante, and judging from my personal observation of the man, not for one second do I believe he was trying to bribe anyone. He just happens to be a simple man overflowing with kindness.

THURSDAY, DECEMBER 15, 1960   ■   Liberalism, once the cachet of the Scripps-Howard newspapers, is gone forever. This newspaper chain was founded by good old E. W. Scripps, who died in 1926. He was an eccentric, a boozer, a great journalist and so much of a liberal that when he became rich he refused to join a country club for fear he would soak up the prejudices of the wealthy.

Roy W. Howard bought into the chain, which became the Scripps-Howard Newspapers, and after Scripps died their tone began to change. Roy, my ultimate boss at the *World-Telegram*, was a different breed of cat. Still is. He likes to hang around country clubs and go sailing on his yacht and he believes he helps elect Republican Presidents. Recently he told one of our reporters that he had not ridden a subway train in many years. How, then, can he know anything about the values and attitudes of the people to whom he wants to sell newspapers?

Joseph Medill Patterson had something of Scripps in him. In 1919 he founded the *New York Daily News*, the first successful tabloid in the history of American journalism and even after he piled up his gelt he hung around street corners in this city to listen to the things people were talking about. But Roy—!

Suddenly I remember something that happened a few years ago. A third tube was being dug for the Lincoln Tunnel beneath the Hudson River, to connect New York and New Jersey. A wall collapsed and some sandhogs were trapped 60 feet below ground. I galloped to the scene, where I found some wet and weary sandhogs safe on dry land. I began questioning two of them. They said they swam to safety.

Incredulous, I asked: "You *swam*—60 feet underground?"

"Yeah."

Eager to be sure I correctly understood them, I pantomimed the motions of a swimmer doing the Australian crawl. "You mean you actually *swam?*"

"Hell, yes!" snorted one sandhog, looking at me in disgust.

Okay. Now I knew for sure. I phoned this unusual feat to my office.

When I returned to the city room I was approached by the city editor, who wore a cynical smile.

"Ellis," said he, "you know damned well that sandhogs don't swim!"

Grinning at him, I said: "Oh! You got the word from 230 Park Avenue?"

"Yeah. I heard from Roy."

So, sitting in his golden tower, the great Roy Howard had issued a fiat: Sandhogs don't swim. That afternoon the *World-Telegram* published this headline: SANDHOGS WADE TO SAFETY.

In the other afternoon newspapers the headline was: SANDHOGS SWIM TO SAFETY.

FRIDAY, DECEMBER 16, 1960 ■ This morning I was at my desk in the office when I heard a murmur among staff members. Then I heard that two planes had crashed. I cleared off my desk, for I thought I knew what was about to happen—but I had no way of foreseeing the magnitude of the tragedy I was to cover.

Art Williams called Bill Longgood and me to the city desk and said, "There's a plane down in Staten Island. We don't yet know just where. You two get out there fast and call me when you reach the other side. By that time we should know the exact site of the crash and can direct you there. Get going!"

I told Bill I had to go to the bank across the street and would meet him in front of it. Other reporters were being sent elsewhere in the city. As I ran out of the city room I heard that a second plane had crashed in Brooklyn.

I dashed across the street, hammered at a cashier's window, yelled that there had been a plane crash and I had to have change. The people in the bank are accustomed to this demand by reporters. Nothing is so frustrating to a reporter as to be on a fast-breaking story and then find himself far from the office without the correct change for a telephone. The cashier opened his window and gave me $10 in change.

Charging out of the bank, I met Bill on the street and we got a cab. I wore galoshes, a brown cashmere sweater, a tweed jacket and trench coat. With a wry smile Bill said he had not worked on a big spot story in a long time. He writes many series on solemn subjects. I like and admire Bill. When our cab got us to South Ferry I bought two candy bars because I didn't know when I'd be able to eat again.

Bill and I hopped on a ferry moments before it sloshed out into the upper bay. Seeing cops walking down to a lower deck, we followed them. To my surprise I found that on this deck there was a disaster unit from Bellevue Hospital: three ambulances, 10 doctors, 10 nurses and two attendants. Also four squad cars jammed with six cops each. Bill and I crawled into the rear of the second ambulance, crowded with doctors and nurses. The ferry nosed into a pier on Staten Island and the seven vehicles glided away—an impressive cavalcade.

Away we roared—red lights flashing, sirens screaming, snowchains slamming into the fenders of the ambulance in which I rode. The drivers knew the location of the crash site, so Bill and I were lucky enough to get a ride directly there. After our fast, noisy trip we arrived at what I soon learned was Miller Field, an army airport used by light military aircraft. Our cavalcade screeched to a halt, the siren screams falling to a growl. We were at the end of a dead end street. A hole had been cut in a wire fence around the field.

My first chore was to tell my office the exact location of the downed plane. Bill and I jumped out of the ambulance and ran in opposite directions. Not until the end of the day did I see him again. This often happens when reporters cover catastrophes. I ran to a house and threw questions to a teenage boy in the front yard. His parents came out of the front door. They told me what the plane sounded like as it fell onto the field in front of their house. They pointed. I looked and in the distance saw twisted hunks of metal, black against the snow. I asked the man and wife whether I might use their phone. They said it had been commandeered by the police. Walking to the rear of the house, I found some cops. How many dead? Always the first question. Maybe 15 dead—but they were not sure. I turned and ran down Boundary Avenue, which separates the communities of Grant City and Midland Beach. On the Midland Beach side I saw a woman sitting on her stoop. Running up, I said I was a reporter and wanted to use her phone. She invited me inside.

Her husband led me into a bedroom and pointed. Snatching up the receiver, I dialed my office. Waiting for the connection, I talked to the man. When he and his wife looked through a window and saw the plane falling, they threw themselves onto the floor. On the phone I heard a voice say, "City room." I spoke to an editor, who gave me a rewrite man, to whom I spouted what little I knew. Then I gave the man two dollars, saying I might want to use his phone again.

Outdoors again, I took my press card from my wallet. It would not stay in place in my hatband because the band was too narrow. I raced to a hole in the fence, showed the cops my press card in my hand, crawled out onto the field. The snow was a foot deep.

A few yards inside the field I saw part of the fuselage of the plane, shapeless as driftwood. Then I saw blood on the snow. It looked like red pepper on mashed potatoes. Already on the scene were ambulances, police cars and army trucks. Someone found a man's wristwatch. It had stopped at 10:35. I had arrived about noon. Fifty feet from the fuselage nine bodies lay in a row. They were covered with khaki army blankets. One figure was so small it had to be the corpse of a child. I gulped. An army helicopter whirred down onto the snow. Out tumbled GI's carrying blankets and other gear. The air pulsated with the whines of sirens.

I spoke to a couple of soldiers near a truck. It held five blanket-draped bodies. The soldiers said four army trucks had arrived and already one had left with 10 bodies. While no one knew exactly how many had been killed, I realized this was a major catastrophe.

About 500 feet from the body of the plane I found one of its engines. It gouged a hole into the earth three feet deep. Its oil and flames had blackened the snow for a radius of eight feet. Wading deeper into the field, I felt glad I wore galoshes. Three hundred feet farther I found the tail of the aircraft. On a rudder in red numbers against a silver background I read 907-N69070. Sticking out from broken walls in the middle of the plane were tufts of yellow felt. Scattered here and there were double seats covered with green monk's cloth. The seats were ripped and charred and flecked with blood.

I saw a man in black who looked like a priest. When I walked over to him, he said he was not a priest but a brother, one of the 22 members of a class in canon law in the St. Charles Seminary not far away. In their classroom they had heard the roar of the plane and turned and looked through windows as it fell. Their instructor dashed onto the field to administer last rites while they fell to their knees, stared through windows in horror and chanted *Hail Mary*. Then each prayed by himself. I knew I had a little colorful sidebar story.

By now I was so far inside Miller Field that I decided to cross to the other side to find a phone, rather than turning back. Crossing New Dorp Lane, I knocked at a door and an elderly couple said I could use their phone. At my office the switchboard was so jammed I had trouble getting through to the city desk. Again I delivered the news I had. Then I thanked the couple, gave them a dollar and ran back onto the field.

Soldiers were picking up human meat. Using sticks, they raked entrails and livers from the snow. They used twisted pipes from the wreckage of the plane. They deposited hunks of flesh in white mattress covers and pieces of cardboard and blankets. The soldiers had haunted eyes. Dangling from the charred end of an airplane seat were two feet of intestines. I'm scheduled to fly to Chicago next Friday but, no—I won't go! Rigid with shock, I watched . . . here a liver . . . there a red pudding of brains . . . a severed muscle . . . a calf torn from a leg . . . the red blood and white snow . . . the red blood and white snow. Shivering, I wept . . .

After wiping my eyes and blowing my nose, I got an idea. I walked from one group of GI's to another until I found three men who had been in combat. Good! How did this tragedy compare with their battlefield experiences? Softly, very softly, all three said that this was far worse than anything they ever saw on a battlefield. So! Now I had another story.

I left to try to find a phone. Pity had drained me of energy, so instead of running I walked slowly. I went back to the house I had just left. Another long wait to be connected with the city desk. Holding the phone, I ate the candy bars. I was surprised to be able to eat anything after all I'd seen, but knew I had to renew my energy. There was much more to be done, with no way of knowing how many hours I'd be kept busy.

Standing in the warm house, munching candy, pausing long enough to be able to think, the memory of that carnage on the field brimmed up inside me and almost spilled over a second time. When Robin Turkel came on the wire my voice broke as I began speaking to him. Only by a wrench of will was I able to prevent myself from sobbing. My legs trembled.

Then, out of the house and out on the field again. Personal belongings had been taken from the corpses and piled in a heap. Cops had put wooden horses around this grisly pile. I stared at the tangled items—a rosary dangling from a belt . . . a black briefcase with gold letters D.T.B. . . . a pamphlet with blue letters on red paper saying "Buyers' Guide" . . . a brown briefcase . . . a newsletter from a WVKO radio community club . . . a salesman's book saying "You get (blank) word-sell spots per week" . . . a wet book with its covers open . . .

A cop stood close to these fragments, so I asked him to read the inscription I saw on the flyleaf of the book. It was charred and it was a Bible. The cop read aloud: "Arthur Swenson, 24 Brookfield Drive, Glastonbury, Conn." Another policeman said, "I saw a piece of paper on the snow and picked it up. It was a page from the Bible. I looked at it. The first words I saw were: 'Deliver me to the Prophet—' I dropped the thing right there!"

At a distance I saw a Red Cross truck with uniformed women serving coffee and sandwiches. I admire Red Cross workers, whom I find at every disaster. I walked over and was served coffee and a ham and cheese sandwich. I must have looked cold, for one woman suggested I crawl into their station wagon to get warm, and I did so—gratefully.

Now it was four o'clock. I had to plan my next move. I decided to get to the morgue on Staten Island, for I'd heard that that was where the bodies were being taken. But—I had no idea of the location of the morgue, said to be a part of Sea View Hospital, and in that remote area of Staten Island no cabs were available. When I mentioned my plight to a Red Cross woman she said they were expecting another car, and when it came they would drive me to the morgue.

The car arrived. Two women drove me to the morgue. All day long I was lucky about getting transportation. When we reached Sea View Hospital I learned that Bellevue Hospital in Manhattan had sent 50 wooden coffins there. They were stacked up outside a room in which the bodies were being examined. No reporter was allowed to enter that room. A police captain told me that never before had the Staten Island morgue been taxed beyond capacity. A sad-eyed cop said a head had been found on a street.

No relative or friend could see any corpse on Staten Island. They would have to go to Bellevue. Eight of us reporters and photographers conferred and decided we had better get back to Manhattan and over to the morgue at Bellevue Hospital. A *New York Post* reporter said he had a station wagon that could hold all of us.

The car was full of the objects of daily life. With Bill Ray, a *Life* photographer, I squeezed into the rear, the two of us draping ourselves over a baby buggy. Because the roads were icy, and because the *Post* reporter drove fast, I worried about the car veering off and crashing. Having seen the remains of human beings, this thought terrified me. When we reached the Staten Island ferry landing the air was so cold and clear that across the upper bay the tip of Manhattan looked like an enchanted castle in an illustration by Maxfield Parrish.

During that wild ride, and even after the station wagon eased aboard a ferry, all of us in the car listened to the news on the radio. The disaster was worse than I had imagined. After all, I was covering only one part of it. Two commercial airliners had collided over the upper bay at about 10:30 this morning. One was a United Air Lines DC-8 jet from Boston with 84 passengers. It plunged into the Park Slope section of Brooklyn, causing a seven-alarm fire that destroyed 10 brownstones, a funeral home and a church. The other plane was a TWA Super-Constellation from Dayton and Columbus, carrying 44 passengers. It was fragments of this plane which I had seen on Staten Island.

When we arrived in Manhattan I changed my mind about going to Bellevue. Surely my office already had sent a reporter there. Getting out of the car at the post office near the *World-Telegram,* I walked the rest of the distance. It was 6 P.M. when I entered the city room.

A colleague said my wife had called and wanted me to call her back at her office. For the first time today I remembered she was with our friend Andy Kane. I dialed her number and when I heard the voice of the person I love most in this world, I almost fell apart. In a choked voice I described some of the horrors I had seen. Ruthie was very sweet. She urged me to meet her and Andy so that she might console me. An editor came to my desk and interrupted me to say that, after all, I was being sent to Bellevue, so I told Ruthie I would meet her at the east side airlines terminal near Bellevue.

After hanging up, I walked to the city desk and spoke to Norman Harrington in a voice that trembled. He was kind. Then I left and rode a cab to the terminal, where my wife and Andy soon joined me. He was due to fly out of town tonight and this alarmed me, although I said nothing about my fears. After kissing Ruthie, after gulping down a rum and Coke, I said I had to get going.

When I reached Bellevue and entered the morgue, I found other reporters there. Still affected by all I had seen, I spoke to a couple of detectives in a voice so faint they had to lean forward to hear me. Soon we were joined by Michael J. Ambrose, the superintendent of all city morgues. He remembered me from that night about a year ago when I covered the story of the workers burned to death in a loft fire. He is a gentle person.

I asked whether he would let us reporters go downstairs where the bodies were being identified. Okay. Six of us followed him to the basement.

The first thing we saw were two men examining dental work in the mouth of a dead woman. One held a small dental X-ray plate up to a light. The other man used a tiny mirror at the end of a metal rod to poke around in her mouth. Irrationally, I resented what I considered the roughness of the man poking here and there but, of course, the woman was dead and felt no pain.

We entered another room. Lying on rolling tables were 17 bodies or parts of bodies. They were only partly covered with blankets. I saw a woman's head so smashed that her brains seeped onto the table. In her face there remained only one eye. It stared at me. Heaped on another table was a shapeless heap of flesh. Nearby lay the corpse of a man with only half his skull left. His mouth was open. He seemed to be screaming a silent scream.

My knees turned to Jello. I glanced at the faces of the other reporters. Trying to control themselves, their faces were as empty and hard as cement. My belly fluttered as though a tiny bird were trapped inside. Never in my life had I fainted, but now I felt I might. Half-listening to Ambrose talking, I planted my feet far enough apart to brace myself and not slump to the floor. I had had enough, more than enough. More than I ever care to see again in my entire life. I thanked Ambrose and all of us trooped back upstairs. So far I had not had a chance to talk to any relatives. I asked Ambrose whether it would be all right if I tried to find some, and he said sure. Slipping around a corner, I found myself in a reception room.

There I saw seven Puerto Ricans. Earlier in the day they had waited at La Guardia Field for a relative named Juanita. Born in Puerto Rico, she had become a nurse and then moved to Dayton, Ohio, for further training. There she met a young man who ran a grocery store. She was Catholic, he a Protestant, but for love of him she became a Presbyterian. They were married January 24, 1959. Three months ago a baby girl was born to them. Today all three died in the snow, the bloody snow of Staten Island.

The man who told me the story of Juanita showed me her wedding picture. I said if he would let me publish it in my paper I would be sure to return it to him and I wrote down his home address.

Then I caught a cab and began riding down around the southern tip of Manhattan toward my office at West and Barclay Streets. I slumped in the back seat, my hat pulled down over my eyes, my chin on my chest. I sat and thought and hurt. It seemed to me that after today my life would never again be the same. I had seen the core of reality, the very marrow of horror. All day long I had lived with death—and death is the ultimate reality. All else is appearance. Sunrise and laughter and roses and children and food and drink and sunset and stars and warm flesh—ultimately, all come to the same end, which is nothingness, the void. Does anything remain after the body dies? Who knows? I don't. Is it possible that spirit survives physical death? While I am unable to make any absolute statement about anything, perhaps—just perhaps, spirit survives. Or is this wishful thinking? Huddled in the cab, oblivious to the passing lights, brooding about death, aware of my ignorance, I realized that I know nothing, positively nothing! No, hold on! I love my wife. This is a fact. This is reality. This is a truth.

It was 10:30 P.M. when I again reached the office. I wrote a story about Juanita and her husband Cecil and their little girl and the fact that now all three are dead. My cheeks felt starched. I gave my story and the wedding picture to Drew Phillips and rode a cab home.

Entering my apartment at midnight, I found Ruthie asleep in bed with the TV still turned on. On the phone she had said she wanted to wait up so that she might take care of me. A couple of minutes after I got inside she awakened. She looked at me. I looked at her. She held out her arms. Taking her into my arms, I kissed her mouth and cheeks. Her flesh was warm. She is alive.

1961

THURSDAY, FEBRUARY 23, 1961   ▓   In the office today Ed Wallace and I discussed Allen Ginsberg, who worked as a copyboy here at the *World-Telegram* in 1953. Having just read Ginberg's poem called *Howl*, solemn-faced Wallace said; "Ginsberg might become immortal—if Robert Frost beat him to death with a wet squirrel."

THURSDAY, MARCH 2, 1961   ▓   Yesterday an editor gave me a book written by a Park Avenue psychiatrist and asked me to read it because I have a date to interview the doctor. The editor added that Dr. H. is a close friend of Roy Howard, our ultimate boss. I got the message.

Because of my interest in psychiatry, and my own therapy, I was eager to read this new book, but it turned out to be fifth-rate, compared with some books on this subject that I own. Now I felt apprehensive. How could I write honestly about a man who writes platitudinously but who happens to be one of Roy's white elephants?

Today at 4 P.M. I arrived at the doctor's office. He was not in. Fifteen minutes later he appeared, said he had missed lunch, asked whether I would mind waiting. He didn't ask whether I would care to have a cup of coffee with him. Annoyed, I loitered in his reception room, dimly lit, stocked with heavy furniture and decorated with huge paintings.

At last the psychiatrist joined me. Announcing that he had just appeared on a TV show, he added with a smug smile that he had quoted poetry. I thought: Big deal! His secretary listened with rapture to his every word. I couldn't decide whether her enthusiasm was real or faked. She trilled, "You know, Doctor, you're a ham!" Then she turned to me and said, "I always say that Dr. H. is a ham!" I thought, Yeah, Dr. H. sure as hell is a ham!

Turning back to her boss, she said: "You had me scared there for awhile when you were on camera. I thought you were going to say, as you often do, 'Virginity is just a state of mind!' "

Deep inside myself I groaned.

Dr. H. ignored her. He told me that once he had been called before the board of some medical society to face charges that he got his name in the papers too often. Grandiosely he informed me that he had defeated all his critics.

"You know," he said, "everyone should have the right to face his accusers, but they didn't even give me this chance. Anyway, I told the board members they didn't know what the hell they were talking about, and it wound up with all of them apologizing to me."

"Doctor," said the secretary, "your name was misspelled in a paper again yesterday."

"You mean they dropped the final letter from my name?"

"Yes."

"Well," burbled the modest egomaniac, "they save type that way!" Laughing, he looked at me. I mustered a bleak smile.

I was leaning against a wall. The secretary said: "Maybe Mr. Ellis would like to sit down."

The doctor led me into his office. It had the ambience of a chapel in a medieval cathedral because of its stained-glass windows, oak-panelled walls, massive carved furniture and soft lighting. Beautiful. He sat down at his handsome desk and I took a seat near a lamp so I could take notes.

From his desk he picked up a hearing-aid he said cost $600, but he did not put it on his deaf ear, so he had trouble hearing my questions. I knew he was 74 years old, but he looked only 65. Vigorous, radiating theatrical charm, he babbled on and on, obviously trying to soften me up. When he paused for breath, I broke in, saying:

"Doctor, every reporter works differently. Now, I have picked one passage from your book which I'd like to have you amplify. If we stick to just this one topic, I think we can get a story that—"

"First," he interrupted, pointing a finger at me, "what did you think of my book?"

The moment I had dreaded.

"Shall I be diplomatic or honest?"

"Honest—by all means!"

"Well, frankly, doctor, I didn't think too much of it."

Shock, like a tiny earthquake, registered in his face. Then, instead of asking me why I didn't like his book, he ticked off the names of people he said *do* like it—and very important names they were, too. I sat with a fixed smile, wondering why this man, this psychiatrist, was so defensive. The answer was obvious: Despite his age and profession and renown, he still is insecure.

At last I led him back to the topic I wanted as the theme for my story, but was unable to hold him there. He rambled. He talked, talked, talked. I was forced to conclude that he has a disorderly mind. Weak of ego, needing to impress others, he uses his babble as a pillow held over the face of an opponent to smother opposition. Violating the therapist's first rule of confidentiality, he said he had treated John Barrymore, gangster Frank Costello, and one of the world's richest women—whom he named. He also named one of Hollywood's most famous comedians, saying the man had come to him with a sexual problem.

Now the doctor was airing his own opinions about morality. He said he had heard society women playing bridge and using four-letter words that shocked him. Sighing, he said: "This is a sign of degeneracy—"

Perhaps noting a flicker of surprise on my face, he quickly added:

"—not that I'm a prude! Although I take my pleasure wherever I can find it, I wouldn't think of asking a woman, 'May I fuck you?!'"

I couldn't resist murmuring, "What gentleman would?"

"But I might ask her, 'Would you like to see the bluebird?!' "

The *bluebird?* Ohhh, brother!

"Then, if she didn't understand, I might ask whether she would like to enjoy ecstasy with me!"

He turned his glittering eyes to me. I smiled—wanly, I hope. Again I tried to lead him back to the point of the story I had to write, but he kept meandering all over the landscape of his life. Now he was criticizing bullfighting. Leaning over the right side of his chair, he made a pass with an imaginary cape. Then he fumbled for the name of the pass. "With the—what's it called?"

"The Veronica."

"Ah, yes," he echoed. "The Veronica!"

Next—and don't ask how he got there—he was in Vienna, sitting in the office of the great Freud, whom he denounced. "Why, Freud told me, straight-faced, that he was a genius!"

Then, to my utter amazement, I heard this psychiatrist say scornfully, "This theory about the unconscious—you can't touch it, feel it, smell it, hear it."

The doctor, to state it scientifically, had bats in his belfry.

Now he said he used the Rorschach ink-blot test before Hermann Rorschach even thought of it, and he had taken the Rorschach three times, with three different results. Well, so much for Rorschach. Then there was the time that "Eddie and Liz"—Eddie Fisher and Elizabeth Taylor—had looked at his house with the intention of renting or buying it.

"I told Eddie I wondered what would happen to him if I were to cut his vocal cords, and Eddie said, 'I wouldn't be able to earn twenty-five dollars a week!' "

The doctor looked at me in triumph. I didn't say a word. Why did he say such a thing to a professional singer? I repressed a shudder. I had no idea what this was supposed to prove.

Next it was a story about the first time he testified as an expert at a criminal trial, and how he was pitted against the man who once was his instructor.

"I won, and now when I'm on the witness stand the judges—they all know me—the judges caution attorneys not to let me take the questioning away from them. And if I so much as pull out a pack of cigarets while I'm there on the stand, why the judge will notice it and ask me if I'd like a recess so I can go out and smoke."

This was followed by a story about the Catholic cop who went berserk. Other psychiatrists were unable to discover what was wrong with the man, but our hero soon found out: "Who insisted upon contraceptives being used in your marriage?"

"You," the doctor said the cop said, "are the first person to put your finger on my problem!"

Was I supposed to scream in delight like a bobby-soxer listening to Sinatra, or applaud politely like an opera fan? At last the doctor went to work on me.

"With all my years of experience," he purred, leaning back, eyes half-closed, a knowing smile on his lips, "it's easy for me to tell a lot about people, just as I did about that cop. Now, take yourself: You're clean, neat, intelligent—highly intelligent!—have a forceful personality—"

And *you*, I snarled to myself, refraining from vomiting, are a stupid, egotistical, fraudulent, rigid, sadistic, insecure, opinionated son-of-a-bitch—and I want to get the hell out of here!

As I left, he said: "Remember me to Jack!"

That further enraged me. He meant Jack Howard, son of Roy Howard, my boss. Many celebrities try this ploy with Scripps-Howard reporters. Anyone with any sense knows we don't mingle socially with either Roy or Jack Howard. Then this maniac topped even himself by mentioning the time he went yachting with Roy Howard and Gene Tunney.

Marvie! At last I managed to escape. When I reached the sidewalk on Park Avenue the air was so fresh, so clean, so unpolluted . . .

CHAPTER 13

Steve Hannagan was a press agent with an office on Park Avenue and a business so successful that he was listed in Who's Who in America *in the 1940's. He also was a colorful character with Hollywood contacts and had a mistress who was a movie queen. I never met him. After he died in 1953 my wife's boss, William E. Robinson, left the* Herald Tribune *and bought Hannagan's business, retaining his staff of associates. They liked her, told her stories about Steve, which she repeated to me, so at last I decided to write a biography of the man.*

FRIDAY, MAY 19, 1961 ■ This morning I was writing in my study on Riverside Drive when the phone rang. Picking up the receiver, I said "Hello."

A male voice said: "This is Cary Grant."

I almost scoffed: Yeah? . . . And I'm Napoleon! However, in a split-second I remembered I had written to Cary Grant to say I was coming to Hollywood to interview Steve's friends there, and I'd like to ask him some questions. Besides, the voice on the phone *was* that of Cary Grant.

"Yes, Mr. Grant," I said, trying to keep my voice even.

"I just flew into town," said the movie star "and I'm stopping at the Plaza. I should have replied to your letter to me long before now, but just didn't have the time."

"That's okay," I said. "I appreciate your call. I'd like to interview you about Steve."

"Well," said Cary Grant, "actually I didn't really know him. Met him a couple of times, but that was about all. Nice guy. Wish I could help."

"Perhaps if I came to your suite I could ask questions that might jog your memory."

"I really don't think it would," said Cary Grant. "Awfully sorry!"

In the spring of 1961 I took a four-month leave of absence from the World-Telegram *and began my research by flying to Hollywood and elsewhere.*

CALIFORNIA, SATURDAY, JUNE 17, 1961 ■ The San Fernando Valley shimmered in heat as Sandy and I drove toward the home of Clark Gable. The king of Hollywood died of a heart attack last November 16 at the age of 59. Now my daughter and I were en route to his ranch to talk with his widow, because many years ago she had worked for Steve Hannagan. This appointment had been made for me by Ned Moss, formerly one of Steve's bright young men. On the phone Mrs. Gable had told Ned she was willing to help me with the book I plan to write about Hannagan.

My beautiful 19-year-old daughter lives in Los Angeles, and now that I was there she was acting like my chauffeur. In the past few days Sandy had listened as I interviewed several Hollywood celebrities, but now she confessed she felt nervous for the first time.

While it was unnerving enough to her to know we would be received in the home of the man considered the most famous male screen star in the world, there was further excitement in the possibility that we might see his son, now regarded as the most famous baby alive. Last March 20 the widowed Mrs. Gable gave birth to a son she named John Clark Gable, and stories about the child appeared all over the world.

Before leaving New York I had done my homework about Mrs. Gable. Her maiden name was Kathleen Williams. After modelling in Manhattan she went to Hollywood and became a starlet with Metro-Goldwyn-Mayer. Her friends called her Kay. She dated Clark Gable the first time in 1944 when she was 25 years old; they did not marry until 11 years later. Five days after their 1955 wedding they moved into his ranch home.

This 22-acre estate had been owned by Gable since the late 1930's. It is located at 4525 Petit Avenue in suburban Encino in the San Fernando Valley. Ned Moss had told me how to get there. We would see an iron fence, he added, and if I pressed a button and spoke into the intercom system, the electrically operated gate would open to admit us.

This happened as Ned said it would, and Sandy drove through the opened gate and into an estate so large she took a wrong turn and followed a road ending at the stables. She turned around and drove to the house, where we were met by a butler. He ushered us into the cool interior and there, standing a few feet inside, was Mrs. Gable, burping her baby.

Neat and crisp, she wore a blouse, white shorts and handsome leather sandals. Her exquisitely groomed hair was golden, her eyes the color of bluebells, her figure strikingly beautiful. Her cheeks had the scrubbed look of a child. Her radiant smile, friendly manner and spirited conversation soon proved that besides being a great beauty she also is intelligent and fun-loving.

Walking into the living room she put her son on pillows on the sofa, and when she saw the excitement in Sandy's eyes she urged her to play with him. Did we care for a drink? No, too early in the day. The Gable home is not grandiose, not overpowering, but truly comfortable and thoroughly masculine in its decor. Mrs. Gable said her husband had occupied the ranch during his marriage with Carole Lombard. As I gazed around, I wondered how many movie stars had drunk and laughed in this very room.

Mrs. Gable and I sat down on a sofa that was quite the most comfortable I ever felt. When I took out my tape recorder she said she would put her baby to bed and then return to chat with us. For the next hour and a half we conversed without interruption, except for one brief call from Reno. Because of her excellent memory, spiced with wit, I obtained from her much more information about Hannagan than I got from Jack Benny a couple of days ago.

As Sandy and I arose to leave, Mrs. Gable told us about a device she bought to help keep her baby asleep during his nap. Then she led us into his bedroom. He was asleep in his crib. On a table at the head of the crib was a small machine making a sound like an amplified heartbeat. *Flubb-dubbb!* *Flubb-dubbb!* Mrs. Gable said she didn't know whether this sound really works, but doctors have theorized that since a baby is accustomed to hearing its mother's heartbeats while it is in the womb, the machine's sound may be soothing.

She said that since the birth of her son she has received more than 20,000 letters. Leading us into a study, she showed us cartons overflowing with letters. Also there was the canvas chair Clark Gable used during the filming of his last picture, *The Misfits.*

Although Kay Williams was his fifth wife, he'd never had a child, and when she became pregnant he became ecstatic. Then he was felled by a coronary thrombosis and rushed to a hospital, where he rallied for days. His wife slept on a cot at the foot of his bed and then in an adjoining room. One day a doctor handed him a stethoscope with which he heard the heartbeats of his unborn child. His eyes glowed as he listened. He died, however, about four months before the birth of his only child.

Saying good-bye to Mrs. Gable, Sandy and I walked outdoors where the sun smote our eyes and made them smart. Or was it the sun?

NEW YORK, SATURDAY, NOVEMBER 25, 1961   ▨   A couple of weeks ago I sent Billy Rose a copy of my manuscript about Steve Hannagan. They knew one another, so I wondered whether Rose had anything to add. Furthermore, I wanted to ask Rose to let me write his biography. Today, when I telephoned, he invited me to his home.

For years I have been fascinated by this small, colorful razzle-dazzle showman called the Bantum Barnum, Mighty Midget and Basement Belasco. He became an over-achiever because he was born poor and because he said, referring to his height, "It's tough to be five three in a five nine world." When I moved to New York in 1947 one favorite tourist trap was Billy Rose's Diamond Horseshoe. The only time I ever saw him was the day he and Eleanor Holmes began divorce proceedings in the state courthouse on Foley Square. That divorce cost him more than a quarter million dollars.

I did some homework before visiting Billy Rose today. He was born William Samuel Rosenberg in the Bronx, of parents so poor that he and his two sisters often went to bed hungry. As a boy he excelled as a sprinter—by jumping the gun without detection, so I've read. When he grew to five feet three he stopped growing. He studied shorthand, became the world's champion, worked as secretary to Bernard Baruch, challenged President Wilson to a shorthand contest in the White House.

When he discovered that some songwriters earned more than secretaries, he taught himself how to write lyrics. He spent months in the public library studying the patterns of popular novelty songs. Most had silly syllables, the very silliest sound being *ooooo*. With this in mind, he wrote the words to *Barney Google*—"with the goo-goo-googly eyes." When it became a hit he shortened his name to Rose and began making money writing lyrics to songs such as *More Than You Know, Without a Song, That Old Gang of Mine* and *It's Only a Paper Moon*.

Next he opened one night club after another and then began producing Broadway shows such as *Jumbo* and *Carmen Jones*. In 1939–40 he ran the Aquacade at the New York World's Fair. After having been married and divorced several times, he now was single again and lived alone in his mansion.

Rose paid $430,000 for the white marble 45-room five-story town house at 56 East 93rd Street. When I got there today and stepped out of a cab, I gazed in awe at its splendor. At the ornate front door I was met by a butler wearing street clothes. He asked me to wait in the foyer.

The floor of the foyer was made of white tile and had a black border. To the right was an elevator. I saw a life-size statue of a maiden with her head held back and her lips parted to offer a kiss.

When I got home I checked and learned that this statue is entitled *Song* and was sculpted by an American named Hugo Robus. Standing face to face and almost lip to lip with the marble maiden in the mansion, I felt like leaning forward and kissing her.

The butler entered the foyer to say Mr. Rose would receive me. I had to dismiss my cab, walked outdoors to do so, and when I turned around I saw Billy Rose on the threshold of his palace, hand outstretched. He led me past a rack of canes in the foyer, through an imposing reception room and then up a wide and winding stairway between walls hung with paintings by old masters. I followed him into a room two stories high. I'll call it a card-room because, among other things, it contained a round poker table.

Suddenly I saw a big ebony bust and cried: "My God! That's George Gershwin!" Seemingly pleased because I had recognized the composer, my host said it was carved by Noguchi. At one end of the room there was an enormous fireplace. Although there were many heavy leather chairs and sofas, Rose sat down at the poker table, so I joined him there.

Now I had a chance to study Billy Rose. He is indeed short. I thought he was 61 years old but he said 62. His forehead was wrinkled, his dark eyes hooded, his nose blunt, his ears big, his lips thick, his chin small. Hardly a handsome fellow. His hair was long and straight and streaked with gray. He wore a dark blue suit and when I saw it was rumpled I felt better because my own shirt had a slight tear under the collar and I felt I did not look my best. Billy Rose also had dirty fingernails. He said he had spent part of the day in an art gallery, so he may have handled dusty objects.

He asked what I wanted to drink and I told his butler a rum and Coke. I wasn't surprised when Rose asked for nothing alcoholic, for I had read he never drinks liquor. However, he lit one cigaret after another. After the butler brought my drink Rose said he had chosen Maurice Zolotow to write the story of his life. I admire Zolotow's literary portraits of theatrical celebrities. Rose said he had produced a 500-page manuscript.

"It was a good solid job, all right," Rose said, "but it was on the pedestrian side. What I need is a fun guy to write about my tinsel-and-thunder career."

I thought: Hey, that's a pretty good phrase. But Rose liked it so much that he kept repeating it, like a child rubbing the golden fuzz off the wings of a butterfly.

He said that after he rejected the manuscript, he paid Zolotow handsomely for his time and work and injured ego. Now he is considering Ben Hecht or Alexander King for his biography. "Ben can make words jump through hoops!" Rose exclaimed. Familiar with books by Hecht, I agreed. However, I remembered that Harry Hansen, editor of the World-Almanac and a friend of Hecht in their Chicago days, once told me that Hecht is careless with the truth.

Rose said several film companies want permission to produce a movie about his life.

"That would bring me at least a couple of hundred thousand dollars—and without any book—so there's no reason for my sharing this with any writer."

He said he is retired but has a ticker-tape machine in one room and spends his days playing the stock market. He still owns two theaters, seldom visiting them "since I run them practically by osmosis." I thought, Billy, you *do* need a writer. *Osmosis* ain't the right word, man! Proudly he said that these days his major interest is the establishment in Israel of a museum to which he will leave most of his works of art. It will take two years to complete this project, and only then does he want a book written about him.

I said he may have been too busy to read my manuscript about Steve Hannagan, but he said he had read part of it. Although he said I had done a good job, the flatness of his voice revealed that this was qualified praise.

"Hannagan was a fun guy and, like me, he was a tissue-paper character. I think that any book about him—just like any book about me—should be full of tinsel and thunder."

Again that phrase. I said that, yes, Hannagan was a fun guy, but I am a serious, hard-digging, fact-finding biographer who tries to get behind the scene and beneath the skin of the man in an attempt to evaluate his character and his impact upon society.

Actually, Billy Rose did not give me much of a chance to talk. I had read about his titanic ego. Now I was discovering that although his manner was gentle and his voice soft, the sound of his own voice almost hypnotized him. The only time he asked me a single question was after I mentioned that Hannagan had slept with three famous Hollywood actresses, whom I named.

Eagerly he asked: "Who else did Steve sleep with?"
I told him.
"Oh," said Rose, lighting another cigaret, "all of us guys sleep around."
No doubt they do, but as I sat in one of the 45 rooms of the Rose mansion I sensed that no one else was there except his butler. The silence was like the silence in a pyramid. Billy Rose was all alone—a rich man, an old man, a small man, a sad man.

Walking out of the card room I stopped to stare at a statue eight feet tall.
"Rodin!" I cried.
"Yes. That's his *Adam.*"
I said Rodin is my favorite sculptor and then I asked Rose whether he knew that Rodin had sculpted pornographic statues. He said this was news to him. Then he pointed across the hall at a huge statue of a woman with

thick thighs, her arms clasped behind her back. He identified it as *Chained Liberty* by Aristide Maillol.

As my host led me down the majestic stairway he said he hoped I would not feel he was behaving arbitrarily in rejecting my request to write his biography. I was surprised by compassion from a man renowned as a bully.

"No," I said, "I'm not hurt. After all, you are a friend of Ben Hecht and Alexander King, and I'm aware I have nothing like the reputations they enjoy."

When I got home I realized our entire living room is smaller than Billy Rose's card room, but it is alive with love.

Billy Rose died February 10, 1966. Neither Hecht nor King wrote a book about him. Newspaper stories said that Hecht called Rose "a kind of slum poet and Jack the Ripper rolled into one." Billy Rose became the biggest single stockholder of AT&T securities. Between October of 1963 and February of 1964 his investments earned him almost $9,000 every hour the New York Stock Exchange was open. He left an estate of about $50 million.

MONDAY, NOVEMBER 27, 1961 ■ This morning an editor told me I had a 3 P.M. date to interview Joan Sutherland. I almost panicked. I hadn't even heard her name until I found the morning papers full of stories about her debut last night at the Metropolitan Opera house in *Lucia di Lammermoor*. Her performance in the mad scene was so thunderously received that she made 14 curtain calls.

I know nothing about opera, care nothing about opera. Of all art forms, this is the one that fails to move me. Why was I assigned to cover Miss Sutherland? The *World-Telegram* has a music critic and, furthermore, rewriteman Jack Ferris is an opera buff. Why me?

I dashed into the morgue and asked for data about Miss Sutherland. She was born in Australia in 1926, specializes in lyric-coloratura roles in Italian operas, is renowned for her *bel canto* phrases sounding like "crystal bubbles of sound," has appeared in England and much of Europe. She married a childhood friend, Richard Bonynge, a pianist and authority on Italian opera, who quit his own career to promote hers.

Still nervous, I left with photographer Phil Stanziola and went to the Hotel Navarre at 112 Central Park South. This was to be a mass interview. Other reporters and photographers waited in the lobby as Miss Sutherland finished lunch. After she left the dining room I squeezed into an elevator with her, rode to the third floor, walked to Suite 3-B. There I was astonished to see the diva herself carrying chairs from the bedroom into the living room, helped by a woman press agent for the Met. I sprang to their assistance.

It was the photographers, of course, who first sprang into action. They yelled: ". . . Joan, look this way! . . . Joan, please sit on the piano bench! . . ." Their behavior irked me. After all, last night Miss Sutherland received one of the greatest ovations in the history of the Metropolitan Opera House. While waiting in the lobby I had been told by an Australian correspondent that journalists considered her difficult. Difficult? Moving chairs around, tolerating the photographers?

When they had all the pictures they wanted, she sat down to my right. Before I left my office I read she stands five eight and a half and weighs 170 pounds. In my notebook I began caricaturing her ski-nose and jut-jaw, then feared she might happen to see the picture and feel hurt. Her dark red hair was spun into the shape of a beehive on top of her head. She has gray-green eyes, wore a powder-blue suit with a three-strand pearl necklace and her fingernails were unpainted. Tinglingly aware of my ignorance about her art and career, I was afraid I might be the only reporter to ask a gauche question. I needn't have worried. A woman reporter asked:

"Miss Sutherland, who does your hair?"

Miss Sutherland replied that she had a young Mexican hairdresser. Silence.

Glancing left and right, I saw that the other reporters were as nervous as myself. Were they also ignorant about opera? Why didn't someone say something? Fumblingly, I began questioning the diva. She gave me direct answers but did not elaborate and uttered nothing newsworthy.

Hating the editor who had sent me to this slaughter, I asked banal question after banal question. Then I felt guilty about dominating this mass interview, and shut up.

But when I stopped asking questions, no other reporter asked anything, so more than a dozen of us sat in icy, brittle silence. Hoping to melt the situation, I resumed my interrogation and again Miss Sutherland gave me polite pointed answers. I thought: I'll bet she thinks we're a bunch of dumb bastards! Again I stopped speaking. Again everyone sat like a stalagmite. With my genius for the obvious, I asked where her husband was, and she beckoned and he walked forward to perch on an arm of her chair. He is a slim and handsome man with dark hair. I asked him a couple of non-Pulitzer Prize questions.

At last I arose and thanked Miss Sutherland and her husband for their time and courtesy, then walked to the rear of the room in the hope that the other alleged reporters would carry on the interview. Another chilly silence. It was broken at long last by a United Press International reporter who began asking some really intelligent questions. I thought: Where the hell were you when I needed you? Then I heard a female reporter interrupt his creative interrogation with a demand to know all about Miss Sutherland's wardrobe.

Finally I slunk out, unhappy with myself, sorry for Miss Sutherland.

WEDNESDAY, DECEMBER 6, 1961 ■ Shortly after I reached the office Norman Herrington said he wanted John Miller and me to cover President Kennedy's visit to the city today. Kennedy was scheduled to speak in the Waldorf-Astoria to delegates to the 66th annual congress of the National Association of Manufacturers. I began by telephoning the NAM headquarters to ask a series of questions, having learned that a few phone calls can provide me with necessary background and save me unnecessary steps. Now I discovered that a copy of the text of the President's address could be obtained in NAM press room in the Waldorf. John left for the Stanhope Hotel where he hoped to find Kennedy's press secretary, Pierre Salinger, and I departed for the Waldorf.

In the NAM press room I was given Kennedy's speech and I sat down to underline those passages I considered most significant. Then I phoned my office with the expectation of delivering to some rewriteman, only to be told by Al Salerno that the wire services already had moved the text. Later I discovered that the entire text was in the city room before I left it.

I left the Waldorf and rode a cab to the Hotel Carlyle at 76th Street and Madison Avenue, where Kennedy stays whenever he is in New York. The lobby was filled with reporters wearing special green press cards issued by the police department for the President's visit. And there I found John Miller, who said Salinger was not at the Stanhope but with the President in his suite in the Carlyle. I noticed Alistair Cooke, the celebrated British correspondent, who wore a sweater under his jacket.

John and I agreed that it might be wise for me to leave the Carlyle and return to the Waldorf, for traffic could get sticky once the Presidential cavalcade began to move. I hailed another taxi. My hat band was too narrow to hold the special press card, so from the cab driver I borrowed a rubber band to fit around my hat and keep the card in place. Some people believe reporters behave melodramatically by wearing press cards in their hats, but the fact is that this insignia enables newspapermen to move quickly through police lines.

Back at the Waldorf I spoke to a Secret Service man who said that Kennedy would be driven inside the hotel at its 50th Street entrance, so I took up a position there. The weather was sunny but so chilly I felt grateful to Ruthie for the knee-length sox she bought me. At 12:11 P.M. the Kennedy limousine rolled through the hotel entrance and when I saw members of the Washington press corps break through police barricades to press closer, I dashed after them. Kennedy got out of his car and stood for a couple of minutes about a dozen feet away from me. He was hatless, as usual, and a lock of hair protruding at the back of his head gave him a boyish look. Then the President, the others and myself surged through the door into the Waldorf. Kennedy was ushered into a waiting elevator. I took a second one.

I phoned my office to announce that the President had arrived and then walked to the Astro Gallery where correspondents were being served a buffet luncheon. I chose sea food, which proved to be delicious. I ate at a table facing a closed-circuit television set that showed Kennedy walking into the main ballroom. Murray Kempton, the sharp-tongued columnist for the *New York Post*, was looking for a place to sit, so I invited him to join me. He was pleased when I said I own a copy of his book called *A Part of Our Times*. Murray is a lean, bespectacled, pipe-smoking, sandy-haired, articulate fellow. Aware that he hated Joe McCarthy, I began talking about ultra-conservatives.

When I finished eating I walked to the main ballroom. I had been told that on one of its balconies a table had been reserved for the press. There I encountered Carlton Kent, a red-faced white-haired Washington correspondent whom I knew in Oklahoma City. In those days we called him Bill. He sat beside Bill Lawrence, an ABC correspondent I've seen on television many times. Bill Kent said he was glad to see me again and we chatted about old times until Murray Kempton joined us.

Deciding that the press table on a second balcony was too far away from the lectern where the President would stand as he spoke, I wandered down to a lower balcony and found a chair from which I had an unobstructed view of the stage. Marguerite Piazza, clad in a dramatic red dress, sang three songs as she stood spot-lighted on a lower balcony directly across the ballroom from me.

At exactly 1:30 P.M. the President was introduced by John W. McGovern, president of the NAM. In appearing before this organization Kennedy was, of course, speaking to a slightly hostile audience. Everyone arose when he was introduced and he received 15 seconds of applause. I know, because I timed it with my watch. Kennedy wrung laughter from the 2,300 luncheon guests by quipping: "I recognize that in the last campaign most of the members of this luncheon group supported my opponent, except for a very few who were under the impression that I was my father's son."

Watching from a distance of 75 feet, I saw him indulge again and again in three gestures: 1) his clenched right hand descending down toward the lectern without quite hitting it; 2) index finger of the right hand held out and stabbing toward the lectern; 3) this same finger ticking off points on the fingers of his left hand.

Since I was following his speech from an advance text, I was able to note when he departed from it. He ad-libbed often, at length, and extremely well. But after each ad-lib he would return to his prepared remarks so skilfully that I doubted whether the audience was sure which were spontaneous comments and which were prepared. During his talk he was applauded only three times, and then but briefly. He spoke 48 minutes, finished at 2:18 P.M., received 25 seconds of applause.

I threaded my way to the third floor press room where I phoned my office again. Since our story about Kennedy already had been written from the wire service text of his speech, and since it was now rather late in the afternoon for an afternoon paper, Al Salerno wanted nothing more from me. So today I covered President Kennedy without getting a line about it in the paper.

TUESDAY, DECEMBER 19, 1961 ■ I plan to write a series of articles about the charming streets in this city. One of them is Patchin Place in Greenwich Village, a quaint cul-de-sac, a notch in the belt of W. 10th Street between Greenwich and Sixth Avenues.

In magazines I have seen photographs of high fashion models posing in boy-hipped nonchalance under the antique lamp hanging near the iron gate at the entrance to Patchin Place. The past few days I have gone there again and again to let its ambience soak into my mind. Walking through the gate I felt transported to some back-street in London. There are flagstone walks, black iron fences, three-story oyster-gray houses more than a century old, several ailanthus trees, also known as the Tree of Heaven.

Down through the decades Patchin Place has been the haven of famous writers, painters and sculptors. Ever since 1925 house No. 4 has been the home of E. E. Cummings who, along with Robert Frost, has been called "the finest lyric poet of this century." The other day I wrote Cummings to ask whether he would receive me and tell me the history of the street. Because he is shy, I doubted whether he would agree.

Today I knocked at other doors there. In one house I found William Brinkley, a friendly ginger-haired novelist who wrote a very successful novel called *Don't Go Near the Water* and has just published another entitled *The Fun House*. He suggested I speak to Cummings. I said I'd already written to him. At that moment Brinkley said: "There's Mrs. Cummings now!" I reached her just as she was about to enter her house, and identified myself. Smiling, she said she remembered I had written her husband. Yes, she said, he would be pleased to see me today at 3 P.M.

Cummings fascinates me. A rebel, a Bohemian, he never held any salaried job—or so I've read. Of course, he paid a price for his independence. He wrote: "I have always been poor and never gotten used to it." His parents were introduced to one another by philosopher and psychologist William James—which ain't a bad start in life. His father was a Unitarian minister and an assistant professor of English at Harvard. Cummings himself studied the classics at Harvard and won a master's degree in 1916.

Before the U.S. got into World War I, E. E. Cummings drove an ambulance for the French army. Because he associated with another American regarded with suspicion by the French, and because he refused to say he hated the Germans—saying, instead, that he loved the French—Cummings spent three months in a French concentration camp. That experience gave him the material for his first novel, called *The Enormous Room.* It was a literary success but a commercial failure.

While Cummings is a novelist, playwright and painter, he is best known as a poet. In fact, he is renowned for the eccentricities in his poems, his use of slang and wild typographical oddities. These earned him the nickname of Peck's Bad Boy of American poetry. Nonetheless, some critics call him "the greatest innovator in modern poetry" and place him near Thoreau and Whitman in "the pantheon of American letters." He also is regarded as one of the great love poets of the English language. I am especially fond of this:

> be of love (a little)
> More careful
> Than of everything

So at three o'clock this cold rainy day I knocked at his front door. It was opened by Mrs. Cummings, his third wife, a former fashion model. Photographer Edward Steichen once called her "the best fashion model I ever worked with." She is tall and willowy and has an oval face. Standing in the hallway of the first floor she picked up a hand-bell and rang it. Puzzled, I soon realized she was signalling to her husband in his third-floor studio that company had arrived. I was in the living room when he entered.

Extending a slim hand, he put his heels together and bent over as we shook hands. In this mannerism there was a hint of the ritualistic courtesy of a Chinese mandarin. He is 67 years old, weighs only 120 pounds and is shorter than his wife. He looks like Henry Miller, the novelist, whose face is familiar to me through photographs. Cummings sat down in a straight-back chair to my left while his wife sank into a more comfortable chair near windows fronting upon Patchin Place.

He would be all bald but for the crescent of fuzz fringing his head. His long lean face slopes down and forward, ending in a pointed chin beneath taut lips. I always look at faces with the eye of a caricaturist. The day was drab and the room dim, so I could not see his eyes, which are small, close-set and seemingly lacking eyelashes. His naked eyelids and the fact that his skin was drawn drum-tight over high cheek bones lent an Oriental cast to his countenance. He has big ears. He wore a light blue shirt, a darker blue sweater buttoned down the front, a loosely knotted yellow tie and rumpled pants. Despite the informality of his attire, though, he had an aura of elegance, for he was the soul of courtesy.

When I interview people I talk little and listen a lot, but having read that Cummings is shy, I tried to prime his conversational pump by speaking more than usual. I began by saying I'd heard that all his life he has done exactly what he wants to do.

"Yes," he said, his eyes suddenly Puckish, "I read that too—and afterwards I was afraid people would assault me on the street."

He clapped a hand over a grin.

While waiting for him to come downstairs, I had told his wife about *The Iconography of Manhattan Island*. This is a six-volume set of books that is the granddaddy of all history books about New York City. Now she asked me to repeat what I had said to her. Cummings said he never had heard of the *Iconography*, but was interested and asked how the volumes were bound. Mrs. Cummings said she had read about a technique used by thieves in public libraries when they want to tear a page out of a book. They chew a piece of string until it is soggy and then lay it along the bound edge of a page, which then becomes moist and can be pulled out easily and noiselessly.

I had compiled a list of celebrities who may have lived on Patchin Place and told Cummings I wanted to check with him. Theodore Dreiser? . . . No. John Masefield? . . . No. John Reed? Ah, yes! John Reed, a Harvard man and poet, life-gulping, icon-smashing. He went to Russia as a journalist, wrote a classic about the Russian Revolution, died in Moscow and was enshrined in the Kremlin.

Mrs. Cummings mentioned Mrs. Lydia Corkery, an elderly resident of Patchin Place with whom I chatted yesterday. She had told Mrs. Cummings that when John Reed lived in the court at No. 1, he had tacked a red blanket on a wall and in the middle of it had hung a picture of a man with a small pointed beard.

I guessed, "Lenin?"

Cummings and his wife laughed. Yes, Lenin! They were amused by the fact that to Mrs. Corkery he was just a bearded man, not the architect of the Russian Revolution. I knew that in 1932 Cummings himself had visited Soviet Russia and became so revolted by its system that he wrote a scathing book called *Eimi*. Cummings detested all institutions, never joined any political party or clique. Forever true to himself, he once wrote:

> i am a little church (far from the frantic/world with its rapture and anguish) at Peace with nature.

I resumed reading from my list: Harry Kemp? . . . Yes, Kemp once lived on Patchin Place. Deep-chested, ruddy-faced Harry Kemp, the Hobo Poet, who proclaimed: "I need women for my body, I need women for my soul, I need women for poetic inspiration!"

Cummings asked whether Kemp is still alive. I don't know.

I said I was sure another one-time resident of Patchin Place was English-born John Cowper Powys, also a writer. Yes, said Cummings, Powys had occupied the very house in which we now sat. I said I had read about a visit paid by his brother and fellow writer, Llewellyn, to this enclave, and I began reading aloud Llewellyn's description of an ailanthus tree with "leaves that in April open out like the webbed feet of goslings."

My voice faltered. I became self-conscious about reading aloud to a famous poet. What gall, Ellis! Or, as Ruthie might express it, what *chutzpa*! But Cummings was so attentive I resumed reading.

Had Cummings really said he'd move out of Patchin Place if anyone cut down that ailanthus tree?

"Yes, that's true . . . I have to be able to see a tree to write well. You can understand this because you're a writer, but not many people can. This is the only place in any city I've ever seen where I can work. It's relaxed and quiet here. It's almost as though nobody were here. I've never owned a radio or television machine, and I never answer the telephone."

He said in winter the first floor of his house is comfortable because it is over the oil furnace, but the upstairs rooms are cool and after midnight have no heat in them at all. So, at times he has to go to bed when he really wants to continue writing or painting. He added that he alternates between these two activities. Then, despite all he had said about the quietude of Patchin Place, he now told me that a new building is being constructed nearby, and that blasting and drilling awaken him early in the morning.

"This is forcing a mechanical rhythm of living upon me. Since I'm neurotic, or whatever you call it, I now find I have to take sleeping pills."

I said he's lucky he doesn't have to get up early to go to work in an office. Agreeing, he added that if he worked in an office he would miss the fascinating attempts made to penetrate his isolation. On languid summer days college boys and girls, heady with wine and his poetry, peek into his windows. Sight-seeing guides bring tourists to Patchin Place to point and spiel about him, but he has not yet been able to hear what they say.

"I must, some day!" he cried. Again he blotted a grin with his hand.

"Is it true," I asked, "that you never held a salaried job in all your life?"

"Once," the poet replied, "I worked for Collier's Publishing Company and they paid me the munificent sum of fifty dollars a week. They also gave me a two-week vacation—but that was a bribe!" When he spoke the word *bribe* he hushed his voice into a conspiratorial whisper, and his eyes twinkled. Then he shook in silent laughter. I didn't understand what he meant, and he didn't explain.

I was enjoying him so much I wanted to remain longer but did not wish to out-stay my welcome, so I said I had better leave. First, though, might I caricature him. He assented.

Begging his pardon, I moved a lamp at his left so that it shone upon his right profile. Now I saw he has blue eyes. Talking, to keep him at ease, I began drawing with a pencil upon a manila folder and in a couple of minutes had a rather good caricature of him. I asked whether he would autograph it.

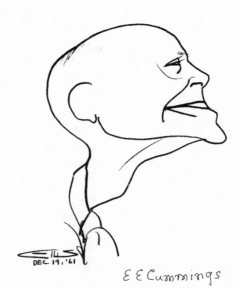

DEC. 19, '61

E E Cummings

Nodding yes, he took the picture from me and grinned at his image. His wife walked across the room to see it, made a face, said she disliked it and wished he would not sign it. Despite her, he signed E E C u m m i n g s— with three capital letters and with no two letters joined.

I thanked him. Then I asked: "I should use capital letters in writing your name, should I not?"

"Oh, yes," he said casually. "I always sign my name in capitals. This business of lowercase for my signature—people just made it up."

Saying good-bye, tingling with exhilaration, I left and walked a few paces to the home of William Brinkley. When he opened the door I cried: "Hey, Bill! Lookit what I have!" And I held up the autographed caricature.

He yipped: "My God!" Taking one quick look at the caricature, he said: "I'll give you a hundred bucks for it, Eddie!"

I shook my head no. Bill poured us Scotch and water and as we drank we talked about E. E. Cummings. Bill speculated that I may have been the first reporter to interview the poet in the past 15 years or so. I'm not sure. From a shelf Brinkley took a copy of *The Fun House* and on the fly-leaf wrote: "To Eddie Ellis—a great reporter who scored the scoop of the decade by interviewing my neighbor, Mr. e e cummings. With all best regards, Bill."

1962

MONDAY, JANUARY 8, 1962 ▓ Today I got this letter:

4 Patchin Place
New York City
January 5, '62

Dear Mr. Ellis—
thanks most kindly for the note & tear-sheet; as well as your gener-ous wish on behalf of Patchin Place. Let me only add that my wife & I were, & are, very pleasantly surprised by your story

—Happy New Year!
E. E. Cummings
(signed in red crayon)
He died September 3, 1962, about a month before his 68th birthday.

MONDAY, JANUARY 15, 1962 ■ The *World-Telegram* has an elderly police reporter with only a fourth-grade education. His name is Mike and he is stupid, monumentally stupid, creatively stupid. No one believes any story he phones from police headquarters, where he is stationed. According to a legend, decades ago Mike did a favor for Roy Howard, our boss, who told another editor that Mike was never to be fired, and then forgot him. Hilarious anecdotes about Mike's ignorance are kept in a file by our managing editor. Here's one:

Mike called the city desk to say a woman had fallen or jumped to her death in front of a subway train at Times Square. He was switched to a rewriteman, who typed notes as Mike talked. An editor shoved a paragraph from the Associated Press in front of the rewriteman, who had trouble getting Mike to shut up long enough to listen.

"Mike, listen! AP says the woman was decapitated. Was she?"

"How da hell do I know?" Mike replied. "Dey ain't found her head yet."

FRIDAY, JANUARY 26, 1962 ■ An editor walked toward my desk and in his eyes I read this message: *Boy, do I have an assignment for you!* He knows I work on series of stories that keep me from taking spot assignments. Right now, in fact, I'm writing the fourth article in my series about the Metropolitan Museum of Art.

The editor said he wanted me to go to the Waldorf Towers to see General Douglas MacArthur, who became 82 years old today. I dislike the general because of his autocratic attitude and ultra-conservatism. In 1932 Franklin D. Roosevelt, then governor of New York, said that next to Huey Long, the most dangerous man in the nation was Douglas MacArthur. However, months ago when I wrote a long obituary about the general, my research revealed how brilliant, daring and dynamic he is.

Al Ravenna was the photographer picked to go with me. Under a gray sky Al drove us up the East River Drive and parked near the Waldorf. I asked how many times he had photographed MacArthur.

"Oh, God, half a dozen times in just the last year, I'd say. He's a cold fish, a very cold fish. He'll never pose, never do anything the photographers want him to. Just stands there!"

We walked into the north entrance of the Waldorf Towers. Waiting in a small lobby under crystal chandeliers were other cameramen and reporters. An army officer emerged from an elevator and said: "Some of your colleagues already are upstairs. You can go up, if you like. It's Suite 37-A."

Six of us entered the elevator. As we were wafted up, one photographer said moodily: "Boys, you might as well forget trying to pose MacArthur."

He won't do a thing. The guy just stands there, not moving a muscle.

When I got to the suite I put my hat and coat on the floor in the corridor and then walked into a large foyer. One corner held a huge urn thick with walking sticks.

The living room held about 25 members of the media. Two lights on tripods had been set up in the northeast corner. A tall bald reporter who works for the Associated Press asked me how long I thought the room was, so I said I'd pace it off, and did. From east to west the room was 50 feet long, and it looked 20 feet wide.

The decorations were Oriental. Japanese scrolls and cloth paintings hung between the two windows on the east wall, the two on the west and the four on the south. Along the north wall was a mahogany table holding a gold baton. It was inscribed: *General Douglas MacArthur. Field Marshal. Philippine Army, June 18, 1936*. To the right of the baton lay a silver box, while on the left was a large vase holding red and yellow flowers. I bent over to smell them. They were made of wax. At the extreme right end of the table there stood a bunch of red roses. I smelled them and they were real.

The ceiling was white. The AP reporter and I agreed that the walls could be described as blue-gray. Actually, it was some exotic tint, but this was as close as we could come to identifying the color. I wish I were an amateur painter and knew more about colors. An enormous mirror covered the wall between the two windows on the east end of the room. Near it stood a waist-high green urn, and a little further away, a nest of end-tables, all hand-carved. I counted two sofas and 12 easy chairs, but the Oriental art treasures were so numerous I lacked the time to inventory them.

Into the room came a ruddy-cheeked officer in a greenish uniform, Lt. Col. Joel Stephens, information officer at West Point. He was leading four cadets. In his hands he held copies of a press release. I took one. The colonel protested in alarm when the AP man reached for another, crying that they were limited in number. Deny the Associated Press, when you want publicity? How silly. This press release had the words of congratulation to be spoken by the cadets to the general, and also their names and home towns.

The colonel told the photographers he would stand on the spot where the general would stand, so they could focus their lenses. Television men stretched measuring tape from TV cameras to the colonel. Frantic last-minute adjustments were made to lights. Cables snaked over the floor. Chairs had been pushed aside. The cameramen slowly formed a half-moon around the colonel.

I walked to the right tip of this half-moon of men because I wanted to be near MacArthur when he entered. Reporters are like football players because they always try to stay near the ball, close to the center of action. My elbow hit a statue on a ledge and I held my breath lest I knock it off. It remained in place.

The cadets wore the gray dress uniform of West Point, gold buttons in a double row down the tunic, gold trimmings. Birthday greetings were to be read by James R. Ellis of Birmingham, Alabama, a brown-eyed youth who is first captain and brigade commander at the Point. The colonel rehearsed him in his lines. Cameramen babbled contradictory orders until Ellis blurted:

"I don't want to be breathing down the general's throat when this thing begins! They'll have to get their pictures as well as they possibly can."

A man in a brown suit walked over to the colonel to help him. I guessed correctly that this was MacArthur's friend and aide, Maj. Gen. Courtney Whitney. He is short and pink and has a moustache and a halo of white hair on his otherwise bald head.

Someone shouted: "He's coming!"

In walked MacArthur. The time was 12:34.

Going to the spot indicated by the colonel, the general cried: "Good day, gentlemen!"

There was a chorus of welcomes.

MacArthur now stood near Cadet Ellis, who began reading:

"Dear General MacArthur: The United States Corps of Cadets expresses—"

From the photographers came muffled oaths and the thud of shoulder against shoulder as they vied for positions.

"—its heartfelt best wishes to you on this, your eighty-second birthday. Few of us have ever met you, yet we of the Corps feel particularly close to—"

The muttering became louder, the jostling worse. It was hard to hear what the cadet was saying. I felt ashamed to belong to such an ill-mannered group.

"—you, for we associate your service with all that we cherish. Your name and feats in both World Wars and Korea have been long known to all of us. Since joining the Long Gray Line—"

Now the muttering had become almost an uproar. Cadet Ellis never lifted his eyes from the document he held. MacArthur stared stonily into the lights.

"—we have come to appreciate even more the extent and meaning of your great contributions to our Alma Mater, our Army and our Nation. Indeed, the impact of your brilliant leadership—"

Ellis and the other cadets towered over the general. He was not so tall as I had expected. He wore a dark suit, trousers without cuffs, a light blue shirt, a blue-and-black tie, a white handkerchief in his breast pocket. No decorations. He held his hands in the pockets of his jacket with only his thumbs protruding. He still has much of his hair, more dark than gray, and he wears it parted on the right and plastered flatly over his head. With hooded brown eyes he stared straight ahead.

"—from your days as Cadet First Captain, throughout your distinguished career, is felt in our daily lives. Sir, it is—"

One photographer after another elbowed me aside. I gave way because, after all, this was a photographic session, not a press conference. MacArthur stood as still as a wooden Indian—except for his thumbs, which trembled. Maybe he kept his hands in the pockets to hide this tremor.

"—with deep humility, tremendous pride and high esteem that we join in celebrating your birthday."

The general accepted the document from the cadet. After holding it a moment, he turned and placed it on a table behind him. He faced into the lights again. He shook hands with Cadet Ellis. For the first time, the room was bleached by silence.

"I'm grateful, deeply grateful, to the Corps for the warmth of this birthday greeting—"

In my notebook I scribbled as fast as possible in the bastard shorthand I taught myself.

"I've reached the age when every birthday represents something of a triumph. It is a pleasure to me to express my thanks and appreciation for this unprecedented gesture—"

Two TV reporters were on their knees in front of the general, too low to be seen by cameras, both holding up microphones. His voice was firm.

"Of all the honors that have been bestowed upon me, I prize most highly, and am most grateful to be a graduate of West Point, to belong to the Long Gray Line, whose motto is 'Duty, honor, country!' "

His voice was becoming stronger. His hooded eyes seemed to look inside himself rather than toward the people gathered in his honor. Now his mouth moulded each word, gave it resonance, his lips opening wider with each sentence. Once again he was the commanding officer, the old war horse, the hero.

"Please give the Corps my affectionate greetings, from its older First

Captain to its youngest First Captain, and let me again thank you personally for bringing me this message."

Then he stepped forward and shook hands with each cadet. Each said
crisply: "Congratulations, sir."

Now the photographers howled for him to get in line with the cadets and,
to my surprise, he did so without protest. When he locked his right arm
through the left arm of Cadet Ellis, the cameramen murmured approval.
Now I could see his hands—mottled with age. Also, his dusky face was
flecked with tiny chocolate spots common among old people. As flash after
flash fired in his face he stood like a rock.

At last he said: "I don't know what you boys do with all the pictures you
take. Later I look at the papers and I just see one picture on page 43. You
never want to take people as they are, but as you think they ought to be."

He tempered his rebuke with a smile.

A photographer said: "Our editors want as many shots as we can get."

Lapsing into silence, the general continued to pose with the cadets, his
nose like the bow of a ship pointing into the sun of the light from the
cameramen. To my amazement and annoyance, I saw a TV cameraman
poke his lens four feet from the face of the general, and grind away, grind
away. I shuddered at the man's audacity. I also wondered how long the
hero could hold that pose and his temper under such close scrutiny. He
broke—stepping back a little.

A TV reporter asked: "General, did your remark about cameramen
apply to television, as well?"

I winced.

MacArthur gave him a cold smile and said: "Let's not get into controversy."

From the far right came the kind of question that makes me ashamed of
my colleagues: "General, what do you think about the state of the world?"

Icily, he asked: "What do you want me to do? Write a book?"

Then the colonel cried: "That's it, gentlemen!"

Two members of the press shook hands with MacArthur. So did I.

"Congratulations, general," I said.

As his eyes locked on my eyes, I felt the man's dynamic leadership—or
was I seeing him through the prism of the books I've read about him? One
thing I know for sure: He still has one helluva strong handshake!

*General Douglas MacArthur died in Washington, D.C., on April 5, 1964,
at the age of 84.*

TUESDAY, FEBRUARY 6, 1962 ■ Nick's bar is where we hang out. It's two
blocks from the *World-Telegram*, at 232 Greenwich St. in lower Manhat-

tan, and its formal name is the Greenwich Tavern. It was there, in the 1930's, that Heywood Broun and other journalists met to form the American Newspaper Guild.

This bar and restaurant is owned by Nick Settaducati, a fat man so very kind that all of us like him. If a guy is short of money Nick will lend him ten, twenty bucks. Mary, his plump and pleasant wife, stands at the cash register. Their grown sons, Mike and Tony, tend bar. Our favorite waitress, also plump and pleasant, is Agnes; we call her Aggie. In the bar room one wall is covered with the caricatures I drew of my colleagues, so we call Nick's the downtown Sardi's, known for its caricatures of theater people.

The other day Mike and Tony were so absorbed in an old movie on television that they didn't hear a man ask for a glass of beer. Thus does TV change an important institution—the workingman's bar.

Today I worked through my lunch hour, so I didn't get to Nick's until 2:30 P.M. The TV set was blasting so damned loud that I cupped my ears with my hands.

Nick asked, "What's wrong, Eddie?"

"That goddam television! Nick, I'm going to picket your place, I'll swear! I'll go elsewhere to eat."

"C'mere," said Nick. Taking my elbow, he led me into the dining room, empty, silent, sat me at a table and closed the door to the bar.

"You'll be all right here," he said. "And try my chicken cacciatore!"

I did and it was delicious and I felt better. Aggie came over to drink iced tea as I finished my meal. I said I want to buy a knitting bag to hold my wife's embroidery, and asked whether I could find one at Macy's. She said she thought so and then brought out a needlework magazine to show me the design of the afghan she is knitting. Reporter talks needlework with woman while the boys in the bar watch violence on television.

On the next page is my self-caricature that hung on the wall at Nick's bar.

SUNDAY, FEBRUARY 11, 1962 ▪ I'm preparing to write a series of articles about Staten Island. Today I had a date with Loring McMillen, director of the Staten Island Historical Society Museum, and when I called and said my wife is free he asked me to bring her with me. Ruthie and I dressed in warm clothes because the weather was very cold. After an interesting day on Staten Island, we caught the 6 P.M. ferry back to Manhattan.

I stood outside on the deck to give myself to the magic of a winter night and watch the golden lances of light that the city threw on the darkling water. Ruthie stood just inside a door, watching me through its glass panel.

I wore my heavy Russian leather cavalry coat, a suede jacket beneath it, and a fur cap, so my body was relatively comfortable, but the coldness, like

the coldness between stars in space, almost paralyzed my cheeks. Above me I saw a crescent moon pinning together the blueness of the night. I felt poised on the rim of the cosmos.

Standing with my feet braced far apart, hearing the *chunk!—chunk!—chunk!* of waves against the bow, I faced the wind and bared my teeth. . . . Ecstasy! For the first time in a long time I sensed again my kinship with nature, felt swaddled in infinity, seemed ageless and almost eternal. When I turned and saw my wife smiling at me, I was warmed by my awareness of her love for me. The water and wind and night and sky and moon and stars and cold washed me clean of my sins, blessed me with the feeling that in this crystal-sharp second I could expire blissfully.

This mystical mood is called the *oceanic experience.* The phrase was coined, I believe, by William James. A couple of times earlier in my life I had lived through moments such as this. It happened to me during World War II when I was based on Okinawa and survived a typhoon with a wind velocity of 200 miles an hour. It happened in Chicago when I worked for the United Press and lived with my wife Lee and our baby daughter Sandy.

She was about three months old when it happened. Late one cold night she began crying in her crib. Her mother was asleep, exhausted from taking care of her. Tip-toeing into the bedroom, I picked up the baby, wrapped her in blankets and carried her into my study. There I sat down in a swivel chair by my rolltop desk to rock her back and forth, her head on my left shoulder. In her hair I smelled that fragrance so characteristic of infants. I agree with the Greek philosopher who said that pleasure is gentle motion; Sandy immediately fell asleep again.

And then it happened:

I was thinking of nothing, absolutely nothing. Instead of thinking I was feeling. No, I was not even feeling, I was just—*being*. At first I was unaware of what was happening, but soon sensed something unusual about my mood. Although I knew who I was and where I was and what I was doing, in a vague sort of way I also sensed that my consciousness had drifted outside of me, that my essence was meshing with the souls of other people, with all the people in the city and world and even the cosmos. The silence was absolute. Space and time took on a different texture.

So I sat in my study in my apartment in Chicago, yes, and I also seemed suspended in space, in touch with infinity, simultaneously living in the past, the present and the future. Everything had come together in one cosmic flash. While I retained my own identity, I also shared the identities of all other human beings. This was not frightening. It was exhilarating! My cells and pores and heart and mind and soul flowered and expanded until I was One with All and All were One with me. I rejoiced, for it seemed I had come home—with a capital H.

I also was at home in Chicago with my wife and daughter, who were safe and well. In a kind of illuminated state I held my baby and wanted nothing. Really? Wanted *nothing?* My curiosity dented the beautiful bubble of the moment. True, I wanted nothing because I had what I wanted, and wanted what I had, and this is happiness. This is what Buddha said will happen with the death of desire.

Now I was in New York. Now I stood in the cold on the deck of a ferry in another mystical mood, and behind that door stood Ruthie, the woman I love, so I walked inside and took her in my arms.

In April of 1962, an editor gave me tickets to a new Broadway musical called I Can Get It for You Wholesale. *He asked me to pay close attention to the show's comedienne because I have a date to interview her. Her name is Barbra Streisand.*

Ruthie and I saw the musical, liked it, agreed she was very funny. Two days later I went to a press agent's office, where Miss Streisand and I were introduced, and then she and I walked to Downey's Steak House at 705 Eighth Avenue, at the western edge of the theater district. We were alone together.

She was 19 years old. I was 51. Instead of giving me honest answers to my questions, she lied to me, toyed with me, tried to manipulate me. For example, she insisted she was born on the island of Madagascar, although I knew she had been born in Brooklyn. This made it difficult for me to write about her. Since she told me almost nothing of value about her life, I based my story upon her performance in the musical.

In my diary I said briefly that she was talented and might go far. How far is far, oh Dumbhead Prophet? It never occurred to me that she would become a super-star.

Anyway, my feature story, published in the New York World-Telegram *on April 9, 1962, was one of Barbra Streisand's first pieces of publicity.*

FEMALE GUNGA DIN
FINDS GILT BUCKET
By Edward Ellis
World-Telegram Staff Writer

In the new musical, "I Can Get It for You Wholesale," a female Gunga Din strikes back.

She's a secretary to a clothing manufacturer. Although she's as frowsy as a scarecrow in a hurricane, she has the frightening efficiency of an IBM computer on a Benzedrine jag.

Like the water-bearer in Kipling's poem, she does everything for everybody until she becomes the indispensable person.

Din! Din! Din! You 'eathen, where the mischief 'ave you been?

Cursed with the sticky name of Miss Marmelstein, she is pulled at like taffy, others crying: Miss Marmelstein! Miss Marmelstein! Miss Marmelstein! Take this letter! Pay this bill! Zip this dress!"

Finally, in act II, scene 2, flopping into a chair like a stricken ostrich, she decides she has had it up to the top of her scrawny neck.

And, night after night, the song she sings stops the show. The role of Miss Marmelstein is played by Barbra Streisand, 19, who is making her first appearance on Broadway. Remember the new volcano that grew to great heights in Mexico a few years ago? That's the way she is shooting up.

In fact, her performance has won her a nomination for a Tony Award as featured actress in a musical.

The day Miss Streisand auditioned for the part she was beat, having stayed up late the night before. In a so-what mood, she sang the song slumped in a chair. The director was so amused he not only hired her but insisted she continue to lounge in the chair after the play opened, which it did March 22.

She'll tell you she's no Elizabeth Taylor, and she's right. Her haystack hair, her beanpole figure, the way she lopes across the stage like a camel with a snootful—these are among her assets as a comedienne.

She refuses to have plastic surgery on her nose, as some well-meaning, ill-advising friends suggest. She wants to be herself, although just what this is eludes her at present.

Her brief biography in *Playbill* says she was born in Madagascar and reared in Rangoon, but this is just gooniness in which she delights.

Actually, she was born in Brooklyn. *Playbill* does add that she went to Erasmus Hall High School, which is true. She put that in. She hopes her Broadway success will be noted by former classmates who may remember her only as a kookie kid wearing purple lipstick.

Her curious spelling of her first name is a part of her who-am-I routine. On stage, though, she ceases to be Barbra from the mysterious East, and becomes the disjointed, frenetic, lovably awkward Miss Marmelstein.

As voices on and off-stage caterwaul: "Miss Marmelstein! . . . Miss Marmelstein! . . . Miss Marmelstein!" she casts her blue eyes skyward in a piteous appeal to heaven.

Nobody, she warbles, thinks of calling her Baby Doll or Honey Dear or Sweetie Pie. And she continues her lament: ". . . Even my first name would be pre-fer-able, though it's terr-ible. It might be betta—it's Yetta!"

By the end of the wail of this woeful frail she's still on her chair— but you may have fallen off yours.

THURSDAY, APRIL 12, 1962   ▓   This morning an editor told me that at 3:30 P.M. I would be covering a press conference called by Roger M. Blough, chairman of the United States Steel Corporation, at 71 Broadway.

In our city room there is a teletype called the Public Relations News Wire. Robert Knight, a press agent for U.S. Steel, had put on this wire a four-line announcement of the press conference. I called him to say I would be covering the event and to point out that since the *Telly* is an afternoon paper, I would be fighting the clock. Would there be a handout I might see before Blough began talking at three-thirty? Yes. I would have permission to study it but could not phone it to my office until the appointed hour. I asked about telephones. Knight said 12 extra phones were being installed near the auditorium on the ground floor, where Blough would appear. Knight added I might bring someone with me to hold a wire open until I could deliver to my city desk.

Reporting to my editor, I suggested a copyboy be sent with me. Picked for the job was Stan Wolfson, because he is young, and aggressive. Stan and I left our office at 2:30 P.M. I felt keyed up because I knew Blough's press conference was one phase of a tug-of-war between the President and big business. On April 10, Blough announced that his company planned to increase its steel prices an average of six dollars a ton. That was four times greater than the wage increase just won by steel workers. Other major steel producers then said they would institute similar price hikes. Kennedy's reaction, in the words of his staff, was one of "controlled fury." At a press conference of his own yesterday the President called these price increases "unjustifiable and irresponsible."

As we entered the lobby at 71 Broadway, another company press agent said the release wasn't ready and he wasn't sure it would be finished before Blough began speaking. This news distressed me.

When Stan and I reached the foyer of the auditorium I was surprised when two secretaries asked our names and wrote them down. TV technicians were setting up equipment. More and more reporters arrived. Among them were my friends, Bud Nossiter of the *Washington Post* and Kevin Delaney of CBS. Then I saw Walter Cronkite of CBS walk in with Murray Kempton, the columnist for the *New York Post*.

I found a phone and took possession of it. Calling my office, I said no press release had been given out. Then I handed the receiver to Stan and told him to keep the line open to the city desk, to guard it but not to get feisty about it. Next I found another company press agent—friendly, fatuous and inefficient. He introduced me to his boss, who had booze on his breath. How could he drink at a moment so critical to his company?

I looked at the auditorium. It was long, narrow, and altogether too small for a press conference of this magnitude. It became jammed with 100 members of the press and company officials. Tension seemed to crackle through the air.

At 3:12 P.M. a man took the stage at the western end of the hall and asked that everyone with any kind of a bag open it for inspection. I was thunderstruck. Except for the 1960 session of the United Nations that brought together more heads of state than ever before in history, I never had known this kind of request to be made. Nor was I alone. Murray Kempton shouted: "But this is America!"

I ran out, grabbed the phone from Stan and told my office about this surprise development. Then other reporters and I found Robert Knight and demanded to know what the hell was going on. He and his aide tried to minimize the significance of the request. It had been the head of building services for the company who made the announcement, and now we were told he merely was concerned about the safety of the building. We asked whether Blough had received a bomb threat. Knight said no. Bud Nossiter and I pressed Knight for a specific answer to the question of whether the bags were ordered opened because of fear of a bomb. At last he conceded that this was the real reason.

Company officials had behaved stupidly in their failure to anticipate the way reporters would react to that order. Moments later the fatuous press agent came to me with a counterfeit smile and said the order had come from the police. I sensed he was lying but lacked time to check this out.

At 3:20 P.M., while I was on the phone with my office, a man came into the foyer with copies of Blough's six-page statement. I snatched a copy from his hands and so did Stan. On the other end of my line was Tom McCabe, a rewriteman famous for the speed of his typing. When I told him I had a copy of the handout, he asked me to start delivering. I said I was pledged not to phone it in until 3:30 when Blough began speaking.

Stan hammered my left arm. When I looked up, he pointed. Eight feet away I saw a *Journal-American* reporter with a press release in his hand and reading it to his office. I snarled at him that we were supposed to wait until 3:30. Snapping at me, he went on reading. I yelled to a company press agent that since the agreement had been violated, I was going to deliver.

First, though, I wanted to scan the pages to find the guts of what Blough was about to say, so I handed the receiver to Stan to hold. This was one of those split-second high-pressure moments in which a reporter is tested. As my eyes raced over Blough's sentences, I was unable to find a single hard sentence that would make a bulletin for my paper.

Picking a paragraph, I took the receiver from Stan and began reading it to Tom. Soon he complained it didn't say much. I agreed. I said the entire six pages had nothing that could be condensed into a single sharp news item. Tom typed the rest of the paragraph I had chosen, then a second graf, then got off the phone to write a bulletin. We were near deadline.

Mike Mok, another rewriteman, came on the line. He took more quotes from me and then, like Tom, commented that Blough said nothing important. After delivering the essence of the statement, such as it was, I gave the receiver to Stan and ran back into the auditorium.

By this time Blough was reading aloud from his press release. Checking the text in my hand, I noted that he had reached the third page. I was unable to see him. He didn't stand on the platform, where he would have been visible to all; instead, he stood on the floor in front of the platform. At 3:47 he finished reading.

Reporters shouted: "Mr. Blough! . . . Mr. Blough! . . ." Walter Cronkite managed to put the first audible question to him. I was screened from the steel tycoon by a wall of backs and TV equipment. I scribbled questions and answers as fast as I could.

Blough's answers were as vague as his written remarks. The reporters were unable to elicit a single clear comment. Whenever I heard anything even mildly significant, I dashed back to the phone to deliver to other rewritemen. One was Drew Phillips, who dryly commented: "The questions are great, but the answers are lousy!"

Suddenly I realized I might be covering a press conference without even seeing its spokesman. What if a rewriteman asked me to describe Blough? Finding a table in the middle of the auditorium, I climbed on top of it. From there I could look over the heads of the reporters and see Blough.

He stood behind a lectern so thick with microphones it looked like a bramble bush. He wore a blue suit, blue tie, and his hair was parted on the left side of his head. Unsure of himself, he spoke in faltering tones. Whenever he finished giving a weak answer to a strong question, a dozen correspondents would bellow his name to try to attract his attention. While many questions were excellent, some were too complex.

Blough said the steel increase would have little effect on the costs of the ordinary family: A refrigerator would cost 65 cents more, a gas oven 70 cents, a washing machine 35 cents, a toaster three cents, a standard size car $10.64.

I didn't even try to question Blough because he was being bombarded with questions from other reporters, because I was too far away from him, and because I am weak in economics. Anyway, I lacked the guts to ask the one question I ached to ask: "Mr. Blough, since we consumers will be hurt by this increase in the price of steel, will you please tell us your annual income?"

None of the lectern's microphones was attached to the public address system—a big mistake made by company press agents. I had trouble hearing Blough. To make matters worse, a TV cameraman kept whispering hoarsely to a blue-jacketed motorcycle courier at his side. A couple of us reporters snarled at him to shut up, but he ignored us.

It was sad to see a spokesman for big business make an ass of himself in public. Wrong though I considered Blough, I would have preferred to see a strong man stand his ground, but he actually looked afraid. I think he knew that besides having the President of the United States as an antagonist, public opinion was against him. As he evaded question after question, the reporters became hostile. At 4:27 he cut off all questions.

When I took the phone from Stan to tell my office that the man was ducking the questions, a nearby secretary glowered at me and recorded my remarks in shorthand. I suppose all company employees consider the press the enemy.

Soon thereafter U.S. Steel and all the other big steel producers cancelled their proposed price increases.

FRIDAY, APRIL 27, 1962 ▪ Ed Wallace strolled over to my desk to tell me of a lead by Tony Shannon that did not get into today's paper. Later I walked over to Tony's desk to ask him about it. He said that the moment his story reached the city desk there was a burst of laughter from Norm Herrington, followed by a raucous explosion from Walt MacDonald, and then a rumble of guffaws. Tony had written: "British Prime Minister Harold Macmillan toured the International Auto Show at the Coliseum today and indicated that any one of the lovely models on display would be a suitable replacement for the heap he pushed around back home . . ." Tony told me: "Somehow, in the back of my mind, I felt there was something a little wrong with my lead, but I couldn't think what it was and I was in a hurry, so I shoved it through."

For self-protection, every newspaperman *must* be dirty-minded.

SATURDAY, MAY 19, 1962 ▪ Today Ruthie and I flew home from Puerto Rico, where we had vacationed. All 168 seats on the Transcaribbean plane were filled; we were lucky to get two seats in the second row from the front. I sat by the window, Ruthie in the middle, a Puerto Rican woman in the aisle seat. Glancing to the left, I saw that the man across the aisle was Adam Clayton Powell, Jr., the Harlem minister and Congressman. Eager to chat with him, I asked the lady whether she would exchange seats with me; she was glad to do so because that gave her the window seat.

As a reporter I knew much about Powell; after getting home I read more about him in a couple of books. He was born in 1908, the son of a Baptist Minister. Young Powell earned his bachelor's degree from Colgate University, his master's from Columbia University, and in 1937 he succeeded his father as pastor of the Harlem Abyssinian Baptist Church. It had 13,000 members, making it probably the largest church congregation in the world.

He was such a political activist that he was called "Mr. Civil Rights." In 1939 he picketed the Empire State Building to force the management of the New York World's Fair to give jobs to Negroes. He founded and edited a weekly newspaper called *People's Voice*, which he declared was the largest Negro tabloid in the world. In 1941 he became the first black man elected to the New York City Council. In 1944 he was elected to the House of Representatives, but when he reached Washington D.C., he was unable to rent a room in the downtown district.

Today, as I sat a few feet from Powell, I soon realized that he is indeed a charismatic man. He is tall and handsome, with curly black hair and a moustache, light-skinned, friendly, erudite. I believed him when he said he uses the Library of Congress more than any other Representative. He had been reading a book when I introduced myself. Upon learning that I am a reporter for the *World-Telegram*, he gave me total attention.

Off the record, he told me, he favors the establishment of gambling casinos, although publicly he denounces this issue. I did not quite understand why this difference. Of course I was aware, as were all New Yorkers, that Powell is a worldly minister who enjoys drinking and night clubs. His wife is Hazel Scott, the brilliant pianist and singer.

There on the plane, Ruthie joined our conversation. Powell said he had gone to Europe three times with "Jack Kennedy." He declared that Mayor Robert Wagner "has no balls." An engaging raconteur, Powell told us a couple of mild racial jokes, to our surprise. When I said I plan to write a history of New York City, he suggested I send him an envelope marked *Private*, and he will ask the Library of Congress to send me whatever data I need. I was impressed by this kind offer.

Ruthie bit into a candy—and broke off a front tooth. Fortunately she did not swallow it; thankfully there was no pain. Powell graciously offered her a slug of brandy from a flask in his briefcase, but she declined with a smile that had a hole in it.

Powell's downfall had begun two years before I met him. In 1960 he had refused to pay a judgment against him for defamation of the character of a Harlem woman; appearing on a TV show he had said bad things about her. Later found guilty of criminal contempt of court, he had fled to the Bahamian island of Bimini to avoid arrest. After serving in Congress for 11 terms, he was excluded from his seat on the charge that he had misused public funds. He was re-elected in 1968, and three years later the U.S. Supreme Court ruled that his exclusion had been unconstitutional. He developed cancer and died in Miami in 1972.

THURSDAY, MAY 31, 1962 ■   It was almost 5 P.M. when I was called to the city desk to talk with Ed Easton, an assistant city editor. He is pleasant and bright and a friend of mine.

"Eddie," he began, "as you know, the ticker tape ran late at the stock exchange the other day. We just got a call from Roy Howard, who wants a three-part series about the operations of the stock market and an explanation about the tardy tape."

Holding out my hands to beg for pity, I said: "Ed, you know damned well that I'm ignorant about business and financial matters. We've got a staff of financial writers. Why don't you give this assignment to one of them?"

"Because," said the editor, "much of the time they write gobbledygook. No, you have to do this—and the series has to begin next Monday."

I winced. Then I asked whether he, at least, would let me work at home with my reference books. Yes. I left the office with a sinking heart.

FRIDAY, JUNE 1, 1962 ■ A *World-Telegram* promotion man called me at home to ask about my forthcoming series on the New York Stock Exchange. Hell, I haven't even begun to write it! The PR guy said he is preparing a big advertisement about the series.

SATURDAY, JUNE 2, 1962 ■ I wasn't sure the New York Stock Exchange would be open on Saturday but took a chance and called and spoke to John Maloney, manager of its news bureau. Telling him about the series I'd been ordered to write, I threw myself upon his mercy. Too many reporters pretend to know something they really don't know; I always admit my ignorance and have found that this evokes sympathetic help. Maloney said that if I came down to Wall Street at 1 P.M. he'd show me around the place.

I took Ruthie with me. John is a nice guy. I asked him many questions as we sat in his office and then when we lunched in Fraunces Tavern. When we walked back to the exchange he took us down onto the trading floor and then up to the ticker room on the fifth floor.

Today's *World-Telegram* published a quarter-page advertisement about my stock market series, scaring the hell out of me because I still have not written a line. However, the series begins on Tuesday, not Monday. The condemned man ate a hearty meal.

SUNDAY, JUNE 3, 1962 ■ Here at home I wrote the first draft of the first article in my three-part series about the stock market. It was hard going. I'm so nervous about the series that I walk around the apartment with a frown on my face.

MONDAY, JUNE 4, 1962 ■ Today I began my 16th year as a staff writer for the *World-Telegram*. After rewriting my first piece about Wall Street, I called John Maloney of the stock exchange and read it aloud, begging him to point out my mistakes. There were only a few mistakes and I was surprised to hear John say he likes my story a lot.

TUESDAY, JUNE 5, 1962   As Ruthie and I were dressing we had the radio turned on and heard a *World-Telegram* commercial promoting my Wall Street story. I glanced nervously at my wife. When I reached the city room I saw that my first piece was published in today's paper. I also saw the editor of our business staff reading it with a sour face.

WEDNESDAY, JUNE 6, 1962   This morning I was in the office when all of us heard a siren howling from a cop car. We rushed to windows. Apparently the siren was stuck. I found myself at a window near Dick Peters, our new executive editor, here very recently.

"Oh!" he said to me. "I meant to give you this."

He handed me a tear-sheet of Tuesday's split-page. Over the top of my Wall Street piece he had written: "Ellis—Damned well done. Even I could understand it."

Then, a twinkle in his eyes, he said he'd had a complaint about me from our financial department. Someone there asked him to insert a box in my series to say: "This was written by an amateur for amateurs." He said he'll tell the boys in the financial section that they have their steady readers of the financial page, but my series would attract new readers, which would mean more money, which would mean that the financial boys could remain in business. Looking at him in surprise, I thought: Here's a guy with guts!

THURSDAY, JUNE 7, 1962   Another radio commercial about my stock market series. The third piece ran today. In the office I ran into Wes First, our managing editor, who said very seriously that I had written the series exactly as he had wanted it. Amazing.

FRIDAY, JUNE 8, 1962   I wrote a letter to G. Keith Funston, president of the New York Stock Exchange. I said I wanted to thank him for all the help I had received from John Maloney and others in the exchange's news bureau.

TUESDAY, JUNE 12, 1962   Today I received this letter from G. Keith Funston:

THIRD SECTION
WEDNESDAY
JUNE 6, 1962

New York World-Telegram
and
The Sun

THIRD SECTION

TOUR BONUS
COUPON - 6/6

13 Steps: How You Sell Share of Stock

1800 Private Phones, 75 Teletypes Speed Exchange Floor Deals

By EDWARD ELLIS
World-Telegram Staff Writer

You're right down on the floor of the Stock Exchange. Photo was taken after hectic session of May 28.

Dear Mr. Ellis:

Your kind letter of June 8 anticipated one that I planned to write to you.

The evening your first article appeared my driver said that I ought to read the piece about the Stock Exchange—that the author had made it so clear even he could understand it. I read your article at once and the subsequent two articles and thought that they were excellent indeed.

I'm glad to know that our people were helpful in feeding information to you. They are the first to tell me that they give equal data to many but, somehow or other, few have the capacity to make as much of it as you did. Many thanks for your kind commendation of them, which not only they, but also I, appreciate tremendously.

Sincerely yours,
G. Keith Funston

Soon I received an offer from the New York Stock Exchange. If I would accept a job as one of its press agents, I would be paid double what I was making at the World-Telegram—from about $8,000 a year to more than

$16,000. *Puffed with pride, I ran home to tell my wife.*

"No," said Ruthie, looking at me with soft eyes. "No, no, Eddie! That's not for you."

"But, Ruthie—! That's a lot of money!"

"I know, dear, but within three weeks you'd have an ulcer."

True. Very Goddamn true. *So I turned down a job that, over the years, might have left me financially comfortable. However, I am inquisitive, not acquisitive.*

MONDAY, JUNE 18, 1962 ■ The Mendoza bookstore is near the *World-Telegram* in downtown Manhattan, so I spend uncounted noon-time hours there pawing through books, buying books, adding to my private library. The city editor let me write a feature about the shop and the owner liked my story so much that he hung it in a front window, where it remained for years. This is what I wrote:

OLDEST USED BOOK SHOP HAS
AURA OF BEWHISKERED ERA
By Edward Ellis
World-Telegram Staff Writer

For a moment the other day a visitor to the city's oldest used book-shop thought he'd found one of Shakespeare's autographs.

The collector was an age-ripened gentleman of starchy dignity. It was his first visit to the 68-year-old Isaac Mendoza bookstore at 15 Ann St., on the northern fringe of the financial district.

Maybe he was attracted by the weatherbeaten sign in front. Perhaps it was the quaintness of the recessed open entrance. Anyway, by walking inside he seemed to step into a bygone century.

Although the bookstore has electric lights, two gas mantles hang from the tin ceiling. On the left is an old-fashioned standup desk. A hand-winding clock a half-century old perches on a bookshelf. A musty smell pervades the interior of this 142-year-old building.

The stranger was approached by the late Isaac Mendoza's last surviving son, David, 60. He's a foot taller than the Harvard Classics, a man of absent-minded affability, rumpled hair, gingerbread eyes and a Puckish sense of humor.

In muted eagerness, the visitor asked: "Have you something rare?"

Silently, the glint of his glasses hiding his Foxy Grandpa look, Mr. Mendoza turned around. With elaborate care he pulled out a brown book. It was a legal tome written in Latin and published in 1607. Its leather cover was crumbling into what looked like grains of brown sugar.

Opening the book to its flyleaf, Mr. Mendoza pointed. In a voice like the flourish of a trumpet, he cried: "Look!" There, scribbled in ink, was the shaky signature: William Shakespeare.

"How much," the visitor quavered, "do you want for it?"

"Oh . . . $10,000."

"I'll let you know," said the stranger. And he left, breathing heavily.

Laughing about this a few days later, Mr. Mendoza told a friend there is no known copy of any book ever inscribed by Shakespeare. The autograph in this tome, which really is ancient, probably is the work of William Henry Ireland (1777–1835), an infamous forger of Shakespeare's name.

Mr. Mendoza said that if the customer had taken his joke seriously he would, of course, have told him the signature is a fake.

Isaac Mendoza, the son of British immigrants, was born on the Lower East Side in 1864. After clerking for book dealers, he opened his own shop in 1894 at 17 Ann St. Later he moved into a six-story red brick building at 15 Ann St.

Just around the corner from Park Row, once the city's publishing center, and not far from Wall St., the shop became the haunt of many famous persons.

Mark Twain browsed there. So did rich Hetty Green, "the Witch of Wall Street." A brash young reporter named Gene Fowler bought a history of Egyptian embalming and thereafter became a steady customer.

A. A. Milne, the British author, would look in during visits from England. And Christopher Morley spent many a noon hour in the shop.

Just above the stand-up desk of Isaac Mendoza, who died in 1937, perches a photograph of bearded Mr. Morley. It is inscribed: "As Goethe said: 'Mehr Licht!' (More light!) With love to the Mendoza Boys from C. M."

Two of the Mendoza boys, Aaron and Mark, loved the book business as much as their father. Not so the youngest, David.

But Isaac gently cajoled him into entering the store. And before a year had passed David felt the love of books entering into his veins.

One day as young David was unpacking books from Jersey, one volume fell out. His father saw the title, pounced on it, tore it up.

David later learned it was *Fanny Hill*, a classic of pornography.

Mark died in 1956 and Aaron in 1960. Now the sole owner of this quaint and famous shop, David carries on in the tradition of his father and brothers.

In addition to random browsers, he has a hard core of about 100 customers who visit his shop at least once a week.

Until about four years ago an eccentric professor from New Jersey would stop by now and then. He looked like a bum. He wore a rope around his waist instead of a belt. But he was listed in *Who's Who* and he corresponded with Albert Einstein.

Mr. Mendoza doesn't specialize. His stock of 100,000 volumes includes every kind of subject. For 50 cents you can buy an 1899 horror called *Fred Fearnot's Desperate Ride—or—A Dash to Save Evelyn*. For $500 you can purchase a Latin Bible printed in 1482.

Not for sale, though, is one of Mr. Mendoza's pet possessions. It's a clipping from the *New York World* of 1899. The story is about a bookworm his father found. Book dealers often see the damage the worms do without discovering the worms themselves.

This particular worm was gorging itself on *The Memoirs, Correspondence and Miscellanies from the Writings of Thomas Jefferson*. The elder Mr. Mendoza consulted some scientists. They figured it would have taken the bookworm 1,284 days to eat its way through Jefferson's life.

After the death of David Mendoza, the store was taken over by his widow, Gilda, whom I knew and liked. In 1972 she sold it to Walter Caron, whom I met just once. What she sold him was the business, not the six-story building; it was owned by someone else. In 1985 the building was sold for $550,000. That was at a time when Manhattan real estate prices were exploding. The very next year the building was sold again for $750,000. Then came a plan to auction it off for perhaps $1.2 million. The rent increases became just too much for Caron, so on February 28, 1990, he closed the city's oldest used bookshop.

TUESDAY, JUNE 19, 1962 ▩ Ruth and I arose at 5 A.M. because we planned to spend the day on Ellis Island. I intend to write a five-part series for my paper about this former immigration station, this renowned gateway to the New World. Taking cameras, food and drink, we rode the subway to the Battery at the southern tip of Manhattan.

The Coast Guard had arranged for one of its cutters to take us to the island, which lies in the upper bay one mile southwest of the Battery. The sun was hot, the air hazy. Aboard the cutter we met James Tiegland, 61, once an engineer in the power plant on the island, now its only guard.

As our craft left the dock I pulled out a notebook in which I had written facts about Ellis Island. When New York City was called New Amsterdam it consisted of three acres, was used by the Dutch as a picnic ground and was called Oyster Island. Later it was named Bucking Island. In 1765 a pirate named Anderson was hanged there, so the name was changed to Gibbet Island. In the 18th century it was bought by a New York business-man, Samuel Ellis, who gave it his name. After he died it passed to John A. Berry, who in 1808 sold it to the state of New York.

Soon the state sold the isle to the federal government, which first used it to store ammunition. Fort Gibson was built there in 1814. Then the U.S. decided to use the island as an immigration station and restored the name Ellis Island. The station opened in 1891, but six years later fire destroyed most of the buildings. Between 1898 and 1905 the government put up 28 new buildings and enlarged the island to 27 acres by dumping soil and rocks there.

A total of 1,285,349 aliens landed there in 1907, the peak year of immi-gration into the U.S. On some days 5,000 bewildered men, women and children were processed by immigration officials. Fiorello H. La Guardia, who later became the mayor of New York City, worked there as an inter-preter.

As our cutter knifed through the pearl-gray water, Ruth and I stared beyond the bow to watch the approach of Ellis Island. It is not a solid land-mass but three tiny islands, three rectangles held together on the west near the shore of New Jersey. Some of the red brick buildings are capped by red-and-green onion-shaped spires in the Byzantine architectural style.

The cutter nosed into a ferry slip and the three of us hopped ashore. The guard walked toward his room in the abandoned power plant. Ruth and I looked around, seeing high weeds and tall trees. Silence . . . except for the lapping of waves. We decided to explore, starting at the north end and working our way south. Squeezing under barbed wires, we climbed onto a long wharf and walked along its rim, hanging onto a wire fence two inches from our noses. Wherever I walked or crawled, Ruthie followed fearlessly—not bad for a gal soon to become 53 years old. For a long time we stood by a stone balustrade to gaze through the golden haze at the jag-ged skyline of Manhattan, soaking up sunshine, smiling at our seeming isolation from the entire world.

Ruth had provisioned us with sandwiches, cookies, a thermos jug of milk, two bottles of frozen Coke and a frozen can of tomato juice. After eating in the open air, we walked to the dead power plant to find the watchman. I asked him many questions. He introduced us to his dog, a Doberman-Pinscher named Millie, who laughed and wriggled like a worm to entice us to pet her.

When Ruthie and I resumed our wanderings we reached the huge administration building at the north end of the island and found we could get inside. We had brought along a flashlight but didn't have to use it much. In a room on the first floor we saw several 1954 calendars. Time seemed to have stopped that year. With Millie frisking at our heels, we picked our way through dozens of deserted rooms, laughingly agreeing that this was quite the largest haunted house we had ever seen. It was an eerie feeling crunching across littered floors, here and there finding old documents, many kinds of records, a Kafka-like nightmare of a bureaucracy gone mad.

Stooping over, I picked up something from the floor. Made of iron, it looked like a paperweight, was about four by three inches, had a handle on top and five holes in the bottom. It may have been a kind of stamp used to imprint wax seals on documents. Wanting a souvenir from Ellis Island, I brought it home to hold down the pages of a book from which I copy.

My wife and I climbed to the second floor of the administration building and found ourselves in an enormous hall. I had read about it. One of its pillars was called the Kissing Post because it was there that immigrants were greeted by relatives and friends who had arrived here earlier. Of course, Ruth and I didn't know which post was the legendary one.

Enfolded in absolute silence, smelling musty yesteryears beyond reckoning, we stood and stared. What thousands, what *millions* of people had stood beneath this very ceiling with its high arch, stood and waited to be processed and thus become Americans. As a reporter who has covered many American Legion conventions and listened to scores of Fourth of July speeches, I am hostile toward plasticized patriotism, the bangs of drums and bursts of oratory, but now that my wife and I stood on such hallowed ground, I felt more patriotic than ever before in my life. America is a nation of immigrants from every corner of the earth, from valleys and wetlands and mountains and tundra and forests and hamlets and towns and cities. Brave people pulled up their roots and surged toward a place promising progress and freedom, the United States of America, a lamp of hope, and many had passed through the hall in which Ruthie and I now stood. My blood quickening, my mind reeling backward in time, I harkened to those days when folks in odd clothes, speaking strange tongues, held in their hearts the honey of great expectations.

I glanced at Ruth. She looked transfixed, as though in religious ecstasy, and I realized she also remembered her roots in the thunderous silence of the hallowed hall. Her parents came here from Austria before she was born. My paternal grandfather was born in England of Welsh parents and arrived here as a boy of sixteen. Alone. I never saw him because he died before I was born, but I believe I resemble him more than any other member of my family. So now the daughter of Austrian-born parents and the grandson of an English-born Welshman stood where they once stood.

Standing at attention, I yelled:

"Sadie Kraus!"

The name of Ruth's mother cleaved the hush of the hall.

"Isaac Kraus!"

The name of her father echoed from wall to wall.

Both died before I met Ruth, but here and now I sensed I knew them very well. My wife's eyes sparkled with tears.

"John Ellis!"

The name of my grandfather throbbed through the chamber and I seemed to see him, a teen-age boy, partly brave, partly scared.

Wildly, excitedly, exultantly, in a way I am unable to explain, I felt a mystical bonding of our two families, almost a second wedding uniting us. We were opening our hearts to the past, to the people who gave us life, seeking to draw strength from their strength. Sadie and Isaac and John were gone, but Ruthie and Eddie were giving them the very best of themselves by giving them total attention.

Now I know what it means to be an American.

As I researched Ellis Island I discovered many current ideas about how the site might be used. One promoter hoped to buy it before the public learned what was happening and then erect a kind of city within the city. When I got him on the phone he begged me not to disclose his impending deal. At long last he agreed to meet me.

When we met in a posh restaurant of his choice, I showered him with questions, and then he asked me one: What would I like done with Ellis Island? Evasively, I said I was a reporter who wanted to write an objective series about the island—its past, present and future. The promoter urged me to express a personal opinion. Finally, I said that as a citizen and as the grandson of an immigrant who entered America through Ellis Island, I preferred that it remain federal property and perhaps be converted into a shrine. He became angry. After a heated discussion, we agreed to part as "friendly enemies."

He had told me that Frank Lloyd Wright, the great architect, had drawn a sketch of his plan for the island. Now, despite our dispute, he promised to let my paper publish it. He shook hands to seal his promise. Immediately afterward, he broke his promise. I never was able to reach him by phone and he never sent me the sketch—if, indeed, it existed.

I suggested to my editors that the World-Telegram crusade to urge the government to convert the island into a national shrine. Nothing was done about this.

One editor after another pressured me to get the Wright sketch. I explained the hostility of the promoter, tried phoning him again, never reached him again, explained again to the editors. Meantime, the promoter called the city editor to complain about me.

One day, to my astonishment, the tall city editor reared up to his full height and tongue-lashed me at the top of his voice, in full view of everyone in the city room. I was astonished because in our office editors and staffers were usually soft-spoken. Now, however, the city editor berated me for angering the promoter by expressing a personal opinion. I wondered: Whose side is he on?

I said that the man had asked for my opinion, and then I added that just because I am a reporter I am not disenfranchised as a citizen. But, crimson-faced with fury, the city editor cursed me in vile language. My own anger, slow to erupt, now spewed out like lava. Standing nose to nose with him, I called him every name I could think of, roared I had no respect for him, finally told him to go to hell.

I quit. It was July 12, 1962.

After being a reporter and feature writer for 35 years, the last 15 years at the World-Telegram, I ended my career in journalism.

In the next few moments half my colleagues called me an idiot for sacrificing perhaps $5,000 in severance pay, while the other half praised what they called my guts. Most of them disliked the city editor. When I called my wife to tell her what I'd done, she cried: "Wonderful!"

Before walking out I made sure that I got letters of recommendation from other editors, two of them higher in rank than the city editor.

Soon a wave of relief washed over me. Deep down in my unconscious something said I had done the right thing. I thought so then and I think so now. Had that editor and I never engaged in a shouting match, I'm sure I would have left him at some distant date.

I had done almost everything a reporter can do, including two very brief stints as a foreign correspondent. Because I read history and biography, psychology and philosophy, I had become impatient with the superficiality of *journalism. Roy Howard, our ultimate boss, had decreed that he wanted lots of brief stories in the paper at the expense of some long ones, and I thought he was wrong. People read lengthy articles if they are well-written.*

I also wanted to write books, to leave something of value when I die. For years I had been enchanted with the phrase "place one pebble on the pyramid of culture." I forget where I read this line. Already I was co-author of Traitor Within, *a study of suicide published in hard-cover and favorably reviewed by the* New York Times. *However, it did not sell well. I had completed my biography of Steve Hannagan, the prince of press agents, but was unable to sell it.*

Editor after editor asked, "Who was Steve Hannagan?" That taught me a lesson: Pick a big target. I decided to write a history of New York City.

During my last years on the paper I wrote many five-part series about the city, its tiny islands and old mansions and stately lighthouses, but lacked the space to include all the facts I gathered. I had saved my notes and now planned to use them in a book. My wife and I had wondered whether we could afford to let me stay home to write it, and at last she said: "I'll earn the money. Your job will be to write." I could have kissed her. Well, fact is, I did kiss her. But had I known then what I know now, namely that only a few authors can live off their royalties, I might have lacked the courage to quit the paper.

The day after I resigned I found a literary agent willing to represent me. When I spoke to a reporter who had quit before I did, he warned that the first couple of weeks I'd feel like a deep-sea diver brought to the surface too abruptly, and thus getting the bends. An apt description. That's how I felt.

As for Ellis Island, it did not fall into the hands of that slick promoter, for which I am grateful. In 1965 it became a part of the Statue of Liberty National Monument. Then came a restoration project costing $156 million, paid for by corporate and private donations. The result was the Ellis Island Immigration Museum, the kind of shrine I had envisioned. When it was dedicated on September 9, 1990, Vice President Dan Quayle called Ellis Island "nothing less than the triumph of the American spirit."

When I left the World-Telegram *I knew it was losing money. So was the* Journal-American, *so was the* Herald Tribune. *These three papers merged as the* New York World Journal Tribune *and began publication September 12, 1966. Soon the money ran out, though, so the hybrid paper ceased publication May 5, 1967.*

In the year 1900 New York City had 15 major daily newspapers. Now it was left with only three—the Times, Daily News *and* Post.

Before the merger Herb Kamm became managing editor of the World-

Telegram *and urged me to come back to the paper. That made me feel good, but I had a book to write.*

Ruth continued to work as an executive secretary while I engaged in massive research, consulting some 1,100 books and writing thousands upon thousands of pages of notes.

When I was halfway through my book Ruthie ended her own career to stay home and help me. No writer could have had a better assistant. Without her I would have been unable to produce The *Epic. Our bedroom became our office. I had my rolltop desk while she had her own desk with its electric typewriter. Because I can dictate as fluently as I write, I dictated the last half of my history, but I'll bet no reader can detect the place where I switched to dictation. We wrote almost 1,000 pages of manuscript.*

1963

THURSDAY, JANUARY 10, 1963   ▨   Now that I'm writing a huge history of New York City I appreciate something said by John Steinbeck in his book *Travels With Charley:* "When I face the desolate impossibility of writing five hundred pages a sick sense of failure falls on me and I know I can never do it. This happens every time. Then gradually I write one page and then another. One day's work is all I can permit myself to contemplate."

MONDAY, JANUARY 21, 1963   ▨   I'm working hard on my narrative history called *The Epic of New York City.* Today I labored on the very first paragraph in the book, rewriting it 18 times.

TUESDAY, JANUARY 22, 1963   ▨   I agree with Nathaniel Hawthorne, who said: "The greatest possible merit of style is, of course, to make the words absolutely disappear into the thought."

TUESDAY, APRIL 9, 1963   ▨   In the *Herald Tribune* I read a review of *Boswell: The Ominous Years.* James Boswell (1740–95) was a Scottish lawyer and author who kept a diary from 1761 until his death.

The *Trib's* critic, Maurice Dolbier, said in part:

"This is one of the greatest works of self-revelation in the history of world literature. Pepys had more important public events to relate and Rousseau had more influence on the future course of public events, but Boswell's is one of the frankest and most disturbing confessional documents that, in Leonard Bacon's words, 'ever ran down the nib of a pen.'"

My own diary, now in its 36th year, already is longer than the Boswell diary. I wonder whether any parts of my journal ever will be published?

MONDAY, APRIL 22, 1963 ▣ The morning papers said that within the past 24 hours the city fire department answered 1,000 fire alarms—the greatest number in the history of the city. Most of those calls came from Staten Island, where brush fires destroyed 85 homes.

WEDNESDAY, APRIL 24, 1963 ▣ The federal government has declared Staten Island a disaster area because of brush fires that destroyed 116 buildings worth $2 million and left hundreds of people homeless. In New Jersey other fires charred 450 buildings at a loss of $20 million, caused six deaths and left hundreds of folks without shelter.

FRIDAY, JULY 12, 1963 ▣ It was a year ago today that I resigned from the *World-Telegram*. Except for the first couple of panic-stricken weeks, I never have regretted this decision. These past 12 months I have worked harder than ever before in my life and enjoyed it immensely. Each morning I come to my work as a bridegroom goes to his bride.

This afternoon I went to a mid-Manhattan hotel to see Joy, a New Orleans friend, who is passing through the city. Many years ago when I went to New Orleans to work for the Associated Press, she was the first friend I made in that southern city. Joy is several years older than I, but so intelligent, cultured and charming that I spent much time with her while also dating women my own age. Because of her age and sophistication, Joy felt free to criticize my attire and behavior, and I continue to feel gratitude toward her for smoothing out some of the wrinkles in my manners.

Born in Louisiana, she has lived all her life in the deep South. In her hotel suite today she said she had known William Faulkner, who died last year. Then she told me that when she worked for a university, she had an administrative superior, a professor who happened to be a Negro. She did not mind calling him *Professor* or *Doctor*, but was unable to bring herself to call him *Mister*.

"Why not?" I asked.

"I don't know . . . isn't that silly?"

Nodding my head yes, I said: "If you happen to know a Negro who is brilliant, who has several college degrees, who obviously is cultured and gentle and a man of good character—wouldn't you consider him your equal?"

"Not really," Joy confessed. "I honestly don't know why. It's just that I can't get away from my background."

Smiling at her, I said: "That's silly! You're an intelligent woman. Of *course* you can break with your past!"

"No . . . I just can't help it."

"Don't you Southerners know you're going to lose this thing?"

"Of course!" she cried. "No question about it."

"But you're going to fight a rearguard action against civil rights and in so doing you're going to tear this nation in two."

Joy trilled that golden laughter I know so well. "Oh, no! We're not the ones who are sundering this nation. It's you Yankees—you New Yorkers!"

And she waved gracefully toward the windows of her hotel suite, out toward the millions of Yankees living below.

Here sat Joy and I, friends the past 28 years, but despite our friendship and our politeness, we were unable to discuss a social issue of transcendent importance. Joy thinks of me as a Yankee. I suppose I am, but I never think of myself as a Yankee—just as a human being. In my heart I felt winter.

FRIDAY, SEPTEMBER 27, 1963 ▪ Before noon I left the apartment and subwayed to Fourth Ave. to buy books. My first stop was at the Fourth Avenue Bookstore, 138 Fourth Ave., where I saw a smashingly handsome 25-volume set called *The Historians' History of the World*, which I had known about for some time. Before deciding to buy it, I continued to Schulte's Bookstore at 80-82 Fourth Ave., where I bought nine books about New York City for a total of $19.76. Then back to the first shop, which is owned by a man and his wife. He wanted $50 for the history set, which was a bargain, but I demurred. Then his wife said that since I am a writer they ought to let me have it for $37.50. To that I agreed. The man was tying up the set when his wife became aware for the first time that it consists of 25 volumes. Chagrined at having let it go at that price, she nonetheless went through with the sale. I was so excited my fingers trembled. Besides this set, I also bought three books about the city at that shop. Had to take a cab to bring home my haul. Altogether I spent $66.76 on books today. In the eleventh edition of the *Encyclopedia Britannica* I found this evaluation of my new history set:

> *The Historians' History of the World*, edited by Dr. H. Smith Williams, (1908) is a compilation from the works of eminent historians of all ages, and the value of its various parts is therefore that of the historians responsible for them. Its chief merit is that it makes accessible to English readers many foreign or obscure sources which would otherwise have remained closed to the general reader. It also contains essays by notable modern scholars on the principal epochs

and tendencies of the world's history, the texts of a certain number of treaties, etc., not included as yet in other collections, and comprehensive bibliographies.

Apart from the scholarship, which is most important, this set is quite the most beautiful I own. Each out-sized volume numbers more than 600 pages, is bound in green covers and rich gold-embossed leather, and its title page was designed by Tiffany & Co.—something new to me. The man who sold me the set said it would cost $15 per volume to duplicate it today, and I believe him. The pages are uncut. The rest of this hot day— the temperature hitting 83 degrees—I put away this set, glanced through a couple of volumes, and set the apartment straight for our visitors this evening.

FRIDAY, NOVEMBER 8, 1963   ■   Today my psychiatrist gave me this Thanksgiving thought: "The Pilgrims thanked God for saving them from the Indians. We thank God for saving us from the Puritans."

MONDAY, DECEMBER 23, 1963   ■   At about 6:00 P.M. my Doubleday editor, Tom McCormack, arrived, stamping snow from his rubbers, hatless, his face flushed with cold. Today he read more chapters of my history of New York. He is unadulteratedly enthusiastic. He said such things as, "I forgot I was reading and began living. What a sense of drama you have! 'The tornado slammed into the city with the crack of a wet bullwhip'—Eddie, a great phrase! Yet wisely, you don't overdo images. The book gets better and better. I'm thinking of other books for you to write, thinking and discarding, waiting until I get just the right kind of book for you. . . . There's no reason at all why you can't wind up a recognized author and get enough money to live comfortably. You always should write about human beings, since you handle them so graphically. You know how to build suspense and tension most dramatically . . ." On and on went Tom McCormack, Ruthie and I practically hugging ourselves in glee. When he first let loose with this string of compliments Ruthie was out in the kitchen preparing dinner, and I yipped for her to race into the living room. Tom, for that matter, said he wanted her to hear. It did my heart good to hear this editor confirm everything that Ruthie has thought and felt and said about me and my writing. The truth is, I was so taken aback by this unstinting praise, I can't remember everything Tom said. Now, as never before, I believe in my ability as a writer. It wasn't enough for me to hear the favorable remarks of my wife and sister and friends. It only really registered when I heard them from a man who has no vested interest in me—or hadn't. Surprising to me was the statement that editors look for writers as much as writers look for editors. I hadn't realized this. When I showed Tom my study he grinned and said: "You know, this looks exactly like the kind of study I would expect to find for a guy who is writing a history of New York City."

CHAPTER 14

1964

TUESDAY, JULY 24, 1964 ■ My half brother Jack is visiting us. He is an engineer who owns his own business, an inventor with several patents to his credit. He lives in Chicago and came here on business, flying his own plane. Since I have been relatively poor all my life, it seems odd to have a brother who owns an airplane.

This afternoon he asked us whether we'd like to take a ride with him. When we agreed we then decided to fly to Montauk Point at the eastern end of Long Island. Today's weather was almost perfect for flying—sunny, warm, cloudless. We rode a cab to Butler Field at La Guardia Airport.

Jack paid $11,500 for a nine-year-old Beechcraft Bonanza, model 35-F, weighing 2,600 pounds, a single-engine craft with underslung wings and a fuselage 30 feet long. The cabin holds four people. The seats are upholstered in soft white leather.

Because I wanted Ruthie to see the instrument panel, I urged her to sit beside Jack, while I took a rear seat. He said that yesterday at Butler Field there were 360 *movements*—take-offs and landings. This evening we were seventh in a line of private planes waiting to lift off.

Air-borne at 6:35 P.M., we headed east along the north shore of Long Island. Although Jack is a seasoned pilot who flew the Hump during the war, I know from experience that he is reckless, so I was tense until we reached our cruising altitude of 5,000 feet. Then I relaxed and gawked at the scene below us.

After leaving the city and flying over the suburbs, the Long Island landscape looked like a verdant wonderland, thick with foliage. I was surprised by the great numbers of inlets and creeks and coves and lakes lacing the island. Thousands of small boats were beached along the shore or tucked inside coves. From our height the boats moving along the blue surface of Long Island Sound left wakes like zig-zag hairpins.

We were flying over some of the richest estates in the country. Here and there I saw blue-gray pockmarks I knew were swimming pools. The further east we flew the higher reared the sandy cliffs along the north shore of the island. I saw a huge diamond-shaped island that may be owned by a single family, for it contained only one neat complex of buildings. What isolation so near the city!

It was 7:23 P.M. when we first saw the lighthouse at Montauk Point. It looked much as I knew it from photographs—a tall cylinder encircled by one wide white stripe, a brown stripe, then another white stripe. It commands a majestic view of the Atlantic Ocean perched on a high cliff and down below the waves creaming and curdling at the base of the cliff. To give us a great view, Jack made a vertical turn over the lighthouse at an altitude of about 2,000 feet. The scene was so beautiful, so awesome, I held my breath.

We landed on a small runway and taxied to a parking area near a half-dozen other planes. The only people there were a woman and three children awaiting the arrival of the children's grandfather. It was 7:35 P.M. when we put down, which meant we had flown from the city to the east end of Long Island in exactly one hour. I marvelled at this swift transition from asphalt streets to sand dunes.

When the airport manager arrived, Jack refuelled the plane. He already had telephoned for a cab to drive us the three miles from the air strip to the lighthouse. I saw rabbits running along the highway, noted the lack of fences on each side, was surprised by the thickness of the undergrowth in the fields.

Our taxi was not allowed to drive close to the lighthouse. It stopped at the top of a hill, where we got out. Soon we found sightseeing binoculars mounted on metal stands, so we inserted coins to scan the horizon. In the distance we saw Rhode Island. We got back into the cab to head back to the air strip as the elderly driver pointed out interesting sites such as the mansion once owned by Anthony Biddle Duke, a member of the wealthy Duke family.

Years ago our cab driver had worked for Carl Fisher, the real estate promoter who turned Miami Beach into a playground and then tried to do the same thing at Montauk Point. Jack and I were fascinated, for our father knew Fisher in Florida. During the Florida land boom of the early twenties, Dad bought a lot from Fisher, watched it rise in value until it became worth perhaps $250,000, refused to sell, held on too long, saw the boom peak and then crash. Had our father not been so stubborn, Jack and I might have been the sons of a rich man.

The cabbie let us off at the Flying Fish restaurant across the road from the air strip. Its plain exterior belied its interior, which was handsome. The huge dining room opened on three sides overlooking sand dunes and ocean. Because the air strip has no lighted runway, we knew we had to leave before the fall of darkness, so we bought sandwiches to eat in the plane.

It was 8:47 P.M. when we took off. This time Jack flew along the south shore of Long Island. Soon he discovered his instrument panel would not light up. Using a flashlight, Jack began experimenting. Since light in the eyes of a pilot makes it difficult for him to see objects in the dark, he was careful not to let the beam of flashlight, or any reflection from it, get into his eyes.

Besides the sandwiches, we had been given a cardboard container of pickles. After we ate the pickles Jack cut off the bottom of the container to try to convert it into a hood for his flashlight, but it kept falling off. He put his fingers over the end of the torch, but this didn't work. I handed him a handkerchief to dull the glow. When none of these improvisations helped, I began worrying. I remembered that when Jack was training to become a pilot during World War II, he cracked up a plane in Denver—walking away unhurt.

Although I know nothing about planes, I am aware that a pilot must be able to see his instruments when he lands—especially at night. Jack was his usual cool self. Ruthie displayed no fear.

With anxious eyes I peered down on Long Island, now so different in appearance from the way it looked earlier this evening. Except for pin-pricks of light, the land was black while the water had the color and texture of hammered pewter. As we approached the suburbs east of the city we saw strings of light, like diamond necklaces, along the highways. Each separate suburb might have been heaps of diamonds spilling onto black velvet on the counter of a jewelry store. The western sky glowed a dull orange, with one cloud smearing the horizon like a slash of burnt cork across a rouged cheek.

Jack kept experimenting with his flashlight. I found myself rolling a handkerchief back and forth between wet palms. To myself I admitted I was frightened. Remembering Hemingway's definition of courage as grace under pressure, I hoped I was behaving well. Ruthie was alert, chatty, undisturbed. I recalled her crisp courage one murky night over St. Louis when our commercial plane had to circle the airport more than an hour.

As Jack left the south shore of the island and angled toward the north-west, he asked whether I'd like to fly over Manhattan before we landed at

Butler Field. I felt like saying no—but said yes. So our plane described a wide circle over the George Washington Bridge linking New York and New Jersey, began skimming down the Hudson River, pulled out into a left vertical turn over the Empire State Building, over the neon noon of Times Square, turned back toward New Jersey, winged over again and made a slow steep dive directly over the Statue of Liberty. I don't know how many aviation rules Jack broke.

I thought: Well, if we die we will plunge to death in the very heart of the most beautiful scene ever to gladden my eyes. Not the Grand Canyon by moonlight, not twilight-tinged Paris seen from Montmartre, not the spectacular sunrise I saw from the ship bringing me back from Okinawa— none of those glorious scenes could compare with this magic moment, this aerial ecstasy, the godlike view of this glittering metropolis seen through the prism of a perfect night.

Jack turned toward La Guardia. Picking up a hand mike to his left, he called the control tower. Then, switching off the mike a moment, he told Ruthie and me he was unable to identify La Guardia Field because it was surrounded by so many other lights. I stiffened when he added that this would be the first time he ever landed at La Guardia at night.

Jack and the man in the control tower talked in businesslike tones. The man would ask for a certain reading . . . pause . . . Jack would aim the flashlight at the instrument panel a split-second, then turn it off lest he be blinded . . . then he would speak into the mike to give the man the requested data . . . question . . . long pause . . . answer . . . question . . . long pause . . . answer . . . Jack told the man he was unable to pick out the runway at Butler Field . . . a note of puzzlement crept into the voice of the man . . . at last, in a flat voice, Jack confessed he had no lights on his instrument panel . . . pause . . . the next time the man spoke I sensed an iron control masking anxiety . . . now he talked with greater frequency, talking Jack toward a runway he was unable to locate with his eyes . . . we circled Butler Field . . . once . . . twice . . . lower and lower . . . at last we saw the landing strip . . . Jack was approaching it from the east . . . coming down lower and lower as he headed west.

I braced myself. I hoped Ruthie was doing the same. In addition to my fear of dying a painful death in a wrecked plane, I wanted to live many more years with my wife and finish my book. My work was not done. I knew I had many more books to write. Lower and lower . . . then, with the skill born of thousands of hours in the air, Jack swooped down gently and surely, our wheels touching the runway at 10:02 P.M. One bounce. A very slight bounce—and that was that.

Or was it?

The man in the tower asked whether we were off the runway. Jack said he thought so. This did not satisfy the controller. He checked and then told Jack he was not on Butler Field, used by all aircraft, but in a busy part of La Guardia used by commercial planes. He was sending two trucks to guide us to a safe area. Jack began easing his plane over to one side. The man in the tower saw this movement and curtly told Jack to stay put until the trucks arrived. Soon they appeared—galaxies of flashing red lights, oceans of screaming sirens.

As one truck wheeled to the right its driver beckoned Jack to follow. The man in the tower came back on the radio to tell Jack to lengthen the distance between this lead truck and his plane. Jack slowed down. We were led to a parking area and safety. The man in the truck got out and used two red batonlike flashlights to conduct Jack into a proper parking position.

We stepped out of the plane. The concrete felt softer than a welcome mat. I spoke to the man who had waved us in, learning that he wasn't even a regular ramp attendant because of a strike at Butler Field. When I said I was surprised at his skill in maneuvering this complex area, he laughed and said he hardly knew the place. I did not laugh.

Just then I heard Ruthie exclaim that the danger had added a thrill to our flight. Although I said nothing, I imploded in anger. I admit that my wife is braver than I am. However, since she never was a reporter, since she never witnessed auto accidents or plane crashes, since she never waded through blood or heard the screams of dying people, she cannot imagine the horrors I endured. This was a great adventure to my wife, but not to me. My memory is salted with images of jagged bones. In that moment I hated the woman I love.

THURSDAY, SEPTEMBER 3, 1964 ▪ In researching and writing *The Epic of New York City* I have almost reached the place where I must explain how headquarters of the United Nations came to be located in New York City. However, the other day I realized, in mild alarm, that I lack all the data I need.

I knew that one of the prime movers in this historic event was William Zeckendorf, board chairman of Webb & Knapp, probably the most influential and certainly the most flamboyant real estate man in this country. When I was a reporter I saw Zeckendorf at various banquets in Manhattan, but I never had met him. Today I telephoned his press agent, Werner Renberg, and asked whether he would hand to his boss a list of my questions. Renberg suggested instead that perhaps I might like to sit down with Zeckendorf to ask him myself. Surprised and pleased, I accepted. Minutes later the press agent called back to say I had a date today at 2:30 P.M. with Zeckendorf in his private office on the twelfth floor at 383 Madison Avenue.

I asked Ruthie to accompany me to take notes. She and I dove into books and clippings to learn as much as possible about Zeckendorf before meeting him.

Like myself, he was born in Illinois—Paris, Illinois—in 1905. When he was three his family moved to Long Island. He attended New York University, played on its football team, quit college after his junior year. He had an uncle in real estate who gave him a job. When Zeckendorf was only 25 he earned a $21,000 commission on a $3 million sale of property—and was off and running. In 1938 he joined the sedate real estate management firm of Webb & Knapp and soon shook it up with his daring and unorthodox methods of doing business. Because of his monumental wheeling and dealing he soon became known as "Wild Bill" Zeckendorf. In 1954 he tried to buy the Howard Hughes empire. One day while conferring with President Eisenhower he interrupted their conversation to take a phone call. The *New Yorker* magazine delighted in publishing wry cartoons about the eccentricities and power of this multimillionaire.

When Ruth and I reached Renberg's office he showed me the company files about the United Nations and let me select whatever items I wanted. Zeckendorf was so proud of the part he played in bringing the UN here that his stock certificates bear an engraving of UN headquarters. At 2:30 P.M. Renberg ushered us into Zeckendorf's private office, which is so unusual that it has become a legend in the business community.

It is a circular room so huge that it reminded me of a bull ring. The ceiling is a skylight. The curved wooden walls seem three-dimensional because they are studded with protrusions like the tips of triangular diamonds. In the center of this circular room there was a circular desk and at the desk sat Bill Zeckendorf whose bull-like bulk enhanced the impression of a bull ring. Bald and barrel-chested and weighing perhaps 250 pounds, he radiated energy. His moon-shaped face was expressive and he smiled a lot. Suffering from a summer cold, from time to time he raised a menthol inhaler to his nostrils.

The moment we met he unleashed a hurricane of words, a monologue so overwhelming I was afraid I might lose my conversational bearings. Politely interrupting, I said I knew much of the story about the United Nations but wanted to fill in the gaps in my knowledge by asking him questions about specific episodes. Zeckendorf quieted down. No doubt he is accustomed to ordering around subordinates and perhaps even peers.

From my briefcase I took a reprint of an article in the May 1947 issue of *Reader's Digest* that tells the origin of the UN building. Zeckendorf scanned it, then declared it was inaccurate. I asked him to point out the errors. After reading it a second time, he conceded it erred only in its omissions. I told Zeckendorf what I wanted to know and he then gave me specific and helpful answers. Weaving together what I already knew and what he now was telling me, I learned this story:

The first two years of its existence the United Nations held its sessions at Hunter College in Manhattan and at Lake Success on Long Island. In 1945 the UN created a commission to choose a site for a permanent headquarters. William O'Dwyer, the mayor of New York City, invited the UN to settle here and appointed a committee of prominent citizens to try to woo the UN here. Chairman of the city committee was Robert Moses, and among its members was Nelson Rockefeller.

Zeckendorf had won options to buy 17 acres of land in the Turtle Bay area of the east side of Manhattan. This property was bounded on the south by 42nd St., on the north by 49th St, on the west by First Avenue, and on the east by the East River Drive. Since the days of the Civil War this area had been a ghetto of slum dwellings, slaughterhouses, packing plants and cattle pens—one of the most unsightly parts of the city.

Zeckendorf planned to raze the place to the earth and then erect a series of high-rise buildings which would be self-contained, or almost so—a city unto itself, much like the Rockefellers' Radio City. For the time being he called his dream "X City." However, he had trouble obtaining the $150 million necessary to begin this monumental project, and his options were about to run out.

Meantime, neither the UN commission nor the city committee had made any progress in locating a site for UN headquarters. At last the UN set December 11, 1946, as the deadline for making a decision.

Nelson Rockefeller convened an emergency meeting at noon on December 10 in his father's office in Rockefeller Center. Among those present was Wallace Harrison, an intimate of the Rockefellers and a prominent architect. Zeckendorf already had chosen Harrison as the principal architect for his "X City." Harrison now suggested that perhaps Zeckendorf's property along the East River might be a suitable site for UN headquarters.

The UN deadline was only hours away. Nelson Rockefeller asked Harrison how much he thought Zeckendorf might ask for his land. About $8.5 million, Harrison guessed. Nelson called his father, John D. Rockefeller, Jr., at his father's Park Avenue apartment and explained the situation to him. At last the elder Rockefeller said he would give the United Nations $8.5 million to pay Zeckendorf for his property. When Nelson got off the phone he excitedly told Harrison to find Zeckendorf to ask whether he would sell for that sum.

Now it was evening. No one seemed to know where Zeckendorf was. With much difficulty Harrison finally was able to trace him to the Monte Carlo nightclub, which Zeckendorf owned. With his partner, Henry Sears, their wives and friends, Zeckendorf was holding a party. The architect rushed from Rockefeller Center to the nightclub, carrying a block-by-block city plan of the Turtle Bay area.

Harrison tingled with a sense of mission, for he thrilled to the idea of locating the United Nations in New York City and thus realizing the hopes of the Rockefellers and O'Dwyer and Moses and other influential New Yorkers. As the architect sat down at a table with the surprised Zeckendorf, he wanted to feign nonchalance, but was bursting with such excitement that instead he blurted: "Would you sell your Turtle Bay property for eight and a half?"

Zeckendorf said yes.

He and Sears and Harrison moved to another table, where they spread out the real estate map. The architect had to raise his voice above the blare of the band as he explained the Rockefeller offer and as they discussed the site. Soon Zeckendorf pulled out a pen and on the map scribbled this option: "8.5 million — United Nations only. December 10 for 30 days."

When Zeckendorf reached this part of his story he pressed a button under his desk and in walked his gray-haired secretary. He gave her an order and soon she came back with a five-foot by four-foot blow-up of the map on which he had scribbled the option. He propped it against a chair. I sat down on the rug to dictate the exact wording of the option to Ruthie, who had her steno book open.

In all the time we spent with Zeckendorf he was blunt and honest, responsive and helpful. After we left, Ruthie praised the way I handled him. Only then did I realize that unconsciously I had used on Zeckendorf the gentle art of jujitsu. I had used his superior strength to control him. I am almost unknown. He is prominent and powerful. I wanted something from him. He wanted something from me. I wanted information. He wanted glory. Because I could put his name in a book that might last many years, all I had to do was give a slight tug and he gave me everything I wanted. Fair enough. He deserves his place in history.

Since I deeply appreciated the help Zeckendorf gave me, I am sorry to have to add that when I finished writing The Epic of New York City, *it was so lengthy that I had to cut out more than 300 pages, and in this cutting the story of the United Nations was sacrificed. In 1966 Zeckendorf went broke. In 1970 he published his autobiography. In 1976 he died. Long Island University now has a campus called the Zeckendorf campus.*

SUNDAY, OCTOBER 11, 1964 ■   This morning when Ruth and I awakened we realized that after three and a half years of hard work we would finish writing *The Epic of New York City* today, today, today!

While showering and shaving, I heard the radio playing *Autumn in New York*, which seemed appropriate. After barely glancing at the Sunday *Times* we walked into the study to begin working. Ruthie sat at her typewriter desk to take dictation directly on her electric typewriter. I sat at my rolltop desk, feet cocked up, notes in my hands, sometimes reading them, sometimes staring north out of a window of this 26th floor apartment and thinking so hard I really did not see the Hudson River nor the George Washington Bridge.

We took a short break for lunch. Ruthie was so emotional she almost wept. Back to our desks. Tense, misty-eyed, she made a few mistakes. Exactly at 2:15 P.M. Ruthie typed THE END at the bottom of page 933. She charged out of her chair, I charged out of mine, we collided in the middle of the study and hugged hard.

Sometimes I surprise myself. In some dramatic moments I feel strangely calm, like the eye of a hurricane, and this is how I felt today. During the years it took to write this book, I had been forced to discipline myself so rigorously that I suppose I still held myself in. But Ruthie let all of herself out—trembling and laughing and weeping because we actually had finished this monumental work.

We carried the pages of the manuscript into the living room, golden with sunshine, to gloat over what we had wrought. These 933 pages weigh eight pounds and form a pile of sheets four and a half inches thick. Ruthie estimated that we produced about 300,000 words.

Yesterday, anticipating the event, we put a few bottles of champagne into the refrigerator. Now I opened a split, which we instantly downed, but it had no effect upon us. I was beginning to come out of shock, so both of us were venting emotions stronger than the energy that comes out of a bottle. I opened another split and we drank and drank, laughed and laughed. Ruthie toasted me for my persistence in completing this huge history, while I toasted her for her help and for making me a whole man. Bursting with joy, becoming tipsy and playful, we left to join our friend

Lucy Wind in her apartment on Sutton Place South to continue our celebration. The—book—is—done!

MIAMI BEACH, FRIDAY, OCTOBER 23, 1964   ■   Now that we have finished writing *The Epic of New York City* we are exhausted and need a vacation, so we have flown down to Miami Beach to relax. This morning when I awakened in our hotel room I peered at her in confusion and yipped: "—and don't forget the Black Tom explosion!" My dream-soaked mind was still working on my history book.

This afternoon while Ruthie visited with a friend, I strolled onto the beach and out into the water until I stood ankle-deep looking at the ocean—really looking at it. To stand on the rim of the sea is to stand on the rim of the world. Puckering my eyes because of the sunshine, I peered toward the horizon and dreamily realized that far, far beyond me, infinitely beyond my line of vision, there lay continents and cultures and masses of people waiting to be explored by my mind. Which lands, which people, would I visit?

I saw huge waves hunched like sprinters at the starting line, stooping down, muscles bunched in a spasm of expectation, then suddenly lift and lunge toward the shore, splitting open upon the strand, snarling as they retreated. Big waves spawned little waves, creamy and languid, opening like lace fans upon the sand, hissing like snakes as they were sucked back into the deep.

I saw sand pipers stalking prey along the lip of the water, their fast-scissoring legs blurring my vision, birds that almost were caught by the ivory fingers of the shoremost reach of the ocean, little living things existing on the edge of eternity like the rest of us. I stood and stared and suffered faint vertigo as the water inhaled seaward, tugging at my ankles, luring me back into that brine from which all of us came, erasing my footprints, depositing seaweed at my feet. I mused that I must again read *The Sea Around Us* by Rachel Carson, then winced with the realization that she is dead. I know nothing about the ocean. When I was 16 years old I knew all the answers to everything. Now I know I know nothing. Life, the world, the universe, everything, is much more complex than I had imagined. Chinese boxes within Chinese boxes. My ignorance is as limitless as the cosmos itself.

Along the beach I saw more of those blue air-puffed creatures Ruthie and I previously had noted. What are they? Some form of marine life, of course, but I don't know what. Overhead there now came pelicans, pinned to the wind, flying in military formation just above the surface of the water like bombers on submarine patrol. I stood in the hem of the sea, a nothing, a human grain of sand, just one among billions of people, my heart hushed in awe by the enormity and mystery of this world, this cosmos, suddenly saddened by the thought that others and I live in eye-batting brevity, while the ocean rolls and heaves and bashes at distant shores forever and ever, Amen.

1965

My wife died of a heart attack on August 4, 1965.

It happened so fast and I hurt so much that I suffered writer's block for the first and only time in my life. My daughter Sandy, then 22 years old, flew in from California. She adored her stepmother Ruthie. After the funeral Sandy stayed to take care of me.

Ruthie had helped me write The Epic of New York City *and now I had a contract with a book publisher, but had been asked to pare the manuscript down from 1,000 pages to 600 pages. This meant I would have to rewrite the entire book. But, as I told my daughter, I simply was unable to write. Not even my diary.*

Alarm in her eyes, Sandy said my entire life was based on writing. I said I knew, but . . . Sandy said I owed it to Ruthie to get our book into print. I said yes but . . . After Sandy flew back to California I realized she was right, that I did owe it to Ruthie to finish the book. Before I could do that, though, I knew that I could overcome writer's block only by resuming my diary.

On August 21 I took a deep breath, sat down at my typewriter, began pounding the keys and in one stressful afternoon told the story of my wife's death. Then I collapsed. I had written without any thought of style. It felt like slapping raw hunks of beef onto a butcher's block.

My half brother, Jack, and his wife, Virginia, had come here with their two small children.

Here is what I wrote:

WEDNESDAY, AUGUST 4, 1965   ▓   Jinny came to our apartment this morning with the children. Jack had gone to Long Island on business. Ruthie was awake when the visitors arrived. Wearing pajamas, she walked from her bed to the chaise lounge. Three days ago she felt exhausted and massaged the fourth finger of her left hand, which alarmed me.

After all, ten months after we met she had a heart attack that almost killed her, one that kept her in a hospital a long time. This time, over her protests, I called our family doctor, who confirmed my suspicion that indeed she had suffered an acute attack of angina pectoris. He said if she were no better within a couple of days he would put her in the hospital again. Meantime, he prescribed medicine and warned Ruthie that she had to remain quiet, very quiet. When she shrugged off his warning, sternly he said she had the choice of obeying his orders or killing herself.

I served orange juice, coffee and doughnuts to Ruthie, Jinny and her kids. When they left to go sightseeing, I ordered Ruthie to remain in the chaise and put everything she needed within easy reach. Then I went into the study to write.

In the early part of the afternoon I sat near Ruthie in a chair beside our western window, overlooking the Hudson River and New Jersey. I read the newspapers to her and we chatted. Her sister, Ann Goldschmidt, arrived about 4 P.M. with flowers for Ruth. As the sisters chatted I was glad to note that my wife was alert and bright-eyed. Ann said Sol had told her to stay only 15 minutes, but Ruthie was so animated that Annie remained an hour.

After Ann left I said to Ruthie, "Honey, you've been sitting on your can all day. Maybe you'd like to get up and walk across the floor?"

To my surprise, she smiled, shook her head and replied: "I don't think so, Eddie."

About 5:30 P.M. Jinny returned with the kids and told us about their day of sightseeing. From time to time Ruthie's right hand fluttered up to her chest. I watched nervously. As Jinny was about to leave, Ruthie tried to say something—but couldn't. She sat in a kind of a daze, a smile trembling on her lips.

I jumped up, ran across the room, got a green pill the doctor had prescribed, ran into the bathroom for a glass of water, darted back. When I handed her the pill she pantomimed she was unable to swallow anything. Jinny and I sat with frozen muscles, watching Ruthie. In a few moments she smiled up at me, so I gave her the pill and held her head as she swallowed it. With the reflex of a reporter I glanced at the clock by my bed. The time was 6:05 P.M.

Ruthie's hand flew to her chest again.

"Do you hurt a lot?" I asked.

She nodded yes.

I ran into the study, grabbed the phone, called our doctor. What I got was a voice saying he was out of town, but if I needed a doctor I could call Dr. R.—whom I did not know. Calling him, I identified myself, said my wife was having a heart attack and I wanted him here immediately.

"I can get there in thirty minutes," he said.

"Now!" I barked. "I want you here *now!*"

The doctor promised to hurry. I told him to bring everything necessary to treat a person suffering from a heart attack, then I hung up and ran back into the living room.

Ruthie was in such agony that she had drawn her knees up against her chest. Jinny, who is a registered nurse, was comforting her. Then Jinny ordered her two children to go to their room in this apartment hotel and I caught a glimpse of their frightened faces. Ruthie twisted and turned in the chaise. She was unable to speak. She had trouble breathing. The color drained from her face, leaving her cheeks grayish green. I felt so sorry for her that my chest hurt. I held her hand. Every few seconds Ruthie would open eyes that had been bunched in pain, then stare about, looking for me. When she was able to focus on my face she would smile a tiny smile.

I sobbed. Jinny, who held her fingers on the pulse in Ruthie's wrist, stared me in the face and ordered me with her eyes to remain in control of myself. Suddenly Jack was in the room. I ran back to the study to call our hotel switchboard operator and tell her to get a doctor, any doctor! When I got back in the front room I saw that Jack had brought Ruthie a bouquet of flowers that now lay across her lap. Wanting no weight on her body, I threw the flowers into a chair.

Even in her agony Ruthie had greater presence of mind than I. "There's oxygen," she gasped, "in my closet."

I shouted to Jack to look for it. Soon he found a small oxygen tank and a plastic mask. With trembling fingers I held the mask over my wife's nose. Jinny rhythmically pushed a lever that activated the tank and sent oxygen gushing into the mask in tempo with Ruthie's breathing. Everything was happening fast, chaotically.

Jack is an engineer. Huskily he said, "That tank won't last long. I'm going out for another one!" He dashed out.

Jinny and I worked over Ruthie. Sweat rolled down her forehead, cheeks and chest. I wiped her with my handkerchief, kissed her forehead, stroked her hair. I whispered: "I'll take care of you, darling! The doctor is on his way. Jack has gone out for more oxygen . . . I'll take care of you . . . I'll take care of you . . . I love you, sweet Ruthie!"

With effort, she lifted a fluttering hand for me to hold. Her grasp was weak. I was more frightened than ever before in my life. Jinny softly suggested I find woolen pajamas or something to absorb Ruthie's perspiration. With Jinny still pumping the lever, I lunged for Ruthie's bureau and pulled out pajamas—or something—which Jinny and I tucked over Ruthie's heaving chest.

Jack was back. Jinny and I pulled the oxygen tank away from Ruthie and held a second mask to her face. Jack yelled that we weren't pushing the plunger in tempo with her breathing. He bent over her. I bolted for the study and again called Grace on the switchboard.

"Get a doctor!" I screamed. "Get a doctor! I don't care where the hell you get him! Just get a doctor! My wife is having a heart attack and she's dying!"

"Mr. Ellis," said Grace, "I just can't find a doctor!"

"Call the police!" I bellowed. "Get the emergency crew! Get oxygen, lots of oxygen! Get it!"

Grace performed magnificently.

I ran back to the front room. Ruthie's color was hideous. Her throat was contracting. She was about to vomit. I ran to the kitchen and got a pot. I handed it to Jinny. I knew the sight of Ruthie vomiting would make me vomit, so I looked away, my face quivering.

I whimpered. Jinny shot me another look. She is a dear lady. I managed to control myself. Jinny was feeling Ruthie's pulse in the wrist, then in the ankle. My wife was gasping. She almost died in that contour chair. Her eyes were closed and her skin was the color of death. Gray. She did not vomit. I took her hand again. I was afraid the second oxygen tank would not last long enough.

Then the cops arrived. Four of them. They tip-toed into the room.

"Over here!" I yelled.

They had a huge oxygen tank, which made me feel better.

In only a second or two a burly cop had another mask on Ruthie's face. He had no place to sit. She lay on the left side of the chair, her dear legs dangling. Jinny gently swung them back onto the footrest. I urged the cop to sit down on the right side of the chair and he did. The big oxygen tank hissed louder than the small ones we had been using.

I sat on an end table to the left of my wife and held her hand. The oxygen brought her back to consciousness. She opened her eyes. The first thing she did was to gaze into my eyes. Then she smiled at me. I tried to smile back. She looked to her right and was surprised to see a policeman. A certain look entered her hazel eyes.

"Gentlemen," I said to the cops, "my wife is trying to thank you for helping her."

She smiled again and nodded ever so slightly.

In the pit of her agony all she did was groan a couple of times. I would have been screaming. Leaving her with the cop, I again ran into the study and snatched up the phone and screamed at Grace to get a doctor.

"He's here!" Jack shouted.

I ran back to the front room. There was Dr. R.—young and slim and grave of face. Then I was surprised to see a white-jacketed ambulance driver standing there impatiently. He muttered that he couldn't tie up his ambulance any longer. Did I want him to take my wife to Knickerbocker Hospital?

"No!" I snapped. "St. Luke's! . . . But we're not going to move her until the doctor says so!"

The doctor worked too slowly to please me. Ruthie was in extreme agony. Now she vomited. Too fast for Jinny and the doctor, she vomited all over the end table on which I had been sitting. Jinny mopped up.

To the doctor I shouted: "Give her something! Give her a shot!"

He took out a syringe and pulled Ruthie's pajamas away from her right hip. I turned my head. He plunged the needle into her flesh.

I whimpered: "God! . . . God! . . . God!"

I doubt whether she heard me. The doctor said something to her I didn't hear. She kept on writhing in pain. I begged the doctor to give her another shot. He said he'd have to wait five minutes. After taking another close look at her, though, he prepared another syringe.

He told the ambulance attendants to get ready. They didn't have a stretcher. They had one waiting on the 25th floor. The elevators rise only to the 25th floor, and our apartment is on the 26th floor. The men said they would carry her down that one flight in her chair. I grabbed an aluminum terrace chair with a yellow facing—one I call Ruthie's Golden Throne. It was light. The ambulance men said it was just the thing. I tossed it into the middle of the floor. There were so many people in the room and so much was happening that things were getting knocked over.

The men lifted Ruthie's limp figure into the terrace chair and began carrying it down our long corridor, lined with book shelves. Books thudded to the floor.

"Damn the books!" I yelled. "Hurry!"

I followed as they carried her in the chair down the steps. They did the best they could but sort of dumped her out of the chair and onto their stretcher. Her face was gray. Jack held open the door leading into the corridor on the 25th floor and then darted past the men to get an elevator.

They carried her inside an elevator cage. Jack, the doctor and I followed, Jack pressed the down button. The elevator door closed a third of the way—and then stuck! I had a horrible vision of all of us getting stuck between floors in a cranky elevator, watching my wife die.

"Get the other elevator!" I screamed at Jack.

He did. The men took Ruthie out of the first elevator and carried her into the second one. I held my breath as we began descending. No one spoke. I watched Ruthie's face. She seemed unconscious.

Lobby. The men carried her across the tile floor. Glimpses of startled faces of other tenants. Jock, my 13-year-old nephew, standing there with a white face. Men lifted Ruthie into ambulance.

On the sidewalk Jack said he and Jinny and the kids had better leave for a Pennsylvania motel, where they had reservations. I stared at him dumbfounded. Surely he knew Ruthie was dying? Surely he wouldn't leave me alone on the worst day of my life? But—no time for words. Get her to the hospital!

Glancing at the ambulance I saw that Ruthie was about to vomit again. If I rode with her then I, too, would vomit and thus be in the way. I jumped into the front seat of the ambulance. Turning, I looked through a window and saw Ruthie. An attendant sat beside her, an oxygen mask at the ready.

As from a great distance, I heard the doctor say: "I'll follow in my car."

The ambulance driver got in and asked: "St. Luke's?"

"Yes," I moaned.

On West 104th Street a car got in our way and I froze in fear of having our path blocked. I hoped the ambulance driver would use his siren, but he didn't. He sneaked around the end of the auto. The ambulance picked up speed. All life had become a blur to me.

I remembered hearing the doctor say he had a private room ready for my wife. It's only a few blocks from the Hotel Master to St. Luke's Hospital. I looked back at Ruthie and felt sorry for the attendant. He was unable to decide whether to put the mask on her face because she looked as though she were ready to vomit again.

We reached the hospital. A man emerged and opened one side of the double door at the rear of the ambulance. I jumped out and began opening the other half. The man said they could get the stretcher through a single door. The men lifted Ruthie out of the ambulance and put her on a gurney and began rolling it down a corridor. Then to the right. Elevator out of order. What is it with elevators today? Down some steps to another elevator.

I started to dash into the elevator behind Ruthie. A man at a desk shouted at me to stay. He said he wanted to ask me some questions. I thought: Fuck you! A young man walked up and took my arm. The man at the desk tried to soothe me, saying: "They'll take good care of her! This will take only a moment."

I shouted at him: "What room?"

"Room 1325. That's on the third floor. Only a moment!"

I let them wheel Ruthie out of my sight. I let the young man lead me into an office. My chest was heaving. Asked questions, I kept my eyes on the elevator that had taken Ruthie from me, and I snapped out answers— sullenly. In a few minutes the man said I could go.

I rode an elevator to the third floor. I ran down a corridor, searching for room 1325. When I found it, I lunged inside. Ruthie lay on a bed. With her was a doctor I'd never seen before.

"Who are you?" he barked.

"Her husband!"

"Well, get out! You'll only be in the way!"

Aware that this was true, I backed out, staring at Ruthie. Her legs were doubled up in pain, but I don't think she was conscious. I ran down a corridor and bit my left wrist to keep from screaming. I felt the hair in my mouth. I wanted my wife and I wanted her alive. In that hospital corridor the lights seemed fuzzy at the edges. Why? Oh, yes! Because I was crying.

Before leaving home I had grabbed a little telephone book. In the third floor lounge I found a phone booth. I wanted to get in touch with Ruthie's sisters, Ann and Helen. I dialed. No answer at either apartment. I heard someone moaning—and realized it was myself. A couple of people heard me. I couldn't stop.

Lucy Wind! Our dear friend Lucy! I dialed her number. She answered. My voice was so thin that at first she did not recognize it.

"Ruthie's in St. Luke's Hospital! She's very bad! Come! Oh, come, come, come!"

"Where in the hospital?" Her voice was wooden.

"Third floor lounge."

"I'll be right there."

I ran back to room 1325 and looked inside. Now Dr. R. was there with the other doctor. They had a needle stuck in Ruthie's left arm. In a gentle tone, Dr. R. told me to go away but I walked to the left side of the bed and leaned down and kissed the forehead of my wife. Dr. R. now ordered me out. As I walked out I turned and got a glimpse of Ruthie through a crack in a door. That was the last time I ever saw her alive. She was unconscious.

I stumbled down a corridor moaning like an animal. I heard a nurse gasp: "Who let him in here again?"

A slim black girl, perhaps a nurse's aide, put her arm around my waist, spoke softly, sweetly, coaxingly, and led me back into the lounge. I told her she was a dear. She offered to get me fruit juice but I said I couldn't drink anything. She left.

I walked out onto a terrace there on the third floor. It was screened in and had columns painted black and I entwined my arms around one column and then another and hammered them with my fists again and again as I whimpered:

"No, no, no, no, no! . . . God! . . . Don't let her die! Don't let her die! . . . Ahhhh, Ruthie! . . . Ruthie! . . . Ruthie! . . . Ohhhh! . . ."

Then I thought of something. I ran to the elevator and rang and when the elevator operator opened the door I said I was expecting a friend named Lucy Wind and he must—he simply must!—let her come to me. He looked at me in a strange way. I have no idea what my face looked like. The man promised.

Suddenly—confusion! People were running down the corridor. They came from all directions, they ran at top speed, and I knew they were heading for Ruthie's room. As I later learned, there were fifteen of them, each a specialist of some kind, and they comprised an emergency cardiac unit that perhaps is the best in the nation. Wherever they go in the hospital they carry pocket radios. An alarm had been sounded and now they came on the double, the triple. Grim-faced men trundled various machines past me.

I ran after them, but stopped at the corner. There were many people in Ruthie's room. One of the machines had been parked just outside the room. It was an oscilloscope with a round green face and a yellow dot of light slowly bouncing along a line. No one had to tell me that this revealed Ruthie's heartbeat. Well, at least she was alive.

I stood and wept. A gray-haired nurse comforted me and then had to leave. A man walked out of a nearby room. He was husky and swarthy. He put his hand on my shoulder and spoke softly to me. As I turned to trudge back to the lounge, he followed me. He said his name is Al and he sells cars and his wife was in the hospital for a minor operation tomorrow. His bulk and face made him look like a prizefighter, but his voice and eyes were soft. He said he was 27, but he looked much older. I kept forgetting his name.

I said I'd tried to reach my wife's sisters but couldn't get in touch with them. Al invited me into his wife's room to use her phone. The telephone cord stretched across the lap of his pretty wife and, not knowing the nature of her illness, I was afraid it might hurt her. Gently she told me not to worry. Again I rang Ann and Helen but, again, no answers.

I stumbled back to the lounge and out onto the terrace. I paced and wept. Click! The elevator—and Lucy was with me. Folding her arms around me, she murmured: "Baby . . . baby . . . baby!"

"She's dying!" I cried. "She's dying and there isn't one Goddamn thing I can do to save her."

Lucy is tall and willowy, sophisticated and witty. Ruthie and I always said she reminded us of "Auntie Mame."

Lucy and I walked out onto the terrace. A light rain was falling.

"Ruthie would like this," said Lucy. "Even the sky is weeping for her."

Dr. R. appeared. A nearby clock said the time was 8:14. Always the reporter. The doctor said that two minutes after he got to Ruthie's side here in the hospital her pulse stopped. It was then that he signalled for the emergency cardiac team. Now he said that Ruthie had been dead techni-cally since—I don't remember. I was confused about everything.

"But I saw her heartbeat on the oscilloscope!"

The doctor explained: While it was true that her heart continued to emit electrical impulses, it no longer pumped her blood. The crew would continue working on her. I asked how long. He said awhile.

"Then . . . you mean that when the crew quits, she's dead?"

He nodded yes.

"Tell me before you quit. Tell me—so I can be with her when she dies. She would want it that way. You'll tell me?"

He promised.

"But there's no hope?"

"There's always hope," said the doctor.

"Look! I'm a realist . . . Tell me the truth: Does she have one chance in one thousand of living?"

"No more than that . . . I'll come for you before we give up."

I turned to Lucy and said: "She's going to die."

For the first time, I guess, Lucy really believed it. I saw pain in her eyes. In a strangled voice, Lucy said: "I'd give my heart to save her."

I wailed: "Now I have nothing to live for!"

Lucy put her hands on my shoulders and gently shoved me away so that she could look me in the face as she cried: "That's wrong, Eddie! You have to go on living for Ruthie's sake! That's the way she would want it. You've got to live and write books, lots of books, for Ruthie! You've got to become a smashingly successful author, in memory of Ruthie!"

I actually smiled. "God, Lucy! Of course you're right! You couldn't have said a better thing. Of course I have to go on living for Ruthie!"

"After all the work she's done for you," Lucy added, "helping you with your books! Of course you have to go on."

Glancing up, I saw Al. I introduced Lucy to him. Folding and unfold-ing his hands, speaking softly, he said he and his wife have their differences, but now that she was about to have an operation, and now that he had seen my love for my wife, he realized how much his wife meant to him. He talked about their two little girls.

I told Al that soon I would have to walk into a room and watch my wife die. He said he would wait to drive me wherever I wanted to go. I told him not to wait but was glad when he said he intended to stay.

The doctor walked up to me. He said the cardiac crew had been unable to do anything for my wife. Now was the time to come and be with her if that was what I wanted. However, he said, he'd better tell me what to expect: She had all kinds of tubes and instruments in her and—

I stopped him. I thought a moment.

"No," I said. "I don't want to see her that way."

I felt strangely calm, maybe like the eye of a tornado, maybe like a reporter. I shot question after question at the doctor. Had the team done all it could for Ruthie? . . . All? . . . All? . . . Was there no hope? He replied that the crew usually works only an hour over a person who is technically dead, but this team had worked over Ruthie more than two hours. No, there was no hope. I asked about her heart. Didn't it still have electrical energy in it? Yes, but that was all. After I had made damned sure that everything possible had been done for Ruthie, after realizing there truly was no hope, I felt my face turn to stone.

"All right," I said quietly. "Let the crew stop—and please thank them for all they've done."

I felt like an executioner.

Lucy and I walked back to the lounge. Al still sat there. His eyes searched mine. Then a group of men and women in white frocks walked past me. I realized they were members of the cardiac team. Jumping up, I thanked them. Their first reaction was surprise. Then each one gave me a little nod of the head.

I walked back down the corridor and around a corner. I saw the doctor in an office sitting at a desk and writing on a piece of paper. When he saw me he arose and said: "The official time was 10:40."

A nurse approached me, holding out her hand. On her palm there lay Ruthie's wedding ring, the one made for her by her sister Hilda. My tears magnified its size. I thought I might faint. I thanked the nurse, thanked the doctor, walked away. He followed me.

"Mr. Ellis, back in your apartment when your wife came back to consciousness, I said to her: 'My dear, you're not so badly off as you think. Your husband and relatives have frightened you.' Well, with the massive dosage I had given her, your wife was able to speak. She looked up at me and said: 'I know this is the real thing and—I—am—not—afraid!' "

1966

WEDNESDAY, JANUARY 19, 1966 ■ I awakened at 6 A.M. and was unable to fall asleep again. I loafed, read magazine articles, took a walk, ate pancakes, bought groceries, came home, began reading a biography—and then saw Ruthie's bust on the TV set.

It reminded me of last August 4 when she lay dying in the contour chair. Instantly I felt lonely, oppressively lonely. I was drained of all wish to work, felt heavy with fatigue, wept. The tears did not help. I made a couple of phone calls, but no one was home. All by myself in this world, so it seemed, I sat in that very contour chair and ached and sobbed and felt irrational. At last I telephoned my former therapist, who checked his list of patients and then said he could see me at 5:30 P.M.

Twenty minutes before that time I arrived at his apartment building on West End Avenue but tarried in the lobby. When I reached his office I sat down on the sofa and burst into tears. I told Lionel that P. had said I am immature because I can't control myself, but he declared I would be immature if I did *not* grieve for the woman I love.

When I reported that P. prides herself upon being a Stoic, and feels I should remain in control at all times, Lionel grumbled: "Dumbbell!" He said the concept of the stiff upper lip is all nonsense, and that I should give in to grief whenever I felt like it. I saturated three handkerchiefs while with Lionel, who said softly, "Each tear is a tribute to Ruthie."

I said I must be mature because I did not kill myself after Ruthie died, and he agreed. I added that had I not gone through therapy with him I might have taken my life and, solemn-eyed, Lionel said that might have happened. Although I have used work as therapy, today I found myself fearful that never again may I be able to work. He assured me that I'll be able to work if I do *not* keep a safety-valve on my emotions.

When I told him that of my two closest women friends, one is out of the country while the other is married, Lionel said: "Well, Eddie, I'm your friend, am I not? And you can come to me any time you like." He did warn me that women will get tired of hearing about Ruthie and about my love for her.

I said I did not believe I am idealizing Ruthie just because she is dead. Lionel smiled and said: "It isn't necessary, is it, Eddie? She was great enough as she was in life."

This reminded me that I had received a note from Ceci Norris, who declared that Ruthie was the only person she ever knew who had *total integrity.*

And then, my voice quavering, I said: "Know what, Lionel? The night before Ruthie died she moaned: 'Oh, Eddie, I adore you!' "

In this excerpt I have changed a few of the facts about the background and career of a lovely lady to protect her identity. If she is alive and reads this book, she will realize I am talking about her, but no one else will know.

SUNDAY, MARCH 13, 1966 ■ I was awakened by a telephone call from Rachel, who asked me to meet her in her Fifth Avenue apartment at 12:15 P.M. We have not seen one another in many, many years. I wonder how much she has changed. I wonder what changes she will see in me. I know I've lost ten pounds since Ruthie's death.

Last week I visited my friends in the city room of the *World-Telegram* and one of them told me about Rachel's fabulous career and the fact that now she has an apartment in Manhattan. I met her when I worked in Chicago, we became good friends and one evening began kissing and almost wound up in bed together. The man who mentioned her to me also knew her and has followed her career. She is so intelligent, energetic and ambitious that she rose high in the business world, had her picture published in *Time* magazine, married a multi-millionaire who owned a sixty-foot yacht, was deliriously happy for seven years—and then he died of a heart attack. At the suggestion of my friend I had called her a couple of days ago.

Today when I entered her apartment I was pleased to find that Rachel has not changed very much, either in appearance or personality. She greeted me effusively and waved me into her apartment, one so huge that I was impressed. Among other things, it has two terraces, each 100 feet long. When I told Rachel I wanted to take her to Reuben's for brunch, she happily agreed and donned a mink coat.

After we arrived in the restaurant and took a seat in a booth I began asking Rachel about her life, and she answered freely. Her father died a few months before she was born in Texas, and her mother moved to Tennessee, where she served as a maid in a private home. In those days they were achingly poor, and Rachel vowed that some day she would become rich and give her mother a home of her own.

Rachel wanted to become an actress but realized the odds were against anyone succeeding on the stage or in movies, so with money from her mother she went to college and took practical courses. After graduation her first job was as a secretary and when she began to understand the way business works, she decided that that was the way to wealth. She is so very bright and she worked so very hard that she rose fast into the stratosphere of business and politics.

Before accepting a high-profile position in Washington, D.C., Rachel told me, she carefully decided upon the kind of image she wanted to project. She wore severely tailored suits and conducted business with men in a brisk and efficient manner, meanwhile keeping her private life very private.

"I became a Dr. Jekyll and Mr. Hyde," is the way she expressed it to me. I think she meant she did enjoy love affairs—but very discreetly.

When she was 41 she met a man of 57 who was rich and recently widowed. They fell in love and got married.

"Rachel," I asked, "since you never knew your own father, were you attracted to your husband as a father-image?"

She looked at me, surprise in her blue eyes.

"Yes, Eddie! Yes, that's true, but you're the first person who ever made this point with me. Yes, he was my father, my husband, my lover, my brother—everything in the world to me! And after he died of a heart attack I've wondered whether I was wrong in not insisting that he have regular physical examinations. When he died my world fell apart and for the next ten months my friends kept constant vigil over me for fear that I might harm myself."

She stopped, fixed me with a wry smile and exclaimed that I had turned the tables on her, since it is her habit to get the other person talking. We agreed that few people are good listeners. We returned to her apartment.

She changed into canary-yellow slacks and a yellow and white blouse. She is five feet four, has kept her figure, has pale blue eyes and sharp features and talks very fast. Because she is a widow and I am a widower, we discussed grief. Fumblingly, she tried to express the fact that no one is equipped to deal with this emotion.

I said, "There is no prep school for grief."

Laughing aloud, playfully hitting my shoulder, Rachel cried: "There! You've done it again! With your ability to handle words, you've summed up in one short sentence what I was trying so painfully to express."

She stretched out on a sofa and pulled a light blanket over herself.

"Do you mind background music?" she asked, her hand at the radio beside her.

"Not now," I replied, "although in the first few months after Ruthie died I was unable to listen to music. It did not seem fair for me to enjoy beauty she was unable to share."

Peering at me, Rachel turned on the radio to soft music, then remarked, "Exactly so! That's the way I felt in my own grief."

She asked what I wanted to drink and I suggested a screwdriver. She poured herself Cutty-Sark and water.

I began talking about my diary. I said that after I heard she has an apartment here I looked back in my journal to find out what we had done in those long-ago days in Chicago.

"What we did?" she asked with a smile, then sipped her drink.

"Yeah!" I said. Then it hit me like a hammer: "Don't tell me you've forgotten that we dated!"

With her free hand she pulled the blanket over her face and I saw her body bounce as she laughed.

"You rat!" I roared playfully.

Emerging from the blanket, she grinned and said: "Eddie, tell me what we did."

"You have destroyed my masculine ego by forgetting," I groaned.

Pleading that she has a bad memory, rolling back and forth in amusement, this wealthy woman fell off the sofa and crawled on hands and knees across the soft rug to the chair where I sat and crouched with her head bent low, laughing and begging forgiveness. I chuckled, placed my hand upon her head and said I granted her absolution. When she returned to the sofa I took our playfulness one step further.

"Why, Rachel, you don't even remember whether we went to bed together, do you?"

She burst into another fit of spangled laughter. When at last she won control of herself, for a second time she crept over to me. This time she put her head on my shoulder and encircled me with her arms. Still throbbing with laughter, in a muffled voice she asked:

"Well, did we?"

"No," I said. "Dammit! But we did kiss and we did engage in some heavy necking, and you swabbed one of my ears with your tongue. First time any woman ever did that to me."

Now the two of us rocked together in laughter.

After awhile she warmed up a stew for us and as we ate, our mood changed. I began talking about Ruthie and at last, against my will and judgment, I began weeping softly.

"Come over here and sit beside me," Rachel said in the softest tones I'd heard from her all day.

I stumbled across the room and sat down on the rug by the sofa. When I was unable to control my crying, she opened her arms and led my head to her breast.

"Go ahead and cry, Eddie," she whispered. "Let it out. It will do you good."

I buried my nose in her flesh as she stroked my hair and patted me with soft hands. Now came a change over this kind lady. No longer was she the crisply efficient businesswoman, no longer the playful unrememberer, but instead a woman who now was all woman, gently kissing my cheeks and hugging me tighter. I kissed her lightly upon her neck and cheeks and then her mouth sought my mouth and, to my amazement, she tongued me. My tongue gently explored her tongue but despite the fact that my caresses were soft she began breathing hard. In that moment I realized that it was likely I could become intimate with her.

But—I held back.

I'll admit that in flashes as fast as lightning, I fantasized about bedding and later marrying a woman so rich that all the rest of my life I could write books without worrying about money. But—

But much though I like and respect Rachel, much though I am attracted to her, I recalled that as we ate brunch she had talked about her home in Acapulco and the need of new drapes in her Fifth Avenue apartment and about the cooks and maids she hires and about that party for a member of the Cabinet. She had not bragged. Success had not spoiled her. She had simply talked about her life, which happens to be in the big league, and I do not want that kind of life. Besides, how in hell do I know whether she would want me?

Now, on her sofa, we held one another awhile. She said: "I feel sleepy." This was not a hint that I take her to bed. Previously she had told me that due to her grief she has extreme difficulty falling asleep, so I was grateful to hear her words. As I arose to leave, she began to struggle off the sofa to see me to the door, but gently I pushed her back down, whispering that I wanted her to stay where she was and drift into sleep. Then I tiptoed out of her apartment.

FRIDAY, JULY 22, 1966 ■ When Ruthie died I weighed 155 pounds; now I weigh 145. I gave her a plant that she loved and tended carefully. Now I feel like the character in the short story called "The Last Leaf" by O. Henry; if this plant dies, I may die. During the recent hot spell I gave it lots of water but today it looked exhausted, which frightened me.

SUNDAY, JULY 24, 1966 ■ Nearly one year has passed since Ruthie died, and perhaps the only change is that now the pain is more chronic than acute. Time, said my analyst, time is the only healer. He warned me that from 18 to 24 months would have to transpire before I would begin to feel like myself again. Well, only one-half this predicted period has passed, and he must indeed be right, for I still feel as though I were drowning. Perhaps this figure of speech—drowning—is as apt as any I can adduce. I seem to suffocate in sorrow and often feel as though I am going down and under for good. On the average, I suppose, I weep every other day. At times my heart hurts, my limbs feel weak, I am listless, and much of the time I am emotionally paralyzed. Because the outside world seems to menace me, I remain huddled within my apartment far too much and only by a wrench of will can I dress and get out of here. But when I leave—where do I go and what do I do? To be in a crowd only enhances my loneliness.

I have socialized with a succession of women, but none pleases me very long. I realize that this is my fault, more than it is theirs, but Ruthie's near-perfection set such a high standard that every other woman fails to satisfy me. While Ruthie was alive I adored her and worshipped her and told her so a dozen times a day, but now that she is dead and I remember her many wonderful attributes and read in my journals of her never-failing kindnesses and sweetness, I realize with a sense of shock that she was even more precious than I knew. The other day on the phone one woman said to me: "Eddie, face it: Maybe you've had the only great love of your life. Maybe you never can find it again— or anything like it." In a dull voice, I replied: "If I thought this were true, I'd kill myself immediately."

TUESDAY, OCTOBER 18, 1966 ■ The editors at Coward-McCann, my publishers, forwarded a letter they received from Allan Nevins, the scholarly historian and biographer, winner of two Pulitzer Prizes. He also edited the diaries of Philip Hone and John Quincy Adams. At the top of the letter he wrote: "Use this as you like."

Dear Sirs:
Let me congratulate you heartily upon Edward Robb Ellis's *The Epic of New York City.* For many years I have desired to see this particular gap filled. It has been done, and done in a way that will delight scholars and general readers alike. Mr. Ellis's volume is admirably planned and proportioned, is accurate and full, and is written in a vibrant, graphic style that proves him a gifted author. New Yorkers and many others elsewhere will find the book a rich

feast of facts, informative anecdote, and spirited scene painting and portraiture. It deserves the widest sale.

Sincerely yours,
Allan Nevins

I wish Ruthie had lived to read this letter.

1967

MONDAY, APRIL 3, 1967 ■ The other day I got a call from a secretary working for Robert Moses. She said he read my *Epic of New York City* and likes it and wants to see me. I agreed to visit his apartment today at 5 P.M. She did not explain why Moses wants to see me and I did not ask, but I felt deeply puzzled.

While the name of Robert Moses is familiar to all New Yorkers, I may know more about him than most people. This is so because when I worked for the *World-Telegram* and wrote very long obituaries about very famous people, I produced a 15-page biography of the man. One evening in 1959 I met Moses at Jones Beach, which he created, but I did not expect him to remember me. Now that I was about to meet him again at his invitation, I turned to my library to refresh my memory of his career.

Robert Moses is an extraordinary man. He is the greatest public builder in the history of the United States. He has transformed the physical appearance of New York State and New York City more than any other man who ever lived. Often he is compared with Baron Georges Eugene Haussmann, who changed the face of Paris in the last century under the autocratic rule of Napoleon III.

For more than four decades Robert Moses has wielded more power than any governor of this state or mayor of this city. Simultaneously he held 12 state and city titles. He forced his will upon six governors, seven mayors and three Presidents, even defeating Franklin D. Roosevelt when F.D.R. wanted to take away one of his titles. He is said to have written most of the speeches delivered by Governor Alfred E. Smith. Sometimes he would get a note from Mayor Fiorello H. La Guardia, saying: "Dear Bob: You're right—you always are."

Moses created a public works empire, employed more than 70,000 workers, oversaw the expenditure of more than $25 billion for the construction of parks and beaches and highways and the like. He helped bring the United Nations headquarters to New York City. He was a prime mover in the creation of Lincoln Center. His unique stature is celebrated in verse by Margaret Fishback:

> The Park that flanks the Hudson is
> A veritable bed of roses.
> It fills my heart with pride that this
> Is Gotham. Glory be to Moses.

Why should such a famous and powerful man wish to meet me? Maybe I found the answer in one of the books I consulted. Called *Working for the People* and published in 1956, it is a collection of articles and speeches by Moses. In the preface he says that publishers often ask him for his autobiography. Was this it? Had he decided to produce his memoirs? I called Patricia Soliman, my editor at Coward-McCann. When I said Moses wants to see me, and when I theorized about his reason for doing so, she became excited. She said that for years Coward-McCann had wanted a book from him.

Maybe Moses wants my help in writing the story of his life? But why should he need me? All I have is a bachelor of journalism degree from the University of Missouri, while Moses is a certified egghead. He went to Yale, was elected to Phi Beta Kappa, graduated in 1909—two years before I was born. He attended Oxford, became president of its debating society, in 1914 won another degree in jurisprudence, with honors. He also attended Columbia University, where in 1914 he earned a doctorate degree with a thesis called *The Civil Service of Great Britain*. He holds 20 honorary degrees from various colleges and universities. He is a fluent speaker and formidable debater, a graceful writer and pungent phrasemaker whose articles appear in prestigious magazines and newspapers.

I felt like David about to meet Goliath this afternoon as I rode a cab from Manhattan's west side to its east side. Moses lives at One Gracie Terrace on the East River at E. 82nd Street. I felt nervous as I rang the buzzer to his eighth-floor apartment at exactly 5 P.M. His wife opened the door and invited me inside. Last year, after his first wife died, Moses married one of his secretaries, Mary Grady. She and Ruthie knew one another.

Mrs. Moses led me across a long rectangular room to a picture window overlooking the East River and Welfare Island. I told her that the small stone lighthouse at the northern tip of the island was built years ago by an inmate of the insane asylum there. I had learned this fact while working for the *World-Telegram* and preparing to write a series of articles about Welfare Island.

Robert Moses entered the room and strode toward me with his hand held out and a grin on his face. His wife repeated what I had told her about the lighthouse. He said he hadn't known that. He waved me into a chair as his wife asked what I would like to drink. Vodka? Yes, they had vodka, and she poured me a drink—very strong. Then she handed her husband a highball. Wearing glasses, he held his eyeglass case in his left hand and used it from time to time to rub his nose.

At the age of 78 Moses still is dynamic. His scant hair juts forward. His olive-hued skin is peppered with the tiny brown dots that come with age. He has black eyebrows, a strong nose and firm jaw. His thick wrists are matted with black hairs. His strong hands have tapering fingers. He radiates supreme self-confidence and his dark eyes are piercing. Today he wore a fawn-colored jacket, sports shirt and dark slacks. I had read that Moses can behave imperiously or charmingly, and now he was turning on the charm. Whenever he smiled, which he did often and easily, his dark-lashed eyes almost disappeared in amused crinkles. Speaking in a loud voice, he flitted conversationally from subject to subject, but never aimlessly, for he ended each anecdote with a punch line.

I said I met him a few years ago at Jones Beach at a party he gave for the Seraphic Secretaries of America, adding that my late wife had been a member. When I saw the blank look in his eyes I realized he is a little deaf, so thereafter I spoke louder.

He said he is buying a summer home on Long Island. Remembering something I'd read about him, I said I was amused by the resistance he met from rich Long Islanders when he was building parkways the length of the island. Some even complained that the highways would cause their hounds to lose the scent in fox hunts. Chuckling, Moses said the rich people out there haven't learned a damned thing.

I laughed and said: "To them Robert Moses probably is the devil incarnate!"

Rubbing his nose with the back of his left hand, he chortled: "That's exactly their opinion of me—the devil incarnate!"

Then we engaged in a wide-ranging discussion of the use of public property, corruption in politics, the danger that some day some press agent might elevate some dumbbell to the Presidency. I did not quite catch a remark he made about the Kennedy family and its lavish use of money in winning elections.

I said I'm surprised by the fact that Moses is a Republican, since most of his opinions sound like those of a Democrat.

Grinning, he said; "No, I'm a Republican, all right—a little to the left of center, maybe—but a Republican. I began, as you know, as a Progressive

Republican, but most of my life I worked for Democrats."

He knew I was familiar with his career because I had written about him admiringly in my *Epic of New York City*. I was well aware that Moses had been very close to Governor Alfred E. Smith, a Democrat. Now my host told me he might have become mayor of New York City were it not for Judge Samuel Seabury, who let his prejudice against Al Smith influence his attitude toward Moses.

I blurted: "But what the hell—! You were able to do more for the city and state without holding office!"

Moses cried: "Best Goddamn thing that ever happened to me—not being elected!"

I said that years ago the Sunday *Times Magazine* published an article in which 75 historians rated all American Presidents. The consensus was that the five greatest Presidents, in order of importance, were Lincoln, Washington, Franklin D. Roosevelt, Wilson and Jefferson.

"Considering your long-standing feud with F.D.R.," I added, "I wouldn't expect you to agree about him in that category."

Slowly, Moses said: "No, I *do* agree . . . I agree that Roosevelt was a great President. He promised too much—Democrats always promise too much—and this is one reason why I remained a Republican, but he was the right man at the right time."

Mrs. Moses asked whether I would like another drink. I accepted but asked for less vodka this time. Not only was I feeling the liquor, but I also sensed a strange mood engulfing me. What was it? Well, in addition to the respect I felt for this man of enormous accomplishments, I liked him more than I had anticipated. Why? As I talked with Moses, part of my mind analyzed this question. At last I understood: Robert Moses was beginning to seem like a father figure to me. All my life I have looked for some older man to serve as a substitute for the father I never really had. Moses is old enough to be my father. He is strong and dynamic, brilliant and articulate, certainly an authority figure. Had he really been my father I would gladly have accepted him as a model.

Or would I? When his wife gave him his second drink he did not thank her, and that bothered me. Then I remembered my therapist and laughed inside myself. So my mother wanted me to be perfect, so I expect myself to be perfect, so I demand that the father figure be perfect? Nuts!

Anyway, by now I had been with Moses an hour and not one word had been uttered about why I was there, so at last I said: "Mr. Moses, I had better warn you that I am not going to leave this room without making a pitch to write a biography of you."

His face darkening, throwing up his left hand, he cried: "No! No! No!" He was not smiling. "No, I simply won't have any biography written! I—"

Interrupting, his wife said: "Why don't you tell Mr. Ellis that we do want his help, though."

"Yes," he said, quieting down . . . Pause . . . "I read your book and liked it and felt you were the right man to help me with something. I have a sort of a book in mind. I've got a helluva lot of stuff thrown together—oh, maybe fifteen hundred pages—and I don't know what the hell to do with it."

Then he tried to describe the kind of book he had in mind, but I was unable to understand. A couple of times Moses even confessed "—not that we really know just what the hell we're doing or where we're going!"

Did he have a contract with a publisher? Yes. One of the biggest.

"But now," Moses growled, "the editor-in-chief is giving me trouble, and I'll be damned if I'll let some little pipsqueak editor think he can change my stuff to convert it into a regular autobiography. I don't want that. I want to tell what happened on my jobs, but I do not consider it an apologia or a confession or a sensational story of any kind. God knows, I know all kinds of behind-the-scenes stuff, but I don't care to spill it in public. Mary and I have pulled together a lot of data and we wondered whether you'd consider looking it over and telling me what you think of it."

"But you have all those editors at that publishing house ready to do this very thing for you!"

"Yeah—but I don't trust them. No, I don't want them, but I would appreciate your help and, of course, I'd want to pay you."

"Oh, no!" I cried. "No . . . I couldn't take any money from you, Mr. Moses, but I'd be happy to do whatever I can to help."

Then I thought, Ellis, you must be crazy! Why wouldn't I accept money to perform a service for Moses? Why? Why? Ah, ha! Now I see: If Moses is a father figure, what I want from him is not money, but love. Okay, Ellis, so you figured that one out.

The unwitting father figure said: "No, I don't want to be obligated to you. Maybe you'd be willing to take this stuff and look it over?"

I asked: "Do you have dupes, as well as top-copy? I wouldn't for one second accept the responsibility of taking any of your papers out of your home—and then maybe get hit by a truck."

He assured me he has copies of everything. I asked whether he wanted a written report from me. He said he would like that. His wife added that perhaps we could get together over lunch to discuss the project. She brought two huge piles of papers into the room and put them on a sofa. Then she said their chauffeur would drive me home.

I walked toward the door with Moses at my heels. He pointed at a carved wooden figure of a woman that was about two and a half feet tall.

"Sukarno of Indonesia gave this to me when he visited me," Moses said. "Tough little bastard! Came with his bodyguards."

I've forgotten to report that earlier Moses had described a visit from Mayor John Lindsay. The old man told me that the boyish-looking mayor stood at the picture window and talked in something like a trance while gazing outdoors. Moses, ducking his head mischievously, added: "Lindsay was addressing an audience of three sea gulls. I know because I looked out the window and counted them."

The chauffeur arrived. Mrs. Moses told him to carry the papers to the car. After she shook my hand in farewell, Moses said he would accompany me to the elevator. As we waited, I asked him how he feels about Lindsay, for earlier he had said the new mayor broke a promise to him.

"Well, I really don't know," Moses replied. "Let's just say I'm hopeful about him."

When the elevator door opened, Moses and I shook hands, he grinned a final grin, I stepped inside and the doors closed. Emerging from the lobby, I found the chauffeur waiting. He bowed me into the back seat of a Cadillac and soon I was being driven home through the streets of Manhattan. Mildly high on vodka, euphoric about my visit with Moses, I leaned back in the limousine and envisioned a boy in the backyard of a house on the prairie and reflected that he had come a long way in life because now his advice was being solicited by the great Robert Moses.

TUESDAY, APRIL 18, 1967 ■ At noon a driver for Robert Moses picked me up at my residential hotel on Riverside Drive. He helped me put into the car a metal drawer from one of my file cabinets; I had filled it with Moses' papers. I also carried a briefcase crammed with documents I had prepared to help guide Moses as he structures his book.

I was driven through Harlem, across a bridge over the East River, out onto Randall's Island, lying between Manhattan and Queens. One of the first parks developed by Moses was on Randall's Island. Now it also has offices of the Triborough Bridge and Tunnel Authority, which he heads. I was met by Harold J. Blake, administrative assistant to Moses. He escorted me into a hall displaying models of public works projects with which Moses currently is engaged.

Soon I was joined by William S. Lebwohl, counsel to the Triborough

Authority. A balding, fleshy, cheerful man of 56, he has worked for Moses about 30 years. He asked a waitress to bring us drinks and when they came we sat down to talk. He confessed he is unable to understand the kind of book Moses wants. I pulled out one of my reports to Moses and showed it to Lebwohl, who said he liked many of my suggestions and felt they would help "the boss." He said Moses is so vain and opinionated that he is difficult, but also so brilliant and creative that it has been a pleasure working for him.

When I asked whether the present Mrs. Moses still works as a secretary to her husband, Lebwohl replied she sure as hell does because Moses uses everybody. Laughingly, he added: "I'll bet the boss can't even put on his clothes without Mary's help!" I said I'd read there was a time when Moses had five or six secretaries. Lebwohl grunted: "Still has!" Then he said Moses admires blunt honesty in the men with whom he deals, but nonetheless becomes angry when contradicted.

This remark sharpened my apprehension that I was about to enter into a confrontation with Robert Moses. Impressed though I am with his mind and achievements, I am unimpressed with his murky approach to the writing of a book. While laboring at home with his documents—those he had sent along with his chauffeur, and some he later had delivered to me—I was forced to conclude that he lacked a viewpoint, a theme, and therefore has no idea how to structure his volume. In analyzing his data and writing reports for him, I had been honest, not diplomatic. The man is paying me for my opinion, so he deserves the truth—as I see the truth. There also is the matter of my own integrity and, lastly, no longer was I under the spell of him as a father figure, which I was when we first met.

In walked Mrs. Moses. She came across the room, smiled and shook hands. Then she led us into her husband's inner office. Moses greeted me with a grin and a strong handshake. Turning to the Authority's counsel, he said he had just left a meeting with Governor Rockefeller and went on to tell what had happened, tossing around phrases about millions of dollars. While they discussed business, I strolled about the office looking at color photographs of bridges and other structures built under the direction of Moses.

The four of us sat down at a table some distance from the desk used by Moses. Just before he took his seat he stripped off his jacket and held it in his fist, his arm parallel to the floor, until his wife took it from him and hung it up. I'd never seen such a haughty gesture. She sat down to my left, Lebwohl to my right, and Moses and I sat across the table from one another.

Staring into my eyes, Moses grinned again and asked: "Well—what do you think?"

Saying I had prepared several written reports, I took them out of my briefcase and handed them to him. He put on dark glasses topped with visors and instantly took on a kind of Satanic look. Because he is deaf he talks in a loud voice, so the rest of us did, too.

As Moses began reading what I had written, from time to time he interrupted himself to bend over some current documents to his left and make check marks on them. Obviously, he was thinking on two levels at the same time. I had begun one report with a comment on the title he wants for his book—*Public Works: A Dangerous Trade*. My first paragraph started this way:

"*Dangerous Trade* is a bad title. I am afraid it would expose you to ridicule because public service is not dangerous in the sense that spaceflights and deep-sea diving and jungle warfare and the defusing of time bombs are dangerous—"

Moses snorted. He jerked up his head. He did not look at me but at his wife. In a booming voice he declared that public service *is* a dangerous trade, and that is exactly what he will call his book!

I had suggested 17 alternative titles, which Mrs. Moses now saw as she glanced over the shoulder of her husband. Down through the decades Moses bellowed that critics build nothing, so I led off with the title *Critics Build Nothing*. She said she thought this an excellent idea. In studying the Moses papers I had found a remark made by Adlai E. Stevenson to Moses: "When you drop off that crocodile skin, leave it to me." Taking this as my cue, I also suggested that Moses call his volume *My Crocodile Hide*. After all, throughout his life he has pretended that no critic ever dented his skin. Lebwohl said he liked *My Crocodile Hide*, but Moses angrily wagged his head back and forth in massive rejection of both titles.

Two or three times his wife and Lebwohl tried to side with me, only to have Moses slap down every idea I advanced in my written reports. Then I detected a subtle shift. Slowly they backed away from my suggestions and began siding with Moses. At first this alienation surprised and disappointed me, but then I realized both of them have to work with Moses day in and day out, while I never have to see him again.

He continued reading my opinions, continued shaking his head left and right, and then he arose and began pacing. Every so often he would stop and stand and talk down to us, then move to a window to stare outdoors and keep on talking, although his back was toward us.

I asked a couple of questions. When he answered, I was astonished to see that he did not look at me, but at his wife or his associate. Was he snubbing me? Or was he avoiding eye contact lest he reveal his anger toward me? Whatever his motivation, the great man was no gentleman. While he may be a genius, he was behaving like a cross between a petulant child and an arrogant member of royalty. I once interviewed an emperor's son, who courteously lit my cigaret.

Abruptly I asked: "Mr. Moses—tell me: What's going to be on page one of your book?"

Caught off guard, he stammered. To help him recover, I tossed him the eight-page table of contents I had drawn up to give structure to his book. Under the heading "Chapter 1" the first line read: "Moses meets Al Smith for the first time."

Glancing at the line, Moses agreed to begin with Al Smith.

I said, "You seem to shy away from the idea of writing a forthright autobiography. In your tribute to Al Smith you said: 'I confess to a settled dislike, I might almost say contempt, for ghostwritten speeches, messages and autobiographies.' I can understand your contempt for *ghostwritten* autobiographies, but surely there is nothing wrong about a public man writing his own autobiography. Do you feel this literary form smacks of vanity? Are you afraid it might reveal too much about yourself? Well, all of us are vain in some degree or another, and your vanity will shine through your book regardless of the form you give it. Furthermore, *any* book about one's life and career is a form of self-exposure. Mr. Moses, what does your publisher say about your plan of procedure?"

He did not answer this question. Instead, he said that in reading my reports he had agreed with my suggestion that he use exact dates whenever possible. Then he added:

"But never—never—never will I write a straightforward autobiography! Rather than do that, I'd dump all my papers into a garbage pail!"

My face betrayed horror. Delighted at having provoked such a strong reaction from me, Moses repeated himself with even greater vigor. Twice—perhaps three times—he said gruffly: "I don't want to say that I built the pyramids and look—aren't they grand! Of course, if people want to say I built the pyramids—that's something else again."

I thought: How interesting that he uses the image of *pyramids*.

I said I had read the autobiography of Trygve Lie, the former secretary-general of the United Nations, and in his book he gives Moses credit for being the first person to suggest that UN headquarters be located in Manhattan.

Now Moses looked at me. "He did? Well, he should, because that's the way it was."

I think I know why Moses won't write an autobiography. When artists write about themselves they tend to confess. When men of action write about themselves they tend to brag. Moses is a man of action. Because he knows he is vain, he may fear that his vanity might peep through his words.

In 1970 McGraw-Hill published a 952-page book by Moses called—you guessed it!—Public Works: A Dangerous Trade. A Newsweek review said: "His overfed volume is remorselessly inclusive: letters, book reviews, memoranda, updatings, speeches . . . It is all too much." Other reviews were downright savage. I bought a copy and was not surprised to find I was not among the 31 persons whom Moses thanked for their assistance. However, he paid me, as promised.

In 1974 Alfred A. Knopf published a book of 1,246 pages entitled The Power Broker: Robert Moses and the Fall of New York. It was written by Robert A. Caro, formerly an investigative reporter for Newsday. His research was breathtaking, his structure solid, his style deft. Caro cited my Epic of New York City in his selected bibliography and quoted from it here and there in his huge volume. In 1975 it won the Pulitzer Prize for biography.

Moses held power from 1924 to 1968. Although Caro criticizes Moses, he nonetheless calls him America's greatest builder. He certainly was the most powerful non-elected public official in American history. He died on July 29, 1981. He is still remembered in books and also by the things named for him.

In northern New York State there is the Robert Moses Parkway, the Robert Moses Power Plant and the Robert Moses Dam. On Long Island there is the Robert Moses State Park and the Robert Moses Causeway.

After the death of my wife it hurt to live alone in the apartment we had shared on Riverside Drive, so I moved. In 1967 a friend found me a place in the Chelsea area of the lower west side of Manhattan on a street lush with trees and bright with flowers.

My current home is on the third floor of a five-story brownstone built about 1854. Sometimes I wonder about the people who lived here during the Civil War. My apartment has four rooms and a bath, two carved marble fireplaces, high ceilings, handsome moldings on every wall, and seven windows—one a huge casement window in the bedroom. In every direction I look I see trees and flowers.

In 1966 my father died and left me a little money, so I was able to furnish my home in Victorian decor, like the house in which I was born. I hired a carpenter to build book shelves in every room, floor to ceiling, then filled them with my thousands of volumes. Visitors say my place looks more like a house than an apartment, while an English lady declared it resembles a London flat. This is quite the most charming home I ever had.

The Epic of New York City *got great reviews in newspapers and maga-zines from coast to coast, but did not earn me much money. For reasons I still do not understand, my publisher did not reprint my book when the first edition sold out. Fred Bass, owner of the famous Strand used-book store, told me again and again he could sell many more copies of my work. Only years later was the* Epic *reprinted by another publisher. However, soon I got a contract to write a narrative history called* A Nation in Torment: The Great American Depression, 1929–1939.

1968

THURSDAY, APRIL 4, 1968 ▨ Three friends were in my kitchen and I was in the front room listening to the radio when I heard a bulletin that sent me flying to the rear of the house yelling, "Martin Luther King has been shot!"

Someone had gunned him down in Memphis. His condition was not yet known.

After my guests left I turned on the eleven o'clock TV news—and heard that King had died! I stiffened. CBS-TV broadcast a commercial-free pro-gram until 12:30 A.M. about Dr. King, his life and the way he was killed. Early this evening he was shot from a distance as he leaned over a railing outside his room at the Lorraine Motel in Memphis. Soon afterwards he died in a hospital. Police are searching for a white man seen driving away from the scene in a Mustang.

A white man! God! Even more than the assassination of President Kennedy, the assassination of Dr. King is a watershed in the history of America. The relations between blacks and whites before King's death were one thing; our relations in the future will be something else. The murder of the Negroes' moderate leader may bring black militants to the foreground, and as of this day no man can foretell what lies ahead of all of us.

The United States of America, not yet 200 years old, may be torn apart and done to death by racial strife, by ignorance. In the future historians may note that no nation in the history of the world ever rose so high so fast—and then fell so swiftly. As I lay in bed watching the CBS special I wept twice. My muscles were tense. At the end of the program I felt as though my entire body was black and blue. This was how I felt after the death of my wife. A person in pain keeps his muscles tight in an uncon-scious defense against the hammer blows of fate, so when he does relax he feels sore all over.

The Reverend Dr. Martin Luther King, Jr., winner of the Nobel Prize for peace, was a great man in the tradition of Ghandi—brilliant, sincere, compassionate, dedicated, single-minded and one of the greatest orators of all time. His loss simply cannot be measured.

On the radio I heard that rioting has broken out in several cities across the land and that Mayor John Lindsay was chased out of Harlem by black extremists.

FRIDAY, APRIL 5, 1968 ▪ This morning on the radio I heard further reactions to the murder of Dr. King. Then, weeping, I wrote his widow this note:

Dear Mrs. King:
Words mean nothing now,
but let my heart try to speak.
You have lost a husband, your children
have lost a father, the nation has lost a
leader, the world has lost a great man and I—
a white man—have lost a friend. I weep for all of us.
Later I received a dignified thank-you card from her, as did everyone else who wrote to her.

This afternoon at Broadway and 35th St. I saw an informal parade of people protesting King's murder and heading for City Hall to demonstrate. Most of them were in their late teens or early twenties, gaudily clad, looking like hippies. Some beckoned to me to join them, but I hung back. They carried signs, one saying:

WHITE HOUSE RACISM KILLED KING

I couldn't march under this banner because it wasn't true. President Lyndon Johnson appointed Thurgood Marshall, a black man, to the Supreme Court, the first Negro so honored. One day when I was a reporter I spoke with Marshall on the phone.

Now I heard chanting: "Martin Luther King died to save you!"

To my left I heard: "He didn't die to save *me!*" Turning, I saw a weak-faced kid of about 19, a white boy, who soon scooted away.

This evening I watched a TV special about King, and also late TV news. Fires are raging in Washington, D.C., and in Chicago. Where will this end? Unable to sleep, I ambled into the front room to sit and smoke and worry.

SATURDAY, APRIL 6, 1968 ▓ On the radio I heard that violence continues to flare in several cities, with Chicago and the national capital being hardest hit. Firebombs tossed into stores started blazes that kept firemen busy—sometimes under sniper fire! I feel helpless. This is war. Here and now war between blacks and whites has begun in earnest.

SUNDAY, APRIL 7, 1968 ▓ Leaving home about 3:30 P.M., I subwayed to Central Park West and 72nd St., where I walked into Central Park to join the thousands of people gathered to honor the memory of Dr. King.

The center of the ceremony was the band shell, but the crowd was so enormous I got no closer than perhaps two blocks from it. Loudspeakers amplified the words of the speakers, and some folks carried radios on which we could follow the proceedings. Trees were bright in white and yellow blossoms. The weather was sunny, windy and cool, with a new moon in the eastern sky. Some women wore spring hats. Everyone was orderly, respectful, quiet. I did not see a single ugly incident.

While I had heard the singing of "We Shall Overcome" on radio and television, never before had I heard it sung in my presence, as now was happening. Since I do not know the words, I did not try to sing with the others. To my left stood a middle-aged black woman wearing a bright bonnet. She knew all the words and sang softly and movingly, her voice so rich and her mood so tragic that I wept. Those acres of people in the park also sang softly, while on the stage in the distance the celebrities held hands to form a line gently swaying with the music. And as the benediction was spoken, all the people hummed the song—a lovely effect.

TUESDAY, APRIL 9, 1968 ▓ I turned on TV to watch the funeral of Dr. King and watched it most of the day. The white people of Atlanta, where the service was held, may have been surprised by the magnitude of the audience and the presence of so many famous people. I was struck by the similarities between King's assassination and funeral, and those of President John F. Kennedy—the martyred man, the majestic widow, the bereaved children, the international mourning.

I felt that the Rev. Ralph Abernathy was a little too full of himself, too eager to win acceptance as the new leader. At the request of the widow, Dr. King's last tape-recorded speech was played in the church, and when again I heard that organlike voice with its message of shining promise, I wept.

I wept again when Mahalia Jackson sang—sang from her guts, sang with torture in her black eyes. Then the masses of mourners on the lawn of Morehouse College began singing "We Shall Overcome," and deep inside myself I hurt like hell. God, may this tragedy help integrate the races, bring peace between blacks and whites!

MONDAY, APRIL 15, 1968 ■ I got a call from a friend who is an assistant professor at a southern university, and when I learned that he and his wife are in town I urged him to bring her here to visit. He said they were staying with a married couple in an apartment in Greenwich Village, so he invited me to join them there.

When I arrived his wife greeted me with a smile and kissed me. She and her husband are much younger than I. They introduced me to their hostess, the wife of a business executive, a shapely redhead with an ample bosom. She wore bells on her ankles because she is studying Oriental dancing. The conversation somehow came around to drugs and I said that here I am, 57 years old, but never had tried marijuana.

Smiling at me with soft eyes, the professor's wife said she had some grass, so now I could try it, if I wished, in a safe environment. I agreed. She brought out a small bottle containing pot. The odor of the marijuana reminded me of the mint that grew in the back yard of my grandfather's home—a pleasant association. The wife rolled a joint, lit it, took a couple of drags, handed it to me.

I was afraid. I gave the professor a slip of paper on which I had written the name and phone number of a woman friend, asking him to get in touch with her, should I become disoriented. He accepted it, smiled, said I might not feel anything after finishing the joint. Always the reporter, I saw by a wall clock that it was 4:50 P.M. when I took my first drag. The others told me to inhale deeply and then hold the smoke in my lungs. The wife, hostess and I shared the first joint. The professor drank a highball, watching me in kindly amusement.

When the women and I finished the joint, I felt unchanged. I asked for a second joint, declaring that I wanted to go all the way so that I might learn what it feels like to be high on pot. I was given a second one to smoke by myself. I sat in a big chair and dragged on the second joint and watched my reactions like a psychologist in a laboratory.

Nothing—

—until I finished the second joint. Then, as I shifted my weight in the chair, suddenly I felt dizzy and found my arms and legs seemed lighter. Grinning, I said: "Well, it hit me!"

But it did not hit the way a second or third highball hits one. No heavy jolt. I just felt weightless. Surely there had to be more to grass than weightlessness. I asked for a third joint. The professor said one reaches a plateau of intoxication with pot, never rising to any peak but remaining at that level. Okay, but I wanted to make sure I got stoned, so how about a third joint? This, too, I smoked by myself.

Then I felt a new sensation. Checking the clock, I saw that it hit me 30 minutes after my first drag on the first joint. The backs of my eyeballs seemed to smart. Not unpleasant. Now came a swift succession of eerie feelings.

Our hostess had begun dancing some kind of East Indian dance in her bare feet, the little bells on her ankles tinkling. Dreamily I reflected that instead of staring at her sinuous movements, my attention kept gliding away from her to focus on other things in the room, my gaze alighting here and there like a vagrant butterfly. She danced in front of a big white refrigerator and suddenly I felt filled with mirth at the incongruity of an Oriental dance near an Occidental appliance. Then the incongruity itself faded from my mind and the refrigerator itself became an amusing object. Intellectually I know there's nothing funny about a refrigerator but—dammit!—emotionally I found it hilarious. I put my hand over my mouth to hide my silly grin.

My attention wandered . . .

I, who can pound a typewriter for five hours, now found it difficult to focus on any one thing for more than a few seconds. However, I did not feel anxious about my wandering attention. Soon I found myself acting out a kind of paradox, for now I began to stare a long time at a single object, then glide to another, another, another. Short attention span. Long attention span. Curious!

The professor's wife sat to my right, her eyes luminous, and I leaned toward her and said something. She replied. I was about to make another remark—but it slipped away. I simply could not recall what I had intended to say. Then I *saw* my comment hanging in space a split second, *saw* my unspoken words, stared in astonishment as my remark whipped around one end of a sheet of aluminum four feet high and 20 feet long, an aluminum banner rippling as though someone were shaking it. My words zipped around the near end of the strip, changed into musical notes on the lines of sheet music, then disappeared like a comet.

An hallucination! Yeah, I saw it. Surprised though I was, I did not feel threatened. I may have ducked my head. I wondered whether the others in the room were watching me, censuring me. But when I glanced up and saw they were not paying total attention to me and my wonderful experience, for a moment I felt petulant. I seemed terribly important to myself.

Still, the others also seemed very important to me.

The professor's wife sat in her bare feet. I wanted to tell her she had the most beautiful feet I ever saw, but it took what seemed like hours before I could muster the courage to say this to her. When I did, she accepted my compliment with a smile. To have her understand me seemed more important than anything in the world, unless it was my wish to understand her with all my heart. We talked in soft voices. I would make a remark and instantly forget it. When she spoke I asked her to repeat what she said. Curious about my motor reactions, I arose and walked across the room, feeling dizzy, perhaps swaying.

Sitting down again I asked the wife how I looked. She replied that I looked younger than ever, the lines gone from my face, my skin lighter. I wasn't sure whether I believed her, although I certainly felt relaxed. Like a patient seeking a second opinion from a doctor, I looked across the room at her husband, who sat on a bar stool with a highball in his hand. I asked what he saw in my face.

He chuckled: "You're stoned!"

"I am?"

"*Stoned*, man!"

So this was it . . . I was stoned on marijuana. Eager to record this experience, I pulled sheets of paper from a pocket, fished for a pen, began scribbling notes. I am looking at those notes as I write my diary and consider it significant that the letters and words are easy to read. Had I written them after three highballs, they would not be so legible.

We were joined by a brilliant young Englishman who sailed his boat alone across the Atlantic. He said he tried pot three times but felt nothing, so today he wanted to experiment again. A fourth joint was lit. By this time I had all the grass I wanted, but to be sociable I took several more drags. At least, that's what I told myself. At first the Englishman complained mildly that he felt no odd sensation, but after we finished the joint he exclaimed: "I say! I must admit that I feel jolly well disposed toward the entire world!"

I turned to the professor's wife and asked: "Has my beech—"

I meant to ask, "Has my *speech* been thick?" I think that was the only time I got my words twisted up.

She held out a tray of *body gems*, as she called them. The size of stamps, they consisted of glittering pieces of paper in the shape of circles, triangles, etc. When she asked me to take one, it seemed very important that I make the right choice, so I hovered over the tray before selecting a triangle. She moistened it with her tongue and stuck it on my forehead—reminding me of the "third eye" or "third ear" mentioned by some psychoanalysts. Absurdly, doggedly, I believed there was some deep significance in my choice of a triangle. Soon everyone else wore glinting symbols on their foreheads.

All of a sudden I realized that although I was stoned on marijuana, had anyone offered me heroin or LSD I would have fled screaming from the room. Now I was learning firsthand that it is not necessarily true that smoking grass leads one to use hard drugs. Although this may happen with a teenager whose character is not yet formed, I am too old to be led astray.

Now my mind began returning to daily reality. About 8 P.M. I said I wanted to go home. They asked me to stay but I said I just felt like being home alone and they smiled and said they understood. The professor went downstairs with me, waited until I got a cab, asked whether I could make it home alone. I said I was okay.

TUESDAY, APRIL 16, 1968 ▓ Last night I dreamed I sat in a strange living room watching a lamb frolicking about on the rug. There is no mistaking this symbolism: Turning on with grass is a gentle experience.

1969

FRIDAY, MAY 30, 1969 ▓ The moment I awakened I realized that this is Memorial Day. This intensified my sorrow for Ruthie, enhanced my loneliness of these past months. Tens of thousands of New Yorkers have poured out of town, leaving the streets relatively empty at a time when I have a hole in my heart. Nonetheless, I worked on my new book about the Great Depression, writing four and a half pages about migrants. In fact, my writing went so well that I finished work at 2:45 P.M.—and the rest of the day stretched ahead of me like a dark and endless tunnel.

I knew I simply had to take some action. Dressing carefully, I left the apartment, rode the subway to midtown and for awhile wandered around there. At last I thought about going to Roseland Dance City at 239 West 52nd Street. Admission was $2.25. I had been there once before since Ruthie's death. Today the most I hoped for was temporary relief from loneliness.

Roseland is famous, in its own way. It has a huge dance floor, is clean and orderly and its decor is not too corny, except for a metal American flag with light bulbs that flash on and off, just above the bandstand. Today it was crowded with people—none of them young, most of them middle-aged, some so old they had gray hair. Lots of them are regular customers who have been coming here for years.

They seemed to be enjoying themselves. A majority of them danced very well indeed to music that is square, by the standards of the youths of today. The first half-hour I just sat and watched, taking pleasure in the overt pleasure of the dancers. Standing or sitting, here and there, were single women, some of them over-dressed, a few almost hags, many with faces betraying anxiety under the scrutiny of men trying to decide whether to ask them to dance.

Some were pathetic in their eagerness to be asked, to be wanted. One woman walked over and positioned herself only six inches from my right side, so close I thought I felt the warmth of her body, but after one peek at her face I knew I did not wish to ask her to dance with me.

I walked away and then began strolling back and forth, as is the custom at Roseland, to look at the single women. At last I saw one woman younger and prettier than many others, so politely I asked her to dance. She accepted. As we took the floor I told her that although I had been a good dancer in college, now I was older and unsure of myself. However, she is such an excellent dancer that soon I was performing with a degree of my grace of former years.

She is five feet two, has a lovely slim figure and beautiful legs, electric blue eyes with laugh crinkles at their corners. She smiled easily, sang tunefully as we danced and was fast at repartee without being a smart-alec. When I asked whether she cared to have a drink she said yes, so we walked to the bar where she ordered gin and tonic while I asked for a screwdriver. Her name is Caroline, her husband died six years ago, she has two teenage sons, they live in Queens, she works as a secretary and she came to Roseland alone. The fact that she has had five years of therapy, I believe, helps explain why she has an open personality.

Back on the dance floor I enjoyed the grace of her dancing, her wit and especially the fact that she made me laugh. Then we sat down for more drinks and conversation. She said that for two years she had a lover but broke with him six months ago because he wanted to get married, while she did not. Nonetheless, she freely confessed her loneliness. I asked whether she would have dinner with me. She accepted.

I said I'd like to take her to an Italian restaurant near my home and then show her my apartment—promising she need not fear me. Smiling, she said: "I'm not afraid."

Leaving Roseland, we rode in a cab to the Crane restaurant on West 23rd Street and then walked to my Chelsea home. Recently I have spent quite a bit of money buying antiques, mostly Victorian, and when she saw them she gasped and cried that they are beautiful. Her late husband owned an antique shop on Madison Avenue, so she knows something about furniture and decor. Making coffee laced with rum, I settled down to listen to the story of her life.

She adored her parents, who were born in Russia, but now both are dead. For twenty years she was married, but because her husband slowly died of a heart condition they were unable to make love his last five years. He urged her to take a lover. She refused. As Caroline talked, all gaiety faded from her eyes and voice. We sat together on a sofa. Gently pulling her into my arms, I urged her to relax, saying that because my wife died I understand her grief.

Her body remained rigid because, she explained, last night she had an experience that left her shaken and disappointed in herself. She had a third date with a man she met through friends and, willingly, she went to his apartment.

"And do you know what he did? He said, 'I want to screw you!' Those were his words. That's how he talked."

"What did you do?" I asked.

"Well! I was so Goddamn angry that I jumped up and stripped naked before him, but he did not get an erection. In fact, he didn't even touch me. I don't know why."

She seemed to be blaming herself for not being a womanly woman and, I thought, consciously or unconsciously she was appealing to me to reassure her that she was desirable, which she truly is, so I took her to bed.

MONDAY, JUNE 2, 1969 ▪ Today I bought *Journal of a Novel* by John Steinbeck. It consists of letters he wrote to the late Pascal Covici, his friend and editor at Viking Press. The act of writing those letters was Steinbeck's way of warming up each day before he turned to the novel on which he was working—*East of Eden*. He called this "getting my mental arm in shape to pitch a good game." I liken my diary to a composer who warms up by playing the scales before turning to his creative work.

This book reminded me of something that happened a year or so after Ruthie's death. I saw Steinbeck on Fifth Avenue. He stood at the northeast corner of Rockefeller Center talking with a man and woman about his age. His craggy face, his eyes, his beard, his black thornstick cane—Steinbeck! I went into mild shock. As a reporter I had interviewed several world-famous authors—among them Thomas Mann and Sinclair Lewis—but never did I speak to Ernest Hemingway or John Steinbeck. Now I had no newspaper, no institution giving me power. Did I dare to speak to Steinbeck? Would I let this golden moment pass?

As I pondered, the traffic light changed and Steinbeck and his friends walked east across Fifth Avenue and then faced north toward St. Patrick's Cathedral. I followed, taking up a position four feet behind the author. I spoke impulsively:

"Mr. Steinbeck."

"Yes-s-s . . . ?" Turning around, he looked at me with annoyance.

"I just want to thank you, sir, for all the pleasure you have given me with your books down through the years."

He beamed, like the sun emerging from behind a cloud.

"Well, thank you! Thank you! Thank you!"

And he clapped my shoulder with a heavy hand. I felt as though I had been knighted by a king.

SUNDAY, JULY 20, 1969   ■   I stayed in bed all day to watch on television as two men landed on the moon. This event is so significant that I am incapable of saying anything of value. Perhaps this is the most historic day in the history of humanity. It marks the beginning of a new era. Life will never again be quite the same. Human behavior, international relations, science, philosophy—all will change because of this remarkable achievement.

I am glad I lived long enough to witness this event. Because I am 58 years old, I can remember when a neighbor in my home town used a kitchen match to light the carbide headlights in his car, when my grandmother used kerosene lamps, the thrill I felt at the age of 24 when I took my first airplane ride in a single-wing plane.

Now I have lived long enough to see two American astronauts actually walk upon the moon. During my own lifetime, science and technology have developed faster than in all the previous ages of man. Along with billions of other people I am a beneficiary or victim—we cannot yet be sure which it is—of this explosion of knowledge. Never again can a single man such as Aristotle or Francis Bacon know all there is to know.

Now, weighed down with trillions of facts, we are being suffocated by data. We may die for want of synthesis. The generalist is losing power to the specialist, the layman to the scientist. I am afraid our fate lies in the hands of those who worship matter while ignoring spirit. Means are befouling ends. We do some things just because technically it is possible to do them, not because it is desirable that they should be done.

So we have put two men on the moon—but *why*? Will this help us understand the origin of the cosmos and life itself? Is this the first step toward interplanetary travel? Why should anyone wish to go to another planet? Today's moon landing has given us more questions than answers.

Nowadays every answer breeds a dozen new questions. Is this 20th century—as Oswald Spengler believed—a Faustian age, with man selling his soul to Satan for technology he doesn't need?

I kept my TV set tuned to CBS-TV and Walter Cronkite. In mid-afternoon, riding in a lunar module, Neil A. Armstrong and Colonel Edwin (Buzz) Aldrin, Jr., brought their craft close to the surface of the moon and I stared at the TV screen, my palms wet, holding my breath, sometimes gasping in fear, until they actually touched down at 4:17 P.M. Cronkite kept saying breathlessly: "Oh, boy! Oh, boy!" At the moment of touchdown he was speechless.

The next great moment came at 10:56 P.M. as a TV camera outside the craft showed Armstrong climbing down and putting his left foot upon the moon. My mind reeled. The fact of his presence on the moon, the fact that I was seeing it as it happened—this was too much to absorb. After Aldrin joined Armstrong and after they put a TV camera 50 feet away, I watched as they carefully tested the surface of the moon, adjusted to the fact that the moon has only one-sixth the gravity of earth, began bouncing around like skylarking schoolboys.

I saw them, I heard them, I listened as President Nixon congratulated them—but I was unable to absorb all that was happening. My brain felt like a fuse that has been blown due to an overload of electricity. William James said the human mind is a kind of filter. Every second of one's life a shower of stimuli impinge upon the individual. If the mind did not function like a sieve, sorting out stimuli and letting only a few reach the brain, one would go mad because of overload.

This is how I felt today, and I believe that something of the same sort was experienced by the 600 million other people said to have been watching. I tried to identify the essence of this event, but couldn't. I do not even suppose I will live long enough or become wise enough to understand all of this historic event. My mind is too puny, the occasion too monumental.

TUESDAY, AUGUST 5, 1969 ▪ Ruthie died four years ago yesterday. This morning when I awakened I felt a sense of relief because I had not fallen apart on that dreaded anniversary. Today's *New York Times* had a feature article about poet Conrad Aiken, who became 80 years old today, and it quoted the last lines of one of his poems:

> Separate we come. Separate go.
> And this be it known is all that
> we know.

This comment is like one made by another poet, Edwin Arlington Robinson:

> It's all nothing.
> It's all a world where bugs and emperors
> Go singularly back to
> The same dust.

I have copied a paragraph about grief written by Robert Payne in his biography of Lenin:

> When a man suffers a death in the family, it sometimes happens that he spends the rest of his life at the mercy of his grief. He goes through the motions of living, he marries, brings up children, pursues his ambitions, gives every appearance of leading a normal life, while some part of him remains stunned and nerveless.

SUNDAY, DECEMBER 21, 1969 ■ Today I read *The Man From Monticello: An Intimate Life of Thomas Jefferson*, written by Thomas Fleming. When Jefferson's wife died in 1782 at the age of 33, he lost consciousness and for several weeks his friends feared he might go mad. There is some consolation in the knowledge that I am not the only man almost killed by grief.

1970

FRIDAY, MAY 8, 1970 ■ Today I received the first copy of my third book called *A Nation in Torment: The Great American Depression, 1929–1939*. It is 576 pages long and is published by Coward-McCann.

KEWANEE, WEDNESDAY, MAY 19, 1970 ■ I have returned to Kewanee, the town in which I was born, so that I might visit my mother. I had not seen her in almost three years. Now she is 84 years old, hard of hearing and almost blind. For the first time in my life I heard her swear. She said, "It's hell to be old!"

With us was my sister Doris. Our conversation came around to Miss Molly Peterson, who taught me history when I was in the seventh grade. I always have liked her. When I asked whether she is still alive, Mother said yes, that she is about 87 years old, totally blind and so crippled she is confined to a wheelchair in the hospital. I said I'd like to see her. Doris offered to drive me there.

A nurse led me into Miss Peterson's room and left me alone with her.

She was a pathetic figure: A lump of flesh huddled in a wheelchair, her eyes sightless, her head hanging down.

Approaching her, I said, "Miss Peterson, I don't expect you to remember me, but my name is Edward Ellis, and when I was in the—"

"I remember you, Edward," she said in a muffled voice.

I thought she was just being diplomatic, but then she added: "And I remember your sisters—Kathryn, Frances and Doris."

"Well, I'll—!"

I was at a loss for words. Despite her extreme age, her mind still is keen. Stepping closer, I took her right hand in both of my hands.

"I'm surprised and delighted that you remember us, Miss Peterson. When my mother told me you were in the hospital I wanted to come see you because I have something to say to you: You were my favorite teacher. You were an exciting teacher. You brought history alive for all of us. I can recall that when you were teaching us about George Washington crossing the Delaware, you had us kids place chairs at the front of the room to simulate his boat—and that helped me get the feel of that historic event.

"Well, Miss Peterson, I want you to know that you inspired me, that you generated my interest in history. Now I am an historian. I have written two long narrative histories, one about New York City, the other about the Great Depression. Just recently my history of the Depression won a major literary award, and I could not have done this without you, Miss Peterson. I just had to stop by to thank you—and I do thank you! Very much!"

Before I could stop her, she kissed my hand.

I walked away choking on tears.

NEW YORK, SATURDAY, JUNE 27, 1970 ■ I was asleep. The phone rang. I fumbled for the receiver and heard the voice of my editor at Coward-McCann, Mrs. Patricia Soliman, a very excited Pat. She said today's *New York Times* has a rave review of *A Nation in Torment*. Thanking her, I ran downstairs for my copy of the paper and read the review written by Thomas Lask. At first I felt stunned. Then I wept. Ever since I was a kid of 14 I have fantasized about becoming an author and getting a rave review in a big paper, and now my fantasy had become reality. But, oh, how I wish my dear Ruthie had lived to share this day with me!

I made a publicity tour of several cities in the East and Midwest.

CLEVELAND, OHIO, FRIDAY, JULY 10, 1970 ■ I rode a cab to station WEWS-TV, where I was greeted by Mrs. Dorothy Fuldheim. I had been told that she is an independent-minded old gal and a celebrity in Cleveland. When she met me her face was expressionless, but soon she warmed up and I began liking her. As I later learned, she is 77 years old.

Soon I found myself seated at a round table with her in a studio with lights blinding me to everything but the surface of the table and the face of my hostess. Sticking up from the center of the table was a microphone as thin as a pencil. Since Mrs. Fuldheim's show is a public service program, there were no commercials, so we talked without interruption for 28 minutes.

She kept her pale blue eyes on my eyes so steadily and hypnotically that I almost forgot I was on television and spoke freely, even emotionally. Moments before we sat down she had told me that during a recent broadcast she confessed she had wept when she saw a picture of a father grieving for his daughter, who was one of the four students killed by national guardsmen at Kent State University on May 4. Since then, hate mail and frightening phone calls had poured into the station. She told me that never again will she feel quite the same.

During our broadcast she said she felt that currently not enough is being said about love, and I thought I saw tears in her eyes. Heartily agreeing, I said I would welcome an invitation from her to return and go on the air again to discuss love for a couple of hours. Then, somehow, I began talking about the grief I felt when my wife died—and it was then that I almost forgot I was on public view.

End of program. Lights dimmed. Mrs. Fuldheim and I continued to sit at the table in the studio, chatting with one another. When we were on the air she had said she liked my bright jacket and long hair, so now with the show over, I said in all sincerity that I had enjoyed being interviewed by her. At last we arose and walked to her office and when it was time to say good-bye I became impulsive, stooping to kiss the cheek of this short and lovely lady, but she turned her face so that our lips met.

In later years Dorothy Fuldheim became a favorite of Johnny Carson, who had her on his television show again and again. She died in 1989, at the age of 96.

1971

ILLINOIS, WEDNESDAY, MARCH 31, 1971 ■ I spent last night with my brother, Jack, and his wife, Jinny, in their home in Bloomingdale, about 30 miles from Chicago. This morning I dressed carefully because I was about to receive my award. As Jack drove Jinny and me into Chicago I noticed the ugliness of the prairie landscape, the houses and factories along the industrial approach to the city. At 11 A.M. Jack parked the car in the basement of the Lake Shore Club on Lake Shore Drive, a club that was once the bastion of Chicago's plutocracy. The marquee bore the words FRIENDS OF AMERICAN WRITERS.

As we entered the foyer of the grand ballroom I heard a man speak my name. He is Jim Tabler, a sales representative of my publisher, Coward-McCann; he had a camera slung from his neck. As we chatted, I was approached by Mrs. Carl E. Smith, the awards chairman, a pleasant-faced woman of about 60 with a stocky build. I liked her on sight.

A bearded man stood behind a table piled high with copies of all the prize-winning books, including many of mine. In addition to my first prize, six other awards will be distributed. Woman after woman bought copies of A Nation in Torment and asked me to autograph them. Today I signed more autographs then ever before in my life.

A slim woman approached. When I saw her face I gasped, for she and her husband, Terry, are friends of mine. She is Mrs. Ceci Norris, she once was Ruthie's secretary, and more than once she told me that Ruthie was the greatest single influence in her life. Since she and Terry now live in Wisconsin, she had to arise at 4 A.M. today to drive to Chicago to be with me. Gratefully, I kissed her.

Next I saw Millie and Clem Hathaway, who came from their suburban home in Elmhurst. Finally I caught sight of Bill MacQueen, an elderly attorney from Detroit, a kind of self-appointed fan of mine. There were so many demands upon my attention that I was unable to chat with these friends who rallied around me on my big day.

Half an hour later Mrs. Smith lined up all of us prize-winners so that we might march into the ballroom. Assembled there were about 250 people — literary critics, book editors, authors, book salesmen, television personalities and the like. I was surprised to note that I did not feel nervous.

I was seated to the left of a handsome old lady with white hair. Mrs. Smith introduced her to me as Fanny Butcher. I knew her name. When I was a kid in Kewanee I read her literary reviews in the Chicago Tribune. Now she must be in her early eighties.

We slid into a conversation about books and authors. We found we had a mutual friend in Harry Hansen, the author and critic. She knew Hemingway all his life and even now when she goes to New York she stays with his widow Mary. Miss Butcher said that when she was 10 her father made her set aside one-tenth of her pocket-money for church tithing, so she decided to put aside another tenth to buy books. She said she simply cannot understand people who do not read. She resents the fact that the Trib-

une forced her to retire when she reached 65. A widow, she now lives alone with one servant. She said that Carey Orr, the famous editorial cartoonist for the *Tribune*, died two years after he had to retire—her implication being that he withered away when he no longer had work to do.

Friends of American Writers was established in Chicago in 1938 to help two kinds of authors—those born in the Midwest or those who wrote about the Midwest. The first prize is $1,000. Among the writers who had won in previous years were such notables as Paul Engle, Kenneth S. Davis and A. B. Guthrie, Jr. I felt proud to join their ranks.

I may have been more nervous than I realized, for I ate almost nothing but was delighted by the dessert, champagne ice, a delicacy new to me. Jack and Jinny and my friends sat at a front table, with Jack snapping pictures of me every now and then. A *Sun-Times* photographer coaxed me off the stage and led me into a hall to take several shots of me. I was back in place in time to hear the six other prize-winners being introduced; each gave a short talk.

Then came my turn. As Mrs. Smith introduced me, my mind flashed back to Ruth, who made this possible, who would have been excited and proud had she lived to see this day. Grief grabbed my throat and began choking me. I was afraid I might weep but I took a deep breath and won control of myself.

During my 35 years as a reporter I covered hundreds of speeches, maybe thousands, and what annoyed me about some speakers was their self-importance, lack of humor, reliance upon a script, their insensitivity to the boredom they created. I had no manuscript, no notes. Leaning forward, propping one arm on the lectern, I spoke into the microphone in a conversational tone of voice.

I began by saying I was reminded of Bertrand Russell. One night he did some heavy drinking with friends and then quipped: "I'm drunk as a lord—but I *am* a lord, so I suppose it's all right." I said that all my life I wanted to be a writer, and now that Friends of American Writers had certified me as an actual writer, I felt drunk with excitement—but supposed it was all right.

They laughed. The audience was so friendly that I quelled my nervousness, made myself the butt of a couple of jokes, talked about the need for honest communication among everyone, spoke 15 minutes, sat down. Several women approached the dais to ask me to autograph their copies of my book. One amused me with the declaration that I am a deep thinker. Or did she say—*stinker?* Several women announced that they were members of the committee that had chosen my book. Admiration shone in their eyes. Never before had I been lionized.

My friend Ceci had to leave for home, but Bill MacQueen led Jack and Jinny, Clem and Millie and me to the nearby Drake Hotel and into a soothingly dark cocktail lounge. When our drinks came, Bill arose and, in his best courtroom manner, asked the others to get to their feet, which they did, and then all of them toasted me. I hid my face in my hands, thinking of Ruthie.

FRIDAY, APRIL 2, 1971 ■ Again I dressed carefully because today I was scheduled to appear on two television shows in Chicago. Again Jack drove Jinny and me into town, this time to the Merchandise Mart, once owned by President Kennedy's father. A gust of wind blew my hat off my head and down upon railway tracks 60 feet below. Finding a ladder there, I climbed down to retrieve it, my brother laughing that I am pretty agile for a 60-year-old guy.

We entered the huge building and rode an elevator to the 19th floor and walked into an NBC suite. Soon I was being made up for color television. Then we were led into a studio where the host, Irving Kupcinet, was interviewing Black Panther leader Huey Newton. Tall and handsome, Newton wore a para-military uniform, carried an officer's swagger stick and behaved outrageously.

He was rude to another black man on the show, Jay Parker, who wore an American flag pin in his lapel and is associated with something called Young Americans for Freedom. Newton pretended Parker did not even exist. Newton's followers near me in the rear of the studio sneered at Parker and whisperingly called him "Mickey Mouse." At the end of the taping session Newton strode back to his loyalists. One of them draped a long military cloak over his shoulders, and then Newton marched out, flicking his swagger stick.

Years ago when I was a Chicago reporter I knew the host, Kup, but only slightly. Of Polish descent, he is tall and raw-boned and friendly. A newspaper columnist, he now has a television show with an audience of four million people. He and I chatted briefly before he began his 3 P.M. taping session.

I was one of several guests. Kup began the show with a question about Lt. William Calley, who has just been found guilty of massacring civilians at My Lai in Vietnam. Instantly the program was thrown into an uproar by a sneering remark made by Florence Kennedy. She is a black attorney from New York, a leading feminist, co-author of a book called *Abortion Rap*, a fiery and hyperbolic lady.

She yelled: "Americans dig killers!"

What she meant, I suppose, is that thousands of Americans have written letters demanding that Calley be freed. I would prosecute the bastard to the full extent of the law.

Miss Kennedy is tall and lean, has long fingers and long fingernails, wore slacks and boots. Now she launched into a shrill filibuster. I felt she cared nothing about any of us on the panel but only sought to enhance her image with the black people who would watch the show. For the first half-hour she monopolized all the attention. Kup failed to restrain her so that the rest of us might speak. I wondered whether he preferred sensationalism to truth.

Another guest was Irving Stone, the noted author. He has just published his 24th book, a biographical novel of Freud, called *The Passions of the Mind*. Stone, who had told me he is 70 years old, has a curious squint in his eyes, was neatly dressed and very self-assured. Irritated by Flo Kennedy, he made several comments—or tried to. She interrupted him, snarling and sneering at him, and when he snapped that he hoped she at least would manifest good manners, she rasped: "Oppressed people don't have to have good manners!"

I leaned forward, gazed into her eyes and asked: "What is it you want?"

This seemed to puzzle her. I explained that it is possible to learn much about others by eliciting their basic wishes. Flo Kennedy jousted with me on camera, put me down a couple of times, but during a break in the taping she warmed up to me. Later, back on camera, she smiled at me and asked: "Ed, don't you find that it is fun to write?"

Smiling back, I said yes I enjoy the mental and physical act of writing, but when I work on a book I sweat through five or six T-shirts a day.

Only toward the end of the show did Kup ask about my book so I had time to tell only one story—about the Bonus Army and its march on Washington. Happening to see myself in color on a TV monitor, I thought I didn't look too bad. I felt completely at ease. I don't know why, but I am more comfortable in front of a TV camera than a radio microphone.

Irving Stone seemed to have taken a liking to me—perhaps because I broke Flo Kennedy's filibuster with a question. He nodded and winked at me.

When we finished taping the entire show, I walked to the rear of the studio where I found Miss Kennedy donning her coat. Reaching out to help, I said: "I hope a leader of Women's Lib doesn't mind letting a man help her with her coat."

The militant black woman smiled and said: "You're very kind, dear."

Then I strolled over to Irving Stone to say I'd learned the two of us would appear this evening on Robert Cromie's television program called

Cromie's Circle. I also told him I own and have read several of his books. Beaming, he suggested that after the Cromie show we go out for drinks.

This evening Jack, Jinny and I arrived at station WGN-TV on the west side of Chicago. While waiting in a cafeteria, we discussed Women's Lib. I walked out into the hall to get a drink of water and saw a short man with silver hair who looked like Studs Terkel, the author and radio personality, so I followed him into the makeup room. Yes, it was Terkel.

I introduced myself. He greeted me effusively, shaking my hand a second time as he congratulated me upon winning that literary award. This was generous of him, for his book and mine are in competition. Or are they? Both our books are about the Depression. His consists of tape-recorded interviews with folks who lived through those *Hard Times* — the title of his work. It was published a couple of months before mine, took much of the play away from my volume, and now it sells well. He told me he was to be one of the panelists this evening on *Cromie's Circle.* Studs — as he insisted I call him — wore a loud lumberjacket shirt, no tie, and seems to be an original.

We were ushered into a studio to watch Cromie tape a segment of his show. Irving Stone sat down by me, patted my knee and whispered: "God! You sure took care of that dame today!" He meant Flo Kennedy.

I said: "Oh, hell! I don't think I *took care* of her. I just wanted to find out what it is she wants."

Cromie's Circle takes its name from the fact that Bob and his guests sit on a round sofa — very comfortable, I may say. When I told him that in 1946 he and I were fellow reporters in Chicago, he smiled and said: "I thought your face was familiar and wondered where I'd seen you before."

This evening his other guests were Irving Stone, Studs Terkel, and a concert pianist named Charles Rosen. This TV show, too, was in color. There were three cameras. Again I felt relaxed. Cronie is a literary critic, a mature man with a smiling face. He asked Terkel to review my book. On the air, as he already had done in print, Studs called it "an encyclopedic beauty." He's really a helluva nice man. I hadn't even heard the name Charles Rosen, who now impressed me with his brilliant mind. Because of Irving Stone's book about Freud there was much discussion of the founder of psychoanalysis.

When someone wondered whether Franz Liszt was born before Freud, I murmured: "Freud entered the lists later." My pun almost perished in the cross-talk, but Cromie caught it and liked it so much that when he got silence he repeated it for the benefit of the television audience.

I happen to have a sharp, barking kind of laugh. After the show my brother said Cromie enjoyed hearing it and turned and grinned at me every time I laughed. Once he fondly tapped the back of my hand with his finger. On this show we did not have to contend with anyone like Flo Kennedy, so the conversation was general and genial.

Rosen, who has fair hair and brilliant eyes, delighted me with his sparkling conversation. After I told my favorite story about Gladstone and Disraeli, he told us another. He said that as the former British prime minister lay dying, it was suggested that Queen Victoria be brought to his bedside. Looking up, Disraeli said sharply: "Ah, no! She would only want to give me a message for Albert."

From Chicago I went by train to my home town to see my mother. Since she was very old I feared that this might be the last time I would see her alive — and my apprehension was correct.

KEWANEE, SUNDAY, APRIL 4, 1971 ■ The last few years my mother has been fortunate enough to live in the Whiting Home. This is not a gray, impersonal institution, but a big, beautiful white house that once was home to members of the Whiting family. Mother is one of seven or eight elderly ladies living there, each with her own furniture in her own room. Mother's room has five windows overlooking the green lawn of the Congregational Church.

After arriving here by train and checking into the Kewanee Hotel, I walked down to the Whiting Home. Mother was waiting for me in the parlor. Although she is 85 years old, bent and wrinkled and flabby, traces of her former beauty linger in her face. Now she has lived longer than both her parents. I embraced her, greeted the other old ladies, then helped her to her room, where she sank into an easy chair.

Conversation was difficult. Mother is so deaf I had to put my lips close to her ears so that she could hear me. Her sight is so dim that she could see my face only when it was a yard away from hers. Like many sightless persons, she sat and stared ahead of herself. I noted her old habit of nervously rubbing together the thumb and first finger of her right hand. Able to concentrate upon a given subject for only a few minutes, she switched abruptly from topic to topic.

The *Kewanee Star-Courier*, the local paper where I began my career as a reporter, had published two or three articles about my life and that award I received from Friends of American Writers. Some women in the Whiting Home had read them aloud to Mother, who now was eager to hear all that happened to me in Chicago. I began telling her, but soon her mind wafted away. She gossiped about Kewanee residents, trying to identify them for me, attempting to make me understand that Mrs. Thus-and-Such lived two doors south of Mrs. Thingamabob. Since I left home when I was 18, and because I have a poor memory, I was unable to keep track of the folks she discussed.

A small town housewife all her life, Mother never saw much of the world, seldom read books. As she surely must do when alone, she now sat near me thinking and rethinking her life, her lips puckered in disappointment.

I was glad she was unable to see me well, for tears began filling my eyes. Slowly rocking back and forth, her face etched in anxiety, her gingerbread brown eyes looked not at me but at all her yesterdays.

She cried, "All I can do is lie on that bed and see visions of John Ellis and the Depression! I wish I could think of something else!"

I hurt. This old lady who is my mother wastes all her time torturing herself about her unhappy marriage to my father, and about the torment she endured during the Depression.

"I never loved your father," she said.

Softly I asked: "Then why did you marry him?"

"I really don't know, Edward."

There is a maxim that says blessed is he who knows why he does what he does.

"Well, did you consider him handsome?"

"No!"

"Personable?"

"No!"

"Was there nothing attractive about him?"

"Well," said mother, "he did sing well."

Then she added that he had studied voice in Chicago with some famous teacher.

"Well, why did you marry him?"

"Well, because he was rich and because I was afraid that no one else would ask for my hand."

I thought: At the age of 18, you dear woman? I have seen many pictures of Mother as a girl, and she was strikingly beautiful.

"But surely you must have learned whether you liked or loved John Ellis when he kissed you?"

"He never kissed me! Not before we were married! Never even afterwards!"

I remembered my kind stepmother telling me that when my father married my mother he knew nothing about sex. Oh, those damned Victorians!

Years ago my mother told me that her mother told her nothing about sex. What idiocy.

Now my mother was speaking again:

"But before I met your father I did date one man, and one night in my parents' house he slobbered all over me!

"Slobbered?"

"Kissed me."

I sat there with gray light seeping through windows and I looked at the handsome old woman whose life is flickering out and I mourned because she never really understood the life she is about to lose. She has nothing but four children.

"My father and mother," said my mother, repeating a story I had heard a hundred times, "always said I was a good and obedient girl."

Stifling a sob, I remembered Emerson's dictum that whosoever would be a man must be a non-conformist.

Was Mother content to live her life only in terms of what her parents said was good and bad? Obviously. How tragic. I stared at the broken old woman and remembered when she was a young mother, bursting with energy, bubbling with laughter, exceedingly beautiful, squealing and shivering when I, as a small boy, kissed the back of her neck.

She sat and rocked and thought. Suddenly she shrieked, "Tell me, Edward! Tell me why it is that I have suffered all my life? I tried to be good. I tried to do everything my parents wanted me to do. I tried to be a good wife and mother—but everything went wrong. Tell me! What did I do wrong?"

Paralyzed by pity, my throat hardening, blinking back tears, I wished with all my heart that I were wise enough to be able to say something to comfort my mother. One thought did occur to me, but she is too old to understand it. I thought, the only kind of success I recognize is that of the person who becomes his true self. Much though I yearn to become a famous author, I prefer to know myself and love myself. Mother never found out who she is. She let her parents identify her. She never learned that it is in the nature of nature for the offspring to outgrow the parents by becoming himself or herself.

Since I myself am now a parent, I have the right to declare that the child owes his parents nothing, while owing everything to his own children. Such is the law of psychological and social progression, each generation nurturing the succeeding generation. I learned this concept a year or so ago when I read that George Washington did not love his mother.

The very best I can hope for my dear daughter Sandra is that she will find her genuine self. She owes me nothing. I owe her everything. Most of all, I owe it to her to let her develop in her unique way. Mother never understood any of these things and now she was waiting for some answer from me, since her questions had been genuine, not rhetorical.

I stammered something to the effect that perhaps everyone feels he has been a failure, and must learn to forgive himself. Mother did not seem to hear my reply. Slowly she said, "Edward, lately I have been thinking about you. There has been so much in the paper about your life as a reporter and now as an author, and I find there is very little I knew at the time of your career—or perhaps my memory fails me. It may be that I had two little girls to care for, and poor health and home worries to think about. I am so sorry that I did not grasp everything you were doing, even though I loved you so much. Now that my life is nearly over, I begin to realize I did not have the brains to comprehend what my children were doing while away from me. I feel I have been a failure! Forgive me! Please forgive me!"

I bit my fist to keep from screaming. In mind and body I ached for that poor old woman who sat in front of me, my mother, rocking her way to the grave with puzzled eyes. Pulling out a handkerchief, I wiped my eyes and my hand and then patted her hand as I said:

"There's nothing to forgive, mother. Nothing at all to forgive!"

That was the last time I saw her alive. She died April 10, 1972, at the age of 86. Of course, I returned to Kewanee to attend her funeral.

The need for parental approval is a universal need. After the death of my mother I was impressed by something I read in a biography of Carl Jung. When he was an old man, decades after the death of his father, a friend asked what was the most moving event of his entire life. Jung replied, "I can tell you right away. Some time ago, I went sailing on a Sunday on the lake. It was about noon. No one was around for miles and miles. Clear blue sky. I dozed off. Suddenly my father comes up and pats me on the back, saying: 'Thank you, son. You have done well!' "

TUESDAY, MAY 18, 1971 ■ Ed Wallace of the *Daily News* telephoned and we indulged in the kind of nonsense we enjoy. He talked about one of our former *World-Telegram* colleagues, a reporter who won a Pulitzer Prize. Ed said our friend is in the psychiatric ward of a hospital and recently talked to its psychiatrists about Napoleon's penis being preserved here in America. The patient's remarks convinced the doctors that he truly was mad. He wrote an excited letter to Ed begging for proof of all he had said. They had discussed this matter in the past. According to Ed, although I never read it in any book, it is a fact that Napoleon's organ was amputated after he died, was embalmed, was brought to this country and has been sold many times. Ed obtained a notarized statement testifying to these facts and sent it to our hospitalized friend. The former reporter then waved the document beneath the noses of the psychiatrists, declaring that—see! He was not mad, after all. I told Ed he should write a book about his own journalistic career and call it *Napoleon's Pecker*.

SUNDAY, JULY 4, 1971   ■   Alone, alone, alone this Fourth of July, this birthday of my dear dead wife, I strolled south to Greenwich Village and into Washington Square so that I might be near people, if not with them. The weather was a benediction. The sun was a copper penny against the blue velvet of the sky and a breeze stroked the city like the wings of a lark. The holiday streets were almost devoid of cars and people and thereby hushed and almost holy. The city was like one of Prince Potemkin's fake villages along the Volga River after Catherine the Great had passed by, a series of theatrical flats flanking a site where all action had ceased. Or—to change the image—a village in which the vicar had died and the parishioners glided to and fro on soft and respectful feet, hearts heavy with grief.

Washington Square itself was oddly empty, considering the fact that this is a Sunday and a holiday. Two or three string combos twanged and thumped and jumped. A young black man and a young white man threw a Frisbee back and forth. A pretty, painted white girl, the queen bee of a half-dozen black men shooting craps, watched them bang the cubes against a low concrete wall. Not a cop in sight. No need for one. Muted laughter and innocent merriment among all the gaudily dressed naked-bellied beer-guzzling frolickers.

High in the sky five planes ditted-dotted white bursts of smoke spelling out GOD BLESS AMERICA. Yes, America needs a blessing, needs it badly. This Fourth of July is an intermezzo, a lush and lulling interlude between war and revolution, a stressless here and now, a rare respite from strife, a slow-motion perception of men and women and children as they really are—loving and gentle, giving and generous. No ugly incident marred the peace of this oasis, no voice shrieked in anger, hardly so much as a scowl snaked across the face of anyone.

Lifting my face to the sun I felt its warmth like honey on my skin and sensed within my heart a quietude so achingly absent in my months of mourning. Then I remembered that yesterday as I read an essay by the great Montaigne I found this wisdom: "The greatest thing in the world is to know how to belong to yourself."

TUESDAY, JULY 6, 1971   ▓   The more I write the better I understand that dramatic effects can be created by consciously leaving out certain words. Robert Louis Stevenson said that the art of writing is the art of leaving out. Less is more. This was understood by Ernest Hemingway and it also is understood by his biographer, Carlos Baker. Today I finished reading Baker's book about Hemingway which, of course, ends with his suicide. Here is the last sentence in the book: "He slipped in two shells, lowered the gun butt carefully to the floor, leaned forward, pressed the twin barrels against his forehead just above the eyebrows, and tripped both triggers." My imagination supplied the roar of the explosion.

In 1971 I was researching and writing a narrative history about what happened here in the United States during World War I. I was astonished to learn that during Woodrow Wilson's administration the repression of freedom was so widespread and cruel that it constituted a reign of terror. No history school book told me anything about this matter. Eager to check the facts, I made a date with Roger Baldwin, the grand old man of the American Civil Liberties Union.

WEDNESDAY, SEPTEMBER 22, 1971   ▓   This morning I walked to 282 West 11th Street in Greenwich Village to visit Roger Baldwin, who is 87 years old. In 1905—six years before I was born—he got a master's degree from Harvard. In World War I he became a conscientious objector and chose to go to jail for a year rather than bear arms. After his release he helped found the American Civil Liberties Union, becoming its director in 1920.

The past 40 years he has lived in a white brick four-story town house— and a lovelier place I never saw. The living room has tall French windows and a fireplace with heavy wooden carvings, while an even more ornate fireplace commands the sitting room in which we began chatting. The sun-soaked windows overlook a patio surfaced with fieldstones, an oasis lush with trees and shrubs and here and there a bench seducing one to sit down to meditate. The moment I met the man I was surprised by his muscular handshake and instantly felt at ease with him. I liked the informality of his home; the chair on which I sat had a sock draped over it. Baldwin is about five feet ten and still stands erect despite his age. Except for snowy locks over his ears, his hair remains brown. He has blue-gray eyes and a ruddy face that is wrinkle-free but craggy. His voice is firm, his hearing only slightly impaired. He wore a dark rumpled suit and vest.

Since I did not expect him to know anything about me, I showed him copies of two of my books—*The Epic of New York City* and *A Nation In Torment.* He marvelled at their bulk. Then he read the first page of *Nation* and exclaimed that I know how to use details dramatically. I told him the kind of book I intend to write about World War I, then asked whether he knew of another exactly like it. After reflecting a moment, he said no.

I asked whether the war hysteria of 1917–18 was as bad as the McCarthy era. To my surprise, Baldwin said it was much worse. He explained that McCarthyism was concerned with only one issue—communism—whereas several different issues combined to create the fear and hysteria of the earlier period.

I said I felt World War I was unnecessary and our participation in it pointless. Baldwin quoted Woodrow Wilson as saying—in a remark I already had read—that "the seed of war in the modern world is industrial and commercial rivalry."

Then why, I asked, did President Wilson do so little to protect Americans from the violence of super-patriots? With a grin, Baldwin said because Wilson was a Presbyterian, hard on himself and therefore hard on others. I'd never thought of that.

Baldwin met Wilson several times. He said the President was not professorial in his demeanor, but more like a polished lawyer—persuasive, reasonable, folksy. My eyebrows shot up. *Folksy?* Yes. Baldwin said Wilson enjoyed jokes and limericks and could be charming.

I asked Baldwin whether he ever met Wilson's postmaster general, Albert S. Burleson, whom I detest because of the harsh measures he imposed. Yes, he and Norman Thomas spent an hour in Burleson's office, trying to persuade him to lift his ban on socialist magazines and other journals, but they hardly got in a word because the postmaster general monopolized their time telling stories. When they insisted upon being heard, Burleson dismissed their complaints about violations of civil liberties. He made the vague remark that "this is war and these things happen."

Did Baldwin ever meet Colonel Edward House—Wilson's closest friend? Yes, a few times. The colonel was cool and courteous and listened well, but said almost nothing and never took notes.

It was thrilling to listen to a man who had met several of the men whom I knew about only by reading histories, biographies and memoirs. I remembered I once met Bertrand Russell who, as a child, had been in the presence of Queen Victoria. Links in the chain of causation.

I told Baldwin I will end my book with an epilogue stating that World War I changed all American institutions. He did not wholly agree. For one thing, he said, the First World War was "a trial run into internationalism," after which we withdrew awhile from the world scene.

I said that these days I feel pessimistic about our national condition, for every institution is under attack. With the smile of a wise man, Baldwin declared that we jolly well need to tear down all our institutions and then rebuild them.

"But I don't feel hopeless," he told me. "I believe that the instinct for human survival will carry us through, that the human race won't commit suicide. The human race is a lot better than it appears to be."

As we talked we stared into one another's eyes and I felt fortunate to be in his presence, because all my life I have sought the chance to sit at the feet of such a man. When I asked whether he has written his autobiography, he said no. Then I told him about my diary. This excited him so much that he cried I must try to get it published immediately. I said my agent and editor keep telling me to wait until I am famous, but Baldwin snapped: "No! If it has intrinsic value, then it is valuable in and of itself!"

He said that Thoreau wrote *Walden* mostly from his own diary. I added that it was Emerson who persuaded Thoreau to keep a journal. Baldwin mused that perhaps he himself does not keep a diary because he has an excellent memory that seems to improve with age. I laughed that I have a lousy memory—which may help explain why I keep my journal.

I said I believe an intelligent man can retain his brilliance into very old age unless he suffers physical damage to his brain or is crippled by emotional problems. Baldwin agreed. He said he still enjoys camping and always has five or six different projects going on at the same time. Since he is quick to smile and laugh, I think his sense of humor has helped him to age gracefully. I liked him and sensed that he liked me.

President Jimmy Carter presented Baldwin with the Medal of Freedom, the nation's highest civilian honor. Roger Nash Baldwin died August 26, 1981, at the age of 97.

1972

WEDNESDAY, MARCH 8, 1972   ▦   Last autumn I got a call from a woman who once worked with Ruth. She said an effort is being made to raise $300,000 to restore the Chapel of Our Lady at Cold-Spring-on-the-Hudson. The chairman of the committee of sponsors is Helen Hayes, who lives on the Hudson River in Nyack.

One day as Ruth's friend discussed this project with Miss Hayes, the actress said she plans to write a book about New York City with her friend Anita Loos, the screen writer and author of *Gentlemen Prefer Blondes*. When this woman told Miss Hayes about my *Epic of New York City*, she said she would like to read it. Would I please send the actress a copy of my book? I said I would be pleased to do so.

This evening a fund-raising cocktail party was held in the Colony Club, a rendezvous for rich women. At the corner of Park Avenue and East 62nd St., it is a six-story limestone and red-brick building in the neo-Georgian style. Very handsome. Ruth's friend invited me to the party to meet Miss Hayes.

I had not seen the woman in eight years, and from the moment we met this evening she behaved so archly that I began thinking of her as Mrs. High Hat. Instead of leading me into the room where the guests were gathering, she shunted me into the club's library. Two stories high, it had dark oak walls, many lamps and easy chairs, and thousands of books—many matching those in my private library. Time passed. At last I wondered what the hell I was doing alone in the library while everyone was socializing in another room. Then it dawned upon me that Mrs. High Hat regarded me as a sort of country cousin, not the equal of the others; on the phone she had said that some of the city's most influential people would attend.

I sauntered out of the library and encountered Mrs. High Hat, who nervously introduced me to a few folks as an author. She had said that Robert Moses would attend the party. Thus alerted, I had brought along a copy of the book I wrote about the Depression, called A Nation in Torment. I wanted to give it to Moses, who once paid me to work on his memoirs.

Most guests were old and rich and socially prominent. Declining the scotch offered me by a waitress, I accepted a glass of sherry. From time to time Mrs. High Hat pointed out this and that celebrated guest, but to myself I harrumped that as a reporter I had talked with American Presidents and Nobel laureates and movie stars.

Mrs. High Hat whispered that Helen Hayes had arrived. Then she led me over to introduce me to the first lady of the American theater, identifying me as the author of The Epic of New York City. When Miss Hayes heard this she withdrew her hand from mine so that she might grab my left arm. Why, only this very morning, she told me, she had found the copy of the Epic I had mailed to her and she was eager to read the note I slipped inside the pages.

"Miss Hayes," I said, "I understand that you and Miss Loos are writing a book of your own about New York City. What is your approach?"

"Well," she replied, "perhaps Anita and I were foolish to try to write such a book because all we did in it was to talk about the places we know well."

"What are you calling your book?"

I believe she said New York on the Loose.

As we chatted, Miss Hayes kept her eyes on my eyes. She behaved as naturally as an old friend. She said she and Miss Loos have been unable to persuade any magazine to publish excerpts from their book. What a pity, said I, since this is where a writer gets the big money. She agreed. I said I knew she wrote one book that was serialized in the *Saturday Evening Post*. Correcting me, she said she had published two books, both on the best-seller list for months.

Miss Hayes stood to the right of a man who seemed to be the head of the campaign to restore the chapel. Every now and then women and men would shake his hand, then the hand of the actress, who in turn introduced me to them: "This is Mr. Ellis, an author."

I told her that years ago when I was a reporter I spent an afternoon with her late husband. He was Charles McArthur, a merry journalist and playwright. Suddenly I realized that I had melted into the receiving line without meaning to. Abashed, not wishing to intrude, I stepped back a pace and watched Miss Hayes greeting guests.

Born in 1900, only five feet tall, she held herself very erect, as do many short people. She has full breasts and a thickening waist. She wore an elegant brocaded dress with glinting gold and silver threads. Her grayish-brown hair was pulled back and held in place by a little black ribbon. Although she is 72 years old, she retains much of her youthful beauty because of the regularity of her features. In real life she is less wrinkled than she seems on the movie screen. Animated, friendly toward everyone, her eyes sparkled. When I heard her mention some books she has been reading, I was impressed by her taste in literature.

At last I thought I had better get entirely away from her, so I left the reception room and walked into a hall, where I picked up my glass of sherry. Standing nearby was Mrs. High Hat, who sniffed that she had seen me get into the reception line. I begged her pardon, explaining this had happened accidentally. Darkly I thought: What the hell does she want me to do—commit hara-kiri?

Turning around, I began chatting with a woman who was short, thin and dark. When a waitress offered her a drink, she declined, saying she had to drive Miss Hayes back to Nyack. I realized she is a companion to the widowed actress. She said she is Miss Benlian, and when I asked her to spell it she did so, adding that she is an Armenian. She and Miss Hayes live alone, except for a housekeeper. Miss Benlian ate a tongue sandwich and sipped soda water. I told her I admired the simple behavior of Miss Hayes, adding that as a reporter I discovered that many of the world's greatest people are natural people. Miss Benlian agreed. She said that through Miss Hayes she has met all of the real celebrities in the theater, and all were completely themselves. I thought—except Tallulah Bankhead.

Suddenly I saw a tiny woman approaching, and in a flash I recognized her as Anita Loos, the famous scenario writer and author. Now 79 years old, she is a living legend, for she worked with the immortal D. W. Griffith and wrote more than 200 screen plays starring giants such as Douglas Fairbanks, Mary Pickford, Constance Talmadge and Lionel Barrymore. Although she has been writing since she was 15, she never learned to type. During the twenties she was the original Flapper. When she whacked off part of her hair, so did millions of other women.

As Miss Loos came closer I saw her fabled bangs on her forehead under a black hat the shape of a helmet. She walked up to Miss Benlian, who introduced us. Because she is an inch short of five feet, because she still has a good figure and because of the dim light in the hall, Miss Loos looked like a teenager.

I told her I am reading *The Godfather* and wonder whether it is a true picture of sex in Hollywood. I'm aware that she knows Hollywood as well as anyone alive. She said that not long ago she found herself alone in Atlantic City, bought *The Godfather*, began reading and was unable to put it down. Yes, she told me, everything that Mario Puzo said about sex in Hollywood is correct. I said I own a copy of her autobiography with the amusing title *A Girl Like I*, and she smiled with pleasure.

Miss Hayes glanced into the hall, saw Miss Loos, walked out and pulled her inside the reception room. When Miss Benlian and I were alone again I said I supposed the two women have known one another a long time. Oh, yes, she replied—something like 40 years. I asked how they collaborated on their book about New York. Miss Benlian said they had revisited places they knew well, and they also consulted many guidebooks. She added that their own book—and she held two fingers close together, is not very thick.

I was startled to see Mrs. High Hat dart toward a tall youth with a camera slung from his neck. Her eyes were angry. She was about to throw him out when someone said he had been hired to take pictures of Miss Hayes with some guests. Just then the actress emerged, sensed the situation at a glance and smiled so sweetly at him that his pique melted. Miss Hayes, who was munching a sandwich as he lined up his first shot, stopped chewing only long enough for him to snap his camera, then resumed chewing.

One after another, three or four celebrities were photographed with the affable actress. In throwing an arm around her a tall man spilled his cocktail down her dress, but she made no fuss. I held out a clean handkerchief but Miss Benlian got there first and wiped Miss Hayes dry.

For awhile a man who seemed in charge of everything stood near Miss Benlian and me, introducing me to others as an author, and when a waitress took his empty glass he grabbed a full one and downed it in one gulp. Tipsy by the time we walked into an inner room to start the meeting, he began by saying that everyone knows an event such as this is floated on liquor.

The architect restoring the chapel by the river described the work as slides were shown by a projector. Then the bibulous chairman announced that not only had Helen Hayes become the loving spirit of this restoration, but she also had donated $10,000. When she was introduced she stood up, self-composed, and spoke briefly. She said that in this cruel world there are only two things that give her courage and peace—her religion and the Hudson River. Then she read a poem by E. E. Cummings.

Robert Moses did not appear, so at the end of the session I stepped forward to hand Miss Hayes a copy of my narrative history of the Great Depression, *A Nation in Torment*. She accepted it graciously. Because of what she had said about her love of the Hudson River, I told her that the New-York Historical Society quarterly had asked me to review a book by Roland Van Zandt called *Chronicles of the Hudson*.

She said she, too, had been sent a pre-publication copy, which she read and liked. However, she added, she thought that actress Fanny Kemble was too rhapsodic as she described her feelings about the beauty of the river. Then, for the first time today, I saw Miss Hayes turn into the great actress she is—dramatically pressing the back of her right hand to her forehead and striking an arch pose as she mocked Miss Kemble. Very amusing!

When I left, walking down the club's broad stairway, I found myself behind Miss Hayes, now clad in a brown fur coat. We said goodnight to one another. She was clutching my book to her bosom. As I stood on Park Avenue trying to find a cab, I saw Miss Benlian drive up in a long black limousine. Miss Hayes got in and slid to the middle of the front seat, while Miss Loos took her place to the right of the actress.

The sight of Helen Hayes holding my book at her breast has to be one of the great moments of my life.

Years later I received this letter:

Dear Mr. Ellis:

I'm only four years late in writing this letter. I came upon your letter in the drawer of the desk. It had accompanied your book *The Epic of New York City*.

In the intervening years I have read your book with wonder and fascination. I am deeply apologetic that I lost track of your letter.

What a monumental and extraordinary work you have created and I thank you with all my heart for making it known to me. As a New York lover, I am so grateful.

Sincerely,
Helen Hayes

Helen Hayes died in 1993 at the age of 92.

TUESDAY, NOVEMBER 21, 1972   ▦   Today I did something so eccentric that I was reminded of my father, the eccentrics' eccentric. A pianist and organist, he lacked mechanical dexterity. In his apartment on the near north side of Chicago he had a heavy, standard, manual typewriter. Whenever its ribbon had to be changed, he would carry the machine aboard a streetcar, ride to the Loop, enter a typewriter store, place the thing on a counter and tell an astonished clerk to replace its ribbon.

I'm just as bad. Today I had to change a fuse in the basement of the brownstone in which I live. I am so ignorant and fearful of electricity that I broke into a cold sweat. I went to the basement and found my two fuse boxes and tried to unscrew this and that fuse but became terrified lest I electrocute myself.

I left the building with the intention of going to the local hardware store to ask the son of the owner to come help me. However, on the street I ran into Arnold Anderson, the black carpenter who built the bookcases in my apartment. Shame on my face, I explained my problem. Too much of a gentleman to smile at my imbecility, Mr. Anderson accompanied me to my basement, where I left him while I ran out to buy new fuses. He found the blown-out fuse and replaced it and I felt so grateful I not only tipped him but thanked him again and again.

No one is totally sane unless he can laugh at himself.

1973

TUESDAY, JANUARY 2, 1973   ▦   I am so anguished and angered by the American bombing of North Vietnam that I've written letters of protest to President Nixon and our New York Senators.

It's possible that some time in the future some one may ask what I did to try to stop such horrors, and I want to be able to say that I lifted my voice against them. In fact, I'm urging all my friends to write similar letters.

■ Here I am with other reporters and photographers, surrounding impresario Billy Rose in front of the New York State Supreme Court. I am looking over his right shoulder. His wife, the famous swimmer Eleanor Holm, was just granted a divorce. This was on September 10, 1952. Years later, on November 25, 1961, I met with Rose in his lonely mansion on the upper east side of Manhattan. THE BETTMANN ARCHIVE.

■ My colleagues were the brightest, most colorful people I ever knew. Here we are at a farewell party for Delos (Doc) Lovelace in the city room of the New York World-Telegram on October 10, 1952. I wore a green eye-shade.

■ In 1952, I wrote a series of articles about lighthouse keepers in the New York City vicinity. This one worked in a New Jersey lighthouse built in 1862. Because I am a loner, I've often fantasized about living in a lighthouse.

■ Here I am on Robin's Reef lighthouse in the upper bay of New York harbor. The Manhattan skyline appears behind my left shoulder. A picturesque place.

■ Here near Wall Street is a statue of George Washington, on the very site where he was sworn in as the first President of the United States. While writing about that first inaugural for my book The Epic of New York City, I wept. The statue was sculpted by J. Q. A. Ward.

■ Here I am with Grace Kelly in the lobby of her apartment house on Fifth Avenue just after her engagement to Prince Rainier III of Monaco was made public. It was early on the morning of January 11, 1956. I was angry with the editor who sent me there because I doubted whether Miss Kelly would talk—and she didn't really. Nonetheless, she was polite and pleasant.

■ Irving Berlin, the great composer, disliked interviews, but I was fortunate enough to spend the afternoon of July 11, 1957, with him in his office in Manhattan. We drank a little whiskey, I got a little tight and actually sang one Irving Berlin song to Irving Berlin.

By 1957, *my diary volumes, piled on top of one another, reached up to my head. This picture was taken by Dick Kraus, Ruthie's nephew, in our apartment at the Hotel Master at 310 Riverside Drive. At that time, I called my journal* Briefly I Tarry. RICHARD KRAUS.

■ Whenever President Harry Truman was in New York City, he stayed at the Hotel Carlyle. Several times I accompanied him, along with other reporters, during his morning walks. One day, saying he would speak only off the record, he expressed contempt for Senator Joseph P. McCarthy.

■ *I liked and admired President Truman very much. Here I am interviewing him aboard the SS Independence on May 26, 1958, just before he left for a European vacation. When he returned, on July 9, 1958, I interviewed him again, and wrote about it in my diary. It pleased me when he remembered my face and greeted me in a friendly way.*

■ In 1958, Ruthie and I flew to California to visit my daughter, Sandra, then fifteen years old. Ruthie snapped this picture of us by our hotel pool. Later, the three of us drove to Hollywood, where a press agent took us to a studio to meet and be photographed with several actors.

I was so cocksure about being a good dancer that when I met Ruthie, I worried lest she not be in my class. Ha, she danced even better than I did!

This is my favorite picture of my late wife, Ruth Kraus Ellis. It shows her natural charm and vivacity. She is aboard Malcolm S. Forbes's yacht called the Highlander *in July of 1960.*

■ *The bearded young man on the right is the famous actor Jason Robards, Jr. The gentleman on the left is his father, also an actor, although not as well known as his son. I interviewed them on September 18, 1958, in the Hotel Van Rensselaer, 17 West 11th Street, and wrote about them in my diary. My editor disliked my story because the elder Robards declined to discuss his temporary blindness.*

■ *This is a* World-Telegram *advertisement that showed me being plucked out of Jamaica Bay by a Coast Guard helicopter—just to get the feel of a rescue. Yes, I did walk up a cable on the Brooklyn Bridge. That was during my meeting with Fred Bronnenkant, which I wrote about in my diary on March 23, 1949. I did break my right foot covering a subway accident. I still wish our advertising manager had depicted me as a serious reporter.*

DARING
YOUNG MAN

SO FAR Edward Ellis hasn't swung on a flying trapeze for the World-Telegram—but he's risked all four limbs in various other precarious situations to get his story. He's been hoisted out of Jamaica Bay by helicopter, when his assignment was to find out what it feels like to be rescued by the Coast Guard. Covering a subway crash, Ed Ellis jumped down on to the tracks and managed to survive injury more serious than those suffered by any of the 75 passengers hurt in the crash. Walking up a Brooklyn Bridge cable was his own idea. He wanted to "get the feeling" of a feature story about a man who keeps the bridge in repair. Ed Ellis is another shining example of just how far World-Telegram reporters go to satisfy the intelligent curiosity of alert New Yorkers—to give readers the news *and* the story behind the news.

TODAY'S NEWS <u>TODAY</u> in the

NEW YORK
World-Telegram and Sun
A SCRIPPS-HOWARD NEWSPAPER

This advertisement appears in the May 3rd issue of:

NEW YORK HERALD-TRIBUNE
NEW YORK WORLD-TELEGRAM & SUN
NEWARK NEWS
NEWSDAY
LONG ISLAND PRESS
LONG ISLAND STAR-JOURNAL
STATEN ISLAND ADVANCE

MOUNT VERNON DAILY ARGUS
NEW ROCHELLE STANDARD-STAR
WHITE PLAINS REPORTER-DISPATCH
YONKERS HERALD-STATESMAN
PORT CHESTER DAILY ITEM
MAMARONECK DAILY TIMES
OSSINING CITIZEN-REGISTER

TARRYTOWN NEWS

■ *This picture was taken at 12:28 p.m. on September 17, 1959, in Herald Square in Manhattan. It shows Soviet Prime Minister Nikita Khrushchev's cavalcade heading east on 34th Street. I am standing behind a police barrier, checking my watch, an old-time reporting habit.*

■ *Here I am with Bernard M. Baruch, an advisor to American presidents, in his home at 4 East 66th Street. It was taken on August 18, 1960, the day before his ninetieth birthday. I wrote about him so often that he once sent me a letter of thanks.*

■ I loved the view of downtown Manhattan from the southwest balcony of our apartment on the twenty-sixth floor of the Hotel Master. This picture was taken in 1964. I guess I'm smiling because Ruthie and I loved that apartment very much.

■ Ruthie took this picture of me on June 18, 1962, aboard the Coast Guard cutter that carried us to Ellis Island. Formerly the main gateway to America from Europe, it now was empty and silent. On that hallowed spot my wife and I felt the presence of our dead ancestors who landed there decades before.

■ In 1980, the University of Wyoming offered me the use of fireproof vaults for the safekeeping of my diary. While I retained legal title to the diary, the University kept it for a decade. This picture shows me in front of the cartons containing the diary volumes when they were returned to New York. It was sort of a birthday present for me, since this was taken on February 20, 1991, just two days before I turned eighty. CHRISTOPHER BURKE, QUESADA BURKE, NEW YORK CITY.

■ *I became diary consultant to Letts of London, Ltd., the world's oldest and largest manufacturer of diaries, in 1988. This picture was taken at the Letts booth on Fifth Avenue during a book fair in September 1989.* COURTESY OF RITA ROSENKRANZ.

If millions of Americans were to do this, and if a tally were kept in the basement of the White House, perhaps Nixon might get our message.

In my letter to Senator Jack Javits I said that for the first time in my life I am ashamed to be an American.

SATURDAY, JANUARY 20, 1973   ■   One day, a few years ago, I told myself that in every country in every century a majority of the people were mad. I meant 51 per cent or more. By *mad*, I meant more or less out of touch with reality. The next moment, feeling shocked, I thought maybe I was mad for saying such a thing.

But then I read Voltaire, who called the world an insane asylum and declared: "History is a pack of lies, agreed upon." Then I read Leo Tolstoy, who believed that nine of every ten people are mad. Then I read Bertrand Russell and D. H. Lawrence and Arthur Koestler and others, who reached the same conclusion.

At present I am researching a book I plan to write about what happened in the United States during World War I. President Woodrow Wilson himself said that there was no logical reason for that war. Logic, in fact, plays almost no part in history. In 1915 the world was flooded with stories of the alleged atrocities committed by the Huns. Most Americans believed these stories because it is easier to believe than to think. Later it was proved that perhaps 90 per cent of the stories were propaganda and lies.

Former President Theodore Roosevelt was eager for the United States to get into the war in Europe—largely because he never matured, because he considered war *romantic*. Imagine! In the preface of my new book I will quote Sir Arthur Keith, the Scottish anthropologist: "The course of human history is determined . . . by what takes place in the hearts of men." I also may use a line by Carl Jung: "What is the fate of great nations but a summation of the psychic changes in individuals?"

I'm calling my new book *Echoes of Distant Thunder: Life in the United States, 1914–1918*.

TUESDAY, MAY 22, 1973   ■   We are in the grip of Watergate, a morality play of such significance that I need all my will-power to stay away from the TV set so that I can do my work. The day James McCord took the stand I became so hypnotized that I didn't even try to produce my daily quota of words. Time and again I gasped as he produced one verbal link after another in the chain of events that will lead to the White House.

How strange it feels to be part of an era in which there is growing talk of impeachment of the President of the United States. There has been nothing like the Watergate investigation since the McCarthy-Army hearings, an event that jolted me into an awareness that television, after all, does possess great merit. Nonetheless, the Watergate trail was not found by electronic journalists but by two old-fashioned print reporters, Bob Woodward and Carl Bernstein of the *Washington Post*. I saw them on the Dick Cavett show and was impressed by their intelligence and sense of balance.

MONDAY, AUGUST 6, 1973 ■ I dreamed that Edna St. Vincent Millay walked into the kitchen of some house in which I lived and asked to borrow some kitchen matches. Only one interpretation suggests itself, an interpretation so vain that I dislike mentioning it, but shall: Miss Millay wanted me to give her a match, which means a fire, which means insight and inspiration—imagine! I wonder, he wondered, whether there is any known cure for egomania.

MONDAY, AUGUST 13, 1973 ■ On the Op-Ed Page of the *New York Times* I read a column by Anthony Lewis about American actions in Cambodia— and I flinched. Among other things, he said: "We transported whole populations in order to make the destruction of their villages easier. We set up a program to assassinate leaders suspected of sympathy with the other side. We allowed, and sometimes participated in, the systematic torture of prisoners. We wantonly killed civilians. We bombed hospitals."

I lack the language to express the disgust I feel about this American bestiality. And, as Lewis pointed out, "the Nazis made evil commonplace, banal, so much a part of the social order that the respectable people simply learned to live with it." He was echoing Hannah Arendt. When I contemplate the condition of the world, I feel almost totally hopeless. I simply believe our civilization is committing suicide.

Society is disintegrating so fast I doubt whether we'll ever be able to put the pieces together again. What we are witnessing is the most precipitous decline of a civilization since the fall of the Roman empire. No nation ever rose so fast and then came down so swiftly as the United States.

No longer is there a national vision—if, indeed, there ever really was one. And, as the Bible says, where there is no vision the people perish. Ignorance, madness and greed are begetting anarchy, with this small group and then that one violating the rights of others in pursuit of their own selfish ends. Lies blossom, truth withers.

MONDAY, SEPTEMBER 24, 1973 ■ I entered a shoe repair shop to get my shoes shined. Staggering around inside was a black woman muttering to herself and calling everyone a "mother-fucker!" She was drunk, drugged or psychotic. I saw anxiety in the eyes of the three white men at work in the shop, and also the black man polishing my shoes. None knew how to handle her without causing a scene. She put her hands on my knees without being aware of it and without looking at me. She mumbled: "People ain't shit!" Of course not. Poor woman!

SATURDAY, NOVEMBER 10, 1973   ▓   Years ago when I ended therapy, my doctor smiled and said he hoped I would continue to analyze myself the rest of my life. I have tried to do so, and often it has been painful. Nikos Kazantzakis, best known to Americans for the film made of his novel *Zorba the Greek*, wrote in his memoirs, *Report to Greco*, "I look down into myself and shudder." When I read this, the very first sentence in the book, my mind exploded.

While I do not wish to make too fine a point of it, I must say that smoking grass is an extension of therapy for me. I will not argue that this is true for everyone. What I do know is that it works well for me, and Carl Jung said that the *actual* is that which *acts*. The fact that I know nothing about the neurological reaction induced by pot is a problem I leave to neurologists, pharmacologists and Puritans.

Alone in bed this evening, I lit a joint that had a *brown* taste, which in itself was puzzling. Then my mind took off like a rocket, lifting my awareness into the metaphysical stratosphere. I cannot produce a chronological narrative of the events that followed because I was not thinking in a structured way but boundlessly, like a comet in space. Ideas and symbols and visions burst beyond the horizon of normal thinking, a series of fiery pinwheels exploding in every direction. I whizzed through chaos.

At first I kept my eyes shut without being aware that they were closed, and then I seemed to see against the inside of my eyelids a phantasmagoria of celestial effects, discs that whirled, lights that glowed, ladders that reached to the sky in thinning lines due to long perspective. The radio was on a coffee table to the right of my bed, but I did not so much *hear* the music as *see* it, shimmering lines, the pulsation of the universe. Although at that time I did not think of it, later I recalled Einstein's remark that in the end, everything may be only vibrations.

Suddenly I recalled that last week when I was stoned I jumped up and yelled: "Yes, goddamit! Space *is* curved!" I didn't know then, and I don't know now, why I said that.

Now, tonight, I opened my eyes but continued to lie still, very still, stoned in the sense that my body felt like marble. I had no wish to move so much as a muscle. I have read that heroin addicts call heroin *Mother* because it satisfies their every wish, making them feel as though they were back in the womb, warm and safe, devoid of desire for food or drink or sex. Some people proclaim that the use of marijuana leads to the use of heroin or cocaine, but I disagree. While some thrill-seeking teenagers may go from grass to hard drugs, I believe that mature individuals will stop at pot.

So as I lay still in my bed, it now seemed as though my brain was a huge cell generating a form of life unknown to me, a surrealistic vision locked within my unconscious all my years and only now rising into consciousness. Glancing around my bedroom I saw lights and shadows assume strange forms and relationships—here a very high castle, there a charming garden, then a seascape and a vast patch of sky, each hallucination lasting but a fraction of a second and followed by images that changed so fast they seemed to overlap one another.

Presto, and I saw a rainbow rich in the glory of its colors, a rainbow that arched from the upper right down to my left and then, from behind my right shoulder, there shot a beam of white light, thin at first and then thickening into a luminous cone shining against a distant tent, a beam that grew brighter and brighter and became so dazzling I was afraid it might hurt my eyes. The light seemed to symbolize a message I was unable to understand. I flinched. I jerked my head to look to the right, convinced that in a real sense there actually was a light shining over my shoulder, but all I saw was my radio with one dim beam.

Then, from a distance, I heard a heavenly choir and thought, oh Christ, this is really too much! I'm a ham, sure, but a heavenly choir—? At that moment the wall to my right receded and changed into a tunnel that promised some vague reward at the other end if I had the courage to go through it. . . . Death . . . Was that it? Was I thinking about death? Straight ahead of me I saw a huge arch like the Washington Square Arch in Greenwich Village, an arch of pure whiteness, perfect whiteness, which is to say perfection itself, and although I always had read that death was dark, now I realized that it is white, an opening leading into an existence both flawless and eternal, since it is wholly spiritual. The human body, I told myself, is a bother: all coils and loops and holes and bags and tubes, necessary to sustain physical life, of course, but to be dead is to be free of flesh, free of physical needs and functions and desires, to be liberated from the organic and reach the spiritual, a transcendence of the limitations the body imposes on the mind. When I was a boy I read an Edgar Rice Burroughs novel that ended with a single human brain within a mountain, doing nothing but pulsating and thinking. Now I felt much the same way.

Flash! I turned into an Egyptian priest. I wore a robe and stood at rigid attention, probably praying, within a temple whose walls were made of brown stone blocks, a mysterious chamber lit by a single torch stuck in the rude floor. I had become one of the elect because now I knew all the answers to life, and the answers were so beautiful that I sucked in air in awe.

Next I saw a tall armchair, the kind a scholarly man would have in his study, a father-like chair, but its back was turned toward me. And then—! Then I realized something I never had known. I knew that that chair symbolized my father, the father who left my life when I was only one year old, the father who never gave me the love I wanted from him. The lack of his love left a hole in my heart. It turned me into a neurotic, a disturbed boy, an anxious man. For years I have blamed my mother, but now I realized that all along I had been aware she loved me in her way, although never had I been sure that my father loved me. Bereft of a male model, I felt in my gut that I was fatherless.

It may have been this hollow feeling that led me to do so many crazy things down through the decades, fervently trying to embrace an emotion that forever eluded me, my father's love, getting drunk and misbehaving, striving to become whole because half of me was missing.

Yes, the absence of my father almost destroyed me—but not quite. Why? Because I felt that although my father did not love me, I loved him. Never, of course, had I ever thought this in my conscious mind. I often laughed at my father, called him an eccentric. He was eccentric, to be sure, but he also was much more than that. If I had let my pain blot out my love for my father, then I might have become a psychotic, rather than just a neurotic.

One sign of good mental health is the ability to love, and I had continued to love my father although he never returned my love—at least in the way I wanted it. So my ability to love saved me. There is another way in which I saved myself from madness, and this is the fact that all my life I have tried to communicate with myself. My diary is proof of this effort. My life has been one long monologue. I will go mad only if I am ever unable to talk to myself.

CHAPTER 15

1974

THURSDAY, AUGUST 8, 1974 ■ Janet Steinberg called from her office to say there are rumors that Nixon will resign today. And he did!

At 6 P.M. I turned on my TV set and continued to watch it until 1 A.M., for the networks gave massive coverage to this historic event.

I suppose I was like many other Americans in feeling that this was not happening, that it was some surrealistic experience, for never in the history of this nation had any President resigned from office. For a fleeting moment I wondered whether Nixon would end his resignation speech on TV and then pull out a revolver and shoot himself in the head. The other day this was done by a young woman who worked as a newscaster for some TV station. However, I've always felt Nixon never will take his life. Instead, to quote one commentator tonight, he has committed "psychic suicide." I agree.

Why did Nixon let that tape recorder run when he and his aides were discussing criminal acts? Why did he fail to destroy the tapes after their existence became known? Down through all the years I have seen Nixon on TV—and once shook hands with him—I felt he was a man who did not know himself. He never behaved naturally. His every gesture was calculated, not casual. He is awkward, not graceful. For a long time I have paid attention to his rapid eye blink, which I consider a sign that a man is trying to hide something. Having hidden himself from himself, he worked hard at hiding his true self from the public. The total political animal, he nonetheless managed to protect an image of himself that was accepted as reality by the 47 million Americans who voted for him the last time.

Born in humble circumstances, clawing his way to the top, all his life he may have been plagued with the queasy feeling that at bottom he did not amount to much. Yet, by God, he would show everyone what he could do! But when at last he won the highest honor in the land he may have felt he did not deserve the honor, and so set out on a course ending in self-destruction. At least he may have the satisfaction of having been brought down by his own behavior, rather than by some outside agency. I realize I am indulging in amateur analysis about a very complex man—but why not? His actions practically beg for it.

All his life Nixon has behaved as though he were alone in this world, and to feel all alone is to be mad. Nixon's conscious mind is brilliant, as was Hitler's, and on this level he functioned very well. He sometimes raged that the enemy was the public, but in fact the enemy was his unconscious. Since he seldom glimpsed his soul, he lived his life split down the middle—a schizophrenic. As is well known, many schizophrenics are brilliant.

Suddenly I am struck with a strange thought: In some dim and uncomprehending way, Nixon may have regarded those tapes as his *unconscious*, the part of him seldom seen by himself or others, and maybe he preserved them because he was trying to preserve his sanity, his very life. Although full disclosure of the tapes would destroy him, he clung to them in a compulsion beyond his rational will.

I recalled that famous poster with a leering Nixon and the caption: "Would you buy a used car from this man?" The person who prepared that poster was a close student of human nature. What the American public almost bought from Nixon was fascism. Except for the Joe McCarthy era, never had this nation come so close to totalitarianism as in the last two years of the Nixon administration. This evening some TV commentators declared that today's event proved that our political system works, that the checks and balances among the three branches of government proved adequate to the crisis, but I wonder why we let ourselves get this close to a dictatorship.

As I lay in bed watching the final act in the fall of the most powerful person on earth, I recalled the times when Ruthie and I watched crises together, such as the assassination and burial of President Kennedy.

At 9 P.M. Nixon appeared on TV, speaking from the White House. I wrote notes on a clipboard as I watched: . . . Nixon's face was a ruin . . . his cheeks sagged . . . his voice quavered at times . . . he was close to tears . . . he looked very old . . . a few times he smiled a weak smile . . . he was barely holding himself together . . . never natural, he now looked more artificial than ever . . . he has ugly hands, and with his right hand he made little chopping motions on the top of the desk . . . he said he had made errors of judgment, confessed to no crime, extolled his record as President, especially in foreign affairs . . . trying to the very end to sound like a statesman, he sounded instead like a madman in a mental hospital insisting that he is

Napoleon . . . once the idol of millions of people, Nixon now is so power-less that he finished by talking to himself.

He spoke for 16 minutes and at the end his lower lip quavered. I would not be surprised to learn that the next moment he burst into tears.

Then came the comments on television. Some of the TV reporters who covered Nixon tried so hard not to gloat over his fall that they went to the other extreme and called his speech "majestic." Majestic? It was cheap. Nixon said: "I have never been a quitter!" No? He quit today.

1975

FRIDAY, JANUARY 17, 1975 ■ Mrs. Lillie Sherer is a friend who lives in my neighborhood and teaches at the Hudson Guild Head Start Nursery School at 459 W. 26th St. in the Chelsea area of Manhattan. This school has such a good reputation that it is known far beyond New York.

Lil has taught there many years. Monday through Friday she is with girls and boys three to five years old. Fond of children, delighted with their direct perceptions and unconscious humor, she writes notes about the funny things they say.

A little boy named Peter said to his small friend: "My mother has a waf-fle iron at home." Paul said: "My mother doesn't have a waffle iron. Her iron just irons clothes, not waffles."

Amy boasted: "I'm four and three-quarters!" Mary huffed. "Well, I'm older! I'm four and six dimes!"

Two kids wondered whether Audrey was Spanish. Lil said: "No, Audrey is not Spanish. She is Chinese." Michelle sniffed: "Well, I'm not Chinese! I'm Capricorn!"

Nancy accidentally scratched another child with a toy. Elana pointed her finger at Nancy and cried: "If you do that again, God is going to come down and take you up there!" Nancy thought this over and then said: "No, He won't! Because my mother won't let me go!"

David told Lil: "My brother Jonathan's teacher got married and she's living with her wife." Lil said: "You mean with her husband." David: "Oh, whatever you call it!"

A five-year-old boy said: "I want my mommy to buy me a diarrhea so I can write in it every day like my big brother."

After a lesson about polar bears, Nicole cried: "I know why they're called polar bears! Because they came from Poland!" Carla piped up: "Then I must be French because I was born in French Hospital."

After a child mentioned death, Rebecca moaned: "I wish my mommy, daddy and sister wouldn't die!" Lil said comfortingly: "Your mommy, daddy and sister will be around for a very long time." Rebecca: "You mean it takes a long time to die?"

Two little girls were talking face-to-face. Loaiza yelled: "Stop spitting at me, Betina!" Betina said: "I'm not spitting at you! I just have a juicy mouth."

One of Lil's pupils became an actress and now is known to the world as Whoopi Goldberg.

SUNDAY, FEBRUARY 2, 1975 ▪ As I do every Sunday morning, I drank coffee while reading the *Times* and then came into this study to write my diary. To my surprise, my fingers stumbled over the keys. My mind was dull. I felt so dizzy I thought I might faint—something that never happened to me in my life. I was disoriented. I was not hung-over. I'd never felt like this before. Aware I would be unable to work on my book, I just loafed all afternoon and evening.

At midnight I was awake when I got a call from Eugene, Oregon. No, it was not my daughter calling, but a friend of hers named Barbara Smith, whom I'd never met. In a hesitant voice she said Sandy had been in a terrible auto accident, a three-car crash, and is badly injured. Even as Barbara spoke, Sandy was in a hospital undergoing emergency surgery. I felt as though a sledgehammer had hit my heart. My voice trembling, I asked Barbara whether Sandy might die. Barbara replied that she will live, but I detected a note of uncertainty in her voice. I began weeping. This alarmed Barbara, who urged me to get someone to stay with me.

I went into shock. Nine years ago my wife died. Now my daughter may be taken from me. Sitting like a lump on the edge of the bed I wailed aloud . . . confusion . . . mind blank . . . fear . . . I started to feel cold . . . losing control . . . slipping into hysteria. To be a writer is a curious thing because a part of me stands back to watch the other part. My mind collapsed like a heap of strings.

Shaking all over, I called relatives and friends. Time passed—I don't know how much. Then, beginning to get a hold of myself, I called the hospital in Eugene and spoke to the surgeon who had attended Sandy. She had been in the operating room two and a half hours.

EUGENE, OREGON, JUNE 10–JUNE 25, 1975 ▪ Sandy's doctors decided that she should recuperate awhile before undergoing reconstructive surgery. When I learned that this operation was scheduled for June 11, my sister Kay and I flew to Oregon to be with Sandy for the operation. The two weeks I've been away from home I've been unable to keep my diary, so what I now write is only impressionistic.

I was shocked when I saw my daughter. She has a hole in her forehead. At the back of the hole a thin membrane can be seen throbbing with the pulsations of her brain. To my horror she said her surgeons warned her that when she emerged from the operation she might be paralyzed from the neck down.

The day before the operation Kay and I sat with Sandy in her hospital room. Two surgeons and an anesthetist came into the room, one after the other. Sandy asked a series of intelligent questions. Each said that while the threat of paralysis was slight, none could guarantee that she might not wind up totally paralyzed.

No soldier entering battle was more courageous than my daughter. In mounting admiration, I watched as she held herself together, never giving in to hysteria, only a couple of tears trickling down her gashed cheeks. I felt I would explode. As the third doctor left the room, Kay started to say something, but I waved her away and when my daughter and I were alone I took her into my arms to try to comfort her.

Her operation was set for 7:45 A.M., June 11. Since none of us would be allowed to see her that morning, I did not reach the hospital until 11:30. I was driven there by Sandy's friend, Barbara Smith. Kay was waiting in a room set aside for relatives and friends of patients undergoing surgery. Soon we were joined by Sandy's husband, Victor Emelio.

We sat . . . waited . . . sweated. At a desk sat a kind white-haired Red Cross lady who kept telephoning to check on the condition of Mrs. Emelio. Sandy was still in surgery. . . . Noon . . . one o'clock . . . two o'clock . . . two-fifteen. Barbara's eyes were wet. She and Victor drank coffee from plastic cups that shook in their hands. The operation was supposed to last only three hours. Had something gone wrong?

At 2:25 P.M. the Red Cross lady reported Sandy was out of surgery and okay. We sighed in relief.

A couple of hours later they let us go to Sandy's room. Her head and eyes were covered with a bandage as thick as a turban worn by a sultan. She lay on her back, taking glucose intravenously in her left arm. Her cheeks were stained with what looked like iodine. *And she was not paralyzed!*

She lay very still. She wafted in and out of consciousness. Dehydrated, when awake she wanted water. To her face I held a glass of water with a bent plastic straw in it. Confused and stubborn, Sandy insisted upon holding the glass. She tilted it so far to one side that she almost spilled the water. Then she wanted a cigaret. I walked into the hall to check with a nurse, who said it would be all right. I lit a cigaret and held it to her lips. She insisted upon holding it herself. She was unable to see because her eyes were bandaged and because she was groggy from the anesthetic. When I gave her the cigaret she pulled it to her chin, rather than her lips. Leaning forward, I guided it to her mouth. Then she passed out.

When she returned to consciousness, she murmured; "I feel like a Buddhist flower-pusher."

I didn't know what she meant and doubted whether she did. But because she was out of surgery and free of paralysis, my heart soared.

Days later we took her home.

One evening when Sandy and I were alone I told her something: I said that had she been left paralyzed, and had she wanted me to do so, I would have killed her with a revolver. If she had been unable to speak, we could have worked out a series of eye-blinks. One blink of her eyes would mean *yes*. Two blinks would mean *no*. Three blinks would mean *let me think it over*. Now, what did Sandy think about that? She agreed that she would have wanted me to kill her. She certainly would not care to live paralyzed from the neck down.

Staring into her eyes I said: "Honey, you know of course that had you wanted me to shoot you, and had I done so, the next instant I would have turned the gun on myself." My daughter said: "I know."

After the death of my wife I saw a lot of our mutual friend, Selma Seskin Pezaro. I had met Selma through her brother Steve, whose bookstore near the World-Telegram was a favorite haunt of mine. In many ways she was like Ruthie because she was mature and sweet-tempered, reliable and hard-working, and she also happened to be a non-religious Jew.

Selma had been matured by tragedy. When she was 21 she married, soon discovered her husband had cancer, and at night she tied her ankle to his so if he stirred she would awaken and take care of him. They had been married only a year and a half when he died. At first she cowered alone in her apartment, as I had done, but a husband and wife persuaded her to join a family-oriented nudist colony in New Jersey. There, among people ranging from babies to grandparents, she began to recover her emotional balance.

Irrationally, she felt she had not done enough to save her husband when, in fact, she had done everything possible. Now the widow resolved to save the new widower—me. She tolerated my black moods, made sure I ate well, typed notes for the books I wrote, was totally generous of her time and money. She even coped with me when I felt suicidal. One day in her apart-

ment I picked up a sharp letter-opener and held it in my hand while staring melodramatically at my belly. Selma just sat and stared at me. Over the years I came to love her—not in the way I loved Ruth, of course, and Selma understood. Our favorite recreation was sitting behind her apartment building to watch children at play.

At times Selma could be witty. At one party I started to tell a joke, forgot the punch line, shrugged and said: "Well, I guess I'm just no raconteur."

Selma added, "Not only that, Eddie! You don't tell jokes very well."

WEDNESDAY, JULY 2, 1975 ■ After publication of a story about my diary in our neighborhood paper, the *Chelsea Clinton News*, I got a letter from a man who lives in a housing project a few blocks south of my home. After saying he is impressed by my journal, he offered to give me some books. I wanted to call, but there is no number listing him in the Manhattan telephone directory. I walked to the project and met James F. McShea.

What an original! A retired elevator operator, he now does almost nothing but sit alone in his home reading the 2,000 books in his private library. His hobby is educating himself.

He was born in Hell's Kitchen on the west side of mid-Manhattan, an area known for producing gangsters, not scholars. Both his parents were born in Ireland. There his father walked to school in winter in bare feet, getting an education so scant that even as an adult he had trouble writing letters.

After emigrating to New York City, the father worked in a slaughterhouse and the family was so poor that little Jimmy had to go to work after only six years of schooling. One teacher was so impressed by his yearning for learning that she lent him a children's book called *Teddy and Carrots*. He read it 15 times. To this day he remembers its plot and characters.

When he was 14 and working as an office boy he attended a high school graduation ceremony because his best friend was valedictorian. Jimmy McShea wept. He felt ashamed of his ignorance. He vowed that, despite everything, he would educate himself.

He opened the doors of carriages stopping at stores on 5th Avenue, did menial work on a ship sailing around the world, served in the army 14 months, became an elevator operator.

When he retired more than a decade ago he took a small apartment in Chelsea and settled down to his books. Divorced, he lives alone. A small man with the map of Ireland on his face, he has thinning gray hair, grizzly eyebrows, blue-gray eyes and so much energy he almost hums like a dynamo.

He built his own bookshelves and the swinging book-rest attached to the left side of his deep chair. Nailed to this book-rest is an empty can of Campbell's chicken rice soup, to hold his pencils and pens, for he underlines as he writes. He has a 100-watt bulb in an overhead lamp, wears glasses and has his eyes checked once a year. There are dark patches under both eyes.

Existing on Social Security, he cooks his meals to save money. With his time his own, free of interruptions because he refuses to own either a telephone or television set, he reads all day long, seven days a week. He gets through three to five books each week.

He told me that thinking is almost as important to him as breathing. His favorite subjects are history, politics, international affairs, business and finance. He is fond of the works of the late John Maynard Keynes, the British economist, and also dotes on books by the American economist Eliot Janeway. Sir Winston Churchill's style fascinates him because, he says, Churchill wrote majestically but simply. He has read every word of Karl Marx's monumental *Capital* but had trouble finishing *The Wealth of Nations* by Adam Smith.

Politically, McShea says, he is neither a reactionary nor a radical, but something in between. Like Harry Truman and some other self-educated people, McShea sometimes mispronounces some of the words he uses correctly. He has an extensive vocabulary.

I asked whether he would agree with my wife's definition of an intellectual as someone excited by ideas. His eyes lit up and he cried that yes he agrees, but quickly added that he is too modest to apply this definition to himself. He confessed that his voracious reading and his dislike of small talk have left him rather isolated. He scorns non-readers or those who read trash. He declared he never is lonely. Why? He said he can't explain this even to himself.

He gave me as many books as I could carry, telling me to return to pick up more. Before he dies he wants to give his books only to someone who appreciates them. That's me, me, me!

As I began to run out of money I knew I had to find a part-time job. I got in touch with Dr. Louis M. Starr, director of the Oral History Collection at Columbia University. He remembered me because when I worked for the World-Telegram I wrote a long article about this worthy project.

It was started in 1948 by Allan Nevins, a great historian. He reasoned that people of the present write fewer letters than the people of the past, so to preserve the memories of famous men and women it would be helpful to tape-record interviews with them. The interviews are conducted by historians and journalists. The words then are transcribed and made available to scholars and authors writing biographies and histories.

I asked Dr. Starr to let me interview Alger Hiss, and he agreed. Years ago I met Hiss at a cocktail party, but that night we did not discuss his celebrated case. Instead, we talked about publishing, for he was completing a book telling his side of the story. Dr. Starr made an appointment with Hiss for me. To prepare myself, I spent days rereading the dozen books I own about the Hiss-Chambers case.

For folks too young to remember, let me sketch the background of this case: In 1948 Whittaker Chambers, a senior editor of Time *magazine and a self-confessed former spy for the Soviet Union, publicly accused Alger Hiss of belonging to an underground communist cell in Washington, D.C., and of stealing federal documents. That was when Hiss was a high official in the State Department. By the time Chambers made this accusation Hiss was president of the Carnegie Endowment for International Peace.*

In 1948 Hiss denied these charges before a federal grand jury in New York. Then he was indicted on two counts of perjury. The first count said he lied when he denied giving federal documents to Chambers. The second count said he also lied when he denied having conversed with Chambers in, or about, February and March of 1938.

In 1949 Hiss stood trial and got a hung jury. In 1949–50 he stood trial a second time and was convicted of perjury. He was sentenced to five years in prison. He insisted he was innocent and, like millions of other Americans who followed this celebrated case, I believed him.

Now Hiss agreed to Dr. Starr's request that I interview him. I must point out that since I was working for the Oral History Collection, I cannot reveal in this book what Hiss told me on tape. Everyone who is interviewed may stipulate the date when his revelations may be made public. Trust in the integrity of those connected with the project is paramount to its existence. However, there is nothing unethical about reporting my impressions of Hiss the man.

WEDNESDAY, JULY 9, 1975 ■ Alger Hiss walked into the restaurant. I was waiting for him in the Chelsea Steak House at 248 Eighth Avenue near West 23rd Street. Glancing up, I saw the lean six-footer peering around, so I stood up and snatched off my glasses to gesture with them toward Hiss. He saw me and smiled and walked over and sat down.

His face was quite unlined for a man of 70. He was carrying a *New York Times* and a big envelope and after we shook hands he put them on the floor. When a waiter asked whether we cared to order a drink we both declined. Since I always begin an interview with small questions, I asked Hiss whether he had used the subway to come uptown this sweltering day and he said he had, adding that he likes heat so he did not feel bothered. Then he picked up the menu, which has a map of my neighborhood on its cover.

Hiss, born in Maryland, said he would like the soft shell crabs if they were fresh, not frozen. Fresh, said the waiter. Hiss also ordered ice tea. The waiter kept forgetting his tea and every time he asked Hiss what he wanted to drink, Hiss repeated his order with no trace of annoyance.

He asked what college I attended. When I said the University of Missouri, he said his friend Edgar Snow had taken his journalism degree there. Snow went to China and became friendly with Mao Tse-tung. Hiss said that on the radio he had heard Mao quoted as saying nice things about Richard Nixon. I said I was surprised. Hiss said he was only mildly surprised, since American leaders and Red China have entered into detente. Aware that Nixon had been instrumental in ruining the life of Hiss, I asked what he thinks about Nixon's mental health. Hiss replied that he dislikes dealing in personalities.

I was sensitive to the fact that I was with a man who figured in one of the most celebrated trials in American history. Hiss asked what form my interview would take when we reached my apartment. I said that of course I would go into his case in great detail, I also would ask his opinion of the great men with whom he had worked in the federal government.

We finished eating. The waiter brought the check, and I took it. Hiss put out his hand and said we must go Dutch, for this has been his habit since his days as a young New Dealer, because he never wanted to feel obligated to anyone. I said that during my career as a reporter I had been offered several bribes, the first one for $5 and the last one for $35,000. Hiss chuckled. When I said that not for one second did I feel tempted, he nodded understandingly. Each of us left $7 on the table and walked out.

We were in my neighborhood. On the northwest corner of West 21st Street and 9th Avenue there is a small old-fashioned grocery owned by Louis P. Chavell. Since it is only a half block from my home I have come to know Lou well. Hiss surprised me by saying he knows Lou and wanted to step in to say hello. Lou saw Hiss, held out his hand and said: "Alger! How are you?"

"Fine, Lou. And you?"

The two men exchanged pleasantries. Hiss behaved with Lou just as he had with me—courteously and pleasantly. As we left to walk to my place, Hiss pointed to a brownstone four doors east of mine and explained that he lived there a couple of months after he quit his job with the State Department in Washington and came to New York to take up his position as president of the Carnegie Endowment for International Peace.

We reached my brownstone and climbed the winding stairway to my apartment on the third floor. Hiss walked up slowly, sighing that his son lives in a five-story walk-up. Then he added that his stepson, with whom he is close, is a surgeon, lives in California and owns a private airplane. I said I have a brother who owns a plane, but I've been poor most of my life. Smiling, Hiss said, "I've been poor, too."

Although my apartment is air-conditioned, I suggested that he remove his jacket, which he did, also stripping off his tie. I put the tape recorder on a piano stool in front of the sofa, where I had asked him to sit. The microphone itself I placed on a nearby coffee table. When I asked him to say a few words so that I might test his voice level, I found that his voice was so soft that I wondered how I could get the mike closer to his lips. He offered to hold it. This I resisted, but he insisted. Gently.

Before I began asking questions, I said he knew from our brief telephone conversation that I always have believed in his innocence. However, to do a proper job of interviewing him, I felt I must ask blunt questions and even behave as though I were a prosecuting attorney. Hiss, a graduate of Harvard Law School, agreed.

Alger Hiss has thinning brown hair, a high forehead and a lean face, ears with edges as thin as the rims of shells, few wrinkles in his forehead, a long neck and long slim fingers. When we were in the restaurant I had mentioned that whenever I saw Nixon on TV I had noted his rapid eye blink, which I considered proof that he was trying to hide his feelings. Surprised, Hiss said that only yesterday a friend of his, a psychiatrist, had said the same thing.

From time to time Hiss reached for his tobacco pouch to fill his pipe, although he played with the pipe more than he smoked it. He was so kind and gentle and considerate that I wondered whether I was being taken in by him. No, I decided, I didn't think so. Sitting only a few feet apart, we looked into one another's eyes and he kept his gaze fixed on me with such candor that he almost seemed transparent. I was reminded of the day when one of my friends said I am so frank I seemed to be transparent, that he seemed to be able to see through me. I considered that a compliment. I encourage others to see through me and now believe Hiss does the same thing.

Although I have met Chief Justice Earl Warren and Judge Learned Hand, I doubt whether I ever encountered any judge or attorney with a mind as legalistic as that of Alger Hiss. This, in fact, is what is wrong with the book he wrote in his defense, *In the Court of Public Opinion*. His book was devoid of all emotion.

Now, as he answered my questions, Hiss was emotionless, for the most part. Over-controlled? I don't think so. When he spoke of a woman friend, his voice became warmer. Earlier, when I mentioned my daughter's auto accident, compassion showed in his face as he asked about her present condition. Nonetheless, Hiss remains an enigma to me—a comment, so I've read, made by many of his friends. Courteous in an old-world way, he has a cool personality.

I once saw Whittaker Chambers, the man who wrecked his life. That was in 1951, when Chambers spoke at a *Herald Tribune* forum I attended. Sitting in the front row that day, I drew a sketch of Chambers. This accuser of Hiss had what I regarded as a furtive air about him, even in the presence of an audience in sympathy with him. Today, for more than three hours, I stared into the eyes of Alger Hiss, and if he actually was a Soviet spy, then I know nothing about human nature.

I wonder whether Chambers, a man fragmented and perhaps even demented by the many tragedies in his life, saw in Hiss the kind of man he wanted to be. If this were so, then perhaps the only way he could absorb Hiss into himself was by denigrating and then destroying him.

This noon at lunch I told Hiss I had met Huey Long a few times, studied his life, and now know that a demagogue is one who says out loud what others think but dare not speak. Hiss agreed—but with one qualification. He said my definition of a demagogue also could be applied to sincere and truly great leaders. Thinking of Franklin D. Roosevelt, I agreed. So the difference between the demagogue and the statesman is the difference between evil intentions and good ones.

At the end of the interview this afternoon, Hiss asked how much more time I wanted from him. I said I'd like to see him a couple of more times. He said he has had two heart attacks that have left him unsteady on his feet—something I had noticed as we walked here—and now he must hoard his energy. With a smile he agreed to meet me for two more sessions. He said he dislikes being interviewed, but had liked my voice on the phone, liked the letter I wrote to him, and so he will join me a couple of more times.

"I'm doing this just for you," he said.

I hope he didn't see me wince. Was he sincere? If he was, I'd feel pleased, but I had hoped he would consent to further sessions for his own sake and that of the Oral History Collection—and therefore posterity. As regards these interviews, I am nothing but an instrument.

WEDNESDAY, JULY 30, 1975   ■   For a second time I met Alger Hiss in the Chelsea Steak House. When I asked whether his work as a salesman for a stationery firm takes him out of the office much, he said he is outside half the time and inside the other half.

A few days ago about 5 P.M. he went to a 21-story building on 42nd Street to call on a client. He was the only passenger in the elevator. As it rose it suddenly shot to the top of the elevator shaft and stuck there. Finding the squawk-box in the elevator, he called the guard in the lobby, who said he would send for help. Thanking him, Hiss asked that he call his customer to report his predicament and say he would be late. Aware he had to spend time in the hot elevator, Hiss sat down on the floor, opened his *New York Times* and began reading.

Afterwards, some friends said they would have panicked. Hiss said he knew he would be rescued, and besides he does not suffer from claustrophobia. An elevator repair man—"a nice young man from Brooklyn," as he put it—arrived and released him within an hour. I asked whether that experience reminded him of the years he spent in jail. He did time in the federal penitentiary at Lewisburg, Pennsylvania.

He told me that when he entered prison he resigned himself to reality. In fact, he appreciated the silence, since by nature he is a rather solitary person. Over the prison's radio network he heard symphonic music an hour a day. Since few other prisoners liked this kind of music, one hour of it was all he could hear.

In his cell he studied the Babylonian Talmud. I had not known that the Talmud was a part of Babylonian culture. When I expressed surprise that such a book was in prison, Hiss said it probably was there because of some Jewish organization, since the people of ancient Israel were taken into exile by the Babylonians.

Other prisoners, aware he is an attorney, asked him to become their "jailhouse lawyer," so he helped them with their appeals.

"How could I not," he asked rhetorically, "help men whose only hope lay in winning freedom?"

I said I enjoy solitude, but if I were ever imprisoned, I might kill myself. While behind bars, had he ever thought of suicide?

"Oh, never!"

Hiss's reply was so intense it almost was passionate—a surprise because usually his voice is soft, his manner cool. He said he used his time in prison to peer deeply within himself in the hope of discovering his motives for his general behavior. This reminded me of a profound remark by the German mystic, Meister Eckhart: "The eye with which I see God is the eye with which God sees me."

Hiss smiled and said he did not understand. He asked me to explain. I said I consider this remark so deep it cannot be explained; it can only be felt after one has studied mysticism.

Hiss said my next book should not be about history but philosophy. I said that if I live long enough I will write a book about the history of mysticism. Then I added that the more I study history the better I realize that all history begins and ends in psychology and philosophy. Agreeing, Hiss said every great historian works from philosophical premises.

Since Hiss had told me he suffered two heart attacks, I asked about his present health.

"It's not good."

His reply was so casual I wanted to be sure I had heard him correctly, so I asked him to repeat what he had said.

"It's not good."

He said that since his condition is irreversible, he accepts it. I said I hope he lives long enough to clear his name. His face lighting up, Hiss said that tomorrow, for the first time, he and his lawyers will see three of the microfilms that Whittaker Chambers hid in a pumpkin on his farm.

When we got to my home, Hiss took off his jacket and tie and sat on the sofa while I perched in a big chair in front of him. Before leaving to meet him, I had set up the tape recorder, but now when I pressed the button it would not run. Then I realized I had forgotten to plug in the machine, and I laughed at my usual ineptitude.

After my first session with Hiss I had played back a part of the recording we made that first day; it contained burbling sounds. After some reflection I remembered he had toyed with his pipe as he talked, and sometimes he also shifted the microphone he held in his hands. This taught me a lesson; put the mike on a table where it will remain immobile. Explaining this, I took the mike from his hand.

By the light from a window I saw again that his face is not very lined for a man his age. His blue-gray eyes are sunk even more deeply within his skull than I had remembered. Again as we talked he kept his eyes on mine with such intensity that at last my eyes tired and I wanted to shift them to ease them, but did not wish to violate our rapport.

Perhaps because he now knows me a little better, Hiss seemed more relaxed and his face became more animated. Previously I had wondered whether he is over-controlled. He is not. Always he simply is *controlled*.

"A sentimentalist," he said, "is unable to feel genuine affection."

The truth of his remark hit me so hard that instantly I thought of an old woman I know who is sentimental and cruel.

Hiss then said something to the effect that he is an intellectual—adding, with a smile, that he cannot be sure he is one. I said my wife defined an intellectual as one who is excited by ideas.

At lunch today Hiss had told me he once lectured in a city in upstate New York where there were many members of the John Birch Society, which I regard as a loony bin of mindless wild-eyed anti-communists. When the session was opened to questions, some Birchers grabbed the microphone on the floor of the auditorium and peppered him with loaded questions. At the end of the evening a few Birchers remained and his friend asked whether he would like to meet them. "Sure!" Hiss replied, but when he approached them they turned and fled. His friend laughed and said: "Look, you have to realize that to them you are the devil incarnate!"

Today, for a second time, Hiss and I discussed the nature of demagogues. He said he was reminded of the late Senator Robert R. Reynolds of North Carolina, whom he called a demagogue, but one who did not advocate violence. I remembered having read that during one campaign Reynolds told an audience of farmers that his opponent "had a sister who went to New York and became a *thespian!*"

Hiss laughed, "That's the man!"

Now, alone with me in my apartment, Hiss told me exactly how he hopes to clear his name. In surprise I realized he was revealing his entire legal strategy. I said I was astonished at his frankness. He said: "Well, I hope you won't use any of this information for a year or so—until after the case is decided."

At last we reached the crucial question of whether Hiss lost his second trial because of alleged "forgery by typewriter." He went into a long complex explanation. As an interviewer, I had to do five things at the same time:

— make sure the tape recorder was working properly
— maintain rapport with Hiss by keeping my eyes on his
— truly listen to everything he said
— write more questions on the paper on my clipboard
— find certain passages in the many books about the Hiss case that lay open near me.

Hiss said he had tried without success to find a copy of *A Nation in*

Torment, my narrative history of the Great Depression. Saying I wanted to show my appreciation for all the time he has given me, I found a copy, autographed it and gave it to Hiss. Thanking me, he said he will use it when he writes his history of the New Deal.

WEDNESDAY, AUGUST 6, 1975   ■   The *New York Times* said today that Alger Hiss has been reinstated as a lawyer in Massachusetts by order of that state's highest court. I wrote him a note of congratulations.

WEDNESDAY, SEPTEMBER 17, 1975   ■   For the third and final time, Hiss came here and again I interviewed him for three hours. In total, I was alone with him for nine hours. Today I got him talking about all the famous people he knew: Justices Holmes, Brandeis and Cardozo; Franklin and Eleanor Roosevelt; Adlai E. Stevenson, John Foster Dulles, James F. Byrnes, Harry Hopkins, Arthur Vandenberg, Tom Connolly, Dean Acheson, et al.

On April 20, 1994, the New York Times *published a picture of Hiss and a four-paragraph piece about a birthday party given for him by some 70 friends. He was born in Baltimore on November 11, 1904, but his 90th birthday was celebrated in advance. Almost every big dictionary and encyclopedia includes an article about Alger Hiss.*

FRIDAY, DECEMBER 19, 1975   ■   The other night at a cocktail party I met a man from New Jersey named Arnold Tversky. He is assistant superintendent of the Dover High School, which has 1,100 students. We chatted together a long time. I liked him and he said he found me so interesting that he invited me to speak to his students. Surprised and flattered, I agreed. This morning he came in his car to drive Selma and me to New Jersey.

In his office he introduced me to Ray Schwartz, a young man with brown eyes and a bubbling personality, who teaches English. In the first of three appearances today, I was supposed to talk to his English class. Ray warned me that his students would look at me as though I were a TV set. This remark disturbed me.

Selma and I were led into the library. Wire cables snaked over the floor because my talk was to be broadcast on closed-circuit television. About 40 boys and girls sat in silence. Holding up a copy of *A Nation in Torment,* Ray identified me as its author, said he had read my book and liked it, then gave me a long and flattering introduction. When he finished I arose and said I'd like to meet the man who sounded so important. Not a snicker.

Two boys and two girls had been chosen to ask me questions. All looked scared—perhaps because of me, perhaps because they knew they were on television. None asked any sharp, significant, provocative questions. For 35 minutes I talked, ending with the story of how some Jewish boys being taught to read by their elders are told to lick a drop of honey off the cover of a book so that they would associate sweetness and learning. No response from the kids.

At the end of this first session we went to the cafeteria where Ray said he flipped when I told this story because he came from an orthodox family and this very thing happened to him. Arnold Tversky, I learned, liked to be called "Mr. T." He, Ray, Selma and I wondered why these days children are so non-verbal. Why don't they read? Why are they emotionally flat? I told these educators that they are competing with the deadening influence of an ignorant society lying just outside the school doors. They agreed.

Then I was led before two more classes, and both times I was met with an aloofness that was palpable. Straining for rapport with the children, I drifted away from the subject of writing and began talking about life itself. Nothing I said evoked any reaction from the kids. I felt as though I were slogging through a swamp, my boots mired in ignorance and indifference.

In desperation I told the students I wanted to give them a demonstration of curiosity. Then, without pausing for breath, I rattled off perhaps 30 questions about the dimensions of the room, the kind of wood in their chairs, the material used to make the handbags the girls carried, etc. I did hear a murmur of amazement—but that was all.

During my third appearance of the day I asked a girl in the front row to come sit with me so that I might show her how reporters interview people. Shyly, she stepped forward. I asked questions about her life. When she said she wants to design women's clothes, I cried that already she must sew well.

"No, not really," she said hesitantly.

"I won't let you get away with that," I told her. "You said you want to design women's clothes and I know you sew, so surely you must sew well. There's nothing wrong with admitting it. You do sew well, don't you?"

A little startled, the girl said: "Well, yes, I do."

In the second row I saw an Hispanic girl. I asked what she likes to do best.

"Read poetry." she replied.

Taking heart, I praised her. Perhaps because of her Spanish heritage, I remembered that my daughter had spoken to me about a Spanish poet named Lorca, and asked the girl whether she had read him. Her black eyes blazing with joy, she said yes she has read him. I told her she was ahead of me because I never have read Lorca.

But those were the only sparks I lit in the eyes staring at me. I thought, to these kids I *am* only a substitute for a television set. Day after day they sit and watch TV. There is neither the opportunity nor necessity for them to communicate with the images they see on the screen. I was bombing and knew it. Taking a deep breath, I said: "Hey, tell you what, all of you who find me boring, please hold up your hands. I promise I won't get angry, and I'll ask your teacher not to rebuke you. Now, how many of you think I'm boring? Let me see your hands!"

Not a hand went up. I thought: Oh, my god! I can't even elicit a negative response from these kids.

Heavy-hearted, I left the room. Ray said I got to his students. I scoffed that I didn't believe him. He said that although none asked any questions, at least they gave me their full attention—which is more, he added, than he gets from them. This made me feel even worse. Television is turning our children into zombies.

1976

TUESDAY, AUGUST 17, 1976 ▓ Today I rode a bus to Washington, D.C. Getting out in the bus terminal, I caught a cab to take me to Arlington, Virginia, to visit my sister Kay and her husband, Bob Burton. My cab driver was a young black man. He asked whether I wanted Ford or Carter to win the election. I said Carter.

Then I asked the cabbie whether he wished the Democrats had chosen Barbara Jordan as their candidate for Vice President. Miss Jordan is a black Congresswoman from Texas, a penetrating thinker and hypnotic orator. The black driver replied that—no—he did not want any woman in that position.

I snorted: "Why, you black male chauvinist! I'm sure you complain when people call you *nigger*—but you're a bigot about women!" Leaning forward, playfully I poked his ribs. He looked sheepish.

MONDAY, SEPTEMBER 13, 1976 ▓ Saturday night as a woman and I were leaving mid-Manhattan, we had to run to catch a subway car at 42nd Street. Because of my momentum I almost lost my balance, automatically put out my hand, felt it touch a man's shoulder, murmured an apology. The man was black, perhaps in his fifties, not badly dressed but quite drunk. Instead of accepting my apology, he glared at me and began ranting, asking again and again how I dared to touch him, shouting that he was going to get a gun. My companion smiled at him. I whispered to her to stop smiling and to look away from him, for he was a ticking bomb ready to explode.

1977

WEDNESDAY, MAY 25, 1977 ■ When I was in high school and yearning to become a writer, there was no author in my home town to whom I might turn for guidance. Now that I have had four books published I decided to try to find some youngster who might like to have me as his mentor. Although I am poor and cannot help anyone financially, perhaps I can help another by sharing my experience and talent.

I began by writing a letter to an old friend of mine in Kewanee, Mrs. Shirley Jones Shilgalis, the wife of the local postmaster. Shirley and I went to high school together. Telling her what I want to do, I asked her to ask some local English teacher if there is a boy or girl who wants above all things to become a writer. Should such a child be chosen, then I would require that his or her parents grant me permission to correspond with the youngster. Shirley spoke to Mrs. Dorothy Johnson, head of the English department at Kewanee High School. Subsequently, Mrs. Johnson wrote to me, saying:

"It gives me great pleasure to inform you that we have selected a student from Kewanee High School to take advantage of your generous offer. The student is— — —. Her ambition is to become a writer and she often brings stories and poems to school for her friends and teachers to read. She is the kind of eager, responsive and questioning student any teacher would enjoy having in her class, and she is thrilled to have an opportunity to correspond with a professional writer."

Well, this girl and I began corresponding. However, she did not write to me very often and she failed to send me some of her stories or articles so that I might critique them. Puzzled, I asked by mail what was wrong. She had asked how old I was and I had told her. Did she feel strange corresponding with an old man? She did not reply. That was the end of our communication. Having so badly wanted a protégé, I feel disappointed.

SATURDAY, MAY 28, 1977 ■ Selma Selkin Pezaro, Edna Paul and I dined this evening in the West Boondock Restaurant on Tenth Avenue. Owned by a black man, featuring boss soul food, the restaurant is patronized by blacks and whites alike. The sawdust on the floor and candles on the tables are part of its colorful ambience.

We were surprised to see our white waitress take a candle from a table and get down on her hands and knees in the sawdust to search for something. A lost contact lens? No. She said an expensive dental bridge had popped out of her mouth. Selma grabbed another candle and went down on all fours to help in the hunt. The black chef came out of the kitchen to look. I got into the act.

Two black couples arrived, asked what was the trouble, began poking through the sawdust. Two French-speaking white couples wanted to know what was happening, and then they began searching with the rest of us. Still other customers came over with candles and cigaret lighters.

Suddenly it occurred to me that here was a group of strangers of varying races and backgrounds now united in a common cause—that of helping a waitress. A kind of impromptu United Nations. The search continued almost an hour and with all the help she had the girl found her missing bridge. Some out-of-towners mouth the platitude that while New York is a great place to visit, they would not care to live here. I am proud to be a resident of New York City.

SATURDAY, JUNE 18, 1977 ▨ While at the New York Public Library today, I discovered an exhibit on diaries. I saw a pocket diary kept by Dickens when he visited America, written in script so small I was unable to read a single word. I saw the typed diary of William Inge open to a page in which he tells about the acceptance of his play *Come Back Little Sheba* for production in a theater. Gazing at that wondrous collection of diaries, for the first time in my life I felt a sense of immortality: Years from now, long after I am dead, my own journal may be on display. The *New Orleans Item*—now the *States-Item*—just celebrated its 100th anniversary. The fat centennial edition contained an article about one-time *Item* reporters who later became authors, and along with Lafcadio Hearn, O. Henry, Carl Carmer, et al., there was a paragraph about me. Scary.

I have completed seven chapters of my book called *The Watchdogs*. One concerns Mike Johnson of the *New York Sun* and his 1948 exposé of waterfront conditions, for which he won a Pulitzer. I knew Mike. His son Haynes is assistant managing editor of the *Washington Post* and also a Pulitzer winner. Haynes sent me data about his dad, which I used to write my chapter. I sent Haynes a copy to check my errors. Yesterday he replied in such complimentary phrases that I've kept his letter. Since I seem unable to win monetary rewards for my writing, at least I get other kinds of satisfaction.

Now that I have been freed of jury duty I have slogged along at my work, attaining that momentum so necessary to the production of a big book.

Right now I am researching William Lloyd Garrison and Elijah Lovejoy. My book is almost half done. The deeper I get into writing about freedom of the press, the more I believe in the value of this book. It would make one helluva great TV series. With guidance from John Cushman, I have written Coward-McCann to ask that all rights to *The Epic of New York City* revert to me, now that it is out of print. John will try to sell it as a paperback.

My agent wasn't able then to sell a paperback of Epic, *and my history of freedom of the press was not published either. In 1989, a new hardcover edition of* Epic *was finally published.*

WEDNESDAY, JULY 13, 1977 ■ This evening Selma and I were in my apartment watching Merv Griffin on television. We were surprised to see the images on the screen flicker and zig-zag. It was a hot evening. Through the casement window we saw heat lightning. Selma left for home moments before 9:30 P.M. She had been gone only about three minutes when the television set went blank. I knew what had happened: another power failure!

Snapping off the set, I rushed into the kitchen to switch off the air conditioner lest electrical power suddenly return and blow out the machine. Then I worried about Selma. Had she reached home safely?

Selwyn Raab, a reporter for the *New York Times*, is a friend of mine. I dialed the number of the *Times* with the intention of telling him there was a power failure in the Chelsea area. I thought only my own neighborhood was affected, for when I looked out a window I saw lights still glowing atop the Empire State Building. Five minutes later they went dark. A woman reporter at the *Times* said Selwyn was not there. I told her about the blackout in my area. She said the *Times* also was affected. In fact, she continued, lights were out all over the city and even on Long Island.

Before calling the paper I had tried to reach Selma by phone, getting no answer. I tried again but the line was busy. Seconds later she called to say she was all right. She had reached the corner of Ninth Avenue and West 22nd Street when the street lights began fading, section by section. She felt a little afraid because nearby she heard some youths whooping. But she picked her way to a bus stop a block away and soon was back at her apartment building. The doorman gave her a candle to light her way as she walked up three flights to her apartment. I felt relieved. In somber voices we talked about the people who may be trapped in elevators and on subway cars. Since I suffer from claustrophobia, I think I might panic were I caught in a stalled elevator in a high-rise building.

By now I had taken a flashlight from a drawer and lit a candle. I was grateful to be home. I was home alone during the previous blackout shortly after Ruth's death. This evening I thought the cool air in my bedroom might remain awhile even with the air conditioner off, but soon I felt warm and opened windows. At 10:30 P.M. rain began falling. I prayed for a hard rain to break the heat wave, but I also worried about people in the open who would get soaked. The rain was light and barely cooled the city.

I sat by an open window in the front room, surprised to see stars amidst the occasional flicker of lightning. I hung my bare legs out the window and pointed my flashlight at the Episcopal Theological Seminary across the street. It consists of an entire block of buildings of various shapes and sizes and ages, some with towers and turrets and sloping roofs which now stood silhouetted against the sky.

The block on which I live looked eerie. Except for headlights of passing cars, the street was dark—although not black. Pedestrians carried flashlights. Some walked dogs. I heard people calling to one another. Fireworks exploded in the distance. The batteries in my transistor radio were dead, so I had no way of knowing what was happening elsewhere in the city. I felt oddly isolated in a metropolis of nearly eight million people.

From apartments behind my brownstone I heard sounds of partying. Candles flickered here and there in windows. I thought: A recent trend in movies is the production of films about catastrophes involving thousand of people, and now here we were in the very middle of one.

I was unable to hear radio music. I could not read because I wanted to save my flashlight batteries. So Abraham Lincoln educated himself by reading in the light of a candle or fireplace? Good for him—but what toll did that take on his eyesight? God bless Thomas Edison for giving us electricity! Holding the flashlight in my left hand, I put my right hand in front of the beam and then saw a gigantic shadow of my hand on the ceiling . . . Menacing . . . What was life like before there was artificial light? Small wonder that primitive people feared darkness. How much we take for granted our technological civilization. How fragile it is in fact! This savage summer our society slides faster and ever faster down the slope toward nihilism.

THURSDAY, JULY 14, 1977 ▨ When I awakened at 8:30 A.M. I found that electricity had not been restored. What should I do? How long would this condition last?

I decided to go outdoors to look around. As I left my apartment I carried my flashlight because the stairway was dark. When I reached the street I saw other people with torches. The sun was hot and bright. Another day of searing heat—92 degrees. No traffic lights working. At other intersections motorists and pedestrians had to work out their own patterns of avoidance, which they did with mutual respect. However, in crossing streets I was more careful than usual.

I hoped to get a *New York Times* at the newsstands at 23rd and 8th, but they were closed. Then I saw a young man sitting in a car parked in front of a building. The car radio was spewing out news. I asked whether I might listen to the news with him. He invited me into the front seat. He works for the firm that owns the building where he was parked, and he said he drove here from Jersey to make sure the place was okay. We heard bulletins about looting here and there in the city after lights went out. Some merchants lost everything. Cops and firemen had been injured. Fires had been set.

Close at hand was a radio shop and I hoped to buy a transistor radio or some batteries, but the place was closed. I strolled to a restaurant on Eighth Avenue. Closed. I walked to my favorite stationery store, where I found the owner standing behind his barred gate. Max Strum said he drove from Brooklyn into Manhattan to check on his place, and Brooklyn's Flatbush Avenue had been so badly looted it looked as though it had been bombed. Max told me that his son had left for a Florida vacation and he hoped Ken would not fly back to be with him when he hears the news about New York.

Seeing a pedestrian with a copy of the *Times* I asked where he got it and he said on Eighth Avenue at West 29th Street, so I began walking north. On the sidewalks knots of people stood with bewildered expressions on their faces. The Cornish Arms on 23rd has many old people. Most of them were outside, leaning on canes and rockers and crutches. How hot and dark and lonely their rooms must be!

At one newsstand I found no *Times* but did see a fat volume of the collected letters of Thomas Wolfe, which I bought for only 50 cents. At another stand I saw some *Times* and bought two copies, for today's edition is sure to become a collector's item. The paper had two front pages—its regular one and a special one concerning the blackout. Spread across the top of the paper was this banner:

POWER FAILURE BLACKS OUT NEW YORK:
THOUSANDS TRAPPED IN THE SUBWAYS:
LOOTERS AND VANDALS HIT SOME AREAS

Tucking the book and papers beneath my sweating arm, I began walking home. I was hungry. The corner grocery store was open but since there was no power Lou was unable to make coffee. I bought a roll and walked to the lawn of the ILGWU housing complex to sit and eat and read until the radio store opened—but it never did.

SUNDAY, AUGUST 21, 1977 ▨ Needing exercise, I walked down to Greenwich Village and into Washington Square. It was crowded.

Suddenly I saw a face I knew. It was David Dubinsky, the famous labor leader, long-time president of the International Ladies' Garment Workers' Union. Just now in my study I checked and found that he was born in Poland in 1892, which means that he is 85 years old. He is short and squat and looks his age. He still has all his hair, which is totally white and worn in a pompadour. His face is mottled with brown spots. He wore a black-and-white checked shirt, dark trousers, and shuffled along in black "space shoes."

Our eyes met. When he saw that I recognized him, he grinned. Stepping up and shaking his hand, I said that when I was a reporter for the *World-Telegram* I often wrote about him. How is his health? Good, good, he replied. I recalled that he knew Franklin D. Roosevelt, among other notables. Dubinsky was pleased by the fact that I knew who he is and wanted to talk to him.

As he strolled away I sat down on a bench to engage in my favorite sport—people watching. Along came a young woman handing out reprints of a *New York Post* editorial backing Ed Koch for mayor. She kept announcing that within minutes Koch would arrive at the square to speak. A man to my left took the campaign literature and sneered: "That bleedin' liberal! Wants to get unions for prisoners!"

Then Koch approached. He is very tall, mostly bald, with a tanned face and big nose, wearing a striped shirt open at the throat and with his sleeves rolled up. Koch is a Democrat with a career as a city councilman and congressman. He moved along a line of benches shaking hands with people. When he reached me and our hands met, I asked: "Have you read my book called *The Epic of New York City?*"

"No," he replied, "I did not."

I saw in his eyes that he thought I was a nut.

My feelings were not hurt. However, I was surprised that a man running for mayor of this town had not read a book considered the standard one-volume history of New York.

On election day I voted for Ed Koch.

FRIDAY, SEPTEMBER 2, 1977 ■ Anthony Perkins lives a few doors west of my building. During the years I have lived in Chelsea I have become a Perkins-watcher. However, the actor is so pathologically shy that he even avoids eye contact with passersby lest they stop to talk to him. Every week or so I see him walking or bicycling along my block, his lips grim.

This hot and humid day I stopped in the Two Sisters ice cream parlor for a malted milk. I had just sat down at a table with four chairs when I saw Tony Perkins enter with his wife and their son of about four. They took stools at the counter. Arising, I offered them my table, but the film star thanked me and said they were okay where they were.

This was the first time I had had a chance to sit and look at Perkins at close range. He wore a T-shirt, tan slacks and mocassins. A few white hairs are visible in his short cropped hair. His glasses have temples made of wire. He wears his wristwatch on his right hand, which may mean that he is left-handed. His wife is tall and blonde and beautiful, the bone structure of her face finely sculpted. Her eyes are blue. Perkins and his wife looked into one another's eyes as they talked and laughed. Their son sat between them, and Perkins absently and fondly rubbed his hair.

MONDAY, SEPTEMBER 12, 1977 ■ The *Times* published an interview with 85-year-old Alfred A. Knopf, the famous publisher of good books. He said something with which I agree: "The state of the Western world is so bad that I think we are living through the beginning of the end of a great civilization. You can sum up the reason in a five-letter word: Greed."

FRIDAY, SEPTEMBER 16, 1977 ■ In a book about Lyndon B. Johnson by Eric F. Goldman, I learned that in a speech in Manchester, N.H., LBJ once said: "When we retaliated in the Tonkin Gulf, we dropped bombs on their nests where they had their PT boats housed, and *we dropped them within thirty-five miles of the Chinese border.*" (My italics.)

I wonder how Americans would react if Red Chinese planes dropped bombs in Canada only 35 miles north of the U.S. border? The ranting of anti-communist reactionaries cannot erase the fact that at times our own nation has behaved in an aggressive manner. Disgusting! Democratic Senator J. William Fulbright of Arkansas was correct when he spoke of "the arrogance of power."

THURSDAY, NOVEMBER 22, 1977 ■ Aware that I have a drinking problem and need help, I telephoned Alcoholics Anonymous. The phone was answered by a soft-voiced woman named Pat. I said I'm not sure whether I am an alcoholic, but possibly may be one, and I want to attend an AA meeting, preferably one near my neighborhood. When she learned where I live she said a meeting is due to begin at 7:30 P.M. in the Christian Lutheran Church at 355 East 19th Street.

This one, she said, is for beginners. To my astonishment I learned that each week more than 1,200 AA meetings are held in the New York area. Each of them, Pat added, has its own special flavor. She said that AA is a non-profit group that pays its own way, and I will not have to pay anything, although a collection plate will be passed.

Ask any question you wish, she told me. Identify myself however I wish. I had to wait four hours before leaving for the meeting. Pat asked whether I wanted an afternoon session. Laughing, I explained that I am a spree drinker and do not have an hourly problem.

After hanging up, I wondered whether I actually would have the guts to go, and then sensed to my surprise that I truly felt eager to attend. This is one measure of my awareness of my problem. Because I was unsure of the location of the church, and because a light rain began falling, I hailed a cab. The driver may have been unfamiliar with this part of town, or he may have been trying to cheat me, but he took me in the wrong direction. I steeled myself not to explode in anger since I did not wish to enter that AA meeting in an emotional mood. I just refused to tip the cabbie.

The meeting, held in the basement of the church, was already under way when I arrived. About 40 people were present. At the door I was met by a black man who greeted me with a smile. Tiptoeing to the back of the room, I sat down but was unable to hear the speaker clearly, a woman in her sixties, who sat at a small table at the front of the room, so I walked around and took a chair in the front row to her left.

She called herself Fritzi. Not knowing what to expect, I found my palms were sweaty. Fritzi—bless her heart!—proved to be intelligent, articulate and very amusing in the way she poked fun at herself. Nonetheless, she told horrible stories. She would lie in bed for days, her body and linen dirty, drinking, drinking, drinking. She was afraid to walk alone through Grand Central Terminal. When she began a vacation she did not leave town but stayed in bed to drink.

Finally deciding to go to an AA meeting, she arrived with an air of superiority and hostility. Here is how she characterized her attitude: "You see, I'm so Goddamn cultured I thought that all of you were just a bunch of slobs!" The audience laughed *with* her. "Now," she continued, "I don't much care for swearing, since I love our language and consider it rich in meanings, but just this once I'll let myself go a little. So I said to myself:

'Ah, fuck it!'—and came to my first meeting." A roar of approval. Fritzi had them in the palm of her hand.

She chain-smoked, and soon I saw that almost everyone was smoking. Okay, so it's hard enough to give up one vice, let alone two at a time. Fritzi has shapely hands. She said that one of the best things she got that first night was touching, people reaching out to touch her physically. That, she declared, was what she most needed because she thought she was just about the worst human being ever born. I sighed in relief. My latest drinking spree had left me marinated in guilt. Fritzi tried to make some distinction I did not understand, so when she threw the meeting open to questions I stood up.

"My name is Eddie, and I may or may not be an alcoholic. This is my first AA meeting and I don't know whether I am allowed to ask questions, but I do have one for you."

Fritzi turned, looked into my eyes, smiled and said: "Of course, welcome!" However, she was unable to clarify the distinction I sought, so my confidence in her sagged.

Questions came from other people. They wore white badges showing their first names and most seemed to know one another. A pretty mother in her thirties said she drank so much that for three years she refused to look at herself in a mirror. When a young man aired his problems without making much sense, I was struck by the fact that everyone in the room gave him total attention. Slowly I realized it has been years since I had attended any kind of gathering where everyone paid strict attention. Fritzi said something kind to every questioner. My confidence in her was restored when she said that we must learn to love ourselves first and foremost.

Then she arose and the others stood up and before I knew what was happening she took my right hand in her left hand and the entire audience began reciting the Lord's Prayer. An agnostic, I stumbled through it, not having recited it in decades. After a fervent Amen! Fritzi turned to me and said: "I think I just have to kiss you, since this is your first meeting." And she put her arms around me and kissed my cheek. I was speechless.

Two men charged at me. One was burly and roughly dressed. Grinning, he held out his hand and said: "I'm Bill. Welcome!" At about that moment I was reached by the other man, who wore an expensive leather jacket, was handsome and had a deep voice. He said: "I'm Ben. Welcome!" They were so open and simple I felt comfortable. Ben said he'd like to serve me a cup of coffee, so we walked to the rear of the room where a huge coffee urn stood on a table.

Because of Ben's resonant voice, I asked whether he is an actor. He said no, but did not identify his occupation. I realized I had goofed. Looking around, I was astonished to see so many happy smiling faces. Everyone seemed to like everyone. Although it was obvious that this AA group consisted of people from every social class, they mingled easily. Some were articulate, some silent but smiling. Suddenly a second meeting began in the room.

This time the speaker was a well-dressed man in his late fifties who said he had been a salesman. His story was even worse than Fritzi's. Due to his drinking he blew two marriages and several jobs. Once he lived In Chicago, prowling the streets and hanging out in bars, fantasizing that he was an FBI agent. He actually carried a .38 in a holster under his left arm. When his second wife left him he decided to kill her and then himself. He did not do so. Instead, one morning he awakened with a clanging hangover in a strange city in a cheap hotel called Paradise Inn. The audience howled at the name of the inn.

Maybe I had expected AA members to be dull, straitlaced folks who sat around never cracking a smile. Well, I was wrong. I found them casual and open and quick to laugh and forgive. They have the habit of confessing to one another. I thought, hey, this is for me! Because I have been psychoanalyzed, because I read a lot about therapy, and because I constantly confess in my diary, I felt drawn to others willing to admit to others how weak they are, or had been. All evening long I heard no word of censure. The only *ought* was that one *ought* not to take that first drink.

During the first session of the evening I had sat near a man with a craggy face who said he was a Texan. Well, during the second session a young black man in tattered clothes wandered in, obviously drunk, and began talking in a loud voice. The Texan said quietly, "If the gentleman will wait until the end of this session, then it might be better." The black man subsided. Next I saw Tex get up and fetch coffee for the black man. I thought, Jesus, if AA also can break down the color barrier, then it surely is some organization!

When the salesman finished speaking and opened the session to questions, I listened awhile and then raised my hand. He nodded toward me. I said that since this was my first meeting perhaps I was wrong to speak so much, but he smiled at me and said: "Since this is your first visit here, that makes you the most important person at this meeting. Please ask away."

I thought, hold it! What kind of crap is this?

However, I asked what a sponsor does and how one finds one. I was told that a sponsor is a person who will help an alcoholic whenever he feels he just has to have a drink. And the way to get a sponsor is to walk up to someone and ask him. Of course, a member may decline to act as sponsor because he may have prior commitments. Nonetheless—just ask. Then I asked whether one may call his sponsor as late as midnight. General laughter. I was told that a sponsor will answer his phone at any hour of the night.

A man who sat across the room said, "I'd just like to say to our newcomer that he looks one helluva lot better than I did my first visit to AA, and I hope he believes all that we're saying."

Then the session ended.

As I arose I was approached by a tall woman in her forties with clear eyes and smooth skin. Smiling, she said, "And if you don't believe us, my name is (she gave me her real name) and my number is (and she gave me her real phone number), and you may call me at any time!" My jaw sagged. She added, "Here, let me write it out for you." I had been given an envelope of AA literature, so I handed this to her and she wrote down what she had just said.

Then she told me that one night she got a call from a man who said he needed help, and he gave her an address she knew was in the South Bronx—a very dangerous place. She also thought the man was black. Nonetheless, she went to the address he gave her, a shabby tenement, and sure enough, the man was black and had other black men with him, but they treated her like a queen. She went back again and again and now considers them "family."

A quiet man stood to my right as she talked and before I left he smiled and said he'd like to give me his name and phone number, too. He wrote them down on my envelope and said, "Call me at any time." Never had I made so many friends so quickly—courtesy of AA.

A man named Charlie, who seemed in charge of the meeting, bustled up and flashed a grin at me through a thick moustache. By now Ben had attached himself to me, and he and Charlie poked fun at one another. We only tease people we like. The two men invited me out for coffee, saying some of the best AA work is done in coffee klatches after the end of evening sessions. We were joined by a young man who appeared to be gay, for there were references to the fact that he lives with another man who also is an alcoholic but was attending another AA meeting elsewhere this evening.

The four of us strolled to a delicatessen on Third Avenue. The gay guy said that before he and his partner joined AA, their bill at their local liquor store was $6,400 a year. Wow! Ben said he too is saving money. He had been drinking a fifth a day and went to his first AA meeting so drunk that later he remembered nothing of it. Ben graduated from the Wharton School of Business, which I know ranks with the Harvard Business School. He joined AA only 40 days ago and has attended meetings 40 successive days.

I said I was unable to believe the remark that I was the most important person at tonight's session. All three men grinned. Charlie then explained that without new members AA would die. They need new blood. They need others to whom they may impart what they have learned from older members.

The woman who gave me her phone number had said that tomorrow night she would attend a meeting in the Murray Hill section of Manhattan, and invited me to go there. With a wry grin, she had added that that group was one of the liveliest in town, whereas some other groups are too square for her. Ben now said he plans to attend that meeting. Charlie said he had a date on the Bowery.

When I was not asking questions the three men were plying me with remarks—some of them platitudinous, or so I felt—but when they saw skepticism in my eyes, they vowed there is truth in those commonplace expressions. Again and again they said they don't know why AA works. All they know is that it *does* work and has helped at least a million people. I asked whether I ever will be able to understand why I am unable to stop after just one drink. Charlie said no. Ben said yes. Then they laughed and agreed it really doesn't matter whether or not I understand, provided I can resist taking that first fatal drink.

The gay guy turned over his glass of water, pouring the last few drops into an ash tray on the table. He said he learned from AA that he must empty his mind just as he now had emptied his glass. I said this sounded like Zen. In fact, I feel that AA blends several attitudes, disciplines, faiths and techniques—elements of Christianity, borrowings from Zen, a pinch of Christian Science, a touch of mysticism and much of psychotherapy.

AA is loosely structured. In fact, it is the most loosely structured organization I have ever encountered. More than once I was told it has no big shots, that it is wholly democratic. I like this lack of rigidity. No one asked me to sign anything. No one begged me to attend a second meeting. Everyone said that whatever I want to do with my life is my business, but if I consider myself an alcoholic, they are there to help me whenever I want help.

I told the three men that, nonetheless, I may have some difficulty with AA, just as I had trouble, at first, with psychoanalysis. The day I met the doctor who became my beloved therapist, he said he preferred I read no psychoanalytic literature while in treatment with him. Stiffening, I snapped I would let no one hobble my curiosity. The doctor had smiled and held out his hands in gentle surrender.

My coffee klatch friends smiled, shrugged and said okay. Do anything I wish. Think whatever I wish. Charlie said they believe that alcoholism is physical, mental and spiritual. Whenever one becomes a drunkard, his spirituality vanishes first, his power of reasoning next, and his body last. Recovery follows in reverse order: First the body gets better, then the mind, finally one's spirit.

Charlie said one new member had trouble with the idea of praying to God. Charlie suggested he try praying to a door knob, if he wished, and the man did and later reported the door knob seemed to help. All that AA members care about is what works. They are the ultimate pragmatists. Ben said he has received so much help from AA in only 40 days that now he believes in it with blind faith. I said I doubted whether I could do that.

Ben shrugged and said: "Okay. But just don't take that first drink."

I asked whether it would be dangerous to go to cocktail parties—not that I attend many. They agreed it is best to avoid them. They said cocktail parties bore them, and I agreed. Both in the AA meeting in church and now in the delicatessen, all the talk was about stuff that matters, what lies close to the heart. AA members hold their own little parties in their homes, serve soft drinks and otherwise behave like others.

As regards sponsors, Charlie explained that even though he might dislike me personally, if I asked him to become my sponsor and called him at three o'clock in the morning, he would be at my apartment within a half hour. Not—mind you!—if I had taken that first drink. When he saw a question in my eyes, he vowed he would do this to help himself, more than to help me.

Enlightened selfishness, Bertrand Russell calls this attitude.

I did attend a few more AA meetings but at last stopped going to them. However much I admire this movement, and I do, I am the sort of guy who has to do everything by himself. A matter of temperament or stupidity—take your pick. In any event, I completely broke myself of the habit and have not had a single drink in many years. And, no, it does not bother me to be with people who do drink.

TUESDAY, NOVEMBER 29, 1977 ▪ My friend Janet Steinberg is a very funny woman. She wanted to become a comedienne but was side-tracked into a career in business. She delights in telling the story of how ignorant she was when she first began working.

In 1940, at the age of 20, she became secretary to M. Garfunkel, who owned his own millinery store on 5th Avenue near 57th Street. One day he gave her a check and told her to go to the bank and deposit it for him. The bank was near her office. She walked in, went up to a teller and handed her the check. The teller asked questions she was unable to answer.

"You must have this okayed by an officer," said the teller, "and then bring it back to me."

This sounded strange to Janet but, following orders, she left the bank and walked up to a cop who was directing traffic at 5th Avenue and 57th Street. The time was 12:30 P.M., so the traffic was thick, the noise loud. Janet held out the check to the policeman.

"I don't understand this," she said, "but at the bank they told me that you have to okay this check."

The cop, continuing to direct traffic, cried, "I don't understand!"

Then a light dawned in Janet's mind: *Bank* officer, not *police* officer!

After Janet told me her story, she added, "And if that cop is still alive, I'll bet he's still talking about that dumb blonde who walked up with a check!"

CHAPTER 16

1978

WEDNESDAY, FEBRUARY 22, 1978 ■ This is my 67th birthday. Now I am older than Abraham Lincoln and Ernest Hemingway lived to be. Now I am about one-third as old as this republic. During my lifetime the American population has more than doubled.

Like other people, I suppose I half-expected to live forever but, instead, am taken by surprise to find I am an old man. What have I learned? What do I know? I do not even know whether I know enough to realize that I know nothing. Never in my life have I had an original thought. The artist creates nothing; all he does is rearrange the pieces of reality that were born when the universe was born. Truth slumbers within everyone. I have awakened only enough to express old truths in new forms, to coin maxims. My daughter likes them so much she urges me to publish them in a thin volume. If I do, I'll call it *Infinity and Three Doors Beyond*.

Here's a finite sampling of my maxims:

The secret of eternal youth is curiosity and enthusiasm . . . ignorance is the root of all evil . . . one who accepts himself is sane while one who rejects himself is mad . . . love is communication . . . true lovers copulate with their eyes . . . anger masks pain . . . guilt is grief over a lost ideal . . . fear is borrowed pain . . .

A violent person is a spiritual weakling . . . only the brave can be wise . . . only the wise can be good . . . a coward is a person afraid to be himself . . . a selfish person cannot be happy . . . mysticism begins where logic ends . . .

What cripples us are the secrets we don't know we're keeping from ourselves . . . secrets divide while truth unites . . . a friend is one who urges you to be yourself . . . an institution is a fossilized insight . . . science is rules, technology is tools, knowledge is facts, while wisdom is knowledge of oneself . . . guilt feels like a wall of eyes . . .

Occasional solitude is as necessary as food and drink . . . teach questions, not answers . . . a genius just pays closer attention than others . . . fear distorts reality . . . try to see a lot in a little . . . love can be contagious . . . if you don't forgive yourself you'll poison yourself . . .

An insight is a bubble bursting on the brim of the unconscious . . . your true identity is not ego but essence . . . the cave of reality is safer than the castle of fantasy . . . we detour through hell to reach heaven . . . some folks assassinate their own souls . . . silence is a bandage on the wound of life . . . greed counts but never reckons . . . never measure yourself against your parents . . . let no one else identify you . . .

Yesterday was once tomorrow . . . if you feel you're okay, then you are okay . . . everyone is a card-carrying god . . . satire is praise of that which you despise . . . sarcasm camouflages pain . . . the truth is obvious— come to think of it . . . sex is physics . . . love is metaphysics . . . he who sins is sick . . . dare to stare at evil . . .

The more love you give away the more you have left . . . it is easier to believe than to think . . . life is an interlude between one infinity and another . . . the richest person in the world is the one who wants nothing . . . the intelligent person is eager to change his mind when proven wrong . . . one who is never bored is never boring . . . the only thing that's really shocking is cruelty . . . the way we see things changes them . . .

A radical refuses to ignore injustice . . . a reactionary says that yesterday was better than today . . . a conservative says that everything is okay . . . love is compound interest in one another . . . a marriage license is a pledge to pay attention to one another . . . a clock doles out infinity . . .

Neighbors usually want to borrow a cup of platitudes . . . a success is one who has become himself . . . love is a portable shrine . . . decadence is elegant cruelty . . . some people go mad for fear of going mad . . . the symbol of hope is a seed . . . the most beautiful sound in the world is the laughter of children . . .

To be silly from time to time is to be sane . . . please see through me . . . vanity is sand while pride is rock . . . the only way you can get a firm grip on yourself is by letting go . . . to lie to yourself is to kill yourself piecemeal . . . cope with your pain by being kind to others . . . vice honors virtue by trying to imitate it . . . war is madness sanctified and magnified . . . truth is paradoxical because All is One and One is All . . . society is coming apart because it is a tissue of lies . . .

A dream is a fragment of your unconscious begging to be discovered . . . one kind word can save a life . . . the saint is unaware he is saintly . . . A computer never asks *why?* . . . if you stare long enough you will see everything . . . looking precedes thinking . . . essence is like a waterfall, ever changing, always the same . . . love doubles pleasure and halves pain . . . if you love yourself you cannot be insulted . . . the one who is the first to become defensive is the one who starts the argument . . .

You honor me with your honesty . . . if you want to be impressive, be simple . . . no dogma, no faith, is more precious than a single human life . . . folks who agree for the sake of agreeing are disagreeable . . . to conform to others is to condemn yourself . . . the word *scientific* is not a halo over truth . . .

The only evil is hurting another or yourself . . . you cannot find yourself outside yourself . . . if you fail to become whole you will die of fragmentation . . . a mystery is only an unseen cause . . . creativity follows a feeling of congestion . . . society is a web of agreements . . . science is institutionalized curiosity . . .

Free will is the freedom to decide what to pay attention to . . . most people hide behind words . . . nature is neutral about truth . . . television is the opiate of the masses . . . when one speaks the truth he feels young . . . a genius is like a cathedral . . . let society stutter while you speak the truth . . .

A genius distills data into principles, particulars into universals . . . listening can be more powerful than speaking . . . a good person flunks sadism . . . truth is transparent, falsehood opaque . . . you become yourself by turning yourself inside out . . .

The masses follow those who believe in themselves . . . charisma is self-confidence . . . you delight me by existing . . . accept your lover's fantasies . . . beauty and truth are hypnotic . . . the artist works while the dilettante plays at working . . .

Truth is naked . . . lies are disguises . . . if you will tell me what you think you are, I will tell you what you really are . . . history is an echo chamber in which people call for help . . . you can stay sane if one person listens and understands . . . the reward for living is knowing . . . money is nothing going nowhere . . .

Tragedy is an unfulfilled potential . . . all people are equal when they speak the truth . . . enthusiasm is spirituality overflowing . . . one must love to live . . . when we die we are right back where we started . . . patriotism is collective madness . . . be inquisitive, not acquisitive . . . truth travels at the speed of light . . . to go into oneself is to go out into the cosmos . . .

One is in a state of grace when he loves himself . . . if you play by the rules of society you will lose your own ballgame . . . lies need company while truth can live alone . . . guilt is egotistical . . . pain is a broken connection . . . give your beloved everything except your soul . . . an ideal is a representation of hope . . .

A charming person is one who listens well . . . every act of violence is a confession of failure . . . the unusual usually happens . . . an insight is a conscious awareness of a part of the unconscious . . . reality is unique and irregular . . . you will never get what you want unless you know what you want . . . no one is mature unless he loves himself . . . extreme formality cloaks violence . . . .

Essence is vibrations . . . light holds everything together . . . democracy can work only if people tell the truth . . . an orgasm extinguishes the ego . . . The two worst fears are death and seeing one's true self . . . I give you my all when I give you my attention . . . one can create a work of art by being one's self . . . people who talk fast are afraid others won't listen . . . to be filled with wonder is to be religious . . . would you love me if you knew all my secrets? . . . truth is not an absolute but a relationship . . .

A neurotic is one who lies to himself . . . a psychotic is one who rejects himself . . . the establishment is a conspiracy of the few against the many . . . true love is telepathic . . . the only miracle is reality . . . meditation is spiritual medication . . . strangers thrust their fantasies at you . . . some sick people commit murder to get attention . . .

The Holy Trinity is thesis, antithesis and synthesis . . . capitalism is greed sanctified and institutionalized . . . a masochist is a glutton for punishment . . . wisdom is awareness of ignorance . . . the more one values himself the less he takes himself seriously . . . temporary madness can inoculate one against terminal madness . . .

The liar tries to murder truth . . . when you hear a compliment you see yourself as another sees you . . . a prophet listens not to others but to the voices within himself . . . arrogance is the badge of ignorance . . . silence filters out stimuli . . . compassion is more precious than creativity . . . a cynic is one who looks for ulterior motives . . .

Sex can be a sacrament . . . the best teacher is a mistake . . . lies are obscene phone calls . . . I hurt myself when I hurt others . . . an artist is hot while a mystic is cool . . . an insight is a synthesis . . . there is only one of everything . . .

One starving person is a reproach to all mankind . . . lust possesses while love liberates . . . memory is a boomerang . . . a consumer society is a consumed society . . . fear walks with a limp . . . curiosity is holy . . . the quality of attention determines the quality of thought . . . don't feel guilty about not feeling guilty . . . the only absolute is everything . . . friendship is a dialogue . . . don't put all your eggs in one fantasy . . .

One who is not himself is nothing . . . gossip is pollution . . . trivia is anything that does not magnify the soul . . . he who listens best learns most . . . it is impossible to embellish the truth . . . to think is to define . . . it is normal to be abnormal . . . I pledge allegiance to myself . . .

1979

FRIDAY, MARCH 30, 1979   ■   There is big news: The risk of a reactor core meltdown has arisen at the crippled Three Mile Island atomic power plant in Middletown, Pennsylvania.

Today, at the request of the governor of the state, young children and pregnant women began evacuating an area within five miles of the plant. Also 23 schools were closed and 15 mass-care centers were opened in counties near there. We do not seem to be getting all the truth about this situation from federal officials or utility executives.

On a TV show one utility spokesman horrified me by blandly declaring that "we are not a nation of technological cowards." Oh, no? I'm scared. I would be willing to accept a lower standard of living by closing all nuclear plants now in operation in this nation.

The Faustian hubris of Western man may end in the destruction of our civilization. I distrust some scientists because they seem more concerned with dubious ends attained through nefarious means than with life itself. As I watched two TV documentaries about the developing situation in Pennsylvania, I became aware that all my muscles were tense.

SATURDAY, MARCH 31, 1979   ■   In the *New York Times* I read that 600,000 gallons of slightly radioactive water was released into the Susquehanna River by the Three Mile Island nuclear plant in Pennsylvania. When reporters asked a spokesman for the utility company why this had been done without notifying anyone, he snapped that the company doesn't have to tell everyone everything it does. The bastard. The hell with public safety and health!

Tonight I listened to three television documentaries about the situation in Pennsylvania. There still is danger of a meltdown at the atomic plant.

There is a conservative Washington correspondent named James Kilpatrick who defended the alleged safety records of other nuclear facilities in the U.S. and then sniffed that we should not get excited by "a little accident" at one of them. He accused the press of blowing up the story to unwarranted proportions. He doesn't seem to care that perhaps 10,000 people might be killed.

MONDAY, NOVEMBER 19, 1979   ■   The B. Dalton book store at 666 Fifth Avenue had announced that Norman Mailer would appear there today to autograph copies of his latest book, *The Executioner's Song*, which I have read. I believe I own a copy of every book written by Mailer. When he is at the top of his form he is the greatest living American writer, in my opinion, but he's also like the little girl who had a curl on her forehead. When she was good she was very, very good, and when she was bad she was horrid. That's Mailer.

Back in 1971 when I won a literary award he sent me a two-paragraph letter, which was kind of him, but I've never met the man. I'm intensely curious about him.

He agreed to appear at B. Dalton because, to celebrate the first year of its existence at that site, it promised to give all of today's proceeds to the New York Public Library. I put on a tie for the first time in months and stuffed my briefcase with a copy of his new book, which has received rave reviews, and also a copy of an earlier work, *Of a Fire on the Moon*, about astronauts. I like this the best of all of Mailer's books.

This B. Dalton store occupies the southwest corner of the avenue and 52nd Street. First time I ever saw it. The place has 300,000 books on two levels, the street level and the large basement, both floors pleasantly decorated. It sells only new books.

Descending to the basement I found an area called the *Authors' Plaza*, first of its kind I ever saw. It is a tiny pit, two steps down from the peach-colored rug on the floor of the basement, and only about 20 by 15 feet. Surrounding it is a metal railing. I sat down in a chair and wrote notes of all I saw. In the pit there sat a plain wooden table six feet long. Piled on its right side were many copies of *The Executioner's Song*, while behind the table with its two chairs there was a stack of other copies. Overhead were four recessed lights and one spotlight, all unlit. A tiny row of lights ran around the top of the area.

Suddenly a young woman appeared and said: "May I present Norman Mailer."

Glancing up, I saw him and instantly had two impressions: Short . . . Fat. Although I knew Mailer had put on weight, I was unprepared for the sight of the man with such a thick body. I would have known his face had I passed him on a street—which, in fact, happened to me many years ago.

Stepping down into the pit, Mailer held out his arms, flashed a smile and said: "This is the first time in my life I ever signed books, but I'm glad to do it for such a worthy cause." Meaning, of course, that the proceeds would go to the Public Library.

Mailer is perhaps five feet eight inches tall. He wore a dark jacket, a maroon turtleneck sweater, tan slacks and black Oxfords. I sat 15 feet from him. His rumpled hair is now not just gray but rather the color of silver. It is thinning out at the top of his head. He has grizzly eyebrows, a rutted forehead, electric blue eyes and a ruddy complexion. This morning he must have cut himself shaving, because there was a tiny bandage on the left side of his chin.

A sunburst of laugh wrinkles radiates from his eyes. Mailer is 56 years old. He smiled often and spoke in a soft voice, which somewhat surprised me, for I've seen him ever so boisterous on television. His hands are square, fingernails clean. He held a black pen in his right hand. I know that when he writes he wears glasses, but now he was without them.

Men and women, one after another, stepped down into the pit and walked toward the author, some extending their hands, which he shook in seeming pleasure. He perched on the edge of his chair and sometimes leaned forward to ask the name of the person in front of him, even inquiring how the person spells his name. Today Mailer was being that persona which he seems to dislike—the nice Jewish boy from Brooklyn—but he also is a man who enjoys butting heads with other men. Now, of course, he was The Great Author.

One of the things I like about myself is that I never belittle anyone who deserves his good fortune. Mailer may be our greatest living author, and he works hard and deserves all the acclaim he gets.

He listens well. He would fix his eyes upon the man or woman standing before the desk and bandy words with them. One man handed him an envelope, spoke some woman's name, and then I heard the phrase "fan letter." Mailer thanked him and slipped the envelope into a pocket of his jacket. Many folks carried not only *The Executioner's Song* but also copies of his previous books which they wanted autographed, and Mailer obliged them. In fact, he wrote whatever inscription anyone wanted. Hovering around this scene was a hush like a fog. The awe of Mailer was palpable.

I began to think I'd better get in line myself, but when I arose and walked back along it, I discovered it consisted of more than a hundred people, so I decided to leave without an autograph because I had been privileged to sit near him, to observe him.

1980

SATURDAY, MARCH 8, 1980 ■ I know a 27-year-old man who is a broker in commodity futures. Sometimes he earns $20,000 a month. Last month he bought a house costing $105,000. Last week he flew to Las Vegas where he gambled away $4,000.

This evening when he visited me, he told me about a recent dream he had: He entered a burned-out discount house to buy a towel, but was unable to find one big enough. What did I make of this dream?

"Well," I said, "you are living at such a mad pace that in your unconscious you're afraid you'll burn yourself out. This explains why, in your dream, you walked into a store that had been burned out. And why was it a discount store? Because, at bottom, you don't think you're worth very much. Why did you want to purchase a towel? Because you feel guilty about your sins and want to wipe them away, but because you feel massively guilty there is no towel big enough to do the job."

Looking at me with surprised eyes, he said my interpretation made sense to him.

FRIDAY, MARCH 14, 1980   A new tenant has moved into the studio apartment on the ground floor of the brownstone in which I live. He is Carmen Capalbo, a famous theatrical director and producer. We play chess together and are becoming good friends. Carmen is one of the pioneers of the off-Broadway movement and perhaps is best known for *The Threepenny Opera* that he directed and co-produced at the De Lys Theater at 121 Christopher Street in Greenwich Village. It ran almost seven years and earned him both a Tony Award and an Obie Award. Carmen is 54 years old and has eyes like the eyes of Picasso.

Today Carmen told me about his 1957 production of the play by William Saroyan called *The Cave Dwellers*. This calls for an actor to play the role of a bear—not a phoney bear, but one as lifelike as possible. For this part Carmen chose a tall actor who had appeared in *The Threepenny Opera*.

The man did his research by visiting zoos, where he spent hours watching live bears, studying their movements and even sketching them. However, when Carmen rehearsed him alone, the actor was unable to imitate the swinging gait of a bear, so Carmen went down on all fours to show the man the kind of performance he wanted.

Carmen spent $9,000 crafting a costume for the man to wear. Wanting him to remain in character as soon as he donned this outfit, Carmen told other members of the cast to treat him as though he were a real bear, not a man playing the part of one. The actor threw himself into the role so passionately that when the play opened some members of the audience thought they were seeing a genuine bear.

One day Carmen got a frantic phone call from the wife of the actor. She had a baby, and several times she caught her husband down on all fours, peering at the child and growling. She was afraid he might actually harm their son. Carmen then had the task of moderating the actor's behavior at home without at the same time blunting his performance on the stage.

I got a letter from Dr. Gene M. Gressley, director of the Archive of Contemporary History at the University of Wyoming at Laramie. Somehow he had heard about my diary. Gently he warned me of the danger of fire. I already had thought about this, since I smoked two packs of cigarets a day, until I quit in 1984. Gressley and I began corresponding.

At last he said his archive building not only was fireproof but had a sophisticated smoke detector and alarm system. I decided that if I really wanted to save my journal for use by historians of the future, I had to put it in a safe place. I wrote to Gressley, saying I would let him store my diary in his archive although I would retain legal title to it and might withdraw it at any time. One day in 1980 two truck drivers came to my apartment, packed the volumes of my diary in big cardboard boxes, loaded them onto the truck, then drove away. At that moment I felt the way I guess a woman feels after a stillbirth: Empty.

After Gressley read some of my journal he wrote, saying: "That diary is incredible. It is much more than a history of our contemporary times; it really represents the history of civilization, from one vantage point, by one very erudite and perceptive commentator."

Not only that: Gressley got in touch with the editor of the Guinness Book of World Records *to suggest it might identify my diary as the longest in the world.*

TUESDAY, JUNE 3, 1980   ▉   When I went down for my mail I found a package from the London office of the *Guinness Book of World Records*. Before opening it I dawdled, steeling myself to accept rejection, but in fact I was told there will be an entry about me in the 1981 edition, so now I am world champion about one thing.

I ran back downstairs to tell Carmen. With him was his son Marc, whom I was meeting for the first time. I told Marc that under ordinary circumstances I would ask him questions about his life, but today I was too excited. I told them about *Guinness* as we sat in Carmen's studio under a skylight while a thunderstorm exploded over the city.

I said I did not want to become guilty of hubris, and at that very moment a lightning flash flared through the skylight.

Carmen laughed, pointed toward the sky and said: "Eddie, be careful!"

Putting my hands together as though in prayer, I held them toward the skylight and cried: "Look, gods! Don't take me now! I'm humble, humble, humble!"

Carmen and Marc laughed.

THURSDAY, SEPTEMBER 4, 1980 ■ The other day I visited Lucy Wind in her apartment at Sutton Place South on the East River. Suddenly she pointed at an oil painting flecked with rainbow colors made by the sun shining through a glass vase. We exclaimed at its beauty. I quoted Keats: "Beauty is truth, truth beauty . . ." I told Lucy that while I have felt the force of this statement, I've never been able to explain it to my total satisfaction.

Well, today I let myself sleep as long as I wished, not arising until 1:30 P.M., and when I awakened and sat down in my big chair to drink coffee, I felt unusually well in both body and mind. Opening the casement window, which I had kept closed the past few weeks because of the heat and therefore the need to air-condition my apartment, I gazed out at the trees and appreciated their beauty. Through me there surged a wave of appreciation for this beauty of nature, for the fact that I love leisure, that I am well, that I live alone, that in many ways I am blessed with the good things of life even though I am poor.

I decided to read about beauty in a book that has become my favorite — *Great Treasury of Western Thought.* It was edited by Mortimer J. Adler and Charles Van Doren. I opened it to the meditations of Marcus Aurelius, who said in part: "Everything which is in any way beautiful is beautiful in itself, and terminates in itself. . . . That which is really beautiful has no need of anything."

I blurted out loud, "I've found it! Now, at last, I understand the connection between beauty and truth! Beauty is an *end* in itself. So is truth. Neither is an intermediary, neither is an instrument, neither is a means to an end, but the very end itself! Beauty and truth are the same because they are essence."

Joy overwhelmed me. I'd often said I doubted whether I would be able to understand this before I die, but now, within only a few moments today, I found the answer. Of course I understand that my understanding is not original. The only original thing is the universe itself. People who seek truth may travel many different paths to reach it, but when they arrive they find they stand on the same peak.

1981

THURSDAY, JANUARY 8, 1981   ▦   Today's mail brought a note from Alice, whom I met last month at a Christmas party.

Eddie,
    It was delightful meeting you and spending time with you Christmas weekend. How I love making new friends who are so charmingly stimulating! We should have dinner some time soon —

Alice

This astonishes me. I remember her very well. She is young and soft and round and friendly and vivacious and loquacious. At the party she sat to my left and as we smoked grass my eyes met her blue eyes and we peered deeply inside one another. Why does she want to see an old man?

FRIDAY, JANUARY 9, 1981   ▦   This evening I called Alice, who lives in the Village, and had a long talk with her. She is 32. I am 69. I began by saying I am astonished that a woman as young as she should care to see a man as old as myself. So convincingly did she declare that age makes no difference to her that at last I was forced to believe her.

    She was born in New York of Austrian and Polish ancestry but looks Irish, at 19 began living with a man she later married and was divorced a little more than two years ago. No children. She tried therapy but soon decided she didn't need it. She is a college graduate who made excellent grades and won several prizes, is quick to admit she has a good mind while also confessing she has much to learn. She said that at the party she was attracted to me because I am an intellectual, and she likes intellectuals. I quoted Ruth's definition of an intellectual as one who is excited by ideas. Alice agreed.

SATURDAY, JANUARY 10, 1981   ▦   This evening Alice and I dined in a Spanish restaurant in the Village. She is five one, weighs 108 pounds, has light blue eyes, light brown hair worn short, arms soft and round, beautiful hands and small feet. She is very feminine and gestures dramatically. She is even more intelligent than I had realized. She does not engage in idle chatter. She insists upon being herself and therefore is utterly natural. A witty woman, she laughs easily.

From the restaurant we strolled to her one-room apartment, about the size of my bedroom. She rolled a joint, took a couple of tokes and then urged me to finish it. We sat at opposite ends of her sofa, she an appealing, woman of 32, I a man of almost 70, my face grizzled because I am growing a beard. She likes beards. She has honest eyes. At last I said helplessly that much though I wanted to throw a pass at her, and despite a lifetime chasing women, I did not know how to begin with her.

She asked what I wanted her to do. I said I would like to see her breasts. Smiling, she removed her sweater and bra and leaned back. I gasped. Seldom have I seen such luscious breasts! Full, shapely, beautiful. Alice then began seducing me. Tilting her nude torso slightly, she walked the fingers of her right hand along the back of the sofa toward me, edged forward, brought her breasts within touching distance.

She is very very sensual. She plainly loves sex and is wholly without guilt. After we satisfied one another I felt more peaceful than I had in more than a decade. I had almost forgotten the sensation of romantic love—absolutely the best feeling one can have. No wonder many songs concern love but, of course, romance lasts but briefly and I am old while she is young, so we can share no future.

THURSDAY, JANUARY 15, 1981　Late this afternoon Alice came to my apartment from her office, clad in a long blue-gray dress and wearing pretty pumps on her shapely feet. I poured wine for her and gave myself coffee.

Then I did something daring and perhaps foolish. I let her read what I wrote in my diary about the two of us last Saturday night. I wanted her to check my accuracy. She objected to only one thing: I said her apartment is about the size of my bedroom, but she said it is larger, and she is correct. Other than this, she said I was accurate in my reportage of what happened. She added that it feels romantic to know that a writer is describing her in his diary.

Her father is 70 years old. Bluntly I asked Alice whether she regards me as a father figure. Scornfully, she said no! Nonetheless, I wonder. I'm sure she likes me for myself, but at the same time she may be using me to work out incestuous feelings toward her father, who never displays affection toward her.

Alice said she feels very comfortable with me. In fact, she added she likes me better than any man she has met within the past two and a half years—meaning, since her divorce. When again I mentioned my age, she asked whether on TV I saw Dick Cavett interview the English actress Eva

Le Gallienne. Yes. Well, asked Alice, wasn't she youthful, although she is 82? I had to admit this is true.

Alice is both logical and witty. She squealed in delight when I began scribbling notes about her wisecracks.

Alice often touches her face, a gesture I regard as proof of high intelligence.

After much more conversation, I blurted, "I'm terrified!"

"Why?"

"Because just being with you makes me so happy I'm afraid I'll be punished for feeling happy."

My therapist would have cried, "Eddie! There's that old Midwestern puritanical conscience again!"

SATURDAY, JANUARY 17, 1981 ■ Alice called and asked: "May I sleep with you tonight?"

This evening when she arrived she handed me two joints. We talked a lot. When I got high I said that the better I know her the more I believe that she is, as I expressed it, "a closet mystic." I also said that spiritually we are the same age. This is true of any two persons who are spiritual. We see each other with total clarity. To share a truth is to feel equal.

I like Alice's playfulness. I said: "Happiness is fun!" She remarked: "I've been saying that for years." I reminded her of Plato's doctrine of recollection, which alleges that everyone is born knowing all the big truths. Alice said: "Two people can't be jealous if they're equal."

Alice said she feels very comfortable with me. I said I'm happy to be with her and grateful that fate brought us together.

With mischievous eyes, she cried: "You forget who started this whole thing!" True. It was she who wrote me.

She said if sex was all she wanted she would not have pursued a 70-year-old man. While she lets me know she appreciates me, she never fawns upon me, never flatters me—thank God!

I had to go to the bathroom, and in the mirror I saw the face of an old man and was shocked by the contrast between my physical appearance and my youthful mood.

Alice feels free to disagree with me about values, but never becomes defensive and always tells me plainly what she thinks. Sometimes I agree that she is right and I am wrong. What matters is truth, not who utters it. Alice's perceptions and insights are swift and straight and profound.

"What changes truth," I asked, "if indeed truth can be changed?"

"A different vantage point!" she cried.

Exactly so! Einstein said much the same thing in different words.

I asked Alice whether she is a genius. When she began stammering, I knew she had considered this question without having the courage to declare that, yes, she is a genius. I praised her and coaxed her until at last she admitted that she may be something of a genius. I said I am a magician who wanders around the world, turning people into themselves. She agreed.

Alice feels no compulsion to talk all the time. She often lapses into silence and as I watch her face I observe that she is thinking furiously. Now, however, she launched into a lengthy monologue, telling me all about her life, her parents, her childhood, her attempts to save her marriage, her hopes and dreams and ideals. Out poured this torrent of words until at last I felt that for years she had wanted to tell everything to someone she trusted. I listened. With every cell of my being I drank in her words. Alice ended her confession with shining eyes and the statement that I understand her better than anyone she ever knew, that I see her exactly as she sees herself and thereby augment her love of self. Then she added she is afraid she is falling in love with me.

SUNDAY, FEBRUARY 22, 1981 ■ Today I became 70 years old. My friends gave me a party, and among the gifts were three joints of grass brought by Alice. The hostess held out a cake with one candle, and when I leaned forward to blow out the flame my white beard caught fire. Two women used their hands to put it out while others jeered that, yeah, Eddie will go to any extreme to attract attention! When the party ended I went down to the Village to spend the night with my young mistress.

SUNDAY, MARCH 15, 1981 ■ This morning, as on many other mornings, I awakened in Alice's apartment. Ours is such a sweet relationship that I am bitter—bitter because I am an old man and therefore unable to enjoy a long rapport with her. At times, within my skull, I rant at what—*fate?*

If I were only 20 years her senior, instead of 38, I would beg Alice to marry me. I have told her I could write a novel about an old man falling in love with a young woman, and in part this is what I am doing in my diary. Anyway, today soon after we awakened so did our passion, and so we made love again. Totally open and honest in her sexuality, she turns intimacy into a masterpiece.

After she had another orgasm, she took a shower. I strolled into the bathroom to behold her ripe body. She threw back her head as she stood under the shower and I watched enchanted as ropes of water, like coils of smoke, curled around her breasts and then gushed down her belly to blend into the marsh of the delta above her legs. What beauty! Her breasts are tipped with nipples the color of tea roses. Her back is an architectural wonder. It reminds me of the facade of some noble monument, such as the Washington Arch at Washington Square. No sign of her spine may be seen behind her flesh; instead, her entire back is a sleek ski slope down which my hand glides, from time to time, until it meets the hill of her rump. I adore every part of her body and want to touch it all the time, all the time, all the time!

Alice and I remained romantic friends over the next few years. She told me to continue writing freely about our sexuality in my diary. As soon as I taught her chess she began beating me, game after game. Then she met a good man about her age, decided to marry him and asked me to help her write the vows she would pledge to him during their wedding. I attended the ceremony and when she spoke those words she glanced across the chapel at me. She, her husband and I remain friends and see one another from time to time. Now they have a son and when he was seven Alice brought him to my home and within a half-hour I realized that the boy truly is a genius.

CHAPTER 17

1982

SATURDAY, JANUARY 9, 1982 ▓ Chatting with Carmen Capalbo, I said that last night as I watched a TV drama I became angered by the profusion of commercials interrupting the narrative flow of the movie. I believe it is mainly the fault of television that Americans now have such a short attention span.

He theorized that one prime aspect of contemporary life is *interruption*. Few people can pay attention to any single thing very long, so therefore they welcome interruption. I agreed and said that perhaps this is so because unconsciously they fear that if they are left alone with their own thoughts too long, they might discover how empty-headed they are. Nothing is so terrifying as seeing one's true self. I quoted Carl Jung's dictum that modern man has lost his soul.

Most movies and TV dramas strive to spark excitement, not reflection. Directors like to show cars crashing into one another or tumbling off cliffs. Carmen and I believe that most people have become so insensitive that they need more and more intense external stimulation to enable them to feel anything at all. This is why the media depicts increasingly horrible scenes of cruelty. Many people seem to equate excitement with living, just as they equate money with happiness. The ceaseless impact of thousands of stimuli upon the nervous system is sure to leave it utterly numb, and when this happens we will become a race of zombies.

Carmen told me a fascinating story about his production of *The Three-penny Opera*. In a wedding scene he had many things happening very fast, as in a Marx Brothers film, and when the first-night audience did not react as he had anticipated, he became puzzled. He told his actors that at the next performance he wanted to reverse this scene. Now he stopped everything else while all attention was focused upon but a single event on stage. Next the attention was shifted to a second event, and so on. This worked the way a close-up works in a movie. It worked so well that audiences were enthralled.

The human mind is able to attend to only one thing at a time in full measure, although of course some peripheral events may be partially absorbed. But most people are scatterbrains. They seem to feel they will miss something if they give complete attention to just one thing at a time. A man who knew Napoleon said that the one attribute that distinguished him from others was the absolutely steady quality of his attention.

SUNDAY, MARCH 7, 1982 ▓ Television's madness increases. Now Channel 7 proclaims that its newscasts are "ahead of the times." Well, well! Institutional precognition.

FRIDAY, JULY 16, 1982 ▓ I heard a radio commercial about the Volvo—"a car you can believe in!" Hurrah! In this age of nihilism we can bow down to an object made of metal. Come to think of it, whatever happened to the Golden Calf of the Israelites?

WEDNESDAY, NOVEMBER 3, 1982 ▓ Russell Baker, the *New York Times* columnist, seems to agree with my thesis that mankind is going mad at an accelerating pace. On today's Op-Ed Page, he said: "For five weeks I traveled across beautiful autumnal America. It was like a booby hatch of the criminally insane . . . we all live by the faith that insanity will not prevail . . . the tyranny of a minority that is beyond the reach of reason . . . I was struck by the sense of encroaching madness . . ."
I really don't think he had his tongue in his cheek when he wrote this.

SUNDAY, NOVEMBER 28, 1982 ▓ I have read all 18 volumes of the collected works of Carl Jung. He is my hero of heroes. I regard him as my spiritual father because he is wise, and he is wise because he understands himself. Today, as I had done before, I savored this remark of his: "The great events of world history are, at bottom, profoundly unimportant. In the last analysis, the essential thing is the life of the individual. This alone makes history."

1983

TUESDAY, APRIL 26, 1983 ▓ My friend Carmen Capalbo knows a young Englishman named Peter Cannon, who makes documentary films for Central Independent Television Pic of Birmingham, England. At present Peter happens to be in New York with a TV crew, so Carmen told him about my diary and Peter quickly agreed that I would make a good subject for him. He wants to film me for 30 minutes for a show called *Getting On*, a series about old folks. It is one of the most popular TV shows in the United Kingdom.

This noon Carmen got here before the television people. The first of them to arrive was Tony Budd, a producer and interviewer. In his early thirties, Tony wore a wrinkled shirt and his hair was scraggly, somewhat blowing my stereotype of an Englishman. However, he spoke in a soft voice and behaved in the understated style of the British. Soon I understood he would interview me on camera. I asked whether I should address him as Mr. Budd.

He snorted: "Oh, good God—no!"

Then he began asking me preliminary questions about my diary and the encyclopedia of New York City that I'm compiling. I grinned and said this was an odd reversal of roles, for as a reporter I asked the questions.

Last night I washed my hair, which is so damned fine that it wouldn't stay in place, but when I pulled out a pocket comb Tony laughed and told me to forget the way l look. I wore a short-sleeved golden sports shirt, blue jeans and short boots. This film will be in color. I was glad that this was Selma's free day, so she could share the fun.

Tony said he wanted to ask me on camera what it feels like to be old, so I repeated something I wrote yesterday in a letter to my daughter: "To be old feels like swimming through wool."

My buzzer sounded, and in came Peter and Sheila Ford. She has beautiful eyes and is an assistant producer; Tony began dictating notes to her.

I had spoken to Peter on the New York-Birmingham phone line, but this is the first time we have met in person. He is about 27 years old, tall and handsome and as carelessly attired as Tony. Soon Carmen whispered to me that moments after his arrival Peter had told him: "This is a magical flat!"

Then in trooped four men—the cameraman, assistant cameraman, sound engineer and his assistant. Three have the first name of John. When the one wearing a blue windbreaker asked about the fuses in the boxes in the basement, I called him "Blue John," which somehow seemed to amuse the others.

Tony asked me to sit in my big chair near the window. The sun shone. Crew members lugged in piece after piece of heavy equipment, lighting me front and back.

Tony sat in front of me. Sheila sat beside him, notebook and pen in hand. The cameraman focused on me and she arose, a clapboard in her hands, held it in front of my face and then clapped it together to signal the beginning of a take.

The clapboard was used before each take.

I yipped: "This is like being in a movie!"

The cameraman growled: "This *is* a movie!"

Dumb Ellis.

For reasons unclear to me, I am unafraid of a movie or TV camera. When Tony began questioning me, I answered without any hesitation, no embarrassment, no fumbling for answers. Of course, I never looked into the lens of the camera. The film in its magazine has a running time of ten minutes. After the first ten-minute take I asked Tony whether my answers were too long. No, if anything, they were too short. I said I would watch his eyes and if I thought I saw the beginning of boredom, I'd shift to another subject.

The camera was reloaded four times, which means, of course, that 50 minutes of film was exposed. I talked easily and time glided by and soon it was after five o'clock. Then I asked Tony whether I had sounded egotistical. Not at all, he reassured me.

Suddenly the sound engineer asked all of us to be silent. He ran film through his audio machine. I asked why. He said every room has its unique silence—a fact I had not known.

Tony said he wanted to return tomorrow. Would 10 A.M. be all right? Sure.

WEDNESDAY, APRIL 27, 1983 ▪ This morning I walked downstairs and found the British TV crew in front of this brownstone. Peter, taking over as director, said he wanted a shot of me emerging from my building.

Tony walked up, put his arm around my shoulder and said: "Eddie! Yesterday was magical! My questions weren't very good, but your answers were great."

I was wearing my Walt Whitman hat. This is what I call it because of its broad brim. I shook hands with all the crew members and, without exception, they were friendly, quiet and polite.

The camera was placed on the sidewalk in front of the building, facing the front door. Under Peter's guidance, I walked back inside and then emerged as the camera ground away. Then I was asked to walk west on 21st Street, turn around, await a signal, walk back east toward my brownstone. At first this was done with the camera on my side of the street. Then it was placed across the street.

Next I was asked to walk to the corner grocery store on 9th Avenue and then saunter back home while a shot was taken with a telescopic lens. I looked through the viewfinder of the camera and was astonished to note its clarity and magnification. The other day when the crew was filming in the

South Bronx, the camera was able to get a clear view of the World Trade Center towers at the southern tip of Manhattan.

Sheila had obtained permission to shoot inside the quadrangle of the General Theological Seminary, an Episcopalian institution just across the street to the south of my building. This quadrangle is a pleasant place. It looks a little like Oxford, which I admire endlessly.

Under Peter's direction, I strolled from behind a clump of bushes, came into view, gazed up at the sun-lit trees, sat down on a stone bench by the chapel and took off my hat. Then came close-ups. Peter now wanted his cameraman to walk along while pointing up at the leaves of the trees above my head. I said I had seen this technique used dramatically in one of the best TV movies ever made.

Peter cried: "Sure! . . . *An Occurrence at Owl Creek Bridge!*"

I was astonished that this young Englishman knew what show I meant. It was based upon a story by Ambrose Bierce, the caustic American writer.

All of us returned to my apartment.

This time the camera was put in the bedroom, looking into the kitchen. I sat at my heavy kitchen table, prepared to read aloud from pages of my diary. Tony would ask the questions. He sat close to me but out of range of the camera. I had shown him some excerpts and he chose one about a dream in which I felt I had seen the soul of my dead wife.

Before the camera started I said I was not sure whether I could get through this take without breaking down. I began reading. As I went deeper into this sad experience my throat hardened and my voice quavered. Steeling myself, from time to time glancing into Tony's steady blue eyes, I managed to get through this selection. On Tony's face I saw such compassion that I knew he was suffering along with me. At the end of the passage I knew I would be unable to continue speaking, so I waved my hands in front of my face to signal—*no more!* Tony touched my wrist. The crew members were silent.

FRIDAY, SEPTEMBER 23, 1983   ▣   Today I finished reading *Justice at Nuremberg* by Robert E. Conot, whose style is a bit untidy. When Justice Robert Jackson summed up for the prosecution, he said:

"It is common to think of our own time as standing at the apex of civilization. The reality is that in the long perspective of history the present century will not hold an admirable position unless its second half is to redeem its first. These two-score years in the twentieth century will be reported in the book of years as one of the most bloody in all annals.

"Two World Wars have left a legacy of dead which number more than all the armies engaged in any way that make ancient or medieval history. No half century ever witnessed slaughter on such a scale, such cruelties and inhumanities. The terror of Torquemada pales before the Nazi inquisition.

"If we cannot eliminate the causes and prevent the repetition of these barbaric events, it is not an irresponsible prophecy to say that this twentieth century may yet succeed in bringing the doom of civilization."

And then tonight, so help me God, on TV I heard three racial bigots raving about killing all Jews and black people! One of these crackpots heads an Idaho group called the Aryan Nation. They are as demented and dangerous as the Nazis. One young nut who murdered three persons and was sentenced to death in an Ohio courtroom stood up and actually gave the Nazi salute. My belly soured.

A couple of days ago James Watt, Reagan's secretary of the interior, said that members of a new commission he heads consist of "one black, one woman, two Jews and one cripple." Even leading Republicans are calling upon the President to fire Watt.

TUESDAY, OCTOBER 25, 1983 ■ I was in the kitchen making coffee when on the radio I heard that U.S. troops had invaded Grenada. Invaded *what?* I had to pull out a volume of the *Encyclopedia Britannica* to learn that Grenada is a tiny oval-shaped island of 133 square miles about 100 miles north of the coast of Venezuela in the eastern Caribbean Sea. It has a population of 85,000. What the hell are we doing there?

President Reagan said he had "no choice" but to invade Grenada to save the lives of American medical students there, although other people said they never were in danger. Whenever I hear a politician say he *has no choice but . . .* I run for the cyclone cellar. In 1979 a left-wing party staged a bloodless coup and took control of the island. Reagan said the new government is turning Grenada into an outpost of Castro's Cuba, so he sent in 7,000 GI's.

What will the rest of the world think about the giant, the United States of America, crushing an ant of an island? Our hubris is becoming Faustian and may end in our decline and fall. The U.S. is a bully!

WEDNESDAY, OCTOBER 26, 1983 ■ This morning Carmen Capalbo came upstairs to drink coffee with me and discuss our noble invasion of Grenada. Both of us were very depressed. Americans are impatient and believe in the quick fix. They do not know history. They have been raised on a diet of movies in which the hero wins and the villain loses in the last three minutes.

The U.S. has troops stationed all around the world. We seem to believe we have the right and might to police everyone everywhere. In fact, we do not have such a right, and now it's possible that no longer do we have the necessary might.

Around the world most nations are condemning our move into Grenada. Here in New York City protest marches have been held in front of the United Nations headquarters and also in Times Square.

That invasion led to the deaths of 19 American soldiers and sailors, 110 Grenadian militia and 71 Cubans, many of them armed construction workers with no formal military training. During 1983–85 U.S. and Caribbean peacekeeping forces were gradually withdrawn and democracy was re-established. Years later declassified Defense Department documents proved that the medical students were not in danger and that the invasion suffered from poor planning and a lack of equipment. Nonetheless, the Pentagon awarded 9,802 decorations, including 813 Bronze Stars.

1984

TUESDAY, JANUARY 24, 1984 ■ Here in Chelsea my favorite restaurant is R. J. Scotty's, on the east side of 9th Avenue a few steps south of 23rd Street. It has a soothing ambience, the cuisine is Italian, the portions are enormous and I have become fond of its owner, who also is the chef.

Everyone calls him Ray. This is because they have trouble remembering his real name—Renato Lesizza. He named the place after his son Scotty. One afternoon he told me the story of his life.

He was one of three children born to a poor couple in Trieste. When he was six months old his father deserted the family. His mother had such trouble feeding her kids that when he was six she gave him to a farmer.

For the next ten years he toiled in the fields for the farmer, receiving no wages, and mostly bread for food. He never went to school a single day in his entire life. He couldn't even spell his own name until he was fifteen. He hated his father, hated his mother, hated farm work, hated his poverty and ignorance.

When World War II broke out and the Nazis occupied Italy, Ray joined an underground band of partisans—Italians, Englishmen, New Zealanders, Americans. They taught him how to blow up bridges behind Nazi lines. Each of the 15 men in the group carried 20 sticks of dynamite as they walked three to five weeks through the mountains on the way to their targets.

In four years of underground work Ray blew up ten bridges. Much later, when he saw the film *For Whom the Bell Tolls*, when he watched Gary

Cooper dynamite a bridge, Ray broke out in a sweat. To him, destroying the bridges wasn't the bad part.

The really bad part of the war for Renato Lesizza was that he killed some men called Nazis. Not at a distance. Not with a carbine so far away that he couldn't see their faces. No, he was a guerrilla, and his killing had to be done up close—flesh to flesh.

That bothered him then and for years and years afterwards.

After the war Ray became a cook on a Canadian vessel, and when it reached Baltimore he jumped ship and made his way to New York City. All he had was eight dollars.

His first job was washing dishes six days a week in a coffee shop for $22 per week. He worked hard. He did nothing but work. New Yorkers watched the Italian kid work 15 to 18 hours a day and were impressed by his ambition.

Ray, now 65 years old, told me: "Ambition had nothing to do with it. It was a compulsion. It was rage and guilt. I couldn't talk to anyone. I couldn't sleep. I worked hard to try to forget that my father left me, that my mother gave me away, that I never had a chance to go to school, that I killed men with my own hands."

Ray said he became schizophrenic. On the one hand, he was successful with everything he touched, opening one profitable restaurant after another. On the other hand, he drank to forget, and became an alcoholic.

A man six feet tall, he let his weight balloon to 230 pounds. He was married and divorced—twice. He thought about suicide all the time. But at last he let a friend persuade him to enter therapy, and it truly helped.

Ray found that his father was living on Staten Island, married again and with more children, but Ray did not try to take revenge. Although he saw his father twice, he did not identify himself as his son.

He has forgiven his father and mother and that farmer and the war that led him to kill. Best of all, he has forgiven himself. No more nightmares.

Now that he owns the restaurant and the three apartments above it, he could sell everything for perhaps $2 million.

"So I could sell this place!" he cried. "So what? I've been poor. I've been hungry. I've suffered. But now—thank God!—I understand myself!"

SUNDAY, FEBRUARY 26, 1984 ■ This sunny day Selma and I walked to Greenwich Village. In the past few years I often visited Martin's book shop, a hole-in-the-wall at 162 West 4th Street. Today a sign in the window said the shop soon will close. Walking inside, I spoke to Mrs. Ethel Lader;

she and her husband have run this bookstore for 40 years. Last December he died in his sleep, so now she is selling out. These days, she lamented, no one buys books.

I usually carry pen and paper, but had neither today, so I asked for writing material to make notes so that I can write about her in my diary. Sitting in the shop was a man who began chatting with us. When I started to identify myself he said he remembered having read about me and my diary. He was so articulate and interesting that I invited him to eat brunch with Selma and me at a nearby diner.

His name is Peter F. Skinner. He was born in England 45 years ago, the son of a dental surgeon. After attending a private boarding school, he served two years in the Royal Navy and then studied at Oxford University, where he earned a master's degree in modern history. In 1961 he moved to the United States and later became an American citizen. He taught history in two private schools in Manhattan, married and divorced, and took up freelance writing. In 1979 he became an executive in a medical center in Manhattan.

After we finished eating he led Selma and me to his apartment on Macdougal Street across from Minetta Tavern. I gasped in admiration when I saw his private library of 4,000 books. A true bibliophile, Peter told us story after story of how he bought this or that volume. His private library is the best I've ever seen in New York. At present he is using an electric typewriter to write a brochure about the neighborhoods of this city. Peter is a brilliant man standing about five feet ten, with wavy light brown hair, wearing glasses and so closely shaven he looks squeaky-clean. I like him.

Peter and I quickly became close friends and remain friends to this day. We speak on the phone almost daily and see one another at least once a week. One evening in a restaurant I asked whether he would consider editing my diary after I die; Peter said he would feel honored to become my editor. He introduced me to Rita Rosenkranz, a literary agent I soon chose to represent me. Early in 1993 she put me in touch with Philip Turner, a senior editor at Kodansha America, and he gave me a contract for this book you are reading. A chain of causation.

THURSDAY, MARCH 15, 1984   ■   I read that Samantha Smith, a bright 11-year-old, asked civil rights leader Jesse Jackson whether he could describe himself in three words. He couldn't. This I can do easily: *I am curious.*

MONDAY, MAY 14, 1984   ■   Early this evening I decided to go out to get ice cream. When I emerged on West 21st Street and looked east, I gasped.

There was the moon—and such a moon! It was a full moon, huge and saffron-colored, hanging only a few degrees above the horizon at what seemed like the east end of my street. It was one of the most majestic, most beautiful sights I ever saw.

Standing at the corner was Joyce Ostrin, who owns the shop called Early Halloween, and I yelled at her to look and she did and she appreciated this enchanted sight as much as I. I was so hypnotized by the beauty that a car almost hit me, and would have, had Joyce not pulled me to safety just in time. Although I do not belong to any religious organization, I am a religious man by nature, and now I worshipped with my eyes. I called out to pedestrians to look at the moon and I'm sure some thought I was moonstruck. Well, I was.

TUESDAY, JULY 17, 1984 ■ Today I read an analysis of Lincoln's Gettysburg Address. It has 194 words of one syllable, 53 words of two syllables, 13 words of three syllables and seven words of four syllables. This is further proof of my belief that the best writing is simple writing.

WEDNESDAY, SEPTEMBER 5, 1984 ■ I dreamed that in a bed of mud I found several pairs of glasses that I own. Here is what I think the dream means: The mud symbolizes my ignorance. The spectacles symbolize my wish to learn.

1985

On June 15, 1985, I got a call from a woman in West Hollywood, California. She identified herself as Miss Akiko Nishizawa, production coordinator of the Kyodo Television Company, which is affiliated with Fuji Television of Toyko, Japan.

She said a two-hour TV show will be built around 20 winners in the Guinness Book of World Records, and she invited me to fly to Tokyo to participate, all expenses paid. I asked if this were a joke. No, she laughed, she meant everything she said.

She asked me to bring my diary. I explained that it is much too bulky to carry, but I promised to bring her some excerpts. She said this program will be seen all over Japan. She asked me to leave New York via Japan Air Lines on July 17. My ticket will be sent to me. I will be in Tokyo until July 23, will be shown around the capital, will have my hotel room and meals and everything else paid for.

The next few days I did some homework. I learned that Tokyo is 5,887 air miles from New York, that Japan Air Lines flies one plane out of JFK Airport each day, that it leaves at 1:30 p.m., that it is a 747 jumbo jet seating 286 passengers, that it flies non-stop to Tokyo in 14 hours, that round-trip tourist class costs $1,305 and first-class $3,540.

I mailed some excerpts from my diary to Miss Nishizawa in California, then had passport pictures taken, renewed my passport, obtained a visa from the Japanese consulate in New York.

The lady called again to say the producer of the TV show in Tokyo will pay to have one volume of my journal mailed to him. I said I can't do this because it might get lost and also because it contains confessions too intimate for others to see.

WEDNESDAY, JULY 3, 1985 ■ This afternoon I received yet another call from Miss Nishizawa of California. She said that Tsuneyasu Suzuki, the Tokyo producer of the forthcoming TV show about Guinness winners, wants me to bring one or more volumes of my diary so that he might show their bulk to the Japanese viewers.

I said I already had explained that I will not do so for fear they might get lost and because they are too intimate to be seen by anybody else. She said she understood. However, in a voice betraying anxiety and embarrassment, softly she said her producer insisted. It was obvious he had told her to confront me with an either/or decision.

"Well," I said, "if this means taking my diaries to Japan or not going, then I will not go."

She apologized—again and again and again. She said she wished she might come to New York to apologize in person, whereupon I said that if she ever got here I would be delighted to receive her in my home. She berated herself for acting unprofessionally. I said the fault was not hers. I realized she was stressed because she had been ordered to say what she had said.

I said, "Look, my dear. I am an old man and I have suffered many disappointments and frustrations during the course of my long life. Of course I should have liked to visit your country, but this turn of events does not devastate me. You are a perfect lady. You have behaved professionally. I accept your apology. This is not your fault. Please do not suffer on my behalf."

In a voice almost laced with tears, she crooned: "Ahh, you are so kind!"

1986

MONDAY, JANUARY 20, 1986 ■ Today was the first federal holiday honoring Dr. Martin Luther King, Jr. All the media paid massive attention to this great man, who was assassinated in 1968. I rejoice in these tributes, for King was to the United States what Ghandi was to India. Seeing his image on the TV screen again and again today, hearing again his deep and eloquent voice, I felt tears brimming my eyes. In Atlanta his widow stood beside Vice President George Bush as they and others sang "We Shall Overcome"—an ironic touch, I thought, since Bush seldom was overcome with sympathy for the rights and plights of black people.

SUNDAY, FEBRUARY 2, 1986 ■ I dreamed an important dream: It seemed that I sat conversing with President Reagan, he looking into my eyes, and I into his, and I sensed he liked me and realized I liked him. What makes this dream important is the fact that *it proves that the unconscious can lie!*

Until now I had assumed that the unconscious never lies, however bizarre one's dream, however vague the symbolism. If there is one thing I know for sure, it is that I dislike Reagan, do not respect him, scorn him for his ignorance.

To understand Reagan it is necessary to know that there is a vast difference between sentimentality and compassion. Reagan is a sentimentalist, a man who can become misty-eyed with patriotism but hard-eyed when he looks at the poor.

My dream was ridiculous, for I am incapable of liking that man. My dream was worse than ridiculous, for it was a flagrant lie.

SATURDAY, FEBRUARY 22, 1986 ■ My paternal grandfather, John Ellis, died May 15, 1902, at the age of 73. My maternal grandfather, Samuel Robb, died October 22, 1933, at the age of 74. Today I became 75 years old, which means that I have lived longer than both my grandfathers—an eerie feeling.

THURSDAY, JUNE 19, 1986 ■ Last night I had a big dream. Carl Jung, who met and studied some American Indians, said that when a medicine man had a dream he felt was significant, he would summon the tribesmen, and when they had gathered he would say he had had a big dream he wanted to share with them. I want to share my big dream with you.

In my dream I had a wife about to give birth to a baby. I never saw her face but knew I loved her very much. People began to gather to watch this birth and the setting seemed to be a small town. From the very beginning of the dream I was aware that these people were hostile toward my wife, our expected baby and myself. I did not know why. Some called me her lover, rather than her husband, which angered me. Others sneered at her, and this infuriated me.

I saw my wife's father with four or five other men, and was astonished because he seemed indifferent to what was happening. The audience grew bigger and bigger. Peddlers sold cheap binoculars to folks wanting a close look at the birth of my first child. They also hawked scorecards so people could keep a record of the coming event.

Somewhere in the background, out of sight, was my wife, my suffering wife. I worried about her. It seemed that something kept me at a distance from her.

The horde of people, becoming larger by the hour, hardly could wait for the birth of the child, so that they might scorn it. I knew this was the way they would greet it. No one was protecting my pregnant wife. Bigger and bigger became the mob. The people had ugly faces because they had ignorant minds. I was afraid of what they might do to my wife and child, so I set out on a journey to try to find help from someone.

After many adventures, which I have forgotten, I came at last to a luxurious hotel, and in its lobby I saw a fat man wearing expensive clothes. He was ringed by a group of admiring men. I walked up to the fat man and asked whether he was the most influential person present. His toadies came toward me with the intention of throwing me out, but he stopped them with a gesture.

He seemed to know me and he also seemed to know that my wife was about to have a baby. In fact, he asked one of his henchmen the latest news from my wife, and he was told that her labor had begun and the baby was partly out of her body. When I heard this I said I had better hurry back to her because her doctor had said that if the child did not emerge all at once, it would die and my wife would die. I said I had to return to get the dead body of my wife.

In the dream I had managed, until then, to control myself despite the hostility of the people and the danger to my wife. Now, however, I let out a scream so anguished and high-pitched that it sounded like the scream of an animal. This scream crossed the border of my dream into the real world, for in reality I was screaming as I lay in bed, and the scream awakened me. I lay there, panting. What was happening? Why did I dream this horrible nightmare? What did it symbolize?

I thought and thought and thought and at long last I understood:

This coming July 4 Americans will celebrate the 100th anniversary of the Statue of Liberty. The past few months the media has been full of stories about the renovation of the statue and the fireworks display to be held in the presence of the President.

During those same months I read other stories about the fact that in this world there are only a few democracies, about the use of torture as an official policy in scores of nations, about the growing number of homeless people here at home, about Reagan's reactionary attitudes, about senseless wars and the spread of madness, about the arms race and the threat of nuclear disaster. So why are we about to celebrate Liberty?

I had dreamed a parable. Life is horrible and becoming worse. Civilization is collapsing. Ever since I was a boy and began reading history and became interested in "progress," I had expected Liberty to bring forth freedom and compassion. I had faith in her. I loved Liberty. She was my wife. She had become a symbol of the hope of all mankind, which explains why a crowd gathered when they heard that my wife was expecting.

But the people had lost their innocence and virtue and pity. No longer is there democracy in the United States. The high cost of getting elected to office, the proliferation of political action committees, the presence in Washington of hundreds of lobbyists, the pressures from corporations and wealthy people—all these factors, along with others, now make it impossible for the common people to obtain real representation in Congress and elsewhere. Money and greed and drugs and ignorance are ripping civilization to tatters.

There never was any golden age in all history, as some people like to believe, but during my 75 years of life I have witnessed the worsening of everything. And so my dream symbolized the end of civilization.

Dr. Rollo May, the noted therapist, said in his book *Love and Will* that "we find the artists expressing the conflicts in the society before these conflicts emerge consciously in the society as a whole."

Perhaps black people and the people of other minorities in this land might agree with me when I suggest this: On the Fourth of July we should hang a huge sign on the Statue of Liberty, and this sign would have just one word:

Miscarriage!

SUNDAY, JULY 27, 1986 ▦ In 1837 Abraham Lincoln said: "At what point shall we Americans expect the approach of danger? . . . I answer, if it ever reach us, it must spring up amongst us; it cannot come from abroad. If destruction be our lot, we must ourselves be its author and finisher."

THURSDAY, SEPTEMBER 25, 1986   ■   On a street in Chelsea I saw actress Geraldine Page, who recently won an Oscar for her great talent. She wore a wool cap and sweater and almost looked like a bag lady. Previously, I'd chatted with her in the supermarket, and she is wholly simple, natural, kind. She and her actor husband, Rip Torn, live on the north side of West 22nd Street between 9th and 10th Avenues, and they have a mailbox beneath the words TORN PAGE.

1987

SUNDAY, JANUARY 11, 1987   ■   This evening on television I saw singer Eartha Kitt being interviewed. With her was her daughter, a model in her twenties. This interested me because when her daughter was an infant I played with her. I was a reporter for the *World-Telegram* and Miss Kitt was appearing in the Persian Room of the Plaza Hotel. I went to her suite in the Plaza to interview her.

When I arrived she was talking business with some man, so I wandered through an open French door into the bedroom, for I saw her child on a blanket on the floor. I stretched out on the floor to talk to the baby and suddenly became aware of an enormous silence. Glancing up, I saw Miss Kitt beaming down at me. I had read that she was difficult to interview, but I found her altogether sweet.

She asked whether I was married. Yes. Did my wife and I plan to attend her opening show tonight in the Persian Room? Yes. She then invited us to join her in her suite after the first show.

As I left that afternoon, I said: "Thank you, Miss Kitt."

With glittering eyes, she said: "You may call me Eartha!"

FRIDAY, JANUARY 16, 1987   ■   A rocking chair sat in a window of the Salvation Army store in my neighborhood, so I went inside to look at it. Brand new, of Colonial design, very heavy, very masculine, it has a tall back and curved arms. A salesman took it out of the window and I sat down in it. A woman shopper blurted: "Buy it! You look great in it!"

So I bought it and had it carried home by a young man.

It seemed proper for me to buy a rocking chair now that I am 75 years old. I recalled that an ancient Greek philosopher said that pleasure is gentle motion. Wickedly, I decided that should someone ask whether I exercise, I'll say: "Yeah, I gallop like hell in my rocking chair!"

SUNDAY, MARCH 16, 1987 ■ Three homeless men sat with their backs against the dime store at the corner of 23rd Street and 8th Avenue. Two were white, one black. Walking up to them, I said I had a couple of coats I would give them if they could wait ten minutes. The young black man said he sure needed another coat; the tattered coat he wore was held together with a safety pin.

I walked a block to Selma's apartment, where I had left my coats. As I walked back toward the homeless men I heard one say: "Here he comes!" I guess they hadn't believed me. I gave the heavier of the two coats to the black man, who thanked me and said: "God bless you!"

When I was descending in the elevator in Selma's building, I had been alone in the car with a little old man who stared at me. At last I grinned and said: "I'm not a thief. These are my coats, which I left with a friend, and now I'm going to give them away."

Smiling, he said: "Oh, not that! It's just that you look like Santa Claus."

In fact, I do. I have ruddy cheeks because of my Welsh heritage, a full white beard, and now that I've stopped smoking I have a potbelly—dammit! A week earlier I had been standing in front of the stationery store when a mother and her three-year-old son stopped in front of me. He whispered to her. She smiled at me and said: "He thinks you're Santa Claus."

Willing to play the part, I leaned down and asked: "Have you been good this year?"

The kid didn't know what the hell I meant!

WEDNESDAY, APRIL 15, 1987 ■ My block has many tiny front yards filled with flowers. Today I saw that someone had torn up the flowers in one yard and scattered them around, leaving shoe-prints in the soil. What kind of person would murder flowers? A drunk? A madman? My spirits drooped. Then they revived when I turned a corner and saw a kid with a wonderful toy. He was pushing what looked like a small lawnmower, but with each revolution of the wheels it shot out 20 to 30 bubbles, glistening bubbles, glorious bubbles! 1 was so fascinated I walked the block with him and his mother.

SUNDAY, JUNE 14, 1987 ■ Listening to TV news, I learned that Geraldine Page died yesterday in her home on West 22nd Street, just one block north of me. She was only 62. She was praised by actor Richard Chamberlain, who said her acting was "incredibly real." For years I have been inveighing against misuse of the word *incredible,* but this is quite the worst misuse I ever heard. The word means *that which cannot be believed.* What Chamberlain said is that her acting was so real it could not be believed—a contradiction in terms. At the present time this is the most over-worked, wrongly used word in America.

WEDNESDAY, JULY 15, 1987   ■   When Ruth and I lived on the 26th floor of the Hotel Master on Riverside Drive at 103rd Street, the man who lived on the floor above us was Joseph Nathan Kane.

He is a famous author. He has written some of the best reference books ever published in the U.S. Most notable is his *Famous First Facts*, first published in 1933 and never out of print since then. Second best known, I suppose, is *Facts About the Presidents*. It came out initially in 1959, and whenever a new President takes office Joe updates his book. He has produced other reference works, as well.

Today Joe came down to Chelsea to visit me. Since he was born January 23, 1899, he now is 88 years old, pot-bellied, a bit shaky on his feet, but still active. He told me something that happened last year.

One evening he was walking home when he was mugged by three white kids. One threw an arm lock around his neck. Another bashed his face, breaking his teeth. The third kid grabbed his briefcase. Joe fought back. Managing to free himself, he snatched back his briefcase. When the punks saw people approaching, they ran away.

I asked: "Joe, what was so valuable in the briefcase?"

"Nothing."

"*Nothing!* Then why did you fight those jerks?"

"Because," Joe harrumphed, "I am a citizen and a human being and a man!" Then, blue eyes twinkling, he added, "—a rather foolish man." His dental bill was $700.

We often discuss the fact that both of us are workaholics. Even in deep old age, Joe works seven days a week, every holiday and on every vacation—*alleged* vacation.

"Work," he declares, "is my medicine! If I were unable to work I'd die—one, two, three—like that!"

Every morning he gets up at 7:30 and immediately begins his day's labor. Once or twice a week he will visit one of the 15 or 16 libraries here in the city that he patronizes on a regular basis. Each year he delivers some 25 lectures, and as he flies around the country he always works on some manuscript. Whenever he visits friends in their homes in other cities he appreciates it when they say they want to show him the town, but prefers to stay in their houses so that he might go on working.

"Hey, Joe!" they'll cry. "Relax! Why kill yourself working? Your heirs won't appreciate what you're doing! Why don't you have some fun?"

Fun? This man has found happiness, so why should he bother with fun? Happiness is having what you want and wanting what you have. He also has found fame, for copies of his books are in every major library on the face of the earth. They also may be found in American consulates around the world.

Today Joe said to me: "I admit I work too hard, too long, too compulsively. I violate all the rules of good health. I get my annual checkup — every five years. The only exercise I get is attending the funerals of young doctors who tried to tell me how to live. Seriously — look, I know the value of work. When I work I concentrate so hard I lose all track of time and don't feel all the aches and pains of old age. I meant it when I said that work is medicine."

In 1994, as I prepared this book for publication, Joe Kane was 95 years old and working as hard as ever.

SATURDAY, SEPTEMBER 12, 1987 ■ Writing a letter to my granddaughter Orion, who lives in Oregon, I quoted some lines from Arabic literature I've liked for many years. I think I remember them correctly:

He who knows not, and knows not he knows not, he is ignorant — shun him.
He who knows not, and knows he knows not, he is a student — teach him.
He who knows, but knows not he knows, he is asleep — awaken him.
He who knows, and knows he knows, he is wise — follow him.

SATURDAY, OCTOBER 3, 1987 ■ Turning the pages of a book called *The Wisdom of Israel*, I read a maxim so profound that it jolted me. I guess I've known it for many years, but never saw it expressed so well:
The highest wisdom is kindness.

THURSDAY, DECEMBER 24, 1987 ■ In *Newsday* I read an article that almost made my heart stop beating: "A single-volume encyclopedia of New York City, with contributions from 150 scholars and experts, will be published in 1991, the New-York Historical Society and Yale University Press announced."

This hit me hard because for ten years I have worked seven days a week doing research for a one-volume encyclopedia of this city. As I slogged along at this labor I often became tired but never bored, for this city is fascinating. I was helped enormously by Selma, who clipped and filed and assisted in organizing my tens of thousands of pages of notes.

Years ago, after publication of my narrative history called *The Epic of New York City*, I realized there is a need for an encyclopedia of our town. I know of only one encyclopedia of any city—London—published by Macmillan about five years ago. I own a copy. It is excellent—except for one major and puzzling omission: It contains no biographies.

Newsday says the editor-in-chief will be Dr. Kenneth T. Jackson, a history professor at Columbia University. He will be helped by a managing editor and 20 associate editors. This project has a budget of $700,000.

A couple of years ago I wrote 200 pages of my own encyclopedia to get a sense of proportion and style. As part of my research, I looked at every page of every volume of the *Encyclopedia Americana* and the *Encyclopedia Britannica* and, of course, my own library includes hundreds of books about this city.

1988

SUNDAY, JANUARY 17, 1988 ■ The *New York Times* had a long story about the forthcoming encyclopedia of New York City. It will be 2,000 pages long. I wanted my volume to be 2,000 pages long. It will sell for about $50. I wanted mine to sell for about $50. Lucy Wind called to ask whether I'd seen this story. Aghast, she cried, "I can't believe it!"

TUESDAY, JANUARY 26, 1988 ■ I telephoned Dr. Kenneth Jackson at Columbia University. The moment I spoke my name he said he knows who I am because he has read my *Epic of New York City*; in fact, he added that I write well.

After telling him I spent the last decade doing research for my own encyclopedia of this city, I said I now surrender because I cannot compete with 150 scholars and 20 associate editors. A pleasant man, he sympathized with me and we enjoyed a long talk. I said I had compiled tens of thousands of notes, which he might find helpful.

He said, "I'm overwhelmed by your generosity!"

Trying to put a smile into my voice, I said: "Well, please don't be, because I want to sell my notes to you."

He said he does not plan to build a library of literature about New York City because he has the resources of the Historical Society at his disposal. However, he added, he might appoint me an associate editor and hired me as a consultant at $150 an hour.

"You can be helpful," he assured me.

He urged me to keep my files, and after he names a managing editor the two of them will come here to see what I have. The encyclopedia project hasn't even started yet.

Dr. Jackson said: "You'll probably want to write lots of pieces for the encyclopedia."

"Yes, I would," I replied. "In particular, I'd like to write a long article about construction of the city's water supply system, an engineering feat that ranks with the construction of the Panama Canal."

Dr. Jackson said no one will get rich writing for the encyclopedia because payment will be only ten cents a word. However, each piece will be signed.

"I'm delighted to bring you on board," said Dr. Jackson.

SUNDAY, MARCH 13, 1988   ▪   Early this morning I awakened and lay in bed listening to news on the radio and heard of the death of Romare Bearden, an old friend of mine. He had been ill with bone cancer for a year and a half, and suffered a stroke yesterday, dying in New York Hospital at the age of 75. In the 1950's Ruthie and I often socialized with Romie, and then with his wife Nan; we visited his studio and they came to our apartment. The last time I saw him was in 1965 just after Ruthie's funeral. He ran toward my car as I was leaving, waving to show me he had been there. For a couple of years after her death I was mad, and somehow Romie and I drifted apart, but only recently I wrote to him and he replied. Today the *Times* and *Newsday* published long obituaries of Romie, who became one of America's leading artists and certainly the most famous person who was a close friend of mine. Among other things, he was honored by Presidents Carter and Reagan. I'll copy the obits and include them in this diary.

March 15, 1988

Dear Nan:

Although I am a writer I do not know what words to use to say how sorry I am that Romare is gone. I remember him as one of the most gentle men I ever knew.

Twenty-three years ago when Ruthie died I went a little crazy for a couple of years, and so I did not continue seeing you and Romare. However, as you know, a few months ago I wrote to him, and he replied.

Some day soon someone will approach you to say he wants to

write a biography of your husband. When he does, you must tell him about my diary—now in its 61st year. I am 77 years old. Back in the 1950's when you and Romare, Ruthie and I socialized a lot together, I always wrote about it in my journal. He was such a great raconteur that in my diary I reproduced some of the stories he told. A lot of his life is related in page after page.

Because of my age, and because I have emphysema, I do not know how long I will live. Nonetheless, if I am dead when a writer plans Romare's story, with this letter I hereby grant the writer of your choice access to my diary, provided he or she does not use any portion of passages concerned with my intimate life.

My dear lady, I know in part what you now suffer and will suffer awhile. My heart aches for you. I loved, really loved, your husband.

In sorrow,
Eddie Ellis

THURSDAY, APRIL 14, 1988 ▪ In the mail I received *Diarist's Journal,* a magazine of diarists, by diarists and for diarists. It is the brain-child of Edward Gildea of Lansford, Pennsylvania. It consists of excerpts from the diaries of various living people. A monthly periodical, its first issue was published last January.

In that issue Gildea wrote an article beginning with this question: "Who is the most prolific diarist of all time?" Then he suggests this might be Arthur Crew Inman, whose diary contains 17 million words. However, Gildea added that "Edward Robb Ellis of New York City is still writing and he's not too far off Inman's pace . . ."

I happen to own *The Inman Diary,* edited by Daniel Aaron and published in 1985 in two volumes by Harvard University Press. Inman was born in 1895, kept his diary from 1919 until 1963 when he killed himself. The editor calls it "the autobiography of a warped and deeply troubled man whose aberrations call for psychiatric probing." As for style, the editor speaks of "the turgid, highfalutin language that sometimes marks his writing."

I wrote Gildea to say that my diary now has an estimated 18 million words, so I may have exceeded Inman. I enclosed some excerpts from my journal.

SATURDAY, APRIL 23, 1988 ▪ Ed Gildea sent me a three-page letter glowing with praise of me. He called me "the world's champion diarist of all time," although I doubt it and know of no way to prove it. Gildea said: "You write crystal clear English with style and flair, setting experiences regarded as mundane aglow, illuminating both the outstanding and the mundane . . ." He said he plans to devote his entire July issue to me and my diary.

MONDAY, MAY 9, 1988 ▪ My diary was cited for the first time by the *Guinness Book of World Records* in its 1981 edition. The 1982 edition has a photograph of me and a picture of my diary volumes spread out on a long line of tables at the University of Wyoming. Today I attended the first "convention" ever held for Guinness winners.

The site was the 42nd floor penthouse of the new Hotel Parker-Meridien at 118 West 57th Street. I was met by Cyd Smith, assistant editor, who handed me a lapel sticker that said "Edward Robb Ellis . . . Longest Diary."

As the suite filled with people, I walked to a window to gaze down upon the green glory of Central Park. There I stayed. Reporters and photographers thronged the suite. A pleasant man approached me and began asking questions. His name is Gregory Jaynes, and he is a reporter for the *New York Times*. He asked intelligent questions and wrote down all my answers. I thought he would leave in a few minutes, but instead he sat and talked with me for half an hour.

Slowly it became evident that this alleged convention was a publicity stunt staged by Roma Food Enterprises. The firm is owned by Lorenzo Amato, who is in *Guinness* because he made the largest pizza in the world. I saw Morris Katz, the most prolific painter in the world, knock out a painting in about 30 seconds. Near me stood Sal Piro, a pudgy non-achiever, whose claim to fame is that he has seen the *Rocky Horror Show* more often than anyone else in the world.

Two men played harmonicas—one the largest harmonica in the world, the other the smallest. Suddenly, into the cone of my vision there strode a man dressed to look like General George Patton. The place swarmed with egomaniacs hungry for attention. Paul Tavilla, the world's champion catcher-of-grapes-in-his-mouth, took up a position at some distance from a grape thrower, and at that moment I asked myself what I was doing in such a nutty place, so I walked out and came home.

WEDNESDAY, MAY 11, 1988 ▮ Today's *New York Times* published a column by Gregory Jaynes, and more than half of it was about me. He produced a tongue-in-cheek story about all the nuts at the Guinness convention, then depicted me sitting alone at a window gazing down at Central Park.

This evening I got a call from David Boehm, the American editor-in-chief of the *Guinness Book of World Records*. I assumed he had read the piece in the *Times* and wanted to harangue me for my cynical attitude toward his alleged convention. Instead, he said he wants to reproduce one page of my diary in the 1989 edition of Guinness, and perhaps I'd like to write about that gathering last Monday. Taking a deep breath, I confessed I had not been thrilled by the party and do not care to write about it for his book. Nonetheless, he said he wants one page of my diary. I agreed to provide him with one page about a subject of my choice.

SATURDAY, MAY 28, 1988 ■ Waiting for Ed Gildea to arrive from Pennsylvania I felt like a kid waiting for the circus. I knew he was bringing the July issue of his magazine *Diarist's Journal*, with all of its 16 pages devoted to me.

Looking out a front window I saw a man on the sidewalk. He asked, "Eddie?" I asked, "Ed?"

I walked downstairs and we shook hands and then sat down on the stoop. Ed is 59 years old, stands about five seven, has a slim build, blue eyes, glasses and the face of an Irishman. On the phone I had detected an accent, but now told him I couldn't place it, so he said it probably came from the coal mining region of Pennsylvania, where he lives. Ed is Irish and Welsh. His wife, the former Dolores Lanzos, is of Spanish origin. They have seven children ranging in age from 28 to 18.

We walked up to my apartment and continued talking. Ed and his wife live in a house in Lansford, Pennsylvania, at 102 W. Water Street. This is a depressed area because most of the local coal mines are closed. Ed's father was a newspaperman and until recently Ed worked on several papers. Now he has a well-paid job in a brewery.

He heard about me from Mrs. Kay Post, who lives in the Bronx. She is a diarist and although we never have met face-to-face we have talked on the phone several times.

Last January he launched *Diarist's Journal*, a monthly of 16 pages printed on newsprint. He said it has been profitable from the start. With its motto of "true things happening to ordinary people," it publishes excerpts from the diaries of many people. When Ed writes his own journal he stuffs the pages into a breadbox. Then, in each issue of his magazine, he publishes selections under the standing headline NOTES FROM THE BREADBOX.

Usually he prints 500 copies a month, but this time he made 700, so that he might give me 200 copies. He had brought them upstairs in two bundles, which now sat at my feet, and although I was aflame with curiosity I did not look at them until Ed and I had talked long enough to know one another. He is intelligent and sensitive, polite and quiet.

At last I cut open one bundle and pulled out a single copy of the magazine. The front page startled me. It had two headlines:

EDWARD ROBB ELLIS: 60 YEARS, 18 MILLION WORDS . . . AND COUNTING

THE WORLD'S CHAMPION DIARIST OF ALL TIME
IS STILL LIVING, AND WRITING, IN NEW YORK CITY

The bottom half of the front page had a photograph of me sitting at my typewriter.

The 16 pages contained selections from my diary, Ed's reaction when he first heard about me, photographs of me, and an article that Selma wrote about the way I taught her how to keep a journal. When I reached page 12 I burst into tears, for half the page consisted of the wedding picture Ruthie and I had made that April 29, 1955. Dear Ruthie! Now I have given her some of the attention and respect she so richly deserves. Ed sat silently as I wept. I felt no shame.

I told Ed I want to give some copies to Selma, who lives only four blocks away, and I hoped he would accompany me. I explained how helpful Selma has been since the death of Ruthie, explained that now she suffers from Parkinson's disease and hardly can utter a sentence.

After we reached her apartment I introduced them and then told her all about Ed's magazine. First I showed her the front page, then the article she wrote, and finally a picture of the two of us. This was the first time in her life that something she wrote has appeared in print, the first time in her life that her picture has appeared in a magazine. Her eyes gleamed like twin suns. I believe that this recognition of her is as helpful as medicine.

SATURDAY, JUNE 4, 1988 ■ I sent copies of the magazine to my daughter in Oregon. This evening on the phone she was wildly enthusiastic about it, crying: "I can only talk about you in superlatives!" This is a rich reward for a father.

MONDAY, JUNE 6, 1988 ■ Dr. Kenneth Jackson, editor-in-chief of the new encyclopedia project, was supposed to come to my apartment tomorrow afternoon, but this morning he called to ask whether he might come today instead. I called Selma and spoke to both her and Mavis, asking Mavis to take dupes of documents about Selma to her social worker. I did not wish to risk having Selma lose her standing with Medicaid.

Today's weather was perfect. Jackson arrived at 2:15 P.M., bringing with him Mrs. Deborah Gardner, whom he appointed managing editor of this project. She is a former student of his at Columbia University, where he teaches history and where she earned her doctorate. Her hands are tiny and beautiful. The moment the professor entered my apartment, he shed his coat, loosened his tie and told me to call him Ken. He stands about five feet ten, has sandy-colored hair parted on the left, blue eyes and a light complexion. Born in Memphis, he obtained his doctorate at the University of Chicago and came to New York only 20 years ago. Upon arriving, one of the first things he did was to read my *Epic of New York City*. Ken is an enthusiastic man; this is a quality I admire.

As for the encyclopedia of New York City, it will not be 2,000 pages long, but only about 1,200. Articles will be short, Ken saying that one of a thousand words will be considered long. I was disappointed to learn that the magnitude of the book will be less than first mentioned in the *New York Times*. Ken would like to have it priced at only $35. I am still disappointed that Ken will not buy my mountains of notes; I had dreamed about asking for $50,000 for them. For one thing, Ken's office in the building of the New-York Historical Society is too small to hold my notes. For another thing, about the only activity in that office will be editing, for Ken intends to hire specialists to write the articles. He said that I know more about this city in a general way than anyone else. He definitely wants me to work as an associate editor and consultant, at $150 per day. I don't suppose there will be very many such days; Ken said that the project still is trying to raise funds.

Time after time this afternoon I mentioned facts unknown to either Ken or Deborah. Example: William Randolph Hearst once lived on Riverside Drive in the largest apartment in the world, and in it he had an enormous bathtub once owned by President Taft. When Ken said I should lecture about the history of this city, I said I already have done so. He suggested that I write another book about New York City. I responded by saying that I probably have only two or three more years to live, and during this time I want to write a history of mysticism. Ken surprised me by reporting that there now is an encyclopedia about the city of Cleveland. He is familiar with the encyclopedia of London and shared my annoyance because it leaves out people. I impressed upon both Ken and Deborah that I am poor. He said that although he would not promise anything, he will try to do all he can to help me. Very impressed by my library, he asked whether I care to sell all of it, or part of it. Well, I hesitated, now that I am old my library sustains me intellectually and emotionally. He said he understood. I asked whether he had received copies of *Diarist's Journal*. No. I gave copies to the two of them, then explained that my last hope to make money is by selling my journal to some institution in New York City. Ken said that the New-York Historical Society lacks funds and is failing, but the New York Public Library has lots of money. This is due, of course, to Mrs. Brooke Astor.

Ken, Deborah and I had been sitting close to an open window in my front room, Ken saying he appreciated the breeze, and then he said he wanted to look around, so I led them first into my study. These academics, both with doctorates, were astonished by my library. While I'm on this point, I might add that both are intelligent, of course, but I am at least equally intelligent. They also are pleasant people with whom I felt relaxed. At 4:15 P.M. they left, so I walked to Selma's to tell her what happened. Then I felt tired. Perhaps, more than I realized, I had been nervous about meeting Ken, but my nervousness had vanished because he is so informal. A good man. I walked to the Regal restaurant to eat meat loaf, then came home to sit by the window.

SATURDAY, JULY 2, 1988 ▦ This is Selma's 72nd birthday, so Janet and Lil and I went to the hospital to visit her. We gave her presents, of course. She was sitting up when we arrived. Her condition is so bad that she seldom speaks. Hoping to draw her out a little, I began that joking litany we know so well.

I said: "You're evil, aren't you?"
"Yes." Her eyes glinted with merriment.
"And you do wicked things, don't you?"
"Yes."
"And you're sorry, aren't you?"
"No."

Although she did not laugh, it was obvious that she was amused. Suddenly I realized, as never before, that Selma truly is senile and never again will be her true self. I feel so very, very sorry for this kind woman, this generous woman, this loving woman. When I took her hand, she kissed my hand. I almost wept. Why do bad things happen to good people?

When I asked her doctor about Parkinson's disease, and whether she will suffer, he replied, "No, she will not be in agony. She will be as happy as a clam. You and her relatives—you're the ones who will be in agony."

THURSDAY, AUGUST 11, 1988 ▦ Peter Skinner called as I was browsing through a dictionary, so I asked the origin of the word *pandemonium.* Aloud, he began sorting through Greek roots, but I interrupted, saying: "Oh, Peter! You only went to Oxford, so what the hell do you know!" Then I told him that when John Milton was writing *Paradise Lost* he coined the word *Pandemonium* as a synonym for Hell: All demons.

SATURDAY, AUGUST 13, 1988 ▦ Vice President George Bush is seeking the Republican nomination for President, so he often is on television. Tonight on TV news I heard him declare that he never called Reagan economics "voodoo economics." Moments later we were shown an earlier TV appearance of him calling Reagan economics "voodoo economics." That lying bastard!

TUESDAY, AUGUST 23, 1988 ■ While I did not listen to President Reagan's speech at the GOP convention, today I read what he said: "Facts are stupid things."

Only to stupid people, Ronnie!

SUNDAY, AUGUST 28, 1988 ■ Today I was on the phone with a woman I've known many years. She was the kind of liberal I am. Today, however, she said: "I have no sympathy for the homeless! I've worked hard all my life. Fuck the homeless!"

TUESDAY, SEPTEMBER 13, 1988 ■ Ed Gildea told me there is a British firm called Letts of London that makes blank diaries sold around the world. Its American branch office is in Hauppauge, Long Island. I called and spoke to Phyllis Calderaro, marketing services manager, telling her about my diary and the mention of it in the *Guinness Book of World Records*. She said she would like to know more about me, so I sent her excerpts from my journal and some publicity stuff. She visited me, reported to the president of the company and then said he is interested in doing business with me. His name is David Hall. Phyllis arranged for us to meet here in Manhattan.

When I awakened rain was falling. This worried me because due to my sick lungs, if I get wet and catch cold I might come down with pneumonia. Nonetheless, I had to go. My financial future depends upon it. The meeting was scheduled for 11 A.M. The rain stopped and I got a cab right in front of my house. A lucky beginning.

I went to the office of a public relations firm on Madison Avenue, where I was met by a man with the breezy demeanor of a press agent. Then in strode David Hall of Letts. He is 49 years old, about six feet tall, with broad shoulders and a potbelly even bigger than mine. His hair is thick and black and curly, his beard showed just beneath his skin although he had shaved closely, and his dark brown eyes are crinkly at the corners because he laughs a lot. I knew he had been born in the United Kingdom, but he looks more Spanish than English.

As we shook hands, I asked: "Are you an Oxonian or Cambrigian?"

That's what I get for trying to be clever instead of just sincere! This evening on the phone with a friend, I learned that a graduate of Cambridge University, is called a *Cantabrigian*.

David Hall, gentleman, ignored my error. A pleased smile spreading over his face, he replied: "Well, *akkshully*, I went to Oxford."

He earned a master's degree at Oxford, like my friend Peter Skinner, and both sound the same way. I'm just guessing now, but it seems to me that in addition to what I regard as the standard British accent, on top of this they have an Oxford accent. I have yet to find the person who can explain this to me.

Phyllis Calderaro came late because of traffic congestion. Her boss and I sat beside one another at a conference table. When he called me Edward, I suggested Eddie instead, so he told me to call him David. He is remarkably intelligent and has a dynamic personality; the way he talks reminded me of Niagara Falls. I was astonished to learn that this business executive reads three to four books a week. We exchanged impressions of various authors, quoted favorite lines and witticisms, coined some of our own jokes and then both of us laughed uproariously.

He said, "Eddie, you are an interesting man!"

I said: "David, never in my life have I met any businessman like you!"

I meant it. Our mutual curiosity was what seemed to connect us.

When we got down to business, we discussed three subjects: First, David wants to hire me as a diary consultant. Second, he suggested that I design a diary for Letts. Third, he might want an option to buy my diary with the thought of perhaps publishing it.

Then we went to lunch. Leaving the building, we had to walk six blocks and the humid air hurt my lungs so I had to slow down. The restaurant was Russell's American Grill at 100 East 37th Street, just off Park Avenue South. Elegant decor. Efficient waiters. Other diners old and rich and bored. We were given a table by ourselves at one end of the room and when the others ordered drinks I asked for a Coke with a twist of lemon.

Letts of London has a long and honorable history. In 1796 a man named John Letts opened a stationery shop in the British capital. He paid attention to detail, used sturdy paper, insisted upon fine hand-craftsmanship, and thus began producing the first of many Letts goods. In 1812 he incorporated calendars into his journals, thereby creating the first modern diary. For almost 200 years Letts diaries have been used by famous people such as King Edward VII, novelist Charles Dickens, explorer David Livingstone and, here in America, members of the Roosevelt family.

Charles Letts & Co. has headquarters in London and branch offices in Edinburgh, Toronto, Sydney and New York. There is only one Letts factory, located in Dalkeith, Scotland, seven miles southeast of Edinburgh. It remains a family-owned and family-operated business. Now it is in the hands of the sixth generation of Lettses. On December 18, 1987, in a ceremony held in London at 10 Downing Street, Anthony Letts, chairman of the company, presented Prime Minister Margaret Thatcher with the 20 millionth diary produced by Letts.

THURSDAY, OCTOBER 6, 1988   ■   Phyllis Calderaro and I attended a party held by the *Guinness Book of World Records* on the concourse level in the basement of the Empire State Building on 5th Avenue at 34th Street.

The first Guinness book was published in the United Kingdom in 1955 and the American edition came out the following year. Now there are 262 editions in 35 languages, and more than 60 million copies have been sold. This means that, next to the Bible, it is the best-selling book in the world.

When Phyllis and I entered the Guinness Exhibition Hall I was handed a name tag to pin on my lapel. It said ROBB EDWARD ELLIS. So much for the accuracy of Guinness. The hall is a hodgepodge of artifacts and statues and models and videos and sound effects and multi-screen computer banks. Amazing—and confusing. Winding through the various rooms was the longest soft toy in the world, a plush pink caterpillar with 1,000 legs, 250 feet long, weighing 300 pounds.

We stood near a stage as various world champions displayed their skills. One was a sword swallower who calls himself Count Desmond. It made me ill just to watch him, so I turned away. I did watch David Stein, who uses a special wand to create enormous soap bubbles. Then I saw a man who looked like Einstein, later learning that he is the actor who appeared at the Guinness convention last May looking like General Patton. He's great at make-up!

A woman employed by Guinness gave me a hardcover copy of the 1989 edition, and on page 133 I found a reproduction of one page of my diary. *This—was—thrilling!*

Suddenly I heard my name announced from the stage by the man acting as master of ceremonies. Taken aback, wearing shoes in which I do not feel comfortable, I stumbled onto the stage. The MC asked no questions. He strolled to the side of the stage and left me there in the center with my face hanging out, so I made a few remarks about my diary, saw boredom on the faces of the listeners, bumbled off stage and contemplated suicide.

After several world champions were introduced, I found myself within a group of people in front of the stage while a bevy of reporters and photographers and TV cameramen interviewed and photographed many winners. I spoke briefly into perhaps three radio microphones and was televised twice. I asked one TV reporter for whom he worked. He said Moscow Television. I cocked an eye at him because he had almost no accent, but he convinced me he came from Russia.

At long and weary last Phyllis and I left and rode a cab back to my neighborhood to eat lunch in Scotty's restaurant. There we sat from 1 to 3 P.M.
Phyllis is a lovely lady—physically attractive, mature, stylish, intelligent,
interested in spiritualism. She kept her gray eyes on my eyes.

She was telling me something about her life when abruptly she stopped,
saying she realized that whatever she told me might go into my diary and
then, at some later date, perhaps be read by her boss.

I said I had thought about this, and it does pose a problem. If I refused to
keep her remarks out of my journal, then she would become wary and
stilted. Therefore, I continued, I promise not to include in my diary
whatever personal things she might wish to say to me. Phyllis thought a
moment. Then, with a smile on her shapely lips, she said it is okay to
include anything she tells me. Brave lady.

1989

MONDAY, JANUARY 2, 1989 ■ Poor Selma! Ill with Parkinson's disease, she
stays home all the time with two attendants taking care of her 24 hours of
the day. Because of my emphysema and sometimes the weather, I do not
walk the four blocks to visit her as often as before. Whenever we phone she
cannot speak much, so I do most of the talking and often try to amuse her
by dreaming up extravagant lies.

When I called today she asked what I did New Year's Eve. I said there
are eight beautiful ladies madly in love with me, and they hired a blimp
for the night, stocked it with champagne, and had the name EDDIE
spelled out in lights on the sides of the craft. I told her I warned them not
to sail too close to her apartment lest she look out a window and see me
with all those beautiful bimboes. From Selma I heard a faint chuckle.

FRIDAY, JANUARY 6, 1989 ■ I own more than two dozen dictionaries.
Today, flipping through one of them, I learned the origin of the word *fornicate:* In ancient Rome a fornicate was a vaulted underground dwelling.
Because poor people and prostitutes lived there, early Christian writers
called it a brothel, and later the word took on the meaning of sexual intercourse.

SATURDAY, JANUARY 14, 1989 ■ Some of my best and worst ideas occur to
me as I awaken or fall asleep. This zone of consciousness is called the
hypnagogic state. At those times my will has relaxed its grip on my con-

scious mind, thus enabling patches of the unconscious to come to my attention. Then I think of fascinating phrases, or how to structure whatever I am writing. But—some guilty feelings also wound me while I fall asleep or come to consciousness. My attention wanders around until it finds one of my many sins, zooms in, confronts me, disturbs me as I recall how I hurt someone or made a fool of myself.

FRIDAY, JANUARY 20, 1989 ▒ David Hall paid me a compliment I really appreciate: He said I am the most curious person he's ever met.

THURSDAY, JANUARY 26, 1989 ▒ Today I was reminded of something that happened after my mother died. I flew back to Illinois and my three sisters and I held a wake in a funeral parlor in Kewanee. As I stood in the center of the room, I slowly became aware of the eyes of a woman who stood in a corner. She was staring at me. I began walking toward her and as I peered at her face I realized that she and I had slept together when we were teen-agers—but I could not recall her name. Only a year or two younger than myself, she still was attractive and she was dressed in a quiet stylish fash-ion. As we shook hands I thanked her for coming and she called me Eddie but gave me no hint of her identity. The more we spoke the more positive I was in my belief that we had been intimate, and I cursed myself for for-getting her name. At last she said she had to leave, so I escorted her to the door. When I told my sister Frances what had happened, she suggested we look at the guest book. We did—but she had written her name as Mrs. John Smith. I'll go to my grave without remembering who she is.

Not so, Ellis! As I read the early years of my diary, to prepare this book, suddenly I saw a girl's name. Alone in my apartment, I yelled aloud: "Yes!"

SUNDAY, FEBRUARY 19, 1989 ▒ A lengthy and terrifying nightmare: A group of capitalists got control of a newspaper for which I worked as a reporter. Right away they began regimenting the writers, telling them what they might and might not write, putting desks in absolutely precise rows, letting all employees know that they were our total rulers. Standing up, I openly defied them. From all directions the hard-faced men glided up to me and surrounded me and berated me and inundated me. Over-whelmed, I screamed for help—but no one helped me. It seemed that I drowned beneath the weight of their bodies and ignorance. I also dreamed that I walked into a public toilet in a public building made of marble, and on the floor I saw a hissing serpent. This is the sort of nightmare I take somewhat seriously, since I believe that madmen and artists sometimes can foresee the future. As our society becomes evermore fragmented, there is the danger that people will want law and order at the expense of liberty, and will pick leaders with dictatorial tastes. No need to talk about the future: Today's *Times* reports that down in Louisiana David Duke, a former grand wizard of the Ku Klux Klan, has just been elected to the state legislature from the New Orleans suburb of Metairie, which has about 99 per cent white voters. In the 1970's he was photographed wearing a Nazi uniform. But those Goddamn ignorant voters chose him to represent them!

SATURDAY, MARCH 4, 1989 ■ I'm reading the second volume of *The Decline and Fall of the Roman Empire*. One footnote says that Homer used the word *purple* as a vague but common epithet for *death*. This is interesting because all my life the mere sight of anything *purple* has disturbed me emotionally.

FRIDAY, MARCH 10, 1989 ■ It was 10:30 A.M. and I was dressing when the phone rang and I picked up the receiver. I heard a man's voice:
"Eddie?"
"Yes."
"Eddie, this is Nace Strickland."
I damn near fainted. When I was in college, a couple of centuries ago, Nace was my roommate. I graduated from the University of Missouri a year ahead of him and for some reason neither of us can understand, we did not keep in touch with one another. In fact, we have not heard one another's voice in 55 years!
Nace was calling from Atlanta. I asked how the hell he discovered where I live. He said he read about me in the *New Yorker* magazine. In its March 6 issue, in the Talk of the Town section, there was a story about *Diarist's Journal*, publisher Ed Gildea and me.
Within my mind, as we spoke on the phone, I saw an image of Nace—short and dark and handsome, a dreamy sort of fellow with a poetic nature, very tense, very intelligent. He and I drove a car to California and hitchhiked back. I asked whether he had become an architect, as planned. Yes, and among other things, he designed bank vaults. However, now he wishes he had become a writer, instead, and currently he is writing a novel that began as a memoir. Like myself, he is a non-drinking alcoholic. He is 76 years old and recently had a multiple bypass heart operation.
"I want to confess something, Eddie," he said on the phone. "One day when you were not in our room, I saw your diary on your desk and opened

it and read it. A week or so before this happened I had introduced you to the St. Louis girl I was dating, and in your diary you said you didn't like her. I felt furious as hell toward you but couldn't do anything about it because I had no right to read your diary."

With a laugh, I said: "Oh, hell, Nace! You don't have to apologize. Sure I remember Marjorie. Whatever happened to her?"

Said Nace, "I married her."

I realize that this sounds like low comedy, but it's the truth.

SUNDAY, APRIL 2, 1989 ■ I visited Selma, who was in bed. The woman who takes care of her said she is so weak she cannot get in or out of bed by herself. It is so difficult for her to speak that we cannot have a dialogue. Instead, I engage in a monologue, telling her what I've been doing, trying to be funny. Because she suffers from Parkinson's disease, I don't know how well she understands me. After awhile today I stopped speaking and watched Selma lying there staring at the ceiling. On her face there was an expression, or lack of expression, I cannot describe. I asked what she was thinking. After a moment or two, softly she said "nothing." Because I believe she is dying, I wondered whether she "saw" something perhaps otherworldly. I've read about some men and women who "died" for a few moments, then recovered and later wrote what they saw. Mostly, this is light. Although Selma is not in pain, thank God, her life is so constrained and she is so helpless that for her sake I wish she would die. Staring at her, I felt pain in my belly.

WEDNESDAY, APRIL 26, 1989 ■ His Royal Ignorance, George Bush, hopes the Supreme Court will outlaw abortion. The man is all eloquence. In other contexts he speaks of "this vision thing" and "the contra thing." I wish I could tax bad syntax.

MONDAY, JUNE 26, 1989 ■ Today I reread a part of the biography of Ernest Hemingway by Carlos Baker. Here is a masterful Hemingway sentence:

In the late summer of that year we lived in a house in a village that looked across the river and the plain to the mountains. In the bed of the river there were pebbles and boulders, dry and white in the sun, and the water was clear and swiftly moving and blue . . .

WEDNESDAY, JULY 5, 1989 ■ John Gotti is the head of the Gambino orga-nized-crime family and has his headquarters in the Bergen Hunt and Fish

Club in Ozone Park, Queens. Every Fourth of July he gives a block party for his neighbors, and every year his men shoot off fireworks, although they are illegal.

This year he was told by the police that he simply must not use fireworks. Yesterday some 3,000 people attended his party, where everything was free. When darkness fell his henchmen touched off rockets and starbursts from rooftops, where they had been hidden, while on the street people yelled: "Gotti! Gotti! Gotti! . . . You're the greatest . . . You're number one! . . ."

This adulation, remember, was for a Mafia gangster who kills people and deals in drugs and does other wicked things. But, as always, what the masses want is bread and circuses.

THURSDAY, AUGUST 17, 1989 ▣ This morning as I read a dictionary I learned that light travels about 16 billion miles per day, 115 billion per week, 500 billion per month and 6 trillion miles per year. Now, Ellis, I hope you feel properly insignificant.

FRIDAY, AUGUST 18, 1989 ▣ I am outraged by Malcolm Forbes, publisher of *Forbes* magazine and a man worth about $500 million. To celebrate his 70th birthday, he is flying 585 celebrities in three jet planes to Tangiers for the weekend at an estimated cost of more than $2 million.

Now do you understand why I hate capitalism? With thousands upon thousands of homeless people in the U.S., this egomaniac squanders money and indulges in conspicuous consumption on a greater scale than even could have been imagined by the man who coined the phrase— Thorsten Veblen.

Furthermore, Ruthie knew Gertrude, secretary to the father of Malcolm Forbes, and Gertrude often told Ruth that she was grossly underpaid.

WEDNESDAY, SEPTEMBER 20, 1989 ▣ Ruthie has been dead for 24 years, but last night I missed her as acutely as I did in the days after her death. I sat in my living room swaddled in silence and thoughts, and a vision of her dear face came back to me. It is difficult for me to believe that any human being could be so unselfish and compassionate as she was.

Years ago I made heroes of men and women with brilliant minds. Now I admire people who are compassionate. It is for this reason that I regard Mother Teresa of India as a 10 on my scale of excellence. Now the dear lady is ill herself. I consider myself a compassionate man, but for years she has held dying people in her arms. Obviously, she is superior to me in a moral sense.

THURSDAY, SEPTEMBER 21, 1989 ▦ Donald Trump, the flashy real estate man, is supposed to be worth $1.6 billion. *The People's Almanac* says that if a person spent $1,000 a day, every day since the birth of Christ, even by this date the billion dollars would not have been exhausted.

SATURDAY, SEPTEMBER 23, 1989 ▦ Irving Berlin died in his sleep yesterday at the age of 101 in his town house on Beekman Place. I have a special place in my heart for him because a quarter-century ago I spent an afternoon with him and liked him a lot. The *New York Times* story about him began on the front page and then broke inside to one full page.

SATURDAY, OCTOBER 7, 1989 ▦ General Alexander Haig, chief of staff to President Nixon, was the subject of Russell Baker's column in today's *Times*. Baker said Haig is known as "The Butcher of King's English." Once he told a congressional committee: "There is a conscious castration of America's eyes and ears around the world." I wish he would read Gray's *Anatomy*.

MONDAY, OCTOBER 30, 1989 ▦ The glory is gone from the leaves in the backyard. Their colors, that looked the way an organ sounds, have faded into whispers.

THURSDAY, NOVEMBER 9, 1989 ▦ History exploded today in Europe! The government of East Germany lifted restrictions on emigration or travel to the West, and soon thousands of East Germans swarmed across the Berlin Wall to celebrate their freedom. There were television shots of some East Berliners dancing atop the wall near the Brandenburg Gate, while Tom Brokaw of NBC-TV was talking just a few feet away. The wall was built in 1961. It was a spectacular end to 28 years of communist repression. In East Germany the communist regime has disintegrated so fast that almost everyone has been surprised. What a turbulent era!

TUESDAY, NOVEMBER 14, 1989 ▦ Now that the trees are bare of leaves I ask my annual question: Will I live until next spring to see new leaves? It feels odd to be old. Time changes. Perspectives change. My past is like a long spectrum of light, my present thin as a thread, my future a fragile filament. Each morning I sit in my rocking chair to enjoy gentle motion, to appreciate the beauty of my apartment, mainly to think nothing and feel nothing and so soak up serenity. Far from raucous traffic jams and pneumatic hammers and arguing people, I avoid stress. Increasingly I understand and value the Void, so much appreciated by thinkers from the Far East. When one is without desire one becomes both wise and rich. The only thing I really want is to own my own soul, and increasingly I do own it.

THURSDAY, DECEMBER 7 1989 ▨ In the mail I received a medical emergency alert necklace made of metal, 2 1/4 inches long and hanging from a thin chain. I had sent it to an engraving center at Kennedy Airport to be engraved. Now it says *emphysema* and gives my name and phone number, together with those of my daughter and physician. Wearing this around my neck will make me feel safer because if I collapse on a street my ailment will be known, my daughter and doctor can be reached, and this alert necklace will show that I am not a homeless person. Hospital emergency rooms have become horrors.

This afternoon I read further in the new biography of Lewis Mumford, a man I cannot admire because he was so selfishly centered on himself that he hurt his wife and daughter and mistresses.

Early this evening I waited at the Moonstruck restaurant for Peter Skinner. He came out of the cool of the night with no hat covering his curly hair, his blue eyes bright beneath broad eyebrows and behind gold-rimmed glasses. My English-born friend never wears any headgear. If I did what he does, I would have a cold within 10 minutes, the flu 30 minutes later, pneumonia 15 minutes after that, and soon my daughter would be thanking people for the flowers they sent to my funeral. Other than that I'm perfectly fine, perfectly fine! Peter's face always has a scrubbed, squeaky-clean look to it.

I said I had something serious I wanted to discuss and I hoped he would let me monologize awhile. The other day I was struck by an idea that still appeals to me, although it remains amorphous and therefore in need of structuring and completion. Bumbling, stumbling and fumbling in my speech. I said I know damned well that Letts never will buy my diary, and two years hence the company may not renew my contract as a diary consultant. Were this to happen, I then would be 80 years old and moneyless. Coming to my central point, I said I would feel a lot safer if Peter were to edit my journal and otherwise take control of it after I die. To my astonishment, Peter said that several times he had thought about this, but did not care to force himself upon me. Then he went on to say that nothing would make him happier than to have this huge project to work on. Thunderstruck, wishing to make sure I had heard him correctly, I asked him to repeat what he had just said, and he did, his face and eyes solemn. I nearly exploded in excitement. Here we sat, each wanting the same thing!

I had ordered the turkey dinner, but whenever I'm excited intellectually I lose my appetite, so I just picked at the gravy-drowned white meat on the plate in front of me. I asked Peter whether he ever wondered if some day I would make this proposal to him. Yes, he had wondered.

I asked whether he shares my belief that my diary has historic value and that some day it may become a commercial success. Yes and yes. Now, the other day I said to myself that perhaps Peter might create a small consortium of people willing to invest a little money in me to keep me alive so that after I die they might publish my diary in several volumes and make a profit. I can manage to live on $10,000 to $20,000 a year the two or three years left to me. Peter, to my astonishment, suggested this very thing tonight. I said that if such a partnership were formed, I would want him have at least 51 per cent of the power. Thanks to his friendship for me, together with his manifest interest in my diary, that would make me feel safe. I trust him totally, of course. He and I might need some legal contract spelling out our arrangement, and he said he has a lawyer in mind. For one thing, if and when my diary gets back here and into that warehouse three blocks from here, I want Peter to have the right to enter the vault and take out the diary when I die. What I am getting from Peter as I deepen in age and weaken in energy is a kind of a protector, one passionately concerned about my welfare. He is the correct age for this role; next February 25 he will become 52 years old. He owns a house in Newport, and I said I had visualized him there, working at editing my diary for publication. Peter, thank God, has both publishing and academic connections. After all, it was he who persuaded Barnes & Noble to reprint my *Epic of New York City*. Peter said that it is given to few men to be handed a project as valuable as it is massive. I doubt whether, in scouring the world, I could have found a guy better qualified to become the editor-in-chief of my diary.

When we left the restaurant Peter walked home with me under a half-moon whose mountains I could see. As I walked I breathed heavily, of course, and in the frigid air my breath looked like a bouquet of white roses. Upon reaching the stairway inside my house, I took my time inching up the steps. I gave him an inventory of the items held for me at the University of Wyoming, promised to give him many pages of excerpts from my diary, and the two of us agreed that there is much more we must discuss in the near future.

1990

SATURDAY, JANUARY 13, 1990 ▨ This evening I was disgusted by something I saw on NBC-TV News. To promote a film called *Texas Chainsaw Massacre III*, an actor wearing a grotesque mask used a chainsaw in a studio to split open soft models of human heads. On the radio I heard that in Greenwich Village a woman and a man were slashed on their faces by razors or knives wielded by members of a passing gang. The woman is Viveca Lindfors, 69, the Swedish actress; it took 28 stitches to repair her left ear. Five minutes earlier and three blocks away, a man of 36 was cut so badly he needed 40 stitches.

SUNDAY, JANUARY 14, 1990 ▨ Czechoslovakia has a new president, Vaclav Havel, an author and playwright. He has uttered a great truth: "We have become morally ill because we are used to saying one thing and thinking another." Someone should write a novel in which everyone on earth agrees that as of January 1 all will speak the truth. What would happen?

SUNDAY, JANUARY 21, 1990 ▨ The line between reality and fantasy is becoming blurred. NBC is promoting a silly new morning show. In one episode an ordinary American family attends a Presidential press conference in the White House and some of them ask questions of President Bush. Clips from genuine Bush press conferences have been edited into this comedy show, making it appear that he was responding to the family questions. Another example: A company that sells furniture paid for a radio commercial structured to sound like a real news story, using phrases such as "informed sources say . . ." Some TV commercials try to attract attention by flashing onto the screen NEWS BULLETIN! Whenever I see these words I know the copy was not written by anyone who once worked for a newspaper. In real journalism it's just BULLETIN.

THURSDAY, JANUARY 25, 1990 ▨ President Bush is adding to the confusion between reality and fantasy with his inept use of the language. Regarding a secret trip made by an administration official to China, he said: "I notice now that some of the critics who were so opposed and using this fantastically, diabolically anti-me language, they come up now saying, 'Well, if you get A, B and C, then it will be all right or then we'll understand.' Let them just stay tuned in."

I see his point as clearly as I see a black cat on a pile of coal at midnight on a moonless night.

SUNDAY, JANUARY 28, 1990 ▉ My friend Peter Skinner remarked that these days most people give less and less attention to more and more things. True! This explains the superficiality of modern life. I told Peter that I pay more and more attention to less and less, then explained that I believe all reality is One, as has been said in several religions and philosophies.

Last autumn Letts of London had a booth on 5th Avenue as part of the New York Is Book Country fair. It contributed to the New York Public Library by raffling off tickets. The individual who bought the most tickets won first prize—me. The prize was lunch for the winner and me in the Four Seasons restaurant.

THURSDAY, MARCH 8, 1990 ▉ The *New York Times* has said that the Four Seasons is the city's most glamorous restaurant. It is in the prize-winning Seagram Building on Park Avenue between East 52nd and East 53rd Streets. Both the building and restaurant were designed by Philip Johnson, the famous architect.

Aware that I was about to encounter elegance, I dressed carefully for the first time in a long time. The luncheon date was for 1 P.M. I caught a cab whose driver did not even know the location of the Seagram Building, one of the most famous in town. Leaning forward, I looked at his license and saw an Arabic name. Too many new cab drivers do not speak English well or know the city as they should.

As I rode across mid-Manhattan I saw that many streets and buildings look tawdry, although a new skyscraper is rising on Broadway. My 79-year-old mind told me that this town is for the young and middle-aged, but not for elderly persons such as myself. I recalled that when I was a reporter for the *World-Telegram* I brimmed with energy and dashed hither and yon. The city has changed, and so has my opinion of it. Now I am not so fond of New York as I was when I moved here in 1947.

When I reached Park Avenue memories of Ruthie washed through my mind. There is a plaza with two fountains in front of the Seagram Building, which is set back from the avenue, and Ruthie and I liked to stroll there to gaze at the fountains. Upon entering the restaurant the first thing I saw was an enormous Picasso on a wall. Turning left, I approached the Pool Room, which the *Times* has described as "romantic and plush." At the door I was met by the maitre d', and when I told him my name he smiled and said he was expecting me. He escorted me to a table in the northwest corner of the restaurant near a window overlooking Park Avenue.

I was early and glad of it, for now I had time to pull out a pen and pad and scribble notes about the Four Seasons. Its square pool is illuminated and bordered in white marble. The north and west walls consist of towering windows, the east wall is finished in beautiful walnut panels, while the south wall is made of some composition finished in a creamy color. The windows' "curtains" are made of long strands of tiny chains drooping toward the center of each window, and the slightest breeze makes them shiver and shine.

The room was only half full and very quiet. I saw no celebrity. At one table a man sat alone talking into a telephone. The floor was covered with a thick patterned rug. Hanging from the ceiling were three wooden planters filled with plants and flowers. Metal wine buckets stood here and there. The waiters wore olive jackets, red ties, red cummerbunds, and all responded eagerly, so it seemed, to the slightest signal of a finger.

Asked what I chose to drink, I ordered a Coca-Cola in a tall glass with lots of ice and a slice of lemon. When I asked whether I might have a menu to take home, the answer was a polite yes. Studying it, I was stunned by the prices. As I glanced up I saw a waiter leading a woman to my table and realized she was my luncheon companion. Holding out my hand, I said: "We must stop meeting this way."

She smiled. She is Mrs. Mildred Marmur, a literary agent and a friend of my own agent, Rita Rosenkranz. Mildred—we were soon on a first-name basis—is of medium height with dark hair cropped close, brown twinkling eyes behind round glasses, very little make-up, and over her shoulders she wore a colorful scarf—an accessory I like on women.

I am glad she won the Letts lottery because she is intelligent and personable. Usually it is I who ask the first questions, but today she peppered me with probing questions about my diary. She knows how to ask questions and, better yet, she also knows how to listen. Few people listen well.

She was born in this city of Jewish parents born in Russia. Even as a child she knew that books would play an important role in her life. She speaks French, Yiddish and some Hebrew. To escape from some pressures at home, she did not go to college here but attended the University of Minnesota, where she earned a master's degree in French.

Upon returning here she began working for various book publishers and rose fast because she labored hard and has a superior mind. Rita had told me that one reason for admiring Mildred is the fact that she does not think just in linear fashion but can analyze problems three-dimensionally. I understood Rita's remark because when I smoked grass I often thought in three dimensions simultaneously.

So Mildred became the president of Scribner's publishing company, its first woman president and first Jewish president. She is, quite properly, proud of this accomplishment. Although she is an atheist, as was Ruthie, she likes to observe Jewish customs and holidays. I said that Carl Jung taught me the value of ceremonies.

Mildred knew A. Bartlett Giamatti, the brilliant president of Yale, and when he was named the commissioner of baseball she urged him to keep a diary. He said he would, but procrastinated, and a few months ago he died. Mildred understands the value of journals.

As regards our luncheon, I ordered "a service of shrimp," consisting of three large shrimp and costing $16. Everything was a la carte. As an entree I wanted a filet mignon, the most delicious I ever ate, but it cost a screaming $36.75. I got a baked potato that cost $5.50. For dessert I chose chocolate cream pie, a rather slim slice priced at $6.50. I don't remember what Mildred ordered, but I did find out that this luncheon for two, plus tip, cost Letts $174.

This is immoral! It came to me as culture shock. Back in the days of the Depression, back when I was a cub reporter in Orleans, I ate for one dollar a day. I remember reading that Margaret Mead, the celebrated anthropologist, said that in her opinion the cultural gap is not between young and old, but rather between those who lived through the Depression and those who didn't. I agree. In many ways my mind still is stuck back there.

WEDNESDAY, MARCH 14, 1990 ■ I rode a cab to the Biography Bookshop at 400 Bleecker Street in the Village, arriving at 12:50 P.M., ten minutes before it was due to open. I waited across the street in the sunshine, leaning on a shoulder-high mailbox, and on top of it I found a key, seemingly a key to a house, and I thought that if I wrote mystery novels this would be a good way to begin one. Come to think of it, my 63-year-old diary is peopled with thousands of characters, plots for scores of short stories and dozens of novels.

TUESDAY, MARCH 27, 1990 ■ Today I read that evangelist Pat Robertson, who ran for President in 1988, said of pro-choice politicians: "They just want to kill. They have a spirit of murder. Abortionists are worse than Ceausescu, worse than Stalin, worse than Hitler." Hearing this, can you doubt my declaration that the world is going mad? Whenever I see Robertson's smiling face on television I am reminded of a line in Shakespeare's *Macbeth*: "There's daggers in men's smiles."

FRIDAY, MARCH 30, 1990   ■   Today I was on the phone with John (Mickey) McGuire, a colleague from my days on the *World-Telegram* who now owns his own house in Brooklyn. When I said my emphysema is worse and I may live only a year or so, Mickey paused a moment and then paid me a great compliment: "Well, Eddie, your body may disintegrate, but we'll have to beat your mind to death!"

THURSDAY, APRIL 12, 1990   ■   I was sitting at the front window when Pete Hamill appeared on the sidewalk below me. After buzzing him in, I leaned over the railing on the third-floor landing to chortle that he had arrived exactly at 11:30 o'clock, as planned. Walking up the winding stairs, he joked that he was three minutes late by his watch. As we shook hands I said it was odd that we had not met before, since we are in the same business. He agreed.

Years ago, in his column in the *New York Post*, he had praised my *Epic of New York City*, which pleased me. Given the fact that he was born here and has written much about this town, Pete is practically Mr. New York. Recently I read somewhere that he plans to write a book about the way the city was in 1955, so I called to say I would let him see my 1955 diary and also would give him some of my books about New York.

As he walked into the front room I saw his eyes dart toward the books on shelves on three walls, floor to high ceiling. He wore a sports jacket and slacks and carried a metal briefcase. Pete Hamill is 54 years old, about five feet ten inches tall, with a stocky build and meaty shoulders that must have served him well when he worked as a longshoreman. He has light brown wavy hair, a brown beard less than abundant, piercing blue eyes, shapely hands and a resonant baritone voice.

He has an open and honest personality. He is self-assured without being arrogant, with a flashing mind, acute curiosity and palpable enthusiasm. He is one of those rare conversationalists who knows how to listen. Although he is a celebrity, he is utterly natural, unlike actors I've known who worked hard at being "sincere."

I was quick to tell him that I wear a beret to keep my head warm in old age, not because I was trying to look Bohemian. On the coffee table in front of the sofa, where he sat, I had placed a copy of the reprint of my *Epic of New York City* and now said it was my gift to him. Picking it up and looking at it, he seemed pleased with my inscription: "For Pete Hamill, whose style is a laser beam."

We talked a lot about writing, agreeing upon the value of details and simplicity. I said that some writer or philosopher, I forget who, declared that "God is in the details." I added that I think the guy meant that reality resides in details. Agreeing, Pete said that he and his friends like my *Epic* because it is full of colorful details.

He told me that many young men who want to become novelists do not read very much, and when he suggests they study Conrad or Henry James, they don't even know the names of these authors. Pete said he learned a lot about how to structure a novel by reading a book about the notes kept by Henry James. As for youths who want to become journalists, Pete continued, they can't even spell correctly but expect to get a column of their own within weeks after taking a newspaper job.

It was obvious to me that Pete works hard at his writing. He writes three columns a week for the *New York Post*, staying only one column ahead, produces long articles for *New York* magazine, turns out movie scripts and now is at work on his non-fiction book about this city in 1955. It takes him from one to three hours to pound out one of his columns. Sometimes, when his thinking gets tangled in knots, he takes a nap and while asleep will find the solution to his problem of syntax. I remember Bertrand Russell said in his memoirs that his unconscious often produced answers as he slept.

When I asked Pete how many books he has written, he said eight. Seven are novels. His first book was a collection of his columns under the title *Irrational Ravings*. That was the phrase used by former Vice President Spiro Agnew, that genius, to characterize Pete's liberal thinking. Or perhaps it was Agnew's speech writer, William Safire, who coined this phrase.

Recently Pete bought a computer and taught himself how to use it in only three weeks. I marvel at this! The mere sight of a computer hurts my belly. Neither Pete nor I learned touch-typing, but he reported a great quote: "Hands have memories of their own."

Pete smiles a lot and when he does the sunburst of wrinkles at the edges of his eyes deepen and lengthen. I said it was a helluva lot of fun for two old newspaper guys to shoot the breeze and talk shop. I had a dim memory of some connection Pete had with the famous bank robber, Willie Sutton. I covered the first day of his trial.

Pete said that after Willie had served part of his sentence, Pete wrote a column urging that he be released, since he never had done anything violent, and Governor Nelson Rockefeller actually let him out of prison. Willie was not called "The Actor" for nothing. Appearing at parole hearings, he looked like a weak little Dan, but the day he came out from behind the bars (and as Pete told this, he acted it out) he expanded his chest, held his head high and marched away.

I mentioned Norman Mailer and when Pete said he has known Norman about 30 years, I exclaimed it's a pity Pete never kept a diary, so that his anecdotes about Mailer might be remembered. Pete chuckled that had he kept a diary and Norman found out about it, Norman might have knocked him on his ass. Pete and I agreed that Mailer's Egyptian novel, *Ancient Evenings*, was a failure.

As Pete and I continued to discuss books and writing, he said he lived with Shirley MacLaine for five years and helped her with her writing. He added that although they broke up, they continue to be good friends. I've read a couple of her books and in one of them she expressed appreciation for the writer who helped her.

I urged Pete to keep a diary. Admitting that his life has not been exactly dull, he agreed he really should but said he writes all the time, and besides, his columns pretty much tell him what he was doing when. Grinning, I said I might begin to nag him a little. I showed him my maroon-bound diary of 1955 with its 737 typed pages, and he seemed impressed. When he finds time he'll return to examine it at length to decide what excerpts he might want for his book.

THURSDAY, APRIL 26, 1990 ▓ Pete Hamill's column in the *New York Post* today begins this way: "In the past month, there has been a distinct odor of collapse and doom around the city. I've never heard so many otherwise optimistic citizens talking in such pessimistic language. . . . 'I just can't take this town anymore,' one old New Yorker said. 'I just don't want to live like this. I'm sick of it.' "

It's obvious I'm not the only one who feels this way.

SUNDAY, MAY 6, 1990 ▓ In volume 12 of the majestic *Historians' History of the World,* I found this statement: "There is nothing better proved by a course of historic study than the strange fact that the people on the very verge of change and revolution have no idea that anything is about to take place. A nation is always taken by surprise when its institutions are overthrown."

Always?

SUNDAY, MAY 13, 1990 ▓ About 8 A.M. I got a call from Cora, who takes care of Selma. She said Selma has a fever, her face is red and she has trouble breathing. I dialled 911 and asked that an ambulance be sent to her

building. She was taken to St. Vincent's Hospital in Greenwich Village
and later I received a call from a Dr. Hamid, who said she has pneumonia,
a fever of 104 degrees and now is receiving antibiotics intravenously.
Selma is so weak from her prolonged illness with Parkinson's disease that I
doubt whether her body can shake off the pneumonia. Later I tried to
read, but my worry and sorrow about her made this impossible.

MONDAY, MAY 14, 1990   ■   Because I pity poor Selma, I felt older and more
arthritic today. Leaving the house, I bought six red roses, took a cab to the
hospital. I told a nurse I have emphysema, then asked whether it would be
dangerous for me to see a patient with pneumonia. She said it would be
okay if I just turn my head whenever Selma coughs. I did not feel reassured.

Selma looked like a little ghost as she lay in bed with oxygen tubes in
her nostrils. Her eyes were open and I believe she recognized me. I
touched her hand but did not kiss her. I stood at the foot of the bed to tell
her about Pete Hamill's visit and other events in my life. She did not utter
a word. Her expression never changed—the classic Parkinsonian mask.

TUESDAY, MAY 15, 1990   ■   When my wife died in 1965 it happened so fast I
had no chance to brace myself emotionally, and so I went mad. Now it
seems I am about to lose Selma, too, but this time I will not go mad. I'll
just ache a lot, a lot, a lot.

Today, in an antique shop near my home, I bought a glass globe that
makes a little snowstorm when shaken, and it also plays a tinkly tune. I
took it to the hospital to give to Selma.

She lay scrunched up in a corner of her bed by the window, with tubes
in her to give her oxygen and nourishment, a wan creature, very white,
motionless, a mere wisp of a human being, her hazel eyes half-closed as
though to shut out pain. This time I wasn't sure whether she recognized
me. I wound up the glass ball and held it near her face so she could see the
snow and hear the music. Her face was blank. She did not speak a word.
From time to time her eyelids drooped, so I said I would leave to give her a
chance to take a nap. I wish for her sake she would die!

SUNDAY, MAY 20, 1990   ■   This morning when I called the hospital I was
told that Selma's condition has worsened, and this evening may determine
whether she will live or die. I flinched, partly in sorrow, partly because of a
role I was supposed to play this evening.

The National Stationery Show opened today in the Javits Convention

Center on the west side of mid-Manhattan. There are thousands of exhibitors and Letts of London has a booth there. Anthony Letts, chairman of the board, has flown here from London to attend the convention and also to hold a gala cocktail reception in the Russian Tea Room at 150 West 57th Street. The formal invitation says:

Meet Letts Guest of Honor
Edward Robb Ellis
"Guinness" Diarist Recordholder

Having learned that Selma may be dying, I asked myself how in the world I could attend that party and pretend to be cheerful as she eked out her last breath on earth. If I went to that reception and she died while I was there, I would feel guilty. However, if I failed to attend a party that has been in preparation for weeks, if I, the guest of honor, did not show up, then I would feel guilty about my friends at Letts. I felt torn in half.

After much agonizing, I decided to go to the party but not visit Selma first, because the sight of her would imprint pain on the face I must show to strangers this evening. When I left I took four autographed copies of my *Epic of New York City*. Barnes & Noble has reprinted my 1966 history under the imprimatur of Old Town Books.

For years I had been curious about the Russian Tea Room because it is one of the best restaurants in town, because it has been called a "great New York classic," and because it is a renowned rendezvous for celebrities, especially those in the theater and movies. Because of Selma, when I arrived there this evening, my curiosity was diminished but not extinguished.

The reception was held on the second floor. All year round the place has a red, green and gold "Christmas decor." There were red lamp shades, red leather chairs, a red leather banquette along one wall, red leather on the front of the cocktail bar and a soft burgundy rug. On the walls were paintings and etchings of New York City. The waiters were costumed as Russian dancers. All in all, here was an ambience such as I seldom have seen.

The hostess of the evening was Phyllis Calderaro of Letts, and the moment I met her again I told her about Selma and about how sad I felt, and Phyllis comforted me with soft words and warm hands, for which I was grateful. I also thanked her when I saw two small signs asking people not to smoke.

I gave one copy of my *Epic* to Phyllis, and another to David Hall, who had retained me as a diary consultant. The other two copies I handed to Anthony Letts and Liam Swords from the company's London office.

I sat down upon the red upholstered bench along the wall. Sitting to my left was Mrs. Marianne Jardine of Providence, R.I. She is a 53-year-old college graduate, the mother of four grown children, and she has a flashing smile and asks as many questions as I do. She seemed such a nice person that soon I explained that my best friend was dying, so this would explain any erratic behavior of mine. She put her hand on my hands, looked at me with soft brown eyes and we fell into instant friendship. She stuck by my side all evening. When I told her some of my maxims, she seemed to appreciate them.

I drank soda and nibbled on canapes served by waiters, and thought about Selma. Once I went to the food bar, where I was given red caviar stuffed inside a small pancake. When I returned to the banquette, there was Marianne, waiting to take care of me. Nearby were women who saw copies of my *Epic* and asked about it, and then one of them left the restaurant, walked to a nearby Barnes & Noble bookstore, bought five copies and brought them back for me to autograph.

David asked me to dine with him and other executives, but I was eager to get home so that I might call the hospital. When I phoned I learned that Selma still was alive.

Soon thereafter I wrote Marianne to thank her for her compassion. Quickly she replied, saying in part: "I have never had such an immediate bonding as did you and I in that exceptionally lovely setting, the Russian Tea Room. . . . I treasured our delightful conversation all the way home to Rhode Island, and shared the best parts with my husband Len as we drove. Such as LOVE IS COMMUNICATION!!!"

At long last Selma died on March 29, 1992. She was a good woman. I had urged her to keep a diary and so she did, for 18 years. Now I possess all her volumes.

MONDAY, MAY 28, 1990 ■ In the *Times* I read about a place in Texas where men and boys pay a fee to fire machine guns and other heavy weapons. Some of those macho jerks have cars with bumper stickers saying: "The more people I know the more bullets I need!" Madness seeps around the world like mustard gas.

TUESDAY, MAY 29, 1990 ■ As an old newspaperman I am fascinated by great leads to feature stories, and today I found one written by John Lardner. It is about a famous boxer: "Stanley Ketchel was twenty-four years old when he was fatally shot in the back by the common-law husband of the lady who was cooking his breakfast."

This reminds me that John's father, Ring Lardner, wrote the funniest single line I ever read in any book. The line is spoken by a father scolding his son: " 'Shut up!' I explained."

WEDNESDAY, JUNE 13, 1990   ■   Nace Strickland sent me a letter that included this joke:

Question—What would you get if you crossed a chronic insomniac with an agnostic dyslexic?

Answer—A guy who stays awake all night wondering if there really is a dog.

WEDNESDAY, JUNE 20, 1990   ■   This is the day Nelson Mandela came to town. A South African, a hereditary tribal chief, the living symbol of resistance to apartheid, a man who spent 27 years in prison for his resistance to the white government, now nearly 72 years old, this tall and dignified black man uncorked a mood of celebration that affected most New Yorkers.

The city opened its arms to welcome him. While it is true that in the Queens communities of Howard Beach and Ozone Park some white ignoramuses made rude gestures, the vast majority of the people smiled and grinned and cheered and even wept for joy. The black leader and his wife were given a parade up lower Broadway. Watching this event on television, I saw that they had been seated inside a glass vehicle that looked like an ark, with bulletproof windows, a peaked roof, mounted on top of a flatbed truck.

Years ago when I was a reporter and watched heroes ride triumphantly up Broadway, they sat in open cars, but now there is so much hatred and violence that security measures must be taken. Something else was different, too: No ticker tape. Instead, because of changing technology, thick wads of shredded computer printouts were thrown out of windows to hail Mandela.

I rejoice in the fact that black people now have a hero whose stature is beginning to rival that of Ghandi. Good for them! Good for Mandela!

WEDNESDAY, AUGUST 29, 1990   ■   This brilliant August day I strolled south on Hudson Street in Greenwich Village and became thirsty and walked into a small Mexican restaurant. I sat down at a table in the front near the bar, by a mirrored wall.

A woman sat at the bar. She perched on a tall stool. She may have been in her late thirties. She had short hair the color of honey, blue-tinted sunglasses, and she spoke fluent Spanish to the bartender, although she did not look Latino. She may have been a saleswoman because she showed the bartender a catalog of some sort and pointed out various items in it.

She wore a blouse and a short skirt, very short, and her tan hose held beautiful legs that vanished into sleek shining black pumps with very high heels. Staring at her legs, mesmerized by them, I knew she knew she has beautiful legs and likes to show them, but I was unable to do anything about it.

In the mirror on the wall I saw the face of an old man with white whiskers and long hair, and I also saw the potbelly that precedes me wherever I go. Oh, to be only forty again! Then I was slender and graceful and some ladies said I was handsome, and I liked women and women liked me and almost never was I afraid to speak to a woman, especially a woman who sat at a bar in a short skirt, a very short skirt, a woman who uses her beautiful legs to bewitch men.

Had I been half my present age I surely would have struck up a conversation with this woman whose sensuality flowed out of her like lava. My first remark to her would have been non-threatening, neutral, impersonal, having nothing whatsoever to do with either of us. Because of the space I would put between us conversationally, she would have felt safe enough to make some small comment in reply, and that would have opened a dialogue between us. This technique is one I used again and again and, unless memory fails me, I cannot recall any woman who did not reply with at least a word or two.

But . . . but now the reality is that I am old and fat and ugly and lack the bravura that worked well back in the days when I chased women, especially lava-hot women who wanted to be chased. So I choked down a tortilla and a Coke and reflected that this sadness comes to all men in all places when age diminishes them. So in a Mexican restaurant on Hudson Street in Greenwich Village one sparkling day in August, a tiny tragedy was played out by a man too old to make out.

SUNDAY, SEPTEMBER 2, 1990 ■ In the doorway of a building on 9th Avenue I saw the debris left by some homeless person—including a tattered flower in the neck of an empty wine bottle.

1991

SATURDAY, JANUARY 19, 1991 ■ When I was born in 1911 there were an estimated 1.7 billion people on earth. Now there are about 5.2 billion, which means that during my lifetime the world's population has increased by 3.5 billion. Furthermore, every four days there are one million more mouths to feed. This is scary!

THURSDAY, JANUARY 24, 1991 ■ The social center of my Chelsea neighborhood is the L & S Dairy on the northwest corner of 9th Avenue and W. 21st Street, a half block from my home. Long ago it may have been a dairy, but now it is part grocery, part deli in a two-story structure built in the Federal style in 1831. It is so quaint that an ink sketch of the exterior is in a book called *Nooks and Crannies*.

The interior is small. It has pressed-tin walls, an ancient cash register, old-fashioned ceiling fans and a few tables with red-checkered tablecloths where neighbors sit to nurse cups of coffee, eat sandwiches, do crossword puzzles and gossip. A dog named Wingnut lolls in one window. It is like a country grocery store where one can loaf for hours without feeling uneasy.

Chelsea has a few celebrities, such as Anthony Perkins and Bonnie Raitt, and a sprinkling of intellectuals such as professors and editors and writers. The L & S is their town square, where they meet and mingle on equal terms.

The place is owned and operated by Peter and Carol Howell, who own a brownstone on 21st Street. They are middle-aged college graduates and dropouts from stressful upscale positions. Peter was an American Airlines executive. Carol was in the art publishing world.

Because many customers also are friends, much joking goes on. On a wall behind the counter there usually is a snapshot of the so-called Chelsea celebrity of the week. There also is trust; credit is given. One day when I handed Carol a ten-dollar bill she said: "Thank you, Your Majesty." Keeping my face straight, I said: " 'Sir Edward' will do nicely, thank you." The index card on which they keep track of my credit is not filed under "E" for Eddie or Ellis, but under "S" for Sir Ed. That's what they call me.

One of the countermen is Jose, built like a fire plug. He and I maintain a rapid-fire patter of teasing. Sometimes when I walk in I'll wail: "Jose, try to be good! Please!" His Pancho Villa moustache bristling, he'll bark: "Never! Never! Never!" And then grin.

Today, after finishing work at the L & S, Jose came to my apartment to move some books to provide space for the volumes of my diary, soon to be brought back from the University of Wyoming. He brought milk, orange juice and two muffins as presents for me. For himself he brought four beers, which he drank one after the other.

Jose was born in Puerto Rico 29 years ago. He said he is part Puerto Rican, part Indian, part Sicilian. He is one of 18 children, among whom are five sets of twins. Jose has a twin sister and among his own seven children is one set of twins. When he was two years old his family moved here and found a seven-room apartment, where he still lives.

Jose is five feet six, a burly figure with bulging muscles; he wears a ring in his left ear and always has a stubble of beard on his cheeks in addition to his turned-down moustache. When he was in his teens he became the leader of a gang in Manhattan and has had many fights. Saying he has been shot three times, he pulled up the left leg of his blue jeans to show me the wounds. Adding that he was slashed with razors, he tugged down his shirt to reveal rows of scars. Also, he told me, he had been stabbed in the belly, so he hoisted his shirt to exhibit a scar ten inches long. And he broke his knuckles several times while fighting.

Several times today he declared he is not stupid. I had not even hinted that he is stupid. Repeatedly he called me "Sir"—not the joking "Sir Ed" of the grocery, but a sincere form of address. When I asked whether he calls me this because of the two years he spent in the army in Germany, he said no. He said he likes and respects older people and he called me a good man. To my amazement, he said he felt honored when I asked whether he would do a little work for me.

Jose is a fascinating blend of machismo and Latino courtesy. When I guessed that the thing he wants most is respect, he smiled and said I hit it on the nose. Whenever he wanted another beer I told him to get it from the refrigerator, but he said he would not think of opening anyone's refrigerator. He began to get tipsy.

We were in the kitchen. I wanted him to take books off two tables and put them up on pantry-shelves. Jose stood on a tall stepladder. Because he was getting tight, and because he read aloud the title of every book he handled, he did not accomplish as much as I had hoped. However, it was a help.

We walked to the front room and sat down and I listened as he talked. He invited me to visit his home. Then, as the beer clouded his mind, his brown eyes filled with tears and he said he loves me. When we stood up he gave me a big hug and kissed my cheek, so I kissed his cheek. He knows how to fight and he also knows how to love.

Talk about the Odd Couple! Old man born a WASP in puritanical small town on prairie of mid-America now meets young man born on tropical island who believes in voodoo and carries scars of big city fights.

MONDAY, FEBRUARY 4, 1991 ■ Today I thought about Michelangelo's painting on the ceiling of the Sistine Chapel showing God creating Adam. Their index fingers almost touch. It occurred to me that the tiny gap between their fingers is like a synapse, the tiny space between one nerve cell and another, through which nerve impulses are transmitted.

FRIDAY, FEBRUARY 15, 1991 ■ Harvey Wang is a photographer and a friend of mine. Today he brought over Elizabeth Burke, a tall young woman with a thin face and brown hair; she is a senior producer of Radio 3 of the British Broadcasting Corporation. She is a graduate of Cambridge University, the wife of a barrister and a very intelligent lady.

The moment she entered my apartment she exclaimed that she likes it better than any other she had seen in New York. My books, I suppose. Another Englishwoman once said my place looks like a London flat. Harvey had told Elizabeth about my diary and suggested that she interview me.

She seemed fascinated by the fact that I keep books on pantry shelves in the kitchen. In the front room she had just begun asking questions when bells started ringing from the chapel of the seminary across the street. Instantly she thrust her wand-shaped microphone out of the open window to record the chimes. She was delighted when I told her that the poet Wallace Stevens lived in the apartment above mine many years before I moved here, and he wrote a poem after hearing those bells.

Because of Elizabeth's intelligence, she did an exceptional job of interviewing me. She asked whether I could remember one day that was the happiest day of my life. In a flash, I said yes. It was a day Ruthie and I spent together in Paris. We felt healthy, the weather was beautiful, taxi drivers and waiters were polite, the champagne was delicious, every bite of food was luscious, we were deeply in love and, back in our hotel room, we became very romantic.

Then this BBC correspondent asked a question never before put to me: "Do you regard yourself as an extraordinary man?"

Startled, I thought a moment before replying: "No, I am an ordinary man who has done one extraordinary thing—keep a diary as long as I have."

The BBC interview was broadcast throughout the United Kingdom on June 14. It evoked a few letters. The best came from Mrs. Ruth Arnold, who said in part: "Have you ever felt that when someone was talking, you knew them straight away? This is how I felt listening to you."

WEDNESDAY, FEBRUARY 20, 1991 ■ Today my diary was brought back from the University of Wyoming, where it had been the last decade, and this evening David Hall of Letts of London gave me an 80th birthday party in the Algonquin Hotel.

TUESDAY, APRIL 16, 1991 ■ This afternoon I left my doctor's office on Washington Square West and walked to 6th Avenue, where I hailed a cab. As I opened the cab door I saw an envelope on the street, so in a sweeping motion I picked it up, got into the taxi, closed the door. Not until I reached home did I open the envelope.

It contained two $50 bills. But—it also had the name of a man, his address and phone number. There also was evidence that the money was intended as a donation to a Catholic church in the Village.

I telephoned the gentleman, identified myself, reported that I had found something belonging to him. He sounded very old. He said he is a former actor and now quite ill. In a tremulous voice he said:

"I don't know whether you are a Catholic, Mr. Ellis, but when a Catholic loses something he prays to St. Anthony, so just now, when you called, I was on my knees praying to him."

I'm so damned slow-witted! I should have said, "Yeah, but the money was found by an agnostic!"

I'm sure that gentleman will tell this story for years, sticking in the word *miracle*, and I'll bet that St. Anthony will get top billing.

I have a dear friend who is as conservative as I am liberal, so we never discuss politics. However, one day he wrote a letter that triggered an outburst from me. I wrote him a long reply in which I told him, for the first time, exactly where I stand on politics and economics. Here are some excerpts from that letter.

THURSDAY, APRIL 18, 1991 ■ The single most influential book I ever read, with the exception of one or two by Carl Jung, was *History of Great American Fortunes*. It was published originally in 1910 in three volumes; now it is a Modern Library Giant volume.

It was written by Gustavus Myers, a journalist and historian who spent eight years researching this book. Then it took him nine years to find a publisher brave enough to publish it, but after it came out not a single libel suit was filed against it because it was accurate. Myers had worked mainly from court records.

His theme is that all great fortunes are founded upon crime. For example, back in the 18th century John Jacob Astor dealt in drugs, selling opium, and his western agents got Indians drunk and then bought their furs for almost nothing.

Capitalists declare they want a free market when, in fact, they form monopolies and cartels. They give lip-service to democracy while promoting economic slavery—for the other guy.

Capitalism is an economic system. Democracy is a political system. They are not identical. Some people, especially Republicans, try to equate democracy with capitalism, in the interest of protecting capitalism, but this is a charade. I see through their game.

I dislike capitalism, cherish democracy and hate communism. Capitalism is greed sanctified and institutionalized. I despise Wall Street sharks such as Michael Milken, who made $1.5 million per day, and Dennis Levine, who placed two phone calls and profited by $3 million.

Ted Turner, the media magnate, said, "Business is war." President Calvin Coolidge said, "The business of America is business." Wrong! The business of business is earning a profit. The business of government is helping the people.

Too damned many men and women have lied and cheated and used other corrupt means to obtain their selfish ends—more money, more power. Legislators are bought and sold. As a result, so many Americans have been alienated that only about half of all eligible voters actually vote. The plutocracy practiced by Republican Presidents Nixon, Reagan and Bush has widened the gap between rich and poor—a condition that historically precedes a revolution.

Fortunately, there are a few of us left who realize that government officials are our *servants*, not our *masters.* Too often they lie to us, and when lying becomes chronic, society becomes sick. It is truth that holds society together.

I detest Lenin because he advocated lying to win power. I abhor Stalin because he was a mass murderer. I disagree with Karl Marx because I do not believe that history is only a struggle of class against class; it is this, to be sure, but there also are many other factors.

By daring to say out loud that I dislike capitalism means running the risk of being called a communist. However, Pope John Paul II has criticized capitalism, and I tend to doubt whether he is a communist. Since I prefer cooperation to competition, I wish we had some form of socialism in the United States. There are many kinds of socialism, and I do not know which is best.

What I do know is that Chief Sitting Bull put his finger on capitalism when he told Annie Oakley: "The white man knows how to make everything, but he does not know how to distribute it."

WEDNESDAY, MAY 1, 1991   ■   In Germany and Austria there is a new video game that lets the player pretend he is a Nazi concentration camp manager who earns points for gassing prisoners and selling gold dental fillings. Dear God! The banality of evil, the trivialization of tragedy, the continuing madness!

WEDNESDAY, MAY 15, 1991   ■   This is one of the strangest stories I ever heard about New York City: Last Friday night as Mr. and Mrs. John Brownett of Abbeville, S.C., were riding in a cab along the West Side Highway here, she was bitten on her thigh by a bat. She screamed and flung the bat onto the floor of the cab. It wrapped its wings around her ankle. She and her husband pulled it off and stomped it to death. She was taken to a hospital where she got the first of five painful rabies shots. However, the bat was tested and found free of rabies.

MONDAY, JUNE 17, 1991   ■   This evening Peter Skinner visited me and we talked about many things. I said I define knowledge as a body of facts, and wisdom as knowledge of oneself. Peter said, "Ah, yes! Knowledge is beer. Wisdom is brandy." Brilliant!

THURSDAY, JUNE 20, 1991   ■   The playful side of my personality comes from my maternal grandfather, Samuel Ervin Robb. I wish some musician would compose "Fanfare for a Grandfather." He and my grandmother were happily married partly, perhaps, because he teased her. He teased her often and creatively while I watched and appreciated him.

Once they sat at the kitchen table while she peeled potatoes. He put his hand flat on the table, spread apart his fingers, and dared her to stab the space between them. Irritated, she stabbed—a finger! By mistake. She burst into tears. He burst into laughter.

Every so often Grandma Robb would squeal: "Oh, Erv, stop that!" He never did stop, of course, and everyone in the family knew that had he stopped she would have shrivelled up and died. We only tease the people we love or like.

I thought of this today because I did something horrible.

When I got back from the bank and walked into the foyer of this brownstone, I found the floor being cleaned by my landlady's maid, a pleasant black woman who is the mother of seven successful children. I've known her a long time and like her. When she complained that the front door did not close properly, I said flippantly, "Oh, you're just ignorant about how it works."

Her face froze. She said grittily: *I—am—not—stupid!"*

I think my blood felt cold. In a flash I realized what a stupid, terrible mistake I had made. Aghast, I talked fast as I tried to explain that I was just kidding, just teasing, that I did not mean what I said.

Her face still frozen, she muttered: "I've *been* hurt."

Of course she has. Every black person in the country has been hurt. I walked upstairs to my apartment and felt so fragmented by guilt and shame that I walked back down to the foyer. She took one look at my face.

"You came all the way down here just to apologize again?"

"Yes," I said, taking her hand and kissing it. "Please forgive me. I did a very stupid thing. I'm sorry. I like you, and we only tease the people we love."

She smiled at me.

SUNDAY, JUNE 23, 1991 ■ Louisiana has passed the most repressive anti-abortion law of any state. On TV I heard a Louisiana state legislator bellow, "We're not ashamed to say we love children!" No? Oh, really?

THURSDAY, JULY 4, 1991 ■ Hemingway said: "A writer's job is to tell the truth."

TUESDAY, JULY 9, 1991 ■ Confucius said: "The beginning of wisdom is calling things by their right names."

SUNDAY, JULY 28, 1991 ■ I know a woman who worked in the garment district many years ago. One day she was eating lunch in a restaurant in that area with a clothing manufacturer named Bob. Looking up, he saw three men and spoke to one of them, asking: "How you doing, Tommy?"

The woman looked at the man. He wore a dark coat and dark shirt, a white tie and a big hat and stood with both hands in his coat pockets.

The woman blurted: "Oh, if I were casting for a gangster movie I'd hire you right away because of the way you look!"

The man smiled. When he and the others walked away, Bob turned on the woman, snarling: "You've gotta big mouth! Do you know who that guy is? 'Three Finger Brown,' a killer for 'Lucky' Luciano!"

After hearing my friend's story, I looked into The *Encyclopedia of American Crime*. The man's real name was Thomas Lucchese. When he was eight years old he lost three fingers in an accident and then was called "Three-Finger" after "Three-Finger" Mordecai Brown, a baseball pitcher with the Chicago Cubs. He was, indeed, Luciano's favorite killer and is believed to have been involved in a total of 30 murders. In 1967 he died of cancer.

My friend is still too scared to let me use her name.

SUNDAY, SEPTEMBER 1, 1991   ■   Today I read that Juvenal, the Roman satirist, called the passion for writing *cacoethes scribendi.* That's me, all right!

THURSDAY, SEPTEMBER 19, 1991   ■   This rainy day as I read Peter Ackroyd's biography of Charles Dickens. I learned, to my horror, that Dickens kept a diary every year of his adult life but burned it at the end of each year. What a loss!

SUNDAY, SEPTEMBER 29, 1991   ■   Miles Davis, the trumpeter and composer, died yesterday in California at the age of 65. He once said something about music that I say about writing: "I always listen to what I can leave out."

SATURDAY, OCTOBER 19, 1991   ■   Daniel Boorstin, the historian, says that Americans increasingly live in a "world where fantasy is more real than reality."

SATURDAY, NOVEMBER 16, 1991   ■   Michael Jackson, that sleek and slithering symbol of senselessness and sensuality, has produced another video in which he throws a garbage pail through the window of a house and knocks the glass out of car windows. I suppose this is intended to represent current nihilism.

This very day in the *Encyclopedia Britannica* I read that Mikhail Bakunin, the Russian anarchist of the 19th century, made a statement with which I totally *disagree.* He said: "The passion for destruction is also a creative passion." Wrong!

SATURDAY, DECEMBER 7, 1991   ■   Blaise Pascal, the French genius of the 17th century, once said: "I praise and prize only that writer who tells the truth about men — with tears in his eyes."

SUNDAY, DECEMBER 22, 1991   ■   Although I know I am eccentric, I am not so extreme as the man I read about today in the *Encyclopedia Britannica.*

He was Joseph Beuys, a German sculptor and performer who died in 1986. "He covered his head with honey and gold leaf, wore one shoe soled with felt and one with iron, and walked through an art gallery for about two hours quietly explaining the art therein to a dead hare he carried."

WEDNESDAY, DECEMBER 25, 1991   ■   Christmas. At noon I turned on the TV to watch as Mikhail S. Gorbachev sat at a desk in the Kremlin in Moscow and resigned after six years and nine months as president of the Union of Soviet Socialist Republics. He was forced from office by the creation of a Commonwealth of Independent States, consisting of eleven former republics of the Soviet empire—which died today!

Like millions of other people on this planet, I realized I was witnessing one of the most dramatic events in human history.

In Moscow, at 7:32 P.M., soon after the end of the brief televised talk, the red communist flag with its hammer and sickle was lowered over the Kremlin and up fluttered the white-blue-red Russian flag.

After Gorbachev recounted his achievements, he said in part: "An end has been put to the cold war and to the arms race, as well as to the mad militarization of the country, which has crippled our economy, public attitudes and morals. The threat of nuclear war has been removed."

I never expected to live to see the events of this day.

CHAPTER 19

1992

WEDNESDAY, JANUARY 22, 1992 ■ The January 27 issue of *Newsweek* magazine contains this precise quotation from President Bush as he spoke in New Hampshire the other day: "The guy over there at Pease—a woman, actually—she said something about a country-western song, you know, about a train, a light at the end of the tunnel. I only hope it's not a train coming the other way. Well, I said to her, well, I'm a country-music man. I love it, always have. Doesn't fit the mold of some of the columnists, I might add, but nevertheless—of what they think I ought to fit in, but I love it . . . But nevertheless, I said to them, you know there's another one the Nitty Ditty Nitty City—that they did. And it says if you want to see a rainbow you've got to stand a little rain. We've had a little rain. New Hampshire has had too much rain. A lot of families are hurting."

SUNDAY, FEBRUARY 16, 1992 ■ *Cassell's Encyclopedia of World Literature* has an article on nonsense and quotes one well-known nonsense story. I quote it here to prove that the fact that someone speaks sentences is not proof that the sentences mean anything: "She went into the garden to cut a cabbage-leaf, to make an apple-pie; and at the same time a great she-bear, coming up the street, pops its head into the shop. 'What, no soap?' So he died, and she very imprudently married the barber; and there were present the Picninnies, and the Joblilies, and the Garyulies, and the Grand Panjandrum himself, with the little round button at the top."

WEDNESDAY, FEBRUARY 19, 1992 ■ The *Times* had a story about teenage kids carrying guns. One kid admitted to a reporter that he had shot the folks he robbed, then added: "They were just people. Just people."

SUNDAY, FEBRUARY 23, 1992 ■ This evening on TV I watched *Life Styles of the Rich and Famous* because I like to hiss and boo conspicuous consumption. I was disgusted to learn that cruise ship passengers consumed caviar costing $100 an ounce—in a world of starving people!

SUNDAY, MARCH 1, 1992 ▦ Today I was interviewed about my diary by Gary Tuchman of Cable News Network.

FRIDAY, MARCH 13, 1992 ▦ Elizabeth Burke of BBC called from London to say that my first public reading from my diary and my book *The Epic of New York City* will be aired on radio tomorrow at 8:30 P.M., London time. It will be heard all over the United Kingdom.

SUNDAY, MARCH 15, 1992 ▦ I have a friend who works for an insane boss. Today he told me she was kind, for a change. I asked how this made him feel. He replied: "Well, it's rather like being invited to a picnic by Himmler."

MONDAY, MARCH 16, 1992 ▦ Watching TV news, I saw a man carrying a sign that said GOD SAYS KILL FAGS! This reminds me that the other day I read that William James, the great psychologist and philosopher, said he thinks most people are mad.

THURSDAY, APRIL 30, 1992 ▦ This is a black day in American history, a sad day, a bad day. Because a California jury acquitted four white cops who struck a black man 56 times in 81 seconds, an event of police brutality seen on TV all over this country, outraged black youths rioted in Los Angeles. I watched on CNN as anarchy spread over that city of 3.5 million people. Fires were set, windows were broken, stores were looted, white motorists were dragged out of their vehicles and beaten. No one can be sure, but it appears that 23 people were killed, 700 were injured, 378 were arrested and $100 million worth of property was damaged. It was horrible!

SUNDAY, MAY 10, 1992 ▦ I began reading *Simple Justice* by Richard Kluger and found an anti-black incident so barbaric that it staggered me: ". . . the summer of 1911 when one of the more barbaric lynchings of the era was literally staged in Livermore, Kentucky. A Negro charged with murdering a white man was seized and hauled to the local theater, where an audience was invited to witness his hanging. Receipts were to go to the murdered man's family. To add interest to the benefit performance, seatholders in the orchestra were invited to empty their revolvers into the swaying black body, while those in the gallery were restricted to a single shot . . ."

THURSDAY, MAY 21, 1992 ▇ Today I resumed reading a biography of Robert M. Hutchins, former chancellor of the University of Chicago. He said: "Other civilizations were destroyed by barbarians from without. We breed our own."

SATURDAY, MAY 23, 1992 ▇ In the *Cadillac Modern Encyclopedia* I found an excellent analysis of Hemingway's style: ". . . concreteness; nouns rather than adjectives; active rather than passive verbs . . . simple declarative sentences, avoiding qualifying clauses; coordinating rather than subordinating conjunctions, and above all, repetition . . ."

Although I have not consciously imitated Hemingway's style, perhaps unconsciously I let it guide me.

MONDAY, MAY 25, 1992 ▇ Fisher Ames (1758–1808), a politician and orator, once said: "Democracy is like a raft. It never sinks but, damn it, your feet are always in the water."

FRIDAY, MAY 29, 1992 ▇ Today I remembered something that happened to me when I was a child. I was in the third grade. My sister Kay was in the sixth grade. One day a boy entered our room and spoke to the teacher. She then told me that the sixth-grade teacher had asked her class a question none of her pupils could answer. She said she was sure Kathryn's little brother in the third grade could answer it. So I was led into the sixth-grade classroom, told to stand in front of the class, and then was asked the question . . . Pause . . . At last I whimpered: "I doooon't know!"

SATURDAY, MAY 30, 1992 ▇ I own a book called *Power and Innocence*, written by Dr. Rollo May, a noted psychotherapist. I knew him slightly because he had an office in the Hotel Master, where Ruthie and I lived. Dr. May quotes the poet W. H. Auden, who died in 1973. Auden said it is the duty of the poet "to defend one's language from corruption. And that is particularly serious now. It's being so quickly corrupted. When it's corrupted, people lose faith in what they hear, and this leads to violence."

FRIDAY, JUNE 19, 1992 ▇ Janet Steinberg told me something she saw today on a street: A young white woman walked past a young black man she evidently did not know. He ran after her, stopped her, demanded to know why she had not smiled at him. Thinking quickly, she said she did. Her reply mollified him but, nonetheless, he *ordered* her to smile at him the next time they pass.

FRIDAY, JULY 10, 1992 ■ In the *Encyclopedia Americana* I read that at the Tower of Babel 70 different languages were spoken. Right now, in New York City, more than 100 languages are spoken.

MONDAY, JULY 20, 1992 ■ A worldwide conference on AIDS is being held in Amsterdam. The news is bad: Every 15 to 20 seconds someone in the world gets infected with the AIDS virus. One million of the world's 11 to 13 million infected people contracted HIV in just the past six months. I am reminded of the Black Death that wiped out almost half the population of Europe during the Middle Ages.

SUNDAY, JULY 26, 1992 ■ In my opinion the most amusing word in the English language is *cloudy*. Say it again and again: cloudy . . . cloudy . . . cloudy . . . cloudy . . . cloudy . . .

TUESDAY, AUGUST 4, 1992 ■ My beloved wife died 27 years ago today. I kept myself busy so I would not recall the details of that black day, although this evening I kept peeping at the clock because Ruthie died about 10:30 P.M.

MONDAY, AUGUST 10, 1992 ■ Today I was visited by a young lady named Robin Samson, who is a location scout for Woody Allen. She had heard about the huge studio on the ground floor of this brownstone and wanted to see it, but the owners were not home.

I invited her into my apartment. The moment she entered her eyes widened and she flung out her arms and exclaimed:

"My God! What a great setting for a scene in a Woody Allen film about a scholar!"

As I led her from room to room her interest mounted until at last she said she wants to return with a camera to photograph every square inch of my walls. Then she will give the prints to the man in charge of production for Woody Allen. He pays $1,500 to $2,000 per day for the use of an apartment.

Nothing came of this.

THURSDAY, AUGUST 20, 1992 ■ On TV I heard a black youth express sorrow for a friend beaten to death by a gang that mistook him for someone else. The young black man spoke a somewhat Shakespearian line: "The bottom of my heart seemed to drop out."

MONDAY, SEPTEMBER 14, 1992   ■   Last Saturday actor Anthony Perkins died in Hollywood at the age of sixty. He suffered from AIDS. I mention him because, until a few years ago, he lived on my block. I often passed him when he was walking or bicycling, but he was so pathologically shy that he avoided making eye contact with anyone. At last I stopped saying hello to him. As an actor he is best remembered for his role in the film *Psycho*.

SUNDAY, OCTOBER 4, 1992   ■   I continue to be fascinated by the symbols created by the unconscious. Last night as I lay in bed, half asleep or asleep, I don't know which, I saw something suspended in space. What was it? A moth-eaten check! Yes. A symbol of poverty. Lately I've been worried about my money running out.

THURSDAY, OCTOBER 8, 1992   ■   President Bush and other Republicans are attacking Bill Clinton harshly, unfairly and disgustingly. When Clinton was at Oxford he took a student sight-seeing trip to Moscow, and now Republican Congressman Robert Dornan of California has charged that he was handled by the KGB. Bush then accused Clinton of not telling the truth about his visit to Moscow, although the President admitted he had no evidence of wrong-doing. Character assassination!

MONDAY, OCTOBER 12, 1992   ■   It was 500 years ago today that Christopher Columbus reached land in the Bahamas. While this event was celebrated today across the U.S., it also was criticized. Wishing to refresh my memory about Columbus, I read about him in three encyclopedias and then sided with the revisionist historians.

Columbus was half mad, greedy for gold, wrong about the size of the earth, quick to hang subordinates, and he kidnapped and killed native Americans. In fact, he began slave-trading in this hemisphere.

This evening on TV I watched a documentary about the Pueblo Indians and the harm done to them by Spaniards. White people are guilty of a Holocaust against Native Americans, as well as black Americans.

FRIDAY, OCTOBER 23, 1992   ■   My friend Janet Steinberg is fond of the detective stories written by S. S. Van Dine. His real name was Willard Huntington Wright, he graduated from Harvard, became ill and had to curtail his writing to detective stories. He died in 1939.

In his books he created a detective called Philo Vance, whose sophistication and esoteric learning were characteristics of Wright himself. Janet recently found a copy of *The Greene Murder Case* and copied two pages, which she gave to me today.

In this book Philo Vance told his friend Markham: "Society is ignorant and venomous, devoid of any trace of insight or understanding. It exalts knavery and worships stupidity. It crucifies the intelligent and puts the diseased in dungeons. And, withal, it arrogates to itself the right and ability to analyze the subtle sources of what it calls 'crime,' and to condemn to death all persons whose inborn and irresistible impulses it does not like. That's your sweet society, Markham—a pack of wolves watering at the mouth for victims on whom to vent its organized lust to kill and flay."

These words are like some of the things I've said of late. Now I realize I'm both an elitist and a liberal, afraid of the ignorance of the masses but in agreement with Al Smith's dictum that the ills of democracy can only be cured by more democracy.

SATURDAY, OCTOBER 24, 1992 ▪ In the *Britannica* I read about John Stuart Mill (1806–73), the English philosopher and reformer. It was said that he "combined enthusiasm for democratic government with pessimism as to what democracy was likely to do." This expresses what I feel.

SUNDAY, OCTOBER 25, 1992 ▪ My upstairs neighbors, Rob and Debbie Mounsey, had their car stolen from the street near our house. Today when I telephoned Janet, she told me something that happened about a decade ago: A man and wife had their car stolen from the street where they parked it. However, pinned to a nearby tree was a note saying it had been borrowed by a man who had to rush his pregnant wife to a hospital; he promised to return it. The couple did not report this to the police. Sure enough, the next day their car was back on the street and attached to the steering wheel was a note of thanks, together with a pair of tickets to a Broadway show. Sighing in relief, they attended the show, and when they got back to their apartment they discovered that everything in it had been stolen.

That scam was similar to what happened to me the day of Ruthie's funeral. As was later explained to me by a detective, some thieves read in her obituary in the *Times* that her funeral service would be held at thus-and-such a time and place, so while I was in the funeral home they broke into our apartment. Because of my grief I didn't much care, until I realized they had stolen Ruthie's wedding ring, whereupon I exploded in wrath and I shouted all the foul words I knew.

THURSDAY, OCTOBER 29, 1992 ▪ I thought it was Voltaire, but actually it was Epicurus who said: "If God wishes to prevent evil but cannot, then He is impotent. If He could but will not, He is malevolent."

SATURDAY, OCTOBER 31, 1992 ■ On the radio I heard a political commercial from the Republican national committee that used these exact words: "The Democrats plan to cripple our economy." Now, why in the world would half of all Americans wish to foul their own nest? Madness! Like most Americans, I am sick of this Presidential campaign, sick of lying commercials and speeches, sick of hypocrisy and hyperbole! Instead of campaigns lasting two years, we would do better to employ the shorter British system.

SUNDAY, NOVEMBER 1, 1992 ■ On this next-to-last day of the campaign, Bill Clinton has lost his voice. In the *Times* I read that some religious radicals in the Republican party are saying: "To vote for Bill Clinton is to sin against God." The longer I live the more difficult it is for me to accept the magnitude of the madness in this world.

THURSDAY, NOVEMBER 5, 1992 ■ A lot of people must have sinned against God, because Bill Clinton won 43 per cent of the popular vote and 370 electoral votes to 168 for George Bush.

THURSDAY, DECEMBER 31, 1992 ■ Something reminded me of the evening I watched a TV interview with Peter Ustinov, the actor, writer and intellectual. He was asked whether he has a hobby.

He replied, "Yes . . . I observe things."

Hey, Ustinov, that's my job!

1993

SUNDAY, JANUARY 3, 1993 ■ Last night I dreamed a sad dream. It seemed that, at my present age of 81, I had joined the staff of a newspaper rich in the latest technology, such as computers and the like. Everything was mechanized, everyone dehumanized. There was a very large staff, all of them in motion, some roller-skating here and there, with a general buzzing confusion and seeming lack of order. None paid any attention to me and I noticed that they did not communicate very well with one another. I was trying to find the city editor so that he might give me an assignment and thus enable me to earn my pay, but my wanderings failed to reveal him anywhere. I felt old-fashioned. I also felt annoyed, saying to myself that if they would just let me go out into the city by myself, I could find and report an interesting story. In reality, I could do this very thing. Well, this dream told the truth, because I would feel out of place in a modern city room.

FRIDAY, JANUARY 8, 1993 ■ Elvis Presley stamps went on sale today, much to my disgust. Years ago, when he was being discharged from the army, I was one of many reporters interviewing him. I remember asking him how he could justify his enormous wealth when school teachers were being underpaid. He gave me a non-answer with a smile and extreme politeness.

MONDAY, JANUARY 11, 1993 ■ This evening I called my daughter in Creswell, Oregon. Among other things, I asked whether she still has the *Encyclopedia Britannica* and the *Encyclopedia Americana* that I gave her. Yes, she replied. I told her I had just seen a TV documentary about Oxford University and felt thrilled. Sandy said I'd make a great professor because I explain things so simply. *Bingo!* Her mother divorced me when Sandy was only four years old, and I've always regretted her absence as she grew up, so that I might educate her. Now she has declared that I am a good teacher. Hurrah for me!

FRIDAY, JANUARY 15, 1993 ■ The newspapers are full of controversy about the forthcoming St. Patrick's Day parade. Gays and lesbians of Irish heritage want to join the procession, carrying signs identifying their sexual preferences. I think they are wrong, however much I otherwise side with them. Any group has a right to parade with only people of its own choice. If six of my friends and I wish to march down a street proclaiming our friendship, we do not have to include elevator operators.

SUNDAY, JANUARY 17, 1993 ■ This is from Guy Murchie's book *The Seven Mysteries of Life:* "In the body of an eighty-year-old man 50 million of whose cells are dying off each second, while perhaps only 30 million new ones replace them, muscle has lost 30 percent of its former weight, the brain has shriveled to 10 percent, nerve trunks have shed 25 percent of their fibers, each breath uses 50 percent less air, each heartbeat pumps 35 percent less blood, the blood absorbs oxygen 60 percent more slowly . . ."

Other than this, I feel fine!

Here is what I regard as the beginning of old age: One is old when he stops pursuing pleasure and seeks instead to avoid pain.

Yeah, but I still enjoy looking at beautiful women.

I remember romances—girls won, girls lost—and then in a mirror see my crumbling face and white beard and wonder where my youth has gone, wonder why it passed so fast, so fast, so fast!

MONDAY, FEBRUARY 15, 1993   ■   Last night, dreaming of Ruthie, suddenly I bolted wide awake with the horrifying realization that she is dead. Oh, how I miss my wife!

FRIDAY, FEBRUARY 26, 1993   ■   I was at my desk in the front room, reading the papers and listening to the radio, when suddenly I heard there had been an explosion in one of the twin towers of the World Trade Center in lower Manhattan.

Turning off the radio, I walked into the bedroom and switched on my TV set. Soon it became apparent that a major disaster was in the making.

The blast occurred at 12:18 P.M. in one of the underground garages and its force was so great that it shook the building of 110 stories. On the average working day each tower contains some 50,000 employees of hundreds of companies and then, of course, there are visitors.

Today there were kids from kindergarten classes in the building, and some were trapped in dark elevators for hours. TV cameras on the street in a light snow showed men and women stumbling out of exits, gasping and coughing, the lower halves of their faces blackened with soot. Most of them suffered from smoke inhalation and I, who have emphysema, knew how they felt.

Cops and firemen put oxygen masks on their faces to help them breathe. Some people had blood running down their cheeks. Some were so exhausted after inching their way down from top floors in total darkness, that when they emerged they slumped onto the icy pavement. Others were trapped on upper floors but telephoned TV stations, whose newscasters tried to give them advice and encouragement.

As smoke thickened in offices, men broke windows to let in fresh air. That building, like many new skyscrapers, has windows that do not open at all. Both towers, each 1,350 feet high, are the tallest buildings in New York City. They are human beehives, for they have a daily working population of 100,000 people. Strange though it may sound, they are supposed to have 250 elevators. I don't know for sure, because I've never been inside either building. In my opinion, they are the ugliest skyscrapers in town. They look like gigantic dominoes standing on end.

Today that area became thick with police cars and ambulances and emergency medical vehicles, etc. Watching on TV, never had I seen so many cars of that kind in one place in all my life. I sympathized with the gasping victims as they emerged in the open, listened in apprehension about folks trapped in elevators and on upper floors, thrilled to tales of heroism—such as the helicopter pilot who landed on the roof to evacuate a pregnant woman.

One woman had been blown out of her high-heel shoes five feet into the air. It took some people two and a half hours to feel their way down 60 floors. On the 66th floor there was a woman in a wheelchair, and two men lifted it up and carried her, floor by floor, down to the ground. An enormous hole was blasted at the base of the building, erupting through three floors of reinforced concrete; it may be 100 feet in diameter.

All figures are tentative, of course, because of the chaos and confusion. From five to seven persons were killed and 1,000 injured—most of them suffering from smoke in their lungs. Downtown hospitals were jammed. In lower Manhattan traffic was stalled. After the explosion the police received 19 calls from persons claiming to have bombed the building.

At first it was thought that transformers had exploded, but as the day inched by, officials began to believe that only a bomb could do such massive damage so fast. Terrorists? Have they now targeted New York City? I doubt whether this town will ever be the same again.

WEDNESDAY, MARCH 10, 1993   As I climbed out of bed I became aware that stuck in my mind was one word—*hebephrenic*. Unable to remember its definition, I wondered why I even thought about the word.

Pondering the chain of events of the previous few minutes, I found the answer: In the morning I do not bound out of bed, but lie there awhile, glancing around at my beloved apartment and talking aloud to myself. Today I said in my normal speaking voice: "Ellis, you have to get up!" Then, playfully, I said in falsetto: "But I don't wanna!"

Checking a dictionary, I learned that *hebephrenic* is a word characterizing a disturbed person who engages in silly behavior. I had been silly, ergo: *Hebephrenic!*

I am fascinated by the way the mind works. Let me repeat a wise remark: "Blessed is he who knows why he does what he does."

FRIDAY, APRIL 2, 1993   The other day a friend introduced me to Elizabeth, who is 30 years old and was born in the West. This morning she called to ask whether she might visit me this afternoon and of course I said yes.

She arrived carrying a bag in which she keeps her diary. She asked many questions about my life. Just as I had trouble with my mother, so did she have trouble with her father. When she was a child he told her she was not worth having, not good for anything. How can anyone be cruel to a child?

In her three decades of life Elizabeth still has not overcome her low self-esteem. Recently, here in New York, she went to bed with a man she likes, but later he said he wants her only as a friend, not a lover.

Thinking "nobody on earth gives a shit about me," as she expressed it to me, she went to a bar, put a $20 bill on the counter and told the bartender to keep the drinks coming. At last she staggered home, drunk of course, and awakened with a ferocious hangover.

Smiling at me, she said she calls herself "a Sunday School teacher gone bad."

She is a good woman and is now married.

SATURDAY, APRIL 17, 1993   I dipped into some of my earlier diaries and am astounded by the fact that I have forgotten so many things, some of them important. For example, using photographs, I caricatured Ike and Mamie Eisenhower, Ruthie showed them to her boss, a close friend of the President, her boss took them to the White House, where Ike liked my caricature of him, thought the one of Mamie also was funny, but decided not to show it to her lest it hurt her feelings. How could I forget *this?*

MONDAY, MAY 3, 1993   My favorite pharmacist is Howard Appel of the London Terrace Pharmacy. When I walked in there today he was talking to a beautiful woman of about 20, with no makeup, ivory skin, clean-cut facial features and flashing eyes. I saw him sign a sheet listing various items.

I said to her: "You must work for some pharmaceutical company." Smiling at me, she said: "Yes, in a way . . . I sell condoms." I'm sure she saw my jaw drop.

SATURDAY, MAY 15, 1993   This evening as I watched a comedy channel on TV I heard a comedian trying to make a joke about the assassination of President Kennedy, with the screen showing the film of the moving limousine. Obviously, nothing is sacred! Joan Rivers is a comedienne whose husband killed himself, and when her guest was foul-mouthed radio jock Howard Stern, he joked about the suicide and she laughed. She should have slapped him, ordered him off the set or stormed off herself.

MONDAY, MAY 31, 1993   This evening I was on the phone with my sister Doris in Peoria. She remembered that when she was small I took her to a circus in Kewanee and there I introduced her to Tom Mix, the cowboy film star, whom I had interviewed earlier in the day. He behaved in a cool, distant, ungracious way toward her.

THURSDAY, JUNE 3, 1993 ■ Some days when I feel old I recall a funny line spoken by Selma: "They don't make mirrors the way they used to make them!"

SATURDAY, JUNE 5, 1993 ■ This sunny afternoon I walked to the tiny park on this block and sat down and watched unleashed dogs at play.

One was a male black Labrador toying with a blue rubber ball. The owner was a man in his early thirties, well built, almost handsome, neatly dressed. After the dog frolicked around awhile, its eyes gleaming in triumph as it ran with the ball in its mouth, the man wanted the dog to let go of the ball. The dog refused. The man held it by a chain around its throat and stroked its muzzle and spoke softly and tried to tug the ball out of the jaws of the dog, but the dog was stubborn and refused to open its mouth.

Suddenly I realized I was witnessing a duel between the will of a man and the will of a dog. I thought I saw a streak of obstinacy in the eyes of the dog. Thus far the man had been firm but mild; abruptly he exploded in anger. He tightened the chain around the throat of the dog until its eyes bulged and it choked and was unable to breathe and at last let the ball fall to the ground. Then the man twisted the chain until the dog yelped in pain.

He began walking it away, again and again torturing it by twisting the chain tight, and I stared at him, astounded and helpless, unable to comprehend why a man hurt an animal just because it held a ball in its mouth.

SUNDAY, JULY 25, 1993 ■ The ongoing big story of the day and week and year is the flood in the Mississippi valley, with homes and farms and stores and cars drowned in water, and with rain falling, falling, falling. I feel very sorry for its victims. I was astonished to read a poll that showed one in every five people believe the flood is God's punishment. Folks drown in ignorance, as well as water.

WEDNESDAY, AUGUST 4, 1993 ■ Ruthie, my sweet wife, died 28 years ago today. I still miss her, think of her almost every day, often speak her name aloud, wish she were here to share my tiny triumphs. Time has grown tissue over my wound. She was the best person I ever knew.

When I die my diary will go to New York University. Here are links in the chain of events that led to this end:

A few years ago I got a letter from a woman named Laura Stein, who said she read about me in some paper. She, too, keeps a diary. Her letter was so intelligent that I called her, then she visited me and we fell into instant friendship.

She created "Eat Healthy" workshops based on her method of appetite training. She also wrote The Bloomingdale's Eat Healthy Diet, which became a national best-seller. Although she keeps her maiden name, Laura is the wife of Gene Wolsk, a Broadway producer. When Gene and I met the two of us also became friends. We are amused by the fact that he and I look like one another.

Laura and Gene are friends of Mrs. Naomi Levine, a senior vice president of New York University. They spoke to her about my diary. She spoke to Carlton Rochell, dean of all N.Y.U. libraries. He spoke to Evelyn Ehrlich, humanities bibliographer of the Elmer H. Bobst Library. I was visited by Ms. Ehrlich and George Austin Thompson, also of the Bobst Library and a specialist in the history of New York City.

The process of donating my diary to N.Y.U. was so complex that I turned for advice to Rita Rosenkranz, my literary agent, and my friend Peter Skinner, who will edit my journal after my death.

Ms. Ehrlich wrote me a letter that begins this way: "It is with pleasure that I accept your gift of your 66-volume Diary to be placed in the Special Collections of Bobst Library . . ."

TUESDAY, SEPTEMBER 28, 1993 ▪ Dressing carefully and donning a jacket for the first time in months, I left by cab for Washington Square in Greenwich Village. The weather was cool, so I took my trenchcoat.

I sat down on a bench in front of the Elmer Holmes Bobst Library at 70 Washington Square South on the southeast corner of the square. At 4 P.M. I was due to go inside and be met by Ms. Evelyn Ehrlich, humanities bibliographer. During the 46 years I have lived in this city I have sat in that square hundreds of times, but this time it felt different. Now I am old, now I am disposing of my diary and now death looks like a ship emerging from fog.

Looking at the facade of the library, I saw that it is not handsome because it is a bilious pink, so I wondered about its interior. Then I crossed the street, walked inside and instantly was awed by its atrium. Three guards at three turnstiles looked at the library cards held by students walking inside. I was surprised to see many Asian faces.

Ms. Ehrlich arrived, greeted me warmly and ushered me past a guard. The building, she told me, was designed by Philip Johnson and his partner Richard Foster. Aware of Johnson's reputation, I was impressed. My attention went to the floor, done in black and white marble in a design that made it look three-dimensional. As I stared at it I almost felt hypnotized.

The Bobst Library is one of the major research libraries in the United States. New York University has 47,000 students and this library can seat 4,000 of them at the same time. There are two underground floors and five elevators.

With a smile, Evelyn suggested that she punch a computer to find out how many copies of my own published books are in the library. She did so and reported it has three copies. Next she said she would find out how many American colleges own my book, and she led me to a second computer, but the lady in charge said it was down just then. Later, when it came back on line, Evelyn printed out three pages showing that scores of my books are in dozens of colleges. I gulped in surprise.

Then we took an elevator to the Fales Library, housing English and American literature published since 1750. There I met Marvin Taylor, Fales librarian, who has just transferred here from Columbia University. He is young, wears rimless glasses, is slender and quiet, intelligent and pleasant. As he showed me his office Evelyn left to call their boss, Dean Rochell; he said he would join us after leaving a meeting.

I showed Evelyn and Marvin photographs of myself with Herbert Hoover, Harry Truman, Eleanor Roosevelt and others, to prove that my diary contains data about important people. I also told a few anecdotes about myself to give them the flavor of my journal, but soon felt ashamed because I was doing all the talking.

We three left Marvin's office, walked out into the hall and then through a series of doors, all of which Marvin unlocked. There was one room devoted entirely to Charles Dickens, another to Lewis Carroll, another to Erich Maria Remarque, the German novelist who wrote the World War I classic *All Quiet on the Western Front.* His room has the table on which he wrote, one so huge and handsome I was reminded of the furniture I saw in the Krupp mansion in Essen, Germany.

There also is a Robert Frost room. It has a life-size bust of the poet, whom I saw in the Waldorf-Astoria Hotel many years ago. It also contains his private library; Evelyn explained that it is helpful to researchers to see the books owned by a writer. I asked whether she wants my library of 12,000 volumes. She said she will return to my apartment to see them.

There in the Fales Library we walked on carpets, and everything was sleek and elegant, spick and span. I saw display cases of astounding originality, and I began to feel overwhelmed by the realization that when I die I will become a part of all this. Evelyn said that after my diary is processed, the library's sophisticated bibliographic computer network will tell scholars here and abroad that The Ellis Diary is available, and pages can be faxed to them.

I mused that at long last I have done that which I had hoped to do—deposit my diary where it can be used by historians of the future. I was so excited I almost felt faint. Because of my emphysema, too, the walking had tired me. We returned to the reception room and sat down.

In a moment we were joined by Dean Rochell, a man with southern charm and a penchant for laughter. He has been the dean for 17 years and he lives in the apartment building that once was the home of Eleanor Roosevelt, on the northwest corner of the square. The dean said kind things about his subordinates. When I asked all three whether they enjoy their work, all three said yes in chorus. Good! I thanked the dean for accepting my diary; he thanked me for donating it. The three of them seemed genuinely pleased about getting it.

At 6:30 P.M. I left, spiritually high but physically exhausted. Walking slowly, I made my way to the Minetta Tavern, where I telephoned Peter Skinner in his apartment across Macdougal Street. He asked me to wait for him in a Greek restaurant called Sirtaki. When he arrived I was so keyed-up and winded that it took some time before I could speak, but then I told him everything. Peter congratulated me. This day, I told him, was the most exciting day in my life within the past ten years.

TUESDAY, OCTOBER 5, 1993   ▇   Today I began using a cane.

THURSDAY, OCTOBER 14, 1993   ▇   Today I received a letter from Marvin Taylor, Fales librarian at New York University. Among other things, he said: "I am looking forward to adding your diary to the collection. I think it will be a great resource for future scholars."

FRIDAY, OCTOBER 29, 1993   ▇   This evening I watched a movie on TV and saw actress Sylvia Sidney, exotically beautiful when young, painfully ugly in old age. Last night on the screen I also saw Betty Grable, never much of an actress, but a pinup beauty during World War II. Now she is an old hag. I guess one price I pay for living a long time is watching the decay of my peers. Of course, my mirror lies a lot.

SATURDAY, OCTOBER 30, 1993   ▇   I learned that just before a football game some college coach had a pig castrated in front of his players to excite them. Anyone in the room care to tell me that the world is sane?

MONDAY, NOVEMBER 1, 1993   ▇   This morning as I lay in bed listening to a radio program called *Rambling with Gambling*, I heard a staff member tell this story. Early today he was in front of the WOR building on Broadway at 41st Street talking to a vendor of coffee and doughnuts. A man walked up to the vendor, pointed a gun at him and said he wanted a vanilla frosted doughnut. That's all he wanted. The vendor gave him a doughnut and the gunman sauntered away.

My British-born friends David and Susan Hall have two daughters, Felicity and Amelia. They are only slightly older than my two granddaughters, Shine and Orion Emelio, who live far away in Oregon. From time to time Felicity and Amelia visit me. Both are intelligent, articulate and well-read. I regard them as foster granddaughters and know they like me, perhaps because I listen to them.

TUESDAY, NOVEMBER 2, 1993 ■ This evening I was visited by Felicity Hall. She now works in public relations in London and lives in the London home of her parents. Felicity is 24 years old, about five six, with shoulder-length light brown hair, a creamy complexion, and tonight she wore a sweat shirt, a string of beads, blue-jeans and a long black coat. She is beautiful and brilliant.

We enjoyed a rapid-fire conversation, my eyes locked on her eyes, and then I read aloud a few pages from my manuscript. She actually wept upon hearing one passage. It is gratifying to a writer to know his words can evoke emotion. When I glanced at a clock I saw that it was 9:30 and already dark, of course. I told Felicity she'd better leave because I did not want her on the streets at night. Too dangerous. Agreeing, she got up and left.

About two minutes later I heard a commotion on my third-floor landing. Curious, I opened the door. There stood Rob Mounsey, my upstairs neighbor. He was staring at a woman crouched on a step. She looked old. She was weeping and trembling and it took me a few seconds to realize that, yes, this actually was Felicity! She managed to sob that she had been mugged right in front of my house.

Rob and I helped her inside my apartment. She cringed in a chair, her face in her hands, her shoulders shaking with sobs, and I stroked her hair and back and did all I could to comfort her. I've never seen anyone so frightened. She managed to tell us that the mugger jumped out from under a tree and held a knife to her heart and told her to give him her money. She had about $50, but it was not in her purse; instead, it was in the hip pocket of her jeans and because of her long coat she had trouble reaching it. The mugger raised his blade to her throat.

Her fumbling fingers found the bills and she gave them to the guy, who ran away. She said he may have been Hispanic and looked about 18, but other than this she could not describe him.

Rob called the police and soon we were visited by two pleasant cops. They asked Felicity to get into their squad car and ride a few blocks around the neighborhood to try to find the mugger, and although it was obvious she didn't want to go, she did leave with them. I had said that of course she could spend the night here, but she said she had planned to meet a friend, a banker, so she had called and asked him to pick her up here.

When Felicity returned with the policemen she was somewhat more composed, but still empty-eyed. The young banker arrived and we shook hands solemnly. After Felicity and I had a final hug, she left with him. I was so unnerved by this event that I felt twitchy.

1994

WEDNESDAY, JANUARY 12, 1994   ■   This evening I was visited by my friend Ken Gray, who told me an amusing true story. After World War II his father, an army captain, was stationed in Bremerhaven in the American Zone of Occupation. When he returned to New York he brought back a trophy, a huge Nazi flag, and gave it to his three uncles. One was a lawyer, one a doctor, one a dentist. They never married, but lived together on the upper west side of Manhattan. For awhile they hid the Nazi flag under a bed. Then, fearful that someone might find it, they cut it up into pieces two inches square and over a period of weeks took out the pieces and threw them into garbage cans.

SUNDAY, FEBRUARY 20, 1994   ■   On TV I heard again a phrase I hate: "pre-planned." It is preposterous. Not *pre*-preposterous. Just preposterous. Either something is planned or it isn't. Many people befoul the language because they want to sound important.

I was reminded of an essay written by George Orwell, so off a shelf I took the fourth volume of his collected essays, journalism and letters. In 1946 he sounded an alarm about the decadence of our language in an article called "Politics and the English Language."

He said: "The great enemy of clear language is insincerity."

MONDAY, FEBRUARY 21, 1994   ■   In a volume of the *Encyclopedia Britannica* I found this sentence: "The great test of knowledge is the ability to state what a thing *is*."

TUESDAY, FEBRUARY 22, 1994 ■ This is my 83rd birthday. During my 83 years I have lived:
— 29,930 days
— 718,320 hours
— 43,099,200 minutes.

MONDAY, MARCH 7, 1994 ■ On the Op-Ed Page of the *New York Times* Anthony Lewis devoted his column to an article by Richard D. Kaplan in the February issue of the *Atlantic Monthly*. The article is called "The Coming Anarchy," and it echoes and amplifies what I've been saying about the decline of civilization.

This is an issue which Peter Skinner and I debate endlessly. He believes mankind will muddle through, but I argue that now we are confronted with something new in history—the population explosion. A reasonable man, Peter always says there is lots of empty space for people to use. I've finally found the flaw in Peter's arguments: He is logical but history is illogical. Sad to say, reason has played only a minor role in civilization. Peter assumes that due to the instinct for self-preservation, people will behave reasonably. Much of the time they don't. For example, millions of Americans know that if they smoke cigarets they may suffer from lung cancer, emphysema, etc., but nonetheless many go on smoking. And consider the hundreds of years during which millions of people did cruel and insane things because they believed in this or that god or goddess. Forever and ever, the enemy is ignorance.

Ibn Khaldun (1332–1406) was an Arab historian who wrote a seven-volume *Universal History*. He believed that civilizations rise and fall in constant cycles. Hard work and cooperation bring wealth and luxury, but then selfishness, corruption and decline follow.

Our own John Steinbeck, the American novelist who wrote *The Grapes of Wrath*, once said: "If I wanted to destroy a nation, I would give it too much and I would have it on its knees, miserable, greedy and sick.... I am troubled by the cynical immorality of my country. It cannot survive on this basis."

WEDNESDAY, MARCH 9, 1994 ■ ABC-TV pays reporter Diane Sawyer $19,000 per *day*. This is twice as much as I was paid per *year* when I was a reporter.

TUESDAY, APRIL 5, 1994 ■ Barnes & Noble opened a new bookstore today on the west side of 6th Avenue between 21st and 22nd Streets, and I attended the opening.

Construction of this building, with a Beaux-Arts facade, began in 1900, and for many years it was the Adams Dry Goods Store. It is in the heart of what formerly was called the Ladies' Mile—6th Avenue between 14th and 23rd streets. Barnes & Noble occupies the entire first floor of 35,000 square feet. It is the largest, most beautiful bookstore I have ever seen—and it is on my street!

I entered through a door whose wood gleamed with polish, and stepped onto a parquet floor that is covered, in some places, by soft carpets. The interior is painted white. There are tall, stately columns with Corinthian capitals, a huge rectangular atrium spanned by a bridge with a wrought-iron railing, overstuffed chairs and soft sofas here and there, handsome wooden tables and wooden chairs, flowers on tables, on the mezzanine a cafe and in the air the odor of coffee and the sound of music.

More than 100 people work in the store. On the walls are signs stating the kinds of books displayed in a given area, computers for clerks to find out what is in stock, a children's room with a tiny theater. I appreciated the wide aisles. I rested in a comfortable chair and watched a man who sat opposite me on a sofa talking to himself.

I asked a clerk how many books there are in the store. The answer: 225,000. I chatted with another clerk, a woman born in England, educated in London, named Sandy Weston. She is in her late thirties, copper-haired, bright, pleasant, without makeup, loves books. I had to buy a book to help remember this day, so I chose *Genius: The Life and Science of Richard Feynman* by James Gleick. Years ago on television I saw Feynman (pronounced Fine-man) and was dazzled by his brilliance.

WEDNESDAY, APRIL 13, 1994   ■   In New York City all the minority groups are collectively the majority, with 52 per cent of the population. Now I am a member of a minority.

FRIDAY, APRIL 22, 1994   ■   This evening I was watching Barbara Walters interviewing Louis Farrakkan, the black leader, when the TV program was interrupted by a bulletin announcing the death of Richard Nixon at 9:08 P.M. in New York Hospital. After that Channel 7 broadcast, nothing but news and memories of the former President. I hated that bastard and still hate him! People who praise him for opening relations with Red China forget that years earlier he had belonged to the China Lobby, which was stridently against China.

SATURDAY, APRIL 23, 1994 ■   Today all the media gave maximum attention to the dead Nixon, heaping upon him praise he does not deserve. Why should one speak well of a bastard just because he is dead?

FRIDAY, APRIL 29, 1994 ■   This evening on television I watched excerpts of the 1977 interview that David Frost had with Richard Nixon—the real Nixon, not the mythical hero eulogized at his funeral day before yesterday. Talking to Frost on camera, Nixon lied, temporized, evaded, rationalized, confessed minor mistakes but refused to admit that he broke any law. Again I heard his fatuous line: "When the President does it, then that means it is legal."

MONDAY, MAY 16, 1994 ■   The Andy Warhol Museum opened in Pittsburgh yesterday. It cost $12 million and is the biggest single-artist museum in the United States. It also tries to enoble trivia, for Warhol was not an artist but a con artist, a flimflam man who brainwashed people into believing that the emperor *was* wearing clothes! I am angered at the thought of so much attention given to such a phoney as Andy Warhol.

WEDNESDAY, MAY 18, 1994 ■   Browsing through a volume of the *World Book Encyclopedia*, I read an article about Nathaniel Hawthorne. In two of his finest stories the central characters suffer from intellectual pride. Hawthorne called this "the Unpardonable Sin," described it as the "sin of an intellect that triumphed over the sense of brotherhood with man and reverence with God."

It was this puritanical ethic that led my mother to lecture me about the danger of pride, so it was this which damaged me when I was young. Those Goddamn stupid Puritans! *Everyone* should be proud of himself!

SUNDAY, MAY 22, 1994 ■   Robert Louis Stevenson said: "There are not words enough in all Shakespeare to express the merest fraction of a man's experience in an hour."

MONDAY, JUNE 6, 1994 ■   I have kept my diary more than 24,000 days.

1995

SUNDAY, JANUARY 1, 1995 ■   In one of her poems Emily Dickinson wrote that her soul "closed the valves of her attention"—a marvelous metaphor. Now that a new year has begun, now that I am an old man with death waiting in the wings, I think I'll open the valves of my attention to look at my past, present and future.

How is my health, now that I am almost 84 years old? Well, I suffer from emphysema caused by smoking. Although I gave up cigarets more than a decade ago, the damage has been done. Lung cells were killed; they do not rejuvenate themselves. I am short of breath, become exhausted whenever I shower or climb stairs, lack energy, have difficulty walking, stay home most of the time. Spiritually, though, I do not feel old. I am as enthusiastic as ever and more curious than before.

Am I afraid of death? No, I do not fear the state of non-being. However, I am afraid of a lingering illness and painful death. I think the individual has the right to take his life when he wishes to do so. Certainly, I own myself; no society, no government, no institution owns me.

Do I believe in heaven? Not at all. How about hell? I've been there, while alive. Would I like to live my life over again? Absolutely not! Once is quite enough, thank you.

Am I a skeptic? Yes, because I doubt whether anyone can know the essence of anything. Am I a cynic? No, because I regard every woman as a lady and every man as a gentleman, unless they prove themselves otherwise. As for myself, I get almost sensual pleasure from being polite.

What is my life like now? Pleasant, actually. The past 28 years I have lived in a four-room apartment on the third floor of an ancient brownstone on a tree-lined street in lower Manhattan. The ceilings are high, there are two marble fireplaces and all the walls are covered with books. I decorated my abode in the Victorian mode and beautified it with a marble bust of a nubile maiden, a statue of Shakespeare, an oil portrait of my wife and a collection of glass eggs that catch the light.

Although I live in New York City, I can see trees whenever I look out any of the seven windows in my home. In warm weather I like to loll at an open window in the front room, listening to the sparkling of cool jazz on the radio, watching birds on branches only a few feet from me, listening to their songs, watching my neighbors walking along the sidewalk below me.

Because I lack the strength to put everything back in its proper place, my floors are littered with books and magazines, manuscripts and notes. My visitors fall into two classes: Those who call my home a wonderful colorful Bohemian lair, and those who sniffily call it a mess. One of my friends declares that I am The Last Bohemian. This may be due to the fact that indoors I wear a red beret to keep my ancient head warm.

I regard my private library as a literary smorgasbord. If in this hour a certain book fails to satisfy my appetite, another will. I own dozens of encyclopedias, dozens of dictionaries, and when some friends are searching for an obscure fact, they call me rather than the public library. I'm vain enough to try to find the answer within a minute or two. Some folks ask me to check my diary to find out what I was doing the day they were born.

Although I used to be complex, I am now a simple man with plain tastes. I care so little for food that I wish I could exist without eating. But— I'll confess I'm fanatically fond of chili. In the morning, after awakening, I loll in bed for maybe an hour. I just lie there, day-dreaming, meditating, philosophizing. I rationalize this by telling myself that a philosopher *must* be lazy. Often I talk out loud to myself. Doesn't everybody?

When I was a reporter, I was sent to the Waldorf-Astoria Hotel at least once a week, so I dressed carefully. In fact, I was a neatnik. Now that I am an old geezer and can stay home, I've become a slobnik. Clean, but carelessly clad. I don't care much how I look on the outside. It's the inside that interests me.

It's possible that I'm a two-bit rinky-dink mystic. During my life I've had four or five mystical experiences in which I seemed to melt into the universe, into the One. Then I began turning on with pot and found my mind wandering to distant places, to eternity and three doors beyond. As a result, I have made an intense study of mysticism the past quarter-century.

Am I religious? Oh, yes. I am awed by the universe, awed by the laws of astronomy and physics, awed by sunsets and love and roses and bubbles. To revere nature and beauty, in my opinion, is to be religious. I consider the invisible more significant than the visible. For example—love.

However, I am agnostic. I can neither prove nor disprove the existence of a deity. Perhaps each of us is a god. I accept the bitter fact that I must live in uncertainty. When I was a teenager I scorned people who went to church, but now I know that life hurts, so I understand the need to seek solace from some source.

Descartes said: "I think, therefore I am."

I say: "I hurt, therefore I am."

I agree with Thoreau, who believed most people lead lives of quiet desperation. Yes, all of us hurt. All of us need help. Happiness is a sometime thing. I define happiness as having what you want and wanting what you have. I have not been happy since the death of my wife thirty years ago, although I am often serene.

I have learned much from Buddhism, which teaches that pain is due to desire. Now I have such few wants that I can satisfy all of them. All I want, besides Ruthie, is a roof over my head, a little food, moderate health, fond friends, my books and enough leisure to let me do the work that pleases me. I think I have one big book left in me.

This year Kodansha America will publish excerpts from my journal in a

book called A *Diary of the Century: Tales from America's Greatest Diarist.*
I didn't pick this title. My publisher did. And this year my humongous
diary will be hauled by truck to New York University, where it will be open
to historians and other scholars.

Each day as I write my diary I sit at the typewriter on the kitchen table
under a painting of the ocean and when I pause to seek the precise word I
lift my eyes to see the water and let my mind float. Water is the prime
symbol of the unconscious.

Years ago I quit trying to *impress* people. I just *express* myself. Because I
want to be understood, I write simply. I agree with Robert Louis Stevenson, who said that the art of writing is the art of leaving out. I also agree
with Arthur Schopenhauer, who urged us to use common words to say
uncommon things.

My daughter Sandy writes well. She also is a successful mother. I have
two granddaughters, Shine and Orion, now in their twenties, and neither
drinks liquor, smokes commercial cigarets or gets stoned on pot. It's
Grandpa Eddie who is the sinner—*was* the sinner. Sandy lives far away in
Oregon and Shine lives with her mother. Orion is a photographer on a
luxury liner. I seldom get to see my family, but we are close because often
we are on the phone.

Space and time. As one ages, time flows faster. Once I read an interesting comment upon this fact: If you tell a five-year-old boy he must wait
one year before going to the circus, he has to wait one-sixth of his life. If
you tell me I must wait a year for something to happen, I have to wait only
1/84th of my life.

But apart from an individual's age, these days change *changes* faster
than ever before in history. In my opinion, this acceleration in time is the
chief characteristic of the modern era. It is due to the population explosion and the technological revolution. During my lifetime alone, the population of the United States has more than doubled. Now there are 5.5
billion people on earth and in another fifty years there may be 9 billion,
according to one estimate. The more people there are, the more they
interact, the greater the number of events. One measure of time is the
number of events occurring in a given moment.

In this year of 1995 more than 100 wars are being fought here and there
on earth. Television and computers bare these ugly facts as never before in
history. What with all the other problems we face, we are fed more facts
than we can digest. This overload of information is like a fuse that blew
out. It partly explains the fragmentation to be seen wherever one looks.
We need fewer facts and more synthesis.

But what do I know? Like Socrates, all I know is that I know nothing. I can prove nothing. I cannot even prove that I am alive. When I say "I" and then "am," already I'm hip-deep in metaphysics. I am a mass of ignorance. However, a confession of ignorance is the beginning of wisdom. And, despite what I've just said, there is one thing I know for sure:

The highest wisdom is kindness.

I want to end this book with the only original idea I've ever had. I explained it in an essay published on the Op-Ed Page of the *New York Times* on December 13, 1976:

A National Drawer for Dusty, Yellowing Diaries

I advocate the creation of an institution called the American Diary Repository.

While every civilized nation has libraries and archives and museums, none has a central clearinghouse for the preservation and use of the diaries written by its people.

As this nation enters its third century, we would do well to gather under one roof an untapped body of Americana—the life stories of all sorts of men and women as told in their journals.

History is a subject of diminishing interest to students. While there are many reasons for this condition, one explanation is that most history textbooks are dull. However, there is no dull history; there are only dull historians.

Every good historian is eager to find and use diaries kept during the period about which he is writing. Even the journals of obscure people are valuable, for they mirror the mood of a given era. Honest writing is more precious than precious writing. Historian Carl Becker said that every man is his own historian because he is a sifter and selector of his nation's past.

Mark Twain, a fitful diarist, wrote in his autobiography: "The last quarter of a century my life has been pretty constantly and faithfully devoted to the study of the human race—that is to say, the study of myself, for in my individual person I am the entire race."

Historians writing about 17th century England study the diary of Samuel Pepys, which he kept for nine and a half years. Others researching 18th century England examine the journal of James Boswell, which he kept for thirty years. Those interested in New York City of the last century turn to the diary of George Templeton Strong, which he kept for forty years.

The American Diary Repository could be funded by the federal government, foundations, philanthropists, the American Historical Association, the Organization of American Historians, the American Association for State and Local History, etc.

A building could be put up in Washington, D.C., or the repository could be situated on the campus of some university. However, it should be an independent entity, not an arm of government or a unit of a university. It could be staffed by historians, librarians, archivists and computer operators.

They might formulate criteria for the acceptance of diaries, and others may wish to speak to this point. As for myself, I would welcome all journals because, however modest and humble the diarist, I believe that his or her diary contains something of value. Surely there are historical nuggets in Aunt Minnie's diary in the trunk in the attic.

Donors would not be paid for their diaries, but perhaps they could get a tax break. In the main, their reward would be an awareness that they would be granted a kind of immortality. Never underestimate the power of the ego: Within a few years, the repository would contain tens of thousands of diaries.

The repository could publish exceptional journals. The George Templeton Strong diary, for instance, was edited and published in four volumes. Any diary worthy of publication would yield royalties to be split between the repository and each diarist or his heirs.

If anyone wanted to write a history of Seattle he could apply to the repository, and computers might produce perhaps 67 cards identifying Seattle residents who kept diaries. By using them, the writer could produce a better history of Seattle than otherwise would be possible.

If donors worried lest their diaries embarrass themselves or others, they could stipulate that their confessions might not be examined or used for a stated number of years or decades.

With the establishment of the American Diary Repository, the histories of the future would become richer, warmer, more human. Goethe said: "If you wish to leave something useful to future generations, this cannot but be confession."

INDEX

ABOUT THE AUTHOR

Edward Robb Ellis was born in Kewanee, Illinois, in 1911. At fourteen he knew he wanted to become a journalist and an author. At sixteen he began keeping the diary that is the basis of this book. The *Chicago Tribune* has called Ellis's diary "a jewel of Americana."

In his long newspaper career he worked at the *New Orleans Item*, covering Huey Long, Louis Armstrong, as well as the city's hungry workers and the colorful French Quarter. In the 1930s he joined the *Oklahoma City Times*, writing about the Great Depression, dust storms, and Eleanor Roosevelt. The beginning of World War II found him at the *Peoria Journal-Transcript*, from where he moved to Chicago, where he became a feature writer for the United Press. During the war Ellis edited a navy newspaper on Okinawa. In 1946 the Chicago Newspaper Guild named him the best feature writer in the city.

In 1947 Ellis joined the *New York World-Telegram*, where he remained for the next fifteen years, winning wide attention for his feature stories about world leaders, Nobel laureates, and Hollywood stars. After retiring from reporting in 1962, Ellis embarked on a career as a full-time author, publishing *The Epic of New York City*, which the *New York Times* called "a magnificent modern chronicle." *A Nation in Torment*, Ellis's narrative history of the Great Depression, received the Friends of American Writers Literary Award in 1970. He is also an associate editor of *The Encyclopedia of New York City*.

Mr. Ellis lives in New York City, tending his 15,000-volume library and faithfully recording his life and times in the pages of his epic diary.